Lecture Notes in Computer Science 2500

Edited by G. Goos, J. Hartmanis, and J. van Leeuwen

T0178663

Springer
Berlin
Heidelberg
New York
Hong Kong
London
Milan
Paris
Tokyo

Erich Grädel   Wolfgang Thomas
Thomas Wilke (Eds.)

Automata Logics, and Infinite Games

A Guide to Current Research

 Springer

Volume Editors

Erich Grädel
RWTH Aachen, Mathematische Grundlagen der Informatik
52056 Aachen, Germany
E-mail: graedel@informatik.rwth-aachen.de

Wolfgang Thomas
RWTH Aachen, Lehrstuhl Informatik VII
52056 Aachen, Germany
E-mail: thomas@informatik.rwth-aachen.de

Thomas Wilke
Universität Kiel
Institut für Informatik und Praktische Mathematik
Christian-Albrechts-Platz 4, 24118 Kiel, Germany
E-mail: wilke@ti.informatik.uni-kiel.de

Cataloging-in-Publication Data applied for

A catalog record for this book is available from the Library of Congress.

Bibliographic information published by Die Deutsche Bibliothek
Die Deutsche Bibliothek lists this publication in the Deutsche Nationalbibliografie;
detailed bibliographic data is available in the Internet at <http://dnb.ddb.de>

CR Subject Classification (1998): F.1, F.3, F.4.1

ISSN 0302-9743
ISBN 3-540-00388-6 Springer-Verlag Berlin Heidelberg New York

Springer-Verlag Berlin Heidelberg New York
a member of BertelsmannSpringer Science+Business Media GmbH

http://www.springer.de

© Springer-Verlag Berlin Heidelberg 2002
Printed in Germany

Typesetting: Camera-ready by author, data conversion by Boller Mediendesign
Printed on acid-free paper   SPIN 10870758   06/3142   5 4 3 2 1 0

Preface

A central aim of computer science is to put the development of hardware and software systems on a mathematical basis which is both firm and practical. Such a scientific foundation is needed especially in the construction of reactive programs, like communication protocols or control systems. Characteristic features of such programs are the perpetual interaction with their environment as well as their nonterminating behaviour.

For the construction and analysis of reactive programs an elegant and powerful theoretical basis has been developed with the theory of automata on infinite objects. The main ingredients of this theory are:

- automata as a natural model of state-based systems,
- logical systems for the specification of nonterminating behaviour,
- infinite two-person games as a framework to model the ongoing interaction between a program and its environment.

This theory of automata, logics, and infinite games has meanwhile produced a large number of deep and mathematically appealing results. More important, this theory is intimately connected with the development of algorithms for the automatic verification ("model-checking") and synthesis of hardware and software systems. Numerous software tools have been developed on this basis, which are now used in industrial practice. On the other hand, more powerful theoretical results are needed for the continuous improvement of these tools and the extension of their scope.

In this research, enormous progress was achieved over the past ten years, both by new insights regarding the more classical results and by the creation of new methods and constructions. This progress is so far documented only in conference proceedings or journal papers but not in exhaustive surveys or monographs. This volume is intended to fill this gap. In a sequence of 19 chapters, grouped into eight parts, essential topics of the area are covered. The presentation is directed at readers who have a knowlewdge of automata theory and logic as acquired in undergraduate studies and who wish to enter current research in seminar work or research projects.

In the introductory Part I, the two frameworks of the theory are introduced: automata over infinite words (ω-automata), and infinite two-person games. Part II takes up a central subject of the classical theory of ω-automata, namely determinization procedures. The subsequent two parts deal with fundamental algorithmic questions: the solution of games (Part III) and the transformation of automata according to logical operations, in particular complementation (Part IV). Some core logics to which this theory is applied are the subject of the following two parts (V and VI): the μ-calculus and monadic second-order logic. The last two parts deal with recent extensions to strong logical frameworks: In Part VII, the model-checking problem for monadic second-order logic over "tree-like" infinite transition systems is solved, as well as the solution of infinite games over certain graphs of this kind, and in the final part the logical framework is extended to guarded logics. Each part ends with notes with further references; however, these pointers to the literature are not meant to be exhaustive.

The volume is the outcome of a research seminar which took place in Dagstuhl in February 2001. There were 19 young researchers participating in the seminar; each of them prepared a presentation based on one or several recent articles, reshaping the material in a form with special emphasis on motivation, examples, justification of constructions, and also exercises.

Thanks are due to the International Conference and Research Center of Dagstuhl and the "Gesellschaft für Informatik (GI)" for the support it provided. Achim Blumensath and Christof Löding provided substantial help in technical and editorial matters; we express our sincere thanks to them.

The editors hope that this book will help many readers to enter this fascinating, mathematically attractive, and promising area of theoretical computer science. As an incentive, many open problems are mentioned in the text. The best success which the book could have would be to guide readers to the solution of some of these problems.

Aachen, Kiel, October 2002

Erich Grädel
Wolfgang Thomas
Thomas Wilke

Contents

Part I

Introduction

In this introductory part, the framework of ω-automata and infinite games is presented. This involves two aspects: First, a transition system is used to specify elementary steps which are carried out in a nonterminating process. Secondly, the infinite runs, respectively plays, generated in this way are checked with an "acceptance condition" or "winning condition". Usually these conditions refer to those states or vertices which are visited infinitely often in a run. Different uses of these states lead to a broad spectrum of acceptance and winning conditions. A central purpose of the two chapters in this part is to clarify the expressive power of these conditions (in particular, to exhibit cases where one acceptance condition can simulate another), and, for infinite games, to show how the form of a winning condition affects the form of possible winning strategies.

1 ω-Automata

Berndt Farwer

Fachbereich Informatik
Universität Hamburg

1.1 Introduction and Notation

Automata on infinite words have gained a great deal of importance since their first definition some forty years ago. Apart from the interests from a theoretical point of view they have practical importance for the specification and verification of reactive systems that are not supposed to terminate at some point of time. Operating systems are an example of such systems, as they should be ready to process any user input as it is entered, without terminating after or during some task.

The main topic covered in this chapter is the question how to define acceptance of infinite words by finite automata. In contrast to the case of finite words, there are many possibilities, and it is a nontrivial problem to compare them with respect to expressive power.

First publications referring to ω-languages date back to the 1960's, at which time Büchi obtained a decision procedure for a restricted second-order theory of classical logic, the sequential calculus $S1S$ (second order theory of one successor), by using finite automata with infinite inputs [17]. Muller [133] defined a similar concept in a totally different domain, namely in asynchronous switching network theory. Starting from these studies, a theory of automaton definable ω-languages (sets of infinite words) emerged. Connections were established with other specification formalisms, e.g. regular expressions, grammars, and logical systems. In this chapter, we confine ourselves to the automata theoretic view.

1.1.1 Notation

The symbol ω is used to denote the set of non-negative integers, i.e. $\omega := \{0, 1, 2, 3, \dots\}$.

By Σ we denote a finite alphabet. Symbols from a given alphabet are denoted by $a, b, c \dots$. Σ^* is the set of finite words over Σ, while Σ^ω denotes the set of infinite words (or ω-words) over Σ (i.e. each word $\alpha \in \Sigma^\omega$ has length $|\alpha| = \omega$). Letters $u, v, w, \dots$ denote finite words, infinite words are denoted by small greek letters $\alpha, \beta, \gamma \dots$. We write $\alpha = \alpha(0)\alpha(1) \dots$ with $\alpha(i) \in \Sigma$. Often we indicate infinite runs of automata by $\varrho, \sigma, \dots$. A set of ω-words over a given alphabet is called an ω-language.

For words α and w, the number of occurrences of the letter a in α and w is denoted by $|\alpha|_a$ and $|w|_a$, respectively. Given an ω-word $\alpha \in \Sigma^\omega$, let

$$\mathrm{Occ}(\alpha) = \{a \in \Sigma \mid \exists i\ \alpha(i) = a\}$$

E. Grädel et al. (Eds.): Automata, Logics, and Infinite Games, LNCS 2500, pp. 3-21, 2002.
© Springer-Verlag Berlin Heidelberg 2002

be the (finite) set of letters occurring in α, and

$$\mathrm{Inf}(\alpha) = \{a \in \Sigma \mid \forall i \exists j > i \; \alpha(j) = a\}$$

be the (finite) set of letters occuring infinitely often in α.

The powerset of a set M is denoted by 2^M and $|M|$ denotes the cardinality of M. The i-th projection of an ordered tuple or vector $\mathbf{a} = (a_1, \ldots, a_k)$ is defined for $i \leq k$ and is written $\pi_i(\mathbf{a}) = a_i$.

The class of regular languages is denoted by REG.

1.2 ω-Automata

In classical formal language theory, the notion of acceptance of a word by an automaton is a well-known concept. One defines the notion of **finite computation** or **finite run** of an automaton on a given input word, specifies the configurations (by control states, or by control states and memory contents) which are considered to be "final", and declares an input accepted if a run exists on the input which terminates in a final configuration.

In the present context we are interested only in the acceptance of words by automata (and not in generation of ω-words by grammars). Also we only consider finite automata. The definitions of acceptors and generators for context-free languages and more general language classes have also been adapted to suit the case of infinite words (see for example [113, 36, 37, 38]), or the survey [165]. In the remainder of this chapter we will use ω-*automaton* synonymously for *finite ω-automaton*.

The usual definitions of deterministic and nondeterministic automata are adapted to the case of ω-input-words by the introduction of new acceptance conditions. For this purpose one introduces an "acceptance component" in the specification of automata, which will arise in different formats.

Definition 1.1. An ω-automaton is a quintuple $(Q, \Sigma, \delta, q_I, Acc)$, where Q is a finite set of states, Σ is a finite alphabet, $\delta : Q \times \Sigma \to 2^Q$ is the state transition function, $q_I \in Q$ is the initial state, and Acc is the **acceptance component**. In a deterministic ω-automaton, a transition function $\delta : Q \times \Sigma \to Q$ is used.

The acceptance component can be given as a set of states, as a set of state-sets, or as a function from the set of states to a finite set of natural numbers. Instances of all these case will be presented below.

Definition 1.2. Let $\mathcal{A} = (Q, \Sigma, \delta, q_I, Acc)$ be an ω-automaton. A **run** of $\mathcal{A}$ on an ω-word $\alpha = a_1 a_2 \cdots \in \Sigma^\omega$ is an infinite state sequence $\varrho = \varrho(0)\varrho(1)\varrho(2) \cdots \in Q^\omega$, such that the following conditions hold:

(1) $\varrho(0) = q_I$,
(2) $\varrho(i) \in \delta(\varrho(i-1), a_i)$ for $i \geq 1$ if $\mathcal{A}$ is nondeterministic,
     $\varrho(i) = \delta(\varrho(i-1), a_i)$ for $i \geq 1$ if $\mathcal{A}$ is deterministic.

With the different acceptance conditions defined in the following sections the question arises how they are related in expressive power, i.e. whether there exist transformations from one acceptance condition to another. If such transformations can be established another question naturally arises: what is the complexity for the respective translations?

The size of an automaton $\mathcal{A}$, denoted by $|\mathcal{A}|$, is measured by the number of its states, i.e. for $\mathcal{A} = (Q, \Sigma, \delta, q_I, Acc)$ the size is $|\mathcal{A}| = |Q|$. In addition to the number of states of an automaton the size of the acceptance condition is also of some importance for the efficiency of the transformation. This is usually measured by the number of designated sets or pairs of such. Details are given in the respective sections.

1.3 Nondeterministic Models

1.3.1 Büchi Acceptance

The Büchi acceptance condition has originally been introduced for nondeterministic ω-automata. In this case, the acceptance component is a set of states.

Definition 1.3. An ω-automaton $\mathcal{A} = (Q, \Sigma, \delta, q_I, F)$ with acceptance component $F \subseteq Q$ is called **Büchi automaton** if it is used with the following acceptance condition (**Büchi acceptance**): A word $\alpha \in \Sigma^\omega$ is accepted by $\mathcal{A}$ iff there exists a run ϱ of $\mathcal{A}$ on α satisfying the condition:

$$\mathrm{Inf}(\varrho) \cap F \neq \emptyset$$

i.e. at least one of the states in F has to be visited infinitely often during the run. $L(\mathcal{A}) := \{\alpha \in \Sigma^\omega \mid \mathcal{A} \text{ accepts } \alpha\}$ is the ω-language recognized by $\mathcal{A}$.

Example 1.4. Consider the ω-language L over the alphabet $\{a, b\}$ defined by

$$L := \{\alpha \in \{a, b\}^\omega \mid \alpha \text{ ends with } a^\omega \text{ or } \alpha \text{ ends with } (ab)^\omega\}.$$

L is recognized by the nondeterministic Büchi automaton given by the state transition diagram from Figure 1.1. The states from F are drawn with a double circle.

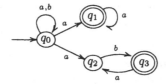

Fig. 1.1. A Büchi automaton accepting the words from $(a+b)^* a^\omega + (a+b)^* (ab)^\omega$

Consider a Büchi automaton $\mathcal{A} = (Q, \Sigma, \delta, q_I, F)$. Using this automaton with initial state p and final state q we obtain a regular language $W(p, q)$ of finite words. An ω-word α is accepted by $\mathcal{A}$ iff some run of $\mathcal{A}$ on α visits some final state $q \in F$ infinitely often. This is equivalent to $\alpha \in W(q_0, q) \cdot W(q, q)^\omega$. Taking the union over these sets for $q \in F$, we obtain the following representation result for Büchi recognizable ω-languages.

Theorem 1.5. *The Büchi recognizable ω-languages are the ω-languages of the form*

$$L = \bigcup_{i=1}^{k} U_i V_i^\omega \ \text{with}\ k \in \omega\ \text{and}\ U_i, V_i \in \text{REG}\ \text{for}\ i = 1, \dots, k$$

*This family of ω-languages is also called the $\boldsymbol{\omega}$-**Kleene closure** of the class of regular languages.*

From this remark one concludes immediately that each nonempty Büchi recognizable ω-language contains an ultimately periodic word.

Let us also note that the **emptiness problem** is decidable for Büchi automata, i.e. there exists an algorithm that decides whether the language recognized by an arbitrary (nondeterministic) Büchi automaton is empty. Given a Büchi automaton $\mathcal{A}$, one computes the set of reachable states, and for each reachable state q from F checks whether q is reachable from q by a nonempty path. Such a loop exists if and only if there exists an infinite word α and a run of $\mathcal{A}$ on α such that q is a recurring state in this run.

1.3.2   Muller Acceptance

The Muller acceptance condition refers to an acceptance component which is a set of state sets $\mathcal{F} \subseteq 2^Q$.

Definition 1.6. An ω-automaton $\mathcal{A} = (Q, \Sigma, \delta, q_I, \mathcal{F})$ with acceptance component $\mathcal{F} \subseteq 2^Q$ is called **Muller automaton** when used with the follwing acceptance condition (**Muller acceptance**): A word $\alpha \in \Sigma^\omega$ is accepted by $\mathcal{A}$ iff there exists a run ϱ of $\mathcal{A}$ on α satisfying the condition:

$$\text{Inf}(\varrho) \in \mathcal{F}$$

i.e. the set of infinitely recurring states of ϱ is exactly one of the sets in $\mathcal{F}$.

Example 1.7. Consider again the ω-language L over $\{a, b\}$ consisting of the ω-words which end with a^ω or with $(ab)^\omega$. The deterministic Muller automaton of Figure 1.2 recognizes L, where the acceptance component consists of the two sets $\{q_a\}$ and $\{q_a, q_b\}$.

We now verify that nondeterministic Büchi automata and nondeterministic Muller automata are equivalent in expressive power.

One direction is straightforward: for a Büchi automaton $\mathcal{A} = (Q, \Sigma, \delta, q_I, F)$ define the family $\mathcal{F}$ of sets of states by collecting all subsets of Q which contain a state from F.

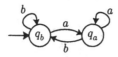

Fig. 1.2. A state transition diagram where the state q_a is reached after reading a and q_b after reading b.

Transformation 1.8. Let $\mathcal{A} = (Q, \Sigma, \delta, q_I, F)$ be a Büchi automaton. Define the Muller automaton $\mathcal{A}' = (Q, \Sigma, \delta, q_I, \mathcal{F})$ with $\mathcal{F} := \{G \in 2^Q \mid G \cap F \neq \emptyset\}$. Then $L(\mathcal{A}) = L(\mathcal{A}')$.

For the converse, a Muller automaton $\mathcal{A} = (Q, \Sigma, \delta, q_I, \mathcal{F})$ is given. The desired Büchi automaton $\mathcal{A}'$ simulates $\mathcal{A}$ and, in order to accept, it guesses the set $G \in \mathcal{F}$ which should turn out to be $\mathrm{Inf}(\varrho)$ for the run ϱ to be pursued. For checking that the guess is correct, $\mathcal{A}'$ makes another guess during the run, namely from which position onwards exactly the states from G will be seen again and again. This claim can be verified by accumulating the visited states in memory until the set G is complete, then resetting the memory to $\emptyset$ and starting accumulating again, and so on. If this reset occurs again and again (and no state outside G is visited), the automaton $\mathcal{A}'$ should accept. By declaring the "reset states" as accepting ones, we obtain the required Büchi automaton.

For an implementation of this idea, we work with the set Q of original states and introduce, for each set $G \in \mathcal{F}$, a separate copy of $Q \cap G$. We indicate such states with index G (and write q_G). The automaton $\mathcal{A}'$ does the two guesses at the same moment, at which time it switches from a state p of Q to a state from $q_G \in G$ and initializes the accumulation component to $\emptyset$. So the new states for the accepting set G will be from $G \times 2^G$, where (q_G, R) codes that q is the current state of $\mathcal{A}$ and R is the set of accumulated states since the last reset (where the R-value is $\emptyset$). So the set Q' of states of $\mathcal{A}'$ is

$$Q' = Q \cup \bigcup\nolimits_{G \in \mathcal{F}} (G \times 2^G)$$

and the set F' of final states of $\mathcal{A}'$ consists of the states $(q_G, \emptyset)$ for $G \in \mathcal{F}$. We do not give a formal definition of the transitions, which should be clear from the description above.

Transformation 1.9. Let $\mathcal{A} = (Q, \Sigma, \delta, q_I, \mathcal{F})$ be a Muller automaton. Define a Büchi automaton $\mathcal{A}' = (Q', \Sigma, \delta', q_I, F')$ with Q', δ', F' defined as described above. Then $L(\mathcal{A}) = L(\mathcal{A}')$.

If Q has n states and $\mathcal{F}$ contains m sets then $|Q'|$ has at most $n + mn2^n = 2^{O(n)}$ states. Summarizing, we obtain the following result.

Theorem 1.10. *A nondeterministic Büchi automaton with n states can be converted into an equivalent Muller automaton of equal size, and a nondeterministic Muller automaton with n states and m accepting sets can be transformed into an equivalent Büchi automaton with $\leq n + mn2^n$ states.*

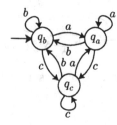

Fig. 1.3. A state diagram where q_x is reached after reading x.

The transformation sketched above transforms nondeterministic Büchi automata into nondeterministic Muller automata and conversely. For a given deterministic Büchi automaton the translation yields a deterministic Muller automaton. On the other hand, a deterministic Muller automaton is converted into a nondeterminsitic Büchi automaton. As we shall see later, this nondeterminism cannot in general be avoided.

1.3.3   Rabin and Streett Acceptance

The acceptance condition for Büchi automata is a positive condition on recurring states for the acceptance of ω-words. In Muller automata the specification by a set F is sharpened, because an accepting set F should contain precisely the recurring states (and not more). There are also formalisms specifying acceptance and rejection criteria separately. The Rabin condition – also called **pairs condition** – is such a condition.

The acceptance component is given by a finite family Ω of pairs (E_i, F_i) of designated state sets with the understanding that the sets E_i should be excluded from an accepting run after a finite initial segment, while at least one state in F_i has to be visited infinitely often.

Definition 1.11. An ω-automaton $\mathcal{A} = (Q, \Sigma, \delta, q_I, \Omega)$ with acceptrance component $\Omega = \{(E_1, F_1), \ldots, (E_k, F_k)\}$ with $E_i, F_i \subseteq Q$ is called **Rabin automaton** if it used with the following acceptance condition (**Rabin acceptance**): A word α is accepted by $\mathcal{A}$ if there exists a run ϱ of $\mathcal{A}$ on α such that

$$\exists (E, F) \in \Omega (\mathrm{In}(\varrho) \cap E = \emptyset) \wedge (\mathrm{Inf}(\varrho) \cap F \neq \emptyset).$$

Example 1.12. The Rabin automaton with state transition diagram from Figure 1.2 and Rabin condition $\Omega = \{(\{q_b\}, \{q_a\})\}$ accepts all words that consist of infinitely many a's but only finitely many b's.

To specify the language consisting of all words that contain infinitely many b's only if they also contain infinitely many a's with a Rabin automaton based on the state graph from Figure 1.2 we have to use $\Omega = \{(\emptyset, \{q_a\}), (\{q_a, q_b\}, \emptyset)\}$. This condition can be paraphrased by saying that each word in the accepted language has either infinitely many a's or it has neither infinitely many a's nor infinitely many b's. It is clear that in the latter case no ω-word can be accepted and the condition could be simplified to $\Omega = \{(\emptyset, \{q_a\})\}$. But in the presence of a third symbol and a third state as depicted in Figure 1.3 two pairs are needed, as the ω-word c^ω must be recognized: $\Omega = \{(\emptyset, \{q_a\}), (\{q_a, q_b\}, \{q_c\})\}$.

The Streett condition is dual to the Rabin condition. It is therefore sometimes called **complemented pair condition**. It can be viewed as a **fairness condition** meaning that for each pair $(E, F) \in \Omega$, if some state from F is visited infinitely often, there has to be a state from E that is also visited infinitely often during an accepting run.

Definition 1.13. An ω-automaton $\mathcal{A} = (Q, \Sigma, \delta, q_I, \Omega)$ with acceptance component $\Omega = \{(E_1, F_1), \ldots, (E_k, F_k)\}$ with $E_i, F_i \subseteq Q$ is called **Streett automaton** if it is used with the following acceptance condition (**Streett acceptance**): A word α is accepted by $\mathcal{A}$ if there exists a run ϱ of $\mathcal{A}$ on α such that

$$\forall (E, F) \in \Omega . (\operatorname{Inf}(\varrho) \cap E \neq \emptyset) \vee (\operatorname{Inf}(\varrho) \cap F = \emptyset)$$

(equivalently: if $\operatorname{Inf}(\varrho) \cap F \neq \emptyset$ then $\operatorname{Inf}(\varrho) \cap E \neq \emptyset$).

Example 1.14. Let $\Sigma = \{a, b\}$. The language consisting of all words that contain infinitely many a's if they contain infinitely many b's can be recognized by a Streett automaton with the state graph from Figure 1.2. The condition can be paraphrased as $|\alpha|_b \neq \omega \vee |\alpha|_a = \omega$, i.e. $|\alpha|_b = \omega \Rightarrow |\alpha|_a = \omega$. In the automaton of Figure 1.2 the two states q_a and q_b indicate that respectively symbol a or b has been read in the previous step. The appropriate Streett automaton is obtained by taking as acceptance component the set $\Omega = \{(\{q_a\}, \{q_b\})\}$.

Rabin automata and Streett automata are transformed into Muller automata by simply gathering all state sets that satisfy the Rabin condition, respectively Streett condition, into a Muller acceptance set.

Transformation 1.15. Let $\mathcal{A} = (Q, \Sigma, \delta, q_I, \Omega)$ be a Rabin automaton, respectively Streett automaton. Define a Muller automaton $\mathcal{A}' = (Q, \Sigma, \delta, q_I, \mathcal{F})$ with $\mathcal{F} := \{G \in 2^Q \mid \exists (E, F) \in \Omega . G \cap E = \emptyset \wedge G \cap F \neq \emptyset\}$, respectively with $\mathcal{F} := \{G \in 2^Q \mid \forall (E, F) \in \Omega . G \cap E \neq \emptyset \vee G \cap F = \emptyset\}$. Then $L(\mathcal{A}) = L(\mathcal{A}')$.

For the converse it suffices to invoke the transformation of Muller automata into Büchi automata, as in the preceding subsection, and to observe that Büchi acceptance can be viewed as a special case of Rabin acceptance (for the set F of final states take $\Omega = \{(\emptyset, F)\}$), as well as a special case of Streett condition (for the set F of final states take $\Omega = \{(F, Q)\}$).

1.3.4 The Parity Condition

The parity condition amounts to the Rabin condition for the special case where the accepting pairs $(E_1, F_1), \ldots, (E_m, F_m)$ form a chain with respect to set inclusion. We consider the case of an increasing chain $E_1 \subset F_1 \subset E_2 \subset \ldots E_m \subset F_m$.

Let us associate indices (called colours) with states as follows: states of E_1 receive colour 1, states of $F_1 \setminus E_1$ receive colour 2, and so on with the rule that states of $E_i \setminus F_{i-1}$ have colour $2i - 1$ and states of $F_i \setminus E_i$ have colour $2i$. An ω-word α is then accepted by the Rabin automaton iff the least colour occurring infinitely often in a run on α is even (hence the term "parity condition").

Definition 1.16. An ω-automaton $\mathcal{A} = (Q, \Sigma, \delta, q_I, c)$ with acceptance component $c : Q \to \{1, \dots, k\}$ (where $k \in \omega$) is called **parity automaton** if it is used with the following acceptance condition (**parity condition**): An ω-word $\alpha \in \Sigma^\omega$ is accepted by $\mathcal{A}$ iff there exists a run ϱ of $\mathcal{A}$ on α with

$$\min\{c(q) \mid q \in \mathrm{Inf}(\varrho)\} \text{ is even}$$

Sometimes it is more convenient to work with the condition that the maximal colour occurring infinitely often in the run under consideration is even. This applies to some constructions in later chapters of this book.

Example 1.17. Consider the parity automaton from Figure 1.4 with colouring function c defined by $c(q_i) = i$.

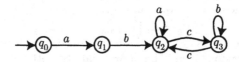

Fig. 1.4. Another ω-automaton

It accepts the ω-words with start with ab, continue by a finite sequence of segments in a^*cb^*c, and end with a^ω; so $L(\mathcal{A}) = ab(a^*cb^*c)^*a^\omega$. For the parity automaton $\mathcal{A}'$ with the same transition graph but colouring c' defined by $c'(q_i) = i + 1$ we obtain $L(\mathcal{A}') = ab(a^*cb^*c)^*b^\omega \vee ab(a^*cb^*c)^\omega$.

It is obvious how a parity condition is cast into the form of a Rabin condition.

Transformation 1.18. Let $\mathcal{A} = (Q, \Sigma, \delta, q_I, c)$ be an ω-automaton be a parity automaton with $c : Q \to \{0, \dots, k\}$. An equivalent Rabin automaton $\mathcal{A}' = (Q, \Sigma, \delta, q_I, \Omega)$ has the acceptance component $\Omega := \{(E_0, F_0), \dots, (E_r, F_r)\}$ with $r := \lfloor \frac{k}{2} \rfloor$, $E_i := \{q \in Q \mid c(q) < 2i\}$ and $F_i := \{q \in Q \mid c(q) \le 2i\}$.

1.3.5   Discussion

The equivalence results obtained above can be summarized as follows:

Theorem 1.19. (1) *Nondeterministic Büchi automata, Muller automata, Rabin automata, Streett automata, and parity automata are all equivalent in expressive power, i.e. they recognize the same ω-languages.*

(2) *The ω-languages recognized by these ω-automata form the class ω-KC(REG),*
   i.e. the ω-Kleene closure of the class of regular languages.

The ω-languages in this class are commonly referred to as the regular ω-languages, denoted by ω-REG.

At this point two fundamental questions arise.

- Are there types of *deterministic* ω-automata which recognize precisely the ω-languages in ω-REG?
- Is the class ω-REG closed under complementation?

Both questions can be answered affirmatively; and both involve tedious work.

The complementation problem can be attacked via several approaches (see Chapter 4 below). One possibility is to work with deterministic ω-automata and thus use a reduction to the determinization problem.

1.4   Deterministic Models

In Chapter 3 below, it will be shown that deterministic Muller automata recognize precisely the regular ω-languages. In the present section, we discuss the relation between deterministic Muller automata and other deterministic ω-automata, and also give some remarks on the complementation problem. We shall see that deterministic Muller automata, Rabin automata, Streett automata, and parity automata are all equivalent in expressive power. Note that the equivalence proof given above for the nondeterministic case cannot be copied: We proceeded via nondeterministic Büchi automata and thus, even from deterministic Muller automata, would obtain nondeterministic Rabin, Streett, and parity automata. As we now verify, we cannot in general sharpen the construction of a Büchi automaton to obtain a deterministic one.

1.4.1   The Büchi Condition for Deterministic ω-Automata

Let us see that Büchi automata are too weak to recognize even very simple ω-languages from ω-REG. The Büchi automaton depicted in Figure 1.5 with $F = \{q_1\}$ accepts those ω-words over the alphabet $\{a, b\}$ that have only finitely many b's.

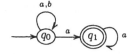

Fig. 1.5. An automaton recognizing $(a+b)a^\omega$

It is easy to provide an equivalent deterministic Muller automaton, using two states q_a, q_b which are visited after reading a, b, respectively, and declaring

$\mathcal{F} = \{\{q_a\}\}$ as acceptance component (see Figure 1.2). Then a run is accepting iff it ends by a sequence consisting of state q_a only, which means that the input word ends with a^ω.

If one would work with the Büchi acceptance condition, using a set F of accepting states, then one has a specification of states which should be visited infinitely often, but it is not directly possible to specify which states should be seen only finitely often.

The argument which shows that deterministic Büchi automata are too weak for recognizing $L = (a + b)^*b^\omega$ works by contradiction: Assuming that the deterministic Büchi automaton $\mathcal{A}$ with final state set F recognizes L, it will on input b^ω visit an F-state after a finite prefix, say after the n_0-th letter. It will also accept $b^{n_0}ab^\omega$, visiting F-states infinitely often and hence after the a, say when finishing the prefix $b^{n_0}ab^{n_1}$. Continuing this construction the ω-word $b^{n_0}ab^{n_1}ab^{n_2}a\ldots$ is generated which causes $\mathcal{A}$ to pass through an F-state before each letter a but which should of course be rejected.

1.4.2   Transforming Muller Automata to Rabin Automata

Let us now show that deterministic Muller automata, Rabin automata, Streett automata, and parity automata all have the same expressive power. We show first the crucial step, namely that deterministic Muller automata can be transformed into deterministic Rabin automata.

We use a technique called **latest appearance record** (LAR). The idea is to use permutations of the states of the given Muller automaton as new states, extended by a **hit position**. So the memory of the new automaton stores *lists* of states from the original automaton; this is in contrast to the construction of Theorem 1.10 which produced a nondeterministic Büchi automaton from a Muller automaton; in that case we stored *sets* of states of the original automaton in the memory of the constructed one.

In a list of (distinct) states, we use the last entry for the current state in the run on the given Muller automaton. The hit position (the position of the marker ♮) indicates where the last change occurred in the record. For every transition from one state p to q in the original automaton, the state q is moved to the last position of the record while the symbols which were to the right of q are shifted one position to the left (so the previous place of q is filled again). The marker is inserted in front of the position where q was taken from. So the positions before the marker are untouched by the transition under consideration.

Transformation 1.20. Let $\mathcal{A} = (\Sigma, Q, \delta, q_I, \mathcal{F})$ be a deterministic Muller automaton. Assume w.l.o.g. that $Q = \{1, \ldots, k\}$ and $q_I = 1$. Let ♮ be a new symbol, i.e. ♮ $\notin Q$.

An equivalent Rabin automaton $\mathcal{A}'$ is given by the following definition:

- $\widetilde{Q}$ is the set of all order vector words with hit position over Q, i.e.

$$\widetilde{Q} := \{w \in (Q \cup \{♮\})^* \mid \forall q \in Q \cup \{♮\} . |w|_q = 1\}$$

- The initial state is $q_I' := \natural k \ldots 1$.
- The transition function δ' is constructed as follows: Assume $i, i' \in Q$, $a \in \Sigma$, and $\delta(i, a) = i'$. Then δ' is defined for any word $m_1 \ldots m_r \natural m_{r+1} \ldots m_k \in \tilde{Q}$ with $m_k = i$. Supposing that $i' = m_s$, define

$$\delta'(m_1 \ldots m_r \natural m_{r+1} \ldots m_k, a) := (m_1 \ldots m_{s-1} \natural m_{s+1} \ldots m_k i').$$

- The acceptance component is given by $\Omega = \{(E_1, F_1), \ldots, (E_k, F_k)\}$, defined as follows:
  - $E_j := \{u \natural v \mid |u| < j\}$
  - $F_j := \{u \natural v \mid |u| < j\} \cup \{u \natural v \mid |u| = j \wedge \{m \in Q \mid m \sqsubseteq v\} \in \mathcal{F}\}$.

Here the infix relation $m \sqsubseteq v$ should be read as "m occurs in v", since m is a single letter.

Consider a run of the Muller automaton $\mathcal{A}$, where the set of infinitely often visited states is, say, $J = \{m_1, \ldots, m_j\}$ This means that in the corresponding run of the Rabin automaton $\mathcal{A}'$, the states of $Q \setminus J$ will eventually reach the first positions and then stay indefinitely in front of the marker. So finally the $\mathcal{A}'$-states will be of the form $u \natural v$ where the $(Q \setminus J)$-elements occur at the beginning of u (or constitute the whole word u). Hence, eventually we will constantly have $|u| \geq |Q \setminus J|$, in other words $|v| \leq |J| = j$. Clearly infinitely often we have $|v| = |J| = j$, since otherwise, from some point onwards we would have $|v| < j$ and thus less than j states would be visited infinitely often.

So infinitely often a state $u \natural v$ with $|v| = j$ is seen but only finitely often a state with $v > j$. Moreover, the states which constitute the word v in the first case $|v| = j$ form precisely the set J.

We can summarize this as follows:

Lemma 1.21. *Let ϱ be an infinite run of the deterministic Muller automaton $\mathcal{A}$ with state set $Q = \{1, \ldots, k\}$ and let $u_0 \natural v_0, u_1 \natural v_1, u_2 \natural v_2, \ldots$ be the corresponding sequence of order vectors with hit, according to Transformation 1.20. Then $\mathrm{Inf}(\varrho) = J$ with $|J| = j$ iff the following conditions hold:*

- *for only finitely many i we have $|v_i| > j$ (and hence $|u_i| \leq k - j$)*
- *for infinitely many i we have $|v_i| = j$ (and hence $|u_i| = k - j$) and $J = \{m \in Q \mid m \sqsubseteq v_i\}$.*

The Muller automaton $\mathcal{A}$ accepts by the run ϱ if the set J considered in the Lemma belongs to $\mathcal{F}$. This means that the run will infinitely often visit a state in the defined set F_{k-j} but only finitely often visit states $u \natural v$ with $|u| < k - j$, i.e. states from E_{k-j}. So the Rabin condition of $\mathcal{A}'$ is satisfied and $\mathcal{A}'$ accepts in this case. The converse implication ("if $\mathcal{A}'$ accepts an input word, then $\mathcal{A}$ does") is shown analogously.

From the definition of the sets E_j, F_j we see that they are arranged in a chain: $E_1 \subseteq F_1 \subseteq E_2 \ldots \subseteq E_k \subseteq F_k$. We can shorten the chain by admitting only pairs where $E_j \neq F_j$, without altering the set of accepting runs. Then we are left with a strictly increasing chain of sets, and thus have defined an ω-automaton which is presentable as a parity automaton.

Altogether we obtain the following result:

Theorem 1.22. *By Transformation 1.20, a deterministic Muller automaton with n states is transformed into a deterministic Rabin automaton with $n \cdot n!$ states and n accepting pairs, and also into a deterministic parity automaton with $n \cdot n!$ states and $2n$ colours.*

Transformation 1.20 is given here for deterministic automata, but it works analogously for nondeterministic automata.

In order to cover also Streett automata it is useful to look at the complementation of ω-languages. Note that the negation of the Rabin acceptance condition

$$(*) \quad \exists (E, F) \in \Omega \ (\mathrm{Inf}(\varrho) \cap E = \emptyset) \wedge (\mathrm{Inf}(\varrho) \cap F \neq \emptyset).$$

is equivalent to the Streett condition:

$$(**) \quad \forall (E, F) \in \Omega \ (\mathrm{Inf}(\varrho) \cap E \neq \emptyset) \vee (\mathrm{Inf}(\varrho) \cap F = \emptyset)$$

Hence, when we transform a deterministic Rabin automaton recognizing L into a Streett automaton by keeping all its components, including the acceptance component, but using it in the form $(**)$ instead of $(*)$, then the resulting Streett automaton recognizes the complement of L.

We can transform a deterministic Rabin automaton into an equivalent Streett automaton by a detour through Muller automata. Namely, the complement of an ω-language recognized by a deterministic Muller automaton is accepted by the same automaton up to the set of designated state sets; this set $\mathcal{F}$ has to be replaced by its complement w.r.t. the set of states Q of the automaton.

Transformation 1.23. Let $\mathcal{A} = (Q, \Sigma, \delta, q_I, \mathcal{F})$ be a deterministic Muller aurtomaton. Then the Muller automaton $\mathcal{A}' := (Q, \Sigma, \delta, q_I, 2^Q \setminus \mathcal{F})$ recognizes the complement of $L(\mathcal{A})$.

Now we can transform a deterministic Rabin automaton $\mathcal{A}$ into a deterministic Streett automaton as follows: From $\mathcal{A}$ construct an equivalent Muller automaton, by copying Transformation 1.15 for the deterministic case. Complement the Muller automaton, and then apply Transformation 1.20 to obatain a Rabin automaton $\mathcal{A}'$ recognizing the compelement of L. Used as a Streett automaton, $\mathcal{A}'$ recognizes L, as desired.

The converse transformation from Streett to Rabin automata works analogously.

As a consequence of the previous constructions we note the following:

Theorem 1.24. *Deterministic Muller automata, Rabin automata, Streett automata, and parity automata recognize the same ω-languages, and the class of ω-languages recognized by any of these types of ω-automata is closed under complementation.*

In this result, the complementation of parity automata would work as follows: Write the parity condition as a Rabin condition, define the complement by reading it as a Streett condition, pass to an equivalent Muller automaton, and obtain from it an equivalent Rabin automaton by Transformation 1.20. This is simplified considerably by the direct approach, which applies the idea of exchanging even and odd colours.

For showing that the complement of a language accepted by an ω-automaton with parity condition is also acceptable by a parity automaton, the colour function has to be modified such that henceforth every word previously not accepted has even parity in its minimal colour value and uneven parity for all previously accepted words.

Transformation 1.25. Let $\mathcal{A} = (Q, \Sigma, \delta, q_I, c)$ be a deterministic ω-automaton with parity condition. Then the complement of $L(\mathcal{A})$ is recognized by the parity automaton $\mathcal{A}' := (Q, \Sigma, \delta, q_I, c')$ where $c'(q) = c(q) + 1$.

So the complementation process is easy (and does not affect the number of states of the automata) if we deal with deterministic Muller or parity automata. For Rabin and Streett automata, the constructions above involve a blow-up of $2^{O(n \log n)}$ (the growth-rate of $n \cdot n!$ as it appears in the LAR construction of Transformation 1.20). The same applies to the transformation of Rabin into Streett automata and conversely. In the next section we will see that this blow-up is not avoidable.

Before turning to these lower bound results, we note a fact about accepting runs of Rabin and Streett automata which will be used there.

Lemma 1.26. *Let $\mathcal{A} = (Q, \Sigma, \delta, q_I, \Omega)$ be an ω-automaton with Rabin condition, and assume ϱ_1, ϱ_2 are two nonaccepting runs. Then any run ϱ with $\mathrm{Inf}(\varrho) = \mathrm{Inf}(\varrho_1) \cup \mathrm{Inf}(\varrho_2)$ is also non-accepting.*

For the proof assume that ϱ_1, ϱ_2 are non-accepting but ϱ with $\mathrm{Inf}(\varrho) = \mathrm{Inf}(\varrho_1) \cup \mathrm{Inf}(\varrho_2)$ is accepting. Then for some accepting pair (E, F) we have $\mathrm{Inf}(\varrho) \cap E = \emptyset$ and $\mathrm{Inf}(\varrho) \cap F \neq \emptyset$. By $\mathrm{Inf}(\varrho) = \mathrm{Inf}(\varrho_1) \cup \mathrm{In}(\varrho_2)$ we must have $\mathrm{Inf}(\varrho_1) \cap E = \mathrm{Inf}(\varrho_2) \cap E = \emptyset$, and also $\mathrm{Inf}(\varrho_1) \cap F \neq \emptyset$ or $\mathrm{Inf}(\varrho_2) \cap F \neq \emptyset$. So one of the two runs ϱ_i would be accepting, contradicting the assumption.

By duality, we obtain the following:

Lemma 1.27. *Let $\mathcal{A} = (Q, \Sigma, \delta, q_I, \Omega)$ be a Streett automaton, and assume ϱ_1, ϱ_2 are two accepting runs. Then any run ϱ with $\mathrm{Inf}(\varrho) = \mathrm{Inf}(\varrho_1) \cup \mathrm{Inf}(\varrho_2)$ is also accepting.*

1.5 Two Lower Bounds

In this section we establish two lower bounds of rate $2^{O(n \log n)}$ for the transformation of ω-automata:

(1) from nondeterministic Büchi automata to deterministic Rabin automata,
(2) from deterministic Streett to deterministic Rabin automata.

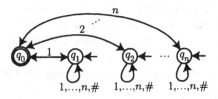

Fig. 1.6. Nondeterministic Büchi automaton $\mathcal{A}_n$

The first lower bound will useful in Chapter 3, where a transformation from Büchi automata to deterministic Rabin automata is presented, using the construction of Safra [158]. The lower bound will show that Safra's construction is optimal.

The second lower bound is of interest in connection with the conversion of Streett automata into Rabin automata (or conversely) presented above. The lower bound result will be taken up again in Chapter 5, where Streett automata are studied in more depth.

1.5.1 From Büchi Acceptance to Rabin Acceptance

The proof idea of the present section is due to Michel [128]. We follow the presentation as given by Löding in [114].

In order to keep the representation of nondeterministic automata small, a set of initial states is used in the examples that follow. It is obvious that the automata can be presented in the usual format by adding just one state and adding arcs from this new state for each arc leaving an initial state of the given automaton.

Example 1.28. Consider the family of Büchi automata from Figure 1.6. This family of automata $(\mathcal{A}_n)_{n \geq 2}$ is defined over the alphabets $\{1, \ldots, n, \#\}$ respectively. (The constraint $n \geq 2$ is introduced for the proof of Lemma 1.29 where two different permutations of symbols from $\{1, \ldots, n\}$ are assumed to exist.)

The languages L_n accepted by these automata can be characterised by the condition: A word α is accepted by $\mathcal{A}_n$ iff there exists k and $i_1, \ldots, i_k \in \{1, \ldots, n\}$ such that each pair $i_j i_{j+1}$ for $j < k$ and $i_k i_1$ appears infinitely often in α. We encode the symbols $1, \ldots, n$ by words over $\{0, 1\}^*$ such that

$$i \text{ is encoded by } \begin{cases} 0^i 1 & \text{if } i < n, \\ 0^i 0^* 1 & \text{if } i = n \end{cases}$$

furthermore we keep $\#$ unaltered. Now we can specify the same family of languages w.r.t. the encoding by the family of automata $(\mathcal{A}'_n)_{n \geq 2}$ over the fixed alphabet $\{0, 1, \#\}$. The size of $\mathcal{A}_n$ (in either of the two versions) is $\mathcal{O}(n)$.

The family of automata from the previous example can be used to prove the following lemma.

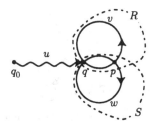

Fig. 1.7. An accepting run of $\mathcal{A}'$

Lemma 1.29. *There exists a family of languages* $(L_n)_{n\geq 2}$ *over the alphabet* $\{0, 1, \#\}$ *recognizable by nondeterministic Büchi automata of size* $O(n)$ *such that any nondeterministic Streett automaton accepting the complement language of* L_n *has at least* $n!$ *states.*

Proof ([114]). Let $n \in \omega$ and $(i_1, \ldots, i_n)$, $(j_1, \ldots, j_n)$ be different permutations of $\{1, \ldots, n\}$. It is clear from the definition of the Büchi automaton $\mathcal{A}_n$ from the previous example that the words $\alpha := (i_1 \ldots i_n \#)^\omega$ and $\beta := (j_1 \ldots j_n \#)^\omega$ are not accepted by $\mathcal{A}_n$. Hence, α and β belong to the complement language $L' := \{1, \ldots, n, \#\}^\omega \setminus L(\mathcal{A}_n)$.

This means that for any Streett automaton $\mathcal{A}'$ accepting $L(\mathcal{A}') = L'$ there have to exist accepting runs ϱ_α and ϱ_β with $R := \mathrm{Inf}\,\varrho_\alpha$ and $S := \mathrm{Inf}\,\varrho_\beta$. Due to the Streett condition of $\mathcal{A}'$ it is sufficient to show that $R \cap S = \emptyset$, as there are $n!$ permutations of $\{1, \ldots, n\}$, thus, leading to an automaton with no less than $n!$ states.

Now, assume on the contrary that there is some state $q \in R \cap S$. Then there has to exist an accepting run ϱ_γ of $\mathcal{A}'$ on a word $\gamma = u(vw)^\omega$ such that u is a subword read on some path from the initial state of $\mathcal{A}$ to the state q and v and w are words read on paths from q to q cycling only through states from R and S respectively. Suppose the infix v of α is given by $i_0, \ldots, i_k \in \{1, \ldots, n\}$ and similarly $w = j_0, \ldots, j_l \in \{1, \ldots, n\}$. This situation is depicted in Figure 1.7.

Since $\alpha \neq \beta$ there has to exist an index in which the two words differ. Let m be the least of such indices, i.e. $\forall x . x < m \rightarrow i_x = j_x$ and $i_m \neq j_m$. But now there have to exist indices $k', l' > m$ such that $j_m = i_{k'}$ and $i_m = j_{l'}$. This leads to a sequence $i_m, \ldots, i_{m+1}, \ldots, i_{m'-1}, i_{m'} j_m, j_{m+1}, \ldots, j_{l'-1}, j_{l'}$ satisfying the characterisation of the words in $L(\mathcal{A}_n)$. So $\gamma \in L(\mathcal{A}_n)$.

We now show that $\mathcal{A}'$ also accepts γ, which contradicts the assumption $L(\mathcal{A}') = \{1, \ldots, n, \#\}^\omega \setminus L(\mathcal{A}_n)$. Namely, for the run ρ_γ we know that $\mathrm{Inf}(\rho_\gamma) = \mathrm{Inf}(\rho_\alpha) \cup \mathrm{Inf}(\rho_\beta)$. Hence, by Lemma 1.27, the $\mathcal{A}'$-run ρ_γ is accepting.

By the duality of Rabin and Streett conditions it is obvious that if there exists an ω-automaton of size less than $n!$ with Rabin condition that accepts L_n then there also exists a deterministic Streett automaton that accepts the complement language $\Sigma_n^\omega \setminus L_n$ with less than $n!$ states. Thus from Lemma 1.29 we conclude the following theorem.

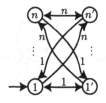

Fig. 1.8. Deterministic Streett automaton $\mathcal{A}_n$

Theorem 1.30. *There exists a family of languages $(L_n)_{n\geq 2}$ over the alphabet $\{0,1,\#\}$ recognizable by nondeterministic Büchi automata of size $O(n)$ such that any equivalent deterministic Rabin automaton must be of size $n!$ or larger.*

1.5.2 A Lower Bound for the Transformation of Deterministic Streett Automata to Deterministic Rabin Automata

The technique of latest appearance records is used for the transformation of various automata into parity automata. Two variants are studied in the literature: state appearance records and index appearance records.

State appearance records have been introduced in Section 1.4.2 for the transformation of Muller automata into Rabin automata. Löding [114] shows that any transformation of a deterministic Streett automaton of size n with r pairs of designated sets into a deterministic Rabin automaton will result in an automaton where the number of states is a factorial in $\min(n, r)$, and by the fact that parity automata are special cases of Rabin automata, a transformation to a parity condition will result in an automaton with at least $\min(n, r)!$ states and $O(r)$ colours. Since the automata used in the proof consist of n states and n pairs, this also proves the optimality of the best known transformation from Muller automata to automata with parity condition.

Due to the duality of Rabin and Streett conditions the result is transferrable to the case with Rabin condition and Streett condition interchanged.

Index appearance records (IAR) are used for example by Safra [159] for the transformation of nondeterministic Streett automata into deterministic Rabin automata. The transformation, to be presented in full detail in Chapter 5 below, takes a deterministic Streett automaton of size n with an acceptance condition consisting of r pairs of designated sets to an equivalent deterministic Rabin automaton of size $nO(r)!$ that uses $O(r)$ accepting pairs.

By Theorem 1.32 we obtain the optimality of the IAR construction. The following example gives the family of automata on which the proof is based.

Example 1.31. Consider the family of deterministic Streett automata $(\mathcal{A}_n)_{n\geq 2}$ from Figure 1.8 with pairs of designated state sets $\Omega_n = \{(E_1, F_1), \ldots, (E_n, F_n)\}$ and $E_i = \{i\}$, $F_i = \{i'\}$.

The language accepted by the automaton $\mathcal{A}_n$ can be characterised by the symbols occurring in odd and even positions of the accepted words. Each word

α in $L(\mathcal{A}_n)$ satisfies the condition that each symbol occurring infinitely often in an odd position must also occur infinitely often in an even position of α.

This family of automata $(\mathcal{A}_n)_{n \geq 2}$ is defined over the alphabets $\{1, \ldots, n\}$, respectively. By encoding the symbols $1, \ldots, n$ by words over $\{0, 1\}^*$ such that

$$i \text{ is encoded by } \begin{cases} 0^i 1 & \text{if } i < n, \\ 0^i 0^* 1 & \text{if } i = n \end{cases}$$

we can specify the same family of languages w.r.t. the encoding by the family of automata $(\mathcal{A}'_n)_{n \geq 2}$ over the fixed alphabet $\{0, 1\}$. The construction is similar to that in Section 1.5.1.

Theorem 1.32 ([114]). *There exists a family of languages $(L_n)_{n \geq 2}$ over the alphabet $\{0, 1\}$ recognizable by deterministic Streett automata with $O(n)$ states and $O(n)$ pairs of designated state sets such that any deterministic Rabin automaton accepting L_n requires at least $n!$ states.*

Proof. The idea for proving Theorem 1.32 is motivated by the observation that for any finite word $u \in \{1, \ldots, n\}^*$ of even length, the word $u\alpha$ is accepted by $\mathcal{A}_n$ iff α is accepted by $\mathcal{A}_n$. It can be shown by induction over n that any deterministic Rabin automaton accepting $L(\mathcal{A}_n)$ must have at least $n!$ states.

The base case for the induction is obvious: Any (Rabin) automaton accepting a proper subset of the infinite words over a 2-letter alphabet with some word having occurrences of both letters needs at least two states.

The induction step relies on the fact that any given deterministic Rabin automaton $\mathcal{A}$ accepting $L(\mathcal{A}_n)$ can be modified to a deterministic automaton over $\{1, \ldots, n\} \setminus \{i\}$ for any $i \in \{1, \ldots, n\}$ by simply removing all arcs labelled by i. Setting the initial state of the modified automaton to any q that is reachable in $\mathcal{A}_n$ by an even number of state transitions we obtain a deterministic Rabin automaton $\mathcal{A}_i^q$.

Because of the characterisation of $L(\mathcal{A}_n)$ given above, it is clear that $\mathcal{A}_i^q$ accepts a language isomorphic up to the renaming of symbols to $L(\mathcal{A}_{n-1})$. The induction hypothesis requires the automaton $\mathcal{A}_i^q$ to have at least $(n-1)!$ states.

For a complete proof the reader is referred to [114].

1.6 Weak Acceptance Conditions

In the previous sections we have defined acceptance by a reference to those states in a run whcich occur infinitely often. For some purposes a "weak acceptance condition" is appropriate. This is a condition on the set of states that occur at least once (but maybe only finitely often) in a run. Recall that

$$\text{Occ}(\varrho) := \{q \in Q \mid |\varrho^{-1}(q)| \geq 1\}$$

is the set of states that occur at least once in the run ϱ. Let $\mathcal{A} = (Q, \Sigma, \delta, q_I, \text{Acc})$ be an ω-automaton.

There are different possibilities to use the set $\mathrm{Occ}(\varrho)$ for acceptance. The analogue to the Muller condition, introduced by Staiger and Wagner [166], uses a family $\mathcal{F}$ of state sets and declares the run ϱ accepting if

$$\mathrm{Occ}(\varrho) \in \mathcal{F}.$$

Other acceptance modes refer to a set F of designated states and require

$$\mathrm{Occ}(\varrho) \cap F \neq \emptyset,$$

(also called 1-acceptance, following [110]), and

$$\mathrm{Occ}(\varrho) \subseteq F,$$

also called $1'$-acceptance.

These acceptance modes are special cases of Staiger-Wagner acceptance. In the first case one collects in $\mathcal{F}$ all sets X with $X \cap F \neq \emptyset$, in the second case the sets X with $X \subseteq F$.

Example 1.33. To accept the ω-words over the alphabet $\{a, b\}$ that have at least one symbol a, we take an automaton $\mathcal{A} = (\{q_a, q_b\}, \{a, b\}, \delta, q_b, F)$, where $F = \{q_a\}$, δ is defined according to the state transition graph of Figure 1.2, and 1-acceptance is used.

The requirement that only the word b^ω should be accepted can be specified with the same transition graph, now with $1'$-acceptance using the set $F = \{q_b\}$. i.e. the only state that may be visited in any successful run is q_b.

In later chapters of the book also the parity condition will be used in the weak sense. The requirement for acceptance is that the minimal (or maximal) colour occurring in a run is even.

We show that acceptance by an occurrence set can be simulated by Büchi acceptance. The idea is to simulate $\mathcal{A}$ and to accumulate the visited states in a separate component of the state, signalling acceptance whenever this component is a set from $\mathcal{F}$.

Transformation 1.34. Let $\mathcal{A} = (Q, \Sigma, \delta, q_I, \mathcal{F})$. The language $L(\mathcal{A})$ recognized by $\mathcal{A}$ with the Staiger-Wagner acceptance condition is recognized by a Büchi automaton $\mathcal{A}' = (Q \times 2^Q, \Sigma, \delta', (q_I, \{q_I\}), F')$ where $\delta'((p, P), a)$ contains all states (p', P') with $p' \in \delta(p)$ and $P' = P \cup \{p'\}$, and where F' contains all states (p, P) with $P \in \mathcal{F}$.

The exponential blow-up can be avoided if only 1-acceptance or $1'$-acceptance are involved. In order to capture 1-acceptance via a set F by Büchi acceptance, one introduces a transition from each F-state to a new state q_f, with a transition back to q_f, which serves as only final state in the Büchi automaton. For $1'$-acceptance, it suffices to take the given automaton and use it as a Büchi automaton (with the same set of designated states).

The reverse transformations are not possible; it should be obvious that an infinity condition in the definition of an ω-language cannot in general be simulated by an occurrence condition. For example, the set L of ω-words over $\{a, b\}$ with infinitely many b is not recognizable by an ω-automaton with Staiger-Wagner acceptance. Assuming such an automaton which recognizes L, say with n states, one would consider an accepting run on the input word $(a^{n+1}b)^{\omega}$. After some finite prefix, say after $(a^{n+1}b)^{k}$, the run would have visited the states which are visited at all. In the succeeding block a^{n+1} the automaton assumes a loop, which can be repeated if the input is changed to $(a^{n+1}b)^{k}a^{\omega}$. So over this input the same states would be visited as in the considered run over $(a^{n+1}b)^{\omega}$. Hence $(a^{n+1}b)^{k}a^{\omega}$ would be accepted, a contradiction.

1.7 Conclusion

We have shown the expressive equivalence of

- nondeterministic Büchi, Muller, Rabin, Streett, and parity automata
- deterministic Muller, Rabin, Streett, and parity automata

The missing link will be provided in Chapter 3 below: Nondeterministic Büchi automata accept the same ω-languages as deterministic Muller automata.

Figure 1.9 gives an overview; it shows the dependencies and known bounds for transformations between different models (including results that are shown in Part II of the book).

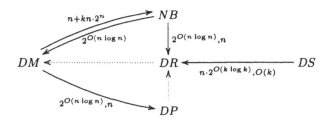

Fig. 1.9. An overview of transformation bounds for ω-automata.

We indicate by D and N the deterministic, respectively, nondeterministic versions and write B, M, R, S for Büchi, Muller, Rabin, Streett, respectively. The noted complexity bounds are given as pairs (n', k') where n' is the size of the constructed automaton and k' the size of the acceptance component, relative to the original sizes (n is the original number of states and k the size of the original acceptance component). Dotted arrows are used for trivial transformations.

2   Infinite Games

René Mazala

Institut für Informatik
Martin-Luther-Universität Halle-Wittenberg

2.1   Introduction

This chapter is meant as an introduction to infinite two-person games on directed
graphs. We will define what they are, how they are played, what exactly a
strategy is, what we mean when we say a game is won by a certain player, etc.
We will introduce fundamental notions such as determinacy, forgetful strategies,
memoryless strategies, and so on. And we will state fundamental results, which
will be proved in later chapters.

2.2   Games

A game is composed of an arena and a winning condition. We will first study
arenas and then add winning conditions on top of arenas.

2.2.1   Arenas

An **arena** is a triple

$$\mathcal{A} = (V_0, V_1, E) \tag{2.1}$$

where V_0 is a set of **0-vertices**, V_1 a set of **1-vertices**, disjoint from V_0, and
$E \subseteq (V_0 \cup V_1) \times (V_0 \cup V_1)$ is the **edge relation,** sometimes also called the set
of moves. The union of V_0 and V_1 is denoted V. Observe that with this notation
the requirement for the edge relation reads $E \subseteq V \times V$. The set of **successors**
of $v \in V$ is defined by $vE = \{\, v' \in V \mid (v, v') \in E \,\}$.

The games we are interested in are played by two players, called **Player 0**
and **Player 1**. We will often fix $\sigma \in \{0, 1\}$ and consider Player σ; if we then want
to refer to the other player, we will speak of him or her as Player σ's opponent
and write Player $\bar{\sigma}$. Formally, we set $\bar{\sigma} = 1 - \sigma$ for $\sigma \in \{0, 1\}$.

Observe that there is no restriction on the number of the successors of a
vertex in an arena. Also, we don't require that (V, E) is a bipartite graph with
corresponding partition $\{V_0, V_1\}$.

2.2.2   Plays

A play of a game with an arena as above may be imagined in the following way:
a token is placed on some initial vertex $v \in V$. If v is a 0-vertex then Player 0

E. Grädel et al. (Eds.): Automata, Logics, and Infinite Games, LNCS 2500, pp. 23-38, 2002.

moves the token from v to a successor $v' \in vE$ of v; symmetrically, if v is a 1-vertex then Player 1 moves the token from v to a successor $v' \in vE$ of v. More concisely, when v is a σ-vertex, then Player σ moves the token from v to $v' \in vE$. Next, when v' is a σ-vertex, then Player σ moves the token from v' to $v'' \in v'E$. This is repeated either infinitely often or until a vertex $\bar{v}$ without successors, a **dead end**, is reached. Formally, a vertex $\bar{v}$ is called a dead end if $\bar{v}E = \emptyset$.

We define a **play** in the arena $\mathcal{A}$ as above as being either

- an infinite path $\pi = v_0 v_1 v_2 \cdots \in V^\omega$ with $v_{i+1} \in v_i E$ for all $i \in \omega$ (**infinite play**) or
- a finite path $\pi = v_0 v_1 \cdots v_l \in V^+$ with $v_{i+1} \in v_i E$ for all $i < l$, but $v_l E = \emptyset$ (**finite play**).

A **prefix of a play** is defined in the obvious way.

Now that we know what arenas and plays are we need to explain what kind of winning conditions we are going to use and how arenas together with winning conditions make games.

2.2.3   Games and Winning Sets

Let $\mathcal{A}$ be an arena as above and Win $\subseteq V^\omega$. The pair

$$(\mathcal{A}, \text{Win}) \tag{2.2}$$

is then called a **game**, where $\mathcal{A}$ is the arena of the game and Win its **winning set**. The plays of that game are the plays in the arena $\mathcal{A}$. Player 0 is declared the **winner of a play** π in the game $\mathcal{G}$ iff

- π is a finite play $\pi = v_0 v_1 \cdots v_l \in V^+$ and v_l is a 1-vertex where Player 1 can't move anymore (when v_l is a dead end) or
- π is an infinite play and $\pi \in$ Win.

Player 1 wins π if Player 0 does not win π.

2.2.4   Winning Conditions

We will only be interested in winning sets that can be described using the acceptance conditions that were discussed in the previous chapter. But recall that these acceptance conditions made only sense when used with automata with a finite state space—a run of an infinite-state automaton might have no recurring state. We will therefore colour the vertices of an arena and apply the acceptance conditions from the previous chapter on colour sequences.

Let $\mathcal{A}$ be as above and assume $\chi: V \to C$ is some function mapping the vertices of the arena to a finite set C of so-called **colours**; such a function will be called a **colouring function**. The colouring function is extended to plays in a straightforward way. When $\pi = v_0 v_1 \cdots$ is a play, then its colouring, $\chi(\pi)$, is given by $\chi(\pi) = \chi(v_0)\chi(v_1)\chi(v_2) \cdots$. So, when C is viewed as the state set of a finite ω-automaton and Acc is an acceptance condition for this automaton (in the sense of the previous chapter), then we will write $W_\chi(\text{Acc})$ for the winning set consisting of all infinite plays π where $\chi(\pi)$ is accepted according to Acc. Depending on the actual acceptance condition we are interested in, this means the following, where π stands for any element of V^ω.

- Muller condition ($\text{Acc} = \mathcal{F} \subseteq \mathscr{P}_0(C)$): $\pi \in W_\chi(\text{Acc})$ iff $\text{Inf}(\chi(\pi)) \in \mathcal{F}$.
- Rabin condition ($\text{Acc} = \{(E_0, F_0), (E_1, F_1), \ldots, (E_{m-1}, F_{m-1})\}$):
  $\pi \in W_\chi(\text{Acc})$ iff $\exists k \in [m]$ such that $\text{Inf}(\chi(\pi)) \cap E_k = \emptyset$ and $\text{Inf}(\chi(\pi)) \cap F_k \neq \emptyset$,
- Streett condition ($\text{Acc} = \{(E_0, F_0), (E_1, F_1), \ldots, (E_{m-1}, F_{m-1})\}$):
  $\pi \in W_\chi(\text{Acc})$ iff $\forall k \in [m].(\text{Inf}(\chi(\pi)) \cap E_k \neq \emptyset \ \vee \ \text{Inf}(\chi(\pi)) \cap F_k = \emptyset)$,
- Rabin chain condition ($\text{Acc} = \{(E_0, F_0), (E_1, F_1), \ldots, (E_{m-1}, F_{m-1})\}$ where $E_0 \subset F_0 \subset E_1 \subset F_1 \subset \ldots \subset E_{m-1} \subset F_{m-1}$): like the Rabin condition.
- Parity conditions (the colour set C is a finite subset of the integers):
  - max-parity condition: $\pi \in W_\chi(\text{Acc})$ iff $\max(\text{Inf}(\chi(\pi)))$ is even.
  - min-parity condition: $\pi \in W_\chi(\text{Acc})$ iff $\min(\text{Inf}(\chi(\pi)))$ is even.
- Büchi condition ($\text{Acc} = F \subseteq C$): $\pi \in W_\chi(\text{Acc})$ iff $\text{Inf}(\chi(\pi)) \cap F \neq \emptyset$.
- 1-winning ($\text{Acc} = F \subseteq C$): $\pi \in W_\chi(\text{Acc})$ iff $\text{Occ}(\chi(\pi)) \cap F \neq \emptyset$.

For simplicity, we will just write $(\mathcal{A}, \chi, \text{Acc})$ instead of $(\mathcal{A}, W_\chi(\text{Acc}))$. To indicate that we are working with a certain acceptance/winning condition, we will speak of **Muller, Büchi, ... games**. We will say a game is a **regular game** if its winning set is equal to $W_\chi(\text{Acc})$ for some χ and some acceptance condition Acc from above, except for 1-acceptance.

Example 2.1. Let $\mathcal{A} = (V_0, V_1, E, \chi)$ be the (coloured) arena presented in Figure 2.1. We have the 0-vertices $V_0 = \{z_1, z_2, z_5, z_6\}$ (circles) and the 1-vertices $V_1 = \{z_0, z_3, z_4\}$ (squares). The colours are $C = \{1, 2, 3, 4\}$. The edge relation E and the colour mapping χ may be derived from the picture, i.e. $\chi(z_4) = 2$ or $\chi(z_0) = 1$. Note that we don't have a dead end in our example. As a winning condition we choose the Muller acceptance condition given by $\mathcal{F} = \{\{1, 2\}, \{1, 2, 3, 4\}\}$.

A possible infinite play in this game is $\pi = z_6 z_3 z_2 z_4 z_2 z_4 z_6 z_5 (z_2 z_4)^\omega$. This play is winning for Player 0 because $\chi(\pi) = 23121224(12)^\omega$ and $\text{Inf}(\chi(\pi)) = \{1, 2\} \in \mathcal{F}$. The play $\pi' = (z_2 z_4 z_6 z_3)^\omega$ yields $\chi(\pi') = (1223)^\omega$ and $\text{Inf}(\chi(\pi')) = \{1, 2, 3\} \notin \mathcal{F}$. Hence π' is winning for Player 1.

When we want to fix a vertex where all plays we consider should start, we add this vertex to the game: an **initialized game** is a tuple $(\mathcal{G}, v_I)$ where v_I is a vertex of the arena of $\mathcal{G}$. A play of such a game is a play of the uninitialized game which starts in v_I.

2.3 Fundamental Questions

There are several obvious questions to ask when one is confronted with an initialized game as introduced in the previous section.

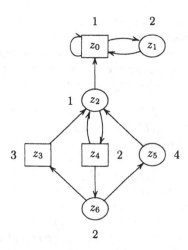

Fig. 2.1. Coloured example arena

First, it would be interesting to know if one of the players can play in such a game that regardless of how the other moves, the emerging plays will be wins for him. This is the question whether the game is "determined". We will formalize this by introducing the notions of strategy and winning strategy, and we will state the fundamental result that every regular game is determined; the result itself will be proved in Chapter 6.

Second, when we consider games on finite graphs these can be input for an algorithm and an obvious question to ask is if one can effectively (and maybe efficiently) determine which of the two players wins the game. This question will be answered in Chapter 7; the complexity of determining the winner heavily depends on the type of the game (the winning condition) one is interested in.

Third, it is not only interesting to know who wins a game, but also how a winning strategy looks like. Clearly, a winning strategy will tell the player what to do next depending on the moves that have been taken thus far. We will be interested in situations where the winning strategies are simple in the sense that the next move of the player does only depend on the current vertex or on a bounded amount of information on the moves that led to the current position—we will be interested in "memoryless" or "forgetful" strategies. We will describe this formally and state the main result that for every regular game there is a forgetful winning strategy and that parity games even allow memoryless strategies.

2.4   Strategies and Determinacy

In order to be able to define formally what it means for a player to win a game, we need to introduce the notion of strategy.

2.4.1 Strategies

Let $\mathcal{A}$ be an arena as usual, $\sigma \in \{0,1\}$, and $f_\sigma \colon V^* V_\sigma \to V$ a partial function. A prefix of a play $\pi = v_0 v_1 \cdots v_l$ is said to be **conform** with f_σ if for every i with $0 \leq i < l$ and $v_i \in V_\sigma$ the function f_σ is defined at $v_0 \cdots v_i$ and we have $v_{i+1} = f_\sigma(v_0 \cdots v_i)$. Note, that this also implies $v_{i+1} \in v_i E$. A play (finite or infinite) is conform with f_σ if each of its prefixes is conform with f_σ. Now we call the function f_σ a **strategy** for Player σ on $U \subseteq V$ if it is defined for every prefix of a play which is conform with it, starts in a vertex from U, and does not end in a dead end of Player σ. When U is a singleton $\{v\}$, we say f_σ is a strategy for Player σ in v.

Let $\mathcal{G} = (\mathcal{A}, \mathrm{Win})$ be an arbitrary game with $\mathcal{A}$ as usual, and f_σ a strategy for Player σ on U. The strategy f_σ is said to be a **winning strategy** for Player σ on U if all plays which are conform with f_σ and start in a vertex from U are wins for Player σ.

Example 2.2. We use the game from Example 2.1.

When Player 1 moves from z_0 to z_0 every time the token is located on z_0, then he will win every play that visits z_0. This means, in particular, that f_1 defined by $f_1(yz_0) = z_0$ and $f_1(yz_4) = z_6$ (or $= z_1$) is a winning strategy for Player 1 on $W_1 = \{z_0, z_1\}$.

Each play that doesn't begin in z_0 or z_1, visits the vertex z_2 at some point. Player 0 should under no circumstances move the token from z_2 to z_0 because his opponent could win as described above. Hence, his only chance is to move the token from z_2 to z_4. The resulting plays will visit z_2 and z_4 infinitely often.

Player 1 should not choose vertex z_2 every time the token visits vertex z_4 because this would result in a play with suffix $(z_2 z_4)^\omega$ which is a win for Player 0. So, Player 1 should once in a while move the token from z_4 to z_6.

The situation for Player 0 in vertex z_6 is a bit more complicated. If he always decides for moving the token to z_3, then the resulting play has the form $\pi = \cdots (z_6 z_3 z_2 z_4 (z_2 z_4)^*)^\omega$ and is a loss for him. Similarly, he will loose if he always moves the token to z_5. But he is able to win if he alternates between z_3 and z_5. To sum this up, consider the function f_0 defined by

$$
f_0(\pi) = \begin{cases}
z_4 & \text{if } \pi \in V^* z_2 \\
z_3 & \text{if } \pi \in V^* z_5 z_2 z_4 (z_2 z_4)^* z_6 \\
z_5 & \text{if } \pi \in V^* z_3 z_2 z_4 (z_2 z_4)^* z_6 \\
z_3 & \text{if } \pi \in (V \setminus \{z_3, z_5\})^* z_6
\end{cases}
\tag{2.3}
$$

This is a winning strategy for Player 0 on $W_0 = \{z_2, z_3, z_4, z_5, z_6\}$.

We say that Player σ **wins** a game $\mathcal{G}$ on $U \subseteq V$ if he has a winning strategy on U.

Example 2.3. In the game from Examples 2.1 and 2.2, Player 1 wins on $\{z_0, z_1\}$ whereas Player 0 wins on $\{z_2, z_3, z_4, z_5, z_6\}$.

When $(\mathcal{G}, v_I)$ is an initialized game, we say Player σ wins it if he wins $\mathcal{G}$ on the singleton set $\{v\}$.

Clearly, every initialized game has at most one winner:

Remark 2.4. For any game $\mathcal{G}$, if Player 0 wins $\mathcal{G}$ on U_0 and Player 1 wins $\mathcal{G}$ on U_1, then $U_0 \cap U_1 = \emptyset$.

Exercise 2.1. Proof the above remark by contradiction.

Given a game $\mathcal{G}$, we define the **winning region** for Player σ, denoted $W_\sigma(\mathcal{G})$ or W_σ for short, to be the set of all vertices v such that Player 0 wins $(\mathcal{G}, v)$. Clearly:

Remark 2.5. For any game $\mathcal{G}$, Player σ wins $\mathcal{G}$ on $W_\sigma(\mathcal{G})$.

Exercise 2.2. Proof the above remark by showing that if $\mathcal{U}$ is a family of sets of vertices such that Player σ wins on each element $U \in \mathcal{U}$, then Player σ wins on
$$\bigcup_{U \in \mathcal{U}} U.$$

2.4.2 Transforming Winning Conditions

In the previous chapter, we have seen how acceptance conditions for ω-automata can be transformed into one another. The same can be done with games. This will be explained in this section.

We first note:

Remark 2.6. For every regular game $(\mathcal{A}, \chi, \mathrm{Acc})$ there exists a Muller winning condition Acc' such that $(\mathcal{A}, \chi, \mathrm{Acc})$ and $(\mathcal{A}, \chi, \mathrm{Acc}')$ have the same winning regions.

The main result says that it is enough to consider parity games. Therefore, parity games are of our interest in the whole volume.

Theorem 2.7. *For every Muller game $(\mathcal{A}, \chi, \mathcal{F})$ there exists a parity game $(\mathcal{A}', \chi', \mathrm{Acc}')$ and a function $r \colon V \to V'$ such that for every $v \in V$, Player σ wins $((\mathcal{A}, \chi, \mathcal{F}), v)$ if and only if Player σ wins $((\mathcal{A}', \chi', \mathrm{Acc}'), r(v))$.*

Proof. The proof will be similar to the transformation of Muller conditions in Rabin conditions for ω-automaton in the previous chapter: We modify the LAR memory with hit position from Transformation 1.20 to contain colours instead of vertices because the acceptance condition for our games was defined for the colour sequence. But we have to keep track of the visited vertices too. This is done in a product construction. We will see that the constructed Rabin condition can be rewritten as Rabin chain or max-parity condition.

Let $(\mathcal{A}, \chi, \mathcal{F})$ be a Muller game, C the (finite) set of colours, and a marker $\natural \notin C$, a symbol not occurring in C. Now set our LAR memory to

$$\widetilde{C} := \{ w \in (C \cup \{\natural\})^* \mid |w| \geq 2 \wedge |w|_\natural = 1 \wedge \forall a \in C(|w|_a \leq 1) \} \ . \tag{2.4}$$

$\tilde{C}$ is the set of all words w over the alphabet $C \cup \{\natural\}$ where $\natural$ and at least one colour are infixes of w and each colour appears at most once.

Now we can define our game $(\mathcal{A}', \chi', \text{Acc}')$. As vertices we choose

$$V' := V_0' \cup V_1' \text{ with } V_0' := V_0 \times \tilde{C} \text{ and } V_1' := V_1 \times \tilde{C} \ . \tag{2.5}$$

The set of edges is given by

$$E' := \{ ((v, q), (v', \varphi(v', q))) \mid v \in V, \ v' \in vE, \ q \in \tilde{C} \} \tag{2.6}$$

where $\varphi \colon V \times \tilde{C} \to \tilde{C}$ is the memory update function that deletes the marker, replaces the colour $c := \chi(v')$ of the given vertex v' by the marker and finally appends c. Formally, φ is defined as

$$\varphi(v', q) := \begin{cases} x\natural yzc & \text{if } q = xcy\natural z \\ xy\natural zc & \text{if } q = x\natural ycz \\ qc & \text{else } (c \text{ is not an infix of } q) \end{cases} \tag{2.7}$$

for each $v' \in V$ and each $q \in \tilde{C}$ with $c := \chi(v')$. The function that transforms the initial vertex can be set to

$$r(v) := (v, \natural\chi(v)) \ . \tag{2.8}$$

The new colouring function $\chi' \colon V' \to \omega$ is defined by

$$\chi'(v, x\natural y) := \begin{cases} 2 * |y| - 1 & \text{if } \{ c \in C \mid c \text{ infix of } y \} \notin \mathcal{F} \\ 2 * |y| & \text{otherwise} \end{cases} \ . \tag{2.9}$$

We conclude the description of the construction by declaring Acc' to be a max-parity condition.

Now we have to prove the correctness of this construction which is similar to Lemma 1.21 in the previous chapter. Let $\pi = v_0 v_1 \cdots \in V^\omega$ be an infinite play in $\mathcal{A}$. The corresponding play π' in $\mathcal{A}'$ is uniquely determined: The projection onto the first component $p_1(\pi') = \pi$ is our original play, and the second component is $p_2(\pi') = q_0 q_1 \ldots \in \tilde{C}^\omega$ with $q_i = x_i\natural y_i$ defined by $q_0 := \natural\chi(v_0)$ and $q_{i+1} := \varphi(v_{i+1}, q_i)$ for each $i \in \omega$. Let $F := \text{Inf}(\chi(\pi))$ be the set of infinitely often visited colours in the play π. Hence, from some point $j \in \omega$ on the marker $\natural$ stays within the last $|F| + 1$ positions: $\forall i \geq j \ |y_i| \leq |F|$. Second, the marker must infinitely often occur in position $|F| + 1$, positions numbered from right to left, because each colour from F is infinitely often moved to the end. That is, $\{ k \geq j \mid |y_k| = |F| \text{ and } y_k \text{ forms the set } F \}$ is infinite. Thus, by construction of χ', we have that the highest colour visited infinitely often in π' has the even value $2 \cdot |F|$ if $F \in \mathcal{F}$ and the odd value $2 \cdot |F| - 1$ otherwise. For finite plays, the situation is even simpler.

In summary, a play π is winning for Player 0 in $\mathcal{A}$ if and only if π' is winning for him in $\mathcal{A}'$. Conversely, every play π' in $\mathcal{A}$ starting in a vertex $r(v)$ corresponds to a play π in $\mathcal{A}$, for which the same holds. So, Player 0 wins the initialized game $(\mathcal{A}, v)$ if and only if he wins $(\mathcal{A}', r(v))$. $\qquad\square$

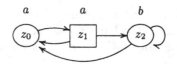

Fig. 2.2. Example for the reduction

Example 2.8. Let $\mathcal{A}$ be the arena in Figure 2.2, and $\mathcal{F} = \{\{b\}\}$ a Muller acceptance condition. The example play $\pi = z_1 z_2 z_0 z_1 z_2^\omega$ is winning for Player 0. The
winning regions are $W_0 = \{z_2\}$ and $W_1 = \{z_0, z_1\}$. The constructed max-parity
game $\mathcal{A}'$ is presented in Figure 2.3. We get

$$\pi' = (z_1, \natural a)(z_2, \natural ab)(z_0, \natural ba)(z_1, b\natural a)(z_2, \natural ab)(z_2, a\natural b)^\omega \tag{2.10}$$

with the colouring $\chi'(\pi') = 133132^\omega$ which is winning for Player 0 too. The
winning region W_0' for Player 0 is the set of all vertices with z_2 in the first
component. W_1' is the complement of W_0'.

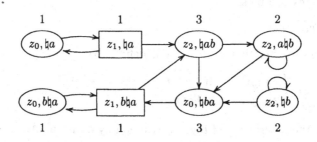

Fig. 2.3. Constructed max-parity game

2.4.3 Determinacy

In all of our example games, the winning regions for Player 0 and Player 1
partition the set of vertices of the game. When a game has this property, we will
say it is **determined**.

Martin (see, e. g., [119], [95]) showed that every game with a Borel type
winning set is determined. In Chapter 6, we will show the following special case
of Martin's theorem.

Theorem 2.9. *Every parity game is determined.*

Together with Theorem 2.7, the previous theorem implies:

Corollary 2.10. *Every regular game is determined.*

2.4.4 Forgetful and Memoryless Strategies

The objective of this section is to introduce some notions that help to explain how complex a winning strategy is.

As a motivation, consider the game from Example 2.1 again. We argued that in order to win it is necessary for Player 0 to alternate between moving the token to z_3 and z_5 when it is on z_6. More precisely, it is necessary not to stick to one of the two vertices from some point onwards. This means that Player 0 has to remember at least one bit, namely whether he moved to z_3 or z_5 when the token was on z_6 the last time. But from our argumentation, it is also clear that it is not necessary to remember more than that. In other words, a finite memory is sufficient for Player 0 to carry out his strategy. We will say Player 0 has a forgetful strategy. The situation is much easier for Player 1. He does not need to remember anything; he simply moves to z_0 every time the token is on z_0. We will say Player 1 has a memoryless strategy.

Let $\mathcal{G}$ be a game as usual. A strategy f_σ is said to be **finite memory** or **forgetful** if there exists a finite set M, an element $m_I \in M$, and functions $\delta \colon V \times M \to M$ and $g \colon V \times M \to V$ such that the following is true. When $\pi = v_0 v_1 \cdots v_{l-1}$ is a prefix of a play in the domain of f_σ and the sequence $m_0, m_1, \ldots, m_l$ is determined by $m_0 = m_I$ and $m_{i+1} = \delta(v_i, m_i)$, then $f_\sigma(\pi) = g(v_l, m_l)$.

Forgetful strategies that don't need memory at all, that is, where one can choose M to be a singleton, are called **memoryless** or **positional**. Observe that a memoryless strategy f_σ has the property that whenever f_σ is defined for πv and $\pi' v$, then $f_\sigma(\pi v) = f_\sigma(\pi' v)$. This allows us to view memoryless strategies as partial functions $V_\sigma \to V$, and, for ease in notation, we will often use this representation.

Example 2.11. In Example 2.2, the strategy f_1 for Player 1 is memoryless. To see this, observe that we can choose M to be a singleton, say $M = \{m\}$, and set $g(z_0, m) = z_0$ and $g(z_3, m) = g(z_4, m) = z_2$. So, Player 1 has a memoryless winning strategy on $W_1 = \{z_0, z_1\}$. Using the simplified notation, we could write $f_1(z_0) = z_0$ and $f_1(z_3) = f_1(z_4) = z_2$.

Player 0 needs to store which one of the colours 3 (occurring on vertex z_3) and 4 (on vertex z_5) he visited last. This can be done with a memory $M = \{3, 4\}$. More precisely, one can choose $m_I = 3$,

$$\delta(v, m) = \begin{cases} 3 & \text{if } v = z_3 \\ 4 & \text{if } v = z_5 \\ m & \text{otherwise} \end{cases} . \tag{2.11}$$

and

$$g(v, m) = \begin{cases} z_4 & \text{if } v = z_2 \\ z_3 & \text{if } v = z_6 \text{ and } m = 4 \\ z_5 & \text{if } v = z_6 \text{ and } m = 3 \end{cases} . \tag{2.12}$$

Thus, Player 0 has a forgetful winning strategy on $W_0 = \{z_2, z_3, z_4, z_5, z_6\}$.

In Example 2.2, we already stated that Player 0 must not move from z_6 to the same successor every time he visits z_6. So, Player 0 can't have a memoryless winning strategy.

We say that Player σ wins a game $\mathcal{G}$ **forgetful** when he has a forgetful strategy for each point of his winning region. Accordingly, it is defined what it means to win **with finite memory, memoryless,** and **positional.**

Exercise 2.3. Give an example for a game $\mathcal{G}$ such that Player 0 wins forgetful on each $\{v\}$ for $v \in W_0$, but he has no forgetful winning strategy on W_0. Can you give an example where $\mathcal{G}$ is regular?

In exercise 2.2, the reader was asked to show that if U is some set of vertices such that Player σ wins a given game $\mathcal{G}$ on every element of U, then he wins $\mathcal{G}$ on U. This is easy to see. In Exercise 2.3, the reader is asked to provide an example that shows that the corresponding statement is not true for forgetful strategies. However, a corresponding statement is true for memoryless strategies under a certain condition:

Lemma 2.12. *Let $\mathcal{G} = (\mathcal{A}, \text{Win})$ be any game with countable vertex set V,*

$$V^*\text{Win} \subseteq \text{Win} \qquad and \qquad \text{Win}/V^* \subseteq \text{Win}, \tag{2.13}$$

where $\text{Win}/V^* := \{\, \eta \in V^\omega \mid \exists w \in V^* \text{ with } w\eta \in \text{Win} \,\}$ is the set of all suffixes of Win. Let U be a set of vertices such that Player σ has a memoryless winning strategy for each element from U. Then Player σ has a memoryless winning strategy on U.

Before we turn to the proof observe that the two conditions on the winning set are satisfied in every regular game: A prefix of a winning play can be substituted by any other finite word; the set of infinitely often visited colours stays the same.

Proof. The proof uses the axiom of choice. For every $u \in U$, let $f_\sigma^u \colon V_\sigma \to V$ be a partial function which is a memoryless winning strategy for Player σ on u. Without loss of generality, we assume that for every $u \in U$ the domain of f_σ^u, denoted D_u, is minimal with respect to set inclusion.

Let $<$ be a well-ordering on U (therefore we choose V to be countable) and $D := \bigcup_{u \in U} D_u$. We have to define a memoryless winning strategy $f_\sigma \colon D \to V$.

For each $v \in D$, let $u(v)$ be the minimal vertex in U (with respect to the well-ordering) with $v \in D_{u(v)}$, and set $f_\sigma(v) := f_\sigma^{u(v)}(v)$. Clearly, f_σ is well defined and memoryless. We have to show that f_σ is a winning strategy on U.

Assume $\pi = v_0 v_1 \cdots$ is a play starting in U and conform with f_σ. In each σ-vertex v_j of the play π, Player σ has to choose the strategy $f_\sigma^{u(v_j)}$. Let i be such that $u(v_i)$ is minimal (with respect to the well-ordering) in the set $\{\, u(v_j) \mid j \in \omega \text{ and } v_j \in D \,\}$. Then, from this moment i on, the strategy f_σ follows the strategy $f_\sigma^{u(v_i)}$. The domain $D_{u(v_i)}$ was minimal with respect to set inclusion, thus, the play $v_i v_{i+1} \cdots$ is a suffix of a play that starts in $u(v_i)$, visits v_i, and is conform to $f_\sigma^{u(v_i)}$. Hence, $\pi \in V^*(\text{Win}/V^*) \subseteq \text{Win}$ by our two conditions, which completes the proof. $\square$

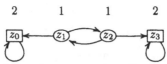

Fig. 2.4. Example for the construction of a memoryless strategy

Example 2.13. Let $\mathcal{A}$ be the max-parity game in Figure 2.4. Clearly, Player 0 wins on each $v \in U = \{z_1, z_2\}$, i. e. with the memoryless strategies

- $f_0^{z_1}(z_1) = z_2$ and $f_0^{z_1}(z_2) = z_3$,
- $f_0^{z_2}(z_2) = z_1$ and $f_0^{z_2}(z_1) = z_0$.

To find a memoryless strategy on U, Player 0 can not set $f_0(z_1) = f_0^{z_1}(z_1)$ and $f_0(z_2) = f_0^{z_2}(z_2)$ because this yields an infinite loop in z_1 and z_2 which is a loss for him. If $z_1 < z_2$ in the well-ordering of U, then we get $f_0 \equiv f_0^{z_1}$. This is a memoryless winning strategy on U.

In Theorem 6.6 in Chapter 6 we will show the following.

Theorem 2.14. *In every parity game, both players win memoryless. This is called **memoryless determinacy of parity games**.*

From this, together with the construction in the proof of Theorem 2.7, we can conclude:

Corollary 2.15. *In every regular game, both players win forgetful. Analogously, this is called **forgetful or finite memory determinacy of regular games**.*

Proof. Let $(\mathcal{A}, \chi, \mathcal{F})$ be a Muller game, $\mathcal{A}'$ the max-parity game as constructed in the proof of Theorem 2.7, and $V' = V \times \widetilde{C}$ the set of vertices of $\mathcal{A}'$ with $\widetilde{C}$ defined in Equation 2.4. The memoryless determinacy of parity games yields memoryless winning strategies f_0' and f_1' on the winning regions W_0' and W_1' with $W_0' \cup W_1' = V'$.

Now the observations in the proof of Theorem 2.7 allow us to construct forgetful strategies in $\mathcal{A}$. The winning regions are $W_\sigma = \{v \in V \mid (v, \natural\chi(v)) \in W_\sigma'\}$ for $\sigma \in \{0, 1\}$. We can use the finite memory $M = \widetilde{C}$ for both strategies. As initial memory state of $(\mathcal{A}, v)$ we choose $m_I = \natural\chi(v)$. The memory update function δ is equal to φ from Equation 2.7. The forgetful strategies g_0 and g_1 are defined by

$$g_\sigma(v, q) := f_\sigma'((v, q)) \tag{2.14}$$

for $\sigma \in \{0, 1\}$, $v \in V_\sigma \cap W_\sigma$, and $q \in \widetilde{C}$.

Clearly, these strategies are forgetful winning strategies because g_σ simulates f_σ'. □

Note that the initial memory state in the previous construction could be chosen arbitrarily.

Exercise 2.4. Using the results from the previous chapter, determine how much memory is sufficient and necessary to win Rabin and Muller games.

Theorem 2.14 states that parity games enjoy memoryless determinacy, that is, winning strategies for both players can be chosen memoryless. It is easy to show that in certain Muller games both players need memory to win. In between, we have Rabin and Streett conditions. For those, one can actually prove that one of the two players always has a memoryless winning strategy, but we will not carry out the proof in this volume.

Theorem 2.16. *In every Rabin game, Player 0 has a memoryless winning strategy on his winning region. Symmetrically, in every Streett game, Player 1 has a memoryless strategy on his winning region.*

This theorem can also be applied to certain Muller automata on the grounds of the following observation. A Muller condition $(\mathcal{F}_0, \mathcal{F}_1)$ can be rephrased as Rabin condition if and only if $\mathcal{F}_1$ is closed under union.

Example 2.17. We got a memoryless strategy for Player 1 in our Example 2.11. His winning condition $\mathcal{F}_1$ is expressible as Rabin condition:
$\{(\{3\}, \{4\}), (\{4\}, \{3\}), (\{1\}, \{2\})\}$. He wins a play if it loops, for instance, finitely often through one of the colours 3 or 4 and infinitely often through the other colour. Note that the winning condition cannot be rephrased as a parity condition, that is, Rabin chain condition (on the same graph).

2.5   Solving Games with Simple Winning Conditions

In this section, we prove special instances of Corollaries 2.10 and 2.15 and Theorem 2.14.

2.5.1   Reachability Games and Attractors

For a start, we consider games which do not really fit into the framework that we have used thus far. Given an arena $\mathcal{A} = (V_0, V_1, E)$ and a set $X \subseteq V$ the **reachability game** $R(\mathcal{A}, X)$ is the game in which a play π (be it finite or infinite) is winning for Player 0 if some vertex from X or a dead end belonging to Player 1 occurs in π. This is different from the games we have studied so far because a dead end for Player 0 does not need to be a loosing position for him. Strategies for reachability games are defined as before, but with the difference that a strategy for Player 0 does not need to be defined for arguments that end in a vertex from X.

Proposition 2.18. *Reachability games enjoy memoryless determinacy.*

Proof. The proof is constructive in the sense that on finite graphs it can be immediately turned into an algorithm which computes the winning regions and the memoryless winning strategies.

Let $\mathcal{A}$ be an arena as usual and $X \subseteq V$. The winning region for Player 0 in $R(\mathcal{A}, X)$ and a memoryless winning strategy for Player 0 are defined inductively. In the inductive step, we use the function $pre\colon \mathscr{P}(V) \to \mathscr{P}(V)$ defined by

$$pre(Y) = \{\, v \in V_0 \mid vE \cap Y \neq \emptyset \,\} \cup \{\, v \in V_1 \mid vE \subseteq Y \,\} \tag{2.15}$$

Inductively, we set $X^0 = X$,

$$X^{\nu+1} = X^\nu \cup pre(X^\nu) \tag{2.16}$$

for all ordinals ν, and

$$X^\xi = \bigcup_{\nu < \xi} X^\nu \tag{2.17}$$

for each limit ordinal ξ. Let ξ be the smallest ordinal such that $X^\xi = X^{\xi+1}$. We claim that $W := X^\xi$ is Player 0's winning region. Clearly, for every $v \in W \setminus X$ there exists a unique ordinal $\xi_v < \xi$ such that $v \in X^{\xi_v+1} \setminus X^{\xi_v}$. By the above definition, we furthermore know that for every $v \in W \cap V_0 \setminus X$ there exists $v' \in vE$ such that $v' \in X^{\xi_v}$. We set $f_0(v) = v'$ and claim that f_0 is a memoryless strategy for Player 0 on W. This can be easily proved by transfinite induction: One shows that f_0 is winning for Player 0 on X^ν for every $\nu \leq \xi$. Hence, $W \subseteq W_0$.

On the other hand, let $W' = V \setminus W$ and assume $v \in W'$. Then $v \notin X$. If v is a dead end, it must be a dead end of Player 0 because all dead ends of Player 1 belong to X^1. But, on a dead end belonging to Player 0, Player 1 wins immediately. If v is no dead end and belongs to V_0, we have $v' \notin W$ for every $v' \in vE$ because otherwise v would belong to W. Similarly, if v is no dead end and belongs to V_1, there exists $v' \in vE$ such that $v' \notin W$ because otherwise v would belong to W. If we set $f_1(v) = v'$ in this case, then f_1 is clearly a memoryless strategy for Player 1. Every play conform with this strategy and starting in W' has the property that all its vertices belong to W'. Since W' does not contain vertices from X or dead ends of Player 1 this play must be winning for Player 1. Hence, f_1 is a winning strategy for Player 1 on W' and $V \setminus W = W' \subseteq W_1$, that is, $W_0 = W$ and $W_1 = V \setminus W$. $\qquad\square$

The winning region of Player 0 in a reachability game $R(\mathcal{A}, X)$ is denoted $\mathrm{Attr}_0(\mathcal{A}, X)$ and called **0-attractor** of the set X in the arena $\mathcal{A}$. A memoryless winning strategy f_0 as described in the above prove is called a corresponding **attractor strategy** for Player 0. 1-attractor and attractor strategy for Player 1 are defined symmetrically, simply by exchanging V_0 and V_1 in the arena.

Exercise 2.5. Let $\mathcal{A}$ be an arbitrary arena, $X \subseteq V$, and $a_X\colon \mathscr{P}(V) \to \mathscr{P}(V)$ the function defined by

$$a_X(U) := X \cup pre(U) \ . \tag{2.18}$$

Show that a_X is monotone with respect to set inclusion and that $\mathrm{Attr}_0(\mathcal{A}, X)$ is the least fixed point of a_X.

Exercise 2.6. Show that in a finite arena with n vertices and m edges the attractor of any set can be computed in time $O(m + n)$.

Exercise 2.7. Let $\mathcal{A}$ be an arena and $Y = V \setminus \text{Attr}_\sigma(\mathcal{A}, X)$ for some $X \subseteq V$. Show that σ cannot escape Y in the sense that $vE \subseteq Y$ for every $v \in Y \cap V_\sigma$ and $vE \cap Y \neq \emptyset$ for every $v \in Y \cap V_{\bar{\sigma}}$.

This exercise motivates the following definition. A **σ-trap** is a subset $Y \subseteq V$ such that $vE \subseteq Y$ for every $v \in Y \cap V_\sigma$ and $vE \cap Y \neq \emptyset$ for every $v \in Y \cap V_{\bar{\sigma}}$. A function which picks for every $v \in Y \cap V_{\bar{\sigma}}$ a vertex $v' \in vE \cap Y$ is called a **trapping strategy** for Player $\bar{\sigma}$.

Remark 2.19. The complement of a σ-attractor is a σ-trap.

The above remark tells us that, without loss of generality, we can assume that arenas have no dead ends. Let $(\mathcal{A}, \text{Acc})$ be an arbitrary game with $\mathcal{A} = (V_0, V_1, E)$. For $\sigma \in \{0, 1\}$, we set $U_\sigma = \text{Attr}_\sigma(\mathcal{A}, \emptyset)$. Then Player σ wins $(\mathcal{A}, \text{Acc})$ on U_σ memoryless. Now, let $V_0' = V_0 \setminus (U_0 \cup U_1)$ and $V_1' = V_1 \setminus (U_0 \cup U_1)$ and consider the arena $\mathcal{A}' = (V_0', V_1', E \cap ((V_0' \cup V_1') \times (V_0' \cup V_1')))$. Clearly, $\mathcal{A}'$ does not have any dead end. Further, for every $v \in V_0' \cup V_1'$, Player 0 wins $(\mathcal{A}', \text{Acc}, v)$ iff he wins $(\mathcal{A}, \text{Acc}, v)$ and, symmetrically, Player 1 wins $(\mathcal{A}', \text{Acc}, v)$ iff he wins $(\mathcal{A}, \text{Acc}, v)$. More specifically, winning strategies for $(\mathcal{A}', \text{Acc})$ can be used in $(\mathcal{A}, \text{Acc})$.

Exercise 2.8. Work out the details of the above argument.

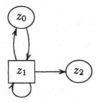

Fig. 2.5. Dead end strategy for Player 1

Example 2.20. In the game depicted in Figure 2.5, Player 1 may prevent an infinite play by moving the token to z_2. This is a dead end for Player 0 and Player 1 wins.

2.5.2 1-acceptance

Using what we have proved about reachability games, we can now easily solve 1-games.

Proposition 2.21. *1-games enjoy memoryless determinacy.*

Proof. Let $\mathcal{G} = (\mathcal{A}, \chi, F)$ and define Y and V' by $Y = \text{Attr}_1(\mathcal{G}, \emptyset)$ and $V' = V \backslash Y$. Let $\mathcal{A}' = (V_0 \cap V', V_1 \cap V', E \cap (V' \times V'))$. Observe that $\mathcal{A}'$ does not contain any dead end of Player 0. We claim that $W := \text{Attr}_0(\mathcal{A}', \chi^{-1}(F))$ is the winning region of Player 0 in $\mathcal{G}$.

Clearly, Y is a subset of the winning region of Player 1. Further, $W \subseteq W_0$, because on this set Player 0 can force the game into a dead end of Player 1 or a vertex in $\chi^{-1}(F)$ and go on forever because $\mathcal{A}'$ does not contain any dead end of Player 0. Remember that V' is a 1-trap, that is, Player 1 cannot escape V'. And on both sets, Y and W we have memoryless winning strategies (attractor and trapping strategies) for the respective players. It is now sufficient to show that Player 1 has a memoryless winning strategy on $Z := V' \setminus W$. Since Z is a 0-trap of $\mathcal{A}'$, Player 1 can use his trapping strategy and the token will then stay in Z forever or stay in Z until it is moved to a vertex in Y, which is winning for Player 1 anyway.   □

Exercise 2.9. Show that for finite arenas, the winning regions of 1-games can be computed in time $O(m + n)$. (See also Exercise 2.6.)

2.5.3 Büchi Acceptance

Obviously, Büchi games can viewed as parity games. So memoryless determinacy follows from memoryless determinacy of parity games, which will be proved in Chapter 6. Nevertheless, we give a straightforward proof along the lines of the proofs that we have seen in the previous two subsections.

Theorem 2.22. *Büchi games enjoy memoryless determinacy.*

Proof. Like in the other solutions, we first describe how to construct the winning region for Player 0 in a Büchi game $(\mathcal{A}, \chi, F)$.

We set $Y = \chi^{-1}(F)$, and define inductively:

$$Z^0 = V , \tag{2.19}$$

$$X^\xi = \text{Attr}_0(\mathcal{A}, Z^\xi) , \tag{2.20}$$

$$Y^\xi = pre(X^\xi) , \tag{2.21}$$

$$Z^{\xi+1} = Y^\xi \cap Y , \tag{2.22}$$

$$Z^\xi = \bigcup_{\nu < \xi} Z^\nu , \tag{2.23}$$

where the last equation only applies to limit ordinals ξ. Let ξ be the least ordinal ≥ 1 such that $Z^\xi = Z^{\xi+1}$. We claim $W := \text{Attr}_0(\mathcal{A}, Z^\xi)$ is the winning region of Player 0.

To prove $W \subseteq W_0$, we describe a memoryless winning strategy f_0 for Player 0 on W. For every $v \in V_0 \cap Z^\xi$, there exists $v' \in vE \cap \text{Attr}_0(\mathcal{A}, Z^\xi)$ and we set $f_0(v) = v'$. For every other $v \in V_0 \cap W$, we know $v \in \text{Attr}_0(\mathcal{A}, Z^\xi)$, and thus we set $f_0(v)$ to the value of a respective attractor strategy. Now, the following is easy to see. First, if a finite play starting in W is conform with f_0, then it ends in a dead of Player 1, which means Player 0 wins. Second, if an infinite play starting in W is conform with f_0 it eventually reaches Z^ξ and from this point onwards it will reach Z^ξ over and over again. But since $Z^\xi \subseteq Y$ (this is because $\xi \geq 1$), the play will be winning for Player 0.

To prove that $W_0 = W$, we argue that Player 1 has a memoryless winning strategy on $W' := V \setminus W$. The winning strategy is defined as follows. For every $v \in W'$ there exists a least ν such that $v \in X^\nu \setminus X^{\nu+1}$. (Note that $X^0 = V$ and $X^{\nu'} \subseteq X^{\nu''}$ for all ordinals ν' and ν'' with $\nu'' < \nu'$.) Since $X^{\nu+1}$ is a 0-attractor, $V \setminus X^{\nu+1}$ is a 0-trap. We set $f_1(v)$ to the value of a trapping strategy for Player 1 if $v \notin Y$. Otherwise, it follows that $v \notin pre(X^\nu)$, and thus, there exists some $v' \in vE \cap V \setminus X^\nu$. We set $f_1(v) = v'$. By induction on ν, it is now easy to show that f_1 is a winning strategy for Player 1 on $V \setminus X^\nu$. It follows that f_1 is a winning strategy on W'. □

Exercise 2.10. Show that for a finite arena, the winning regions of a Büchi game can be computed in time $O(n(m + n))$.

Notes on Part I

The theory of ω-automata started with Büchi's landmark paper [18]. There the Büchi acceptance condition for nondeterministic automata was proposed, and the expressive equivalence of what today are called "Büchi automata" to the monadic second-order theory of the natural numbers with successor was shown.

Further acceptance conditions were introduced in the following two decades, Muller acceptance in [133], Rabin acceptance in [150], and Streett acceptance in [171]. The basic results regarding the power of acceptance conditions (in deterministic and nondeterministic automata), to be discussed in more detail also in Part II of this book, were established by McNaughton [125], Landweber [110], and Rabin [150]. The parity condition was introduced by Mostowski [131] (first without a special name, later called "Rabin chain condition"); the term "parity condition" appeared in [55], where this acceptance mode was proposed independently.

There are by now several surveys on the expressive power of the diverse acceptance conditions of ω-automata, also for more powerful models like pushdown automata or Turing machines. We mention the introductory section of Wagner's paper [192], two articles by Staiger ([164, 165]), and the study of Engelfriet and Hoogeboom [60] on acceptance conditions in automata with diverse types of storage.

General introductions to the field of ω-automata, also discussing the connections to monadic second-order logic and infinite games, are given in the survey articles [179] and [183], the monograph [96], and the forthcoming book [143]. However, several topics which are central in the present volume (mainly from Part IV onwards) are not treated there in depth, for example regarding the interplay between alternating automata and the μ-calculus.

The lower bound of Section 1.6 is due to Michel in an unpublished manuscript [128]. A rather complete analysis of the complexity bounds for the transformation of ω-automata with different acceptance modes is given in [114].

The idea of infinite game arose implicitly in the study of synthesis of digital circuits. An exhaustive survey on the state of knowledge around 1960, with a clear formulation of the central problems, was given by Church [35]. The first to use explicitly the terminology of infinite games in the context of infinite input-output behaviour was McNaughton [124]. The fundamental result providing a solution of Church's synthesis problem (which amounts to solving Muller games over finite graphs) was obtained by Büchi and Landweber in [22]; see also the book [188].

The question of constructing strategies with minimal possible memory was initiated in [55] and [132] where positional (and hence memoryless) winning strategies for parity games were shown to exist (see notes of Part III for more details). The memory structure of "latest appearance record", which fits to Muller games, was used by Büchi in an unpublished manuscript (1981), in [77], and in [126]. As further references on the subject we mention [46, 98, 180, 203].

Applications of the game-theoretic approach to the synthesis of software modules and controllers are treated in many papers. Early work on realizable specifications for state-based systems and on the synthesis of reactive modules is due to Abadi, Lamport, and Wolper [1] and Pnueli and Rosner [144, 145]. As more recent work, also including papers on supervisory control of discrete event systems in the sense of Ramadge and Wonham [152], we mention [177, 104, 118, 2, 3, 101].

Part II

Determinization and Complementation

The transformation of nondeterministic into deterministic automata is one of the key issues of automata theory. In the case of ω-automata, the determinization problem requires quite intricate constructions. The first chapter of this part shows how to transform a nondeterministic Büchi automaton into a deterministic Muller (or Rabin) automaton. This is a cornerstone of the theory of ω-automata. The proof presented here is due to Safra (1988).

Using the transformation to deterministic Muller automata, it is easy to show that the class of Büchi recognizable ω-languages is closed under complementation. The second chapter of this part provides an alternative (and not well-known) method to show this complementation result: one transforms Büchi automata into so-called alternating automata with the weak parity condition for acceptance, and then applies again an easy result regarding their complementation.

The third chapter deals with the Streett acceptance condition of nondeterministic ω-automata, which is a conjunction of fairness conditions. In many practical cases, such conditions occur. An elegant determinization construction, also due to Safra (1992), is presented which transforms nondeterministic Streett into deterministic Rabin automata.

3   Determinization of Büchi-Automata

Markus Roggenbach

Bremen Institute for Safe Systems
Bremen University

For Bene

Introduction

To determinize Büchi automata it is necessary to switch to another class of ω-automata, e.g. Muller or Rabin automata. The reason is that there exist languages which are accepted by some nondeterministic Büchi-automaton, but not by any deterministic Büchi-automaton (c.f. section 3.1).

The history of constructions for determinizing Büchi automata is long: it starts in 1963 with a faulty construction [133]. In 1966 McNaughton showed, that a Büchi automaton can be transformed effectively into an equivalent deterministic Muller automaton [125]. Safra's construction [158] of 1988 leads to deterministic Rabin or Muller automata (c.f. section 3.2): given a nondeterministic Büchi automaton with n states, the equivalent deterministic automaton has $2^{O(n \log n)}$ states. For Rabin automata, Safra's construction is optimal (c.f. section 3.3). The question whether it can be improved for Muller automata is open. Safra's construction is often felt to be difficult. Thus, in 1995 Muller and Schupp [137] presented a 'more intuitive' alternative, which is also optimal for Rabin automata.

Although Safra's construction is optimal for Rabin automata, the resulting automata often contain equivalent states, which can be eliminated. An example for this effect is presented in Exercise3.6. As it is completely open how to minimize ω-automata, it would be quite interesting to develop procedures for 'fine tuning' Safra's construction. Some ideas in this direction can be found e.g. in [153].

Considering the languages recognizable by different classes of automata we obtain the following picture:

nondeterministic Büchi $\Leftrightarrow$ nondeterministic Muller $\Leftrightarrow$ nondeterministic Rabin
$\Uparrow$ $\quad\quad\quad\quad\quad\quad\quad\quad\quad$ $\Updownarrow$ $\quad\quad\quad\quad\quad\quad\quad\quad\quad$ $\Updownarrow$
deterministic Büchi $\;\Rightarrow\;$ deterministic Muller $\;\Leftrightarrow\;$ deterministic Rabin

These relations hold thanks to the following results:

- Obviously the deterministic variant of a class of automata is included in the nondeterministic variant of this class.
- Theorem 3.2 shows that the inclusion of the deterministic variant in the nondeterministic variant is strict for Büchi automata.

E. Grädel et al. (Eds.): Automata, Logics, and Infinite Games, LNCS 2500, pp. 43-60, 2002.

- Safra's construction implies that the class of nondeterministic Büchi automata is included in the class of deterministic Muller automata as well as in the class of deterministic Rabin automata (Theorem 3.6).
- Section 1.3.2 describes how to transform a nondeterministic Muller automaton into an equivalent nondeterministic Büchi automaton.
- Transformation 1.15 of section 1.3.3 constructs an equivalent nondeterministic Muller automaton from a given nondeterministic Rabin automaton.

The above picture also shows how determinization can be used for complementation: given a nondeterministic Büchi automaton accepting a language L, use Safra's construction to obtain an equivalent deterministic Muller automaton with state set Q and system $\mathcal{F}$ of final state sets. With $2^Q \backslash \mathcal{F}$ as system of final state sets, this automaton accepts the complement of L. Applying the construction of section 1.3.2 results in a Büchi automaton for the complement of L.

Another application of Safra's construction can be found in Klarlund, Mukund and Sohoni [99]: they generalize the construction to asynchronous finite automata accepting infinite Mazurkiewicz traces.

This chapter is organized as follows: section 3.1 shows that the inclusion of the deterministic variant in the nondeterministic variant is strict for Büchi automata. Then Safra's construction is discussed and proven to be correct in section 3.2. Finally, section 3.3 deals with the optimality of Safra's construction.

3.1   Deterministic versus Nondeterministic Büchi-Automata

Safra's construction is a refinement of the classical powerset construction as used in the determinization of automata over finite words (c.f. [87]): given an automaton with states Q, the powerset construction uses sets of states from Q – which we call *macrostates* here – as states of the desired deterministic automaton. In order to understand Safra's modifications, it is quite instructive to study why the original construction fails for automata over infinite words.

Example 3.1. Consider the Büchi automaton $\mathcal{A} = (\{q_I, f\}, \{a, b\}, \Delta, q_I, \{f\})$, where

$$\Delta = \{(q_I, a, q_I), (q_I, b, q_I), (q_I, a, f), (f, a, f)\}$$

(c.f. Figure 3.1[1]). This automaton $\mathcal{A}$ accepts the language

$$L := \{\alpha \in \{a, b\}^\omega \mid \sharp_b(\alpha) < \infty\},$$

where $\sharp_b(\alpha)$ denotes the number of 'b's occurring in word α.

The powerset construction for finite automata leads to the deterministic automaton shown in Figure 3.2. The only reasonable Büchi condition would be

---

[1] We follow the convention to depict the initial state by an incoming arc without source, and recurring states of a Büchi automaton by double circles.

$F = \{\{q_I, f\}\}$, which would also accept the word $(ab)^\omega \notin L$. The problem with the corresponding run $\varrho = \{q_I\}\{q_I, f\}\{q_I\}\{q_I, f\}\ldots$ is that – although there are infinitely many macrostates containing f – we cannot extract a run of $\mathcal{A}$ from ϱ exhibiting infinitely many f: at any time when we could choose f from a macrostate in ϱ, there is no transition with label b available in $\mathcal{A}$.

Note that with

- $\mathcal{F} = \{\{\{q_I, f\}\}\}$ as Muller condition, and with
- $(\{\{q_I\}\}, \{\{q_I, f\}\})$ as Rabin condition,

the automaton of Figure 3.2 accepts the desired language L. $\square$

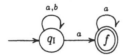

Fig. 3.1. A nondeterministic Büchi automaton.

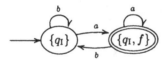

Fig. 3.2. A deterministic Büchi automaton.

It is no accident that in the above example the powerset construction fails in case of Büchi automata. The considered language cannot be accepted by any deterministic Büchi automaton:

Theorem 3.2 (Deterministic versus Nondeterministic Büchi Automata). *There exist languages which are accepted by some nondeterministic Büchi-automaton but not by any deterministic Büchi-automaton.*

Proof. Let $\Sigma := \{a, b\}$. Consider again the language $L := \{\alpha \in \Sigma^\omega \mid \sharp_b(\alpha) < \infty\}$. As shown in the above example, L is accepted by a *nondeterministic* Büchi automaton.

Assume that there is a *deterministic* Büchi automaton $\mathcal{A} = (Q, \Sigma, \delta, q_I, F)$ accepting L. This automaton accepts all words of the form σa^ω, where $\sigma \in \Sigma^*$.

Consider a reachable state $q \in Q$. Any finite word σ_q leading in $\mathcal{A}$ from the initial state q_I to q can be extended to an infinite word $\sigma_q a^\omega \in L$, i.e. some state $f \in F$ occurs infinitely often in its run on $\mathcal{A}$. Thus there must be a *finite* sequence of a-transitions from q to a recurring state.

Let m be the maximal number of a-transitions which are needed in $\mathcal{A}$ to get from a reachable state to a recurring state. Then $\mathcal{A}$ also accepts the word $\alpha = (ba^m)^\omega \notin L$: As $\mathcal{A}$ is deterministic, there exists a run ϱ of $\mathcal{A}$ on $(ba^m)^\omega$. By construction of α, the automaton $\mathcal{A}$ reaches, after each 'b', a recurring state within the next m a-transitions. Thus ϱ includes infinitely many occurrences of recurring states, and α is accepted.   □

3.2   Safra's Construction

The results of the previous section demonstrate that it is indeed necessary to switch to another class of ω-automata in order to find an equivalent deterministic automaton for a given Büchi automaton. But example 3.1 leaves open the question whether the powerset construction might be sufficient to obtain an equivalent Rabin or Muller automaton. This is not the case for Rabin automata:

Example 3.3. Consider the Büchi automaton $\mathcal{A} = (\{q_I, q_1, q_\sharp\}, \{1, \sharp\}, \Delta, q_I, \{q_I\})$ of Figure 3.3.   □

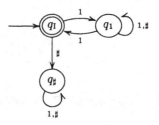

Fig. 3.3. A nondeterministic Büchi automaton.

Exercise 3.1. Apply the powerset construction to the nondeterministic Büchi automaton of Figure 3.3. Prove that there exists no Rabin condition, that allows to accept the same language with the resulting automaton.

Hint: Assume that there exists such a Rabin condition and consider the pair (E, F) which is necessary to accept the word $1(11\sharp)^\omega$.

The weakness of the powerset construction is that the resulting automaton allows for too many 'accepting' runs: given a run of this automaton with infinitely many macrostates containing a recurring state it might be impossible to 'extract' a sequence of states out of this run forming an accepting run of the original nondeterministic Büchi automaton. Safra's key idea is to modify the classical powerset construction in such a way that it allows for such an operation.

3.2.1   Safra's Tricks

Before presenting the construction in detail, we discuss Safra's tricks for extending the powerset construction in an informal way:

Trick 1: *Initialize new runs of macrostates starting from recurring states.*
  Whenever recurring states occur in a macrostate, say M, the successor state of M for some input $a \in \Sigma$ gets an extra component. This component consists of all states which can be reached under a from $F \cap M$, c.f. Figure 3.4. This leads to new concept of states replacing the old macrostates by 'sets' of macrostates. The modified powerset construction can be applied componentwise on these sets of macrostates. This trick corresponds to Step 2 in Safra's construction, c.f. section 3.2.3.
  This idea has the effect that every state included in an extra component has – in the original nondeterministic Büchi automaton – a recurring state as predecessor. Using this information in a clever way allows for constructing an accepting run on the nondeterministic Büchi automaton from an accepting run of the automaton obtained by the improved powerset construction, c.f. Lemma 3.9. See Exercise3.2 for an example illustrating this trick.
  Safra organizes these sets of macrostates as ordered trees with macrostates as labels, the so-called Safra trees. Applying Trick 1 to a leaf gives rise to a son, which increases the *height* of a Safra tree. Applying Trick 1 to a node, which already has a son, gives rise to a younger brother of this son, which might increase the *width* of a Safra tree. In order to obtain a *finite* set of states in the automaton to be constructed this growth in height and width has to be restricted: Trick 2 does so for width, while Trick 3 controls the height.

Exercise 3.2. Apply Trick 1 on the Büchi automaton of example 3.1. How does it prevent the run of $(ab)^\omega$ to be accepting?

Trick 2: *Keep track of joining runs of the nondeterministic Büchi automaton just once.*
  To illustrate this trick we consider two finite runs

$$q_1 q_2 \ldots f q_i \ldots q_{j-1} q_j \ldots q_n q_{n+1} \text{ and } q_1 q_2' \ldots q_{i-1}' q_i' \ldots f' q_j' \ldots q_n' q_{n+1}$$

of a nondeterministic Büchi automaton on the same finite word $a_1 \ldots a_n$, where both runs start in state q_1, end in state q_{n+1}, and visit recurring states f and f', respectively. Figure 3.5 shows, how Trick 1 leads to extra components: the recurring states f and f' give rise to components $\{q_i\}$ and $\{q_j'\}$, respectively. As both runs join in state q_{n+1}, the extra components of the last state are identical and hold the same 'information': state q_{n+1} has – in the original nondeterministic Büchi automaton – a recurring state as predecessor. As there is no need to store this information twice, the second component can be removed. On Safra trees this operation is called 'horizontal merge'. It corresponds to Step 4 in Safra's construction, c.f. section 3.2.3.

Trick 3: *If all states in a macrostate have a recurring state as predecessor, delete the corresponding components.*

Figure 3.6 illustrates this situation: starting in a macrostate M, a finite run leads via Trick 1 to a situation where we have a macrostate M' and extra components $K_1', \ldots, K_k'$. If

$$M' = K_1' \cup \cdots \cup K_k',$$

then all states collected in M' have a recurring state as predecessor. Encoding this situation by marking macrostate M' with a special sign, say '!', all extra components can be removed. On Safra trees this operation is called 'vertical merge'. It corresponds to step Step 6 in Safra's construction, c.f. section 3.2.3.

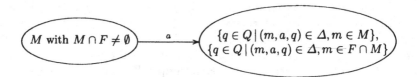

Fig. 3.4. Illustration for Trick 1.

3.2.2 Safra Trees

Given some fixed set of states Q, Safra trees are ordered, directed trees over some vocabulary V of node names, where the nodes have *nonempty* macrostates, i.e. subsets of Q, as labels. Additionally to its macrostate, a node can be marked with the special symbol '!'. Safra trees satisfy the following two conditions:

Condition 1: The union of brother macrostates is a proper subset of their parent macrostate.

Condition 2: Brother macrostates are disjoint.

This has as a consequence that the number of nodes in a Safra tree is bounded by $|Q|$. We prove this claim by induction on the height of Safra trees over Q: For the empty tree with height 0, and also for a tree with height 1, which consists just of a root node, the claim holds trivially. In the induction step observe that the sons of the root define Safra trees of lower height over disjoint subsets Q_i of states (Condition 2). Thus, by induction hypothesis, the number of nodes in the whole tree is bounded by $(\sum_i |Q_i|) + 1$. By Condition 1 we have $\sum_i |Q_i| < |Q|$, and we finally obtain $(\sum_i |Q_i|) + 1 \leq |Q|$.

Interpreting this result in terms of height and branching of a Safra tree we obtain:

- The height of a Safra tree is at most $|Q|$.
- Safra trees are finitely branching, a node has at most $|Q| - 1$ sons.

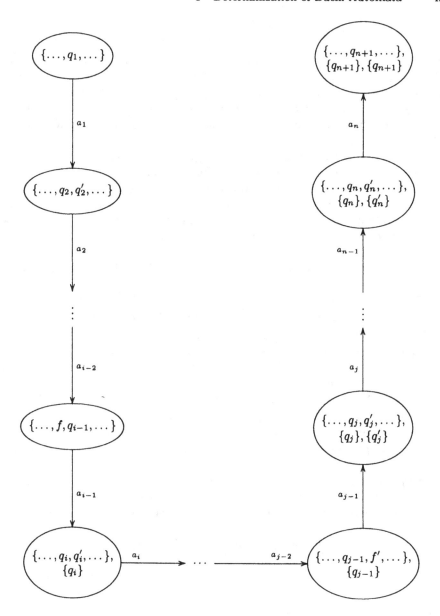

Fig. 3.5. Illustration for Trick 2.

Fig. 3.6. Illustration for Trick 3.

3.2.3 The Construction

Let $\mathcal{B} = (Q, \Sigma, q_I, \Delta, F)$ be a nondeterministic Büchi automaton. Safra's construction yields a Safra tree as an initial state q_I', a set of Safra trees as set of states Q', and a transition function $\delta : Q' \times \Sigma \to Q'$ for the alphabet Σ. To complete the construction a suitable accepting component has to be chosen: either a system of final state sets $\mathcal{F}$ to obtain a deterministic Muller automaton $\mathcal{M} = (Q', \Sigma, q_I', \delta, \mathcal{F})$, or a set of accepting pairs $\Omega = \{(E_1, F_1), \ldots, (E_k, F_k)\}$ to obtain a Rabin automaton $\mathcal{R} = (Q', \Sigma, q_I', \delta, \Omega)$, that both accept the same language as the original nondeterministic Büchi automaton $\mathcal{B}$.

Choose $V := \{1, 2, \ldots, 2\,|Q|\}$ as vocabulary for denoting nodes of Safra trees. This is sufficient, as the number of nodes in Safra trees is bounded by $|Q| = n$, and the computation of a successor of a Safra tree introduces at most n new nodes at intermediate stages (c.f. Step 2).

(1) The *initial state* q_I' is the Safra tree consisting of the single node 1 labelled with macrostate $\{q_I\}$.

(2) The value of the *transition function* $\delta(T, a)$ for a given input $a \in \Sigma$ and a Safra tree T with a set N of nodes is computed as follows:

Step 1: Remove all marks '!' in the Safra tree T.

Step 2: For every node v with macrostate M such that $M \cap F \neq \emptyset$, create a new node $v' \in (V \backslash N)$, such that v' becomes the youngest son of v and carries the macrostate $M \cap F$.

Step 3: Apply the powerset construction on every node v, i.e. replace its macrostate M by $\{q \in Q \mid \exists (m, a, q) \in \Delta : m \in M\}$.

Step 4 (horizontal merge): For every node v with macrostate M and state $q \in M$, such that q also belongs to an older brother of v, remove q from M.

Step 5: Remove all nodes with empty macrostates.

Step 6 (vertical merge): For every node whose label is equal to the union of the labels of its sons, remove all the descendants of v and mark v with '!'.

(3) The set of *states* Q' consists of all reachable Safra trees.

A *Muller automaton* is obtained by choosing the acceptance component as follows: A set $S \subseteq Q'$ of Safra trees is in the system $\mathcal{F}$ of final state sets if for some node $v \in V$ the following holds:

Muller 1: v appears in all Safra trees of S, and
Muller 2: v is marked at least once in S.

To obtain a *Rabin automaton*, one takes all pairs $(E_v, F_v), v \in V$, as acceptance component, where

Rabin 1: E_v consists of all Safra trees without a node v, and
Rabin 2: F_v consists of all Safra trees with node v marked '!'.

We should check first, that – given a Safra tree T and an input symbol a – the transition function δ computes indeed a Safra tree. This ensures that Q' consists of Safra trees, as the initial state q'_I is obviously a Safra tree.

Removing the marks '!' from all nodes of a Safra tree T does not violate Condition 1 or Condition 2, and as all macrostates are nonempty in T, they are also nonempty after Step 1. Thus Step 1 preserves the Safra tree properties.

Applying Step 2 on a Safra tree T with a node v carrying a macrostate $M \subseteq F$, yields a tree violating Condition 1, as v and its youngest son carry afterwards the same label M. Computing new macrostates for all nodes of a tree in Step 3 may lead to even more trouble:

(1) Afterwards, brother macrostates might share a state $q \in Q$, violating Condition 2.
(2) The new computed macrostate can be the empty set.
(3) It might also happen, that Condition 1 is violated, i.e. the union of brother macrostates equals the parent macrostate. This happens for example if in Step 2 a node carries a macrostate $M \subseteq F$.

Step 4, Step 5, and Step 6 deal with these problems, resp.: Step 4 ensures Condition 2 by horizontal merge of brother macrostates. Step 5 removes nodes with empty macrostates. By vertical merge Step 6 fixes situations where Condition 1 is violated. Thus, we finally obtain after all six steps a Safra tree.

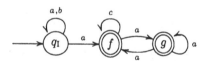

Fig. 3.7. A nondeterministic Büchi automaton.

Example 3.4 (Applying Safra's construction).
We apply Safra's construction to the nondeterministic Büchi automaton shown in Figure 3.7. Figure 3.8 and Figure 3.9 give some examples how to compute the transition function δ: they present the resulting tree after executing a certain step. If a step alters the tree, its name is typed bold. Note that the empty tree ϵ may arise as a result of Safra's construction. The resulting automaton is depicted in Figure 3.10.

To obtain a Rabin automaton, we choose – according to the above described construction – two accepting pairs (E_1, F_1) and (E_2, F_2), where

- $E_1 = \{\epsilon\}$, $F_1 = \{1 - \{f\}-!, 1 - \{g\}-!, 1 - \{f,g\}-!\}$, and
- $E_2 = \{1-\{q_I\}, \epsilon, 1-\{q_I,f\}, 1-\{f\}-!, 1-\{g\}-!\}$, $F_2 = \left\{ \begin{array}{c} 1 - \{q_I, f, g\} \\ \downarrow \\ 2 - \{g, f\}-! \end{array} \right\}$.

Computing $\delta(1 - \{q_I\}, a)$:

Step 1	Step 2	**Step 3**
$1 - \{q_I\}$	$1 - \{q_I\}$	$1 - \{q_I, f\}$

Computing $\delta(1 - \{q_I\}, c)$:

Step 1	Step 2	**Step 3**	Step 4	**Step 5**
$1 - \{q_I\}$	$1 - \{q_I\}$	$1 - \emptyset$	$1 - \emptyset$	ϵ

Computing $\delta(1 - \{q_I, f\}, c)$:

Step 1	**Step 2**	**Step 3**	Step 4	Step 5	**Step 6**
$1 - \{q_I, f\}$	$1 - \{q_I, f\}$	$1 - \{f\}$	$1 - \{f\}$	$1 - \{f\}$	$1 - \{f\}$ - !
	$\downarrow$	$\downarrow$	$\downarrow$	$\downarrow$	
	$2 - \{f\}$	$2 - \{f\}$	$2 - \{f\}$	$2 - \{f\}$	

Fig. 3.8. Steps from Safra's Construction.

Note that we need indeed a 'true' Rabin condition: While it is possible to choose E_1 as the empty set, this is not the case for $E_2 : E_2 = \emptyset$ allows to accept the word $(aaab)^\omega \notin L$.

The construction and discussion of the Muller condition is left as Exercise 3.4.

□

As the above example indicates, the constructed Rabin and Muller conditions are not 'minimal'. For Muller conditions the following restriction might lead to a smaller a system of final state sets (the proof is left for Exercise 3.5):

Remark 3.5 *(Refinement of the Muller Condition).*
Restricting the system of final state sets $\mathcal{F}$ obtained by conditions Muller 1 and Muller 2 to those sets which form a strongly connected component in the automaton leads to an equivalent Muller automaton. □

Exercise 3.3. Apply Safra's construction to the nondeterministic Büchi automaton of Figure 3.3.

Computing $\delta(1 - \{q_I, f, g\}, a)$:
$$\downarrow$$
$$2 - \{g, f\} - !$$

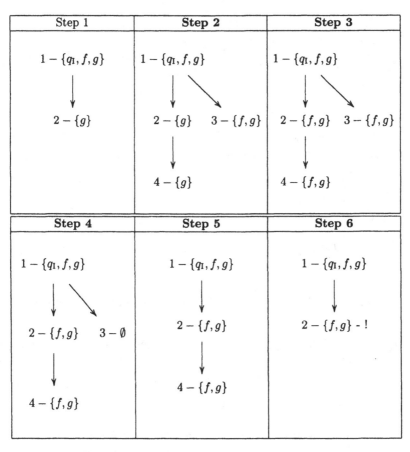

Fig. 3.9. Some Steps from Safra's Construction.

Exercise 3.4. Consider the nondeterministic Büchi automaton shown in Figure 3.7. Figure 3.10 shows the result of Safra's construction. Compute a system of final state sets $\mathcal{F}$ to obtain a deterministic Muller automaton $\mathcal{M} = (Q', \Sigma, q'_I, \delta, \mathcal{F})$.

Argue, why this system $\mathcal{F}$ may be restricted to include only sets, which are strongly connected components.

Exercise 3.5. Prove Remark 3.5. Is it possible to generalize this result to arbitrary Muller conditions?

Theorem 3.6 (Correctness).   *Let $\mathcal{B} = (Q, \Sigma, q_I, \Delta, F)$ be a nondeterministic Büchi automaton. Let $\mathcal{M} = (Q', \Sigma, q'_I, \delta, \mathcal{F})$ be the deterministic Muller and*

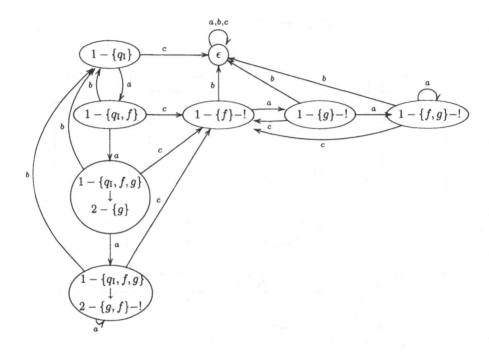

Fig. 3.10. Safra's construction applied on the automaton of Figure 3.7.

$\mathcal{R} = (Q', \Sigma, q'_1, \delta, \Omega)$ *be the deterministic Rabin automaton obtained by Safra's construction. Then*

$$L(\mathcal{B}) = L(\mathcal{M}) = L(\mathcal{R}).$$

Proof. By Lemma 3.7 and Lemma 3.9.   □

Lemma 3.7 (Completeness). *For the nondeterministic Büchi automaton $\mathcal{B}$, the deterministic Muller automaton $\mathcal{M}$, and the deterministic Rabin automaton $\mathcal{R}$ of Theorem 3.6 we have:*

$$L(\mathcal{B}) \subseteq L(\mathcal{M}) \text{ and } L(\mathcal{B}) \subseteq L(\mathcal{R}).$$

Proof. Let $\alpha \in L(\mathcal{B})$. As $\mathcal{M}$ and $\mathcal{R}$ are deterministic and have the same initial state and transition relation there exists *one* run ϱ' on α of both automata. We claim that there is at least one node v in the Safra trees of ϱ' such that

Claim 1: v – from a certain point on – is a node of all Safra trees in ϱ' and
Claim 2: v is marked '!' infinitely often.

Concerning the *Muller condition* this proves that $\text{Inf}(\varrho')$ equals a set in the system $\mathcal{F}$ of final states: condition Muller 1 is true because a Safra tree of ϱ' not including v is not in $\text{Inf}(\varrho')$. As v is marked '!' infinitely often in ϱ' and Q' is a finite set, there exists some Safra tree in $\text{Inf}(\varrho')$ with v marked '!'. Therefore also condition Muller 2 is fulfilled. Thus ϱ' is an accepting run of the deterministic Muller automaton $\mathcal{M}$, and we obtain $\alpha \in L(\mathcal{M})$.

The *Rabin condition* holds trivially for the accepting pair (E_v, F_v) : $\mathrm{Inf}(\varrho') \cap E_v = \emptyset$ is true thanks to Claim 1, Claim 2 implies $\mathrm{Inf}(\varrho') \cap F_v \neq \emptyset$. Thus ϱ' is an accepting run of the deterministic Rabin automaton $\mathcal{R}$, and we obtain $\alpha \in L(\mathcal{R})$.

Claim 1 holds for the root node: As $\alpha \in L(\mathcal{B})$, there exists an accepting run ϱ in the nondeterministic Büchi automaton $\mathcal{B}$. Thus the root of all Safra trees occurring in the run ϱ' is nonempty: the root macrostate of the i-th Safra tree in ϱ' includes $\varrho(i)$ and therefore cannot be removed in Step 5 of the Safra construction. If the root is marked '!' infinitely often, also Claim 2 holds, and we are done.

If the root is not marked '!' infinitely often we need to consider another candidate for v. As the run ϱ of the nondeterministic Büchi automaton $\mathcal{B}$ is accepting, there exists a state $q \in \mathrm{Inf}(\varrho) \cap F$, which occurs infinitely often in the root macrostate of the Safra trees in the run ϱ'. Consider the first occurrence of q in ϱ' after the last occurrence of the mark '!' at the root (if marks existed at all). As $q \in F$, q will be put into the macrostate of the youngest son of the root (Step 2 of Safra's construction). From this point onwards, the states of the run ϱ appear in the macrostate of this son, or (due to the horizontal merge operation in Step 4 of Safra's construction) get associated to older brothers of this son. Such a shift to an older brother can happen only a finite number of times: Due to Condition 2 on Safra trees any node has only finitely many brothers, especially only finitely many older brothers. Step 4 of Safra's construction moves the state of ϱ to an *older* brother, while Step 2 of Safra's construction leads to brothers which are *younger*. Thus eventually the states of the run ϱ remain in some fixed son of the root.

This son is our new candidate for v. It cannot be removed by Step 5 of Safra's construction, as it carries the states of the run ϱ and is therefore nonempty. Furthermore, it cannot be removed by Step 6 of Safra's construction, as the root is no more marked '!'. Thus Claim 1 holds. If this son is marked marked '!' infinitely often, also Claim 2 is true, and we are done.

Otherwise, proceed with this son (in which q occurs infinitely often) in the same way as with the root above. Continuing this way, Claim 2 must hold eventually, since the depth of Safra trees is finite (Condition 1 on Safra trees). □

The following lemma makes use of a result which is known as König's Infinity Lemma (for a proof and further discussion see e.g. [62]).

Theorem 3.8 (König's Infinity Lemma).
An infinite rooted tree which is finitely branching (i.e., where each node has only finitely many sons) has an infinite path.

Lemma 3.9 (Soundness). *For ihe nondeterministic Büchi automaton $\mathcal{B}$, the deterministic Muller automaton $\mathcal{M}$, and the deterministic Rabin automaton $\mathcal{R}$ of Theorem 3.6 we have:*

$$L(\mathcal{M}) \subseteq L(\mathcal{B}) \text{ and } L(\mathcal{R}) \subseteq L(\mathcal{B}).$$

Proof. Let $\alpha \in L(\mathcal{M})$. Then there exists an accepting run ϱ' of the *deterministic Muller automaton* $\mathcal{M}$ on α, i.e. $\text{Inf}(\varrho') \in \mathcal{F}$. Thus there exists some node v such that

- v appears in all Safra trees of $\text{Inf}(\varrho')$, and
- v is marked at least once in $\text{Inf}(\varrho')$.

This has as consequences that

- v – from a certain point on – is a node of all Safra trees in ϱ', and
- in ϱ' Safra trees T_i occur infinitely often with node v marked '!', i.e. ϱ' has the form

$$q'_1 \ldots T_1 \ldots T_2 \ldots T_3 \ldots$$

The same situation is achieved if we consider a word $\alpha \in L(\mathcal{R})$: Then there exists an accepting run ϱ'' of the *deterministic Rabin automaton* $\mathcal{R}$ on α, i.e. there exist a node v and an accepting pair (E_v, F_v) such that $\text{Inf}(\varrho'') \cap E_v = \emptyset$ and $\text{Inf}(\varrho'') \cap F_v \neq \emptyset$. By construction E_v consists of all Safra trees without node v (Rabin 1), i.e. v – from a certain point on – is a node of all Safra trees in ϱ''. As F_v consists of all Safra trees with node v marked '!' (Rabin 2), infinitely many Safra trees T_i with node v marked '!' occur in ϱ''.

Thus we can proceed with the proof independently of the automaton under consideration, taking a run ϱ' on a word α, which is accepted either by the Muller automaton $\mathcal{M}$ or by the Rabin automaton $\mathcal{R}$.

In order to mark the node v with '!' in Step 6 of Safra's construction, it is necessary that – at least during the computation of the transition function δ – v has to be a parent. To become a parent, Step 2 is the only possibility in Safra's construction. Thus in run ϱ' the node v carries *before* any occurrence of a Safra tree T_i a macrostate containing a recurring state $f \in F$ of the nondeterministic Büchi automaton $\mathcal{B}$.

We consider a subrun of ϱ' after the point, where v occurs in all Safra trees, in more detail: Let T and U be Safra trees of ϱ' with node v marked '!', such that in no Safra tree between T and U node v is marked '!'. Let B be a Safra tree between T and U such that v carries a macrostate with $Q \cap F \neq \emptyset$, i.e.

$$T \ldots B \ldots U,$$

say $\varrho'(i) = T$, $\varrho'(j) = B$ and $\varrho'(k) = U$, for some $0 \leq i \leq j < k$. Note that T and B might be identical. Let P, H, R be the macrostate of v in T, B, U, resp.

For the sake of simplicity assume for the moment that B is the only Safra tree between T and U, where v carries a macrostate including a recurring state. Later we will also deal with the general situation.

As ϱ' is a run on α, there exist subwords

$$\alpha[i, j] := \alpha(i)\alpha(i + 1) \ldots \alpha(j - 1) \text{ and } \alpha[j, k] := \alpha(j)\alpha(j + 1) \ldots \alpha(k - 1)$$

of α corresponding to the finite subruns $T \ldots B$ and $B \ldots U$ of ϱ'.

Consider the computation of the successor state of B and the computation of state U from some predecessor state, say X (which might be identical with B), at certain points in Safra's construction of the transition function δ :

Point 1: During the computation of $\delta(B, \alpha(j-1))$ we obtain in Step 2 of Safra's construction a node w with macrostate $H \cap F$ as son of v. This node w remains in all Safra trees before U, as no vertical merge takes place before the computation of U.

Point 2: During the computation of $U = \delta(X, \alpha(k-1))$, the condition of Step 6 of Safra's construction becomes true, i.e., before Step 6 the nodes v and it's son w carry the same macrostate R.

The following picture shows the macrostates of v and w at these points, adds the macrostate of v in T, and shows also the subwords corresponding to the subruns:

node	in T		at Point 1		at Point 2
v	P	$\overset{\alpha[i,j)}{\Longrightarrow}$	H	$\overset{\alpha[j,k)}{\Longrightarrow}$	R
			$\cup\vert$		$\Vert$
w			$H \cap F$	$\overset{\alpha[j,k)}{\Longrightarrow}$	R

As new macrostates on a node are computed in Step 3 by the classical powerset construction, the lower row can be read: for all $r \in R$, there exists a $h \in H \cap F$ and a finite run $h \ldots r$ of the nondeterministic Büchi automaton B on the subword $\alpha[j,k)$. This run can be completed by the upper row: for all $h \in H \cap F$, there exists a $p \in P$ and a finite run $p \ldots h$ of the nondeterministic Büchi automaton B on the subword $\alpha[i,j)$. I.e., for all $r \in R$, there exists a $p \in P$ and a run of B on $\alpha[i,k)$ which leads from p to r while visiting a recurring state. Note that

- there might exist several such run segments, and
- that for any $r \in R$, there exists some predecessor $p \in P$ – but not vice versa.

In general, there might occur several Safra trees between T and U, in which v carries a macrostate including a recurring state. This changes our picture in the way that we have to deal with several 'Point 1'-situations, which might lead to several sons of v. At Point 2 we take the union of all son macrostates. Looking now for the run of B on $\alpha[i,k)$ ending in some $r \in R$, we take the first suitable 'Point 1'-situation to switch from the lower to the upper row. This situation arises, when the predecessor of some state $r' \in Q$ is a recurring state. As all states in the macrostates of the sons of v stem from recurring states, such a situation will always arise.

It remains to combine these finite run segments to a complete infinite run of B : Let $0 < i_1 < i_2 < \ldots$ be the positions of ϱ' at which v is marked '!'. Let $S_0 := \{q_1\}$ and S_j be the macrostate of v at position i_j. Now we construct a directed tree with

- pairs (q, j) as nodes, where $q \in S_j$, $j \geq 0$, and
- as parent of a node $(r, j+1)$ we pick *one* of the pairs (p, j), such that $p \in S_j$ and there exists a subrun from p to r as described above.

Obviously, this is a well formed tree with $(q_1, 0)$ as root. It has infinitely many nodes and is finitely branching. Thus, by König's Lemma, c.f. Theorem 3.8, there exists an infinite path $(q_1, 0)(q_1, 1) \ldots$ in the tree. Collecting all subruns along

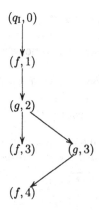

Fig. 3.11. Tree construction for $ac(aac)^\omega$.

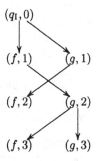

Fig. 3.12. Tree construction for a^ω.

this path, we obtain a run ϱ of $\mathcal{B}$ on α, which visits infinitely often recurring states.   □

Example 3.10 *(Illustrating the Tree Construction for König's Lemma).*
We consider again the nondeterministic Büchi automaton shown in Figure 3.7 and the resulting automaton from Safra's construction depicted in Figure 3.10.
The word $ac(aac)^\omega$ leads to the following sequence of macrostates:

- $S_0 = \{q_1\}$,
- $S_{3i+1} = \{f\}$, $i \geq 0$,
- $S_{3i+2} = \{g\}$, $i \geq 0$, and
- $S_{3i+3} = \{f, g\}$, $i \geq 0$.

Figure 3.11 illustrates that we need indeed Königs Lemma to obtain an infinite path in the tree constructed: The pair $(f, 3)$ has no son, i.e., in node $(f, 3)$ ends a *finite* path of the tree.

The word a^ω demonstrates that there might be indeed a choice between different parent nodes. Here we have as sequence of macrostates

- $S_0 = \{q_I\}$ and
- $S_i = \{f, g\}, i \geq 1.$

In Figure 3.12 one can see that the tree constructed is not uniquely determined: as a parent for $(g, j + 1)$ we have the choice between (f, j) and (g, j). For $(g, 2)$ we choose $(f, 1)$, while $(g, 3)$ has $(g, 2)$ as parent.   □

Exercise 3.6. Apply Safra's construction to the nondeterministic Büchi automaton of Figure 3.1. Compare the result with the automaton of Figure 3.2 – which states of the automaton obtained by Safra's construction are equivalent?

3.3   Safra's Construction Is Optimal

In section 3.2.2 we showed that – given some fixed set of states Q – the number of nodes in a Safra tree is bounded by $|Q|$. Now we refine this result to obtain an upper bound for the number of states necessary in Safra's construction.

Theorem 3.11 (Complexity of Safra's Construction).   *Safra's construction converts a nondeterministic Büchi automaton with n states into a deterministic Muller automaton or into a deterministic Rabin automaton with $2^{O(n*log(n))}$ states.*

Proof. We have already seen that Safra trees consist of at most n nodes, and that it is sufficient for Safra's construction to have a vocabulary of $2n$ elements.

To compute a bound on the number of Safra trees, we describe them in terms of functions:

- Let $\{q_1, \ldots, q_n\}$ be the states of the nondeterministic Büchi automaton. To describe the macrostate labels at all nodes of a Safra tree, it is sufficient to know for any q_i the node v with q_i in its macrostate, which has the greatest hight: by Condition 1 all ancestors of v carry also this state. Due to Condition 2, q_i can not be an element of any other node's macrostate. Thus the macrostate labelling can be captured by a function of type $\{q_1, \ldots, q_n\} \to \{0, 1, \ldots, 2n\}$, where the value 0 is used for the case, that a state q_i is not in the Safra tree.
- The parent relation of a Safra tree can be encoded by a function of type $\{1, \ldots, 2n\} \to \{0, 1, \ldots, 2n\}$, where the value 0 is used for the case, that a node v has no parent in the Safra tree.
- The next-older brother relation can also be captured by a function of type $\{1, \ldots, 2n\} \to \{0, 1, \ldots, 2n\}$, where the value 0 is used for the case, that a node v has no next-older brother in the Safra tree.
- The marks '!' can be encoded by a function of type $\{1, \ldots, 2n\} \to \{0, 1\}$, where 1 stands for 'is marked'. For sake of similarity, we take here a function of the same type as above, i.e. $\{1, \ldots, 2n\} \to \{0, 1, \ldots, 2n\}$.

The number of combinations of such maps (and hence the number of possible Safra trees) is bounded by $(2n + 1)^{n+3*2n} = (2n + 1)^{7n} = 2^{\log((2n+1)^{7n})} = 2^{7n \ \log(2n+1)} \in 2^{O(n \ \log(n))}$.   □

This complexity bound is optimal in the following sense:

Corollary 3.12 (Optimality of Safra's Construction).   *There is no conversion of Büchi automata with n states into deterministic Rabin automata with $2^{O(n)}$ states.*

Proof. We refer to Theorem 1.30.   □

Note that this result holds for *Rabin automata,* and that it is open whether Safra's construction can be improved for *Muller automata.*

4 Complementation of Büchi Automata Using Alternation

Felix Klaedtke

Institut für Informatik
Albert-Ludwigs-Universität, Freiburg i. Br.

4.1 Introduction

Büchi presented in [18] a natural acceptance condition allowing nondeterministic finite-state automata to define languages of infinite words: An automaton accepts an infinite word if there is a run that passes through a final state infinitely often. Such an automaton is called a Büchi automaton. Complementation of Büchi automata is not obvious.

Several constructions for complementing Büchi automata can be found in the literature. For example, Büchi himself gave a construction staying in the framework of Büchi automata [18]. The correctness of the construction involves a nontrivial combinatorial argument. Another construction, proposed by Mc-Naugthon [125] and later sharpened by Safra [158], involves a very intricate transformation to deterministic automata with a more general acceptance condition.

We describe two other constructions for complementing Büchi automata based on [97, 102, 184, 115, 201, 107]. The first construction stays in the framework of Büchi automata [97, 201, 107] and is due to Klarlund. The second construction takes a detour over alternating automata [102, 184, 115, 107]. We show that both Büchi automata obtained by the two constructions are isomorphic [107]. The number of states of the complemented Büchi automaton is $2^{O(n \log n)}$ where n is the number of states of the given Büchi automaton. Hence the constructions described here have the same upper bound as by using the Safra construction [158] (see Chapter 3).

In comparison to Büchi automata, the transition function of alternating automata is more general (in addition to existential choice, universal choice is also allowed). Moreover, we use the "weak version" of alternating automata, i.e., the acceptance condition is defined by mere reachability of some state. An advantage of using alternating automata to show closure under complementation is that much of the complexity of the construction is handled by the existential *and* universal choice of a transition. Complementing an alternating automaton can be done by dualizing its transition function and its acceptance condition. We will use games to show the correctness of this construction. The complementation proof via infinite games sheds some light in the difference between automata over infinite words and automata over infinite trees. In the game theoretic framework, the proofs of closure under complement can be compared by the respective determinacy result. For Büchi automata complementation we only

E. Grädel et al. (Eds.): Automata, Logics, and Infinite Games, LNCS 2500, pp. 61-77, 2002.
© Springer-Verlag Berlin Heidelberg 2002

need a very simple determinacy proof based on a reachability analysis, whereas tree automata complementation require the more complicated determinacy proof for parity games ([183], and also Chapter 8).

The contribution of this chapter is twofold: First, two constructions for complementing Büchi automata are described. Second, alternation is introduced and it is shown that dualizing the transition function and the acceptance condition of an alternating automaton corresponds to complementation. This proof is carried out in a game theoretic setting. Chapter 9 uses similar techniques to show that dualization of alternating automata over Kripke corresponds to complementation.

We proceed as follows. In Section 4.2 we provide background material. In Section 4.3 we describe Klarlund's construction for complementing Büchi automata. In Section 4.4 we define weak alternating parity automata and show that dualization corresponds to complementation. Finally, in Section 4.5 we reformulate the construction in [97] by using weak alternating parity automata.

4.2   Preliminaries

In this section, we provide the needed background material for this chapter. We denote the domain of a (total) function f with $\mathrm{dom}(f)$. If f is a partial function then $\mathrm{dom}(f)$ denotes the set of elements for which f is defined. It will be always clear from the context whether f is a total function or a partial function.

Words

Let Σ be a nonempty alphabet. A **finite word** α of length $m \in \omega$ over Σ is a mapping from $\{0, \ldots, m-1\}$ to Σ. We often represent α as $\alpha(0)\alpha(1)\ldots\alpha(m-1)$. An **infinite word** α over Σ is a mapping from ω to Σ. We often represent α as $\alpha(0)\alpha(1)\alpha(2)\ldots$. With Σ^ω we denote the set of infinite words over Σ. $\mathrm{Occ}(\alpha)$ denotes the set of letters occurring in $\alpha \in \Sigma^\omega$, i.e.

$$\mathrm{Occ}(\alpha) := \{\, a \in \Sigma \mid \text{there exists an } i \in \omega \text{ such that } \alpha(i) = a \,\},$$

and $\mathrm{Inf}(\alpha)$ denotes the set of letters occurring infinitely often in $\alpha \in \Sigma^\omega$, i.e.

$$\mathrm{Inf}(\alpha) := \{\, a \in \Sigma \mid \text{for all } i \in \omega \text{ there is a } j \in \omega \text{ with } j > i \text{ and } \alpha(j) = a \,\}.$$

Büchi Automata

A **Büchi automaton**, **BA** for short, $\mathcal{B}$ is a tuple $(Q, \Sigma, \delta, q_I, F)$, where Q is a finite set of states, Σ is a nonempty finite alphabet, $\delta : Q \times \Sigma \to \mathscr{P}(Q)$ is the transition function, $q_I \in Q$ is the initial state, and $F \subseteq Q$ is the set of final states.

A **run** ϱ of $\mathcal{B}$ on $\alpha \in \Sigma^\omega$ is an infinite word over Q with $\varrho(0) = q_I$ and $\varrho(i + 1) \in \delta(\varrho(i), \alpha(i))$, for all $i \in \omega$. ϱ is **accepting** if a final state occurs infinitely often in ϱ, i.e. $F \cap \mathrm{Inf}(\varrho) \neq \emptyset$. $\mathcal{B}$ **accepts** α if there is an accepting run of $\mathcal{B}$ on α; α is **rejected** otherwise. $L(\mathcal{B})$ denotes the set of words that $\mathcal{B}$ accepts.

Graphs

A **graph** G is a pair containing a set of vertices V and a set of edges $E \subseteq V \times V$. A **path** π in G is a nonempty finite word or an infinite word over V such that $(\pi(i), \pi(i+1)) \in E$, for all $i + 1 \in \mathrm{dom}(\pi)$. A path π is **maximal** if π is infinite, or π is a finite path of length n and $(\pi(n-1), u) \notin E$, for all $u \in V$. A vertex $u \in V$ is **reachable** from $v \in V$ if there is a path $v_0 v_1 \ldots v_n$ with $v = v_0$ and $u = v_n$. If $n \geq 1$ then we say that u is **nontrivially** reachable from v. $R(v)$ denotes the set of vertices that are reachable from v.

We will often use graphs (V, E) together with a set C that contains some information about the vertices in V. We will call the triple (V, E, C) also a graph.

4.3 Complementing Büchi Automata

In this section, we describe a construction for complementing Büchi automata proposed by Klarlund [97]. It is based on the classical subset construction for nondeterministic word automata over finite words (see, e.g. [87]) that builds an automaton describing *all* possible runs of the given nondeterministic automaton on a word. In particular, a state of the constructed automaton that is reached by reading a prefix of the input word, designates the subset of states that the original automaton can reach by reading the prefix. Additionally, the constructed automaton has to ensure that no run of the original automaton visits a final state infinitely often. To show that this is possible, we use *progress measures* which allow to verify locally (i.e., in terms of a single transition) that the global property (i.e., that no finite state occurs infinitely often in any run) holds.

4.3.1 Run Graphs

To complement a Büchi automaton, we analyze all its possible runs on a word. For doing so, we define a graph that embodies all these runs. Let $\mathcal{B}$ be the BA $(Q, \Sigma, \delta, q_I, F)$, and let $\alpha \in \Sigma^\omega$. The **run graph** G of $\mathcal{B}$ for α is a graph (V, E, C), with

(i) the set of vertices $V := \bigcup_{i \in \omega} S_i \times \{i\}$, where the S_is are inductively defined by

$$S_0 := \{q_I\} \quad \text{and} \quad S_{i+1} := \bigcup_{q \in S_i} \delta(q, \alpha(i)),$$

for $i \geq 0$,

(ii) the set of edges $E := \{ ((p, i), (q, i+1)) \in V \times V \mid q \in \delta(p, \alpha(i)) \}$, and

(iii) the set of marked vertices $C := \{ (q, i) \in V \mid q \in F \}$.

Note that each infinite path in the run graph G corresponds to a run of $\mathcal{B}$ on α. From this it follows that $\mathcal{B}$ accepts α iff there is an infinite path in G on which occur infinitely many vertices in C.

Lemma 4.1. *Let $G = (V, E, C)$ be a run graph of the BA $\mathcal{B}$, and let $\alpha \in \Sigma^*$. Then, $\alpha \notin \mathcal{B}$ iff $\mathrm{Inf}(\pi) \cap C = \emptyset$, for all paths π in G.*

We partition the vertices of a run graph $G = (V, E, C)$ in an infinite sequence of sets of vertices $V_0, V_1, V_2, \ldots$ such that V_0 contains the vertices in V that have only finitely many reachable vertices, V_1 contains the vertices in $V \setminus V_0$ that do not have a nontrivially reachable vertex that is in C, V_2 — analogously to V_0 — contains the vertices in $V \setminus (V_0 \cup V_1)$ that have only finitely many reachable vertices, and so on. We show that $\mathcal{B}$ rejects α iff there exists $0 \leq k_0 \leq 2|Q|$ such that $V_k = \emptyset$, for all $k > k_0$. To complement $\mathcal{B}$ we construct a BA that accepts a word $\alpha \in \Sigma^\omega$ iff there exists such a partition of the run graph of $\mathcal{B}$ for α.

We need the following definitions. Let Q be a finite set. A **sliced graph** over Q is a graph $G = (V, E, C)$, where $V \subseteq Q \times \omega$, $C \subseteq V$, and for $(p, i), (q, j) \in V$, if $((p, i), (q, j)) \in E$ then $j = i + 1$. Note that a run graph is a sliced graph.

The sliced graph $G = (V, E, C)$ is **finitely marked** if for all paths π in G, $\mathrm{Inf}(\pi) \cap C = \emptyset$. The ith **slice** S_i is the set $\{ q \in Q \mid (q, i) \in V \}$. The **width** of G, $\|G\|$ for short, is the limes superior of the sequence $(|S_i|)_{i \in \omega}$. In other words, the width of a sliced graph is the largest cardinality of the slices $S_0, S_1, \ldots$ that occurs infinitely often. The **unmarked boundary** $U(G)$ is the set of vertices that do not have a *nontrivially* reachable vertex that is marked, i.e.

$$U(G) := \{ v \in V \mid C \cap (R(v) \setminus \{v\}) = \emptyset \}.$$

The **finite boundary** $B(G)$ is the set of vertices that have only finitely many reachable vertices, i.e.

$$B(G) := \{ v \in V \mid R(v) \text{ is a finite set} \}.$$

$G \setminus U$, for $U \subseteq V$, denotes the sliced graph (V', E', C') with $V' := V \setminus U$, $E' := E \cap (V' \times V')$, and $C' := C \cap V'$.

A **progress measure** of size $m \in \omega$ for a sliced graph $G = (V, E, C)$ is a function $\mu : V \to \{1, \ldots, 2m + 1\}$ satisfying the following three conditions: (i) $\mu(u) \geq \mu(v)$, for all $(u, v) \in E$, (ii) if $\mu(u) = \mu(v)$ and $(u, v) \in E$ then $\mu(u)$ is odd or $v \notin C$, and (iii) there is no infinite path $v_0 v_1 v_2 \cdots \in V^\omega$ where $\mu(v_0)$ is odd and $\mu(v_0) = \mu(v_1) = \mu(v_2) = \ldots$.

Lemma 4.2. *Let $G = (V, E, C)$ be a sliced graph that is finitely marked. If $V \neq \emptyset$ then $U(G) \neq \emptyset$.*

Proof. For the sake of absurdity, assume that $U(G) = \emptyset$. Let v_0 be some vertex in V. Note that $R(v_0) \setminus \{v_0\} \neq \emptyset$ because of the assumption $U(G) = \emptyset$. There is a finite path from v_0 to a vertex v_1 with $v_0 \neq v_1$ and $v_1 \in C$, since $v_0 \notin U(G)$. The vertex v_1 is not in $U(G)$, since it is assumed that $U(G)$ is empty. Repeating this argument we get an infinite sequence $v_0, v_1, v_2, \ldots$ of distinct vertices, where v_{i+1} is reachable from v_i, for $i \geq 0$. Furthermore, $v_i \in C$, for $i > 0$. This contradicts the assumption that G is finitely marked. $\square$

Lemma 4.3. *Let $G = (V, E, C)$ be a sliced graph. For every vertex $v \in V \setminus B(G)$, there exists an infinite path in $G \setminus B(G)$ starting with v.*

Proof. If $R(v) \setminus B(G)$ is infinite then, by König's Lemma, there exists an infinite path in $G \setminus B(G)$ starting with v, since $R(v) \setminus B(G)$ is infinite and $G \setminus B(G)$ is finitely branching.

It remains to show that $R(v) \setminus B(G)$ is infinite. So, for a contradiction assume that $R(v) \setminus B(G)$ is finite. Let

$$B := \{ u \in B(G) \mid \text{there exists a } u' \in R(v) \setminus B(G) \text{ with } (u', u) \in E \}.$$

The set B is finite since $R(v) \setminus B(G)$ is finite and G is finitely branching. Since $B \subseteq B(G)$, we have that $R(u)$ is finite, for all $u \in B$. We have the following equality:

$$R(v) = \left(R(v) \setminus B(G) \right) \cup \bigcup_{u \in B} R(u).$$

In particular, $R(v)$ is a finite union of finite sets. This is not possible since $R(v)$ is infinite, for all $v \in V \setminus B(G)$. □

Let $G = (V, E, C)$ be a sliced graph. We define a sequence of sliced graphs $G_0, G_1, \ldots$ and a sequence of sets of vertices $V_0, V_1, \ldots$ as follows: $G_0 := G$, $V_0 := B(G)$, and

$$G_{2i+1} := G_{2i} \setminus V_{2i}, \qquad V_{2i+1} := U(G_{2i+1}), \qquad \text{and}$$
$$G_{2i+2} := G_{2i+1} \setminus V_{2i+1}, \qquad V_{2i+2} := B(G_{2i+1}),$$

for $i \geq 0$.

Lemma 4.4. *Let $G = (V, E, C)$ be a sliced graph that is finitely marked with $\|G_{2i+1}\| > 0$, for some $i \geq 0$. Then $\|G_{2i+2}\| < \|G_{2i+1}\|$.*

Proof. Since $\|G_{2i+1}\| > 0$ the set of vertices of G_{2i+1} is not empty. From Lemma 4.2 it follows that there is a vertex $v_0 \in U(G_{2i+1})$. From the definition of $G_{2i+1} = G_{2i} \setminus V_{2i}$ it follows that $v_0 \in V \setminus B(G)$ if $i = 0$, and $v_0 \in V' \setminus B(G_{2i-1})$ if $i > 0$, where V' is the set of vertices of G_{2i}. From Lemma 4.3 we can conclude that there exists an infinite path $v_0 v_1 v_2 \ldots$ in G_{2i+1}. Obviously, $v_j \in U(G_{2i+1})$, for all $j \geq 0$. Let $v_j = (q_j, k_j)$. It holds $\|G_{2i+2}\| < \|G_{2i+1}\|$ since each slice of G_{2i+2} with index k_j does not contain q_j. □

Corollary 4.5. *Let $G = (V, E, C)$ be a sliced graph that is finitely marked and let $n = \|G\|$. Then G_{2n+1} is the empty graph.*

Proof. Note that $n \leq |Q|$ assuming $V \subseteq Q \times \omega$ for some finite set Q. Assume that G_{2n+1} is not the empty graph. It holds $\|G_{2n+1}\| > 0$, since $G_{2n+1} = G_{2n} \setminus B(G_{2n-1})$. From the lemma above it follows that $n > \|G_1\| > \|G_3\| > \cdots > \|G_{2n+1}\|$. This contradicts $\|G_{2n+1}\| > 0$. □

Theorem 4.6. *Let $\mathcal{B} = (Q, \Sigma, \delta, q_{\mathrm{I}}, F)$ be a BA and let $\alpha \in \Sigma^\omega$. Then, $\mathcal{B}$ rejects α iff there exists a progress measure of size $|Q|$ for the run graph $G = (V, E, C)$ of $\mathcal{B}$ for α.*

Proof. ($\Rightarrow$) Note that the run graph G is finitely marked by Lemma 4.1. Let $\mu : V \rightarrow \{1, \ldots, 2|Q| + 1\}$ be the function defined by $\mu(v) := i + 1$, where i is the uniquely determined index with $v \in V_i$ and $v \notin V_{i+1}$. From Corollary 4.5 it follows that $1 \leq i \leq 2|Q|$ and thus μ is well-defined. It remains to show that μ is a progress measure.

First, we show that there is no infinite path $v_0 v_1 \ldots$ with $\mu(v_0) = \mu(v_1) = \ldots$ where $\mu(v_0)$ is odd. Assume that $\mu(v_0) = 2i + 1$ for $v_0 \in V$. Then $v_0 \in V_{2i}$. By definition of V_{2i}, the vertices in V_{2i} have only finitely many reachable states in G if $i = 0$ and G_{2i-1} if $i > 0$. Thus, every path $v_0 v_1 \ldots$ with $2i + 1 = \mu(v_0) = \mu(v_1) = \ldots$ must be finite.

Second, for $(u, v) \in E$, it holds $\mu(u) \geq \mu(v)$. This follows from the fact that (i) $u \in U(G')$ implies $v \in U(G')$, and (ii) $u \in B(G')$ implies $v \in B(G')$, for every sliced graph $G' = (V', E', C')$ with $(u, v) \in V'$.

Third, we show by contraposition that if $\mu(u) = \mu(v)$ then $\mu(u)$ is odd or $v \notin C$, for $(u, v) \in E$. Assume that $\mu(u)$ is even and $v \in C$. Since $\mu(u)$ is even, we have that $u \in U(G_{2i+1})$, for some $0 \leq i \leq |Q|$. Since $v \in C$, it holds $u \notin U(G_{2i+1})$. Hence $\mu(u) \neq \mu(v)$.

($\Leftarrow$) Let $\mu : V \rightarrow \{1, \ldots, 2|Q| + 1\}$ be a progress measure for G. Let π be an infinite path in G. Since μ is monotonicly decreasing, there exists a $k \geq 0$ with $\mu(\pi(k)) = \mu(\pi(k + 1)) = \ldots$. By the definition of a progress measure, $\mu(\pi(k))$ must be even and $\mu(\pi(k + i)) \notin C$. Thus, the corresponding run of π is not accepting. Since π was chosen arbitrarily there is no accepting run of $\mathcal{B}$ on α by Lemma 4.1. $\square$

4.3.2   Complementation

The next lemma shows that BAs can check whether there exists a progress measure or not.

Lemma 4.7. *Let $\mathcal{B} = (Q, \Sigma, \delta, q_I, F)$ be a BA. For every $m \in \omega$, we can construct a BA $\mathcal{B}'$ with $2^{O(|Q|+m \log |Q|)}$ states such that $\mathcal{B}'$ accepts $\alpha \in \Sigma^\omega$ iff there exists a progress measure of size m for the run graph G of $\mathcal{B}$ for α.*

Proof. Let Ψ be the set of partial functions from Q to $\{1, \ldots, 2m + 1\}$. Note that the cardinality of Ψ is $|Q|^{O(m)} = 2^{O(m \log |Q|)}$. Moreover, let $f_I \in \Psi$ be the partial function, where $f_I(q_I) := 2m + 1$ and $f_I(q)$ is undefined for $q \neq q_I$. Let $\mathcal{B}'$ be the BA $(\Psi \times \mathcal{P}(Q), \Sigma, \delta', (f_I, \emptyset), \Psi \times \{\emptyset\})$ with $(f', P') \in \delta'((f, P), a)$ iff the following conditions are satisfied:

(1) $q' \in \mathrm{dom}(f')$ iff there exists $q \in \mathrm{dom}(f)$ such that $q' \in \delta(q, a)$.
(2) $f'(q') \leq f(q)$, for $q' \in \delta(q, a)$. Moreover, if $q' \in F$ and $f(q)$ is even then $f'(q') < f(q)$.
(3) If $P = \emptyset$ then $q \in P'$ iff $f'(q)$ is odd, for $q \in \mathrm{dom}(f')$.
(4) If $P \neq \emptyset$ then $q' \in P'$ iff there exists $q \in P$ such that $q' \in \delta(q, a)$ and $f(q) = f(q')$ is odd.

The number of the states of $\mathcal{B}'$ is

$$|\Psi \times \mathscr{P}(Q)| = 2^{O(m \log |Q|)} 2^{|Q|} = 2^{O(|Q| + m \log |Q|)}.$$

Before we prove the correctness of the construction, we give the intuitive interpretation of a state (f, P) occurring in a run: $\mathcal{B}'$ guesses with $\mathrm{dom}(f)$ the slice of the run graph of $\mathcal{B}$, and with $f(q)$ the value of a progress measure for the vertices in the guessed slice. The second component takes care of the global property of a progress measure μ, i.e., that there is no infinite path $v_0 v_1 \dots$ such that $\mu(v_0) = \mu(v_1) = \dots$ and $\mu(v_0)$ is odd.

($\Rightarrow$) Let ϱ be an accepting run of $\mathcal{B}'$ on α, with $\varrho(k) = (f_k, P_k)$, for $k \in \omega$, and let $G = (V, E, C)$ be the run graph of $\mathcal{B}$ for α. Let $\mu : V \to \{1, \dots, 2m+1\}$ with $\mu(q, k) := f(q)$, for $\varrho(k) = (f, P)$. It remains to show that μ is a progress measure for G.

Because of condition (1) it holds for all $k \in \omega$ that $((q, k), (q', k+1)) \in E$ iff $q \in \mathrm{dom}(f_k)$, $q' \in \mathrm{dom}(f_{k+1})$, and $q' \in \delta(q, \alpha(k))$. This can be easily shown by induction over k. Let $(v, v') \in E$. Because of condition (2), $\mu(v) \leq \mu(v')$, and if $v' \in C$ then $\mu(v) < \mu(v')$. Note that $P_k = \emptyset$, for infinitely many $k \in \omega$, since ϱ is accepting. Hence, the conditions (3) and (4) ensure that there is no infinite path $v_0 v_1 \dots$ in G, where $\mu(v_0) = \mu(v_1) = \dots$ and $\mu(v_0)$ is odd.

($\Leftarrow$) Let $\mu : V \to \{1, \dots, 2m+1\}$ be a progress measure for the run graph $G = (V, E, C)$ of $\mathcal{B}$ for α. Note that $\alpha \notin L(\mathcal{B})$, by Theorem 4.6. Let $f_k : Q \to \{1, \dots, 2m+1\}$ be the partial function where $f_k(q) := \mu(q, k)$, for $q \in S_k$, and otherwise f_k is undefined. Let ϱ be the infinite word, with $\varrho(0) := (f_1, \emptyset)$ and for $k \geq 0$, $\varrho(k+1) := (f_{k+1}, P_{k+1})$ with

$$P_{k+1} := \{ q \in Q \mid f_{k+1}(q) \text{ is odd} \},$$

for $P_k = \emptyset$, and

$$P_{k+1} := \{ q \in Q \mid f_k(p) = f_{k+1}(q) \text{ is odd and } ((p, k), (q, k+1)) \in E \}$$

otherwise.

By induction over k it is straightforward to show that ϱ is a run of $\mathcal{B}'$ on α. It remains to show that ϱ is accepting, i.e., there are infinitely many $k \in \omega$ such that $P_k = \emptyset$. For the sake of absurdity, assume that there is an $n \in \omega$ such that $P_n = \emptyset$ and $P_{n+1}, P_{n+2}, \dots \neq \emptyset$. Note that if $q \in P_k$ with $k > n$ then there exists a $p \in P_{n+1}$ such that the vertex (q, k) is reachable from a vertex $(p, n+1)$ in G. Thus, there is an infinite path $v_0 v_1 \dots$ with $v_i = (q_i, k_i)$ for $i \geq 0$, and there is an infinite sequence of indices $i_0 < i_1 < \dots$ such that $q_{i_j} \in P_{k_{i_j}}$ for all $j \geq 0$. Since μ is a progress measure, it is $\mu(v_{i_{j'}}) \leq \mu(v_{i_j})$ for $j' \geq j$. Thus, there exists a $k > n$ such that $\mu(v_k)$ is odd and $\mu(v_k) = \mu(v_{k+1}) = \dots$. This contradicts the assumption that μ is a progress measure. $\qquad\square$

Let $\mathcal{B} = (Q, \Sigma, \delta, q_\mathrm{I}, F)$ be a BA, and let $\overline{\mathcal{B}}$ be the BA from the construction in the proof of Lemma 4.7 for $m = |Q|$. Note that $\overline{\mathcal{B}}$ has $2^{O(|Q| \log |Q|)}$ states. We claim that $L(\overline{\mathcal{B}}) = \Sigma^\omega \setminus L(\mathcal{B})$. By Theorem 4.6, $\mathcal{B}$ rejects $\alpha \in \Sigma^\omega$ iff there exists a progress measure of size $|Q|$ for the run graph G of $\mathcal{B}$ for α, i.e., by the construction of $\overline{\mathcal{B}}$ that $\overline{\mathcal{B}}$ accepts α.

Theorem 4.8. *For any BA* $\mathcal{B} = (Q, \Sigma, \delta, q_{\mathrm{I}}, F)$ *we can construct a BA* $\overline{\mathcal{B}}$ *with* $L(\overline{\mathcal{B}}) = \Sigma^\omega \setminus L(\mathcal{B})$. *Moreover,* $\overline{\mathcal{B}}$ *has* $2^{O(|Q| \log |Q|)}$ *states.*

In the remainder of the text, we reformulate the above described construction by using weak alternating parity automata. Much of the complexity of the construction is handled by the existential *and* universal choice of a transition of an alternating automaton. Complementing an alternating automaton can be done by dualizing its transition function and its acceptance condition. We will use games to show the correctness of this construction. This is an appetizer for Chapter 9 where games are used to show that dualization of alternating automata over Kripke structures corresponds to complementation.

4.4   Complementing Weak Alternating Parity Automata

The idea of alternation is to combine existential branching, as found, e.g., in Büchi automata, with its dual, universal branching. The two kinds of branching are specified by negation-free Boolean expressions over the states. For example, $q_1 \vee (q_2 \wedge q_3)$ intuitively denotes the nondeterministic choice of going either to q_1, or simultaneously to q_2 and q_3.

In this section, we show that a weak alternating parity automaton can be complemented by dualizing its transition function and its acceptance condition. The correspondence between dualization and complementation was first observed by Muller and Schupp in [136] for weak alternating automata over infinite trees. The proof that the dualized weak alternating parity automaton accepts the complement is carried out in a game theoretic setting and is due to Thomas and Löding [184, 115]. The key ingredient is the determinacy result of the games.

4.4.1   Weak Alternating Parity Automata

For a set X, $\mathcal{B}^+(X)$ denotes the set of all **positive Boolean formulas**, i.e., Boolean formulas built from the elements in X, the constants 0 and 1, and the connectives $\vee$ and $\wedge$. A subset M of X is a **model** of $\theta \in \mathcal{B}^+(X)$ if θ evaluates to true for the homomorphic extension of the truth assignment that assigns *true* to the elements in M and *false* to the elements in $X \setminus M$. M is **minimal** if no proper subset of M is a model of θ. $\mathrm{Mod}(\theta)$ denotes the set of minimal models of θ.

A **weak alternating parity automaton**, **WAPA** for short, $\mathcal{A}$ is a tuple $(Q, \Sigma, \delta, q_{\mathrm{I}}, c)$, where Q, q_{I}, and Σ are defined as before for Büchi automata; $\delta : Q \times \Sigma \to \mathcal{B}^+(Q)$ is the transition function and $c : Q \to \omega$ is the parity function, where $c(q)$ is called the *parity* of the state $q \in Q$. For $P \subseteq Q$, let $c(P) := \{ c(q) \mid q \in P \}$.

Because of the universal choice in the transition function a run of a WAPA $\mathcal{A} = (Q, \Sigma, \delta, q_{\mathrm{I}}, c)$ is not an infinite sequence of states but a rooted acyclic graph.

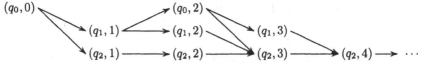

Fig. 4.1. Example of a run dag.

In such a graph the vertices are of the from (q, i), where q is a state and $i \in \omega$. The intuitive meaning of a vertex (q, i) is that $\mathcal{A}$ is in state q before reading the ith input letter. Formally, a **run dag** G of $\mathcal{A}$ on $\alpha \in \Sigma^\omega$ is a graph (V, E), where $V \subseteq Q \times \omega$ with (i) $(q_\mathrm{I}, 0) \in V$, (ii) every vertex v is reachable from $(q_\mathrm{I}, 0)$, (iii) $((p, i), (q, j)) \in E$ implies $j = i + 1$, and (iv) for all $(p, i) \in V$ it holds that

$$\{\, q \in Q \mid ((p, i), (q, i + 1)) \in E \,\} \in \mathrm{Mod}(\delta(p, \alpha(i)))\,.$$

The ith **slice** S_i is the set $\{\, q \in Q \mid (q, i) \in V \,\}$. An infinite path π in G **satisfies** the acceptance condition of $\mathcal{A}$ if the minimum of the set $\{\, c(q) \mid (q, i) \in \mathrm{Occ}(\pi) \,\}$ is even. The run dag G is **accepting** if every infinite path π in G satisfies the acceptance condition. $L(\mathcal{A})$ denotes the set of words for which there exists an accepting run dag of $\mathcal{A}$.

Example 4.9. Let $\mathcal{A}$ be the WAPA $(\{q_0, q_1, q_2\}, \{a\}, \delta, q_0, c)$ with $c(q_0) = c(q_1) := 2$, $c(q_2) := 1$, and

$$\delta(q_0, a) := q_1 \wedge q_2\,, \qquad \delta(q_1, a) := (q_0 \wedge q_1) \vee q_2\,, \qquad \delta(q_2, a) := q_2\,.$$

A run dag of $\mathcal{A}$ on the input word $\alpha = aaa\dots$ is depicted in Figure 4.1. Every run dag on $aaa\dots$ is non-accepting, since the slice S_1 always contains q_2 and $c(q_2) = \min\{c(q_0), c(q_1), c(q_2)\}$ is odd.

Exercise 4.1. The WAPA $\mathcal{A} = (Q, \Sigma, \delta, q_\mathrm{I}, c)$ is **stratified** if for all $p \in Q$ and all $a \in \Sigma$, $\delta(p, a) \in \mathcal{B}^+(\{\, q \in Q \mid c(q) \leq c(p) \,\})$. Show that a WAPA with n states can be transformed in an equivalent stratified WAPA with $O(n^2)$ states.

4.4.2 Dualization and Games

Before we turn to the definition of the games, we define the dual of a WAPA. The **dual** of a formula $\theta \in \mathcal{B}^+(X)$ is the formula $\bar{\theta} \in \mathcal{B}^+(X)$, obtained by exchanging 0 and 1, and $\vee$ and $\wedge$ in θ. Later, we will need the following lemma.

Lemma 4.10. *Let $\theta \in \mathcal{B}^+(X)$. $S \subseteq X$ is a model of $\bar{\theta}$ iff for all $R \in \mathrm{Mod}(\theta)$, $S \cap R \neq \emptyset$.*

Proof. Without loss of generality, we can assume that θ is in disjunctive normal form, i.e. $\theta = \bigvee_{R \in \mathrm{Mod}(\theta)} \bigwedge_{v \in R} v$. It holds $\bar{\theta} = \bigwedge_{R \in \mathrm{Mod}(\theta)} \bigvee_{v \in R} v$. Thus, $S \subseteq X$ is a model of $\bar{\theta}$ iff it contains at least one element from each of the disjuncts. $\square$

The **dual automaton** $\overline{A}$ of the WAPA $A = (Q, \Sigma, \delta, q_\mathrm{I}, c)$ is defined as follows: $\overline{A} := (Q, \Sigma, \overline{\delta}, q_\mathrm{I}, \overline{c})$ where $\overline{\delta}(q, a) := \overline{\delta(q, a)}$, for all $q \in Q$ and $a \in \Sigma$, and $\overline{c}(q) := c(q) + 1$, for all $q \in Q$.

Since a state of A has an even parity iff it has an odd parity in $\overline{A}$ it follows that a path π in a run dag of A satisfies the acceptance condition of A iff π does not satisfy the acceptance condition of $\overline{A}$.

A play in the game, for a WAPA A, $C \subseteq \omega$, and an input word α, is played by two players 0 and 1. The idea is that in the process of scanning the input word α, reading the ith letter of α, player 0 picks in the ith round a set of active states according to the transition function, and thereupon player 1 picks one of these active states that has a parity in C. A play determines a path through a run dag of A on α visiting only states that have a parity in C. Player 0 wins the play if the acceptance condition of A is satisfied on this path, otherwise player 1 wins. The player 0 is often also named A(utomaton) in the literature, since he chooses a model of the formula given by the automaton's transition function, and player 1 is often named P(athfinder), since he determines a path in a run dag.

Formally, a **(weak min-parity) game** $G_{A,\alpha}$ for a WAPA $A = (Q, \Sigma, \delta, q_\mathrm{I}, c)$ and $\alpha \in \Sigma^\omega$ is a graph[1] (V, E, C) that serves as an arena for the two players 0 and 1. The graph (V, E, C) is defined as follows:

(i) The set of vertices V can be partitioned into the two sets V_0 and V_1 with $V_0 = Q \times \omega$ and $V_1 = Q \times \mathscr{P}(Q) \times \omega$.

(ii) The edge relation $E \subseteq (V_0 \times V_1) \cup (V_1 \times V_0)$ is defined by

$$((q, i), (q, M, j)) \in E \qquad \text{iff} \qquad j = i + 1 \text{ and } M \in \mathrm{Mod}(\delta(q, \alpha(i))),$$

and

$$((p, M, i), (q, j)) \in E \qquad \text{iff} \qquad j = i, q \in M, \text{ and } c(q) \in C,$$

for $p, q \in Q$, $M \subseteq Q$ and $i \in \omega$.

(iii) $C \subseteq \omega$ is a finite set of parities with $c(q_\mathrm{I}) \in C$.

We also call a vertex of V a **game position**. Furthermore, we extend the parity function $c : Q \to \omega$ of A to the game positions of $G_{A,\alpha}$, i.e., $c(v)$ is the parity of the state occurring in the first component of $v \in V$. $G^*_{A,\alpha}$ denotes the game (V, E, C) with $C := c(Q)$.

Example 4.11. The game $G^*_{A,\alpha}$, where A and α are taken from Example 4.9, is depicted in Figure 4.2. Game positions that cannot be reached from the game position $(q_0, 0)$ are omitted. A solid outgoing line from a game position represents a possible move of player 0 from that game position. The dashed lines are the edges that correspond to the moves that player 1 can make.

---

[1] Since we do not need to distinguish between *arenas* and *games* as, e.g., in Chapter 2 and Chapter 6, we will only use the notion of a game.

$(q_0,0) \longrightarrow (q_0,\{q_1,q_2\},1)$ $\qquad\qquad\qquad\qquad$ $(q_0,2)$

$\qquad\qquad\qquad\qquad (q_1,1) \longleftarrow (q_1,\{q_0,q_1\},2) \dashleftarrow\dashrightarrow (q_1,2) \quad \cdots$

$\qquad\qquad\qquad\qquad\qquad\qquad\quad (q_1,\{q_2\},2)$

$\qquad\qquad\qquad\qquad (q_2,2) \longrightarrow (q_2,\{q_2\},2) \quad \dashrightarrow (q_2,2)$

Fig. 4.2. Part of a game.

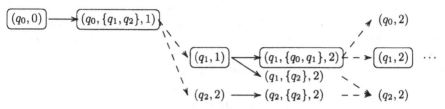

$(q_0,0) \longrightarrow (q_0,\{q_1,q_2\},1)$ $\qquad\qquad\qquad\qquad$ $(q_0,2)$

$\qquad\qquad\qquad\qquad (q_1,1) \longleftarrow (q_1,\{q_0,q_1\},2) \dashleftarrow\dashrightarrow (q_1,2) \quad \cdots$

$\qquad\qquad\qquad\qquad\qquad\qquad\quad (q_1,\{q_2\},2)$

$\qquad\qquad\qquad\qquad (q_2,2) \longrightarrow (q_2,\{q_2\},2) \quad \dashrightarrow (q_2,2)$

Fig. 4.3. Example of a play.

A **play** π is a maximal path in $G_{\mathcal{A},\alpha}$ with $\pi(0) = (q_1,0)$. In the following, let $\overline{\sigma}$ denote the opponent of player $\sigma \in \{0,1\}$, i.e. $\overline{\sigma} := 1 - \sigma$. Player σ **wins** the play π if

- π has finite length n and $\pi(n-1) \in V_{\overline{\sigma}}$, or
- π is infinite, and $\min\{\, c(\pi(k)) \mid k \in \omega \,\} = 2i + \sigma$, for some $i \in \omega$.

A **(memory-less) strategy** for player σ is a partial function $f_\sigma : V_\sigma \to V_{\overline{\sigma}}$ such that for all $v \in V_\sigma$, where v has successors, we have $(v, f_\sigma(v)) \in E$. The play π is played **according** to f_σ if $f_\sigma(\pi(k)) = \pi(k+1)$, for all $\pi(k) \in V_\sigma$ and $k+1 \in \mathrm{dom}(\pi)$. The strategy f_σ is a **winning strategy** if player σ wins every play that is played according to f_σ.

Example 4.12. We define strategies for player 0 and player 1 for the game in Example 4.11. The function $f_1 : V_1 \to V_0$ is defined by

$$f_1(q, S, i) := \begin{cases} (q_1, i) & \text{if } S = \{q_0, q_1\} \text{ or } S = \{q_1, q_2\}, \\ (q_2, i) & \text{if } S = \{q_2\}, \\ (q', i) & \text{otherwise (for some fixed } q' \in S), \end{cases}$$

for $q \in \{q_0, q_1, q_2\}$, $S \subseteq \{q_0, q_1, q_2\}$, and $i \in \omega$, is a strategy for player 1 in the game from Example 4.11. f_1 is not a good strategy because player 0 wins the play if player 1 is playing according to the strategy f_1, and player 0 is playing according to the strategy $f_0 : V_0 \to V_1$ with $f_0(q_0, i) := (q_0, \{q_1, q_2\}, i+1)$, $f_0(q_1, i) := (q_1, \{q_0, q_1\}, i+1)$ and $f_0(q_2, i) := (q_2, \{q_2\}, i+1)$ with $i \in \omega$. The play is depicted in Figure 4.3. The chosen game positions are highlighted by a box.

The strategy $f_0' : V_1 \to V_0$ with $f_0'(q_0, \{q_1, q_2\}, 1) := (q_2, 1)$ and $f_1'(v) := f_1(v)$, for $v \in V_1$ with $v \neq (q_0, \{q_1, q_2\}, 1)$, is a better strategy for player 1 since it is a winning strategy for player 1.

The next lemma shows the tight relation between the acceptance condition of WAPAs and winning strategies for player 0.

Lemma 4.13. *Let $A = (Q, \Sigma, \delta, q_1, c)$ be a WAPA and let $\alpha \in \Sigma^\omega$. Player 0 has a winning strategy for the game $G^*_{A,\alpha}$ iff A accepts α.*

Proof. ($\Leftarrow$) Assume that there is an accepting run dag G of A on α with the slices $S_0, S_1, \ldots$. We define a strategy f_0 of player 0 as follows: Given the game position (q, i) with $q \in S_i$, player 0 picks $M \subseteq S_{i+1}$ with $M \in \mathrm{Mod}(\delta(q, \alpha(i)))$, i.e. $f_0(q, i) := (q, M, i+1)$. For all other game position $(q', i') \in V_0$ with $q' \notin S_{i'}$, $f_0(q', i')$ is arbitrary. In this way, starting from the game position $(q_1, 0)$, player 0 ensures that the play proceeds along a path through the run dag. Since the run dag is accepting, player 0 has a winning strategy.

($\Rightarrow$) A winning strategy f_0 defines an accepting run dag: For $i \geq 0$, the slices S_i are built-up inductively, beginning with the singleton $S_0 := \{q_1\}$. For $i > 0$ and a game position $(q, i-1)$ that is picked by player 1, player 0's strategy prescribes a set of states as the next move. The union of these states defines the next slice S_i, i.e. $S_i := \bigcup_{q \in S_{i-1}} \{ S \subseteq Q \mid f_0(q, i-1) = (q, S, i) \}$. The edges from the vertices in $S_i \times \{i\}$ to the vertices in $S_{i+1} \times \{i+1\}$ are inserted according to the transition function. The run dag is accepting. $\qquad\square$

The next lemma shows the determinacy of the games. For its proof we need the definition of an attractor set of player σ of a set of game positions for a game $G_{A,\alpha} = (V, E, C)$.

The **attractor** of player σ of $X \subseteq V$, $\mathrm{Attr}_\sigma(X)$ for short, contains all game positions from which player σ can force player $\bar{\sigma}$ a visit (after finitely many moves) to a game position in X or to a game position where player $\bar{\sigma}$ cannot make a move.

$$\mathrm{Attr}^0_\sigma(X) := X,$$
$$\mathrm{Attr}^{i+1}_\sigma(X) := \mathrm{Attr}^i_\sigma(X) \cup$$
$$\{ u \in V_\sigma \mid \text{there is a } v \in V_{\bar{\sigma}} \text{ with } (u, v) \in E \text{ and } v \in \mathrm{Attr}^i_\sigma(X) \} \cup$$
$$\{ u \in V_{\bar{\sigma}} \mid \text{for all } v \in V_\sigma \text{ if } (u, v) \in E \text{ then } v \in \mathrm{Attr}^i_\sigma(X) \},$$

and

$$\mathrm{Attr}_\sigma(X) := \bigcup_{i \in \omega} \mathrm{Attr}^i_\sigma(X).$$

For instance, a game position v of player 0 is in $\mathrm{Attr}^{i+1}_0(X)$ if it was already in $\mathrm{Attr}^i_0(X)$ or player 0 can make a move to a game position in $\mathrm{Attr}^i_0(X)$. A game position v of player 1 is in $\mathrm{Attr}^{i+1}_0(X)$ if it was already in $\mathrm{Attr}^i_0(X)$ or all game positions to which player 1 can move are in $\mathrm{Attr}^i_0(X)$. The attractor of player 0 is the union of all $\mathrm{Attr}^i_0(X)$ for $i \in \omega$. Figure 4.4 shows graphically the construction of the attractor of player 0.

Note that for a game position outside $\mathrm{Attr}_\sigma(X)$, player $\bar{\sigma}$ is always able to avoid to visit a game position in X. If it is the turn of player $\bar{\sigma}$, then it is

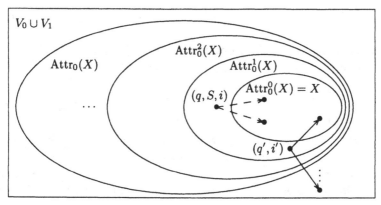

Fig. 4.4. Construction of the attractor of player 0.

possible to stay outside of $\mathrm{Attr}_\sigma(X)$, and if it is the turn of player σ, then it is not possible for him to choose a game position in $\mathrm{Attr}_\sigma(X)$.

Lemma 4.14. *Let $\mathcal{A} = (Q, \Sigma, \delta, q_1, c)$ be a WAPA and let $\alpha \in \Sigma^\omega$. Either player 0 or player 1 has a winning strategy for the game $G_{\mathcal{A},\alpha} = (V, E, C)$.*

Proof. Let $k := \min C$, and let T denote the set of game positions where player 1 can force player 0 to visit a game position from which player 0 cannot make a move, i.e. $T := \mathrm{Attr}_1(\{\, u \in V_0 \mid \text{for all } v \in V \text{ is } (u, v) \notin E \,\})$.

We show by induction over $|C|$, i.e., the number of parities in $G_{\mathcal{A},\alpha}$, that either player 0 or player 1 has a winning strategy. For $|C| = 1$, player 0 has a winning strategy if k is even and $(q_1, 0) \notin T$, and player 1 has a winning strategy if k is odd or $(q_1, 0) \in T$.

Let $|C| > 1$. If $(q_1, 0) \in T$ then obviously player 1 has a winning strategy. Let $(q_1, 0) \notin T$ and assume that k is even (the proof for the case that k is odd is analogous). Moreover, let $U = \{\, v \in V \mid c(v) = k \,\}$.

If $(q_1, 0) \in \mathrm{Attr}_0(U)$, then player 0 has a winning strategy. If $(q_1, 0) \notin \mathrm{Attr}_0(U)$ then we define the game $G'_{\mathcal{A},\alpha}$ by removing the parity k and by deleting the edges $(u, v) \in E \cap V_1 \times V_0$ where u is a game position in U. By the induction hypothesis we know that either player 0 or player 1 has a winning strategy for $G'_{\mathcal{A},\alpha}$. We will show that if player σ has a winning strategy in $G'_{\mathcal{A},\alpha}$ then the player σ has also a winning strategy in $G_{\mathcal{A},\alpha}$.

Assume that player 1 has a winning strategy for $G'_{\mathcal{A},\alpha}$. Playing according to this strategy ensures the players to stay outside of $\mathrm{Attr}_0(U)$ in any play in $G_{\mathcal{A},\alpha}$, as otherwise there would be a game position belonging to $\mathrm{Attr}_0(U)$ in $G'_{\mathcal{A},\alpha}$. Therefore, player 1 also has a winning strategy for $G_{\mathcal{A},\alpha}$.

Suppose that player 0 has a winning strategy for $G'_{\mathcal{A},\alpha}$. If player 0 plays according to this strategy in $G_{\mathcal{A},\alpha}$, then the only possibility for player 1 to give another progression to the play as in $G'_{\mathcal{A},\alpha}$ is to move into $\mathrm{Attr}_0(U)$ if possible. But if player 1 picks a game position in $\mathrm{Attr}_0(U)$, player 0 can force to visit a game position in U. Then player 0 wins the play, due to the choice of U (note that k is even). Therefore, player 0 has a winning strategy for $G_{\mathcal{A},\alpha}$. $\qquad\square$

The next lemma connects winning strategies for the games $G^*_{\mathcal{A},\alpha}$ and $G^*_{\overline{\mathcal{A}},\alpha}$.

Lemma 4.15. *Let $\mathcal{A} = (Q, \Sigma, \delta, q_\mathrm{I}, c)$ be a WAPA and let $\alpha \in \Sigma^\omega$. Player 0 has a winning strategy for $G^*_{\mathcal{A},\alpha}$ iff player 1 has a winning strategy for $G^*_{\overline{\mathcal{A}},\alpha}$.*

Proof. ($\Rightarrow$) Let f_0 be a winning strategy for player 0 for $G^*_{\mathcal{A},\alpha}$. Further, let (q, S, k) be a game position of $G^*_{\overline{\mathcal{A}},\alpha}$. If there exists a play in $G^*_{\overline{\mathcal{A}},\alpha}$ such that (q, S, k) appears in this play, then $S \in \mathrm{Mod}(\overline{\delta}(q, \alpha(k-1)))$. We do not need to define a strategy for vertices that do not appear in any play in $G^*_{\overline{\mathcal{A}},\alpha}$. From Lemma 4.10 it follows that there exists a $p \in S \cap W$, for $f_0(q, k-1) = (q, W, k)$, since $W \in \mathrm{Mod}(\delta(q, \alpha(k-1)))$. We define a strategy of player 1 as $\overline{f}_1(q, S, k) := (p, k)$.

We show that $\overline{f}_1$ is a winning strategy for $G^*_{\overline{\mathcal{A}},\alpha}$. For a play $\overline{\pi}$ in $G^*_{\overline{\mathcal{A}},\alpha}$ played according to $\overline{f}_1$, there exists a play π in $G^*_{\mathcal{A},\alpha}$ played according to f_0 such that $\overline{c}(\overline{\pi}(i)) - 1 = c(\pi(i))$, for all $i \geq 0$. Since player 0 wins π in $G^*_{\mathcal{A},\alpha}$, player 1 wins $\overline{\pi}$ in $G^*_{\overline{\mathcal{A}},\alpha}$.

($\Leftarrow$) Let $\overline{f}_1$ be a winning strategy of player 1 for $G^*_{\overline{\mathcal{A}},\alpha}$ and let (q, k) be a game position of $G^*_{\mathcal{A},\alpha}$. The set $T := \{\, p \in Q \mid (p, k+1) = \overline{f}_1(q, R, k) \text{ with } R \in \mathrm{Mod}(\overline{\delta}(q, \alpha(k))) \,\}$ is a model of $\delta(q, \alpha(k))$ by Lemma 4.10. Let $S \subseteq T$ be a minimal model of $\delta(q, \alpha(k))$. As above, it can be shown that the strategy f_0 with $f_0(q, k) := (q, S, k+1)$ is a winning strategy for $G^*_{\mathcal{A},\alpha}$ for player 0. $\square$

Now, we have all ingredients for proving that the dual automaton accepts the complement.

Theorem 4.16. *For a WAPA $\mathcal{A} = (Q, \Sigma, \delta, q_\mathrm{I}, c)$ it holds that $L(\overline{\mathcal{A}}) = \Sigma^\omega \setminus L(\mathcal{A})$.*

Proof. We show that $\mathcal{A}$ does not accept α iff $\overline{\mathcal{A}}$ accepts α, for $\alpha \in \Sigma^\omega$. By Lemma 4.13, $\mathcal{A}$ does not accept α iff player 0 does not have a winning strategy for $G^*_{\mathcal{A},\alpha}$. By Lemma 4.15, this is equivalent to the case that player 1 does not have a winning strategy for $G^*_{\overline{\mathcal{A}},\alpha}$. By Lemma 4.14, this is equivalent to that player 0 has a winning strategy for $G^*_{\overline{\mathcal{A}},\alpha}$, i.e., by Lemma 4.13, $\overline{\mathcal{A}}$ accepts α. $\square$

4.5 Complementing Büchi Automata by Using Weak Alternating Parity Automata

In Section 4.3 we have complemented a Büchi automaton by constructing a Büchi automaton that checks whether there exists a progress measure. In this section we give another construction for complementing Büchi automata. The BA $\mathcal{B}$ is first transformed in an equivalent WAPA $\mathcal{A}$. The dual automaton $\overline{\mathcal{A}}$ is transformed in an equivalent BA $\overline{\mathcal{B}}$.

4.5.1 From Büchi Automata to Weak Alternating Parity Automata and Vice Versa

Theorem 4.17. *For any Büchi automaton $\mathcal{B}$ we can construct a WAPA $\mathcal{A}$ with $L(\mathcal{B}) = L(\mathcal{A})$. Moreover, if $\mathcal{B}$ has n states then $\mathcal{A}$ has $O(n^2)$ states.*

Proof. Let $\mathcal{B} = (Q, \Sigma, \delta, q_{\mathrm{I}}, F)$ be a Büchi automaton. The desired WAPA $\mathcal{A}$ is $(Q \times \{0, \ldots, 2|Q|\}, \Sigma, \delta', (q_{\mathrm{I}}, 2|Q|), c)$, where $c(q, i) := i$ and the transition function δ' is defined as

$$\delta'((p, i), a) := \bigvee_{q \in \delta(p, a)} \left(\Delta(q, i) \wedge \bigwedge_{0 \le j < i} (q, j) \right),$$

where $\Delta(q, i) := (q, i)$ if i is even or $q \notin F$; otherwise $\Delta(q, i) := 1$.

$L(\mathcal{B}) \subseteq L(\mathcal{A})$: Let π be an accepting run of $\mathcal{B}$ on $\alpha \in L(\mathcal{B})$. The construction of an accepting run dag G of $\mathcal{A}$ on α is straightforward. The slices of G are defined as follows: $S_0 := \{(q_{\mathrm{I}}, 2|Q|)\}$ and $S_k := \{ (\pi(k), i) \mid 0 \le i \le 2|Q| \}$, for $k > 0$. The edges from the vertices in $S_k \times \{k\}$ to the vertices in $S_{k+1} \times \{k+1\}$ are defined according to the transition function. Since π contains infinitely many states of F, each vertex $((p, 2i + 1), k)$ on an infinite path in G does eventually reach a vertex $((q, 2i), k')$. Thus, every infinite path in G satisfies the acceptance condition.

$L(\mathcal{A}) \subseteq L(\mathcal{B})$: Let $\alpha \notin L(\mathcal{B})$. We show that there exists an accepting run dag of the dual automaton $\overline{\mathcal{A}}$ on α. Thus $\alpha \notin L(\mathcal{A})$ by Theorem 4.16. Intuitively, $\overline{\mathcal{A}}$ checks with its transition function the existence of a progress measure for G of size $|Q|$:

$$\overline{\delta'((p, i), a)} = \bigwedge_{q \in \delta(p, a)} \left(\overline{\Delta(q, i)} \vee \bigvee_{0 \le j < i} (q, j) \right).$$

By Lemma 4.6, there exists a progress measure $\mu : V \to \{1, \ldots, 2|Q|+1\}$ for the run graph $G = (V, E, C)$ of $\mathcal{B}$ for α. Let $G' := (V', E')$ with

$$V' := \{ ((q, \mu(q, k) - 1), k) \mid (q, k) \in V \},$$

and there is an edge from $((q, \mu(q, k) - 1), k)$ to $((q', \mu(q', k + 1) - 1), k + 1)$ iff $((q, k), (q', k+1)) \in E$. It is straightforward to show that G' is an accepting run dag of $\overline{\mathcal{A}}$ on α. ☐

Exercise 4.2. Let $\mathcal{B}$ be the BA $\mathcal{B} = (Q, \Sigma, \delta, q_{\mathrm{I}}, F)$, and let $\mathcal{A}$ be the WAPA $(Q \times \{0, \ldots, 2|Q|\}, \Sigma, \delta', (q_{\mathrm{I}}, 2|Q|), c)$ with $c(q, i) := i$ and

$$\delta'((p, i), a) := \begin{cases} \bigvee_{q \in \delta(p, a)}(q, 0) & \text{if } i = 0, \\ \bigvee_{q \in \delta(p, a)}(q, i) \wedge (q, i - 1) & \text{if } i > 0 \text{ and } i \text{ is even}, \\ \bigvee_{q \in \delta(p, a)}(q, i) & \text{if } p \notin F \text{ and } i \text{ is odd}, \\ \bigvee_{q \in \delta(p, a)}(q, i - 1) & \text{if } p \in F \text{ and } i \text{ is odd}, \end{cases}$$

for $p \in Q$, $0 \le i \le 2|Q|$, and $a \in \Sigma$. This construction is from [184]. Prove $L(\mathcal{A}) = L(\mathcal{B})$ without using progress measures.

Exercise 4.3. The natural number m is an **upper bound for the progress measures** for the BA $\mathcal{B} = (Q, \Sigma, \delta, q_1, F)$ if for all $\alpha \in \Sigma^\omega$, $\mathcal{B}$ rejects α iff there exists a progress measure of size m for the run graph. Show that it is PSPACE-complete to decide if $m \in \omega$ is the smallest upper bound for the progress measure for a BA. (Hint: Use the fact that the emptiness problem for WAPAs is PSPACE-complete.)

Theorem 4.18. *For any WAPA $\mathcal{A}$ we can construct a Büchi automaton $\mathcal{B}$ with $L(\mathcal{A}) = L(\mathcal{B})$. Moreover, if $\mathcal{A}$ has n states then $\mathcal{B}$ has $2^{O(n^2)}$ states; and if $\mathcal{A}$ is stratified then $\mathcal{B}$ has $2^{O(n)}$ states.*

Proof. By Exercise 4.1, we can transform $\mathcal{A}$ in an equivalent stratified WAPA $\mathcal{A}'$ with $O(n^2)$ states.

We use a subset construction from [129]. At a given point $k \in \omega$ of a run of the Büchi automaton $\mathcal{B}$, $\mathcal{B}$ saves the kth slice of the run dag of $\mathcal{A}'$. As it reads the next letter, it guesses the next slice of the run dag of $\mathcal{A}'$. In order to make sure that every infinite path visits a final state infinitely often, $\mathcal{B}$ keeps track of the states that owe a visit to a state with an even parity.

Let $\mathcal{A}' = (Q, \Sigma, \delta, q_1, c)$, and let E denote the set of all states that have an even parity. Then $\mathcal{B} := (\mathcal{P}(Q) \times \mathcal{P}(Q), \Sigma, \delta', (\{q_1\}, \emptyset), \mathcal{P}(Q) \times \{\emptyset\})$, where the transition function δ' is defined by

$$\delta'((S, O), a) := \{ (S', O' \setminus E) \mid S' \in \mathrm{Mod}\,(\bigwedge_{q \in S} \delta(q, a)), O' \subseteq S', \text{ and}$$

$$O' \in \mathrm{Mod}\,(\bigwedge_{q \in O} \delta(q, a)) \}$$

and

$$\delta'((S, \emptyset), a) := \{ (S', S' \setminus E) \mid S' \in \mathrm{Mod}\,(\bigwedge_{q \in S} \delta(q, a)) \},$$

for $a \in \Sigma$ and $S, O \subseteq Q$, $O \neq \emptyset$. We omit the proof for $L(\mathcal{A}') = L(\mathcal{B})$. □

Exercise 4.4. Show that there is no linear translation from BAs to stratified WAPAs. (Hint: Use the family of languages $(L_n)_{n \geq 2}$ from Theorem 1.30 in Chapter 1.)

4.5.2 Complementation

Complementing a BA $\mathcal{B}$ can be done in three steps. First, by Theorem 4.17, we can construct an equivalent WAPA $\mathcal{A}$. Second, by Theorem 4.16, the dual automaton $\overline{\mathcal{A}}$ of $\mathcal{A}$ accepts the complement of $\mathcal{B}$. Third, by Theorem 4.18, we can construct a BA $\overline{\mathcal{B}}$ that accepts the complement of $\mathcal{B}$. Suppose that $\mathcal{B}$ has n states. Then, $\mathcal{A}$ and $\overline{\mathcal{A}}$ have both $O(n^2)$ states. Since $\overline{\mathcal{A}}$ is already stratified, $\overline{\mathcal{B}}$ has $2^{O(n^2)}$ states.

The construction can be improved by tuning the translation from the WAPA $\overline{A}$ to the BA $\overline{B} = (P, \Sigma, \delta, q_\mathrm{I}, F)$. The improvement is due to Kupferman and Vardi [102]. Let Q be the set of states of B. Note that $P = \mathscr{P}(Q \times \{0, \ldots, 2n\}) \times \mathscr{P}(Q \times \{0, \ldots, 2n\})$ by the construction of $\overline{B}$. A set $S \subseteq Q \times \{0, \ldots, 2n\}$ is **consistent** if $(q, i), (q, j) \in S$ implies $i = j$. Let $\overline{B}'$ be the BA $(P', \Sigma, \delta, q_\mathrm{I}, F)$, where P' be the set of pairs of consistent sets (S, O) with $O \subseteq S$, and the transition function δ' is restricted to P', i.e. $\delta'((S, O), a) := \delta((S, O), a)$, for $(S, O) \in P'$.

Note that $(S, O) \in P'$ can be represented by the set $\{q \in Q \mid (q, i) \in O\}$ and the partial function $f : Q \rightarrow \{0, \ldots, 2n\}$, where $f(q) := i$, for $(q, i) \in S$, and otherwise f is undefined. It is easy to see that $\overline{B}'$ and the BA obtained by the construction described in Section 4.3 are isomorphic. This was observed by Kupferman and Vardi in [107]. Thus, $L(\overline{B}') = \Sigma^\omega \setminus L(B)$, and $\overline{B}'$ has $2^{O(n \log n)}$ states.

5 Determinization and Complementation of Streett Automata

Stefan Schwoon

Institut für Informatik
Technische Universität München

5.1 Introduction

Several classes of ω-automata have been proposed in the literature, most importantly Büchi automata, Muller automata, and Rabin automata. It has been shown that the expressiveness of all these models is equivalent.

Streett automata were first suggested in [171]. They differ from the other formalisms in their acceptance condition which models strong fairness constraints. Again, their expressiveness is equal to that of Büchi automata; however, for certain properties of ω-words Streett automata can have an exponentially more succinct representation.

Here, we survey results about upper and lower bounds on the problems of determinization and complementation of Streett automata. A relatively simple argument yields a doubly exponential upper bound for determinization; however, Safra [159] found an exponential procedure, involving a transformation from (non-deterministic) Streett automata to deterministic Rabin automata (see Section 5.3), and another transformation from deterministic Streett automata to deterministic Rabin automata (Section 5.4). We present a slight modification of Safra's method and try to provide ample intuition for the method and its proof of correctness. Moreover, the results of [114] lead to lower bounds on these problems; these, together with their proofs, are portrayed in Section 5.5.

5.2 Definitions

A (non-deterministic) Streett automaton $\mathcal{A}$ is a 5-tuple $(Q, \Sigma, \delta, q_0, \Omega)$ where Q is a finite set of **states**, Σ is a finite **alphabet**, $\delta \colon Q \times \Sigma \to 2^Q$ is a **transition function**, q_0 is an **initial state**, and $\Omega = \{(L_1, U_1), \ldots, (L_h, U_h)\}$ is an **acceptance condition** where L_i and U_i, $1 \le i \le h$, are subsets of Q. We call the tuples (L_i, U_i) the **acceptance pairs** of $\mathcal{A}$. For deterministic automata, $|\delta(q, a)| = 1$ holds for all $q \in Q$, $a \in \Sigma$.

For an infinite word $\alpha \in \Sigma^\omega$ of the form $\alpha = \alpha_0 \alpha_1 \ldots$, we say that $\xi \in Q^\omega$ is a **run** of $\mathcal{A}$ over α if $\xi = \xi_0 \xi_1 \ldots$ where $\xi_0 = q_0$ and $\xi_{i+1} \in \delta(\xi_i, \alpha_i)$ for all $i \ge 0$. The **infinity set** $\mathrm{Inf}(\xi)$ is the set of states visited infinitely often by ξ.

A word $\alpha \in \Sigma^\omega$ is **accepted** by the Streett automaton $\mathcal{A}$ if there is an infinite run over α such that the following condition holds for all $i \in \{1, \ldots, h\}$: If some state in L_i is visited infinitely often, then some state in U_i is visited infinitely often, too. The set of infinite words accepted by $\mathcal{A}$ is denoted $L(\mathcal{A})$.

E. Grädel et al. (Eds.): Automata, Logics, and Infinite Games, LNCS 2500, pp. 79-91, 2002.

The acceptance condition can be seen as a model for strong fairness. If, for each i, the states in L_i represent a request for some action and U_i corresponds to the execution of said action, then the condition postulates that every request which is repeated an unbounded number of times is eventually granted.

A **Rabin automaton** has the same structure as a Streett automaton, but with a different interpretation. The Rabin acceptance condition declares a run as accepting if there exists an index i, $1 \le i \le h$, such that L_i is visited infinitely often, but U_i is visited only finitely often.

Since their structures are the same, each Streett automaton can be interpreted as a Rabin automaton, and vice versa. Observe that the Rabin acceptance condition is exactly the opposite of the Streett condition. Hence, in the deterministic case where there is exactly one possible run for every input, the same automaton under the Streett interpretation represents the complement of its language under the Rabin interpretation. We will use this fact in our constructions later on.

Definition 5.1. A set $J \subseteq \{1, \ldots, h\}$ is a **witness set** for $\alpha \in L(\mathcal{A})$ if there is an accepting run over α such that for all indices $j \in J$ the set U_j is visited infinitely often, and for all indices $j' \notin J$ the set $L_{j'}$ is visited only finitely often.

It is easy to see that $\alpha \in L(\mathcal{A})$ exactly if α has at least one witness set. Hence, the problem of checking acceptance of a Streett automaton can be reduced to finding a witness set for the input. The constructions in later sections are based on this idea.

Note also that an accepting run can yield multiple witness sets if there are indices j where L_j is visited finitely often, and U_j is visited infinitely often.

5.3   Transformation of Non-deterministic Streett Automata

Safra [159] showed an exponential complementation procedure for Streett automata. The procedure converts a non-deterministic Streett automaton $\mathcal{A}$ into a deterministic Rabin automaton $\mathcal{D}$ for the same language (and hence a deterministic Streett automaton for the complement of $L(\mathcal{A})$). In this section we present this construction, proving the following theorem:

Theorem 5.2. *Given a non-deterministic Streett automaton $\mathcal{A}$ with n states and h acceptance pairs, one can construct a deterministic Rabin automaton $\mathcal{D}$ with $2^{O(nh \log(nh))}$ states and $O(nh)$ acceptance pairs such that $\mathcal{D}$ accepts $L(\mathcal{A})$.*

The automaton $\mathcal{D}$ simulates, for a given input, all possible runs of $\mathcal{A}$ and tries to find an accepting witness set within these runs. Difficulties arise because the number of potential witness sets is exponential. Therefore, the construction observes only a (polynomial) number of "interesting" witness sets in every step, and these sets change dynamically.

The sets are arranged in a hierarchical structure called a decomposition in [159]. These can also be interpreted as trees (see for instance [94]). Every node in such a tree represents a process that is "hoping" for a certain witness set to be realised. The witness set of a parent node is a superset of that of its child nodes.

A process for a witness set J observes a subset of the possible runs and waits for all the U_j, $j \in J$, to be visited in order. If that happens without visiting any $L_{j'}$, $j' \notin J$, the process "succeeds" and starts over. If some $L_{j'}$, $j' \notin J$, is encountered in a run, the process discards that run. If some process succeeds infinitely often, $\mathcal{D}$ accepts.

Fix a Streett automaton $\mathcal{A} = (Q, \Sigma, \delta, q_0, \Omega)$ for the rest of the section, where $\Omega = \{(L_1, U_1), \dots, (L_h, U_h)\}$. Let $H = \{1, \dots, h\}$. A (Q, H)-**tree** is a finitely branching rooted tree whose leaves are labelled with non-empty subsets of Q and whose edges are labelled by elements of $H \cup \{0\}$. The labels of the leaves are pairwise disjoint and, other than 0, no edge label occurs twice on any path from the root to one of the leaves. Each node bears a name from the set $\{1, \dots, 2 \cdot |Q| \cdot (h+1)\}$. The child nodes of a parent are ordered (from left to right, say). For each parent node, at least one child is connected by an edge with a non-zero label.

The root node represents the "hope" that H is a witness set for the input. If some node n represents witness set J, and an edge labelled j goes from n to a child node, then the child node represents witness set $J \setminus \{j\}$. Informally, the child node has given up on hoping for U_j to occur.

With this intuition in mind, we now present the formal construction of $\mathcal{D}$. We will explain this construction a bit more before we prove its correctness and the size bound.

5.3.1 The Construction

$\mathcal{D}$ is a 5-tuple $(Q', \Sigma, \delta', q_0', \Omega')$ where the set of states Q' is the set of all (Q, H)-trees, and the initial state q_0' is a tree consisting of just the root node, labelled with q_0, and having an arbitrary name.

The transition function is best described as an algorithm which transforms a (Q, H)-tree q' into another tree $\delta'(q', a)$ by a recursive procedure. Whenever we create a new node in the procedure, we assume that it is given a fresh name, i.e. one that does not yet occur in the whole tree. The procedure is parametrized by a set of indices J and a tree t; initially, we set $J := H$, $t := q'$. The procedure consists of the following steps;

(1) If t is a leaf labelled S and $J = \emptyset$, replace S by $\delta(S, a)$ and stop.
(2) If t is a leaf labelled S and $J \neq \emptyset$, then create a child labelled S and remove S from the label of t. Label the edge to the child with $\max J$ and continue at step 3.
(3) If t is not a leaf, assume that its root has l sub-trees $t_1, \dots, t_l$ and that the edges leading to them are labelled $j_1, \dots, j_l$ (from left to right). For all i, $1 \leq i \leq l$, we first apply the procedure recursively for the set $J \setminus \{j_i\}$ and the tree t_i.
Now, let S_i, $1 \leq i \leq l$ be the sets of states occurring in leaves of t_i after the previous changes. If $j_i \neq 0$, then for every state $q \in S_i$ we do the following:

- If $q \in L_{j_i}$, remove the state from its occurrence in t_i and append to t a new child leaf on the right labelled $\{q\}$. The edge to the child is labelled $\max J$.
- Otherwise, if $q \in U_{j_i}$, append a new child leaf on the right, label the edge with $\max((J \cup \{0\}) \cap \{0, \ldots, j_i - 1\})$, and give to the child the label $\{q\}$.

(4) Let $t_1, \ldots, t_{l'}$, $l' \geq l$ be the subtrees of t after the previous changes (labelled $j_1, \ldots, j_{l'}$), and let S_i, $1 \leq i \leq l'$, be the set of states occurring in t_i. Repeat the following for every state q that occurs in two different sets S_i and $S_{i'}$:

- If $j_i < j_{i'}$, remove q from $t_{i'}$.
- If $j_i = j_{i'}$ and $i < i'$, remove q from $t_{i'}$.

(5) Remove any subtrees from t whose leaves have an empty label.

(6) If after the previous steps all edges going from the root of t to its subtrees are labelled 0, then let S be the set of all states occurring in leaves of t. Remove all subtrees, i.e. make t a leaf, with label S.

Acceptance Condition: Let $\Omega' = \{(L'_\nu, U'_\nu)\}_{1 \leq \nu \leq 2|Q|(h+1)}$, where L'_ν is the set of all states (trees) containing a leaf named ν, and U'_ν is the set of all states in which ν does not occur.

Each process (or node) in $\mathcal{D}$ observes a subset of the possible runs of $\mathcal{A}$. However, every state of $\mathcal{A}$ occurs at most once in every tree of $\mathcal{D}$. Basically, this induces an equivalence relation over the runs; for a given prefix of the input, two runs are in the same equivalence class if they end up in the same state after the prefix is consumed. The placement of a state in the tree tries to extract the most useful information (with regard to acceptance) from this equivalence class.

A process with witness set J waits for the runs in its area to pass through all U_j, $j \in J$, in descending order and records their progress. Runs which are waiting for U_j to occur are kept in a child process connected by an edge labelled j. Runs which have passed all U_j are kept below an edge labelled 0. An edge label j going from a parent process with set J to a child process thus has two functions at once: It records the progress that the runs kept in the child have made with respect to J, and it signifies that the child is managing the witness set $J \setminus \{j\}$.

In step 2 of the algorithm, leaves with a non-empty witness set are expanded; all runs are waiting for the highest index to happen. In step 1, the transition function of $\mathcal{A}$ is simulated. In step 3 we check for occurrences of the accepting pairs. If in some process a run is waiting for U_j (i.e. the run is stored below an edge labelled j), and U_j does happen, then the run is transferred to a new child with the next lowest index (or 0, if all indices have been passed). If in some process $L_{j'}$, $j' \notin J$, is seen, we have to remove that run from the process. Recall that children have smaller witness sets than parents. Therefore, if a run is unsuccessful for a parent, it is unsuccessful for its children, too. Moreover, if a parent has a j-labelled edge to a child, then the run is still successful for the parent, but not for the child. So we remove the state from the child and start it over in the parent.

In step 4 we remove duplicate states from the tree. If we have one run that has advanced to index i and another that has gone to i', $i' > i$, then we keep the more advanced one (otherwise we would throw away progress and might miss a

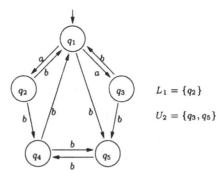

Fig. 5.1. Example Streett automaton.

completed cycle). If two runs are advanced to the same level, we keep the older one, i.e. the one in the leftmost child (otherwise a state might change its position in the tree too often).

In step 5 we clean up "dead" branches of the tree. In step 6, when all the runs observed by a process have succeeded, we reset the process. In this way we limit the growth of the tree.

5.3.2   An Example

Consider the non-deterministic Streett automaton $\mathcal{A}$ shown in Figure 5.1 which has two accepting pairs. For the purposes of this example we will consider the sets $L_1 = \{q_2\}$ and $U_2 = \{q_3, q_5\}$ only. Assume that the automaton has to process input starting with abb.

Figure 5.2 shows the behaviour of the corresponding deterministic automaton. Part (a) shows the steps made by the construction upon receiving the input a. For a better demonstration we assume that the six steps are executed on all leafs simultaneously; the correctness is not affected by this. Diagram (a1) shows the initial state of the deterministic automaton, consisting of the root labelled $\{q_1\}$ and named 1.

Diagram (a2) shows the tree after expansion and simulation of $\mathcal{A}$ (i.e. steps 1 and 2 of the transition function). Diagram (a3) shows the result of step 3; q_2 is in L_1 and is thus "reset"; q_3 is in U_2 and hence advanced to the next index by the root node. Now q_3 appears twice below the root node; this is repaired in step 4, shown in (a4). In the last step, the now empty sub-tree with the node named 3 is removed; the result is in diagram (a5).

Part (b) of the figure shows the processing of the second input character. Diagram (b1) shows the situation after steps 1 and 2. In (b2) the final result is shown: q_5 was advanced to a 0-labelled branch, and the duplicate q_1 was removed from the less advanced sub-tree of the root.

Part (c) demonstrates the third step; again we read a b. Diagram (c1) shows the result of steps 1 and 2. Afterwards, q_5 is removed from the left branch (since it is less advanced), and the occurrence of q_5 in the right branch is advanced to a 0-labelled branch. Since that leaves the label 0 on all edges leaving node 4, the

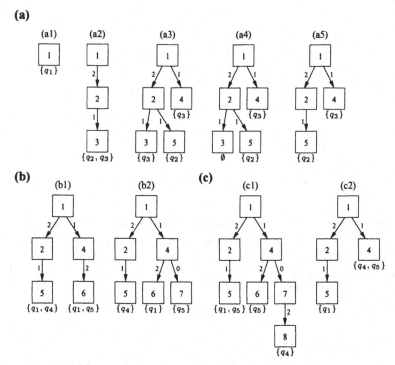

Fig. 5.2. (a) After input a. (b) After input ab. (c) After input abb.

subtrees of that node are collapsed according to step 6 of the transition. The result is shown in Diagram (c2).

5.3.3 Proof of Correctness

We now prove Theorem 5.2 formally, i.e. we show that $L(\mathcal{D}) = L(\mathcal{A})$ and we count the number of states in $\mathcal{D}$.

$(L(\mathcal{D}) \subseteq L(\mathcal{A}))$ Suppose $\alpha \in L(\mathcal{D})$ is accepted by a run $\xi_\mathcal{D}$ where ν is a name such that U'_ν appears only finitely often and L'_ν is visited infinitely often. Then, after some point, every state contains a node n named ν which becomes a leaf infinitely often. If n never disappears after some time, it is the root of a sub-tree whose leaves never become empty, and the witness set J associated with n in the transition function remains the same. Therefore α must have a run $\xi_\mathcal{A}$ in $\mathcal{A}$ that touches states from $L_{j'}$, $j' \in (H \setminus J)$, only finitely often (since these states would be absorbed by one of the parent nodes of n). If n is a leaf in one state, it will create new leaves below itself in the next state unless $J = \emptyset$. In the latter case $\xi_\mathcal{A}$ is accepting because no L_j, $j \in H$, is visited anymore. Otherwise, to become a leaf again, n must first get a child with edge label 0, and for that $\xi_\mathcal{A}$ must visit all U_j, $j \in J$ (in descending order).

$(L(\mathcal{A}) \subseteq L(\mathcal{D}))$ Let $\xi_\mathcal{A} = (\xi_\mathcal{A}^i)_{i \geq 0}$ be an accepting run of $\mathcal{A}$ for α, and let J be its maximal witness set. Consider the unique run $\xi_\mathcal{D} = (\xi_\mathcal{D}^i)_{i \geq 0}$ of α in $\mathcal{D}$. For all

$i \geq 0$, $\xi_{\mathcal{A}}^i$ occurs in $\xi_{\mathcal{D}}^i$. We first wait until $\xi_{\mathcal{A}}$ makes no more visits to any set $L_{j'}$, $j' \notin J$ (which happens after consumption of a finite number of input symbols). From now on, either $\xi_{\mathcal{D}}^i$ becomes a leaf infinitely many times, then $\alpha \in L(\mathcal{D})$. Otherwise we wait until $\xi_{\mathcal{D}}^i$ becomes a leaf for the last time. Thereafter, $\xi_{\mathcal{A}}^i$ always occurs in some sub-tree of $\xi_{\mathcal{D}}^i$. We will see that $\xi_{\mathcal{A}}^i$ can 'migrate' from one sub-tree to another as time goes on, but the number of migrations is finitely bounded: Since all U_j, $j \in J$, occur infinitely often, $\xi_{\mathcal{A}}^i$ is moved to other sub-trees until it eventually ends up in one whose edge is labelled with an element of $(H \cup \{0\}) \setminus J$. From there, $\xi_{\mathcal{A}}^i$ cannot migrate further via steps 3 or 6 of the construction anymore, only via rule 4. But this can happen only finitely often since the set of edge labels is finite, and since there is a leftmost sub-tree of $\xi_{\mathcal{D}}^i$. Eventually, $\xi_{\mathcal{A}}^i$ must end up in some sub-tree which it never leaves anymore. We can repeat the argument recursively for this sub-tree until we arrive at one that becomes a leaf infinitely many times. This recursion is of finite depth because eventually we get to processes for the witness set J. If we do not get a leaf at this level, then $\xi_{\mathcal{A}}^i$ must be in a 0-indexed sub-tree, and some other state must be trapped in a non-0-indexed sub-tree. Thus, if we continue the recursion, the 0-indexed sub-trees containing $\xi_{\mathcal{A}}^i$ have less and less states. In the worst case, we continue until a sub-tree contains only the single state $\xi_{\mathcal{A}}^i$. Since $\xi_{\mathcal{A}}$ is accepting with witness set J, and since all the sets L_j, $j \in J$ occur infinitely often in the accepting run of $\mathcal{A}$, this node must become a leaf infinitely many times.

Let us count how many nodes a (Q, H)-tree can have. A tree has at most $|Q|$ leaves. Suppose a tree has no 0-labelled edges, then the length of a path from the root to a leaf can be at most h. Such a tree can have at most $|Q| \cdot h$ nodes apart from the root. Now consider trees with 0-edges. From the root, there must be at least one path to a leaf without passing a 0-edge, and likewise from each node which is the target of such an edge. So there can be at most $|Q| - 1$ such edges (and nodes). Therefore, in total, a (Q, H)-tree can have at most $m := |Q| \cdot (h+1)$ nodes.

With this knowledge we can determine the size of $\mathcal{D}$, i.e. the number of (Q, H)-trees. Let us consider unlabelled trees without names on the nodes first. According to Cayley's Theorem there can be at most m^{m-2} different trees with m nodes (even ignoring the fact that we are only interested in trees with at most $|Q|$ leaves). We then have no more than $(m-1)^{h+1}$ choices to label the edges, $(2m)!/m!$ choices to name the nodes, and $(|Q|+1)^{|Q|}$ choices to distribute states among the leaves. Taking these results together, we get at most

$$m^{m-2} \cdot (h+1)^{m-1} \cdot \frac{2m!}{m!} \cdot (|Q|+1)^{|Q|} = 2^{\mathcal{O}(m \log m)} = 2^{\mathcal{O}(|Q|h \log(|Q|h))}$$

different states.

5.4 Transformation of Deterministic Streett Automata

The construction from Section 5.3 yields a deterministic Streett automaton for the complement of the language. In order to determinize the automaton, we need another complementation procedure. In [159], Safra shows a conversion of deterministic Streett automata to deterministic Rabin automata. This conversion is exponential only in the number of acceptance pairs of the Streett automaton.

Theorem 5.3. *Given a deterministic Streett automaton A with n states and h acceptance pairs, one can construct a deterministic Rabin automaton D having $n \cdot 2^{O(h \log h)}$ states and $O(h)$ acceptance pairs such that D accepts $L(A)$.*

The construction is based on the idea of "index appearance records" (IAR), also used for conversions from Streett or Rabin automata to other models. In the Rabin automaton, the states record not only the state of the Streett automaton, but also a permutation of the indices of all acceptance pairs. An index j can be moved to the back of the permutation if U_j contains the current Streett state.

Fix a deterministic Streett automaton $A = (Q, \Sigma, \delta, q_0, \Omega)$ with h acceptance pairs for the rest of the section, and consider the Rabin automaton $D = (Q', \Sigma, \delta', q_0', \Omega')$ where

- $Q' = Q \times \Pi \times \{1, \ldots, h+1\} \times \{1, \ldots, h+1\}$ where Π is the set of all permutations of $\{1, \ldots, h\}$;
- For $a \in \Sigma$ and $\pi = (j_1, \ldots, j_h)$ let $\delta((q, \pi, l, u), a) = (q', \pi', l', u')$ such that
  - $q' = \delta(q, a)$;
  - $l' = \min(\{i \mid q' \in L_{j_i}\} \cup \{h+1\})$;
  - $u' = \min(\{i \mid q' \in U_{j_i}\} \cup \{h+1\})$;
  - if $u' \leq h$, then $\pi' = (j_1, \ldots, j_{u'-1}, j_{u'+1}, \ldots, j_h, j_{u'})$, else $\pi' = \pi$.
- $q_0' = (q_0, (1, \ldots, h), h+1, h+1)$;
- $\Omega' = \{(L_1', U_1'), \ldots, (L_{h+1}', U_{h+1}')\}$; for $1 \leq j \leq h+1$,
  let $L_j' = \{(q, \pi, l, u) \in Q' \mid u = j\}$ and $U_j' = \{(q, \pi, l, u) \in Q' \mid l < j\}$.

In a D-state of the form (q, π, l, u), the state q simply records the state that A would be in after the same input. The values for l and u contain information about visits to the accepting pairs. If a set L_j is visited, then its position in the current permutation π is recorded in l. Similarly, if a set U_j is visited, then its position is written to u and additionally the index is shifted to the right in the permutation. If multiple sets are visited in one step, then we choose the one that's leftmost in π.

The intuition behind this construction is that the permutation of the indices maintained by D will take on the form outlined in Figure 5.3. Those indices j for which U_j is visited only finitely often will eventually gather on the "left" side of the permutation whereas the others will be moved to the back infinitely often. If a run satisfies the acceptance condition, then the third component of the D-states must always indicate the right half of the permutation from some point on.

5.4.1   Proof of Correctness

We now prove Theorem 5.3. Clearly, the number of states in D is $n \cdot h! \cdot (h+1)^2$. Moreover, we claim that $L(D) = L(A)$.

$(L(\mathcal{D}) \subseteq L(\mathcal{A}))$ Let $\alpha \in L(\mathcal{D})$. In the unique run of $\mathcal{D}$ over α, there must be an index j such that (a) L'_j is visited infinitely often and (b) U'_j is visited only finitely often. Because of (b), if some L_k is visited infinitely often in $\mathcal{A}$, then k must occur infinitely often at position j or to the right of it in the permutation. Because of (a) we know that no index with this property is allowed to keep its position forever. Therefore it follows that k is also moved back to the end of the permutation infinitely often, and every such move means a visit to U_k.

$(L(\mathcal{A}) \subseteq L(\mathcal{D}))$ Suppose $\alpha \in L(\mathcal{A})$, and consider the maximal witness set J associated with its run. Let $i = h - |J| + 1$. At some point, for all $k \notin J$ all the finitely many visits to L_k and U_k have been made, so k is never moved back in the permutation again. After that, we wait until all indices in J are eventually moved to the back. From now on, all indices on positions left of i are outside of J, so the $\mathcal{D}$-run will never visit U'_i again. Whatever the index k on position i is, it is from now on always an element of J. When $\mathcal{A}$ next visits U_k, $\mathcal{D}$ visits L'_i.

5.4.2   Summary

Let $\mathcal{A}$ be a (non-deterministic) Streett automaton with n states and h accepting pairs. According to Section 5.3 we can transform $\mathcal{A}$ to a deterministic automaton $\mathcal{D}$ accepting the complement of $L(\mathcal{A})$ with $2^{\mathcal{O}(nh \log(nh))}$ states and $2n(h+1)$ accepting pairs. The result of this section lets us transform $\mathcal{D}$ into another deterministic Streett automaton accepting $L(\mathcal{A})$ with the same asymptotic bound on the number of states and $2n(h+1)+1$ accepting pairs.

5.5   Lower Bounds

In [114] many lower bounds for transformations between automata on infinite words are shown. Here we present the results with respect to Streett automata. The results of [114] directly or indirectly prove that the problems of

(1) complementing non-deterministic Streett automata,
(2) complementing deterministic Streett automata,
(3) and determinizing Streett automata

require constructions with at least $n!$ states if the input is an automaton with n states. Hence, the upper bounds by Safra are optimal with respect to the number of states.

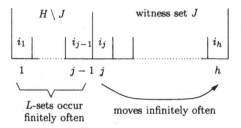

Fig. 5.3. Acceptance behaviour of $\mathcal{D}$.

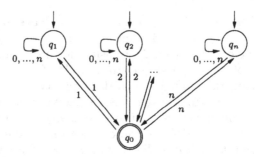

Fig. 5.4. The automaton $\mathcal{B}_n$.

5.5.1   Complementation of Non-deterministic Automata

In Section 3 of [114] a proof is given showing that conversion from a Büchi automaton with n states to a non-deterministic Streett automaton accepting the complement of the language involves a factorial blowup in the number of states. Since a Büchi automaton can be seen as a Streett automaton with a single accepting pair (*non-final states, final states*) the bound also holds for complementation of non-deterministic Streett automata.

Consider the Büchi automaton $\mathcal{B}_n$ over the language $\Sigma_n = \{0, \dots, n\}$ shown in Figure 5.4. $\mathcal{B}_n$ has $\mathcal{O}(n)$ states, and we shall show that there is no Streett automaton accepting the complement of $L(\mathcal{B}_n)$ with less than $n!$ states.

We first observe the following characterization of the language: A word $\alpha \in \Sigma_n^\omega$ is in $L(\mathcal{B}_n)$ exactly if there exist characters $i_1, \dots, i_k \in \{1, \dots, n\}$ such that the sequences $i_1 i_2, \dots, i_k i_1$ occur infinitely often in α. One direction is very easy to show: If such sequences exist, then every occurrence of such a sequence allows us to go through q_0 in $\mathcal{B}_n$, so $\alpha \in L(\mathcal{B}_n)$. For the reverse, assume that $\alpha \in L(\mathcal{B}_n)$, so there is an accepting run ξ. Take any state q_{i_1}, $1 \le i_1 \le n$ that is visited infinitely often in ξ. Whenever ξ leaves q_{i_1} for q_0 (i.e. infinitely often), take note of the state that is visited directly after q_0. One of them, say q_{i_2}, must occur infinitely often. If $i_1 = i_2$, we are done. Otherwise, repeat the argument for i_2 until we get a circle. Since there are only finitely many states, this must happen eventually.

Assume a Streett automaton $\mathcal{A}_n$ accepting the complement of $L(\mathcal{B}_n)$. For every permutation $\pi = (i_1, \dots, i_n)$ of $\{1, \dots, n\}$, let $\alpha_\pi = (i_1 \dots i_n 0)^\omega$. From the characterization of $L(\mathcal{B}_n)$ it follows that $\alpha_\pi \notin L(\mathcal{B}_n)$, hence $\mathcal{A}_n$ has an accepting run ξ_π. There are $n!$ such permutations, and the following proof shows that the infinity sets of all their accepting runs must be disjunct (and thus there must be at least $n!$ states in $\mathcal{A}_n$).

Let $\pi = (i_1, \dots, i_n)$ and $\pi' = (j_1, \dots, j_n)$ be two different permutations, and assume that there is a state $q \in \mathrm{Inf}(\xi_\pi) \cap \mathrm{Inf}(\xi_{\pi'})$. Using this we create a new input α (and an associated run ξ) where we 'interleave' α_π and $\alpha_{\pi'}$, i.e. for all $i \ge 0$ the i-th symbol of α is the i-th symbol of either α_π or $\alpha_{\pi'}^i$. We switch from α_π to $\alpha_{\pi'}$ whenever we pass q in the accepting run and if, since the last switch, we have passed $i_1 \dots i_n$ and gone through all states in $\mathrm{Inf}(\xi_\pi)$ at least once.

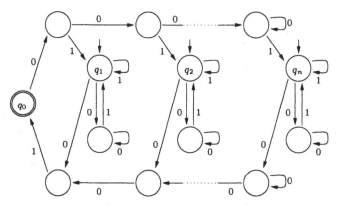

Fig. 5.5. Automaton with a binary alphabet.

Analogously, we switch from $\alpha_{\pi'}$ back to α_π when we have passed the sequence $j_1 \ldots j_n$ and visited the states in $\mathrm{Inf}(\xi_{\pi'})$.

We now derive a contradiction: Clearly, $\mathrm{Inf}(\xi) = \mathrm{Inf}(\xi_\pi) \cup \mathrm{Inf}(\xi_{\pi'})$, i.e. ξ satisfies $\mathcal{A}_n$'s acceptance condition: for every acceptance pair (L_k, U_k) of $\mathcal{A}_n$ such that $\mathrm{Inf}(\xi)$ has a state in L_k, said state must come from either $\mathrm{Inf}(\xi_\pi)$ or $\mathrm{Inf}(\xi_{\pi'})$; and since both α_π and $\alpha_{\pi'}$ are in $L(\mathcal{A}_n)$, $\mathrm{Inf}(\xi)$ also has a state from U_k. So $\alpha \in L(\mathcal{A}_n)$.

On the other hand, one can show that $\alpha \in L(\mathcal{B}_n)$ which is a contradiction. Take the smallest k such that $i_k \neq j_k$. Since i_k must occur in π' later on, there is $l > k$ such that $j_l = i_k$. Similarly, there is $m > k$ such that $i_m = j_k$. Since α infinitely often cycles through π and π', the sequences $i_k i_{k+1} \ldots i_m = j_k$ and $j_k j_{k+1} \ldots j_l = i_k$ happen infinitely often, hence α matches the characterization given above.

Note that the Streett automaton derived from $\mathcal{B}_n$ has only one acceptance pair (albeit one of size $\mathcal{O}(n)$). The alphabet is also of size $\mathcal{O}(n)$. However, the idea can be transferred to a family of automata with a binary alphabet. Such an automaton (still of size $\mathcal{O}(n)$) is shown in Figure 5.5, (which corrects a slight mistake in [114]).

In Figure 5.5 the input characters are replaced with the sequence $a^i b$ for $0 \leq i < n$ and $a^n a^* b$ for n.

5.5.2 Complementation of Deterministic Automata

Another argument in [114] (Theorem 7) shows that even complementation of deterministic Streett automata leads to a factorial blowup. Consider, for $n \geq 2$, the following Streett automaton $\mathcal{A}_n$ accepting a language L_n. $\mathcal{A}_n$ is of the form $(Q_n, \Sigma_n, \delta_n, q_0^n, \Omega_n)$ where

- $Q_n = \{-n, \ldots, n\} \setminus \{0\}$;
- $\Sigma_n = \{1, \ldots, n\}$;
- $q_0^n = -1$;

- $\delta_n(q, i) = -i$ and $\delta_n(-q, i) = i$ for $q, i \in \{1, \ldots, n\}$;
- $\Omega_n = \{(\{-1\}, \{1\}), \ldots, (\{-n\}, \{n\})\}$.

In other words, $\mathcal{A}_n$ switches from positive to negative states and back in every step. After an odd number of steps we are in a positive state, and after an even number of steps we are in a negative state; the ith symbol of the input determines the "absolute value" of the $(i+1)$-th state. The acceptance condition thus states that an input character that occurs in odd positions infinitely often must also be in even positions infinitely often.

For a word $\alpha \in \Sigma_n^\omega$ we denote by $even(\alpha)$ and $odd(\alpha)$ the set of all input symbols which occur infinitely often in even resp. odd positions in the input. If $i \in odd(\alpha)$, this implies that the state $-i$ is visited infinitely often. Hence, α is in L_n exactly if $odd(\alpha) \subseteq even(\alpha)$. Moreover, for a finite prefix u of even length we have $odd(u\alpha) = odd(\alpha)$ (analogously for $even$). In other words, in a deterministic automaton for L_n all the states reachable by reading a prefix of even length are language equivalent to the initial state (in a non-deterministic automaton this need not be the case). We refer to these states as the even-states of the automaton.

We now show that to recognize the complement of L_n, a deterministic Streett automaton $\mathcal{A}'_n$ needs at least $n!$ states. The proof is by induction on n.

Basis. Let $n = n! = 2$. Automata with only one state can only accept either $\emptyset$ or Σ^ω, so we need at least two states.

Step. Let $n > 2$, and let $\mathcal{A}'_n$ be an automaton recognising the complement of L_n. We make the following important observation: While reading the input, we must be prepared for the case that the symbol n never occurs in the input anymore. Then, for the rest of the input, $\mathcal{A}'_n$ must have exactly the same acceptance behaviour as $\mathcal{A}'_{n-1}$ (because $\mathcal{A}'_n$ is deterministic). By the induction hypothesis, this takes at least $(n-1)!$ states, and in particular, this number of states must be reachable (without reading n) from the initial state and from all even-states. Moreover, the analogue holds when some other symbol i stops appearing in the input: The language of the suffixes accepted from now on is isomorphic to L_{n-1}, so from every even-state we can reach at least $(n-1)!$ different states without reading i.

Using these facts, we construct an input α_i for each $i \in \{1, \ldots, n\}$. Each run consists of infinitely many phases, all constructed alike. The first phase starts at the initial state. For α_i we begin each phase by processing an input sequence jj for every $j \in \Sigma$, $j \neq i$, in arbitrary order. Then we continue with arbitrary input (but not i) until we have touched $(n-1)!$ different states and have read an even-sized input. This is possible due to the previous observation; as long as we haven't touched $(n-1)!$ different states, we can reach at least one untouched state from every even-state. Finally, we process the input ji for some $j \neq i$, and continue with the next phase.

For every i, we have $even(\alpha_i) = \{1, \ldots, n\} \setminus \{i\}$ and $odd(\alpha_i) = \{1, \ldots, n\}$, hence $\alpha_i \notin L_n$ and $\alpha_i \in L(\mathcal{A}'_n)$. Since at any point in the corresponding run ξ_i we can still expect to visit at least $(n-1)!$ different states, there must be at least that many states which are visited infinitely often, i.e. $|Inf(\xi_i)| \geq (n-1)!$.

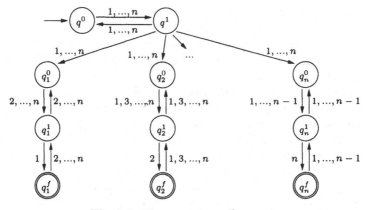

Fig. 5.6. The automaton $\mathcal{B}_n$.

We conclude by showing that $\mathrm{Inf}(\xi_i) \cap \mathrm{Inf}(\xi_j) = \emptyset$ if $i \neq j$. As a consequence, the number of states in $\mathcal{A}'_n$ is at least $n \cdot (n-1)! = n!$. Suppose there is a state $q \in \mathrm{Inf}(\xi_i) \cap \mathrm{Inf}(\xi_j)$ for some $i \neq j$. Using this we could create a new input α (and thus a corresponding run ξ), interleaving α_i and α_j; we switch from one to the other whenever we pass q and have gone through a complete phase since the last change. Hence, on the one hand $even(\alpha) = odd(\alpha) = \{1, \ldots, n\}$, i.e. $\alpha \notin L(\mathcal{A}'_n)$. On the other hand, $\mathrm{Inf}(\xi) = \mathrm{Inf}(\xi_i) \cup \mathrm{Inf}(\xi_j)$, i.e. α is accepted by $\mathcal{A}'_n$ by the same argument as in the previous subsection. We thus have a contradiction.

Note that both the number of states and the number of acceptance pairs is $\mathcal{O}(n)$. The size of the alphabet is also n but can be reduced to a binary alphabet using a similar technique as the one in the previous subsection.

5.5.3 Determinization of Streett Automata

The previous argument leads to the conclusion that determinization of Streett automata is inherently factorial. Consider the Büchi automaton $\mathcal{B}_n$ shown in Figure 5.6 which accepts the complement of the language L_n of the previous subsection.

Recall the acceptance condition of L_n; its complement demands that there is an input character i that occurs in odd positions infinitely often, but only finitely often in even positions. The automaton in Figure 5.6 waits in the states q^0 and q^1 until it non-deterministically decides upon one character i which it expects never to occur in even positions again. If the guess is correct, and if i occurs infinitely often in odd positions, the automaton accepts.

Let Q_n be the set of states of $\mathcal{B}_n$, and let F_n be its final states. $\mathcal{B}_n$ has $\mathcal{O}(n)$ states and an alphabet of size n. Since $\mathcal{B}_n$ can be interpreted as a Streett automaton with one accepting pair $(Q_n \setminus F_n, F_n)$, and since there is no deterministic automaton accepting $L(\mathcal{B}_n)$ with less than $n!$ states we have that determinization of Streett automata has the same lower bound.

Notes on Part II

There is a long sequence of papers with solutions of the determinization problem of Büchi automata (in the sense that an equivalent deterministic Muller or Rabin automaton has to be constructed). The beginning is given by the introduction of the Muller acceptance condition in [133] and the first correct determinization construction by McNaughton [125]. A more transparent approach, the "flag construction", was developed by Choueka [34] (see also [150]); a similar construction was presented in the monograph [50]. In [178] an "abstract" proof was developed which works for both the regular and the star-free ω-languages. For a purely algebraic proof see [157]. A better (however not optimal) complexity bound was provided by a construction of Emerson and Sistla [59].

Safra published his construction in [158]. An alternative approach was developed by Muller and Schupp [137]; it also matches the optimal complexity bound as reached in Safra's proof.

The complementation of Büchi automata has been treated with three different approaches. Historically, the first is a direct construction as developed in Büchi's paper [18] (see, e.g., [179]); it relies on a combinatorial lemma of Ramsey. The two other approaches involve a transformation from Büchi automata to deterministic, respectively alternating automata. In both cases, one can then work with an acceptance condition which itself is closed under complementation (Muller condition for deterministic automata, weak parity condition for alternating automata). The introduction of Chapter 4 above presents the background literature regarding alternating automata.

The determinization and complementation of Streett automata has been analyzed in [159] and [137].

Part III

Parity Games

The parity winning condition is the most fundamental one of all winning conditions for two-player infinite games: every other winning condition can easily be reduced to the parity condition; it can easily be dualized; it is the most expressive one where memoryless strategies always work; and it captures exactly what is needed to evaluate modal μ-calculus formulas.

In this part of the book, we study parity games in detail. In Chapter 6, we show in full generality that parity games are determined and that memoryless strategies indeed always work. In Chapter 7, we describe the most important algorithms known for solving parity games (determining the winner and computing a winning strategy) on finite graphs. All this will later be used over and over again.

6   Memoryless Determinacy of Parity Games

Ralf Küsters

Institut für Informatik und Praktische Mathematik
Christian-Albrechts-Universität zu Kiel

6.1   Introduction

In Chapter 2, parity games were introduced and it was claimed that these games
are determined and that both players have memoryless winning strategies. The
main purpose of this chapter is to provide proofs for this claim.

The determinacy and the memorylessness of parity games is exploited in
various areas inside and outside of game theory. For the purpose of this book,
automata theory, modal logics, and monadic second-order logics are the most
interesting among them.

More specifically, the word and emptiness problem for alternating tree automata as well as model checking and satisfiability in modal μ-calculus [100]
can be reduced to deciding the winner of a parity game. In fact, model checking
μ-calculus is equivalent via linear time reduction to this problem [56, 55, 202].
In Chapter 9 and 10, these reductions are presented.

In addition, parity games provide an elegant means to simplify the most difficult part of Rabin's proof of the decidability of the monadic second-order theory
of the binary infinite tree [148], the complementation lemma for automata on
infinite trees. Although, from Rabin's proof the determinacy of parity games follows implicitly, Rabin did not explicitly use games to show his result. The idea
to use games is due to Büchi [21] and it was applied successfully by Gurevich
and Harrington [77]. In turn, their paper has been followed by numerous other
attempts to clarify and simplify the proof of the complementation lemma; see,
for instance, a paper by Emerson and Jutla [55]. For the proof of the complementation lemma see Chapter 8. We refer to Part VI and VII for more on monadic
second-order logics.

The determinacy of parity games follows from a result due to Martin [119],
who has shown that Borel games, a class of games much larger than the class
of parity games we consider here, are determined. For our purpose, however,
this result does not suffice since the strategies employed there require to store
the complete history of a play, and thus, they require infinite memory. Gurevich
and Harrington [77] showed that finite-memory strategies suffice to win Muller
games, a class more general than parity games, but smaller than Borel games
(see Chapter 2).[1] Later, it turned out that for parity games the winner only
needs a memoryless strategy. This was proved for the first time independently
by Emerson and Jutla [55] and Mostowski [132]. While these proofs were quite

---

[1] Apparently, Büchi was the first to prove the existence of finite-memory strategies in
a manuscript sent to Gurevich and Harrington.

E. Grädel et al. (Eds.): Automata, Logics, and Infinite Games, LNCS 2500, pp. 95-106, 2002.

involved and non-constructive in the sense that the proofs did not exhibit memoryless winning strategies, McNaughton [126] proposed a simpler and constructive proof for Muller games played on finite graphs, from which he could derive an exponential-time algorithm for computing finite-memory strategies. His results also establish the existence of memoryless winning strategies for parity games on finite graphs.

In the present chapter, we follow a proof proposed by Zielonka [203] to show that parity games (on possibly infinite graphs) are determined and that the winner of a game has a memoryless winning strategy. We present both a constructive and a non-constructive proof. In addition, we sketch algorithmic and complexity-theoretic issues. We show that the problem of deciding the winner of a parity game belongs to the complexity classes NP and co-NP. Based on the constructive proof of determinacy, a simple deterministic exponential-time algorithm is derived to compute the winning positions of players along with their memoryless strategies. Jurdziński [92, 93] proved tighter complexity results and developed more efficient algorithms. An in-depth treatment of his results and other approaches for computing winning regions is provided in Chapter 7.

The present chapter is structured as follows. In Section 6.2, some basic notions are introduced. They prepare for the proof of the main theorem of this chapter, which is shown in Section 6.3. Finally, in Section 6.4 the mentioned complexity-theoretic and algorithmic issues are discussed.

We assume that the reader is familiar with the notions introduced in Chapter 2, such as parity games, (memoryless) strategies, determinacy, etc.

Throughout this chapter let $\mathcal{G} = (\mathcal{A}, \chi)$ denote a parity game with arena $\mathcal{A} = (V_0, V_1, E)$ and colouring function χ. The set of vertices of $\mathcal{G}$ will be denoted by $V := V_0 \cup V_1$.

6.2   Some Useful Notions

In this section we introduce and discuss different notions that are used later to show memoryless determinacy of parity games.

6.2.1   Subgames

Let $U \subseteq V$ be any subset of V. The subgraph of $\mathcal{G}$ induced by U is denoted

$$\mathcal{G}[U] = (\mathcal{A}|_U, \chi|_U)$$

where $\mathcal{A}|_U = (V_0 \cap U, V_1 \cap U, E \cap (U \times U))$ and $\chi|_U$ is the restriction of χ to U.

The graph $\mathcal{G}[U]$ is a **subgame** of $\mathcal{G}$ if every dead end in $\mathcal{G}[U]$ is also a dead end in $\mathcal{G}$. In other words, in a subgame no new dead ends may be introduced. Otherwise, winning regions could change. Let us look at an example.

Example 6.1. Figure 6.1 depicts a simple parity game, subsequently called $\mathcal{G}_{ex}$, with the vertices $v_0, \ldots, v_7$ and colours $0, 1, 2$. As in Chapter 2, circles denote 0-vertices and boxes 1-vertices. In this game, $\mathcal{G}[\{v_5, v_6\}]$ is a subgame of $\mathcal{G}$.

However, the subgraph $\mathcal{G}[\{v_5, v_6, v_7\}]$ of $\mathcal{G}$ is not a subgame of $\mathcal{G}$ since, in this subgraph, v_7 is a dead end, whereas it is not a dead end in $\mathcal{G}$.

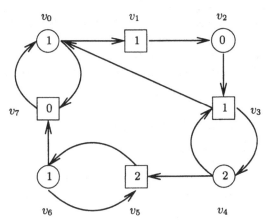

Fig. 6.1. A parity game

One easily shows the following lemma.

Lemma 6.2. *Let U and U' be subsets of V such that $\mathcal{G}[U]$ is a subgame of $\mathcal{G}$ and $(\mathcal{G}[U])[U']$ is a subgame of $\mathcal{G}[U]$. Then, $\mathcal{G}[U']$ is a subgame of $\mathcal{G}$.*

Proof. Exercise.

6.2.2 σ-Traps

The notion of a σ-trap was introduced in Chapter 2. Recall that if a token is in a σ-trap U, then Player $\overline{\sigma}$ can play a strategy consisting in choosing always successors inside of U. On the other hand, since all successors of σ-vertices in U belong to U, Player σ has no possibility to force the token outside of U. In our example, the set $\{v_0, v_7\}$ is a 1-trap, while the set $\{v_0, v_1, v_2, v_3, v_7\}$ is a 0-trap. We summarize some simple properties of σ-traps.

Lemma 6.3. (1) *For every σ-trap U in $\mathcal{G}$, $\mathcal{G}[U]$ is a subgame.*
(2) *For every family $\{U_i\}_{i \in I}$ of σ-traps U_i, the union $\bigcup_{i \in I} U_i$ is a σ-trap as well.*
(3) *If X is a σ-trap in $\mathcal{G}$ and Y is a subset of X, then Y is a σ-trap in $\mathcal{G}$ iff Y is a σ-trap in $\mathcal{G}[X]$.*

Proof. Exercise.

Note that the converse of (1) is not true. In our example, the set $\{v_3, v_4, v_5, v_6\}$ induces a subgame in $\mathcal{G}$, but it is neither a 0-trap nor a 1-trap. Also observe that the equivalence in (3) does not hold for nested traps of different types: If X is a σ-trap in $\mathcal{G}$ and Y is a $\overline{\sigma}$-trap in $\mathcal{G}[X]$, then, in general, Y is not a trap of any kind (neither σ nor $\overline{\sigma}$) in $\mathcal{G}$.

6.2.3 Attractors and Attractor Sets

Attractors and attractor sets were introduced in Chapter 2. Recall that the attractor set $\mathrm{Attr}_\sigma(\mathcal{G}, X) \subseteq V$ for Player σ and set X is the set of vertices from which Player σ has a strategy — and according to Proposition 2.18 a memoryless strategy — to attract the token to X or a dead end in $V_{\overline{\sigma}}$ in a finite (possibly 0) number of steps. In our example, $\mathrm{Attr}_1(\mathcal{G}_{ex}, \{v_2\}) = \{v_1, v_2\}$ and $\mathrm{Attr}_0(\mathcal{G}_{ex}, \{v_2\})$ contains all vertices of $\mathcal{G}_{ex}$.

We summarize relevant relationships between attractors and traps in the following lemma.

Lemma 6.4. (1) *The set* $V \setminus \mathrm{Attr}_\sigma(\mathcal{G}, X)$ *is a σ-trap in $\mathcal{G}$.*
(2) *If X is a σ-trap in $\mathcal{G}$, then so is $\mathrm{Attr}_{\overline{\sigma}}(\mathcal{G}, X)$.*
(3) *X is a σ-trap in $\mathcal{G}$ iff $\mathrm{Attr}_\sigma(\mathcal{G}, V \setminus X) = V \setminus X$.*
(4) *$\mathrm{Attr}_\sigma(\mathcal{G}, X) = V \setminus U$ where U is the greatest (w.r.t. set inclusion) σ-trap contained in $V \setminus X$; U exists since $\emptyset$ is a σ-trap, and by Lemma 6.3, the union of σ-traps is a σ-trap.*

Proof. ad (1): See Exercise 2.7.

ad (2): Let X be a σ-trap. From every vertex in $\mathrm{Attr}_{\overline{\sigma}}(\mathcal{G}, X)$, Player $\overline{\sigma}$ has a strategy to force the token into X or a dead end in V_σ. In either case, from then on there is no way for σ to choose a vertex outside of $\mathrm{Attr}_{\overline{\sigma}}(\mathcal{G}, X)$. Note that all dead ends in V_σ belong to $\overline{\sigma}$'s attractor set.

ad (3): Assume that X is a σ-trap. This means that, starting from some vertex in X, $\overline{\sigma}$ has a strategy to keep the token inside X and that X does not contain a dead end in $V_{\overline{\sigma}}$. Thus, $\mathrm{Attr}_\sigma(\mathcal{G}, V \setminus X) \subseteq V \setminus X$, for otherwise σ would have a way to force the token from some vertex in X into $V \setminus X$. The inclusion in the other direction is trivial.

Conversely, assume $\mathrm{Attr}_\sigma(\mathcal{G}, V \setminus X) = V \setminus X$. By (1), $V \setminus \mathrm{Attr}_\sigma(\mathcal{G}, V \setminus X)$ is a σ-trap. Then, $V \setminus (V \setminus X) = X$ shows that X is a σ-trap.

ad (4): By definition of U, $X \subseteq V \setminus U$. Hence, $\mathrm{Attr}_\sigma(\mathcal{G}, X) \subseteq \mathrm{Attr}_\sigma(\mathcal{G}, V \setminus U)$ (Exercise 2.5). Because U is a σ-trap, (3) implies $\mathrm{Attr}_\sigma(\mathcal{G}, X) \subseteq V \setminus U$. For the converse inclusion, we show that $V \setminus \mathrm{Attr}_\sigma(\mathcal{G}, X) \subseteq U$. By (1), $V \setminus \mathrm{Attr}_\sigma(\mathcal{G}, X)$ is a σ-trap. Moreover, $X \subseteq \mathrm{Attr}_\sigma(\mathcal{G}, X)$ implies $V \setminus \mathrm{Attr}_\sigma(\mathcal{G}, X) \subseteq V \setminus X$. Since U is the biggest σ-trap with $U \subseteq V \setminus X$, it follows $V \setminus \mathrm{Attr}_\sigma(\mathcal{G}, X) \subseteq U$. □

6.2.4 σ-Paradise

Intuitively, a σ-paradise in a game $\mathcal{G}$ is a region (a set of vertices) from which $\overline{\sigma}$ cannot escape and σ wins from all vertices of this region using a memoryless strategy.

Formally, a set $U \subseteq V$ is a **σ-paradise** if

- U is a $\overline{\sigma}$-trap, and
- there exists a memoryless winning strategy f_σ for σ on U, i.e.,
  - f_σ is a total mapping from $U \cap V_\sigma$ into U such that, for all $v \in U \cap V_\sigma$, $f_\sigma(v) \in vE$; and

- for every $v \in U$ and every play p in $(\mathcal{G}, v)$ conform with f_σ, p is winning for σ. (Note that since U is a $\overline{\sigma}$-trap, p only contains nodes in U.)

Note that a σ-paradise is a subset of σ's winning region W_σ. The following lemma shows that the set of σ-paradises is closed under the attractor operation and closed under union.

Lemma 6.5. (1) *If U is a σ-paradise, then so is* $\mathrm{Attr}_\sigma(\mathcal{G}, U)$.
(2) *Let $\{U_i\}_{i \in I}$ be a family of σ-paradises. Then, $U = \bigcup_{i \in I} U_i$ is a σ-paradise.*

Proof. ad (1): By Lemma 6.4, $\mathrm{Attr}_\sigma(\mathcal{G}, U)$ is a $\overline{\sigma}$-trap. A memoryless winning strategy for σ on this attractor set can be obtained as follows: For the vertices $v \in \mathrm{Attr}_\sigma(\mathcal{G}, U) \setminus U$, σ has a memoryless strategy to force the token into U or to a dead end in $V_{\overline{\sigma}}$. In the latter case, σ wins. In the former case, once in U, σ plays according to the memoryless winning strategy for U and wins as well.

ad (2): First note that U is a $\overline{\sigma}$-trap as the union of $\overline{\sigma}$-traps (Lemma 6.3). Let w_i denote the memoryless winning strategy on U_i for σ. A memoryless strategy w on U for σ is constructed in the following way: Fix a well-ordering relation $<$ on I (here we use the axiom of choice to guarantee the existence of such an ordering). Then for $v \in U \cap V_\sigma$, we set $w(v) = w_i(v)$, where i is the least element of I (w.r.t. $<$) such that $v \in U_i$. We need to show that w is a winning strategy on U.

Let $p = v_0 v_1 v_2 \cdots$ be an infinite play conform with w and let, for all k, $i_k = min\{i \in I \mid v_k \in U_i\}$. Obviously, $v_k \in U_{i_k}$. More importantly, the successor vertex v_{k+1} belongs to U_{i_k} as well (either v_k is an $\overline{\sigma}$-vertex and then all its successors, in particular v_{k+1}, belong to the $\overline{\sigma}$-trap U_{i_k}, or v_k is a σ-vertex and then $v_{k+1} = w(v_k) = w_{i_k}(v_k) \in U_{i_k}$). Moreover, $v_{k+1} \in U_{i_k}$ implies that $i_{k+1} \leq i_k$. Since an infinite non-increasing sequence of elements of a well-ordered set is ultimately constant, we conclude that some suffix of p is conform with one of the strategies w_i. Thus, σ wins p.

Let p be a finite play. The dead end, say v, in p belongs to some U_i. Since all vertices of U_i are winning for σ, we can conclude that $v \in V_{\overline{\sigma}}$. Thus, σ wins p. □

6.3 Determinacy

Following Zielonka [203] in this section we show that parity games are determined and that the winner of a parity game has a memoryless winning strategy. Formally, the main theorem of this chapter reads as follows.

Theorem 6.6. *The set of vertices of a parity game is partitioned into a 0-paradise and a 1-paradise.*

Note that the 0- and 1-paradises are the winning regions of the players. We provide two proofs of this theorem. The first proof is non-constructive, whereas the second one is constructive. For parity games on finite graphs, the latter proof can even be turned into a recursive algorithm for computing the winning regions of the players, along with their memoryless winning strategies (see Section 6.4)

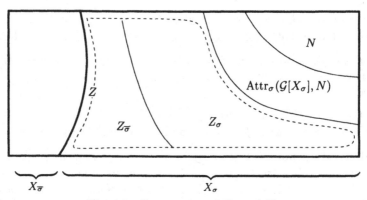

Fig. 6.2. Construction of $X_{\overline{\sigma}}$ and X_σ

Both proofs are carried by induction on the maximum parity occurring in $\mathcal{G}$. The core of the two proofs is summarized in the following three lemmas. The first lemma is the induction basis and the other two lemmas form the main part of the induction hypothesis.

Lemma 6.7. *If the maximum parity of $\mathcal{G}$ is 0, then V is partitioned into a 0- and a 1-paradise.*

Proof. Since the maximum priority of $\mathcal{G}$ is 0, Player 1 can only win $\mathcal{G}$ on dead ends in V_0 or vertices from which he can force the token to such a dead end. That is, the 1-paradise is the set $\mathrm{Attr}_1(\mathcal{G},\emptyset)$ with $\mathrm{attr}_1(\mathcal{G},\emptyset)$ as a memoryless winning strategy. Since $V \setminus \mathrm{Attr}_1(\mathcal{G},\emptyset)$ is a 1-trap and the maximum priority of $\mathcal{G}$ is 0, it es easy to see that $V \setminus \mathrm{Attr}_1(\mathcal{G},\emptyset)$ is a 0-paradise. □

We will now assume that the maximum parity n of $\mathcal{G}$ is at least 1. By induction and Lemma 6.7, we may assume that Theorem 6.6 holds for every parity game with maximum parity less than n. Let

$$\sigma \equiv n \bmod 2 \tag{6.1}$$

be the player that wins if the token visits infinitely often the maximum priority n. Let $X_{\overline{\sigma}}$ be a $\overline{\sigma}$-paradise such that $X_\sigma := V \setminus X_{\overline{\sigma}}$ is a $\overline{\sigma}$-trap. Finally, let

$$N = \{\, v \in X_\sigma \mid \chi(v) = n \,\} \quad \text{and} \quad Z = X_\sigma \setminus \mathrm{Attr}_\sigma(\mathcal{G}[X_\sigma], N). \tag{6.2}$$

Note that since X_σ is a $\overline{\sigma}$-trap, $\mathcal{G}[X_\sigma]$ is a subgame of $\mathcal{G}$. Moreover, as a complement of an attractor set, Z is a σ-trap in $\mathcal{G}[X_\sigma]$, and thus, $\mathcal{G}[X_\sigma][Z]$ is a subgame of $\mathcal{G}[X_\sigma]$. By Lemma 6.2, $\mathcal{G}[Z]$ is a subgame of $\mathcal{G}$. The priorities of $\mathcal{G}[Z]$ are elements of $\{0,\dots,n-1\}$. Thus, by the induction hypothesis, Z is partitioned into a 0-paradise, Z_0, and a 1-paradise, Z_1, say with memoryless winning strategies z_0 and z_1, respectively. The situation described so far is depicted in Figure 6.2.

The set $Z_{\overline{\sigma}}$ is a σ-trap in $\mathcal{G}[Z]$ and Z is a σ-trap in $\mathcal{G}[X_\sigma]$. Thus, according to Lemma 6.3, $Z_{\overline{\sigma}}$ is a σ-trap in $\mathcal{G}[X_\sigma]$. Consequently, $X_{\overline{\sigma}} \cup Z_{\overline{\sigma}}$ is a σ-trap in

$\mathcal{G}$: Once in $X_{\overline{\sigma}}$, σ cannot move the token outside this set; although from $Z_{\overline{\sigma}}$, σ can move the token inside $X_{\overline{\sigma}}$, σ cannot move it outside $Z_{\overline{\sigma}}$ in $\mathcal{G}[X_\sigma]$. Moreover, when playing according to $x_{\overline{\sigma}}$ in $X_{\overline{\sigma}}$ and according to $z_{\overline{\sigma}}$ in $Z_{\overline{\sigma}}$ two cases can occur:

(1) At some moment in a play the token hits the set $X_{\overline{\sigma}}$. Then, from this moment on, $\overline{\sigma}$ plays according to $x_{\overline{\sigma}}$ and wins the play.
(2) The token stays forever in $Z_{\overline{\sigma}}$. Since in this set, $\overline{\sigma}$ plays according to $z_{\overline{\sigma}}$, $\overline{\sigma}$ wins as well.

This shows:

Lemma 6.8. *The union $X_{\overline{\sigma}} \cup Z_{\overline{\sigma}}$ is a $\overline{\sigma}$-paradise.*

This lemma will later allow us to extend $\overline{\sigma}$-paradises. Conversely, if $X_{\overline{\sigma}}$ cannot be extended in this way, one can show that it is not possible to extend $X_{\overline{\sigma}}$ at all and that X_σ is a σ-paradise:

Lemma 6.9. *If $Z_{\overline{\sigma}} = \emptyset$, then X_σ is a σ-paradise.*

Proof. If $Z_{\overline{\sigma}} = \emptyset$, σ wins everywhere on $\mathcal{G}[Z]$ with z_σ.

To win on X_σ, Player σ plays as follows on X_σ: If the token visits a vertex $v \in N$, then σ moves it to any successor vertex v' inside of his winning region X_σ. Note that there is always at least one such successor vertex since X_σ is a $\overline{\sigma}$-trap. If the token visits $\text{Attr}_\sigma(\mathcal{G}[X_\sigma], N) \setminus N$, then σ attracts it in a finite number of steps to N or a dead end in $V_{\overline{\sigma}}$. If the token is in Z, then σ plays according to the winning strategy z_σ on Z.

Formally, the winning strategy x_σ for σ on X_σ is defined as follows: for $v \in X_\sigma \cap V_\sigma$ set

$$x_\sigma(v) = \begin{cases} z_\sigma(v) & \text{if } v \in Z, \\ \text{attr}_\sigma(\mathcal{G}[X_\sigma], N)(v) & \text{if } v \in \text{Attr}_\sigma(\mathcal{G}[X_\sigma], N) \setminus N, \\ v' & \text{if } v \in N \text{ and } v' \in vE \cap X_\sigma \end{cases} \qquad (6.3)$$

Let p be any play conform with x_σ starting at some vertex in X_σ. Then, three cases can occur. First, from some moment on, the token stays forever inside of Z and in this case some suffix of p is conform with z_σ and Player σ wins. Second, the token is moved to a dead end in $V_{\overline{\sigma}} \cap (\text{Attr}_\sigma(\mathcal{G}[X_\sigma], N) \setminus N)$, in which case σ wins as well. Third, the token visits infinitely often the maximal priority n (i.e, the set N) and σ wins by (6.1). □

With these lemmas at hand, the non-constructive and the constructive proofs of Theorem 6.6 are rather straightforward.

A non-constructive proof of Theorem 6.6. Let n be the maximum priority occurring in $\mathcal{G}$. If $n{=}0$, then Theorem 6.6 follows from Lemma 6.7.

Suppose that $n \geq 1$ and let σ be defined as in (6.1). Let $\mathcal{W}_{\overline{\sigma}} = \{W_{\overline{\sigma}}^q\}_{q \in Q}$ be the family of all $\overline{\sigma}$-paradises. Because of Lemma 6.5 we know that $W_{\overline{\sigma}} = \bigcup_{q \in Q} W_{\overline{\sigma}}^q$ is the greatest among these $\overline{\sigma}$-paradises, say with memoryless winning strategy $w_{\overline{\sigma}}$. If we now show that the complement $W_\sigma = V \setminus W_{\overline{\sigma}}$ of $W_{\overline{\sigma}}$ is a σ-paradise, we are done.

We use Lemma 6.8 and 6.9. To this end, we first show that W_σ is a $\overline{\sigma}$-trap. Lemma 6.5 yields that $\mathrm{Attr}_{\overline{\sigma}}(\mathcal{G}, W_{\overline{\sigma}})$ is a $\overline{\sigma}$-paradise. But since $W_{\overline{\sigma}}$ is the greatest such paradise, we know $\mathrm{Attr}_{\overline{\sigma}}(\mathcal{G}, W_{\overline{\sigma}}) = W_{\overline{\sigma}}$. Hence, W_σ is a $\overline{\sigma}$-trap, as a complement of a $\overline{\sigma}$-attractor set (Lemma 6.4).

With $X_{\overline{\sigma}} := W_{\overline{\sigma}}$, $X_\sigma := W_\sigma$ we can apply Lemma 6.8 and obtain that $W_{\overline{\sigma}} \cup Z_{\overline{\sigma}}$ is a $\overline{\sigma}$-paradise. However, since $W_{\overline{\sigma}}$ is the greatest $\overline{\sigma}$-paradise it follows $Z_{\overline{\sigma}} = \emptyset$. By Lemma 6.9, we conclude that W_σ is a σ-paradise, which concludes the non-constructive proof of Theorem 6.6. $\qquad\square$

In the above proof, the winning region $W_{\overline{\sigma}}$ was defined in a non-constructive manner. In the following proof it is shown how $W_{\overline{\sigma}}$ can be constructed by transfinite induction. The construction is mainly based on Lemma 6.8. The set W_σ will be specified as before.

A constructive proof of Theorem 6.6. The base case, $n = 0$, again follows from Lemma 6.7 and for the induction step we assume $n \geq 1$ and define σ as in (6.1).

We construct by transfinite induction an increasing sequences of $\overline{\sigma}$-paradises $W_{\overline{\sigma}}^{\xi}$. The corresponding memoryless winning strategies are denoted $w_{\overline{\sigma}}^{\xi}$. For $\nu < \xi$, $w_{\overline{\sigma}}^{\xi}$ will be an extension of $w_{\overline{\sigma}}^{\nu}$.

Initially, $W_{\overline{\sigma}}^0 = \emptyset$. For a limit ordinal ξ we set $W_{\overline{\sigma}}^{\xi} = \bigcup_{\nu < \xi} W_{\overline{\sigma}}^{\nu}$. By Lemma 6.5, $W_{\overline{\sigma}}^{\xi}$ is a $\overline{\sigma}$-paradise. Since, by induction hypothesis, for every $\nu < \nu' < \xi$ the strategy $w_{\overline{\sigma}}^{\nu'}$ is an extension of $w_{\overline{\sigma}}^{\nu}$, we can define $w_{\overline{\sigma}}^{\xi}$ to be the union of the strategies $w_{\overline{\sigma}}^{\nu}$ with $\nu < \xi$. Now, similar to the proof of Lemma 6.5, (2) one can show that $w_{\overline{\sigma}}^{\xi}$ is a winning strategy on $W_{\overline{\sigma}}^{\xi}$.

For a nonlimit ordinal $\xi + 1$, we define $W_{\overline{\sigma}}^{\xi+1}$ using Lemma 6.8. But first, we set

$$X^\xi = \mathrm{Attr}_{\overline{\sigma}}(\mathcal{G}, W_{\overline{\sigma}}^{\xi})$$

to be the attractor set for $\overline{\sigma}$ on $W_{\overline{\sigma}}^{\xi}$. Lemma 6.5 ensures that X^ξ is a $\overline{\sigma}$-paradise. Moreover, the memoryless winning strategy on X^ξ, call it x^ξ, extends $w_{\overline{\sigma}}^{\xi}$.

Since X^ξ is a $\overline{\sigma}$-attractor set, $V \setminus X^\xi$ is a $\overline{\sigma}$-trap and we can apply Lemma 6.8. We define

$$W_{\overline{\sigma}}^{\xi+1} := X^\xi \cup Z_{\overline{\sigma}}^{\xi}.$$

The set $W_{\overline{\sigma}}^{\xi+1}$ is a $\overline{\sigma}$-paradise and $w_{\overline{\sigma}}^{\xi+1}$, defined as in the proof of the Lemma 6.8, is a winning strategy on $W_{\overline{\sigma}}^{\xi+1}$, and it extends $w_{\overline{\sigma}}^{\xi}$.

This completes the construction of the increasing sequence of $\overline{\sigma}$-paradises $W_{\overline{\sigma}}^{\xi}$. Let ζ be the closure ordinal of the union of the $W_{\overline{\sigma}}^{\xi}$'s, i.e., the smallest ordinal such that

$$W_{\overline{\sigma}}^{\zeta} = W_{\overline{\sigma}}^{\zeta+1}$$

Let $W_{\overline{\sigma}} := W_{\overline{\sigma}}^{\zeta}$. We claim that $W_\sigma = V \setminus W_{\overline{\sigma}}$ is a σ-paradise. Since $W_{\overline{\sigma}}$ is a $\overline{\sigma}$-paradise, this would complete the constructive proof of Theorem 6.6.

We know $W_{\overline{\sigma}}^{\varsigma} \subseteq X^{\varsigma} = \mathrm{Attr}_{\overline{\sigma}}(\mathcal{G}, W_{\overline{\sigma}}^{\varsigma}) \subseteq W_{\overline{\sigma}}^{\varsigma+1} = W_{\overline{\sigma}}^{\varsigma}$, implying that $W_{\overline{\sigma}} = \mathrm{Attr}_{\overline{\sigma}}(\mathcal{G}, W_{\overline{\sigma}})$. Thus, W_{σ} is a $\overline{\sigma}$-trap, as a complement of a $\overline{\sigma}$-attractor.

With $X_{\overline{\sigma}} := W_{\overline{\sigma}}$, $X_{\sigma} := W_{\sigma}$ we can apply Lemma 6.8 and obtain that $W_{\overline{\sigma}} \cup Z_{\overline{\sigma}}$ is a $\overline{\sigma}$-paradise. By construction of $W_{\overline{\sigma}}$, it follows $W_{\overline{\sigma}} = W_{\overline{\sigma}} \cup Z_{\overline{\sigma}}$. Since $Z_{\overline{\sigma}}$ and $W_{\overline{\sigma}}$ are disjoint, we obtain that $Z_{\overline{\sigma}} = \emptyset$. Finally, Lemma 6.9 implies that W_{σ} is a σ-paradise. □

Alternative proofs. We conclude this section with some remarks on yet another proof of determinacy. The proof presented by Emerson and Jutla [55] is a non-inductive proof. The idea is that given a game the set W of winning positions of a player is expressed by a μ-calculus formula φ. Now it is possible to deduce that the complement of W is indeed the set of winning positions for the opponent from the fact that the negation of φ has the same form as φ after exchanging the roles of both players. This shows that from every vertex one of the players has a winning strategy, and thus, the game is determined. Note that the μ-calculus formula and its negation, describing the winning positions of a player and its adversary, respectively, allow to calculate the winning sets of both players independently. In the non-constructive and constructive proofs presented above, we first constructed $W_{\overline{\sigma}}$, and depending on this set defined W_{σ}.

Finally, using a ranking argument, Emerson and Jutla proved (in a non-constructive manner) the existence of memoryless winning strategies.

6.4   First Complexity and Algorithmic Results

In this section, we look at simple complexity-theoretic and algorithmic consequences of Theorem 6.6 for deciding the winner of **finite parity games**, i.e., parity games on finite graphs. These results are presented here to give a feeling for the complexity and algorithmic issues. They are, however, not optimal compared to what is known from the literature. In fact, Jurdziński [92, 93] has proved better results, which are discussed in detail in Chapter 7.

6.4.1   A Simple Complexity Result

Let $\mathrm{WINS} = \{\, (\mathcal{G}, v) \mid \mathcal{G}$ is a finite parity game and v is a winning position of Player 0 $\}$ be the problem of deciding whether, given an initialized finite parity game, Player 0 wins.

As an easy consequence of Theorem 6.6, we obtain the following.

Corollary 6.10. $\mathrm{WINS} \in NP \cap co\text{-}NP$.

Proof. We first show that $\mathrm{WINS} \in \mathrm{NP}$. The following is a non-deterministic polynomial-time algorithm for deciding WINS: (i) Given $\mathcal{G}$ and v, guess a memoryless strategy w; (ii) check whether w is a memoryless winning strategy. We need to show that the second step can be carried out in polynomial time.

The strategy w can be represented by a subgraph $\mathcal{G}_w$ of $\mathcal{G}$. This subgraph coincides with $\mathcal{G}$ except that all edges (v', v'') where v' is a 0-vertex and $v'' \neq$

$w(v')$ are eliminated, i.e., for a 0-vertex we only keep the outgoing edge referred to by w.

Given $\mathcal{G}_w$, we need to check whether there exists a vertex v' reachable from v in $\mathcal{G}_w$ such that a) $\chi(v')$ is odd and b) v' lies on a cycle in $\mathcal{G}_w$ containing only vertices of priority less or equal $\chi(v')$. If, and only if, such a vertex v' does not exist, w is a winning strategy for Player 0. Checking this can be carried out in polynomial time. (We leave the proof as an exercise.) Thus, WINS $\in$ NP.

We now show WINS $\in$ co-NP. By Theorem 6.6, deciding $(\mathcal{G}, v) \notin$ WINS means deciding whether v is a winning position for Player 1. This can be achieved by the above algorithm if we require $\chi(v')$ to be even. (Alternatively, one can apply the above NP-algorithm to the dual game, i.e., the one where 0-vertices and 1-vertices are switched and the priorities are increased by 1). Consequently, WINS $\in$ co-NP. $\square$

Exercise 6.1. Complete the proof of Corollary 6.10.

The result just proved also follows from the work by Emerson, Jutla, and Sistla [56], who showed that the modal μ-calculus model checking problem is in NP $\cap$ co-NP. This problem is equivalent via linear time reduction to WINS. Jurdziński [92] has proved the even stronger result that WINS $\in$ UP $\cap$ co-UP, where UP is the class of languages recognizable by unambiguous polynomial-time non-deterministic Turing machines, i.e., those with at most one accepting computation of length polynomially bounded in the size of the input; as usual, co-UP denotes the problems whose complement is in UP.

6.4.2   Computing Winning Regions

We now present a *deterministic* algorithm, called winning-regions, for computing the winning regions (and corresponding winning strategies) of the two players of a finite parity game. This algorithm is derived in a straightforward manner from the constructive proof of Theorem 6.6, and therefore, its correctness follows immediately.

The algorithm is depicted in Figure 6.3. It uses the function win-opponent (cf. Figure 6.4) as a subroutine. Given a finite parity game, winning-regions returns the tuple $((W_0, w_0), (W_1, w_1))$ where W_σ, $\sigma \in \{0, 1\}$, is the winning region for Player σ and w_σ is the corresponding memoryless winning strategy.

Following the constructive proof of Theorem 6.6, winning-regions first determines the highest priority n occurring in the game. If this priority is 0, paradises as specified in the base case of the constructive proof are returned. Otherwise, for $\sigma \equiv n \bmod 2$, $W_{\overline{\sigma}}$ along with the strategy $w_{\overline{\sigma}}$ is computed using the subroutine win-opponent (explained below). Finally, W_σ and w_σ are determined according to (6.3).

The procedure win-opponent exactly mimics the inductive definition of $W_{\overline{\sigma}}$. First, W is set to the empty set (corresponding to $W_{\overline{\sigma}}^0 = \emptyset$) and w is the empty strategy, i.e., the strategy with empty domain. The loop body of win-opponent follows the definition of $W_{\overline{\sigma}}^{\xi+1}$; since here we deal with finite parity games, natural induction suffices to construct $W_{\overline{\sigma}}$.

---

winning-regions($\mathcal{G}$)
$\quad n := max\{\chi(v) \mid v \in V\}$
$\quad$If $n = 0$ then return $((V \setminus \text{Attr}_1(\mathcal{G},\emptyset), w_0), (\text{Attr}_1(\mathcal{G},\emptyset), \text{attr}_1(\mathcal{G},\emptyset)))$
$\qquad$ // w_0 is some memoryless strategy for Player 0

// otherwise
$\quad \sigma := n \bmod 2$

// compute $W_{\overline{\sigma}}$, $w_{\overline{\sigma}}$
$\quad (W_{\overline{\sigma}}, w_{\overline{\sigma}}) :=$ win-opponent($\mathcal{G}, \sigma, n$)

// compute W_σ, w_σ
$\quad W_\sigma := V \setminus W_{\overline{\sigma}}$
$\quad N := \{v \in W_\sigma \mid n \in \chi(v)\}$ $\qquad$ // see (6.2)
$\quad Z := W_\sigma \setminus \text{Attr}_\sigma(\mathcal{G}[W_\sigma], N)$ $\qquad$ // see (6.2)
$\quad ((Z_0, z_0), (Z_1, z_1)) :=$ winning-regions($\mathcal{G}[Z]$)

$\quad \forall v \in W_\sigma \cap V_\sigma:$ $\qquad$ // see (6.3)

$$w_\sigma(v) = \begin{cases} z_\sigma(v) & \text{if } v \in Z, \\ \text{attr}_\sigma(\mathcal{G}[W_\sigma], N)(v) & \text{if } v \in \text{Attr}_\sigma(\mathcal{G}[W_\sigma], N) \setminus N, \\ v' & \text{if } v \in N \text{ and } v' \in vE \cap W_\sigma \end{cases}$$

return $((W_0, w_0), (W_1, w_1))$

Fig. 6.3. A deterministic algorithm computing the winning regions of a parity game

To analyze the runtime of winning-regions, let l be the number of vertices, m the number of edges, and n the maximum priority in $\mathcal{G}$. Note that, w.l.o.g., we may assume $n \leq l$. We also assume that every vertex has at least one in- or outgoing edge. Thus, $l \leq 2m$.

It is easy to see that all assignments, except for those involving recursive function calls, in winning-regions and win-opponent can be carried out in time $c \cdot m$ where c is some fixed (and big enough) constant: Recall from Exercise 2.6 that attractor sets can be computed in time $\mathcal{O}(l+m)$. If we now denote by $T(l, m, n)$ the worst-case runtime of winning-regions on all inputs $\mathcal{G}$, with $\mathcal{G}$ having the parameters l, m, and n as specified before, and similarly, by $S(l, m, n)$ the worst-case runtime of win-opponent, we obtain the following inequalities:

$$T(l, m, 0) \leq c \cdot m$$
$$T(l, m, n+1) \leq c \cdot m + S(l, m, n+1)$$
$$S(l, m, n+1) \leq c \cdot m + (l+1) \cdot T(l, m, n)$$

Note that win-opponent is only invoked in case $n \geq 1$, thus we do not need to consider $S(l, m, 0)$. More importantly, the recursive call winning-regions($\mathcal{G}[Z]$) in winning-regions is not necessary, since the result of this call coincides with the result of winning-regions($\mathcal{G}[Z]$) in the last iteration step of win-opponent. Consequently, in the inequality for $T(l, m, n+1)$ we can omit the runtime for this call. Solving the above inequality system yields that $T(l, m, n) \in \mathcal{O}(m \cdot l^n)$. This proves the following corollary.

win-opponent$(\mathcal{G}, \sigma, n)$

$(W, w) := (\emptyset, \emptyset)$ // corresponds to $W_{\bar{\sigma}}^0 := \emptyset$

Repeat
  $(W', w') := (W, w)$
  $X := \mathrm{Attr}_{\bar{\sigma}}(\mathcal{G}, W)$
  $\forall v \in X \cap V_{\bar{\sigma}}$:

$$x(v) = \begin{cases} w(v) & \text{if } v \in W, \\ \mathrm{attr}_{\bar{\sigma}}(\mathcal{G}, W)(v) & \text{if } v \in X \setminus W. \end{cases}$$

  $Y := V \setminus X$;
  $N := \{v \in Y \mid n = \chi(v)\}$ // see (6.2)
  $Z := Y \setminus \mathrm{Attr}_{\sigma}(\mathcal{G}[Y], N)$ // see (6.2)
  $((Z_0, z_0), (Z_1, z_1)) = $ winning-regions$(\mathcal{G}[Z])$
  $W := X \cup Z_{\bar{\sigma}}$
  $\forall v \in W$:

$$w(v) = \begin{cases} x(v) & \text{if } v \in X, \\ z_{\bar{\sigma}}(v) & \text{if } v \in Z_{\bar{\sigma}}. \end{cases}$$

Until $W' = W$

return (W, w)

Fig. 6.4. A subroutine for winning-regions computing $W_{\bar{\sigma}}$ and $w_{\bar{\sigma}}$

Corollary 6.11. *Computing the winning regions of finite parity games and the corresponding memoryless winning strategies can be carried out in time $\mathcal{O}(m \cdot l^n)$.*

The best known deterministic algorithm for computing winning regions is due to Jurdziński [93] and is discussed in Chapter 7 (see Theorem 7.25). Unlike the algorithm presented here, Jurdziński's algorithm only needs polynomial space. The following chapter also includes other up-to-date approaches to the problem of deciding the winner of a parity game.

7 Algorithms for Parity Games

Hartmut Klauck*

School of Mathematics
Institute for Advanced Study, Princeton

7.1 Introduction

It is the aim of this chapter to review some of the algorithmic approaches to the problem of computing winning strategies (resp. of deciding if a player has a winning strategy from a given vertex) in parity games with finite arenas and other two-player games. Parity games are equivalent via linear time reductions to the problem of modal μ-calculus model checking (see Chapters 10 and 9), and this model checking problem plays a major role in computer-aided verification. Furthermore we will see that the problem is not too hard in a complexity-theoretic sense, while no efficient algorithm for it is known so far. Also parity games are the simplest of a whole chain of two-player games for which no efficient solutions are known, further underlining the importance of looking for an efficient algorithm solving this particular problem.

We will explain why the problem of solving parity games lies in $\text{UP} \cap \text{co-UP}$, explore its relations to some other games, and describe the theoretically most efficient algorithm for the problem known so far. Furthermore we describe work on more practically oriented algorithms following the paradigm of strategy improvement, for which a theoretical analysis stays elusive so far.

Recall that in a parity game we are given a (finite) graph with vertices labeled by natural numbers. The vertex set is partitioned into vertices in which Player 0 moves and vertices in which Player 1 moves. In an initialized game we are also given a starting vertex. In a play of the game a token is placed on the starting vertex and is then moved over the graph by Player 0 and Player 1, each making their move if the token is on one of their vertices. For simplicity we assume that the graph is bipartite, so that each move from a Player 1 vertex leads to a Player 0 vertex and vice versa. Each player follows some strategy. If the highest priority of a vertex occurring infinitely often in the play is odd, then Player 1 wins, otherwise Player 0 wins. See Chapter 2 for more details.

Exercise 7.1. Show that one can convert any parity game on a nonbipartite game arena into an equivalent parity game on a bipartite arena in linear time.

It is an important (and deep) result that the players may restrict themselves to memoryless strategies (i.e., define their strategy by picking once and for all a neighbor for each of their vertices thus not considering the path on which they arrive there), see Theorem 6.6 in the previous chapter. This also implies that for each vertex one of the players has a winning strategy, so there are no draws!

---

* Supported by NSF Grant CCR 9987854.

E. Grädel et al. (Eds.): Automata, Logics, and Infinite Games, LNCS 2500, pp. 107-129, 2002.

If the players use memoryless strategies, a play of the game leads after a finite number of steps to a cycle in the underlying graph.

Rabin [148] first showed a complementation lemma for parity automata working on infinite trees (while providing a decidability result for a certain logic) implicitly also proving the determinacy result for parity games. The application of games to the complementation problem is due to Büchi [21]. Gurevich and Harrington [77] gave an abbreviated proof of Rabin's result, and Emerson and Jutla [55] another simplified proof by showing equivalence to the modal μ-calculus model checking problem (in which complementation is trivial). Their result also implies that in fact a player who has a strategy so that he wins in an initialized game also has a memoryless winning strategy. See also [126, 203] for further work on these problems.

The first question arising is, of course, whether one can decide the winner in a parity game efficiently, i.e., whether one can find the player who wins if the play starts at a given vertex, given that this player plays optimally. We are also interested in finding winning strategies. The aforementioned result that the players can restrict themselves to memoryless strategies immediately implies that the following trivial approach is successful (using exponential time): for a given vertex go through all strategies of Player 1. For each such strategy go through all strategies of Player 0 and check who wins. If there is a strategy of Player 1 that wins against all strategies of Player 0 declare Player 1 the winner, otherwise Player 0 wins. It is the main purpose of this chapter to review some more efficient algorithms solving this problem.

Why are we interested in this problem? There are at least two reasons. One is that the problem is deeply related to several important topics. First of all the problem is equivalent to the problem of modal μ-calculus model checking [55, 56], which in turn is of large importance for computer-aided verification. So better algorithms for the problem lead to better model checkers, making more expressive types of logical statements about finite systems checkable by efficient algorithms. The modal μ-calculus was defined first by Kozen in [100], see Chapter 10. Parity games are also at the heart of an interconnection between languages defined by automata operating on infinite trees and monadic second order logic [183], see Chapter 12.

Another important reason to study the problem is its current complexity-theoretic classification. It is known [92] to lie in UP ∩ co-UP (and thus "not too far above P", see [142]), but not known to be in P so far, and it is one of the few natural problems so. Trying to find a polynomial algorithm for the problem is a natural pursuit.

In this chapter we describe the best algorithm for the problem known so far (from [93]), show that the problem is in UP ∩ co-UP (following [92]), and discuss other promising approaches to get better algorithms for the problem, mainly the strategy improvement approach first defined in [85], and employed in a completely combinatorial algorithm given in [191].

Further we discuss the connection of the game to other games of infinite duration played on graphs, and see that it is the least difficult to solve of a series of such games all lying in NP∩co-NP. So it is the most natural candidate to attack!

This chapter is structured as follows: in the next section we introduce several games on graphs considered in the chapter and explore some of their properties. In Section 7.3 we deduce a first simple algorithm for the problem based on [204], which is already quite good in both time and space complexity. In Section 7.4 we show why the problem is in UP ∩ co-UP. In Section 7.5 we describe the efficient algorithm due to Jurdziński [93], which yields approximately a quadratically improved runtime compared to the simple algorithm (while maintaining the space complexity). Section 7.6 discusses promising and more practical approaches based on strategy improvement. Section 7.7 collects a few conclusions.

Note that throughout the chapter logarithms are always base two, and that space complexity is measured in the logarithmic cost measure (since we will be dealing with problems involving weights). Regarding time complexity we will stick to the measure in which elementary arithmetic operations cost unit time, however. Also note that we will consider max-parity games throughout the chapter, except in Section 7.5, where we will consider min-parity games to save some notation.

7.2 Some More Infinite Games

To describe our algorithms for the solution of parity games and the containment of this problem in UP ∩ co-UP, we will take a detour via some other two-player games, which will be introduced now. Note that most of these games are no games of chance, so no randomness is used in playing these games, just like e.g. in the game of chess. Picking a good strategy in such a game may only be hard because it takes a lot of time to do so! Also all these are games of full information, in which all relevant data are accessible to both players as opposed to e.g. most card games.

For definitions of infinite games, strategies, winning regions and related notions we refer to Chapter 2.

The first kind of games we consider are parity games as defined in Chapter 2. Recall the memoryless determinacy theorem for parity games, Theorem 6.6 in Chapter 6.

Another natural kind of games are *mean payoff games* [49].

Definition 7.1. A **mean payoff game** is a quadruple $(\mathcal{A}, \nu, d, w)$, where $\mathcal{A}$ is an arena without dead ends, ν and d are natural numbers, and $w : E \to \{-d, \dots, d\}$ assigns an integer weight to each edge.

Player 0 wins a play $v_0 v_1 \cdots$, if

$$\liminf_{t \to \infty} \frac{1}{t} \sum_{i=1}^{t} w(v_{i-1}, v_i) \geq \nu.$$

We also refer to the above limit as the *value* that Player 0 wins from Player 1 after the play.

Exercise 7.2. Extend the above definition so that dead ends are allowed. Do this in a way so that both games are equivalent.

[147] and [92] describe polynomial time reductions from parity games to mean payoff games. We will show how to perform such a reduction in the next section. So parity games are not harder to solve than mean payoff games. Again it is known that memoryless strategies suffice for the players of mean payoff games. Surprisingly the proof is much easier than in the case of parity games.

Theorem 7.2 ([49]). *Let $(\mathcal{A}, \nu, d, w)$ be a mean payoff game. Then Player 0 has a winning strategy from a set of vertices iff Player 0 has a memoryless winning strategy from that set.*

More precisely, for each vertex v_0 there is a number $\nu(v_0)$, called the value of v_0, such that

(a) *Player 0 has a memoryless strategy so that for every play $v_0 v_1 \cdots$ in which he follows this strategy*

$$\liminf_{t \to \infty} \frac{1}{t} \sum_{i=1}^{t} w(v_{i-1}, v_i) \geq \nu(v_0).$$

(b) *Player 1 has a memoryless strategy so that for every $v_0 v_1 \cdots$ in which she follows this strategy*

$$\limsup_{t \to \infty} \frac{1}{t} \sum_{i=1}^{t} w(v_{i-1}, v_i) \leq \nu(v_0).$$

The above theorem allows us to speak of an *optimal strategy*, which means a strategy that ensures for all plays (starting at some vertex v) that the corresponding player wins at least the value $\nu(v)$.

To obtain the above result Ehrenfeucht and Mycielski also introduce a finite variant of mean payoff games in which the play stops as soon as a loop is closed and then the payoff of that loop is analyzed. Both games turn out to be basically equivalent [49].

In the next section we will show how to solve mean payoff games in pseudopolynomial time, i.e., in time polynomial in the size of the graph and the unary encoded weights. Together with the reduction from parity games this yields an algorithm for parity games which is already quite good.

The next games we consider are *discounted* payoff games [204]. Here the importance of the weights decreases by a constant factor each time step in a play. So intuitively only a finite beginning of the play is important. Basically this can be viewed as yet another kind of averaging. The game will be important for technical reasons.

Definition 7.3. A **discounted payoff game** is a tuple $(\mathcal{A}, \nu, d, w, \lambda)$ where $\mathcal{A}$ is an arena without dead ends, ν and d are natural numbers, $w : E \to \{-d, \ldots, d\}$ assigns an integer weight to each edge, and $0 < \lambda < 1$ is the discount.
Player 0 wins a play $v_0 v_1 \cdots$, if

$$(1 - \lambda) \sum_{i=0}^{\infty} \lambda^i w(v_i, v_{i+1}) \geq \nu.$$

We also refer to the above left hand side as the value that Player 0 wins from Player 1 after the play.

The correction term $(1 - \lambda)$ arises to make sure that the value of a game using only edges of weight a is also a.

Zwick and Paterson prove that for each vertex in a discounted payoff game one of the players has a memoryless winning strategy. We will see the reason for this in Section 7.4. Furthermore we will see in that section that mean payoff games can be reduced in polynomial time to discounted payoff games. Note however that the proofs for the facts that memoryless winning strategies exist become simpler with each game defined so far (and that such a result for a more difficult game does not immediately imply the corresponding result for the easier game).

The most general games we mention are the **simple stochastic games** defined by Condon [40]. In these finite games the vertex set is partitioned into three sets of vertices: vertices in which Player 0 moves, in which Player 1 moves, and random vertices, in which a random successor is chosen, plus two vertices in which 1 is paid by Player 0 to Player 1 resp. 0 is paid by Player 0 to Player 1 (and the game ends). The expected amount paid to Player 1 is the result of the game. Zwick and Paterson [204] show that discounted payoff games can be reduced to simple stochastic games. So these are the most difficult to solve of the games considered here. Moreover they are the only games of chance we consider! Still it is possible to decide in NP∩co-NP whether the payoff of Player 1 exceeds a certain threshold. The reduction from parity games to simple stochastic games that results increases the game arena only by a constant factor. Using an algorithm by Ludwig [117], which solves simple stochastic games with fan-out 2, and the reductions we get the following corollary.

Corollary 7.4. *There is a randomized algorithm which computes the winning regions of a given parity game with m edges in expected time $2^{O(\sqrt{m})}$.*

This is the best algorithm we know if the number of different priorities assigned to vertices is larger than $\sqrt{m}$. The algorithm is notably subexponential, if the graph is sparse. The time bound is understood as the expected value of the running time (over coin tosses of the algorithm) in the worst case (over all inputs).

7.3 A Simple Algorithm

In this section we want to describe a relatively simple algorithm for solving parity games, or rather mean payoff games. The approach can also be adapted to solve discounted payoff games.

Let us consider a parity game $(\mathcal{A}, \Omega)$ where Ω assigns d different priorities to the vertices. Our whole objective is to decrease the dependence of the runtime on d, see Section 6.4 for the first algorithm in this direction presented here. Actually, for very large d our algorithms will not be better than the trivial exponential time algorithm testing all strategies. Why do we consider this parameter as important? In applications to model checking this parameter gives us the depth of nested fixed points used in expressions we want to check. The weaker the dependence on d is, the more complicated formulae can be checked, e.g. for all constant d our algorithm is polynomial time, which is not so for the trivial algorithm. To see the effect of this compare with Theorem 10.19. Another concern will be space complexity, which we prefer small as well.

In a first step we give the reduction to mean payoff games as in [92]. Afterwards we describe the algorithm of Zwick and Paterson [204] for these games and analyze its performance for the original parity games. The algorithm will be finding fixed points of a certain natural function, a property which also holds (for a less obvious function) for the more complicated algorithm in section 7.5.

Lemma 7.5. *A parity game on n vertices using d different priorities can be reduced in polynomial time to a mean payoff game on n vertices using weights from the set $\{-n^{d-1}, \ldots, n^{d-1}\}$, and using the same game arena.*

Moreover winning strategies of the parity game are winning strategies of the mean payoff game and vice versa.

Proof. Suppose our parity game is $(\mathcal{A}, \Omega)$. W.l.o.g. the priorities are $\{0, \ldots, d-1\}$. The mean payoff game uses the same arena. An edge originating at a vertex v with priority $i = \Omega(v)$ receives the weight $w(v, u) = (-1)^i n^i$. Let $\nu = 0$. Clearly all weights lie in the range $\{-n^{d-1}, \ldots, n^{d-1}\}$. This defines our mean payoff game $(\mathcal{A}, 0, n^d, w)$.

We claim that the value of the mean payoff game exceeds 0 for a pair of memoryless strategies iff the same strategies lead to a play of the game in which the highest priority vertex occurring infinitely often has an even priority.

W.l.o.g. we may assume that the players use memoryless strategies when playing the mean payoff game, see Theorem 7.2. Then a play corresponds to a path ending in a cycle. In the limit defining the value of the play the weights on the initial segment before the cycle contribute zero. So the value of the game is positive iff the sum of the weights on the cycle is positive. The weights are from the set $\{-n^{d-1}, n^{d-2}, -n^{d-3}, \ldots, -n, 1\}$, assuming for concreteness that d is even. Assume the weight w_{max} with the largest absolute value appearing on the cycle is positive. Then the sum of the weights on the cycle is at least $w_{max} - (n-1)w_{max}/n > 0$, since there are at most $n-1$ edges with weights not equal to w_{max} in the cycle. The maximal weight is on an edge originating from the vertex of highest priority, which must be even. Symmetrically if the weight of largest absolute value is negative, the highest priority vertex must be odd.

So the mean payoff game and the parity game behave in the same way for each pair of memoryless strategies, thus they are equivalent, and have the same winning regions, and the same strategies lead to a win.   □

Now we show how to solve mean payoff games efficiently if the weights are small.

Theorem 7.6. *Given a mean payoff game* $(\mathcal{A}, \nu, d, w)$ *where the arena has* n *vertices and* m *edges, the winning region for Player 0 can be computed in time* $O(n^3 md)$ *and space* $O(n \cdot (\log d + \log n))$.

Proof. It is our goal to find the values of the vertices efficiently. This immediately gives us the winning region. Let $\nu_k(v)$ denote the following value: the players play the game for k steps starting from vertex v (so they construct a path of length k), then $\nu_k(v)$ denotes the sum of the edge weights traversed if both players play optimally.

We want to compute the values $\nu(v)$ as the limit over k of the $\nu_k(v)$. First let us characterize the latter value.

For every $v \in V$:

$$\nu_k(v) = \begin{cases} \max_{(v,u) \in E}\{w(v,u) + \nu_{k-1}(u)\} & \text{if } v \in V_0, \\ \min_{(v,u) \in E}\{w(v,u) + \nu_{k-1}(u)\} & \text{if } v \in V_1. \end{cases} \tag{7.1}$$

Clearly $\nu_0(v) = 0$ for all $v \in V$. Using this recursion we can easily compute $\nu_k(v)$ for all $v \in V$ in time $O(km)$. Recall that we allow arithmetic operations in unit time. Now we investigate how quickly $\nu_k(v)/k$ approaches $\nu(v)$.

Lemma 7.7. *For all* $v \in V$:

$$\nu_k(v)/k - 2nd/k \le \nu(v) \le \nu_k(v)/k + 2nd/k.$$

First let us conclude the theorem from the above lemma. We compute all the values $\nu_k(v)$ for $k = 4n^3 d$. This takes time $O(n^3 md)$. All we have to store are the $\nu_i(v)$ for the current i and $i-1$. These are numbers of $O(\log(kd))$ bits each, so we need space $O(n(\log d + \log n))$.

Now we estimate $\nu(v)$ by $\nu'(v) = \nu_k(v)/k$. Clearly

$$\nu'(v) - \frac{1}{2n(n-1)} < \nu'(v) - \frac{2nd}{k} \le \nu(v) \le \nu'(v) + \frac{2nd}{k} < \nu'(v) + \frac{1}{2n(n-1)}.$$

Now $\nu(v)$ can be expressed as the sum of weights on a cycle divided by the length of the cycle due to Theorem 7.2, and is thus a rational with denominator at most n. The minimal distance between two such rationals is at least $\frac{1}{n(n-1)}$, so there is exactly one rational number of this type in our interval. It is also easy to find this number. We can go through all denominators l from 1 to n, estimate $\nu(v)$ as $\lceil \nu'(v) \cdot l \rceil / l$ and $\lfloor \nu'(v) \cdot l \rfloor / l$, if one of these numbers is in the interval, we have found the solution. This takes about $O(n)$ steps.

Knowing the vector of values of the game it is easy to compute winning strategies by fixing memoryless strategies that satisfy equation 7.1.

Proof of Lemma 7.7. It is proved in [49] that the values of vertices in a mean payoff game and in its following finite variant are equal: the game is played as the infinite mean payoff game, but when the play forms a cycle the play ends and the mean value of the edges on that cycle is paid to Player 0. Also the optimal such value can be obtained using the same memoryless strategies as in the infinite case.

Let f_0 be a memoryless strategy of Player 0 that achieves the maximal values for all vertices (against optimal strategies of Player 1) in the finite version of the game. Let Player 1 play according to some (not necessarily memoryless) strategy. We show that the value of a k step play starting in v is at least $(k - (n-1)) \cdot \nu(v) - (n-1)d$. Consider any play of length k. The edges of the play are placed consecutively on a stack. Whenever a cycle is formed, the cycle is removed from the stack. Since the edges lying on the stack directly before the removal of the cycle correspond to a play which has just formed its first cycle, the mean value of the edges on the cycle is at least $\nu(v)$, because of the optimality of f_0 against all strategies of Player 1 in the finite version of the game. This process continues, until the play is over and the stack contains no more cycles. In this case there are at most $n - 1$ edges on the stack. The weight of each such edge is at least $-d$. Thus the value of the k step play is always at least $(k - (n-1)) \cdot \nu(v) - (n-1)d > k \cdot \nu(v) - 2nd$. So we know there is a memoryless strategy for Player 0, so that he wins at least $k \cdot \nu(v) - 2nd$ in the k step play, no matter what Player 1 does. The other inequality is proved similarly.   □

Note that the above proof uses the memoryless determinacy theorem for mean payoff games [49].

Exercise 7.3. (1) Prove that mean payoff games and their finite variants are equal in the above sense. Hint: Use the above idea with the stack.
(2) Use 1. to show that mean payoff games enjoy memoryless determinacy.

Corollary 7.8. *Given a parity game (A, Ω) where d different priorities are assigned to vertices, the winning region and strategy of Player 0 can be computed in time $O(n^{d+2}m)$ and space $O(d \cdot n \log n)$.*

So there is a rather efficient solution to the problem if d is small. In section 5 we will see how to further reduce the dependence on d.

7.4   The Problem Is in UP ∩ co-UP

In this section we consider the problem from a complexity-theoretic point of view. First observe that the problem of deciding whether a given vertex belongs to the winning region of Player 0 in a given parity game is in NP: simply guess a memoryless strategy for Player 0. Then remove all edges which are not consistent with the strategy. Then one has to determine whether Player 1 can win if Player 0 uses his strategy, which comes down to testing whether there is no path from the designated vertex to a cycle whose highest priority is odd. This is decidable in deterministic polynomial time.

Exercise 7.4. Show that the following problem can be decided in polynomial time: input is a game arena in which Player 0's strategy is fixed (all vertices of Player 0 have outdegree 1) plus a vertex in the arena. Is there a path from the vertex to a cycle in which the highest priority is odd?

Furthermore since each vertex is either in Player 0's or in Player 1's winning region, the same argument gives an NP algorithm for deciding Player 1's winning region, which is a co-NP algorithm for deciding Player 0's winning region. Thus parity games are solvable in NP∩co-NP. This strongly indicates that the problem is not NP-complete, since otherwise NP would be closed under complement and the polynomial hierarchy would collapse (see e.g. [142]).

Now we review a result by Jurdziński [92] saying that the complexity of the problem is potentially even lower. First we define (for completeness) the complexity class UP (see [142]).

Definition 7.9. A problem is in the class UP, if there is a polynomial time non-deterministic Turing machine, such that for each input that is accepted exactly one computation accepts.

The class UP is believed to be a rather weak subclass of NP.

Our plan to put parity games into UP is as follows: we again use the reduction to mean payoff games. Then we show how to reduce these to discounted payoff games. There is an algorithm due to Zwick and Paterson for solving these games in a very similar fashion to the one described in the previous section. This gives us a set of equations whose unique solution is the vector of values of the game. Furthermore using simple facts from linear algebra we prove that these solutions can be specified with very few bits. Thus we get our unique and short witnesses. Again the argument for co-UP is symmetric.

First we state the following observation from [204], which says that a mean payoff game yields always a discounted payoff game of almost the same value, if the discount factor is chosen large enough. The proof is similar to the proof of Lemma 7.7.

Lemma 7.10. *Let $(\mathcal{A}, \nu, d, w)$ be a mean payoff game with an arena on n vertices, played beginning in vertex v. Then rounding the value of the discounted payoff game $(\mathcal{A}, \nu, d, w, \lambda)$ with $\lambda \geq 1 - 1/(4n^3/d)$ to the nearest rational with denominator smaller than n yields the value of the mean payoff game.*

The following characterization of the values of vertices in a discounted payoff game will be useful [204].

Lemma 7.11. *The value vector $\bar{\nu} = (\nu(v_1), \ldots, \nu(v_n))$ containing the values of vertices in a discounted payoff game equals the unique solution of the following system of n equations*

$$x_v = \begin{cases} \max_{(v,u)\in E}\{(1 - \lambda) \cdot w(v, u) + \lambda x_u\} & \text{if } v \in V_0, \\ \min_{(v,u)\in E}\{(1 - \lambda) \cdot w(v, u) + \lambda x_u\} & \text{if } v \in V_1. \end{cases} \tag{7.2}$$

Proof. Let F be a function that maps a vector $\bar{x}$ to the vector $\bar{y}$ such that

$$y_v = \begin{cases} \max_{(v,u)\in E}\{(1 - \lambda) \cdot w(v, u) + \lambda x_u\} & \text{if } v \in V_0, \\ \min_{(v,u)\in E}\{(1 - \lambda) \cdot w(v, u) + \lambda x_u\} & \text{if } v \in V_1. \end{cases}$$

Then we are interested in vectors $\bar{x}$ with $\bar{x} = F(\bar{x})$, the fixed points of F. Let $\|\bar{y}\|_\infty$ denote the maximum norm, then

$$\forall \bar{y}, \bar{z} : \|F(\bar{y}) - F(\bar{z})\|_\infty \leq \lambda \|\bar{y} - \bar{z}\|_\infty.$$

Since $0 < \lambda < 1$ we have that F is a contracting function (with respect to the maximum norm). Thus the limit $\bar{x} = \lim_{n \to \infty} F^n(0)$ exists and is the unique solution to $\bar{x} = F(\bar{x})$.

Now Player 0 can use the following strategy, provided he knows the vector $\bar{x} = F(\bar{x})$: at vertex v choose the neighboring vertex u that maximizes $(1 - \lambda)w(v, u) + \lambda x_u$. Then Player 0 wins at least x_v in a play starting at v. On the other hand Player 1 may fix a strategy analogously so that her loss is also at most x_v. Thus the solution of $F(\bar{x}) = \bar{x}$ is the vector of values of the game.   □

Obviously this lemma leads to a UP algorithm for the solution of discounted payoff games, if the vector of values can be described by short numbers. Then we can just guess these numbers and verify that the equations are satisfied. What is a short number? The number must be representable using a polynomial number of bits in the size of the game. The size of the game is the length of a description of the game, including edge weights and λ.

But first let us note that the strategies obtained from the system of equations are indeed memoryless. The proof of Lemma 7.11 does not presuppose such a memoryless determinacy result.

Corollary 7.12. *Let $(\mathcal{A}, \nu, d, w, \lambda)$ be a discounted payoff game. Then Player 0 [Player 1] has a winning strategy from a set of vertices iff Player 0 [Player 1] has a memoryless winning strategy from that set.*

Lemma 7.13. *The solution of the equations 7.2 can be written with polynomially many bits.*

Proof. Let N be the size of the binary representation of the discounted payoff game. Let $\bar{\nu}$ be the unique solution of the equations. Then this vector can be written

$$\bar{\nu} = (1 - \lambda) \cdot \bar{w} + \lambda \cdot Q \cdot \bar{\nu},$$

where $\bar{w}$ is a suitable vector containing weights $w(v, u)$, and Q is a 0,1-matrix containing only a single one per row. Note that in order to write down this system of equations one has to know the winning strategy.

Assume that $\lambda = a/b$ is a rational included in the game representation, with integers a, b satisfying $\log a, \log b < N$. Let $A = b \cdot I - a \cdot Q$ for the identity matrix I, then A is an integer matrix with at most two nonzero integer entries per row.

The above equation can then be rewritten

$$A \cdot \bar{\nu} = (b - a) \cdot \bar{w}.$$

Due to Cramer's rule the solution of this system can be written as the vector containing $\det A_v / \det A$ on position v where A_v is obtained from A by replacing column v with $(a - b) \cdot \bar{w}$.

The entries of A and A_v are bounded in absolute value by 2^N. This implies that the determinants of the matrices A, A_v are at most $2^{O(N \cdot |V|)}$. But then the solution of the system of equation can be written by using a polynomial number of bits in the length N. $\square$

So we get the following.

Corollary 7.14. *Deciding whether a vertex is in the winning region of Player 0 is possible in UP $\cap$ co-UP for parity games, mean payoff games, and discounted payoff games.*

Exercise 7.5. Formally describe how a nondeterministic Turing machine can solve the decision problem associated to parity games unambiguously in polynomial time.

Exercise 7.6. Devise an algorithm for discounted payoff games similar to the algorithm described in Theorem 7.6.

7.5 A Better Algorithm

Now we describe the best algorithm for the solution of parity games known so far, again due to Jurdziński [93]. The time complexity of the algorithm is $O(d \cdot m \cdot \frac{n}{\lceil d/2 \rceil}^{\lfloor d/2 \rfloor})$ for min-parity games with n vertices, m edges, and $d \geq 2$ different priorities. An algorithm with comparable time complexity has been given by Seidl in [161]. But as opposed to previous algorithms Jurdziński's algorithm uses only space polynomially depending on d, namely $O(dn \log n)$, when achieving this time bound (note that we use the logarithmic measure for space complexity).

The algorithm is fairly simple to describe and analyze after several technical concepts have been explained.

First note that we will apply comparisons in the following to tuples of natural numbers, referring to their lexicographical ordering. Furthermore we will use symbols like $<_i$, referring to the lexicographical ordering when restricted to the first i components of a tuple (ignoring the other components). So e.g. $(2, 4, 3) < (2, 4, 5)$, but $(2, 4, 3) =_2 (2, 4, 5)$. Denote $[i] = \{0, \ldots, i - 1\}$.

For a technical reason in this section Player 0 wins, if the *lowest* priority occurring infinitely often is even, i.e., we are considering min-parity games. The max-parity game can obviously be reduced to this variant and vice versa. Also we exclude dead ends from the game graph, see Exercise 2.8.

Exercise 7.7. How can we reduce min-parity to max-parity games?

Fix a memoryless strategy of one player. This can be regarded as throwing out all edges which are not consistent with this strategy. The remaining game graph will be called a **solitaire game**, since the game is now played by one player only. Obviously it suffices for this player to find a path leading to a cycle in which the lowest vertex priority makes him win the game! So call a cycle **even**, if the lowest priority of a vertex in the cycle is even, and otherwise **odd**.

Furthermore call a memoryless strategy f_0 of Player 0 **closed** on a set of vertices W, if every play starting in W and consistent with f_0 stays in W, i.e., if for all $v \in W \cap V_0 : f_0(v) \in W$ and for all $v \in W \cap V_1$ and all $u \in vE : u \in W$.

Now we see a simple condition that makes a player win:

Lemma 7.15. *Let f_0 be a memoryless strategy of Player 0 which is closed on a set W. Then f_0 is a winning strategy from all vertices in W iff all simple cycles in the restriction of the solitaire game of f_0 to the vertices in W are even.*

Proof. From each vertex either Player 1 or Player 0 has a winning strategy. If Player 1 has a winning strategy, then this can be assumed to be memoryless. So assume Player 0 plays according to f_0 and consider the resulting solitaire game. Then Player 1 can win from a vertex v iff she can fix an edge for each vertex so that the resulting path from v ends in a simple cycle which is odd. If no such cycle exists, Player 1 cannot win (and Player 0 wins). If such a cycle exists, then Player 1 wins iff she can find a path to that cycle. This happens at least for all vertices on that cycle, so there are vertices where f_0 is not winning.   □

The key notion in the algorithm will be a *parity progress measure*. These are labelings of the vertices of graphs with tuples of natural numbers having certain properties. First we consider such labelings for solitaire games.

Definition 7.16. Let $(\mathcal{A}, \Omega)$ be a solitaire game with vertex priorities $\Omega(v) \le d$. A function $\rho : V_0 \cup V_1 \to \mathbb{N}^{d+1}$ is a **parity progress measure** for the solitaire game, if for all edges (v, w):

(a) $\rho(v) \ge_{\Omega(v)} \rho(w)$ if $\Omega(v)$ is even.
(b) $\rho(v) >_{\Omega(v)} \rho(w)$ if $\Omega(v)$ is odd.

The intuition behind the above definition is best explained through the following lemma.

Lemma 7.17. *If there is a parity progress measure for a solitaire game $\mathcal{G} = (\mathcal{A}, \Omega)$, then all simple cycles in $\mathcal{G}$ are even.*

In particular in this case Player 0's strategy used to derive $\mathcal{G}$ is winning.

Proof. Let ρ be a parity progress measure for a solitaire game $\mathcal{G}$. Suppose there is an odd cycle $v_1, \dots, v_l$ in $\mathcal{G}$, let $i = \Omega(v_1)$ be the lowest priority on the cycle, which is odd. Then according to the definition of a parity progress measure $\rho(v_1) >_i \rho(v_2) \ge_i \cdots \ge_i \rho(v_l) \ge_i \rho(v_1)$, which is a contradiction.   □

So parity progress measures are witnesses for winning strategies. It is true that the above condition can also be reversed, i.e., if Player 0 wins from all vertices, then there is a parity progress measure. But an important feature will be that we can show the reverse condition while considering only a suitably bounded number of parity progress measures. We will then be able to replace the search for a winning strategy by the search for a parity progress measure from a relatively small set.

To define this "small" set let $\mathcal{G} = (\mathcal{A}, \Omega)$ be a solitaire game and Ω be a function mapping vertices to $\{0, \ldots, d\}$, and let V_i denote the set of vertices having priority i. By definition there are $d + 1$ such sets. Instead of using $\mathbb{N}^{d+1}$ as the range of values of our parity progress measure we will use a set $M_{\mathcal{G}}$ defined by

$$M_{\mathcal{G}} := [1] \times [|V_1| + 1] \times [1] \times [|V_3| + 1] \times [1] \times \cdots \times [1] \times [|V_d| + 1],$$

assuming for simplicity that d is odd.

Lemma 7.18. *If all simple cycles in a solitaire game $\mathcal{G} = (\mathcal{A}, \Omega)$ are even, then there is a parity progress measure $\rho \colon V \to M_{\mathcal{G}}$.*

Proof. We define the parity progress measure explicitly from the solitaire game $\mathcal{G}$ (as opposed to the inductive proof given in [93]). Let $a_i(v)$ be the maximal number of vertices with priority i occurring on any path in $\mathcal{G}$ starting in v and containing no vertex with priority smaller than i. This value is infinite, if infinitely many vertices with priority i occur on some path with no smaller priority occurring on that path. If v has priority smaller than i or there is no path featuring a vertex with priority i but no smaller priority, then $a_i(v) = 0$.

We then set $\rho(v) = (0, a_1(v), 0, a_3(v), 0, \ldots, 0, a_d(v))$ and claim that this is a parity progress measure with the desired property.

First assume that some $a_i(v)$ is not finite for some odd i. Then there is an infinite path starting at v such that the path contains no vertex with lower priority than i, but infinitely many vertices with priority i. Thus the path must contain some vertex with priority i twice, and we can construct a cycle with least priority i, a contradiction to the assumption of the lemma.

Now we show that we have actually defined a mapping $\rho \colon V \to M_{\mathcal{G}}$. Assume that $a_i(v)$ is larger than the number of vertices with priority i. Due to the definition of $a_i(v)$ there is a path originating in v such that $a_i(v)$ vertices with priority i show up before a vertex with priority smaller than i. If $a_i(v)$ is larger than the number of vertices with priority i, such a vertex occurs twice. Consequently there is a cycle containing as least priority i, again a contradiction.

It remains to show that we defined a parity progress measure. Let (v, w) be any edge and i any odd number. If $i = \Omega(v)$, then $a_i(v) = a_i(w) + 1$. For all smaller odd i we get $a_i(v) \geq a_i(w)$, because the edge (v, w) extended by a path starting in w that contains k vertices with priority i but no smaller priority, yields a path starting in v that contains k vertices with priority i but no smaller priority. Thus for all v with odd priority $\rho(v) >_{\Omega(v)} \rho(w)$ and for all v with even priority $\rho(v) \geq_{\Omega(v)} \rho(w)$. $\square$

The construction allows a nice interpretation of the constructed parity progress measure. The tuple assigned to a vertex contains for all odd priorities the maximal number of times this priority can be seen if Player 1 moves over the graph, until a vertex with smaller priority is seen. Note that this interpretation is not applicable to all parity progress measures.

Exercise 7.8. Find a parity game and a parity progress measure for which the above intuition is not true.

What have we achieved by now? Given a strategy of one player we can construct the solitaire game. Then a parity progress measure for such a graph exists if and only if Player 0 has a winning strategy from all vertices. Also parity progress measures from a relatively small set suffice for this. Our current formulation does not allow to deal with graphs in which both winning regions are nonempty. Secondly we have to extend our notion of a progress measure to deal with game arenas, i.e., to graphs in which Player 1 has more than one option to choose a strategy.

Now consider again the construction of the parity progress measure given in the proof of the above lemma. If we drop the condition that all simple cycles are even, then some of the values $a_i(v)$ are infinite. Clearly, if $a_i(v) = \infty$, then there is a path from v that sees infinitely many odd i and no smaller priorities, so Player 1 might just walk that path and win. If, on the other hand, there is no i with $a_i(v) = \infty$, then Player 1 cannot win from v, because all paths starting in v eventually reach an even priority occurring infinitely often. Note that we excluded dead ends from game arenas in this section. We have a clear distinction of the winning regions in a solitaire game.

So we introduce one more symbol into $M_{\mathcal{G}}$. Let $M_{\mathcal{G}}^{\top}$ denote $M_{\mathcal{G}} \cup \{\top\}$ where $\top$ is larger than all elements of $M_{\mathcal{G}}$ in the order $>_i$ for all i. If we identify all $\rho(v)$ containing the value ∞ at least once with $\top$, we get an **extended parity progress measure** for solitaire games where the vertices with label $\top$ constitute the winning region of Player 1.

To extend the notion of a progress measure to game arenas, we simply demand that for each vertex in which Player 0 moves, there is at least one neighbor satisfying a progress relation.

Definition 7.19. Let $\mathrm{prog}(\rho, v, w)$ denote the least $m \in M_{\mathcal{G}}^{\top}$ such that $m \geq_{\Omega(v)} \rho(w)$, and, if $\Omega(v)$ is odd, then $m >_{\Omega(v)} \rho(w)$ or $m = \rho(w) = \top$.

A function $\rho : V \to M_{\mathcal{G}}^{\top}$ is a **game progress measure**, if for all $v \in V$ the following two conditions hold:

(a) if $v \in V_0$ then $\rho \geq_{\Omega(v)} \mathrm{prog}(\rho, v, w)$ for some edge (v, w).
(b) if $v \in V_1$ then $\rho \geq_{\Omega(v)} \mathrm{prog}(\rho, v, w)$ for all edges (v, w).

Furthermore let $\|\rho\| = \{v \in V : \rho(v) \neq \top\}$.

Let us explain the intuition behind the above definition. A parity progress measure captures the existence of a winning strategy for Player 0 from all vertices in a solitaire game. The key feature of a parity progress measure is that it decreases on edges originating from vertices with odd parity and does not increase on other edges (with respect to some order depending on the priorities of vertices).

In a game arena (as opposed to a solitaire game) the strategy of Player 0 is not fixed, i.e., usually vertices belonging to both players have outdegree larger than one. Also there are usually nonempty winning regions for Player 0 and for Player 1.

A game progress measure is defined with respect to Player 0. For each vertex the above "decreasing" property must hold for *some* edge, if the vertex belongs to Player 0, and for *all* edges, if the vertex belongs to Player 1. So we demand the *existence* of an edge with the "decreasing" property for the multiple edges originating in vertices belonging to Player 0. Furthermore we have introduced the $\top$ element to deal with vertices in the possibly nonempty winning region of Player 1. Note that in case we have assigned the top element to a vertex we cannot demand that an edge leading to that vertex decreases the progress measure. That is the reason for introducing the complications in the prog-notation.

If we restrict a game graph with a game progress measure ρ to the vertices in $||\rho||$, we get a solitaire game with a parity progress measure. Assume that this parity progress measure equals the one constructed in the proof of Lemma 7.18. In this case we get the following interpretation of the game progress measure: the component $\rho_i(v)$ for some odd i and some $v \notin ||\rho||$ contains the number of times Player 1 may force Player 0 to see priority i before some smaller priority occurs, if Player 0 tries to minimize that value and Player 1 tries to maximize it. Unfortunately this intuition does not hold true for all possible parity progress measures as noted before, see Exercise 7.8

It is easy to find a game progress measure by assigning $\top$ to all vertices. This measure does not tell us much. But it will turn out that we can try to maximize the size of $||\rho||$ and find the winning region of Player 0.

First we define a strategy from the measure ρ. Let $f_0^\rho \colon V_0 \to V$ be a strategy for Player 0 defined by taking for each vertex v a successor w which minimizes $\rho(w)$.

Lemma 7.20. *If ρ is a game progress measure, then f_0^ρ is a winning strategy for Player 0 from all vertices in $||\rho||$.*

Proof. Restrict the game arena to the vertices in $||\rho||$. If we now fix the strategy f_0^ρ we get that ρ is a parity progress measure on the resulting solitaire game. This implies that all simple cycles in the solitaire game are even (using Lemma 7.17) and the strategy wins from all vertices in $||\rho||$, if f_0^ρ is closed on $||\rho||$ due to Lemma 7.15. But this is true, since the strategy would violate the conditions of its game progress measure if it would use an edge leading from $||\rho||$ to a vertex labeled $\top$ in the solitaire game. □

So we are after game progress measures with large $||\rho||$.

Lemma 7.21. *For each parity game there is a game progress measure ρ such that $||\rho||$ is the winning region of Player 0.*

Proof. Since each vertex is either in the winning region of Player 0 or of Player 1 we can assume that a winning strategy for Player 0 never leaves his winning set, otherwise Player 1 could win after such a step. Fixing a memoryless winning strategy with this winning region and restricting the vertices to the winning region yields a solitaire game $\mathcal{G}$ containing no simple even cycle. Thus due to Lemma 7.18 there is a parity progress measure ρ with values in $M_{\mathcal{G}}$. If we now set $\rho(v) = \top$ for all vertices outside of $\mathcal{G}$ we get a game progress measure as demanded.   □

We are now almost done. Given a game, we have to find a game progress measure that has a maximal number of vertices which do not have value $\top$. But it is actually not really clear how to compute game progress measures at all, except trivial ones.

So we take the following approach. We consider the set of *all* functions $V \to M_{\mathcal{G}}^{\top}$. Our goal is to find one such function which is a game progress measure, and in particular one with a maximal winning region. First we define an ordering on these functions. Let ρ, σ be two such functions, then $\rho \sqsubseteq \sigma$, if for all $v \in V$ we have $\rho(v) \leq \sigma(v)$. If also $\rho \neq \sigma$, then we write $\rho \sqsubset \sigma$. With this ordering we have a complete lattice structure on our set of functions. We will define certain monotone operators in this lattice. The game progress measure we are looking for is the least common fixed point of these operators.

We start from a function mapping all vertices to the all zero vector and apply the set of operators that "push the function" towards a game progress measure. Eventually this process will actually stop at a fixed point of the operators.

The applied operators work on one vertex label only, and in the worst case during a run of the algorithm the label of such a vertex may take on all its possible values. But then the number of such steps is no more than n times the number of all labels, which is $n \cdot |M_{\mathcal{G}}^{\top}|$.

Let us define the operators now.

Definition 7.22. The operator Lift(ρ, v) is defined for $v \in V$ and $\rho : V \to M_{\mathcal{G}}^{\top}$ as follows:

$$\text{Lift}(\rho, v)(u) := \begin{cases} \rho(u) & \text{if } u \neq v, \\ \max\{\rho(v), \min_{(v,w) \in E} \text{prog}(\rho, v, w)\} & \text{if } u = v \in V_0, \\ \max\{\rho(v), \max_{(v,w) \in E} \text{prog}(\rho, v, w)\} & \text{if } u = v \in V_1. \end{cases}$$

The following lemmas are obvious.

Lemma 7.23. *For all $v \in V$ the operator Lift$(\cdot, v)$ is monotone with respect to the ordering $\sqsubseteq$.*

Lemma 7.24. *A function $\rho: V \to M_{\mathcal{G}}^{\top}$ is a game progress measure iff it is a simultaneous fixed point of all Lift$(\cdot, v)$ operators, i.e., iff Lift$(\rho, v) \sqsubseteq \rho$ for all $v \in V$.*

Exercise 7.9. Prove the lemmas.

Now we have a correspondence between fixed points and game progress measures. We are interested in a game progress measure inducing the winning region. To find such a measure we will be computing the *least* simultaneous fixed point of all the operators. Due to a theorem of Tarski [175] and Knaster such a least fixed point exists and can be computed in the following way (see also Chapter 20 in the appendix):

We start with the function μ assigning 0 to every vertex. Then as as long as $\mu \sqsubset \text{Lift}(\mu, v)$ for some v, apply the lift operator $\mu := \text{Lift}(\mu, v)$.

When the algorithm terminates, it has found the least simultaneous fixed point of all lift operators. This is a game progress measure, and as we have seen it is easy to derive a strategy for Player 0 from it.

Theorem 7.25. *The winning region of Player 0 and Player 0's winning strategy in a parity game with n vertices, m edges, and $d \geq 2$ different priorities can be computed in time $O(d \cdot m \cdot \left(\frac{n}{\lfloor d/2 \rfloor} \right)^{\lfloor d/2 \rfloor})$ and space $O(dn \log n)$.*

Proof. First let us argue that the algorithm actually finds the winning region of Player 0. The computed game progress measure μ is the least simultaneous fixed point of all the lift operators. The strategy f_0^μ induced by μ is a winning strategy on the set of vertices $||\mu||$ due to Lemma 7.20. Therefore $||\mu||$ is a subset of Player 0's winning region. Furthermore $||\mu||$ is the largest set of vertices not assigned $\top$ over all game progress measures. Thus it must be Player 0's winning region due to Lemma 7.21.

Now let us calculate the complexity of the algorithm. The space is very easy to calculate. For each vertex we have to store an element of $M_{\mathcal{G}}^\top$, which consists of d numbers from the set $[n]$. Thus space used is $O(d \cdot n \log n)$.

The time can be bounded as follows. The $\text{Lift}(\rho, v)$ operator can be implemented in time $O(d \cdot outdegree(v))$. Every vertex may be lifted at most $|M_{\mathcal{G}}|$ times, so the time is upper bounded by $O(|M_{\mathcal{G}}| \cdot d \cdot \sum_v outdegree(v)) = O(md|M_{\mathcal{G}}|)$, if we ensure that we can always find a liftable vertex in constant time. This is possible by maintaining a queue of liftable vertices. In the beginning we insert all liftable vertices. Later we get a liftable vertex out of the queue, lift it, and test all predecessors of the vertex for liftability. Liftable vertices are marked liftable in an array, and if they change from non-liftable to liftable they are inserted into the queue. These operations are possible within the given time bound.

It remains now to estimate the size of $M_{\mathcal{G}}$. First assume that priority 0 is used, and also assume that there are vertices with priorities i for all $0 \leq i \leq d-1$. If some priority is missing, we can diminish the higher priorities by 2 without changing the game. Then

$$|M_{\mathcal{G}}| = \prod_{i=1}^{\lfloor d/2 \rfloor} (|V_{2i-1}| + 1).$$

We have

$$\sum_{i=1}^{\lfloor d/2 \rfloor} (|V_{2i-1}| + 1) \leq \sum_{i=0}^{d-1} |V_i| \leq n,$$

because there is at least one vertex with every even priority, and there are at most n vertices. Such a product is maximized when all the factors are equal, and can thus be bounded by

$$\left(\frac{n}{\lfloor d/2 \rfloor}\right)^{\lfloor d/2 \rfloor}.$$

Now assume that priority 0 is not used. Then w.l.o.g. the priorities used are $\{1, 2, \ldots, d\}$. Inspection of the argument shows that it works in this case as well, by switching the roles of the players in the proof and in the algorithm.   □

Now let us mention that one has indeed to specify in which order the Lift operators are applied, leading to a possible improvement by using a suitable such order. But Jurdziński has shown [93] that there is an example where for each such order policy the time bound is basically tight.

Exercise 7.10. Consider the following graph $H_{4,3}$ where quadratic vertices belong to Player 1 and all other vertices to Player 0. The numbers in the vertices are the priorities.

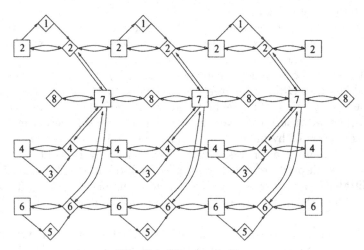

Fig. 7.1. The graph $H_{4,3}$

Show that the vertices with priority 7 are lifted 4^4 times, no matter what lifting policy is used. For this observe that for all vertices except those in the second, indented layer Player 0 has a winning strategy, for all vertices in the second layer Player 1 has a winning strategy, and hence $\top$ is the label assigned to these vertices in the least progress measure. Furthermore show that the Lift operator increases the labels of vertices with priority 7 only to their successors.

Generalize the graph to a family of graphs $H_{\ell,b}$ with $(\ell-1)\cdot(3b+1)+(2b+1)$ vertices and priorities from the set $\{1, \ldots, 2\ell\}$. Show that some vertices are lifted $(b+1)^\ell$ times no matter what lifting policy is used. Conclude that the running time bound of Theorem 7.25 is basically tight, in particular that the running time is exponential in d.

7.6   The Strategy Improvement Approach

In this section we briefly review another promising approach to solve parity games, which should also be useful in implementations. A rigorous theoretical analysis of this approach is missing, however.

The approach follows a quite general paradigm called **strategy improvement**. In this approach one starts with a pair of strategies for Player 0 and Player 1, and applies some simple operation on one player's strategy to "improve" it. Then the other player responds with an optimal strategy given the first player's strategy. This process is iterated. Of course it has to be made precise, what a better strategy is.

Strategy improvement was first proposed by Hoffman and Karp in 1966 [85] for stochastic games. Their algorithm proceeds basically by starting from any pair of strategies, and in each iteration considers a vertex, that can be "switched", in our context a vertex at which changing the strategy "improves" the solution. Then the player whose strategy is not yet changed responds with an optimal strategy according to the other player's strategy. This is done until no such iteration is possible. In this case both strategies are optimal. One has to show in particular, how to compute an optimal response strategy. Furthermore is must be made clear what an improved strategy is (this is easy for stochastic games). It is still unknown whether the Hoffmann-Karp algorithm terminates in polynomial time.

Strategy improvement algorithms for parity games have been proposed by Puri [147] and by Vöge and Jurdziński [191]. Both algorithms can do one iteration in polynomial time, but the actual number of iterations may be large. The algorithm due to Puri has the drawback that it is not a discrete algorithm, but involves linear programming and high precision arithmetic. So we discuss some of the ideas of the algorithm presented in [191]. Note that also the aforementioned algorithm of Ludwig for simple stochastic games [117] falls into this category.

The algorithm follows the approach described above. First a strategy of Player 0 is chosen randomly. Then an "optimal" response strategy is generated. After this the strategy of Player 0 is "improved" by some simple operation. This is done until both steps do not change the strategies anymore.

Instead of dealing with the strategies directly another combinatorial object is considered, and connected to strategies. This object is a *valuation*. Roughly speaking a valuation assigns to each vertex relevant information on a play starting from that vertex. Certain types of valuations correspond to strategy pairs. Furthermore an order is defined on valuations which captures whether one valuation is more valuable than another. This ordering allows to define optimal valuations. Furthermore simple improvement rules can be defined. This gives us all ingredients needed for a strategy improvement algorithm.

The first notion we need captures the kind of information we want to assign to single vertices. Note that we are again considering max-parity games, in which the vertex of highest priority occurring infinitely often is decisive. Furthermore, without loss of generality, we assume that no priority occurs twice.

Definition 7.26. Let $(\mathcal{A}, \Omega)$ be some parity game. Let w_π denote the vertex with highest priority occurring infinitely often in a play π. Let P_π denote the set of vertices encountered in play π before w_π appears first and having higher priority than w_π. Let $l(x)$ denote the size of the set of vertices encountered before w_π appears first.

The triple (w_π, P_π, l_π) is called the **play profile** of π.

A **valuation** is a mapping which assigns a play profile to every vertex.

A valuation is **induced** by a pair of strategies if it assigns to every vertex v the play profile of the play consistent with the strategies and starting at v.

Exercise 7.11. Construct a parity game and a valuation so that no pair of strategies corresponds to the valuation.

Construct a parity game and a valuation so that more than one pair of strategies corresponds to the valuation.

Obviously not all valuations are consistent with strategy pairs. We are looking for some nice conditions under which this is the case.

Consider the play profiles of vertices u, v with $u = f_0(v)$ in a valuation induced by strategies f_0, f_1. Call the plays originating at those vertices $\pi(u), \pi(v)$. Now obviously the most relevant vertex occurring infinitely often in the plays starting at u and at v is the same. We can distinguish three cases.

(1) $w_{\pi(v)}$ has larger or equal priority than v, but is not equal to v. In this case $P_{\pi(u)} = P_{\pi(v)}$ and $l_{\pi(u)} = l_{\pi(v)} - 1$.
(2) $w_{\pi(v)}$ has smaller priority than v. In this case $P_{\pi(v)} = P_{\pi(u)} \cup \{v\}$ and $l_{\pi(u)} = l_{\pi(v)} - 1$.
(3) $w_{\pi(v)} = v$. In this case $P_{\pi(v)} = \emptyset$ and $l_{\pi(v)} = 0$. Furthermore $P_{\pi(u)} = \emptyset$, since there are no vertices on the cycle, which are more relevant than v.

These conditions allow us to define what we call a **progress ordering**. We say that two vertices v, u obey a progress relation with respect to a valuation ϕ if the above conditions hold for the play profiles assigned to the vertices, and write $v \lhd_\phi u$.

The following is straightforward.

Lemma 7.27. *Let ϕ be a valuation satisfying $v \lhd_\phi f_0(v)$ resp. $v \lhd_\phi f_1(v)$ for all $v \in V$, then (f_0, f_1) induces ϕ.*

Our goal is still to give sufficient conditions for valuations which are induced by some pair of strategies.

We call a valuation ϕ **locally progressive**, if

$$\forall u \in V \exists v \in V : v \in uE \wedge u \lhd_\phi v.$$

This characterizes those valuations induced by strategies.

Lemma 7.28. *A valuation is locally progressive iff there exists a strategy pair inducing the valuation.*

Exercise 7.12. Prove the lemma. In particular, first show how to extract a strategy pair from a locally progressive valuation so that the strategy pair induces the valuation. Then show how to compute a locally progressive valuation when given a pair of strategies. Analyze the time needed to do so.

We now have a close connection between strategy pairs and locally progressive valuations. Our original goals were to find a way to get an "optimal" response strategy, and a way to "improve" strategies by some simple operations. We now define these with respect to valuations.

The first thing we need is a total ordering on the valuations. Since we assume that no priority occurs twice, we simply take the order on the priorities.

Next we define another ordering on vertices. Let $u \prec v$, if the priority of u is smaller than the priority of v and v has even priority, and if v has smaller priority than u and v has odd priority. So this ordering tells us how *valuable* vertices are from the point of view of Player 0.

This can be extended to sets of vertices P, Q, saying that $P \prec Q$ if $P \neq Q$ and the highest vertex in the symmetric difference between P and Q is in Q, if even, and in P, if odd.

Now extend the order to play profiles. Let (u, P, l) and (v, Q, r) be two play profiles. Then $(u, P, l) \prec (v, Q, r)$ if $u \prec v$, or if $u = v$ and $P \prec Q$ or if $u = v$ and $P = Q$ and $[l < r$ iff v has odd priority$]$.

This captures how advantageous a play profile may be for Player 0 compared to another play profile. If the most relevant vertex is advantageous, then so is the profile. If the most relevant vertex is the same, then the sets of vertices more relevant but occurring only finitely often is decisive. If these are the same, then the delay until the most relevant vertex appears decides. This is as much as we can see from the play profile, and the profile has been designed to let us see that much from it.

We are now able to state what optimal and improved valuations are.

Definition 7.29. A valuation ϕ is **optimal for Player 0**, if two vertices u and $v \in uE$ satisfy the progress relation $u \vartriangleleft_\phi v$ only if v is the $\prec$-maximal successor of u or if $\phi(u) = (u, \emptyset, 0)$ and $v = (u, \emptyset, k)$.

A symmetric definition **optimal for Player 1**. A valuation is **optimal** if it is optimal for both players.

In other words, regarding the above defined value ordering the progress relation increases only on optimal edges. Strategies inducing the valuation send vertices to optimal neighbors.

Definition 7.30. A locally progressive valuation ϕ is **improved** for Player 0 in the following way: first a strategy for Player 0 is extracted from ϕ so that for each vertex a successor is chosen which is maximal with respect to the $\prec$-order on profiles with respect to ϕ, then a valuation is constructed which is compatible with this strategy.

Note that if a locally progressive valuation is optimal for Player 0, then a strategy for Player 0 can be extracted from the valuation by mapping each vertex to its successor in the progress ordering. This strategy leads from each vertex to a neighbor which is maximal in the value ordering. We can also extract a strategy for Player 1 from the valuation. If Player 1 wins in a play from some vertex v played as determined by those strategies, then Player 1 wins from v also if Player 0 choses a different strategy, since this other strategy cannot lead to vertices with a a more advantageous play profile for Player 0. Hence we can collect the following consequences.

Lemma 7.31. *Let ϕ be a locally progressive valuation which is optimal for Player 0 [Player 1]. Then the strategies which are compatible with ϕ are winning strategies for Player 1 [Player 0] on the set of vertices v whose play profile in ϕ is (w, P, l) with $\Omega(w)$ odd [even], against all strategies of Player 0 [Player 1].*

If ϕ is optimal (for both players) then all strategies compatible with ϕ are winning strategies (from the respective winning regions of the players).

So it suffices to find an optimal valuation! Now we note that improved valuations deserve their name.

Lemma 7.32. *If ϕ is a locally progressive valuation that is optimal for Player 1 and ϕ' is a locally progressive valuation that is improved for Player 0 with respect to ϕ, then $\phi(v) \preceq \phi'(v)$ for all $v \in V$.*

Hence improving a locally progressive valuation cannot lead to a less advantageous valuation. It is also strictly improved until it is optimal:

Exercise 7.13. Show that a locally progressive valuation that is optimal for Player 1, and which does not change when it is improved for Player 0, is already optimal for both players.

Improving valuations is defined in an algorithmic manner via extracting a improved strategies and computing a valuation induced by the strategies. Note that this is possible in an efficient manner due to Exercise 7.12.

Now let us briefly describe the structure of the algorithm.

The algorithm starts with a random strategy for Player 0. Then in each iteration first a locally progressive valuation is computed which is optimal for Player 1. Player 0 responds by improving his strategy as described in Definition 7.29. This is done until the iteration does not change the valuations anymore. Strategies are extracted from the valuations.

Theorem 7.33. *The above algorithm computes winning strategies for Player 0 and Player 1. It can be implemented so that each iteration runs in time $O(nm)$.*

Proof. The first statement follows from the previous lemmas. For the implementation we have to discuss the computation of an optimal valuation for Player 1 given a strategy of Player 0.

For this Player 1 fixes Player 0's strategy and then goes in ascending order over all the vertices in the resulting solitaire game using the "reward ordering" $\prec$. For such a vertex v Player 1 tests, if there is a cycle containing v and otherwise only vertices of smaller priority. If so, then she computes the set of vertices from which v can be reached (and thus also the cycle). Then a valuation is computed on this component alone, and the component is removed, whereupon Player 1 continues with the next v.

To find an optimal valuation for the component from which the mentioned cycle is reachable, notice that it is optimal for Player 1 to go to the cycle, since v is the most profitable vertex which may occur infinitely often. It is her goal to find a path from each vertex that reaches the cycle giving the lowest reward for Player 0. All these computations are possible in time $O(nm)$.

For more details see [191]. □

So we have another approach to find winning regions and strategies in parity games. It is presently unknown how large the number of iterations may be in the worst case, except for an exponential upper bound. Neither examples with a high number of iterations nor good general upper bounds are known. Experiments suggest that the algorithm behaves quite good for some interesting inputs. One possible critique on this algorithm is that it does not make any use of a possibly bounded number of priorities, but rather expands the partial order on vertices induced by the priorities to a total order, resulting in n priorities used.

7.7   Conclusions

We have considered the problem of finding the winning regions of the two players in a given parity game and in several other graph-based games. We have seen that the problem can be solved in polynomial time, if the number of different priorities assigned to vertices is only a constant.

Our interest in the problem comes from its equivalence to model checking in the modal μ-calculus. Furthermore the problem is important as one of the few natural problems in UP ∩ co-UP. We have shown how to prove this complexity theoretic result. It is promising to investigate the complexity of the problem further. One message is at least that the problem is very unlikely to be NP-complete.

Furthermore we have discussed a simple, yet rather efficient algorithm, an algorithm with a quadratically improved time complexity compared to the first algorithm, and an attempt to solve the problem following the paradigm of strategy improvement.

Notes on Part III

The parity condition, also known as Rabin chain condition (see Chapter 1), was introduced by Mostowski [131] in 1984 as an acceptance condition for automata on infinite trees. As a winning condition for games, it was first considered by Mostowski [132] and Emerson and Jutla [55] in 1991. In these papers, it was shown that parity games always allow memoryless winning strategies – determinacy of parity games follows directly from Martin's most general result [119] from 1975 on the determinacy of Borel games.

McNaughton [126] studied infinite games on finite graphs from a more algorithmic point of view; Zielonka [203] gave, for the first time, a very clear and at the same time comprehensive exposition of infinite games on infinite graphs. Both, McNaughton and Zielonka, dealt with the parity condition as one condition of many. Thomas [180, 181, 183] first realized the central importance of the parity condition: it is simple enough so that it can (relatively) easy be solved and at the same time strong enough so that any winning condition can (relatively) easy be reduced to it.

The intimate connection between parity games and the modal μ-calculus was observed by several authors, including Emerson and Jutla [54], Herwig [80], and Stirling [167]. From the memoryless determinacy of parity games it immediately follows that parity games can be solved in NP ∩ Co-NP. The same result can also be obtained from a reduction to stochastic games, which was, for instance, observed by Mark Jerrum (see [167]). Such a reduction also allows to use Ludwig's randomized algorithm for solving stochastic games [117] to solve parity games.

In 1998 Jurdziński [92] improved on the NP ∩ co-NP upper bound and showed that solving parity games is in UP ∩ co-UP. He used a result by Zwick and Paterson [204] which reduces mean-payoff games to discounted mean-payoff games. In subsequent work [93], Jurdziński suggested the algorithm based on progress measures described here, which is the algorithm with the lowest upper bound on the worst-case running time known to date. A similar result was obtained by Seidl [161] in 1996.

Puri in his thesis [147] also saw the connection between parity games and mean-payoff games and opened a new direction in solving parity games by looking at strategy improvement algorithms. Further research led to the algorithm by Jurdziński and Vöge [191].

Algorithms for parity games on infinite graphs are dealt with in later parts of this volume, see, in particular, Chapter 17. For applications of parity games to tree automata and μ-calculus model checking, see Chapters 9 and 10.

This part probably contains the most challenging of all the open problems mentioned in this volume: What is the exact complexity of solving parity games? – As we have pointed out, the best we know is that solving parity games is in UP ∩ co-UP. Proving this problem to be in P or even in ZPP would definitely improve the situation.

As stated in the previous chapter, the strategy improvement algorithm by Jurdziński and Vöge seems to work quite well in practice, but neither nontrivial lower nor upper bounds have been established. In particular, it is an open problem to determine whether Jurdziński and Vöge's algorithm is a polynomial-time procedure.

Part IV

Tree Automata

Most studies of logics in this book follow the approach that logical formulas are translated into equivalent automata, where equivalence means that the models of the formula coincide with the structures accepted by the corresponding automata. The main advantage of this translation is an easier treatment of algorithmic questions in the automata-theoretic framework. For instance, the model-checking problem or a question on satisfiability for logical formulas is converted to the nonemptiness problem of suitable automata. The latter has often a much simpler structure than the original logical problem, since, in many cases, it can be reduced to reachability tests or cycle detection over the transition graphs of automata.

In order to obtain a translation of formulas into automata, the standard approach is to proceed by induction on the construction of formulas. This requires corresponding closure properties of the automata, among them closure under boolean connectives and existential quantification. For nondeterministic automata, existential quantification is easy but complementation difficult; for deterministic or alternating automata, it is the other way round. In all cases, substantial (but very different) automata-theoretic constructions are required.

The following part of the book presents such constructions for the case that infinite trees are the models under consideration: In the first chapter, the theory of nondeterministic automata over infinite trees is developed (originating in the path-breaking work of Rabin). The second chapter presents the (less well-known) approach via alternating tree automata with parity acceptance.

8 Nondeterministic Tree Automata

Frank Nießner

Institut für Informatik
Johann Wolfgang Goethe-Universität Frankfurt am Main

8.1 Introduction

The automaton models introduced so far mainly differ in their acceptance conditions. However, they all consume infinite sequences of alphabet symbols, i.e., they consume ω-words. We therefore call these automata **word automata**. In this chapter we define finite-state automata which process infinite trees instead of infinite words and consequently we call them **tree automata**.

Automata on infinite objects, in general, play an important role in those areas of computer science where nonterminating systems are investigated. System specifications can be translated to automata and thus questions about systems are reduced to decision problems in automata theory. Tree automata are more suitable than words when nondeterminism needs to be modelled.

Furthermore, there are close connections between tree automata and logical theories, which allow to reduce decision problems in logic to decision problems for automata. Such reductions will be thoroughly discussed in Chapter 11. Rabin [148] showed decidability of monadic second-order logic using tree automata which process infinite binary trees. The crucial part in his paper is a complementation theorem for nondeterministic finite-state automata on infinite trees. The proof of this theorem implicitly entails determinacy of parity games. However, Büchi [21] observed that this proof can be much simplified when games are applied explicitly. This approach was successfully implemented by numerous authors, see for instance [77, 55]. Here, we present a game-theoretically based proof of Rabin's theorem according to Thomas [183] and Zielonka [203]. For this purpose we use some results introduced in the previous chapters about infinite games, especially the determinacy theorem for parity games.

Moreover, we consider the emptiness problem for finite-state automata on infinite trees in terms of decidability and efficiency. These observations will be useful in the subsequent chapter about monadic second-order logic.

The chapter is structured as follows. In Section 8.2 we introduce notations and definitions. Section 8.3 introduces two tree automaton models which differ in their acceptance conditions but recognize the same classes of tree languages. We merely sketch the proof of equivalence between the two models. A game-theoretical view on tree automata and their acceptance conditions, together with the main results is given in Section 8.4. Then we are prepared to restate the above-mentioned complementation theorem. The last section, Section 8.5, discusses decidability questions of tree automata. We show that for a particular class of tree automata it is decidable whether their recognized language is empty or not.

E. Grädel et al. (Eds.): Automata, Logics, and Infinite Games, LNCS 2500, pp. 135-152, 2002.
© Springer-Verlag Berlin Heidelberg 2002

8.2   Preliminaries

The **infinite binary tree** is the set $T^\omega = \{0,1\}^*$ of all finite words on $\{0,1\}$. The elements $u \in T^\omega$ are the nodes of T^ω where ε is the root and $u0, u1$ are the immediate (say) left and right successors of node u.

We restrict ourselves to binary trees, since they are sufficient for most applications, see, for instance, Chapter 12.

Let $u, v \in T^\omega$, then v is a successor of u, denoted by $u < v$, if there exists a $w \in T^\omega$ such that $v = uw$.

An ω-word $\pi \in \{0,1\}^\omega$ is called a **path** of the binary tree T^ω. The set $Pre_<(\pi) \subset \{0,1\}^*$ of all prefixes of path π (linearly ordered by $<$) describes the set of nodes which occur in π.

For sets Θ, Σ and a mapping $\mu : \Theta \to \Sigma$, we define the **infinity set** $\mathrm{Inf}(\mu) = \{\sigma \in \Sigma \mid \mu^{-1}(\sigma) \text{ is an infinite set}\}$.

We consider here trees where the nodes are labeled with a symbol of an alphabet. A mapping $t : T^\omega \to \Sigma$ labels trees with symbols of Σ. The set of all **Σ-labeled trees** is denoted by T_Σ^ω (or T_Σ for simplicity, if no confusion occurs). Sometimes we are only interested in the **labeling of a path** π through t. Hence let $t|\pi : Pre_<(\pi) \to \Sigma$ denote the restriction of the mapping t to π.

For n an integer and $1 \le i \le n$, the **projection** onto the i-th coordinate is the mapping $p_i : \Sigma^n \to \Sigma$ such that $p_i((\sigma_1, \sigma_2, \ldots, \sigma_n)) = \sigma_i$. We extend projections to labeled infinite trees. For a $\Sigma_1 \times \Sigma_2$-labeled tree $t \in T_{\Sigma_1 \times \Sigma_2}^\omega$, let $p_1(t) \in T_{\Sigma_1}^\omega$ be the corresponding tree labeled exclusively with elements of Σ_1. Projections can be applied to sets as well. Thus a projection $p_1(\Theta)$ of a set $\Theta \subseteq T_{\Sigma_1 \times \Sigma_2}^\omega$ is defined as $p_1(\Theta) = \{p_1(t) \mid t \in \Theta\}$.

Example 8.1. Let $\Sigma = \{a, b\}$, $t(\varepsilon) = a$, $t(w0) = a$ and $t(w1) = b$, $w \in \{0,1\}^*$.

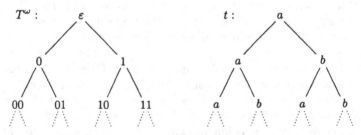

Fig. 8.1. A tree with corresponding labeling

Exercise 8.1. Prove the above-mentioned assertion that binary trees suffice to describe the general case, i.e., describe an encoding of trees with arbitrary finite branching as binary trees.

8.3   Finite-State Tree Automata

The automata seen so far processed finite or infinite sequences of alphabet symbols. They consume one input symbol at a time and thereby enter a successor state determined by a transition relation. It is obvious that we somehow have to modify the automaton models in order to make them running on infinite trees. Since each position in a binary tree has two successors (rather than one successor as in infinite words) it is natural to define for a state out of a set Q and an input symbol from Σ two successor states in the transition relation, that is, transitions are now elements of $Q \times \Sigma \times Q \times Q$. Computations then start at the root of an input tree and work through the input on each path in parallel. A transition (q, a, q_1, q_2) allows to pass from state q at node u with input-tree label a to the states q_1, q_2 at the successor nodes $u0, u1$. Afterwards there may be transitions which allow to continue from q_1 and from q_2, and so on. This procedure yields a Q-labeled tree which we call the **run** of an automaton on an input tree. Such a run is **successful** if all the state sequences along the paths meet an **acceptance condition** similar to the types of acceptance conditions known already from sequential ω-automata.

We start with the description of a **Muller tree automaton**.

Definition 8.2. A Muller tree automaton is a quintuple $\mathcal{A} = (Q, \Sigma, \Delta, q_I, \mathcal{F})$ where Q is a finite state set, Σ is a finite alphabet, $\Delta \subseteq Q \times \Sigma \times Q \times Q$ denotes the transition relation, q_I is an initial state and $\mathcal{F} \subseteq P(Q)$ is a set of designated state sets. A run of $\mathcal{A}$ on an input tree $t \in T_\Sigma$ is a tree $\varrho \in T_Q$, satisfying $\varrho(\varepsilon) = q_I$ and for all $w \in \{0,1\}^* : (\varrho(w), t(w), \varrho(w0), \varrho(w1)) \in \Delta$. It is called successful if for each path $\pi \in \{0,1\}^\omega$ the **Muller acceptance condition** is satisfied, that is, if $\mathrm{Inf}(\varrho|\pi) \in \mathcal{F}$. We refer to Section 1.3.2 for a thorough definition of the Muller acceptance condition. $\mathcal{A}$ accepts the tree t if there is a successful run of $\mathcal{A}$ on t. The tree language recognized by $\mathcal{A}$ is the set $T(\mathcal{A}) = \{t \in T_A^\omega \mid \mathcal{A} \text{ accepts } t\}$.

Example 8.3. We consider the tree language $T = \{t \in T_{\{a,b\}} \mid \text{there is a path } \pi$ through t such that $t|\pi \in (a+b)^*(ab)^\omega\}$. The language can be recognized by a Muller tree automaton $\mathcal{A}$ that guesses a path through t and checks, if the label of this path belongs to $(a+b)^*(ab)^\omega$. For this purpose $\mathcal{A}$ memorizes in its state the last read input symbol. If in the next step the current input symbol varies from that in the state memory, then it gets noticed in $\mathcal{A}$'s successor state, otherwise $\mathcal{A}$ switches back to the initial state q_I. Hence a path label in $(a+b)^*(ab)^\omega$ involves an infinite alternation between a state q_a memorizing input symbol a and a state q_b memorizing b. Therefore $\mathcal{F}$ includes the acceptance set $\{q_a, q_b\}$. It remains to be explained how $\mathcal{A}$ can guess a path. Guessing a path means to decide whether the left or the right successor node of the input tree belongs to the path. In the corresponding run this node obtains the label q_a or q_b, depending on the current input symbol. The remaining node gets the label q_d which signals that it is outside the guessed path.

Formally, $\mathcal{A} = (\{q_I, q_a, q_b, q_d\}, \{a, b\}, \Delta, q_I, \{\{q_a, q_b\}, \{q_d\}\})$. Transition relation Δ includes the following initial transitions $(q_I, a, q_a, q_d), (q_I, a, q_d, q_a)$,

$(q_{\mathrm{I}}, b, q_b, q_d)$, $(q_{\mathrm{I}}, b, q_d, q_b)$. Since we do not care about the situation outside the path guessed, i.e, in a run the left and right successors of a node labeled by q_d will get the label q_d as well, independently of the current input symbol, it follows $(q_d, a, q_d, q_d) \in \Delta$ and $(q_d, b, q_d, q_d) \in \Delta$. If for a node with label q_a the corresponding input label is b, then the automaton enters state q_b, formally (q_a, b, q_b, q_d), $(q_a, b, q_d, q_b) \in \Delta$. Reading an a instead means that there have been two consecutive a's, i.e., we are still checking the label prefix $(a + b)^*$. In this case $\mathcal{A}$ reenters q_{I}, that is, $(q_a, a, q_{\mathrm{I}}, q_d)$,$(q_a, a, q_d, q_{\mathrm{I}}) \in \Delta$. Since the case for node label q_b is symmetrical, (q_b, a, q_a, q_d),$(q_b, a, q_d, q_a) \in \Delta$ and $(q_b, b, q_{\mathrm{I}}, q_d)$,$(q_b, b, q_d, q_{\mathrm{I}}) \in \Delta$.

On the input tree t of Example 8.1 there exists a successful run ϱ that could start with the transitions depicted in Figure 8.2.

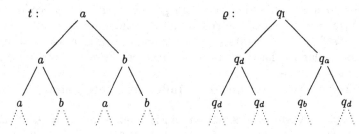

Fig. 8.2. First transitions of ϱ

Exercise 8.2. Define a Muller tree automaton recognizing the language $T = \{t \in T_{\{a,b\}} \mid$ there is a path π through t such that after any occurrence of letter a in π there is some occurrence of letter $b\}$.

In a similar way we can define **parity tree automata**, that is, we adopt the **parity condition**, introduced in [55], to tree automata. It will turn out that this automaton model is particularly useful for the solution of the complementation problem for automata on infinite trees.

Definition 8.4. A parity tree automaton is a quintuple $\mathcal{A} = (Q, \Sigma, \Delta, q_{\mathrm{I}}, c)$ where Q is a finite state set, Σ is a finite alphabet, $\Delta \subseteq Q \times \Sigma \times Q \times Q$ denotes the transition relation, q_{I} is an initial state, and $c : Q \rightarrow \{0, ..., k\}$, $k \in \mathbb{N}$ is a function which assigns an index value out of a finite index set to each state of the automaton. Sometimes the index values are called colors where c is the corresponding coloring function. Again, a run of $\mathcal{A}$ on an input tree $t \in T_\Sigma$ is a tree $\varrho \in T_Q$, satisfying $\varrho(\varepsilon) = q_{\mathrm{I}}$ and $\forall w \in \{0, 1\}^* : (\varrho(w), t(w), \varrho(w0), \varrho(w1)) \in \Delta$. We call it successful if for each path $\pi \in \{0, 1\}^\omega$ the **parity acceptance condition** is satisfied, that is, if $min\{c(q) \mid q \in \mathrm{Inf}(\varrho|\pi)\}$ is even. The tree language recognized by $\mathcal{A}$ is the set $T(\mathcal{A}) = \{t \in T_\mathcal{A}^\omega \mid \mathcal{A} \text{ accepts } t\}$.

Example 8.5. We consider the tree language $T = \{t \in T_{\{a,b\}} \mid$ for each path π through t holds $t|\pi \in a^\omega \cup (a + b)^* b^\omega\}$. The language can be recognized by a parity tree automaton $\mathcal{A}$ that checks simultaneously whether the labels of all paths belong to $a^\omega \cup (a + b)^* b^\omega$ or not. Hence there is no necessity to guess a correct path, i.e, for each state the left and right successor states will be identical.

The automaton starts in the initial state q_I and changes to successor states q_b, q_b if an alphabet symbol b was read and remains in q_I for a symbol a, respectively. We observe that reading a symbol b means we cannot have a label a^ω on the corresponding path. The following initial transitions $(q_I, b, q_b, q_b), (q_I, a, q_I, q_I)$ belong to the transition relation Δ of $\mathcal{A}$. The automaton remains in q_b if the corresponding input is a b, i.e., $(q_b, b, q_b, q_b) \in \Delta$, otherwise it switches both successor states and thus $(q_b, a, q_a, q_a) \in \Delta$. $\mathcal{A}$ behaves symmetrically when its current state is q_a, that is, $(q_a, a, q_a, q_a), (q_a, b, q_b, q_b) \in \Delta$.

While reading a's, $\mathcal{A}$ labels the nodes of his run on t with q_I. An alphabet symbol b signals that from now on the automaton has to verify $(a+b)^* b^\omega$. This is done by using the states q_a and q_b which indicate that the symbol last read was a or b, respectively. On paths which labels belong to $(a + b)^* b^\omega$ the automaton remains, from some point of time, in state q_b and consumes b's exclusively. Thus, if we index the states by $c(q_a) = 1$ and $c(q_b) = 2 = c(q_I)$, we can ensure that only the desired trees are accepted.

Exercise 8.3. Define a Muller and a parity tree automaton recognizing the language $T = \{t \in T_{\{a,b\}} \mid$ any path through t carries only finitely many $b\}$.

Büchi, Rabin and **Streett** tree automata are defined analogously, i.e., we provide the tree automata with a Büchi, Rabin or Streett acceptance condition. For a thorough definition of these acceptance conditions see Chapter 1. Hence a run of one of these automata is successful if and only if for each path of the run the corresponding acceptance condition is satisfied. Büchi tree automata differ from the other automaton models in terms of their generative capacity, i.e., they differ in terms of the language class recognized. We state this fact in the following theorem.

Theorem 8.6. *Büchi tree automata are strictly weaker than Muller tree automata in the sense that there exists a Muller tree automaton recognizable language which is not Büchi tree automaton recognizable [149].*

Proof. The language $T = \{t \in T_{\{a,b\}} \mid$ any path through t carries only finitely many $b\}$ can obviously be recognized by a Muller tree automaton with transitions $(q_I, a, q_I, q_I), (q_I, a, q_I, q_I), (q_I, b, q_I, q_I), (q_I, b, q_I, q_I)$ and the designated set $\mathcal{F} = \{\{q_I\}\}$. (This solves one part of the above exercise.) However, it can not be recognized by any Büchi tree automaton.

Assume for contradiction that T is recognized by a Büchi tree automaton $\mathcal{B} = (Q, \Sigma, \Delta, q_I, F)$ such that $card(Q) = n$. Consider the input tree $t_n \in T_{\{a,b\}}$ which has a label b exactly at the nodes $1^+0, 1^+01^+0, \ldots, (1^+0)^n$, i.e., at positions that we reach by choosing the left successor after a sequence of right successors, but only for at most n left choices. It is obvious that $t_n \in T$. Thus there is a successful run ϱ of $\mathcal{B}$ on t_n. On path 1^ω a final state is visited infinitely often, hence there must be a natural number m_0 so that $\varrho(1^{m_0}) \in F$. The same observation holds for path $1^{m_0}01^\omega$ with m_1 and $\varrho(1^{m_0}01^{m_1}) \in F$. Proceeding in this way we obtain $n+1$ positions $1^{m_0}, 1^{m_0}01^{m_1}, \ldots, 1^{m_0}01^{m_1}0\ldots1^{m_n}$ on which ϱ runs through a final state. This means that there must be positions, say u and v, where $u < v$ and $\varrho(u) = \varrho(v) = f \in F$. We consider the finite path π_u in t_n from u to v. By construction this path performs at least one left turn and thus it contains a node with label b. Now we construct another input tree t'_n by infinite repetition of π_u. This tree contains an infinite path which carries infinitely many b's, thus $t'_n \notin T$, but we can easily construct a successful run on t'_n by copying the actions of ϱ to π_u infinitely often, hence getting a contradiction. $\square$

One can show that Muller, parity, Rabin and Streett tree automata all accept the same class of languages. The proofs are similar to those for sequential automata from the first chapter. This is not a surprising fact because for tree automata the appropriate acceptance condition is applied to each path of a run separately, i.e., to a sequence of states.

Theorem 8.7. *Muller, parity, Rabin and Streett tree automata all recognize the same tree languages.*

Proof. We sketch the transformations of tree automata according to those for word automata described in Chapter 1.

We start with transforming Muller acceptance to parity acceptance. This transformation reuses the modified **LAR construction** already introduced in Section 1.4.2. Let $\mathcal{A} = (\{1, 2, \ldots, n\}, \Sigma, 1, \Delta, \mathcal{F})$ be a Muller tree automaton. The states of the parity tree automaton $\mathcal{A}'$ are permutations of subsets of $\mathcal{A}$'s states together with a marker $\natural$ that indicates the position of the last change in the record. If $(i, a, i', i'') \in \Delta$, then for all states $u \natural v$ where i is the rightmost symbol we have to add transitions $(u \natural v, a, u' \natural v', u'' \natural v'')$ to the transition relation set of $\mathcal{A}'$. The states $u' \natural v'$ and $u'' \natural v''$ are the successor states determined by the rules described in Section 1.4.2. If the states out of

$$\{\, u \natural v \mid |u| < i \,\} \cup \{\, u \natural v \mid |u| = i \wedge \{\, a \in \Sigma \mid a \sqsubseteq v \,\} \notin \mathcal{F} \,\}$$

are colored by $2i - 1$ and the states out of

$$\{\, u \natural v \mid |u| = i \wedge \{\, a \in \Sigma \mid a \sqsubseteq v \,\} \in \mathcal{F} \,\}$$

are colored by $2i$ then $T(\mathcal{A}) = T(\mathcal{A}')$.

Next we transform parity acceptance to a Streett acceptance condition. Let $\mathcal{A} = (Q, \Sigma, \Delta, q_1, c)$ be a parity tree automaton where $c : Q \to \{0, \ldots, k\}$, $k \in \mathbb{N}$. An equivalent Streett tree automaton is defined by $\mathcal{A}' = (Q, \Sigma, \Delta, q_1, \Omega)$ where $\Omega := \{(E_0, F_0), \ldots, (E_r, F_r)\}$, $r := \lfloor \frac{k}{2} \rfloor$ and for all $i \in \{0, \ldots, r\}$ the sets E_i and F_i are determined by $E_i := \{q \in Q \mid c(q) < 2i + 1\}$ and $F_i := \{q \in Q \mid c(q) = 2i + 1\}$.

Next, we transform parity acceptance to a Rabin acceptance condition. Let $\mathcal{A} = (Q, \Sigma, \Delta, q_1, c)$ be a parity tree automaton where $c : Q \to \{0, \ldots, k\}$, $k \in \mathbb{N}$. An equivalent Rabin tree automaton is defined by $\mathcal{A}' = (Q, \Sigma, \Delta, q_1, \Omega)$ where $\Omega := \{(E_0, F_0), \ldots, (E_r, F_r)\}$, $r := \lfloor \frac{k}{2} \rfloor$ and for all $i \in \{0, \ldots, r\}$ the sets

E_i and F_i are determined by $E_i := \{q \in Q \mid c(q) < 2i\}$ and $F_i := \{q \in Q \mid c(q) = 2i\}$.

Next, we transform Streett acceptance to a Muller acceptance condition. Let $\mathcal{A} = (Q, \Sigma, \Delta, q_\mathrm{I}, \Omega)$ be a Streett tree automaton. We define an equivalent Muller tree automaton by $\mathcal{A}' = (\{1, 2, \ldots, n\}, \Sigma, 1, \Delta, \mathcal{F})$ where

$$\mathcal{F} := \{\, G \in \mathscr{P}(Q) \mid \forall (E, F) \in \Omega \,.\, G \cap E \neq \emptyset \vee G \cap F = \emptyset \,\}.$$

Our final transformation transforms Rabin acceptance to Muller acceptance. Let $\mathcal{A} = (Q, \Sigma, \Delta, q_\mathrm{I}, \Omega)$ be a Rabin tree automaton. We define an equivalent Muller tree automaton by $\mathcal{A}' = (\{1, 2, \ldots, n\}, \Sigma, 1, \Delta, \mathcal{F})$ where

$$\mathcal{F} := \{\, G \in \mathscr{P}(Q) \mid \exists (E, F) \in \Omega \,.\, G \cap E = \emptyset \wedge G \cap F \neq \emptyset \,\}. \qquad \square$$

Exercise 8.4. Give an example that shows that the straight-forward conversion of Muller ω-automata to Büchi ω-automata from Chapter 1 does not work for tree automata.

8.4 The Complementation Problem for Automata on Infinite Trees

It is not difficult to prove closure under union, intersection and projection for finite tree automata languages. We leave this as an exercise.

Exercise 8.5. Prove closure under union, intersection and projection for the class of Muller tree automaton recognizable languages.

As already mentioned in the introduction, complementation is the essential problem. We will now show closure under complementation for tree languages acceptable by parity tree automata (and hence acceptable by Muller tree automata).

To simplify the proof we use a game-theoretical approach. We identify a parity tree automaton $\mathcal{A} = (Q, \Sigma, \Delta, q_\mathrm{I}, c)$ and an input tree t with an **infinite two-person game** $\mathcal{G}_{A,t}$ having Player 0 and Player 1 playing the game on t. The rules of the game are the following ones. The Players move alternately. Player 0 starts a game by picking an initial transition from Δ such that the alphabet symbol of this transition equals that at the root of t. Player 1 determines whether to proceed with the left or the right successor. His opponent reacts by again selecting a transition from Δ where the alphabet symbol now must equal the input symbol of the left or right successor node in t and the current transition state has to match the left or right successor state of the previous transition, depending on Player 1's selection. So in general, it is the task of Player 0 to pick transitions and it is the task of Player 1 to determine a direction. Hence, due to Gurevich and Harrington [77], Player 0 and Player 1 are sometimes called automaton and pathfinder. The sequence of actions represents a **play** of the game and induces an infinite sequence of states visited along the path across *t*. Player 0 **wins** the play if this infinite state sequence satisfies the acceptance condition of $\mathcal{A}$, otherwise Player 1 wins. Player 0's goal is it to show that the state sequences for all paths of the corresponding run meet the acceptance condition, i.e., that $\mathcal{A}$ accepts *t*. Player 1 tries to prevent Player 0 from being the winner, his goal is to verify the existence of a path such that the corresponding state sequence violates the acceptance condition of $\mathcal{A}$, i.e., the rejection of *t* by $\mathcal{A}$.

Example 8.8. For our input tree *t* and the parity tree automaton $\mathcal{A}$ introduced in Example 8.5, Figure 8.3 shows the first moves in a play of $\mathcal{G}_{\mathcal{A},t}$. Each arrow is labeled with that player whose decision determines the succeeding position.

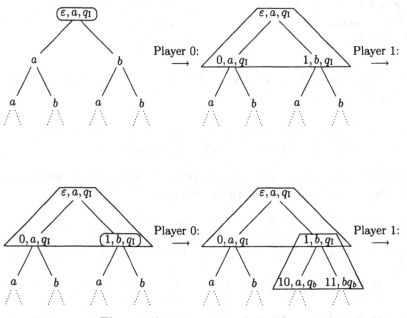

Fig. 8.3. First moves in a play of $\mathcal{G}_{\mathcal{A},t}$

The positions from where on Player 0 or Player 1 have to react are called **game positions**. Thus a play is an infinite sequence of game positions which alternately belong to Player 0 or Player 1. A game can be considered as an **infinite graph** which consists of all game positions as vertices. Edges between different positions indicate that the succeeding position is reachable from the preceding one by a valid action of Player 0 or Player 1, respectively. The game positions of Player 0 are defined by

$$V_0 := \{(w, q) \mid w \in \{0, 1\}^*, q \in Q\}.$$

Player 1's game positions are given by

$$V_1 := \{(w, \tau) \mid w \in \{0, 1\}^*, \tau \in \Delta_{t(w)}\},$$

where for each $a \in \Sigma$,

$$\Delta_a := \{\tau \in \Delta \mid \exists q, q_0', q_1' \in Q, \tau = (q, a, q_0', q_1')\}.$$

In a game position $u = (w, q)$, Player 0 chooses a transition $\tau = (q, t(w), q_0',$ $q_1')$ and thus determines the states belonging to the successors of w. Further-more, by this decision a game position $v = (w, \tau)$ of Player 1 is established. The edge (u, v) then represents a valid move of Player 0. Now Player 1 chooses a di-rection $i \in \{0, 1\}$ and determines from where to proceed, i.e., Player 1 determines wi and thus establishes $u' = (wi, q_i')$ which is again a game position of Player 0. The edge (v, u') represents a valid move of Player 1. The usual starting position of a play is $(\varepsilon, q_\mathrm{I})$ and thus belongs to Player 0. Now we index the game posi-tions with the colors of the states belonging to them, i.e., $c((w, q)) = c(q)$ and $c((w, (q, t(w), q_0', q_1'))) = c(q)$. The games $\mathcal{G}_{A,t}$ then meet exactly the definition of **min-parity games** given in Chapter 4.

Furthermore the notions of a **strategy**, a **memoryless strategy** and a **winning strategy** as defined in Section 2.4 apply to the games $\mathcal{G}_{A,t}$ as well. A winning strategy of a game $\mathcal{G}_{A,t}$ and a successful run $\varrho \in T_Q$ of the corresponding automaton $\mathcal{A} = (Q, \Sigma, \Delta, q_\mathrm{I}, c)$ are closely related.

The run ϱ keeps track of all transitions that have to be chosen in order to accept the input tree t. For any of the nodes (w, q), $w \in \{0, 1\}^*$, $q \in Q$, where $(w0, q_0')$ and $(w1, q_1')$ are the immediate successors, we can derive the corresponding transition $\tau = (q, t(w), q_0', q_1') \in \Delta$. In other words, we know for each node w in each path π through ϱ which transition to apply. Each of these paths is an infinite sequence of states that corresponds to a particular play of the game $\mathcal{G}_{A,t}$. This play is won by Player 0, since the infinite state sequence is a path of the successful run ϱ. The decisions of Player 1 determine the path generated by the current play. Since ϱ determines for each node and each path the correct transition, Player 0 can always choose the right transition, independently of Player 1's decisions, i.e., Player 0 has a winning strategy. Thus if there exists a successful run of $\mathcal{A}$ on t, then Player 0 has a winning strategy.

Conversely, we can use a winning strategy f_0 for Player 0 in $\mathcal{G}_{A,t}$ to construct a successful run ϱ of $\mathcal{A}$ on t. For each game position (w, q) of Player 0, f_0 determines the correct transition $\tau = (q, t(w), q_0', q_1')$. Player 0 must be prepared to proceed at game position $(w0, q_0')$ or at game position $(w1, q_1')$ since he can not predict Player 1's decision. However, for both positions the winning strategy can determine correct transitions such that the play can be continued to a winning play for Player 0. Hence in ϱ we label w by q, $w0$ by q_0' and $w1$ by q_1'. Proceeding in this way we obtain the entire run ϱ which is successful since it is determined by a winning strategy of Player 0. Thus, if Player 0 has a winning strategy in $\mathcal{G}_{A,t}$, then there exists a successful run of $\mathcal{A}$ on t.

We summarize these observations in the following lemma.

Lemma 8.9. *A tree automaton $\mathcal{A}$ accepts an input tree t if and only if there is a winning strategy for Player 0 from position (ε, q_I) in the game $\mathcal{G}_{\mathcal{A},t}$.*

As already mentioned, a game $\mathcal{G}_{\mathcal{A},t}$ which is identified with a parity tree automaton $\mathcal{A}$ and an input tree t meets the definition of parity games. So we can make use of central results about parity games. As is done in Theorem 6.6, it can be shown that these games are determined and that memoryless winning strategies suffice to win a game. Thus from any game position in $\mathcal{G}_{\mathcal{A},t}$, either Player 0 or Player 1 has a memoryless winning strategy.

We are now prepared to focus on our original problem, namely the complementation of finite tree automata languages. Given a parity tree automaton $\mathcal{A}$, we have to specify a tree automaton $\mathcal{B}$ that accepts all input trees rejected by $\mathcal{A}$. Rejection means not accepting an input tree t, or in our game theoretical notation, following Lemma 8.9, there is no winning strategy for Player 0 from position (ε, q_I) in the game $\mathcal{G}_{\mathcal{A},t}$. However, the above-mentioned results about parity games guarantee the existence of a memoryless winning strategy starting at (ε, q_I) for Player 1. We will construct an automaton that checks exactly this.

First of all we observe that a memoryless strategy of Player 1 is a function $f\colon \{0,1\}^* \times \Delta \to \{0,1\}$ determining a direction 0 (left successor) or 1 (right successor). But there is a natural isomorphism between such functions and functions $\{0,1\}^* \to (\Delta \to \{0,1\})$, which, by our definition, are trees. So we can identify memoryless strategies for Player 1 and such trees. We call such trees **strategy trees**, and if the corresponding strategy is winning for Player 1 in the game $\mathcal{G}_{\mathcal{A},t}$, we say it is a **winning tree** for t.

Remark 8.10. Let $\mathcal{A}$ be a parity tree automaton and t be an input tree. There exists a winning tree for Player 1 if and only if $\mathcal{A}$ does not accept t.

Given a parity tree automaton $\mathcal{A}$ and an input t we decide whether a tree s is not a winning tree t using an ω-automaton $\mathcal{M}$ with parity acceptance condition that checks for each path π of t and possible move by Player 0 separately whether the acceptance condition of $\mathcal{A}$ is met. If at least once $\mathcal{A}$'s acceptance condition is met, then s cannot be a winning tree for t and vice versa. Clearly, the automaton $\mathcal{M}$ needs to handle all ω-words of the form $u = (s(\varepsilon), t(\varepsilon), \pi_1)(s(\pi_1), t(\pi_1), \pi_2)\ldots$. Let $L(s,t)$ be the language of all these words.

Example 8.11. Consider a path $\pi = 01100\cdots$ through the tree t. An ω-word $u \in L(s,t)$ determined by π could look like the one depicted in Figure 8.4. Here, every box represents a single alphabet symbol.

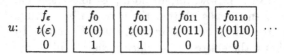

$$u\colon \quad \begin{array}{|c|}\hline f_\varepsilon \\ t(\varepsilon) \\ 0 \\\hline\end{array} \begin{array}{|c|}\hline f_0 \\ t(0) \\ 1 \\\hline\end{array} \begin{array}{|c|}\hline f_{01} \\ t(01) \\ 1 \\\hline\end{array} \begin{array}{|c|}\hline f_{011} \\ t(011) \\ 0 \\\hline\end{array} \begin{array}{|c|}\hline f_{0110} \\ t(0110) \\ 0 \\\hline\end{array} \cdots$$

Fig. 8.4. An ω-word determined by π

Let $\mathcal{A}$ be as usual. The automaton $\mathcal{M} = (Q, \Sigma', \Lambda, q_{\mathrm{I}}, c)$ is designed to handle any trees s and t. So $\mathcal{M}$'s alphabet is defined by $\Sigma' = \{(f, a, i) \mid f \colon \Delta \to \{0, 1\}, a \in \Sigma, i \in \{0, 1\}\}$. So $\mathcal{A}$ and $\mathcal{M}$ have the same acceptance condition. The automaton $\mathcal{M}$ has to check for each possible move of Player 0 if the outcome is winning for Player 0. This is done nondeterministically: for $(f, a, i) \in \Sigma'$, $f \in map_a$, and $\tau = (q, a, q'_0, q'_1) \in \Delta_a$ such that $f(\tau) = i$, $\mathcal{M}$ has a transition $(q, (f, a, i), q'_i)$. Here, for $a \in \Sigma$, map_a denotes the set of all mappings from Δ_a to $\{0, 1\}$.

Lemma 8.12. *The tree s is a winning tree for t if and only if $L(s, t) \cap L(\mathcal{M}) = \emptyset$.*

Proof. "If": Let s be a winning tree. We assume the existence of a path $\pi = \pi_1 \pi_2 \ldots$ such that the corresponding ω-word

$$u = (s(\varepsilon), t(\varepsilon), \pi_1)(s(\pi_1), t(\pi_1), \pi_2) \ldots$$

determined by π is an element of $L(\mathcal{M})$. So there is a successful run $\varrho = q_1 q_1 q_2 \ldots$ of $\mathcal{M}$ on u. This implies for each transition

$$(q_j, (s(\pi_1 \ldots \pi_j), t(\pi_1 \ldots \pi_j), \pi_{j+1}), q_{j+1})$$

that occurs in ϱ the existence of an appropriate transition $\tau_j = (q_j, t(\pi_1 \ldots \pi_j), q'_0, q'_1)$ of $\mathcal{A}$ such that $s(\pi_1 \ldots \pi_j) = f_{\pi_1 \ldots \pi_j}$ where $f_{\pi_1 \ldots \pi_j}(\tau_j) = \pi_{j+1}$. If $\pi_{j+1} = 0$ then $q_{j+1} = q'_0$ otherwise $q_{j+1} = q'_1$ holds. Now we let these transitions τ_j be Player 0's choices in a play of $\mathcal{G}_{\mathcal{A},t}$ where Player 1 reacts by choosing $s(\pi_1 \ldots \pi_j)$. The sequence of states visited along this play is $\varrho = q_1 q_1 q_2 \ldots$ and satisfies $\mathcal{M}$'s acceptance condition. Hence Player 1 loses even though he played according to s. So s cannot be a winning tree for t.

"Only if": Let $L(s, t) \cap L(\mathcal{M}) = \emptyset$. We consider any play of the game $\mathcal{G}_{\mathcal{A},t}$ and assume $(q_j, t(\pi_1 \ldots \pi_j), q'_0, q'_1) \in \Delta$ to be Player 0's choice when $\pi_1 \ldots \pi_j$ is the current node. Player 1 plays according to s. The successor state is determined by $s(\pi_1 \ldots \pi_j)$ as is described above, i.e., $q_{j+1} \in \{q'_0, q'_1\}$. Then we obtain an infinite sequence $\varrho = q_1 q_1 q_2 \ldots$ of states visited along the play. This sequence is as well the run of $\mathcal{M}$ on the corresponding ω-word $u = (s(\varepsilon), t(\varepsilon), \pi_1)(s(\pi_1), t(\pi_1), \pi_2) \ldots$ $\in L(s, t)$. Since $L(s, t) \cap L(\mathcal{M}) = \emptyset$, ϱ is not accepting. The run ϱ is a particular path of $\mathcal{A}$'s run on t which is determined by Player 0's choices. This implies that $\mathcal{A}$ cannot accept t by this run. However, these observations hold for any run, thus $t \notin T(\mathcal{A})$. $\square$

The word automaton $\mathcal{M}$ accepts all sequences over Σ' which satisfy $\mathcal{A}$'s acceptance condition. However, we are actually interested in a tree automaton $\mathcal{B}$ which recognizes $T(\mathcal{B}) = T^\omega_{\Sigma'} \setminus T(\mathcal{A})$. Thus in order to construct $\mathcal{B}$, we first of all generate a word automaton $\mathcal{S}$ such that $L(\mathcal{S}) = \Sigma' \setminus L(\mathcal{M})$. For this we apply Safra's determinization construction to $\mathcal{M}$ as described in Chapter 3. Actually Safra's algorithm applies to nondeterministic Büchi-automata hence, by the methods specified in Chapter 1, we transform $\mathcal{M}$ to a Büchi-automaton. Now Safra's construction yields a deterministic Rabin automaton that accepts $L(\mathcal{M})$. Since a Streett condition is dual to a Rabin condition, we equip the outcome of

Safra's algorithm with a Streett condition instead of a Rabin condition to obtain the desired word automaton $S = (Q', \Sigma', \delta, q'_1, \Omega)$ such that $L(S) = \Sigma' \setminus L(\mathcal{M})$. Note that due to the determinization process, the number of S's states can only be bounded by $2^{O(n \log(n))}$.

Now we are able to construct the desired tree automaton $\mathcal{B} = (Q', \Sigma, \Delta', q_1)$, which runs S in parallel along each path of an input tree. The transition relation of $\mathcal{B}$ is defined by: $(q, a, q_1, q_2) \in \Delta'$ if and only if there exist transitions $\delta(q, (f, a, 0)) = q_1$ and $\delta(q, (f, a, 1)) = q_2$ where $f \in map_a$. Then $T(\mathcal{B})$ accepts $T_{\Sigma'}^{\omega} \setminus T(\mathcal{A})$, as we will prove next.

Theorem 8.13. *The class of languages recognized by finite-state tree automata is closed under complementation.*

Proof. We make use of the constructions given above. It remains to be shown that indeed $T(\mathcal{B}) = T_{\Sigma}^{\omega} \setminus T(\mathcal{A})$.

We assume $t \in T(\mathcal{B})$, i.e., there exists an accepting run ϱ of $\mathcal{B}$ on t. Hence for each path $\pi = \pi_1 \pi_2 \cdots \in \{0,1\}^{\omega}$ the corresponding state sequence satisfies Ω and for each node $w \in \{0,1\}^*$ there are transitions $\delta(q, (s(w), t(w), 0) = q_1$ and $\delta(q, (s(w), t(w), 1) = q_2$ of S where $s(w) \in map_{t(w)}$ and the corresponding transition of $\mathcal{B}$ is $(q, t(w), q_1, q_2)$. This implies that all words $u \in L(s, t)$ are accepted by S and, since $L(S) = \Sigma' \setminus L(\mathcal{M})$, $L(s, t) \cap L(\mathcal{M}) = \emptyset$. Due to Lemma 8.12 and Remark 8.10, s is a winning tree for Player 1 and $\mathcal{A}$ does not accept t.

Now let $t \notin T(\mathcal{A})$. This implies the existence of a winning tree s for Player 1 (cf. Lemma 8.10) such that $L(s, t) \cap L(\mathcal{M}) = \emptyset$ (cf. Lemma 8.12) where $\mathcal{M}$ is the nondeterministic word automaton over alphabet Σ' as is constructed above. It follows $L(s, t) \subseteq S$, i.e., for each path $\pi = \pi_1 \pi_2 \cdots \in \{0,1\}^{\omega}$ there exists a run on the ω-word $u = (s(\varepsilon), t(\varepsilon), \pi_1)(s(\pi_1), t(\pi_1), \pi_2) \cdots \in L(s, t)$ that satisfies Ω. Hence by construction of $\mathcal{B}$ there exists an accepting run ϱ of $\mathcal{B}$ on t, that is, $t \in T(\mathcal{B})$. $\square$

Even though the proof of closure under complement is somewhat lengthy due to some technical details, it should be much easier to understand than the original one presented by Rabin [148]. The proof given above highly benefits from a game theoretical view, especially from the observation, that computations of tree automata can be interpreted as parity games. Specifically, it is the determinacy result for this class of games that induces the aforementioned simplification.

8.5   The Emptiness Problem for Automata on Infinite Trees

Beside the closure properties of sets that are recognizable by nondeterministic finite tree automata, algorithmic properties of the automata themselves are of particular interest. In this section, we present an algorithm that decides whether the language accepted by a parity tree automaton is empty or not. Furthermore, we study the complexity of the algorithm.

In order to prove the decidability result we first of all introduce **input-free tree automata**. As the name suggests, this class of tree automata is defined to operate without any input trees. More precisely, an input-free tree automaton is of the form $(Q, \Delta, q_I, \text{Acc})$ where Q is a finite state set, q_I a designated initial state, $\Delta \subseteq Q \times Q \times Q$ a transition relation, and an acceptance condition. For instance, in case of an input-free parity tree automaton $\mathcal{A}$, a coloring function c would be added. Input-free tree automata can also be defined even without having an acceptance condition. If so, the automata merely consist of Q, a designated initial state and a transition relation $\Delta \subseteq Q \times Q \times Q$.

We call an input-free tree automaton deterministic if and only if for all pairs $(q, q', q''), (q, p', p'') \in \Delta$, $q' = p'$ and $q'' = p''$ holds.

A run of an input-free tree automaton is still a tree $t \in T_Q$, defined in a straightforward manner. If the automaton is deterministic, then t is unique and belongs to a particular class of trees, the so-called regular trees. A tree is called **regular** if and only if it has only a finite number of non-isomorphic subtrees. Formally, this can be defined as follows. Given a tree t and a word $u \in \{0, 1\}^*$, let t^u be the tree defined by $t^u(v) = t(uv)$. Then t is called regular if the set $\{t^u \mid u \in \{0, 1\}^*\}$ is finite.

Exercise 8.6. Prove the above claim that the unique run of a deterministic input-free automaton is a regular tree.

Regular trees can be generated by deterministic finite automata via an additional output function with alphabet $\{0, 1\}$. Let $\mathcal{A} = (Q, \{0, 1\}, \delta, q_I, f)$ be such an automaton where $f: Q \to \Sigma'$ is an additional output function. This automaton generates the tree $t \in T_{\Sigma'}$ defined by $t(w) = f(\delta(q_I, w))$, i.e., the label at node w is $\mathcal{A}$'s output after it has processed w. Note that the root label $t(\varepsilon)$ is the output of $\mathcal{A}$ in its initial state.

Example 8.14. In Figure 8.5 we present a deterministic finite automaton $\mathcal{A} = (\{q_I, q_b, q_d\}, \{0, 1\}, \delta, f)$, where for each state the output function f has the state's index as output, thus generating the regular tree t.

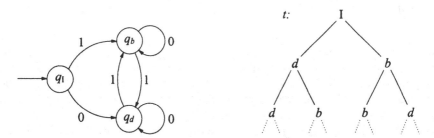

Fig. 8.5. Finite automaton $\mathcal{A}$ generating t

Exercise 8.7. Prove the above claim that a tree is regular if and only if it is generated by a deterministic finite automaton with output function as described above.

Deterministic input-free tree automata without acceptance conditions and deterministic finite-state automata on a binary alphabet are closely related. To see this, we define the state-output pairs $(q, f(q))$ of a deterministic finite automaton $\mathcal{A} = (Q, \{0, 1\}, \delta, q_1, f \colon Q \to \Sigma')$ to be the states of an input-free tree automaton $\mathcal{B} = (Q \times \Sigma', \Delta, (q_1, f(q_1)))$. Furthermore, we identify the inputs $0, 1$ for $\mathcal{A}$ with the left and right branching of $\mathcal{B}$, i.e., for all $q \in Q$, we let $((q, f(q)), (\delta(q, 0), f(\delta(q, 0))), (\delta(q, 1), f(\delta(q, 1)))) \in \Delta$. So $\mathcal{B}$ is deterministic and a run of $\mathcal{B}$ generates in the second component of its states exactly the same tree that $\mathcal{A}$ generates. Hence, in this sense both automaton models have the same expressive power.

Example 8.15. Figure 8.6 presents a run ϱ of the input-free tree automaton $\mathcal{B}$ where $\{(q_1, I), (q_b, b), (q_d, d)\}$ is the state set, $\Delta = (((q_1, I), (q_d, d), (q_b, b)), ((q_d, d), (q_d, d), (q_b, b)), ((q_b, b), (q_b, b), (q_d, d)))$ and (q_1, I) is the initial state.

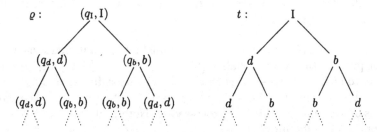

Fig. 8.6. A run ϱ of $\mathcal{B}$ generating t

With respect to the emptiness problem, we now prove the following crucial lemma.

Lemma 8.16. *For each parity tree automaton $\mathcal{A}$ there exists an input-free tree automaton $\mathcal{A}'$ such that $T_\omega(\mathcal{A}) \neq \emptyset$ if and only if $\mathcal{A}'$ admits a successful run.*

Proof. Given a parity tree automaton $\mathcal{A} = (Q, \Sigma, \Delta, q_1, c)$ we construct an input-free tree automaton $\mathcal{A}' = (Q \times \Sigma, \Delta', \{q_1\} \times \Sigma, c')$ which has the required property and behaves as follows. $\mathcal{A}'$ guesses an input tree t in the second component of its states nondeterministically. This can be realized by a suitable modification of $\mathcal{A}$'s transition relation. To be more exact, for each transition $(q, a, q', q'') \in \Delta$ we generate transitions $((q, a), (q', x), (q'', y)) \in \Delta'$ if there exist $(q', x, p, p'), (q'', y, r, r') \in \Delta$. Furthermore, for all states of $\mathcal{A}'$ we define $c'(q, a) = c(q)$. So the behavior of $\mathcal{A}'$ on the guessed input t is identical to that of $\mathcal{A}$ running on t. Hence, if $\mathcal{A}'$ has a successful run, then $T_\omega(\mathcal{A}) \neq \emptyset$ and vice versa. $\square$

With every input-free tree automaton $\mathcal{A} = (Q, \Delta, q_I, c)$, we associate a parity game $\mathcal{G}_\mathcal{A}$ which is won by Player 0 if and only if $\mathcal{A}$ has an accepting run. Clearly, we do not have to keep track of input symbols and tree nodes in the corresponding parity game $\mathcal{G}_\mathcal{A}$. The game positions are states from the state set Q of $\mathcal{A}$ and transitions over $Q \times Q \times Q$. More precisely, $V_0 = Q$, $V_1 = \Delta$, and there are two types of transitions. For every $q \in Q$, and $(q, q', q'') \in \Delta$, we have $(q, (q, q', q'')) \in \Delta$; for every $(q, q', q'') \in \Delta$, we have $((q, q', q''), q'), ((q, q', q''), q'') \in \Delta$. The coloring function maps q and (q, q', q'') to $c(q)$.

Clearly, every strategy for Player 0 corresponds to a run and vice versa, and every winning strategy corresponds to a successful run and vice versa.

Remark 8.17. An input-free tree automaton $\mathcal{A}$ admits a successful run if and only if Player 0 wins $\mathcal{G}_\mathcal{A}$.

Example 8.18. Consider an input-free tree automaton with state set $Q = \{q_I, q_a, q_b, q_d\}$, initial state q_I and transition relation $\Delta = \{(q_I, q_a, q_d), (q_I, q_d, q_b), (q_a, q_a, q_I), (q_a, q_d, q_a), (q_d, q_d, q_b), (q_b, q_b, q_d)\}$. The corresponding game graph is depicted in Figure 8.7.

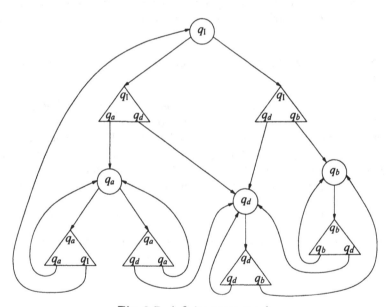

Fig. 8.7. A finite game graph

Since the state set of a tree automaton is finite, the game graph of $\mathcal{G}_\mathcal{A}$ is finite as well and, according to Sections 6.3 and 6.4, the winning strategies for both players are effectively computable. This allows us to solve the emptiness problem.

Theorem 8.19. *For parity tree automata it is decidable whether their recognized language is empty or not.*

Proof. Given a parity tree automaton $\mathcal{A}$, we assume $\mathcal{A}'$ to be an input-free tree automaton that has a successful run iff $T_\omega(\mathcal{A}) \neq \emptyset$. Due to Lemma 8.16, such an automaton exists. Now we identify $\mathcal{A}'$ with the parity game $\mathcal{G}_{\mathcal{A}'}$ and keep in mind that the corresponding game graph is finite because $\mathcal{A}'$ is input-free. From our game-theoretical considerations we know that there is a successful run of $\mathcal{A}'$ if and only if in $\mathcal{G}_{\mathcal{A}'}$ Player 0 wins from some initial position (q_1, a). Since we can effectively compute the winning regions for Player 0 when the game graph is finite, we are able to decide whether there exists a successful run of $\mathcal{A}'$.   □

Corollary 8.20. *If the language of a parity tree automaton is not empty, then it contains a regular tree.*

Proof. We let $\mathcal{A}$ and $\mathcal{A}'$ be defined as in the proof of Theorem 8.19. Now we assume to have a successful run of $\mathcal{A}'$ and a memoryless winning strategy for Player 0 in $\mathcal{G}_{\mathcal{A}'}$ from some starting position (q_1, a). This strategy determines a subgraph of the game graph which is in fact a deterministic input-free tree automaton without acceptance condition. To see this, we just extract the transitions out of the subgraph's game positions for Player 1. The tree automaton can be considered as a part of $\mathcal{A}'$ and generates a regular tree in the second component of its states. Clearly, this regular tree is in $T_\omega(\mathcal{A})$ because $\mathcal{A}'$ behaves exactly like $\mathcal{A}$ does.   □

Figure 8.8 shows an illustrative example of the situation described in the proof above.

Example 8.21. Consider the finite game graph $\mathcal{G}_{\mathcal{A}'}$ depicted in Figure 8.7. We observe the absence of second components in our illustration; just consider the second entry to be the index of the corresponding state. Furthermore, assume the coloring $c(q_1, \mathrm{I}) = 1$, $c(q_b, b) = 2$, $c(q_a, a) = 3$ and $c(q_d, d) = 4$. Thus a winning strategy could determine the subgraph emphasized by solid arcs in Figure 8.8. The regular tree generated by the subgraph is the one depicted in Figure 8.6.

To conclude we give time bounds for solving the emptiness problem.

Corollary 8.22. (1) *The emptiness test for parity tree automata can be carried out in time*

$$O\left(d \cdot r^2 m \left(\frac{rn}{\lfloor d/2 \rfloor}\right)^{\lfloor d/2 \rfloor}\right)$$

where $d \geq 2$ is the number of priorities used in the coloring function.
(2) *The emptiness test for parity tree automata is in UP $\cap$ co-UP.*

Proof. We analyze the proof of Theorem 8.19. Let $\mathcal{A} = (Q, \Sigma, \Delta, q_1, c)$ be a parity tree automaton. Furthermore, let $|\Delta| = m$, $|Q| = n$, and $|\Sigma| = r$. In a first step we have to construct the input-free tree automaton $\mathcal{A}' = (Q \times \Sigma, \Delta', \{q_1\} \times \Sigma, c')$. So this automaton has at most rn states with at most $r^2 m$ transitions. Next we identify $\mathcal{A}'$ with the parity game $\mathcal{G}_{\mathcal{A}'}$ and observe that there exist at most $rn + r^2 m$ vertices and at most $3r^2 m$ edges in this game. The last step invokes

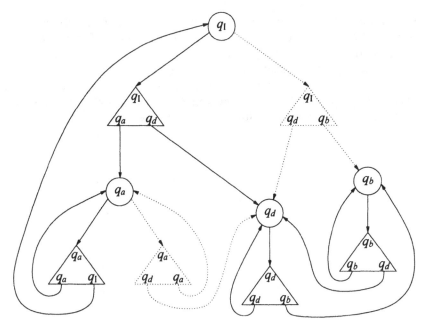

Fig. 8.8. Subgraph determined by Player 0's memoryless winning strategy

an algorithm that computes the winning regions and the winning strategy for Player 0. Here we should apply the best algorithm for the problem known so far (Jurdziński's algorithm [93]) which is thoroughly discussed in Section 7.5. Chapter 6 also presents tight time bounds for this problem, depending on the number of edges, vertices and colors in the game graph. Using this, we get the above bound.

Furthermore, in Chapter 6 it is shown that solving finite parity games lies in the complexity theoretic class UP ∩ co-UP. This proves the second claim. ☐

Exercise 8.8. Use the above corollary to provide upper bounds for the complexity of the emptiness problem for Rabin tree automata.

8.6 Conclusions

In this chapter we have introduced finite-state automata that are able to consume input trees instead of unidimensional structures. We have applied the acceptance conditions presented in Chapter 1 to our tree automata and have obtained that the resulting models are all equivalent with regard to their acceptance capabilities. Büchi tree automata are an exception; they are weaker, even in their nondeterministic version.

Subsequently we have identified a tree automaton and its input tree with an infinite two-person game. This was significant, since it has allowed us to benefit from various results about infinite games, especially in the proof of closure under complementation for sets which are recognizable by finite tree automata. This complementation result is essential to prove the decidability of monadic second-order logic and thus demonstrates the importance of tree automaton concepts. More about this will be presented in the Chapter 12.

We have next studied the algorithmic properties of finite tree automata and have shown decidability of the emptiness problem for parity tree automata by again utilizing results about infinite games on finite graphs.

9 Alternating Tree Automata and Parity Games

Daniel Kirsten

Institut für Algebra
Technische Universität Dresden

9.1 Introduction

Since Büchi's work in 1960 [17], automata play an important role in logic. Numerous different notions of automata provide decision and complexity results in various kinds of logic. Often, one develops a method to translate some given formula φ into an appropriate finite automaton $\mathcal{A}$ such that $L(\varphi) = L(\mathcal{A})$. Such a translation reduces the model checking problem and the satisfiability problem in some logic to the word problem and the emptiness problem for finite automata. Moreover, such a translation provides algorithms to solve the model checking and the satisfiability problems on a computer. Consequently, one is interested in the decidability and the complexity of the word and emptiness problems of automata.

In this chapter, we introduce the notion of alternating tree automata. They have been introduced in [202] to get a better understanding of the modal μ-calculus. Thus, alternating tree automata work on transition systems (Kripke structures). We state complexity results for the word problem, the emptiness problem and complementation.

The notion of parity games and related results play a crucial role within the whole chapter. Parity games provide three advantages:

(1) We use parity games to define the semantics of alternating tree automata, i.e., we define whether an automaton accepts or rejects some transition system by the existence of a winning strategy for Player 0 in an appropriate parity game.
(2) Parity games provide a straightforward, convenient construction to complement a given alternating tree automaton; moreover, the fact that parity games are determined is used to prove the correctness of this construction.
(3) We use parity games to show the decidability of the word problem and the emptiness problem. By applying Jurdziński's result[93], we achieve strong complexity bounds.

The reader should be familiar with parity games as introduced in Chapter 2 and 5. To prove the decidability of the emptiness problem we use various notions of automata on infinite words such as Büchi automata, Rabin- and Streett-automata, parity automata, and transformations between them as introduced in Chapter 1 of this book. We also apply Safra's construction from Chapter 3.

The results from the present chapter will be used to examine the modal μ-calculus in Chapters 10 and 11. In particular, the complexity results of the

E. Grädel et al. (Eds.): Automata, Logics, and Infinite Games, LNCS 2500, pp. 153-167, 2002.
© Springer-Verlag Berlin Heidelberg 2002

word problem and emptiness problem will be used to show complexity results for model checking and satisfiability in the modal μ-calculus.

This chapter is organized as follows: In Section 9.2, we introduce some basic notions. In Section 9.3, we introduce alternating tree automata and their semantics formally. Sections 9.4, 9.5, and 9.6 are devoted to the three main results: The decidability and complexity of the word problem, the complementation of alternating tree automata, and the decidability and complexity of the emptiness problem. Some remarks and exercises close this chapter.

The main ideas presented here are due to [202]. Our complementation of alternating tree automata is based on an idea from [137] with some extensions to our concept of alternating tree automata.

9.2 Preliminaries

We fix a set of **propositional variables** P during this chapter. A **transition system** is a triple $S = (S, R, \lambda)$ where

- S is a set called **states**,
- $R \subseteq S \times S$ is a relation, and
- $\lambda : P \to \mathscr{P}(S)$ is a mapping which assigns a set of states to every propositional variable.

Transition systems are also known as Kripke structures. If we consider the inverse mapping $\gamma^{-1} : S \to \mathscr{P}(P)$, then we can regard transition systems as labeled, directed graphs. For every variable $p \in P$ and every state $s \in \lambda(p)$, we say that p is true in s, and for $s \in S \setminus \lambda(p)$, we say that p is false in s.

For every $s \in S$, we denote

$$sR = \{s' \in S \,|\, (s, s') \in R\} \qquad \text{and} \qquad Rs = \{s' \in S \,|\, (s', s) \in R\}.$$

A **pointed transition system** (S, s_I) is a transition system $S = (S, R, \lambda)$ with an initial state $s_\mathrm{I} \in S$. We call a transition system $S = (S, R, \lambda)$ (resp. (S, s_I)) **finite** iff S is finite and $\lambda(p) \neq \emptyset$ for just finitely many $p \in P$.

9.3 Alternating Tree Automata

Our notion of an alternating tree automaton originates from [202]. An alternating tree automaton is a device which accepts or rejects pointed transition systems by parsing the paths.

In Subsection 9.3.1, we define alternating tree automata formally. In Subsection 9.3.2, we consider their semantics. At first, we discuss an ad hoc approach to define the behaviour of alternating tree automata on pointed transition systems. Then, we present two methods to define formally whether an alternating tree automaton accepts or rejects a pointed transition system. Both of these methods are based on parity games. The first method uses an infinite arena for almost every transition system and is convenient in some proofs, for instance, to show the closure under complement. The second method uses a more compact arena, in particular, a finite one if the transition system in question is finite, and is used to examine the complexity of the word problem. In Proposition 9.2, we show that these two ways to define the semantics are equivalent.

In Section 9.3.3, we show a small lemma which is used to show the complexity of the emptiness problem.

In Section 9.3.4, we discuss a syntactic extension to our concept of alternating tree automata.

9.3.1   Formal Definition of Alternating Tree Automata

To define alternating tree automata formally, we need the notion of transition conditions. For now, let Q be some set of symbols. The **transition conditions** TC^Q over Q are defined as follows:

- The symbols 0 and 1 are transition conditions.
- For every $p \in P$, p and $\neg p$ are transition conditions.
- For every $q \in Q$, q, $\Box q$, and $\Diamond q$ are transition conditions.
- For every $q_1, q_2 \in Q$, $q_1 \wedge q_2$ and $q_1 \vee q_2$ are transition conditions.

Note that this definition does not allow transition conditions like $q_1 \wedge \Box q_2$ or $p \wedge q$ for $p \in P$ and $q \in Q$. Below, we will explain a method to allow these more complex transition conditions without violating our definition. An **alternating tree automaton** is a tuple $\mathcal{A} = (Q, q_{\mathrm{I}}, \delta, \Omega)$ where

- Q is a finite set of **states** of the automaton,
- $q_{\mathrm{I}} \in Q$ is a state called the **initial state**,
- $\delta : Q \to \mathrm{TC}^Q$ is called **transition function**, and
- $\Omega : Q \to \omega$ is called **priority function**.

For convenience, we denote

$$Q_\Box := \left\{ q \in Q \mid \exists q' \in Q : \delta(q) = \Box q' \right\} \quad \text{and}$$
$$Q_\Diamond := \left\{ q \in Q \mid \exists q' \in Q : \delta(q) = \Diamond q' \right\}.$$

For states $q \in Q$ we define $\vec{q} := q'$ if $\delta(q) = \Box q'$ or $\delta(q) = \Diamond q'$. Otherwise, $\vec{q}$ is not defined. For subsets $V \subseteq Q$, we define $\vec{V} := \{ \vec{q} \mid q \in V \}$.

9.3.2   The Behavior of Alternating Tree Automata

Informal Explanation. We examine the behavior of an alternating tree automaton $\mathcal{A} = (Q, q_{\mathrm{I}}, \delta, \Omega)$ on a pointed transition system $(\mathcal{S}, s_{\mathrm{I}})$. At first, we follow a straightforward approach without using parity games:

In every step, the automaton is in some state $q \in Q$, and it inspects some state $s \in S$ of the transition system. We can describe the situation by a pair $(q, s) \in Q \times S$. We call the pairs in $Q \times S$ instances.

In the beginning, the automaton is in the initial state q_I and inspects the state s_I of the alternating tree automaton.

Now, assume that the automaton is in the state q and it inspects the state s, i.e., the current instance is (q, s). The automaton tries to execute the transition condition $\delta(q)$. If $\delta(q) \in \{0, 1\}$, $\delta(q) = p$, or $\delta(q) = \neg p$ for some $p \in P$, then the automaton needs not to take any action.

If $\delta(q) = q' \in Q$ then the automaton changes into the state q', but it does not move to another state of the transition system, i.e., the new situation is (q', s). If $\delta(q) = q_1 \wedge q_2$ or $\delta(q) = q_1 \vee q_2$, then the automaton splits itself into two instances (q_1, s) and (q_2, s). If $\delta(q) = \Box q'$ or $\delta(q) = \Diamond q'$, then the automaton parses the relation R of S. The automaton splits into several instances. These instances are in state q' and inspect the successors of s in S, i.e., for every $(s, s') \in R$ we get an instance (q', s'). Thus, the set of new instances is $\{q'\} \times sR$.

The result of this process is a possibly infinite parse tree with instances as nodes. The main question is how does this tree determine whether $\mathcal{A}$ accepts or rejects the pointed transition system (S, s_I). To answer this question, we try to develop a notion of a "successful instance". If $\delta(q)$ is a propositional variable p and p is true in the state s, then the instance (q, s) is successful. Similarly, if $\delta(q) = \neg p$ and $s \notin \lambda(p)$, then the instance is successful. Conversely, if $\delta(q) = p$ but $s \notin \lambda(p)$ (or $\delta(q) = \neg p$ but $s \in \lambda(p)$), then the instance is not successful. If $\delta(q) = 1$, then the instance succeeds, but if $\delta(q) = 0$, then it does not succeed.

If $\delta(q) = q'$, then we have seen above that the automaton changes its state to q', i.e., the new situation is (q', s). Straightforwardly, we simply say that the instance (q, s) is successful iff (q', s) is successful.

If $\delta(q) = q_1 \wedge q_2$, then the instance (q, s) succeeds iff both the instances (q_1, s) and (q_2, s) succeed. If $\delta(q) = q_1 \vee q_2$, then the instance succeeds iff at least one of the instances (q_1, s) and (q_2, s) succeeds.

The case $\delta(q) = \Box q'$ is very similar to the case $\delta(q) = q_1 \wedge q_2$, above. If $\delta(q) = \Box q'$, then the instance (q, s) succeeds iff for *every* $s' \in sR$ the instance (q', s') succeeds. Finally, if $\delta(q) = \Diamond q'$, then the instance (q, s) succeeds iff there is *at least one* $s' \in sR$ such that (q', s') succeeds.

The automaton accepts the transition system (S, s_I) iff the initial instance (q_I, s_I) succeeds.

If we try to formalize this idea of the notion of a "successful instance" then we will encounter problems:

- If the parse tree is infinite, then successful instances cannot be determined in a bottom-up-fashion.
- If $\delta(q) = q'$, the we simply said that the instance (q, s) is successful iff (q', s) is successful. However, if $\delta(q) = q$, then we end up in an infinite loop.

We resolve these problems by viewing the "evaluation problem" as solving a certain game where infinite plays—that is where we run into problems—are decided according to some acceptance (winning) condition that we have seen in earlier chapters.

Formal Definition. Now, we solve these problems by defining the acceptance of alternating tree automata using parity games.

Let $(\mathcal{S}, s_\mathrm{I})$ be a pointed transition system, and let $\mathcal{A} = (Q, q_\mathrm{I}, \delta, \Omega)$ be an alternating tree automaton. To define the behavior of a $\mathcal{A}$ on $(\mathcal{S}, s_\mathrm{I})$, we consider sequences of pairs from $Q \times S$, i.e., we consider words over the alphabet $Q \times S$.

For a word $v \in (Q \times S)^*$ and a letter $(q, s) \in Q \times S$, the notation $v(q, s)$ denotes the concatenation of v and (q, s).

The **behavior** of $\mathcal{A}$ on $(\mathcal{S}, s_\mathrm{I})$ is the least language $V \subseteq (Q \times S)^*$ with $(q_\mathrm{I}, s_\mathrm{I}) \in V$ such that for every word $v(q, s) \in V$ we have:

- If $\delta(q) = q'$ for some $q' \in Q$, then $v(q, s)(q', s) \in V$.
- If $\delta(q) = q_1 \wedge q_2$ or $\delta(q) = q_1 \vee q_2$ for some $q_1, q_2 \in Q$, then $v(q, s)(q_1, s) \in V$ and $v(q, s)(q_2, s) \in V$.
- If $\delta(q) = \Box q'$ or $\delta(q) = \Diamond q'$ for some $q' \in Q$, then $v(q, s)(q', s') \in V$ for every $s' \in sR$.

We use parity games to define acceptance. At first, we define an arena (V_0, V_1, E). We split the behavior V into V_0 and V_1 to define the locations of Player 0 and Player 1. Some word $v(q, s) \in V$ belongs to V_0 iff one of the following conditions holds:

- $\delta(q) = 0$,
- $\delta(q) = p$ and $s \notin \lambda(p)$,
- $\delta(q) = \neg p$ and $s \in \lambda(p)$,
- $\delta(q) = q'$,
- $\delta(q) = q_1 \vee q_2$ for some $q_1, q_2 \in Q$, or
- $\delta(q) = \Diamond q'$.

Conversely, some word $v(q, s) \in V$ belongs to V_1 iff one of the following conditions holds:

- $\delta(q) = 1$,
- $\delta(q) = p$ and $s \in \lambda(p)$,
- $\delta(q) = \neg p$ and $s \notin \lambda(p)$,
- $\delta(q) = q_1 \wedge q_2$ for some $q_1, q_2 \in Q$, or
- $\delta(q) = \Box q'$.

Clearly, V_0 and V_1 are a partition of V. We complete the definition of the parity game by defining the moves and the priority mapping:

- $E := \{ (v, v(q, s)) \mid v(q, s) \in V, \ v \neq \epsilon \}$
- $\Omega(v(q, s)) := \Omega(q)$ for every $v(q, s) \in V$

As explained above, $(q_\mathrm{I}, s_\mathrm{I})$ is the initial location.

The automaton $\mathcal{A}$ **accepts** the pointed transition system $(\mathcal{S}, s_\mathrm{I})$ iff there is a winning strategy for Player 0 in the parity game $\mathcal{G} = ((V_0, V_1, E), \Omega, (q_\mathrm{I}, s_\mathrm{I}))$. The language of $\mathcal{A}$ consists of the pointed transition systems which $\mathcal{A}$ accepts and is denoted by $L(\mathcal{A})$.

Example 9.1. At first, we consider several very simple alternating tree automata with $Q = \{q_I\}$.

(1) Let $\delta(q_I) = \Box q_I$ and $\Omega(q_I) = 0$. Let $(\mathcal{S}, s_I)$ be any pointed transition system. Player 0 has not any location in $\mathcal{G}'$. However, Player 1 cannot win. He looses every finite play. He also looses every infinite play, because the only priority is 0. Hence, the automaton accepts every pointed transition system.

(2) Let $\delta(q_I) = \Box q_I$ and $\Omega(q_I) = 1$. Again, Player 0 has no location. Let $(\mathcal{S}, s_I)$ be any pointed transition system with some infinite path starting at s_I. Player 1 can win the game by playing along the infinite path.

Conversely, let $(\mathcal{S}, s_I)$ be any pointed transition system in which every path starting from s_I is finite. There are just finite plays in $\mathcal{G}'$. Thus, Player 1 looses every play in $\mathcal{G}'$.

Consequently, the automaton accepts every pointed transition system $(\mathcal{S}, s_I)$ which has no infinite path starting at s_I.

(3) Let $\delta(q_I) = \Diamond q_I$ and $\Omega(q_I) = 1$. This automaton accepts not any pointed transition system.

Exercise 9.1. Construct alternating tree automata for the following languages.

(1) The language of all pointed transition systems where p is true in the designated state.
(2) The language of all pointed transition systems that have an infinite path starting in the designated state.
(3) The language of all pointed transition systems where on each infinite path starting in the designated state p is true only finitely often.

Exercise 9.2. Let $(\mathcal{S}, f_I)$ and $(\mathcal{S}', f_I')$ be two pointed transition systems and assume ρ is a bisimulation between the two systems, that is, $\rho \subseteq S \times S'$ such that the following holds true.

(1) $(s_I, s_I') \in \rho$.
(2) For all $(s, s') \in \rho$ and $p \in P$, p holds in s iff p' holds in s'.
(3) For all $(s, s') \in \rho$ and $\hat{s} \in sR$ there exists $\hat{s}' \in s'R'$ such that $(\hat{s}, \hat{s}') \in \rho$.
(4) For all $(s, s') \in \rho$ and $\hat{s}' \in s'R'$ there exists $\hat{s} \in sR$ such that $(\hat{s}, \hat{s}') \in \rho$.

Show that for every alternating tree automaton $\mathcal{A}$ the following is true. $\mathcal{A}$ accepts $(\mathcal{S}, s_I)$ iff $\mathcal{A}$ accepts $(\mathcal{S}', s_I')$.

An Alternative Formal Definition. A disadvantage of the parity game $\mathcal{G}$ defined is that its arena is possibly infinite, even if $(\mathcal{S}, s_I)$ is finite. Moreover, even if there is no infinite path in $(\mathcal{S}, s_I)$ the game $\mathcal{G}$ can be infinite. We need some more convenient way to define the behavior, in particular, to show the decidability of the word problem, below.

We still assume $(\mathcal{S}, s_I)$ and $\mathcal{A} = (Q, q_I, \delta, \Omega)$ from above. Let $[V] \subseteq Q \times S$ and $[E] \subseteq [V] \times [V]$ be the smallest graph with $(q_I, s_I) \in [V]$ such that for every $(q, s) \in [V]$ we have:

- If $\delta(q) = q'$ for some $q' \in Q$, then $(q', s) \in V$ and $\big((q, s), (q', s)\big) \in [E]$.
- If $\delta(q) = q_1 \wedge q_2$ or $\delta(q) = q_1 \vee q_2$ for some $q_1, q_2 \in Q$, then $(q_1, s), (q_2, s) \in [V]$ and $\big((q, s), (q_1, s)\big)$, $\big((q, s), (q_2, s)\big) \in [E]$.
- If $\delta(q) = \Box q'$ or $\delta(q) = \Diamond q'$ for some $q' \in Q$, then $(q', s') \in [V]$ and $\big((q, s), (q', s')\big) \in [E]$ for every $s' \in sR$.

To define an arena from $[V]$ and $[E]$, we split $[V]$ into $[V_0]$ and $[V_1]$ as above. We simply use the priority mapping Ω and the initial location (q_I, s_I). We define a parity game by

$$\mathcal{G}' := \big(([V_0], [V_1], [E]), \Omega, (q_I, s_I)\big).$$

Let $[] : (Q \times S)^+ \to (Q \times S)$ be the mapping which assigns every word in $(Q \times S)^+$ the last letter. Thus, $[]$ maps locations from V to $[V]$. Moreover, $[]$ preserves edges and priorities, and Player 0's and Player 1's locations are mapped to Player 0's and Player 1's locations, respectively. Consequently, $\mathcal{G}'$ can be obtained by applying $[]$ to $\mathcal{G}$.

Proposition 9.2. *Player 0 has a winning strategy in $\mathcal{G}$ iff Player 0 has a winning strategy in $\mathcal{G}'$.*

Proof. At first, we observe that the mapping $[]$ can be extended to plays by applying $[]$ to every location in the play. Thus, $[]$ transforms plays in $\mathcal{G}$ to plays in $\mathcal{G}'$. If π' is some play in $\mathcal{G}'$, then there is a unique play π in $\mathcal{G}$ such that $[\pi] = \pi'$. Note that π is simply the sequence of all prefixes of π'. A play π in $\mathcal{G}$ is won by Player 0 iff $[\pi]$ in $\mathcal{G}'$ is won by Player 0. Hence, $[]$ is a "winner-preserving" bijection between plays in $\mathcal{G}$ and plays in $\mathcal{G}'$.

To prove Proposition 9.2, we have to show that Player 0 (resp. 1) has a winning strategy in $\mathcal{G}$ if Player 0 (resp. 1) has a winning strategy in $\mathcal{G}'$.

Let $f_0' : [V_0] \to [V]$ be a winning strategy for Player 0 in $\mathcal{G}'$. We define a mapping $f_0 : V_0 \to V$ by $f_0(v) := v f_0'([v])$. Let π be a play in $\mathcal{G}$ which is consistent with f_0. Then, $[\pi]$ is consistent with f_0', and thus, $[\pi]$ and π are won by Player 0. Consequently, f_0 is a winning strategy for Player 0 in $\mathcal{G}$.

Clearly, we can apply a symmetric argument if $f_1' : [V_1] \to [V]$ is a winning strategy for Player 1 in $\mathcal{G}'$. $\qquad\square$

9.3.3 Inflated Transition Conditions

We call transition conditions of the form $q \wedge q$ and $q \vee q$ for $q \in Q$ **inflated**. The following lemma allows to simplify some technical details, later.

Lemma 9.3. *For every alternating tree automaton $\mathcal{A} = (Q, q_I, \delta, \Omega)$ there is an automaton $\mathcal{A}' = (Q, q_I, \delta', \Omega)$ with $L(\mathcal{A}) = L(\mathcal{A}')$ such that for every $q \in Q$ $\delta'(q)$ is not inflated.*

Proof. We define $\delta' : Q \to TC^Q$ for $q \in Q$ by

$$\delta'(q) := \begin{cases} q' & , \text{ if } \delta(q) = q' \wedge q' \text{ for some } q' \in Q \\ q' & , \text{ if } \delta(q) = q' \vee q' \text{ for some } q' \in Q \\ \delta(q) & , \text{ otherwise} \end{cases}$$

Clearly, $\delta'(q)$ is not inflated for $q \in Q$.

Let $(\mathcal{S}, s_I)$ be some pointed transition system. We want to show that $\mathcal{A}$ accepts $(\mathcal{S}, s_I)$ iff $\mathcal{A}'$ accepts $(\mathcal{S}, s_I)$. At first, we observe that $\mathcal{A}$ has the same behavior V on $(\mathcal{S}, s_I)$ as $\mathcal{A}'$. Let $\mathcal{G} = ((V_0, V_1, E), \Omega, (q_I, s_I))$ be the parity game to determine whether $\mathcal{A}$ accepts $(\mathcal{S}, S_I)$.

Let $\hat{V} = \{ v(q, s) \in V_1 \mid \delta(q) = q' \wedge q' \text{ for some } q' \in Q \}$. The locations in $\hat{V}$ have exactly one successor. The parity game

$$\mathcal{G}' = ((V_0 \cup \hat{V}, \ V_1 \setminus \hat{V}, \ E), \ \Omega, \ (q_I, s_I))$$

determines whether $\mathcal{A}'$ accepts $(\mathcal{S}, s_I)$.

The plays in $\mathcal{G}$ are exactly the plays in $\mathcal{G}'$. The locations in $\hat{V}$ cannot be the last location in a play and the priority mappings in $\mathcal{G}$ and $\mathcal{G}'$ are the same. Thus, some play π in $\mathcal{G}$ is won by Player 0 iff π is won by Player 0 in $\mathcal{G}'$.

Let $f_0 : V_0 \to V$ be a winning strategy for Player 0 in $\mathcal{G}$. There is a unique extension $f_0' : V_0 \cup \hat{V} \to V$. Now, assume some play π in $\mathcal{G}'$ which is consistent with f_0'. Then, π in $\mathcal{G}'$ is consistent with f_0, and thus π is won by Player 0.

Conversely, let $f_1 : V_1 \to V$ be a winning strategy for Player 1 in $\mathcal{G}$. Clearly, the restriction of f_1 to $V_1 \setminus \hat{V}$ is a winning strategy for Player 1 in $\mathcal{G}'$.

Consequently, Player 0 has a winning strategy in $\mathcal{G}$ iff he has a winning strategy in $\mathcal{G}'$, i.e., $\mathcal{A}$ accepts $(\mathcal{S}, s_I)$ iff $\mathcal{A}'$ accepts $(\mathcal{S}, s_I)$. □

9.3.4 Complex Transition Conditions

Our definition of transition conditions TC^Q is restrictive. One could imagine more complex transition conditions. For instance, there are situations in which a condition φ like "Change the inner state to q_1 if p is true, otherwise change the inner state to q_2." or formally $\varphi = (q_1 \wedge p) \vee (q_2 \wedge \neg p)$ is convenient although such a condition does not belong to TC^Q.

To model such a condition, we introduce new states q_φ, $q_{(q_1 \wedge p)}$, $q_{(q_2 \wedge \neg p)}$, q_p, $q_{\neg p}$, and we define:

$$\delta(q_\varphi) := q_{(q_1 \wedge p)} \vee q_{(q_2 \wedge \neg p)}$$
$$\delta(q_{(q_1 \wedge p)}) := q_1 \wedge q_p$$
$$\delta(q_{(q_2 \wedge \neg p)}) := q_2 \wedge q_{\neg p}$$
$$\delta(q_p) := p$$
$$\delta(q_{\neg p}) := \neg p$$

This can be easily generalized:

Remark 9.4. Alternating tree automata where transition conditions are built up from 0, 1, p, and $\neg p$ using $\vee$, $\wedge$, $\Diamond$, and $\Box$ in any way are no more powerful than ordinary alternating tree automata.

Example 9.5. We consider the states q_φ, $q_{(q_1 \wedge p)}$, $q_{(q_2 \wedge \neg p)}$, q_p, $q_{\neg p}$ from above, and we complete the definition of δ by $\delta(q_1) = \delta(q_2) = \Box q_\varphi$. We set $\Omega(q_1) = 2$ and we set the priorities of the other states to 1. Let q_φ be the initial state.

The automaton accepts some pointed transition system $(\mathcal{S}, s_I)$ iff every infinite path starting from s_I contains infinitely many states in which p is true.

Exercise 9.3. Describe an alternating tree automaton which accepts a pointed transition system $(\mathcal{S}, s_I)$ iff for any two states $s_1, s_2 \in S$ with $s_1 R s_2$ the variable p is true in s_1 iff p is not true in s_2.

9.4   The Word Problem

In this section, we deal with the word problem, which means to decide whether a given alternating tree automaton $\mathcal{A}$ accepts a given finite pointed transition system $(\mathcal{S}, s_I)$. In Section 10, this result will be used to determine the complexity of the model checking problem for the modal μ-calculus.

We cannot solve the word problem by computing the whole behavior, because the behavior is possibly infinite, even if $(\mathcal{S}, s_I)$ is finite. However, we can reduce the parity game from the previous section to a finite parity game.

Theorem 9.6. *Let $\mathcal{A} = (Q, q_I, \delta, \Omega)$ be an alternating tree automaton with d different non-zero priorities and let $(\mathcal{S}, s_I)$ be a finite pointed transition system.*

(1) *There is an algorithm which computes in time*

$$\mathcal{O}\left(d\,|Q|\,(|R|+1)\left(\frac{|Q||S|+1}{\lceil d/2 \rceil}\right)^{\lceil d/2 \rceil}\right)$$

and in space $\mathcal{O}\left(d\,|Q|\,|S|\,\log\left(|Q|\,|S|\right)\right)$ whether $\mathcal{A}$ accepts $(\mathcal{S}, s_I)$.
(2) *The problem whether $\mathcal{A}$ accepts $(\mathcal{S}, s_I)$ is in UP$\cap$co-UP.*

Before we turn to the proof, let us understand the upper bound on the time complexity stated in the first part of the theorem. Let us consider the transition system complexity, i.e., we fix an automaton $\mathcal{A}$ and consider the complexity in dependence on the pointed transition system $(\mathcal{S}, s_I)$. Then, $d|Q|$ is a constant factor. Clearly, $|R|$ cannot exceed $|S|^2$. Hence, we roughly estimate $|R| + 1$ by $|S|^2$ and simplify the above formula to $\mathcal{O}\left(|S|^2 (|Q||S|)^{\lfloor d/2 \rfloor}\right)$. Roughly spoken, the run-time of the algorithm is proportional to $|S|^{2+\lfloor d/2 \rfloor}$. If for example $d = 2$, then the run-time is proportional to $|S|^3$, i.e., one can determine whether $\mathcal{A}$ accepts $(\mathcal{S}, s_I)$ in reasonable time. However, if $d = 20$ then the run-time of the algorithm is proportional to $|S|^{12}$. Then, the word problem will be practically unsolvable for reasonably big pointed transition systems.

Proof. The complexity of the word problem is in UP$\cap$co-UP, because the problem to decide whether Player 0 has a winning strategy is in UP $\cap$ co-UP as explained in Chapter 6.

To prove the first part, we apply Jurdziński's result to the parity game $\mathcal{G}'$.

To prove the complexity bound of the word problem, we have to examine carefully the number of locations and moves, i.e., we have to estimate $\|[V]\|$ and $\|[E]\|$ (cf. [202]). The set of locations $[V]$ is a subset of $Q \times S$, i.e., there are at most $|Q||S|$ locations. Let $S' \subseteq S$ be the set of states in $(\mathcal{S}, s_I)$ which are reachable from q_I. Every state in S' except s_I has at least one predecessor. Hence, $|R| \geq |S'| - 1$.

To determine $\|[E]\|$, we count the number of successors of every location in $\|[V]\|$. The successors of a location $(q, s) \in [V]$ are $(q, s)[E]$. We have

$$\|[E]\| = \sum_{(q,s)\in[V]} |(q,s)[E]| = \sum_{q\in Q} \sum_{(q,s)\in[V]} |(q,s)[E]|.$$

Let $q \in Q$ be some state. We estimate the sum

$$\sum_{(q,s)\in[V]} |(q,s)[E]|.$$

If $\delta(q) \in \{0,1\}$ or $\delta(q) \in \{p, \neg p\}$, then (q, s) has no successor, and we have

$$\sum_{(q,s)\in[V]} |(q,s)[E]| = 0.$$

If $\delta(q) \in Q$, then every location $(q, s) \in [V]$ has exactly one successor, i.e.,

$$\sum_{(q,s)\in[V]} |(q,s)[E]| \leq |S'| \leq |R| + 1.$$

If $\delta(q) = q_1 \wedge q_2$ or $\delta(q) = q_1 \vee q_2$ for some $q_1, q_2 \in Q$, then we have

$$\sum_{(q,s)\in[V]} |(q,s)[E]| \leq 2|S'| \leq 2(|R| + 1).$$

Now, assume $\delta(q) = \Box q'$ or $\delta(q) = \Diamond q'$ for some $q' \in Q$. For every $(q, s) \in [V]$, we have $(q, s)[E] = \{q'\} \times sR$, i.e, $|(q, s)[E]| = |sR|$. We have

$$\sum_{(q,s)\in[V]} |(q,s)[E]| = \sum_{(q,s)\in[V]} |sR| \leq \sum_{s\in S} |sR| = |R|.$$

To sum up, we have $\sum_{(q,s)\in[V]} |(q,s)[E]| \leq 2(|R|+1)$ and $\|[E]\| \leq 2|Q|(|R|+1)$.

Now, we can apply Jurdziński's algorithm (Theorem 7.25, Section 7.5). □

9.5 Complementation

An advantage of alternating tree automata is the straightforward solution of the complementation problem: Given an alternating tree automaton $\mathcal{A}$, we can effectively construct an alternating tree automaton $\bar{\mathcal{A}}$ which accepts the complement of the language of $\mathcal{A}$. To prove the correctness of the construction we use the fact that parity games are determined in a crucial way. We follow ideas from [137].

Theorem 9.7. *Let $\mathcal{A} = (Q, q_1, \delta, \Omega)$ be an alternating tree automaton. There is an alternating tree automaton $\bar{\mathcal{A}} = (Q, q_1, \bar{\delta}, \bar{\Omega})$ such that $\bar{\mathcal{A}}$ accepts the complement of the language of $\mathcal{A}$.*

The definition of $\bar{\Omega} : Q \rightarrow \omega$ and $\bar{\delta} : Q \rightarrow TC^Q$ is easy: We simply set for every $q \in Q$ the priority $\bar{\Omega}(q) = \Omega(q) + 1$ and

$$\bar{\delta}(q) := \begin{cases} 0 & , \text{ if } \delta(q) = 1 \\ 1 & , \text{ if } \delta(q) = 0 \\ \neg p & , \text{ if } \delta(q) = p \text{ for some } p \in P \\ p & , \text{ if } \delta(q) = \neg p \text{ for some } p \in P \\ q' & , \text{ if } \delta(q) = q' \text{ for some } q' \in Q \\ q_1 \wedge q_2 & , \text{ if } \delta(q) = q_1 \vee q_2 \text{ for some } q_1, q_2 \in Q \\ q_1 \vee q_2 & , \text{ if } \delta(q) = q_1 \wedge q_2 \text{ for some } q_1, q_2 \in Q \\ \Diamond q' & , \text{ if } \delta(q) = \Box q' \text{ for some } q' \in Q \\ \Box q' & , \text{ if } \delta(q) = \Diamond q' \text{ for some } q' \in Q \end{cases}$$

Proof. Let (S, s_I) be a pointed transition system and $\mathcal{G} = ((V_0, V_1, E), \Omega, (q_\mathrm{I}, s_\mathrm{I}))$ be the parity game from Section 9.3.2 which determines whether $\mathcal{A}$ accepts (S, s_I). We show that $\mathcal{A}$ accepts (S, s_I) iff $\bar{\mathcal{A}}$ does not accept (S, s_I).

We examine the parity game $\bar{\mathcal{G}}$ which determines whether $\bar{\mathcal{A}}$ accepts (S, s_I). Intuitively, we simply change the ownership of every location, and we increase every priority by 1. Let $V = V_0 \cup V_1$ be the locations of $\mathcal{G}$ and $\mathcal{G}'$. Let $V' \subseteq V$ be the locations $v(q, s) \in V$ with $\delta(q) = q'$ for some $q' \in Q$. We do not change the ownership of locations in V'. The automaton $\bar{\mathcal{A}}$ accepts (S, s_I) iff there is winning strategy for Player 0 in the parity game

$$\bar{\mathcal{G}} = ((V_1 \cup V', V_0 \setminus V', E), \bar{\Omega}, (q_\mathrm{I}, s_\mathrm{I})).$$

Because parity games are determined (cf. Section 6.3), we have to show that there is a winning strategy for Player 0 in $\mathcal{G}$ iff there is no winning strategy for Player 1 in $\bar{\mathcal{G}}$. The argument is very similar to in the proof of Lemma 9.3. Therefore, it is left as Exercise 9.4. □

Exercise 9.4. Complete the proof of Theorem 9.7:

(1) Assume a winning strategy for Player 0 in $\mathcal{G}$ and construct a winning strategy for Player 1 in $\bar{\mathcal{G}}$.
(2) Assume a winning strategy for Player 1 in $\bar{\mathcal{G}}$ and construct a winning strategy for Player 0 in $\mathcal{G}$.

Exercise 9.5. Theorem 9.7 tells us that the languages recognizing by alternating tree automata are closed under complementation. Show that they are closed under intersection and union as well.

9.6   The Emptiness Problem

In this section, we show the decidability of the emptiness problem for alternating tree automata. As a byproduct, we show that an alternating tree automaton $\mathcal{A}$ accepts a finite pointed transition system if $\mathcal{A}$ accepts at least one transition system. This result is used in Chapter 10 to show that the modal μ-calculus has the finite model property which means that every satisfyable formula in the modal μ-calculus has a finite model.

We fix some alternating tree automaton $\mathcal{A} = (Q, q_I, \delta, \Omega)$. By Lemma 9.3, we can assume that for every $q \in Q$ the transition condition $\delta(q)$ is not inflated.

At first, we give the notion of a tile, which is a graph consisting of states from $\mathcal{A}$ with various properties. We construct a parity game $\mathcal{T}$ from these tiles. In the parity game $\mathcal{T}$, Player 0 can use some arbitrary pointed transition system in $L(\mathcal{A})$ to construct a winning strategy. Conversely, if we assume some winning strategy for Player 0 in $\mathcal{T}$, we can construct some pointed transition system which $\mathcal{A}$ accepts.

9.6.1   Tiles

A **tile over Q** is a graph $\vartheta = (V_\vartheta, E_\vartheta)$ where $V_\vartheta \subseteq Q$, $E \subseteq V_\vartheta \times V_\vartheta$ and

(1) $\forall q \in V_\vartheta : \delta(q) \neq 0$
(2) $\neg \exists q_1, q_2 \in V_\vartheta \, \exists p \in P : \big(\delta(q_1) = p \wedge \delta(q_2) = \neg p\big)$
(3) $\forall q \in V_\vartheta : \quad \delta(q) = q_1 \quad \longrightarrow \quad (q, q_1) \in E_\vartheta$
(4) $\forall q \in V_\vartheta : \quad \delta(q) = q_1 \wedge q_2 \quad \longrightarrow \quad \big((q, q_1) \in E_\vartheta \, \wedge \, (q, q_2) \in E_\vartheta\big)$
(5) $\forall q \in V_\vartheta : \quad \delta(q) = q_1 \vee q_2 \quad \longrightarrow \quad \big((q, q_1) \in E_\vartheta \leftrightarrow (q, q_2) \notin E_\vartheta\big)$
(6) For every cycle in $(V_\vartheta, E_\vartheta)$ the maximal priority of its states is even.

Note that $(q, q_1) \in E_\vartheta$ in (3) (and similarly in (4) and (5)) implies $q_1 \in V_\vartheta$. Further, note that in condition (5) it is possible that both q_1 and q_2 belong to V_ϑ as long as exactly one of the pairs (q, q_1) or (q, q_2) belongs to E_ϑ. For condition (5), it is useful that there are no inflated transition conditions in $\mathcal{A}$.

A **tile with port** is a tuple (ϑ, q) where $\vartheta = (V_\vartheta, E_\vartheta)$ is some tile and $q \in V_\vartheta \cap Q_\diamond$. We denote the set of all tiles and all tiles with port by Θ and Θ_p, respectively.

We call a tile with port $\vartheta_0 = (V_{\vartheta 0}, E_{\vartheta 0}, q_0)$ and a tile $\vartheta_1 = (V_{\vartheta 1}, E_{\vartheta 1})$ (similarly tile with port $\vartheta_1 = (V_{\vartheta 1}, E_{\vartheta 1}, q_{\vartheta 1})$) **concatenable** iff $\overrightarrow{q_0} \in V_{\vartheta 1}$ and $\overrightarrow{V_{\vartheta 0} \cap Q_\square} \subseteq V_{\vartheta 1}$.

Let $g = (\vartheta_1, q_1), (\vartheta_2, q_2), \cdots \in \Theta^\omega$ be an infinite sequence of tiles with port where (ϑ_i, q_i) and $(\vartheta_{i+1}, q_{i+1})$ are concatenable for every $i \in \omega$. We define the **graph of g** in a usual way:

- $\mathcal{V} := \bigcup_{i \in \omega} \{i\} \times V_i$
- $\mathcal{E} := \bigcup_{i \in \omega} \big\{ ((i, q'), (i, q'')) \mid (q', q'') \in E_i \big\} \cup \bigcup_{i \in \omega} \big\{ ((i, q_i), (i+1, \overrightarrow{q_i})) \big\}$
  $\cup \bigcup_{i \in \omega} \big\{ ((i, q), (i+1, \overrightarrow{q})) \mid q \in V_i \cap Q_\square \big\}$

We call an infinite path π in $(\mathcal{V}, \mathcal{E})$ even iff the maximal priority which occurs in π infinitely often is even. We call the sequence g **even** iff every infinite path π in $(\mathcal{V}, \mathcal{E})$ is even.

There can be infinite paths π in $(\mathcal{V}, \mathcal{E})$ which get stuck in one tile, i.e., there is some integer i such that vertices (i', q) for any $i' > i$ and any $q \in Q$ do not occur in π. These paths π are even, because of (6) in the definition of a tile.

Proposition 9.8. *There is a deterministic parity ω-automaton C with $2^{\mathcal{O}(|Q|^4 \log |Q|)}$ states and priorities bounded by $\mathcal{O}(|Q|^4)$ which accepts a sequence of concatenable tiles $g \in \Theta^\omega$ iff g is even.*

Proof. At first, we construct a non-deterministic parity ω-automaton B. Then, we construct C by a determinization and a complementation of B.

The set of states of B are $Q \times \{0, \dots, |Q|\}$. Thus, B has $m := |Q|(|Q| + 1)$ states. The initial state of B is $(q_{\mathrm{I}}, 0)$.

We specify the transition function δ by a set of triples. Let (q_1, i_1), (q_2, i_2) be two states of B, and let (V, E, q) be a tile with port. There is a transition $((q_1, i_1), (V, E, q), (q_2, i_2))$ in B iff

- there is some state $q' \in V$ with $q' \in Q_\square$ or $q' = q$ and $\overrightarrow{q} = q_2$,
- there is some path in (V, E) which starts in q_1 and ends in q', and
- the maximal priority of the states in this path is i_2.

The priority of a state (q, i) is $i + 1$. Clearly, B accepts some infinite sequence of concatenable tiles iff this sequence is *not* even. Finally, we construct C in several steps:

(1) We convert B into a non-deterministic Büchi automaton B_1 with $L(B) = L(B_1)$. This transformation is straightforward. The automaton B_1 has $\mathcal{O}(m^2)$ states.

(2) We apply Safra's construction (see Chapter 4) and transform B_1 into a deterministic Rabin-automaton B_2. The automaton B_2 has $2^{\mathcal{O}(m^2 \log m^2)}$ states and $\mathcal{O}(m^2)$ accepting pairs.

(3) We realize that B_2 is a deterministic Streett automaton for the complement of the language of the Rabin-automaton B_2 (see Chapter 1).

(4) We transform the Streett automaton B_2 into a deterministic parity automaton C (see Chapter 1). The automaton C still has $2^{\mathcal{O}(m^2 \log m^2)}$ states and $\mathcal{O}(m^2)$ priorities. $\square$

9.6.2 Parity Games over Tiles

We denote the set of states of the automaton C by Q^C an its initial state by q_{I}^C.

We construct a parity game T over tiles.

The locations are $\mathcal{V}_0 := Q^C \times \Theta_p$ and $\mathcal{V}_1 := Q^C \times \Theta$.

We define the set of moves $\mathcal{E}$. For every state $q^C \in Q^C$ and every tile with port $(\vartheta, q) \in \Theta_p$, there is a move from $(q^C, \vartheta) \in \mathcal{V}_1$ to $(q^C, \vartheta, q) \in \mathcal{V}_0$.

Let $(q^C, \vartheta, q) \in \mathcal{V}_0$, and let $(q_{\mathrm{I}}^C, \vartheta_1) \in \mathcal{V}_1$. There is a move from (q^C, ϑ, q) to $(q_{\mathrm{I}}^C, \vartheta_1)$ iff (ϑ, q) and ϑ_1 are concatenable and C admits a transition from q^C to q_{I}^C via (ϑ, q). Consequently, a move of Player 0 means to construct a tile, the state q_{I}^C is determined by the automaton C. We can imagine Player 0 and 1 as "tile constructor" and "port selector", respectively.

We define the priority Ω_T of a location (q^C, ϑ) (resp. (q^C, ϑ, q)) as the priority of the state q^C in the parity automaton C.

For convenience, we define a set of initial locations: Every location (q_I^C, ϑ) of Player 0 is an initial location iff $q_I \in V_\vartheta$. As the very first action in a play Player 0 chooses one of these initial locations. A winning strategy for Player 0 has additionally to specify some initial location which Player 0 has to choose to start the game. To know whether Player 0 has a winning strategy in some parity game with multiple initial locations, we calculate Player 0's winning region by Jurdziński's algorithm and check whether an initial place belongs to Player 0's winning region.

Theorem 9.9. *The following three assertions are equivalent:*

(1) *The automaton $\mathcal{A}$ accepts at least one pointed transition system.*
(2) *There is a winning strategy for Player 0 in $\mathcal{T}$.*
(3) *The automaton $\mathcal{A}$ accepts some pointed transition system with at most $2^{\mathcal{O}(|Q|^4 \log |Q|)}$ states.*

Proof. (1) $\Rightarrow$ (2) Let $(\mathcal{S}, s_I)$ be some pointed transition system which $\mathcal{A}$ accepts. We consider the parity game $\mathcal{G}'$ from the proof of Theorem 9.6. Let $f : [V_0] \to [V]$ be a memoryless winning strategy for Player 0 in $\mathcal{G}'$. We construct a winning strategy for Player 0 in $\mathcal{T}$. The winning strategy which we construct is not necessarily memoryless.

At first, we show a mechanism how Player 0 can construct tiles. He construct tiles outgoing from some set $V \subseteq Q$ w.r.t. some state $s \in \mathcal{S}$. Player 0 starts his construction with $(V, \emptyset)$. He chooses some state $q \in V$, and adds new states and edges in order to satisfy the closure properties (3), (4), (5) in the definition of a tile. If for example $\delta(q) = q_1 \wedge q_2$, he adds two states q_1 and q_2 and two edges (q_I, q_1) and (q_I, q_2) to the tile. Then, he has to take care about both q_1 and q_2. For example, let $\delta(q_1) = q_3 \vee q_4$. To satisfy property (5), Player 0 has to choose between q_3 and q_4. He simply calculates $f(s, q_1)$. If $f(s, q_1) = (s, q_3)$, he adds state q_3 and the edge (q_1, q_3) to his tile. Conversely, if $f(s, q_1) = (s, q_4)$, he adds q_4 and (q_1, q_4) to his tile.

Now, we explain a winning strategy for Player 0. At the beginning, Player 0 constructs a tile outgoing from $\{q_I\}$ w.r.t. s_I. Let us call this tile ϑ_1. Player 0 chooses (q_I^C, ϑ_1) as initial location. Next, Player 1 chooses some port, i.e., he chooses a state from $q \in V_{\vartheta_1} \cap Q_\diamond$ and moves to (q_I^C, ϑ_1, q).

Then, Player 0 has to move to a state/tile pair (q_2^C, ϑ_2). It suffices to construct ϑ_2, because q_2^C is determined by C. Let $f(s_I, q) = (s', q')$. Player 0 constructs ϑ_2 outgoing from $\overrightarrow{V_{\vartheta_1} \cap Q_\square} \cup \{\overrightarrow{q'}\}$ w.r.t. s'.

It is easy but technically involved to verify that this technique yields a winning strategy for Player 0.

(2) $\Rightarrow$ (3) Let $f : \mathcal{V}_0 \to \mathcal{V}_1$ be a memoryless winning strategy for Player 0 in the parity game $\mathcal{T}$.

We construct a pointed transition system which $\mathcal{A}$ accepts. Its states are Player 1's locations $\mathcal{V}_1 = Q^C \times \Theta$. We can estimate $|\mathcal{V}_1|$ by $|Q^C||\Theta|$, which is $2^{\mathcal{O}(|Q|^4 \log |Q|)} \cdot 2^{|Q|+|Q|^2}$, i.e., $2^{\mathcal{O}(|Q|^4 \log |Q|)}$.

To define $\lambda : P \to \wp(\mathcal{V}_0)$, condition (2) in the definition of a tile is crucial. For some $p \in P$ and some location $(q^{\mathcal{C}}, \vartheta) \in \mathcal{V}_0$, we let $(q^{\mathcal{C}}, \vartheta) \in \lambda(p)$ iff there is some state $q \in V_\vartheta$ with $\delta(q) = p$.

Let $(q_1^{\mathcal{C}}, \vartheta_1) \in \mathcal{V}_1$ be the location which Player 0 chooses as initial location. This location is the initial state of our pointed transition system. We define the accessibility relation: There is some edge from $(q_1^{\mathcal{C}}, \vartheta_1)$ to $(q_2^{\mathcal{C}}, \vartheta_2)$ iff there is some state $q \in V_{\vartheta_1} \cap Q_\Diamond$ such that $f(q_1^{\mathcal{C}}, \vartheta_1, q) = (q_2^{\mathcal{C}}, \vartheta_2)$, i.e., iff the winning strategy of Player 0 in $\mathcal{T}$ leads to $(q_2^{\mathcal{C}}, \vartheta_2)$.

It remains to show that $\mathcal{A}$ really accepts this pointed transition system. We consider the "small" parity game $\mathcal{G}'$ from the the proof of Theorem 9.6. Let $(q^{\mathcal{C}}, \vartheta, q)$ be some location of Player 0. If $\delta(q) = q_1 \vee q_2$ for some $q_1, q_2 \in Q$, then the winning strategy for Player 0 is determined within the tile ϑ itself. If $\delta(q) = \Diamond q_1$ for some $q_1 \in Q$, then Player 0 simply uses the winning strategy f from $\mathcal{T}$.

(3) $\Rightarrow$ (1) This is obvious. $\qquad\qquad\qquad\qquad\qquad\qquad\qquad\qquad\qquad\square$

Corollary 9.10. *The problem whether some alternating tree automaton accepts at least one pointed transition system is decidable in* EXPTIME.

Exercise 9.6. Let $\mathcal{T}$ be a class of pointed transition systems and $P' \subseteq P$. The cylindrification of $\mathcal{T}$ with respect to P' consists of all pointed transition systems that coincide with some transition system from $\mathcal{T}$ on all propositions except the ones from P'. Show that if $\mathcal{T}$ is recognized by an alternating tree automaton, then so are its cylindrifications.

9.7   Acknowledgements

The author thanks Thomas Wilke for reading and improving a preliminary version of this chapter.

Notes on Part IV

Rabin introduced non-deterministic finite automata accepting labelled infinite complete binary trees in [148], and used them to prove that the monadic second-order theory of the infinite binary tree with two successor functions is decidable. For more on the connection to logic, see Chapter 12. In his paper, Rabin started out with Muller's acceptance condition [133], but in the course of his paper he also defined "dual acceptance": a tree is accepted if for every run there exists a path which satisfies what Rabin's condition. In the same paper, he also considered generalized acceptance, where the acceptance condition is given by an ω-automaton. What we call Rabin acceptance was first defined by Rabin in [150].

With respect to finite automata on infinite trees, Rabin showed in his seminal paper [148] that (1) complementation is effective and (2) emptiness is decidable (elementary recursive). The latter was improved in a serious of papers. Rabin himself [150] as well as Hossley and Rackoff [88] published two algorithms exponential in the number of states and the number of Rabin pairs. Emerson and Jutla [54] and Pnueli and Rosner [144] described algorithms for the emptiness problem with running time exponential in the number of Rabin pairs but only polynomial in the number of states. This bound was improved by Kupferman and Vardi [103]. The best known upper bounds can be derived directly from the best known upper bounds for solving parity games, as described in Chapter 8. NP-completeness is due to Emerson and Jutla [54].

Muller and Schupp were the first to apply the concept of alternation, introduced by Chandra, Kozen, and Stockmeyer [33], to finite automata. They studied alternating tree automata with various acceptance conditions [136]. In their paper co-authored also by Saoudi [134] they introduced the notion of "weak alternation" (which is also used in Chapter 4) and proved that weak alternating tree automata are exactly as expressive as weak monadic-second order logic. From Rabin's work [149] it follows that a language of binary trees is recognizable by a weak alternating tree automaton if and only if the language and its complement are recognized by a nondeterministic Büchi tree automaton. Further work on this was done by Kupferman and Vardi [105].

Extensions of the automaton model used in Chapter 9 will be studied in many of the following Chapters, see, in particular, Chapter 14, where much more powerful transition conditions will be used.

All "efficient" algorithms for checking emptiness of parity tree automata use Safra's construction or any other determinization procedure for ω-automata. It would be interesting to have an explanation for this or to find an algorithm avoiding determinization.

Part V

Modal μ-Calculus

The modal μ-calculus is a fundamental logic for specifying properties of transition systems. It extends propositional modal logic (which can express only local properties) by least and greatest fixed points of monotone operators. The result is a quite expressive logic that subsumes most of the common logical formalisms used in verification, including LTL, CTL, CTL*, and PDL.

In Chapter 10 it is explained how the modal μ-calculus formulas are compiled into alternating tree automata. This is then used to solve the satisfiability and the model checking problem for the modal μ-calculus. In Chapter 11, it is shown how alternating tree automata can be translated into the modal μ-calculus formulas. The thereby established correspondence between the modal μ-calculus and alternating tree automata is then used to prove the modal μ-calculus hierarchy theorem, which states that arbitrary alternation between least and greatest fixed points is necessary to describe all properties expressible in the modal μ-calculus.

10   Modal μ-Calculus and Alternating Tree Automata

Júlia Zappe

Institut für Informatik
Ludwig-Maximilians-Universität München

10.1   Introduction

The modal μ-calculus is a logic that combines simple modal operators with fixed point operators to provide a form of recursion. The modal μ-calculus—as we use it today—was introduced in 1983 by Dexter Kozen [100]. It is well suited for specifying properties of transition systems. For this reason, there is a great interest in efficient solutions of the model checking and the satisfiability problem.

In this chapter these problems will be reduced to the corresponding problems for alternating tree automata, that is, to the problems of acceptance and nonemptiness, respectively. This will be realised by giving a translation which constructs for every formula φ an alternating tree automaton $\mathcal{A}(\varphi)$. Such an automaton accepts a pointed transition system iff the formula φ holds true in this transition system. Solutions of the acceptance problem and the nonemptiness problem were already given in Chapter 9.

The first comprehensive survey about the close connection between fixed point calculi and alternating tree automata was given by Damian Niwiński in [139]. The investigations presented in [139] are rather general and applicable to a number of fixed point calculi. The translation described in this chapter was introduced by Thomas Wilke in [202] and is specific to the modal μ-calculus.

Notation. As in the previous chapters ω denotes the set of the natural numbers. The power set of a set S is denoted by $\mathscr{P}(S)$. Further, we fix an enumerable set P of propositional variables.

With regard to parity games we will use the notations and notions introduced in Chapter 6. In addition, for a parity game $\mathcal{G}$ and a vertex $v \in V^{\mathcal{G}}$ let $\mathcal{G} \downarrow v$ denote the subgame of $\mathcal{G}$ consisting of the vertices of $\mathcal{G}$ reachable from v, having the same edges between them and the same priorities as in the game $\mathcal{G}$.

When proving the correctness of our translation the following lemma about parity games will be useful:

Lemma 10.1. *Let $(\mathcal{G}, v)$ be an initialised parity game, f a memoryless winning strategy for Player 0 in this game and π a play consistent with f. Let $v' = \pi(i)$ for some $i \in \omega$. Then the restriction of f to the vertices of $\mathcal{G} \downarrow v'$ is a winning strategy for Player 0 in the game $\mathcal{G} \downarrow v'$.*

Exercise 10.1. Prove the above lemma.

E. Grädel et al. (Eds.): Automata, Logics, and Infinite Games, LNCS 2500, pp. 171-184, 2002.

Transition systems and pointed transition systems are defined as in Chapter 9. Let $\mathcal{S} = (S, R, \lambda)$ be a transition system, $S' \subseteq S$ and $p \in P$ a propositional variable. The interpretation $\lambda[p \mapsto S']$ is defined by

$$\lambda[p \mapsto S'](p') = \begin{cases} S' & \text{if } p' = p \\ \lambda(p') & \text{if } p' \neq p \end{cases}$$

$\mathcal{S}[p \mapsto S']$ denotes the following transition system:

$$\mathcal{S}[p \mapsto S'] = (S, R, \lambda[p \mapsto S'])$$

The acceptance for alternating tree automata was defined in Chapter 9 in terms of winning strategies in certain parity games. We will write $\mathcal{G}(\mathcal{A}, \mathcal{S}, s)$ for the "simpler" corresponding (initialised) parity game with vertices $V \subseteq Q \times S$ where Q is the set of states of $\mathcal{A}$ and S the set of states of $\mathcal{S}$. This parity game was constructed for finite pointed transition systems in Chapter 9, Subsection 9.3.2, as an alternative definition for the behaviour of an alternating tree automaton, see also Proposition 9.2.

An important notion concerning the complexity of an alternating tree automaton is its **index**. In order to define it we first need the notion of the **transition graph** of $\mathcal{A}$. Let $\mathcal{A} = (Q, q_I, \delta, \Omega)$ be an alternating tree automaton. The transition graph $G(\mathcal{A})$ has the set Q as vertex set. There is an edge from a vertex q to q' iff q' appears in the transition condition $\delta(q)$.

Now we can define the index of $\mathcal{A}$.

Let $\mathcal{C}^{\mathcal{A}}$ be the set of all strongly connected components of $G(\mathcal{A})$. For $C \in \mathcal{C}^{\mathcal{A}}$, let $m_C^{\mathcal{A}}$ be the number of different priorities of states occurring in C, i.e.,

$$m_C^{\mathcal{A}} = |\{\Omega^{\mathcal{A}}(q) \mid q \in C\}|$$

The index of the automaton is defined as the maximum of all these values, i.e.,

$$\text{ind}(\mathcal{A}) = \max(\{m_C^{\mathcal{A}} \mid C \in \mathcal{C}^{\mathcal{A}}\} \cup \{0\})$$

10.2   Modal μ-Calculus

In this Section we introduce the modal μ-calculus. First we give the definitions of syntax and semantics for the modal μ-calculus. Then we introduce the notion of alternation depth of a formula.

10.2.1   Syntax

Definition 10.2. The set L_μ of formulas of the modal μ-calculus is inductively defined as follows:

- $\bot, \top \in L_\mu$.
- For every atomic proposition $p \in P$: $p, \neg p \in L_\mu$.
- If $\varphi, \psi \in L_\mu$ then $\varphi \vee \psi, \varphi \wedge \psi \in L_\mu$.

- If $\varphi \in L_\mu$ then $\Box\varphi, \Diamond\varphi \in L_\mu$
- If $p \in P$, $\varphi \in L_\mu$ and p occurs in φ only positively then $\mu p\, \varphi, \nu p\, \varphi \in L_\mu$.

Remark 10.3. Note that in the definition of L_μ negations can only be applied to propositional variables. However, we will see that the negation of an arbitrary formula can easily be expressed, using de Morgan laws and the following equivalences:

$$\psi_1 \vee \psi_2 \leftrightarrow \neg(\neg\psi_1 \wedge \neg\psi_2) \ , \tag{10.1}$$

$$\Diamond\psi \leftrightarrow \neg\Box\neg\psi \ , \tag{10.2}$$

$$\mu p\, \psi \leftrightarrow \neg\nu p\, \neg\psi[p/\neg p] \ , \tag{10.3}$$

where $\psi[p/\neg p]$ means that in ψ every occurrence of p is replaced by $\neg p$ and vice versa. We defined L_μ in this way (without using auxiliary fixed point variables), because the translation of formulas into automata is simpler for formulas of this form.

The operators μ and ν are called *fixed point operators*. They are viewed as quantifiers. Accordingly, the set $\mathrm{free}(\varphi)$ of free variables of an L_μ formula φ is defined inductively as follows:

- $\mathrm{free}(\bot) = \mathrm{free}(\top) = \emptyset$,
- $\mathrm{free}(p) = \mathrm{free}(\neg p) = \{p\}$,
- $\mathrm{free}(\varphi \vee \psi) = \mathrm{free}(\varphi \wedge \psi) = \mathrm{free}(\varphi) \cup \mathrm{free}(\psi)$,
- $\mathrm{free}(\Box\varphi) = \mathrm{free}(\Diamond\varphi) = \mathrm{free}(\varphi)$,
- $\mathrm{free}(\mu p\, \varphi) = \mathrm{free}(\nu p\, \varphi) = \mathrm{free}(\varphi) \setminus \{p\}$.

The sets F_μ and F_ν of μ- and ν-*formulas*, respectively, are defined as follows:

$$F_\mu = \{\mu p\, \psi \mid \psi \in L_\mu\} \ ,$$
$$F_\nu = \{\nu p\, \psi \mid \psi \in L_\mu\} \ .$$

Formulas from the set $F_\eta = F_\mu \cup F_\nu$ are called *fixed point formulas*.

10.2.2   Semantics

Formulas of the modal μ-calculus are interpreted on pointed transition systems. The modal operators $\Diamond$ and $\Box$ have their usual meaning. In order to define the semantics of fixed point formulas we need the Knaster–Tarski Theorem for the special case of the power set lattice:

Proposition 10.4 (Knaster and Tarski). *Let S be a set and $g : \mathscr{P}(S) \to \mathscr{P}(S)$ a function monotonic with respect to set inclusion. Then g has a least fixed point μg and a greatest fixed point νg. These fixed points satisfy the following equations:*

$$\mu g = \bigcap\{S' \subseteq S \mid g(S') \subseteq S'\} \ ,$$
$$\nu g = \bigcup\{S' \subseteq S \mid g(S') \supseteq S'\} \ .$$

The proof of this theorem and further results on fixed points are summarised in the Appendix of this book, Chapter 20.

Definition 10.5. Let $\mathcal{S} = (S, R, \lambda)$ be a transition system. For a formula $\varphi \in L_\mu$ the set $\|\varphi\|_\mathcal{S} \subseteq S$ is defined as follows:

- $\|\bot\|_\mathcal{S} = \emptyset, \qquad \|\top\|_\mathcal{S} = S$,
- $\|p\|_\mathcal{S} = \lambda(p), \qquad \|\neg p\|_\mathcal{S} = S \setminus \lambda(p) \qquad$ for $p \in P$,
- $\|\psi_1 \vee \psi_2\|_\mathcal{S} = \|\psi_1\|_\mathcal{S} \cup \|\psi_2\|_\mathcal{S}$,
- $\|\psi_1 \wedge \psi_2\|_\mathcal{S} = \|\psi_1\|_\mathcal{S} \cap \|\psi_2\|_\mathcal{S}$,
- $\|\Box\psi\|_\mathcal{S} = \{s \in S \mid sR \subseteq \|\psi\|_\mathcal{S}\}$,
- $\|\Diamond\psi\|_\mathcal{S} = \{s \in S \mid sR \cap \|\psi\|_\mathcal{S} \neq \emptyset\}$,
- $\|\mu p\,\psi\|_\mathcal{S} = \bigcap \{S' \subseteq S \mid \|\psi\|_{\mathcal{S}[p \mapsto S']} \subseteq S'\}$,
- $\|\nu p\,\psi\|_\mathcal{S} = \bigcup \{S' \subseteq S \mid \|\psi\|_{\mathcal{S}[p \mapsto S']} \supseteq S'\}$.

Intuitively, $\|\varphi\|_\mathcal{S}$ denotes the set of states where φ holds true. For a pointed transition system $(\mathcal{S}, s)$ and a formula $\varphi \in L_\mu$ we will write $(\mathcal{S}, s) \models \varphi$ for $s \in \|\varphi\|_\mathcal{S}$.

Note that $\|\mu p\,\psi\|_\mathcal{S}$ and $\|\nu p\,\psi\|_\mathcal{S}$ are the least and greatest fixed points, resp., of the following function:

$$g : \mathscr{P}(S) \to \mathscr{P}(S), \quad S' \mapsto \|\psi\|_{\mathcal{S}[p \mapsto S']}$$

This function is monotonic because of the condition on ψ stated in Definition 10.2 that p occurs in ψ only positively.

Exercise 10.2. Prove the above claim about negating L_μ-formulas, see (10.1)–(10.3).

Let φ, ψ be L_μ formulas. We will write $\psi \leq \varphi$ for "ψ is a subformula of φ" and $\psi < \varphi$ for "$\psi \leq \varphi$ and $\psi \neq \varphi$".

A formula $\varphi \in L_\mu$ is in **normal form** if every propositional variable p in φ is quantified at most once and all occurrences of p are in the scope of its quantification. For a bound variable p occurring in a formula φ in normal form, the unique subformula $\eta p\,\psi$ (for $\eta \in \{\mu, \nu\}$) of φ will be denoted by φ_p. Clearly, for every L_μ formula one can easily build an equivalent formula in normal form just by renaming bound variables, if it is necessary.

Let us now give a couple of examples to indicate how properties of transition systems can be described by formulas of the modal μ-calculus.

Example 10.6. Let $\varphi := \nu p_0(\psi \wedge \Diamond p_0)$. This formula can be read as follows: φ holds true in the current state s_0 iff ψ holds true in s_0 and there is a successor s_1 of s_0 at which φ holds true. By unfolding the formula φ it follows that ψ holds true at s_1 and that s_1 also has a successor s_2 such that at s_2 the formula φ holds true. Since φ is a greatest fixed point, we may loop for ever and we obtain an infinite path such that at each vertex on this path ψ holds true.

Exercise 10.3. Give an L_μ-formula φ such that the following holds: $s \in \|\varphi\|_S$ iff all paths in S starting in s are finite.

Exercise 10.4. Let ψ be an L_μ-formula and $S = (S, R, \lambda)$ a transition system. Find an L_μ-formula φ such that $(S, s) \models \varphi$ iff there exists a state reachable from s in which ψ holds.

Exercise 10.5. Let ψ be an arbitrary L_μ-formula, $S = (S, R, \lambda)$ a transition system and $s \in S$. Give an L_μ-formula φ with the following property: $s \in \|\varphi\|_S$ iff there exists a path π starting in s such that on this path the formula ψ holds true infinitely often, that is, the set $\{i \in \omega \mid \pi(i) \in \|\psi\|_S\}$ is infinite.

Example 10.7. Let $\mathcal{G} = (V_0, V_1, E, \Omega)$ be a parity game as defined in Chapter 6 and $X \subseteq V = V_0 \cup V_1$. Let $S = (S, R, \lambda)$ be a transition system and $p, p_0 \in P$ propositional variables such that the following holds:

- $S = V$
- $R = E$
- $\lambda(p) = X$ and $\lambda(p_0) := V_0$

The attractor set $\text{Attr}_0(\mathcal{G}, X)$ for Player 0 (c. f. Section 6.2 in Chapter 6) can be defined by the following formula:

$$\varphi := \mu p'(p \vee ((p_0 \wedge \Diamond p') \vee (\neg p_0 \wedge \Box p'))),$$

that is, $(S, v) \models \varphi$ iff $v \in \text{Attr}_0(\mathcal{G}, X)$. Here, we use the *least* fixed point operator, because a vertex in X must be reached after a *finite* number of steps and thus, the equation $p' = p \vee ((p_0 \wedge \Diamond p') \vee (\neg p_0 \wedge \Box p'))$ may be applied only finitely many times.

Example 10.8. Let $\mathcal{G}$ be a max-parity game with $|\{\Omega(v)|v \in V\}| = n+1$ (without loss of generality $\Omega(V) = \{0, \dots, n\}$), S a transition system and $p'_0, \dots, p'_n, p \in P$ such that the following holds:

- $S = V$
- $R = E$
- $\lambda(p'_i) = \Omega^{-1}(\{i\})$, $\lambda(p) = V_0$

We give a formula φ that describes the set of winning positions for Player 0 in the game $\mathcal{G}$:

$$\varphi = \eta p_n \, \bar{\eta} p_{n-1} \, \eta p_{n-2} \dots \nu p_0 \left(\bigvee_{i \leq n} (p \wedge p'_i \wedge \Diamond p_i) \vee \bigvee_{i \leq n} (\neg p \wedge p'_i \wedge \Box p_i) \right)$$

where $\eta \neq \bar{\eta}$ and $\eta = \mu$ if n is odd and $\eta = \nu$ if n is even. In order to see that this formula is correct, i.e., $(S, v) \models \varphi$ iff $(\mathcal{G}, v)$ is won by Player 0, one constructs the automaton $\mathcal{A}(\varphi)$ and compares it with the automaton that was constructed in Chapter 9.

Remark 10.9. The interpretation of a formula does not depend on the interpretation of its bound variables, i.e., for a formula φ with $p \notin \text{free}(\varphi)$ and a transition system S the following holds: $\|\varphi\|_S = \|\varphi\|_{S[p \mapsto S']}$ for all $S' \subseteq S$.

Now we define the **graph**, $G(\varphi) = (V(\varphi), E(\varphi))$, of an L_μ formula φ in normal form.

$$V(\varphi) := \{\psi \in L_\mu \mid \psi \text{ is a subformula of } \varphi\}$$

The edge relation $E(\varphi)$ is defined inductively:

- if $\varphi = \bot, \top, p, \neg p$, then $E(\varphi) := \emptyset$,
- if $\varphi = \psi_1 \vee \psi_2, \psi_1 \wedge \psi_2$, then $E(\varphi) := E(\psi_1) \cup E(\psi_2) \cup \{(\varphi, \psi_1), (\varphi, \psi_2)\}$,
- if $\varphi = \Box\psi, \Diamond\psi$, then $E(\varphi) := E(\psi) \cup \{(\varphi, \psi)\}$,
- if $\varphi = \mu p \psi, \nu p \psi$, then $E(\varphi) := E(\psi) \cup \{(\varphi, \psi), (p, \varphi)\}$

For a formula ψ in $G(\varphi)$ let $\text{SCC}_\varphi(\psi)$ denote the strongly connected component of $G(\varphi)$ the formula belongs to.

10.2.3 Alternation Depth

Now we define the notion of **alternation depth** of an L_μ formula, that is, the number of alternations between μ- and ν-operators. We could simply count syntactic alternations between least and greatest fixed point operators, but we prefer to use a more sophisticated definition that was introduced by Damian Niwiński in [138]. This definition yields better complexity bounds, e. g. for the model-checking for the modal μ-calculus.

Definition 10.10. For a formula $\varphi \in L_\mu$ in normal form its alternation depth $\alpha(\varphi)$ is defined inductively:

- $\alpha(\bot) = \alpha(\top) = \alpha(p) = \alpha(\neg p) = 0$
- $\alpha(\psi_1 \wedge \psi_2) = \alpha(\psi_1 \vee \psi_2) = \max\{\alpha(\psi_1), \alpha(\psi_2)\}$
- $\alpha(\Box\psi) = \alpha(\Diamond\psi) = \alpha(\psi)$
- $\alpha(\mu p \psi) = \max(\{1, \alpha(\psi)\} \cup \{\alpha(\nu p' \psi') + 1 \mid \nu p' \psi' \leq \psi, p \in \text{free}(\nu p' \psi')\})$
- $\alpha(\nu p \psi) = \max(\{1, \alpha(\psi)\} \cup \{\alpha(\mu p' \psi') + 1 \mid \mu p' \psi' \leq \psi, p \in \text{free}(\mu p' \psi')\})$

This can be rephrased as follows. Let φ an L_μ formula. Consider the graph $G(\varphi)$ of φ and suppose that the alternation depths of all proper subformulas of φ have already been determined. Let M be the maximum of all these values. If φ is a fixed point formula $\eta p \psi$ and it has a subformula $\eta' p' \psi' \in \text{SCC}_\varphi(\varphi)$ such that $\eta \neq \eta'$, $p \in \text{free}(\eta' p' \psi')$ and $\alpha(\eta' p' \psi') = M$, then $\alpha(\varphi) = M + 1$. Otherwise the alternation depth of φ is $\max(1, M)$. If φ is not a fixed point formula, then its alternation depth is simply M. In particular, the alternation depth of a formula is greater or equal to the alternation depth of any subformula.

Example 10.11. Let φ be the formula from Example 10.6, now letting $\psi = p$, that is, $\varphi := \nu p_0(p \wedge \Diamond p_0)$. By Definition 10.10, the alternation depth of this formula is equal to 1.

Example 10.12. Let $\varphi := \nu p_1(\mu p_2(p \vee \Diamond p_2) \wedge \Box p_1)$. Then $\alpha(\mu p_2(p \vee \Diamond p_2)) = 1$ and because of $p_1 \notin \text{free}(\mu p_2(p \vee \Diamond p_2))$ the alternation depth of φ is 1.

Example 10.13. Let $\psi = \mu p_1((p_2 \wedge p_0) \vee p_1)$ and $\varphi := \nu p_2(\Diamond \psi)$. Clearly, $\alpha(\Diamond \psi) = \alpha(\psi) = 1$. Since $p_2 \in \text{free}(\psi)$, it follows that $\alpha(\varphi) = 2$.

10.3   Translation into Alternating Tree Automata

We now give a translation which for every L_μ formula φ constructs an alternating tree automaton $\mathcal{A}(\varphi)$ such that the following is true:

$$(S, s) \in L(\mathcal{A}(\varphi)) \quad \text{iff} \quad (S, s) \models \varphi$$

As already mentioned in the introduction, by using this translation the model-checking and the satisfiability problem can be reduced to the acceptance and the nonemptiness problem, resp., for alternating tree automata. Thus, the corresponding results of Chapter 9, namely Theorem 9.6 and Theorem 9.9, can be applied.

Since we aim at using the automaton $\mathcal{A}(\varphi)$ to obtain efficient solutions for the above mentioned problems, it is important that our translation is also efficient. In other words, we would like to keep the automaton as small as possible. Beside the size of the state space, another characteristic number for the size of an alternating tree automaton is its index. The translation we are going to present here is such that the number of the states of $\mathcal{A}(\varphi)$ is equal to the number of subformulas of φ and the index of $\mathcal{A}(\varphi)$ is equal to the alternation depth of the formula φ.

10.3.1   Formal Definition

Let φ be an L_μ formula in normal form. The structure of the automaton $\mathcal{A}(\varphi)$ that will be constructed is very similar to the structure of the graph $G(\varphi)$ of the formula. For each subformula ψ of φ the automaton has a state denoted by $\langle \psi \rangle$. The initial state is $\langle \varphi \rangle$ itself. A state $\langle \chi \rangle$ occurs in the transition condition $\delta(\langle \psi \rangle)$ of the state $\langle \psi \rangle$ iff χ is a successor of ψ in the graph $G(\varphi)$. In addition, the transition function reflects the outermost connective of ψ. For example, $\delta(\langle \psi_1 \wedge \psi_2 \rangle) = \langle \psi_1 \rangle \wedge \langle \psi_2 \rangle$ and $\delta(\langle \Diamond \psi \rangle) = \Diamond \langle \psi \rangle$. In the case that $\psi = p$ for a propositional variable $p \in \text{free}(\varphi)$ the automaton has simply to check if in the current state p holds true. Thus, $\delta(\langle p \rangle) = p$. More interesting is the case in which p is a bound variable in φ. Let $\varphi_p = \eta p \, \psi$ be the subformula of φ that binds p. Then $\delta(\langle p \rangle) = \langle \varphi_p \rangle$, that is, when unfolding the equation "$\varphi_p = \psi[p := \varphi_p]$" will be applied. The difference between the least and the greatest fixed points will be expressed by the priority function. Least fixed point formulas obtain an odd, greatest fixed point formulas an even priority. In addition, fixed point formulas with greater alternation depth also have a higher priority.

Definition 10.14. Let φ be an L_μ formula in normal form. We define the alternating tree automaton $\mathcal{A}(\varphi)$ as follows:

$$\mathcal{A}(\varphi) = (Q, q_\text{I}, \delta, \Omega)$$

where

- $Q := \{\langle \psi \rangle \mid \psi \leq \varphi\}$,
- $q_\text{I} := \langle \varphi \rangle$,
- $\delta : Q \to \text{TC}^Q$ is defined by:

$$\delta(\langle \bot \rangle) = 0, \qquad\qquad\qquad \delta(\langle \top \rangle) = 1,$$

$$\delta(\langle p \rangle) = \begin{cases} p & \text{if } p \in \text{free}(\varphi), \\ \langle \varphi_p \rangle & \text{if } p \notin \text{free}(\varphi), \end{cases} \qquad \delta(\langle \neg p \rangle) = \neg p,$$

$$\delta(\langle \psi \wedge \chi \rangle) = \langle \psi \rangle \wedge \langle \chi \rangle, \qquad \delta(\langle \psi \vee \chi \rangle) = \langle \psi \rangle \vee \langle \chi \rangle,$$

$$\delta(\langle \Box \psi \rangle) = \Box \langle \psi \rangle, \qquad\qquad \delta(\langle \Diamond \psi \rangle) = \Diamond \langle \psi \rangle,$$

$$\delta(\langle \mu p\, \psi \rangle) = \langle \psi \rangle, \qquad\qquad \delta(\langle \nu p\, \psi \rangle) = \langle \psi \rangle.$$

- The priority function $\Omega : Q \to \omega$ is defined by:

$\Omega(\langle \psi \rangle) = $ the smallest odd number greater or equal to $\alpha(\psi) - 1$ for $\psi \in F_\mu$,
$\Omega(\langle \psi \rangle) = $ the smallest even number greater or equal to $\alpha(\psi) - 1$ for $\psi \in F_\nu$,
$\Omega(\langle \psi \rangle) = 0$ for $\psi \notin F_\eta$.

Remark 10.15. Since the acceptance for this automaton is defined in terms of the parity game $\mathcal{G} := \mathcal{G}(\mathcal{A}(\varphi), \mathcal{S}, s)$, we now analyse this game. Its initial vertex is $(\langle \varphi \rangle, s)$. The edge relation $E^\mathcal{G}$ is given by

$$(\langle \psi \rangle, s') E^\mathcal{G} = \begin{cases} \{(\langle \psi' \rangle, s') \mid \langle \psi' \rangle \text{ in } \delta(\langle \psi \rangle)\} & \text{if } \psi \neq \Box \psi', \Diamond \psi' \\ \{(\langle \psi' \rangle, s'') \mid \langle \psi' \rangle \text{ in } \delta(\langle \psi \rangle), s'' \in s'R\} & \text{if } \psi = \Box \psi', \Diamond \psi' \end{cases}$$

The priority of a vertex $v := (\langle \psi \rangle, s)$ where ψ is a fixed point formula depends on the alternation depth of ψ and on the outermost fixed point operator; for a μ-formula the priority is odd and for a ν-formula the priority is even.
A vertex $v = (\langle \psi \rangle, s')$ belongs to Player 0 iff

- $\psi = \bot$,
- $\psi = p$, $p \in \text{free}(\varphi)$ and $s \notin \lambda(p)$,
- $\psi = \neg p$, $p \in \text{free}(\varphi)$ and $s \in \lambda(p)$,
- $\psi = p$, $p \notin \text{free}(\varphi)$,
- $\psi = \eta p\, \psi'$,
- $\psi = \psi_1 \vee \psi_2$ for some $\psi_1, \psi_2 \in L_\mu$,
- $\psi = \Diamond \psi'$.

In all other cases, it belongs to Player 1. Note that the structure of the game (the game graph) does not depend on the mapping λ of the transition system $\mathcal{S}$. Further, for $\psi = p \in \text{free}(\varphi)$ the question whether a vertex $(\langle \psi \rangle, s)$ belongs to Player 0 or to Player 1 depends only on λ. For all other formulas it depends neither on φ nor on $\mathcal{S}$.

10.3.2 Correctness

We prove the correctness of the translation presented in the previous section and start with a couple of lemma.

We will write $\mathcal{G}(\psi, \mathcal{S}, s)$ for the game $\mathcal{G}(\mathcal{A}(\psi), \mathcal{S}, s)$.

Lemma 10.16. *Let ψ_1, ψ_2 be L_μ formulas in normal form. Then the following is true:*

$$L(\mathcal{A}(\psi_1 \wedge \psi_2)) = L(\mathcal{A}(\psi_1)) \cap L(\mathcal{A}(\psi_2)),$$
$$L(\mathcal{A}(\psi_1 \vee \psi_2)) = L(\mathcal{A}(\psi_1)) \cup L(\mathcal{A}(\psi_2)).$$

Proof. We only prove the first assertion, the proof of the second assertion being similar.

"$\subseteq$": Let $(\mathcal{S}, s) \in L(\mathcal{A}(\psi_1 \wedge \psi_2))$. By the definition of acceptance for alternating tree automata (cf. Chapter 9) there exists a memoryless winning strategy f for Player 0 in the initialised parity game $\mathcal{G}(\psi_1 \wedge \psi_2, \mathcal{S}, s)$. By Lemma 10.1, it follows that Player 0 has winning strategies for the games $\mathcal{G}(\psi_1 \wedge \psi_2, \mathcal{S}, s) \downarrow (\langle \psi_i \rangle, s)$. Since $\mathcal{G}(\psi_i, \mathcal{S}, s) = \mathcal{G}(\psi_1 \wedge \psi_2, \mathcal{S}, s) \downarrow (\langle \psi_i \rangle, s)$, the claim follows.

"$\supseteq$": Let $(\mathcal{S}, s) \in L(\mathcal{A}(\psi_1)) \cap L(\mathcal{A}(\psi_2))$, that is, Player 0 has winning strategies f_0^1 and f_0^2 for the games $\mathcal{G}(\psi_1, \mathcal{S}, s)$ and $\mathcal{G}(\psi_2, \mathcal{S}, s)$, respectively. Then Player 0 can play in the game $\mathcal{G}(\psi_1 \wedge \psi_2, \mathcal{S}, s)$ as follows: the initial vertex $(\langle \psi_1 \wedge \psi_2 \rangle, s)$ belongs to Player 1 and it has exactly two successors, namely $(\langle \psi_1 \rangle, s)$ and $(\langle \psi_2 \rangle, s)$. If Player 1 chooses $(\langle \psi_1 \rangle, s)$, then Player 0 can play in accordance with f_0^1 and he wins. Similarly, if Player 1 chooses the other successor of the initial vertex, Player 0 can play in accordance with f_0^2 and he also wins. Therefore Player 0 wins the game $\mathcal{G}(\psi_1 \wedge \psi_2, \mathcal{S}, s)$. $\square$

Lemma 10.17. *Let ψ be an L_μ formula in normal form. Then the following is true:*

$$L(\mathcal{A}(\Box\psi)) = \{(\mathcal{S}, s) \mid \forall s' \in sR : (\mathcal{S}, s') \in L(\mathcal{A}(\psi)),$$
$$L(\mathcal{A}(\Diamond\psi)) = \{(\mathcal{S}, s) \mid \exists s' \in sR : (\mathcal{S}, s') \in L(\mathcal{A}(\psi))\}.$$

Proof. We only prove the second assertion.

"$\subseteq$": Let $(\mathcal{S}, s) \in L(\mathcal{A}(\Diamond\psi))$. By the definition of acceptance, Player 0 has a memoryless winning strategy f in the game $(\mathcal{G}, v_0) := \mathcal{G}(\Diamond\psi, \mathcal{S}, s)$. This game has the initial vertex $v_0 = (\langle \Diamond\psi \rangle, s)$ which belongs to Player 0. Further, the following is true:

$$v_0 E^{\mathcal{G}} = \{(\langle \psi \rangle, s') \mid s' \in sR\}.$$

Since f is a winning strategy for Player 0, there is an $s' \in sR$ such that $f(v_0) = (\langle \psi \rangle, s')$. Because of $\mathcal{G}(\psi, \mathcal{S}, s') = \mathcal{G}(\Diamond\psi, \mathcal{S}, s) \downarrow (\langle \psi \rangle, s')$, by Lemma 10.1 it follows that the restriction of f to this subgame is a winning strategy for Player 0. Therefore, for this s' we have $(\mathcal{S}, s') \in L(\mathcal{A}(\psi))$.

"$\supseteq$": Let $(\mathcal{S}, s)$ be a pointed transition system and s' a successor of s such that $(\mathcal{S}, s') \in L(\mathcal{A}(\psi))$; that is, Player 0 has a memoryless winning strategy f in the game $(\mathcal{G}, v_0) := \mathcal{G}(\psi, \mathcal{S}, s')$ (in particular: $v_0 = (\langle \psi \rangle, s')$). Clearly, the following strategy is a (memoryless) winning strategy for Player 0 in the game $\mathcal{G}(\Diamond\psi, \mathcal{S}, s)$:

$$f'(v) := \begin{cases} f(v) & \text{if } v \in V^{\mathcal{G}} \cap \text{dom}(f) \\ v_0 & \text{if } v = (\langle\Diamond\psi\rangle, s) \ . \end{cases}$$

$\square$

Theorem 10.18. *Let φ be an L_μ formula in normal form. Then for every pointed transition system $(\mathcal{S}, s)$ the following holds:*

$$(\mathcal{S}, s) \models \varphi \quad \textit{iff} \quad (\mathcal{S}, s) \in L(\mathcal{A}(\varphi))$$

Proof. We proceed by induction on the size of the formula φ.

Case $\varphi = \bot, \top, p, \neg p$ for $p \in P$. The claim follows directly from the definition of $\mathcal{A}(\varphi)$.

Case $\varphi = \psi_1 \wedge \psi_2$. By induction hypothesis we can assume that the following is true: $(\mathcal{S}, s) \models \psi_i$ iff $(\mathcal{S}, s) \in L(\mathcal{A}(\psi_i))$ for $i = 1, 2$. Thus, the claim follows by Lemma 10.16.

Case $\varphi = \psi_1 \vee \psi_2$. Similar to the previous case.

Case $\varphi = \Box\psi$ We use the definition of the semantics of $\Box\psi$, the induction hypothesis, and Lemma 10.17 to obtain that $(\mathcal{S}, s) \models \varphi$ iff $(\mathcal{S}, s') \models \psi$ holds for all successors s' of s iff $(\mathcal{S}, s') \in L(\mathcal{A}(\psi))$ holds for all successors s' of s iff $(\mathcal{S}, s) \in L(\mathcal{A}(\Box\psi))$.

Case $\varphi = \Diamond\psi$. The proof is similar to the one for $\Box\psi$.

Case $\varphi = \mu p \psi$. Let $\mathcal{S} = (S, R, \lambda)$ and

$$g : S' \mapsto \|\psi\|_{\mathcal{S}[p \mapsto S']} \stackrel{I.H.}{=} \{s' \mid (\mathcal{S}[p \mapsto S'], s') \in L(\mathcal{A}(\psi))\} \tag{10.4}$$

Since

$$(\mathcal{S}, s) \models \mu p \psi \quad \text{iff} \quad s \in \mu g$$

and

$$(\mathcal{S}, s) \in L(\mathcal{A}(\mu p \psi)) \quad \text{iff} \quad \text{Player 0 wins the game } \mathcal{G}(\mu p \psi, \mathcal{S}, s)$$

we have to show that

$$\mu g = \{s \in S \mid \text{Player 0 wins the game } \mathcal{G}(\mu p \psi, \mathcal{S}, s)\} \ .$$

"$\subseteq$": Let S_μ abbreviate the right hand side of the above equation, i.e., S_μ is the set of winning positions of Player 0 in the game $\mathcal{G}(\mu p \psi, \mathcal{S}, s)$.

Since $\mu g = \bigcap\{S' \subseteq S \mid g(S') \subseteq S'\}$, it suffices to show that $g(S_\mu) \subseteq S_\mu$. Let $s \in g(S_\mu)$, that is (cf. 10.4), Player 0 has a memoryless winning strategy f in the game $\mathcal{G}(\psi, \mathcal{S}[p \mapsto S_\mu], s)$. We must prove (cf. definition of S_μ) that Player 0 wins the game $\mathcal{G}(\mu p \psi, \mathcal{S}, s)$, too. In order to show this we study this game more carefully.

The game $\mathcal{G}(\mu p \psi, \mathcal{S}, s)$ has initial vertex $(\langle\mu p \psi\rangle, s)$ and this vertex has an outgoing edge to the initial vertex of $\mathcal{G}(\psi, \mathcal{S}[p \mapsto S_\mu], s)$, i.e., to $(\langle\psi\rangle, s)$.

Further, the game has all the vertices and edges of the game $\mathcal{G}(\psi, \mathcal{S}[p \mapsto S_\mu], s)$. In addition, every vertex of the form $(\langle p \rangle, s')$ has an edge to the initial vertex $(\langle \mu p \psi \rangle, s')$ of the game $\mathcal{G}(\mu p \psi, \mathcal{S}, s')$. All vertices belong to the same Player as in the original game, except for the vertices $(\langle p \rangle, s')$ which are now Player 0's vertices (cf. *Remark 10.15*) .

Now we will show that Player 0 wins this game. At first Player 0 moves the pebble to $(\langle \psi \rangle, s)$. Now he plays in accordance with his memoryless winning strategy f for the game $\mathcal{G}(\psi, \mathcal{S}[p \mapsto S_\mu], s)$ until the play reaches a vertex of the form $(\langle p \rangle, s')$ (if no vertex of this form will be reached, then Player 0 wins, because in this case the resulting play is a play in the game $\mathcal{G}(\psi, \mathcal{S}[p \mapsto S_\mu], s)$ and f is a winning strategy for Player 0 in this game). Such a vertex was a dead end in the game $\mathcal{G}(\psi, \mathcal{S}[p \mapsto S_\mu], s)$. Since Player 0 played with f, this vertex must have belonged to Player 1 in the game $\mathcal{G}(\psi, \mathcal{S}[p \mapsto S_\mu], s)$, that is, $s' \in S_\mu$ $(= \lambda[p \mapsto S_\mu](p))$. By the definition of S_μ, Player 0 has a winning strategy for $\mathcal{G}(\mu p \psi, \mathcal{S}, s')$. Now, he can move the pebble to $(\langle \mu p \psi \rangle, s')$ and then play in accordance with this winning strategy and he wins.

"$\supseteq$": For the converse we prove that every fixed point of g is a superset of S_μ, that is,

$$\text{for all } S' \subseteq S : \text{ if } g(S') = S' \text{ then } S_\mu \subseteq S'$$

Let S' be a fixed point of g and $s_0 \in S_\mu$. Suppose that $s_0 \notin S' = g(S')$. Because of $s_0 \in S_\mu$ there exists a winning strategy f for Player 0 in the game $\mathcal{G}(\mu p \psi, \mathcal{S}, s_0)$. By our assumption $(s_0 \notin S' = g(S'))$, the restriction of f to the vertices of the game $\mathcal{G}(\psi, \mathcal{S}[p \mapsto S'], s_0)$ can not be a winning strategy for Player 0. Thus, there exists a play π_0 in $\mathcal{G}(\psi, \mathcal{S}[p \mapsto S'], s_0)$ consistent with the restriction of f won by Player 1. Comparing the two games one can easily see that π_0 must be finite and its last vertex must be of the form $(\langle p \rangle, s_1)$. Since Player 1 wins this play, it follows that $s_1 \notin S'$. On the other hand, $(\langle \mu p \psi \rangle, s_0)\pi_0$ is a prefix of a play π consistent with f in the game $\mathcal{G}(\mu p \psi, \mathcal{S}, s_0)$ where f is a winning strategy. As $(\langle p \rangle, s_1)$ has exactly one successor in $\mathcal{G}(\mu p \psi, \mathcal{S}, s_0)$, namely $(\langle \mu p \psi \rangle, s_1))$, the sequence $(\langle \mu p \psi \rangle, s_0)\pi_0(\langle \mu p \psi \rangle, s_1)$ is also a prefix of the play π. The play π is consistent with f and so it follows by Lemma 10.1 that the restriction of f is a winning strategy for Player 0 in $\mathcal{G}(\mu p \psi, \mathcal{S}, s_0) \downarrow (\langle \mu p \psi \rangle, s_1) = \mathcal{G}(\mu p \psi, \mathcal{S}, s_1)$. Thus, $s_1 \in S_\mu$.

Now we have a new vertex $(\langle \mu p \psi \rangle, s_1)$ such that $s_1 \in S_\mu$ but $s_1 \notin S'$. As above, it follows that the restriction of f to the vertices of $\mathcal{G}(\psi, \mathcal{S}[p \mapsto S'], s_1)$ is not a winning strategy for Player 0 and we obtain a vertex $(\langle \mu p \psi \rangle, s_2)$ and a (finite) play π_1 in $\mathcal{G}(\psi, \mathcal{S}[p \mapsto S'], s_1)$ consistent with (the restriction of) f such that $(\langle p \rangle, s_2)$ is the last vertex in π_1, $s_2 \in S_\mu$ and $s_2 \notin S'$. Inductively we obtain an infinite sequence of vertices $((\langle \mu p \psi \rangle, s_i))_{i \in \omega}$ and an infinite sequence of (finite) plays $(\pi_i)_{i \in \omega}$ in the games $\mathcal{G}(\psi, \mathcal{S}[p \mapsto S'], s_i)$ consistent with the restrictions of f. Hence, the following play is a play in $\mathcal{G}(\mu p \psi, \mathcal{S}, s_0)$ which is consistent with f and is therefore won by Player 0:

$$\pi = (\langle \mu p \psi \rangle, s_0)\pi_0(\langle \mu p \psi \rangle, s_1)\pi_1(\langle \mu p \psi \rangle, s_2) \ldots$$

Since $\Omega(\langle \mu p \psi \rangle)$ is the maximum priority of the automaton $\mathcal{A}(\mu p \psi)$ and it is odd, we have a contradiction.

Case $\varphi = \nu p \psi$. Let $\mathcal{S}$ and g be as in the previous case. We have to show:

$$\nu g = \{ s \in S \mid \text{Player 0 wins the game } \mathcal{G}(\nu p \psi, \mathcal{S}, s) \} \ .$$

"$\supseteq$": Let S_ν abbreviate the set on the right hand side, i.e., let S_ν be the set of the winning positions for Player 0 in the game $\mathcal{G}(\nu p \psi, \mathcal{S}, s)$.

Due to $\nu g = \bigcup \{ S' \subseteq S \mid S' \subseteq g(S') \}$, it suffices to show that $S_\nu \subseteq g(S_\nu)$. Let $s \in S_\nu$, that is, Player 0 has a memoryless winning strategy f in the game $\mathcal{G}(\nu p \psi, \mathcal{S}, s)$. We have to prove that Player 0 wins the game $\mathcal{G}(\psi, \mathcal{S}[p \mapsto S_\nu], s)$ as well. We show that the restriction of f is a winning strategy for Player 0 in this game. Clearly, every infinite play consistent with the restriction is won by Player 0, because such a play is a play consistent with f in the original game. Let π be a finite play consistent with the restriction of f in the game $\mathcal{G}(\psi, \mathcal{S}[p \mapsto S_\nu], s)$. The last vertex is a dead end in the game $\mathcal{G}(\psi, \mathcal{S}[p \mapsto S_\nu], s)$. If this vertex is also a dead end in the original game then π is a play consistent with f in the original game and therefore won by Player 0. If this vertex has a successor in the original game, then it must be of the form $(\langle p \rangle, s')$. As in the previous case it follows that the restriction of f is a winning strategy for Player 0 in the game $\mathcal{G}(\nu p \psi, \mathcal{S}, s) \downarrow (\langle \nu p \psi \rangle, s') = \mathcal{G}(\nu p \psi, \mathcal{S}, s')$. Hence, $s' \in S_\nu$ and so the vertex $(\langle p \rangle, s')$ belongs to Player 1 in the game $\mathcal{G}(\psi, \mathcal{S}[p \mapsto S_\nu], s)$. Therefore, Player 0 wins also this play.

"$\subseteq$": For the converse, let $s \in \nu g$. Because of $\nu g = g(\nu g)$ for every $s' \in \nu g$ there exists a memoryless winning strategy $f_{s'}$ for Player 0 in the game $\mathcal{G}(\psi, \mathcal{S}[p \mapsto \nu g], s')$. We have to show that Player 0 wins the game $\mathcal{G}(\nu p \psi, \mathcal{S}, s)$.

The initial vertex of the game is $(\langle \nu p \psi \rangle, s)$ and its unique successor is $(\langle \psi \rangle, s)$, the initial vertex of the game $\mathcal{G}(\psi, \mathcal{S}[p \mapsto \nu g], s)$. So, Player 0 moves the pebble to this vertex and then he plays in accordance with f_s unless a vertex $(\langle p \rangle, s_1)$ is reached (in particular, the play is a play in $\mathcal{G}(\psi, \mathcal{S}[p \mapsto \nu g], s)$ consistent with f_s). This vertex is a dead end in the game $\mathcal{G}(\psi, \mathcal{S}[p \mapsto \nu g], s)$. Since this play is consistent with f_s, the vertex belongs to Player 1, that is, $s_1 \in \nu g$. The vertex $(\langle p \rangle, s_1)$ has exactly one outgoing edge that leads to the vertex $(\langle \nu p \psi \rangle, s_1)$. This vertex has also only one successor, namely $(\langle \psi \rangle, s_1)$. Now Player 0 should play in accordance with the strategy f_{s_1} until a vertex $(\langle p \rangle, s_2)$ is reached. After the two trivial steps (to the vertex $(\langle \nu p \psi \rangle, s_2)$ and then to $(\langle \psi \rangle, s_2)$) he should play as given by f_{s_2} and so on. We want to prove that if he plays in this way, he wins. Let π denote the resulting play.

We distinguish two cases.

First case:

$$\exists i \in \omega \forall j > i \forall s' \in S : \quad \pi(j) \neq (\langle p \rangle, s')$$

In this case there exists a $j > i$ such that the suffix $\pi(j)\pi(j+1)\ldots$ of π is an infinite play consistent with $f_{s'}$ in a game $\mathcal{G}(\psi, \mathcal{S}[p \mapsto \nu g], s')$. Since $f_{s'}$ is a winning strategy for Player 0 in this game, he wins π.

Second case:

$$\forall i \in \omega \exists j > i \exists s' \in S : \quad \pi(j) = (\langle p \rangle, s')$$

In this case vertices of the form $(\langle \nu p \, \psi \rangle, s')$ occur infinitely often in π. Their priority, $\Omega(\langle \nu p \, \psi \rangle)$, is the maximum priority in the entire game, it is even and so Player 0 wins.   □

Exercise 10.6. In the above proof, we dealt with the least fixed point operator and the greatest fixed point operator separately. Use Theorem 9.7 to show that it is enough to consider only one of the two fixed point operators.

10.4   Model-Checking and Satisfiability

Now we are able to apply the results of Chapter 9 on the acceptance and emptiness problem for alternating tree automata, i. e. Theorems 9.6 and Corollary 9.10 to solve the model checking and the satisfiability problem for the modal μ-calculus.

Note that the alternation depth $\alpha(\varphi)$ of a formula φ is equal to the index $\text{ind}(\mathcal{A}(\varphi))$ and that the number of states of $\mathcal{A}(\varphi)$ equals the number of subformulas of φ. In the case of the automaton $\mathcal{A}(\varphi)$ the index is equal to the number of its different non-zero priorities.

Corollary 10.19. *Let φ be an L_μ formula with $\alpha(\varphi) \geq 2$ and $(\mathcal{S}, s)$ a pointed transition system. The model-checking problem is solvable in time*

$$\mathcal{O}\left(\alpha(\varphi)|Q|(|R| + 1)\left(\tfrac{|\varphi||S|}{\lfloor \alpha(\varphi)/2 \rfloor} \right)^{\lfloor \alpha(\varphi)/2 \rfloor} \right)$$

and in space

$$\mathcal{O}\big(\alpha(\varphi)|\varphi||S| \log(|\varphi||S|)\big)$$

where $|\varphi|$ denotes the number of subformulas of φ.
The model-checking problem for the modal μ-calculus is in UP$\cap$ co-UP.

Observe that the time complexity bound is exponential in $\lfloor \alpha(\varphi) \rfloor /2$. However, since formulas which specify properties of transition systems are usually not too long and have a rather small alternation depth, this complexity is practically as good as polynomial in the size of the state space of the transition system.

The following Corollary is a straightforward consequence of Corollary 9.10.

Corollary 10.20. *The satisfiability problem for the modal μ-calculus is in* EX-PTIME.

10.5   Concluding Remarks

In this chapter we introduced modal μ-calculus and we proved that for each L_μ-formula one can construct an equivalent alternating tree automaton. From this, together with the results from the previous chapter, we derived reasonable bounds for the complexity of the model checking problem for the modal μ-calculus and a tight bound for the satisfiability problem.

In the following chapter it will be shown that there also is a way to translate every alternating tree automaton into an equivalent modal μ-calculus formula. This will be used to prove that the alternation hierarchy of the modal μ-calculus is strict. The deep connection between modal μ-calculus and monadic second-order logic will be revealed in Chapter 14.

11 Strictness of the Modal μ-Calculus Hierarchy

Luca Alberucci

Informatik und Angewandte Mathematik
Universität Bern

11.1 Introduction

The two main results of this chapter are the translation of alternating automata into the modal μ-calculus and the hierarchy theorem for the modal μ-calculus.

The first main result was initially proven by Niwinski in [139]. He introduces automata on semi-algebras and shows the equivalence with certain fixed point terms on so-called powerset algebras. By using the fact that on binary structures the μ-calculus corresponds to a certain powerset algebra, this result can then be applied to the modal μ-calculus to obtain the equivalence of alternating automata and the calculus, on binary transition systems. We give a direct translation of automata to μ-formulae, using the alternating automata model introduced by Wilke in [202], and discussed in this volume in Chapter 9. The translation will be such that for every automaton there is a μ-formula which is equivalent to it on all transition systems. In this sense the new result we get is a generalization of the original one by Niwinski, since we are not restricting ourself to binary transition systems. By combining our result with Chapter 10, where μ-formulae are translated to alternating automata, we get the equivalence on all transition systems. The established equivalence is such that the alternation depth of the μ-formulae corresponds to the index of the automata.

The second main result was first proved independently by Bradfield in [13] and Lenzi in [112]. Our proof follows the one of Arnold in [5]. We first prove a hierarchy theorem for alternating automata. Then, by using the equivalence result established previously, we get the hierarchy theorem for the modal μ-calculus.

This chapter contains five sections: Section 11.2 reviews the basic notions which will be needed later. Section 11.3 introduces hierarchies, both for μ-formulae and for alternating automata. In Section 11.4 we translate alternating automata into the modal μ-calculus. And in Section 11.5 we prove the hierarchy theorems for alternating automata and for the modal μ-calculus.

11.2 Preliminaries

With regard to alternating tree automata and the modal μ-calculus we use almost the same definitions and the same notation that were introduced in Chapters 9 and 10.

E. Grädel et al. (Eds.): Automata, Logics, and Infinite Games, LNCS 2500, pp. 185-201, 2002.
© Springer-Verlag Berlin Heidelberg 2002

The differences are as follows. First, we use letters X, Y, ... to denote quantified propositional variables in modal μ-calculus. That is, we will write $\mu X \phi$ instead of $\mu p \phi$. Second, in our model of alternating automata, we allow complex transition conditions (which we can do without loss of generality, see Subsection 9.3.4), we fix a finite set P of propropositional variables, which is then explicitly stated in the tuple describing the automaton, and we allow the priority function to be partial. More precisely, it must only be defined on the states that belong to some strongly connected component of the transition graph of the automaton in question.

We also use the following notation. Suppose φ contains propositional variables $X_1, \ldots, X_n$ (we then often write $\varphi(X_1, \ldots, X_n)$) and that $S_1, \ldots, S_n$ are sets of states of a given transition system S. Then we write $\|\varphi(S_1, \ldots, S_n)\|_S$ for $\|\varphi(X_1, \ldots, X_n)\|_{S[X_1 \mapsto S_1, \ldots, X_n \mapsto S_n]}$.

Notice that a transition condition $\delta(q)$ can be interpreted as a modal formula (and hence as a modal μ-calculus formula) over propositional variables in $Q \cup P$, say $q_1, \ldots, q_n$. To indicate that we are interested in this interpretation, we write $\delta_q(q_1, \ldots, q_n)$ for $\delta(q)$.

Recall that the **index**, $\text{ind}(\mathcal{A})$, of an automaton $\mathcal{A}$ is defined as

$$\text{ind}(\mathcal{A}) := \max \Big(\{|\Omega(Q')| \,|\, Q' \subseteq Q, Q' \text{ is strongly connected}\} \cup \{0\} \Big).$$

There are essentially two ways of defining **acceptance** of a pointed transition system (S, s_I) by an automaton $\mathcal{A}$. One option is to proceed as in Chapter 9, with parity games. The second option uses the notion of an accepting **run** of an automaton over a transition system. This is how we proceed in the present chapter.

We first define runs only for automata with simple transition conditions. With the help of Remark 11.1 and Exercise 11.1 the notion of run can then be extended to automata with complex transition conditions.

Let $\mathcal{A}$ be an automaton with state q_0 and S be a transition system with state s_0. We define ϱ to be a q_0-**run on** s_0 of $\mathcal{A}$ on S if ϱ is a $(S \times Q)$-vertex-labeled tree of the form (V, E, ℓ), where V is the set of vertices, E is a binary relation on V, and ℓ is the labeling function. If v_0 is the root of V, then $\ell(v_0)$ must be (s_0, q_0). Moreover for all vertices $v \in V$, with label (s, q), the following requirements must be fulfilled:

- $\delta(q) \neq 0$,
- if $\delta(q) = p$ then $s \in \|p\|_S$, and if $\delta(q) = \neg p$ then $s \notin \|p\|_S$,
- if $\delta(q) = q'$, then there is a $v' \in vE$ such that $\ell(v') = (s, q')$,
- if $\delta(q) = \Diamond q'$, then there is a $v' \in vE$ such that $\ell(v') = (s', q')$ where $s' \in sR$,
- if $\delta(q) = \Box q'$, then for all $s' \in sR$ there is a $v' \in vE$ such that $\ell(v') = (s', q')$,
- if $\delta(q) = q' \vee q''$, then there is a $v' \in vE$ such that we have $\ell(v') = (s, q')$ or $\ell(v') = (s, q'')$,
- if $\delta(q) = q' \wedge q''$, then there are $v', v'' \in vE$ such that $\ell(v') = (s, q')$ and $\ell(v'') = (s, q'')$.

where $vE = \{v' \in V \,|\, (v, v') \in E\}$, similarly for sR.

An infinite branch of a run is **accepting** if the highest priority which appears infinitely often is even. A run is accepting when all infinite branches are accepting. An automaton $\mathcal{A}$ accepts a pointed transition system $\mathcal{S} = (S, s_{\text{I}})$ if there is an accepting q_{I}-run on s_{I} of $\mathcal{A}$ on $\mathcal{S}$ (where q_{I} is the initial state of $\mathcal{A}$).

Let $\mathcal{A} = (Q, P, q_1, \delta, \Omega)$ be an automaton, $\mathcal{S} = (S, R, \lambda)$ a transition system and $\varrho = (V, E, \ell)$ a run. For all $v \in V$ and $q \in Q$ we define

$$S_{vE|q} := \{s \in S \,|\, \exists v'(v' \in vE \text{ and } \ell(v') = (s, q))\}.$$

From the above definition, the following is clear.

Remark 11.1. Let $\mathcal{A} = (\{q_1, \dots, q_n\}, P, q_1, \delta, \Omega)$ be an automaton, $\mathcal{S} = (S, R, \lambda)$ a transition system and $\varrho = (V, E, \ell)$ a $(S \times Q)$-vertex-labeled tree with root v_0. The following two sentences are equivalent:

(1) $\varrho = (V, E, \ell)$ is a q_0-run on s_0 of $\mathcal{A}$ on $\mathcal{S}$.
(2) $\ell(v_0) = (s_0, q_0)$ and for all vertices v which are labeled by (s, q) we have
$s \in \|\delta_q(S_{vE|q_1}, \dots, S_{vE|q_n})\|_{\mathcal{S}}$.

This justifies that we define that a run of an alternating tree automaton with complex transition conditions is required to satisfy the second condition.

Exercise 11.1. Give a direct definition of run for automata with complex transition conditions, without using the notion of equivalent simple automaton. Show that your automaton accepts the same runs as the equivalent simple automaton. (Hint: Use the equivalence established in Remark 11.1.)

11.3 Hierarchies

In this section we introduce hierarchies both for alternating automata and for μ-formulae.

Before we introduce a hierarchy on the formulae L_μ let us define two operators μ and ν on classes of μ-formulae. Let Φ be a class of μ-formulae. We define $\mu(\Phi)$ to be the smallest class of formulae such that the following requirements are fulfilled:

(i) $\Phi \subseteq \mu(\Phi)$ and $\neg\Phi \subseteq \mu(\Phi)$, where $\neg\Phi := \{\neg\varphi \,|\, \varphi \in \Phi\}$.
(ii) If $\psi \in \mu(\Phi)$ then $\mu X.\psi \in \mu(\Phi)$ (provided that each appearance of X in ψ is positive).
(iii) If $\psi, \varphi \in \mu(\Phi)$ then $\psi \wedge \varphi \in \mu(\Phi)$, $\psi \vee \varphi \in \mu(\Phi)$, $\Box\psi \in \mu(\Phi)$ and $\Diamond\psi \in \mu(\Phi)$.
(iv) If $\psi, \varphi \in \mu(\Phi)$ and $X \notin Free(\psi)$, then $\varphi[\psi/X] \in \mu(\Phi)$.

$\nu(\Phi)$ is defined analogously to $\mu(\Phi)$ with the only difference that (ii) is substituted by:

(ii') If $\psi \in \nu(\Phi)$ then $\nu X.\psi \in \nu(\Phi)$ (provided that each appearance of X in ψ is positive).

With the help of the previous definitions we introduce two modal μ-calculus hierarchies. The first one is on the syntactical side, that is, it is a hierarchy of classes of μ-formulae, and the second one is on the semantical side, that is, it is a hierarchy of classes of transition systems.

For all natural numbers n we define the classes of μ-formulae Σ_n^μ and Π_n^μ inductively:

- Σ_0^μ and Π_0^μ are equal and consist of all fixed point free μ-formulae.
- $\Sigma_{n+1}^\mu = \mu(\Pi_n^\mu)$.
- $\Pi_{n+1}^\mu = \nu(\Sigma_n^\mu)$.

All Π_n^μ and Σ_n^μ form the **syntactic modal μ-calculus hierarchy**.

To define the semantical counterpart of this hierarchy, we introduce the class $\|\varphi\|$ for all μ-formulae φ. It consists of all pointed transition systems (S, s_I) such that $s_I \in \|\varphi\|_S$. The **semantical modal μ-calculus hierarchy** consists of all $\Sigma_n^{\mu\,\mathrm{TR}}$ and $\Pi_n^{\mu\,\mathrm{TR}}$, which are the following classes of pointed transition systems:

- $\Sigma_n^{\mu\,\mathrm{TR}} = \{\|\varphi\| \mid \varphi \in \Sigma_n^\mu\}$,
- $\Pi_n^{\mu\,\mathrm{TR}} = \{\|\varphi\| \mid \varphi \in \Pi_n^\mu\}$.

It is obvious that we have

$$L_\mu = \bigcup_{n \in \omega} \Sigma_n^\mu = \bigcup_{n \in \omega} \Pi_n^\mu.$$

Furthermore from the definitions above, we can easily prove that

$$(\Sigma_n^\mu \cup \Pi_n^\mu) \subsetneq \Pi_{n+1}^\mu,$$

and that

$$(\Sigma_n^\mu \cup \Pi_n^\mu) \subsetneq \Sigma_{n+1}^\mu.$$

This clearly shows that on the syntactical side we have a strict hierarchy of formulae. Showing an equivalent result on the semantical side will be the second main result of this chapter.

Lemma 11.2. *The following holds for all natural numbers n:*

- $\Sigma_n^{\mu\,\mathrm{TR}} = \{\|\neg\varphi\| \mid \varphi \in \Pi_n^\mu\} = \{\mathrm{TR} - \|\varphi\| \mid \|\varphi\| \in \Pi_n^{\mu\,\mathrm{TR}}\}$,
- $\Pi_n^{\mu\,\mathrm{TR}} = \{\|\neg\varphi\| \mid \varphi \in \Sigma_n^\mu\} = \{\mathrm{TR} - \|\varphi\| \mid \|\varphi\| \in \Sigma_n^{\mu\,\mathrm{TR}}\}$.

Above, TR denotes the class of all pointed transition systems.

Proof. By Lemma 20.9 in Chapter 20 we have for all transition system S and all formulae φ

$$\|\neg\nu X.\varphi\|_S = \|\mu X.\neg\varphi[\neg X/X]\|_S \quad \text{and} \quad \|\neg\mu X.\varphi\|_S = \|\nu X.\neg\varphi[\neg X/X]\|_S.$$

With this fact we can easily prove the lemma.   □

Let us now introduce a syntactical and a semantical hierarchy for automata. We first introduce the syntactical hierarchy, which consists of the following classes of alternating automata.

- $\Sigma_0 = \Pi_0$ consists of all automata of index 0.
- $\Sigma_n(n > 0)$ contains $\Sigma_{n-1} \cup \Pi_{n-1}$ and all automata of index n where the maximal priority on any strongly connected component of the transition graph of the automaton is odd.
- $\Pi_n(n > 0)$ contains $\Sigma_{n-1} \cup \Pi_{n-1}$ and all automata of index n where the maximal priority on any strongly connected component of the transition graph of the automaton is even.

For the semantical part, if $\|\mathcal{A}\|$ is the class of all pointed transition systems accepted by an automaton $\mathcal{A}$, we define

- $\Sigma_n^{\mathrm{TR}} = \{\|\mathcal{A}\| \mid \mathcal{A} \in \Sigma_n\}$,
- $\Pi_n^{\mathrm{TR}} = \{\|\mathcal{A}\| \mid \mathcal{A} \in \Pi_n\}$.

We conclude this section by stating a lemma, which follows from the Complementation Theorem 9.7.

Lemma 11.3. *For all automata $\mathcal{A} \in \Sigma_n (\in \Pi_n)$ there is an automaton $\hat{\mathcal{A}} \in \Pi_n (\in \Sigma_n)$ such that*

$$\|\hat{\mathcal{A}}\| = \mathrm{TR} - \|\mathcal{A}\|,$$

where TR *is the class of all pointed transition systems.*

Exercise 11.2. Suppose $\mathcal{A} \in \Sigma_n$. Show that there is an equivalent automaton $\mathcal{A}'$ (i.e. $\|\mathcal{A}\| = \|\mathcal{A}'\|$), where the range of the priority function is $\{0, \dots, n-1\}$ if n is even, and $\{1, \dots, n\}$ if n is odd. Formulate and show the analogous claim for Π_n-automata.

11.4   From Alternating Automata to μ-Calculus

In this section we discuss how to translate alternating automata into μ-calculus formulae.

The first lemma deals with simultaneous fixed points of monotone functionals. It is a reformulation of Theorem 20.12 in Chapter 20, in terms of the μ-calculus.

Lemma 11.4. *Assume that Φ is a class of functions which contains μ-formulae $\delta_1(s_1, \dots, s_k), \dots, \delta_k(s_1, \dots, s_k)$ where all s_j $(j = 1, \dots, k)$ appear only positively. Moreover define for all transition systems $S = (S, R, \lambda)$ a functional $\mathcal{F}_S : \mathscr{P}(S^k) \to \mathscr{P}(S^k)$ as*

$$\mathcal{F}_S : (S_1, \dots, S_k) \mapsto (\|\delta_1(S_1, \dots, S_k)\|_S, \dots, \|\delta_k(S_1, \dots, S_k)\|_S).$$

There are μ-formulae $\tau_1, \ldots, \tau_k$ in $\nu(\Phi)$ and $\rho_1, \ldots, \rho_k$ in $\mu(\Phi)$ such that for all transition systems S we have (where $\mathrm{GFP}(\mathcal{F}_S)$ denotes the greatest fixed point of $\mathcal{F}_S$ and $\mathrm{LFP}(\mathcal{F}_S)$ the least fixed point)

$$(\|\tau_1\|_S, \ldots, \|\tau_k\|_S) = \mathrm{GFP}(\mathcal{F}_S)$$

and

$$(\|\rho_1\|_S, \ldots, \|\rho_k\|_S) = \mathrm{LFP}(\mathcal{F}_S).$$

Example 11.5. We illustrate, how we can construct these simultaneous fixed points in the case $k = 2$, i.e., when we have $\delta_1(X, Y)$ and $\delta_2(X, Y)$.

- $\tau_1 = \nu X.\delta_1(X, Y)[\nu Y.\delta_2(X, Y)/Y]$,
- $\tau_2 = \nu Y.\delta_2(X, Y)[\nu X.\delta_1(X, Y)/X]$,
- $\rho_1 = \mu X.\delta_1(X, Y)[\mu Y.\delta_2(X, Y)/Y]$,
- $\rho_2 = \mu Y.\delta_2(X, Y)[\mu X.\delta_1(X, Y)/X]$.

We are now able to prove the main result of this section.

Theorem 11.6. *For any alternating automaton $\mathcal{A} = (Q, P, \delta, q_1, \Omega)$ one can construct a μ-formula $\tau_{\mathcal{A}}$ (over propositional variables $P \cup Q$) such that, for all pointed transition systems (S, s_I), we have*

$$\mathcal{A} \text{ accepts } (S, s_I) \quad \Leftrightarrow \quad s_I \in \|\tau_{\mathcal{A}}\|_S.$$

Moreover, if $\mathcal{A}$ is Σ_n, then $\tau_{\mathcal{A}}$ can be chosen in Σ_n^μ; if $\mathcal{A}$ is Π_n, then $\tau_{\mathcal{A}}$ can be chosen in Π_n^μ.

Proof. The proof goes by induction on the index n of the automaton. We assume for all alternating automata $\mathcal{A}$ that the priority function is defined only on strongly connected components of the transition graph. Moreover, we assume that the cardinality of the range of the priority function of an automaton of index n is also n. This is no real restriction, since all automata are equivalent to one fulfilling these assumptions. There will be two cases for the induction step ($n > 0$):

Case 1: If the maximal priority m is even, we will consider k auxiliary automata of index $\leq n - 1$, in which the states of $\Omega^{-1}[m]$ are moved into variables. Then we will apply the greatest fixed point operator.

Case 2: If the maximal priority m is odd, we consider the complement $\hat{\mathcal{A}}$ of our automaton $\mathcal{A}$. By Lemma 11.3, $\hat{\mathcal{A}}$ can be chosen to have the same index as $\mathcal{A}$, but with maximal priority even. Thus, if we assume that the induction step for Case 1 has been made, we have a Π_n^μ-formula $\tau_{\hat{\mathcal{A}}}$ representing the complement. By Lemma 11.2 we know that there is a formula $\tau_{\mathcal{A}} \in \Sigma_n^\mu$ which is equivalent to $\neg \tau_{\hat{\mathcal{A}}}$. It is easy to check that $\tau_{\mathcal{A}}$ is the Σ_n^μ-formula fulfilling the requirements of the theorem. So, only the induction step for Case 1 has to be carried out.

The informal description above shows that greatest fixed points capture the automata with even maximal priority and the least fixed points, as negations of greatest fixed points, the automata with an odd maximal priority. Before we carry out the induction, let us explain what means 'moving states into variables'. We need to define two transformations for automata:

The first takes an automaton $\mathcal{A} = (Q, P, \delta, q_{\mathrm{I}}, \Omega)$ and a set $X \subsetneq Q$ such that $q_{\mathrm{I}} \notin X$ and defines a new automaton

$$\mathcal{A}_{free(X)} = (Q - X, P \cup X, \delta', q_{\mathrm{I}}, \Omega')$$

where δ' and Ω' are the restrictions of δ (resp. Ω) to $Q - X$. This is the transformation which converts states of the automaton into variables. Notice that the runs of $\mathcal{A}_{free(X)}$ are like the 'beginning' of a run of the automaton $\mathcal{A}$. If we reach a point (s, q), where $q \in X$ the run of $\mathcal{A}_{free(X)}$ stops, whereas if it was a run of the automaton $\mathcal{A}$ it would go on.

The second transformation on automata helps us to deal with the restriction $q_{\mathrm{I}} \notin X$ we had on the first transformation. It takes an automaton as above, a state $q \in Q$ and a new symbol $\hat{q} \notin Q \cup P$ and defines a new automaton

$$\mathcal{A}_{start(q)} = (Q \cup \{\hat{q}\}, P, \delta'', \hat{q}, \Omega)$$

where δ'' is equal to δ on Q and $\delta''(\hat{q}) = \delta(q)$. It is clear, that $\mathcal{A}_{start(q)}$ accepts the same pointed transition systems as $\mathcal{A}$ with initial state q. Moreover, note that for all $X \subseteq Q$, the introduction of $\hat{q}$ makes possible for all automata to do the operation $(\mathcal{A}_{start(q)})_{free(X)}$ (shorter $\mathcal{A}_{start(q)free(X)}$).

Let us now carry out the induction on the index n of an automaton $\mathcal{A} = (Q, P, \delta, q_{\mathrm{I}}, \Omega)$.

$n = 0$: In this case, the transition graph of the automaton does not have any strongly connected component. This means we can easily find an equivalent Σ_0^μ formula as follows. We take $\delta(q_{\mathrm{I}})$ and replace every occurrence of a state q in this formula by the respective transition condition, $\delta(a)$. If the resulting formula still contains states, we proceed in the same fashion. The fact that the transition graph of the automaton does not contain any strongly connected component ensure that the process eventually terminates. The resulting formula must obviously be equivalent to the automaton. We leave the details as an exercise.

$n > 0$: As shown before it is enough to do the induction step only for Case 1. We define U to be the set of states $\Omega^{-1}[m]$, where m is the maximal priority, assuming that $q_{\mathrm{I}} \notin U$; otherwise we consider the semantically equivalent automaton $\mathcal{A}_{start(q_{\mathrm{I}})}$. Suppose $U = \{q_1, \dots, q_k\}$. We consider the automata $\mathcal{A}_{free(U)}$ and $\mathcal{A}_{start(q_i)free(U)}$ for all $i = 1, \dots, k$. It is easy to see that all these automata are of index $\leq n - 1$. So by induction hypothesis, there are μ-formulae $\tau_0(\mathbf{q})$ and $\tau_1(\mathbf{q}), \dots, \tau_k(\mathbf{q})$ in Σ_n^μ (where $\mathbf{q} = (q_1, \dots, q_k)$) such that for all pointed transition systems $(\mathcal{S}, s_{\mathrm{I}})$ we have

$$\mathcal{A}_{free(U)} \text{ accepts } (\mathcal{S}, s_{\mathrm{I}}) \quad \Leftrightarrow \quad s_{\mathrm{I}} \in \|\tau_0(\mathbf{q})\|_{\mathcal{S}}$$

and

$$\mathcal{A}_{start(q_i)free(U)} \text{ accepts } (\mathcal{S}, s_{\mathrm{I}}) \quad \Leftrightarrow \quad s_{\mathrm{I}} \in \|\tau_i(\mathbf{q})\|_{\mathcal{S}},$$

for all $i = 1, \ldots, k$. Now consider the functionals $\mathcal{F}_S : \mathcal{P}(S^k) \to \mathcal{P}(S^k)$ with

$$\mathcal{F}_S : (S_1, \ldots, S_k) \mapsto (\|\tau_1(S_1, \ldots, S_k)\|_S, \ldots, \|\tau_k(S_1, \ldots, S_k)\|_S).$$

By Lemma 11.4 there are μ-formulae $\rho_1, \ldots, \rho_k$ in Π_{n+1}^μ such that for all transition systems $\mathcal{S}$, $(\|\rho_1\|_S, \ldots, \|\rho_k\|_S)$ is the greatest fixed point of $\mathcal{F}_S$. In order to do the induction step let us make the following claim.

Claim. For all pointed transition systems $(\mathcal{S}, s_I)$ and for all $i = 1 \ldots, k$ we have the two following facts:

(1) $\mathcal{A}_{start(q_i)}$ accepts $(\mathcal{S}, s_I)$ $\Leftrightarrow$ $s_I \in \|\rho_i\|_S$.
(2) $\mathcal{A}$ accepts $(\mathcal{S}, s_I)$ $\Leftrightarrow$ $s_I \in \|\tau_0[\rho_1/q_1, \ldots, \rho_k/q_k]\|_S$.

Since $\tau_0[\rho_1/q_1, \ldots, \rho_k/q_k] \in \Pi_{n+1}^\mu$ the claim completes the induction step for Case 1.

We will prove the claim by first showing that (1) implies (2) and then showing the correctness of (1).

Proof that (1) implies (2). Let us remark that by choice of τ_0 and by (1) we have

$$s_I \in \|\tau_0[\rho_1/q_1, \ldots, \rho_k/q_k]\|_S \quad \Leftrightarrow \quad \mathcal{A}_{free(U)} \text{ accepts } (\mathcal{S}', s_I),$$

where $\mathcal{S}' = \mathcal{S}[q_1 \mapsto \mathcal{A}_{start(q_1)}^S, \ldots, q_k \mapsto \mathcal{A}_{start(q_k)}^S]$ and $\mathcal{A}_{start(q_i)}^S$ is the set of states s in S such that $\mathcal{A}_{start(q_i)}$ accepts $(\mathcal{S}, s)$. So it is enough to show

$$\mathcal{A} \text{ accepts } (\mathcal{S}, s_I) \quad \Leftrightarrow \quad \mathcal{A}_{free(U)} \text{ accepts } (\mathcal{S}', s_I).$$

To prove the 'only if' direction let us assume that ϱ is a q_1-run on s_I of the automaton $\mathcal{A}$ on $\mathcal{S}$. We want to convert it into a q_1-run on s_I of the automaton $\mathcal{A}_{free(U)}$ on $\mathcal{S}'$. Let us do the conversion for every branch of ϱ. If we have a branch where there is no state of U, then we do not change anything, otherwise, when we meet the first $q_i \in U$ appearing in the branch, we cut off the rest. The new end point we get is of the form (s, q_i), where by assumption $(\mathcal{S}, s)$ is accepted by $\mathcal{A}$ with new initial state q_i. Using the fact that this automaton is equivalent to $\mathcal{A}_{start(q_i)}$ and that q_i is now a variable, which by definition is true in $s \in S$ (under the valuation λ'), we get the desired result. The proof of the 'if' direction follows similar arguments.

Proof of (1). As before $\mathcal{A}^S$ is the set of all points s in S such that $(\mathcal{S}, s)$ is accepted by $\mathcal{A}$. By definition of ρ_i we have to prove that $(\mathcal{A}_{start(q_1)}^S, \ldots, \mathcal{A}_{start(q_k)}^S)$ is the greatest fixed point of $\mathcal{F}_S$, and so by Tarski-Knaster:

(i) $(\mathcal{A}_{start(q_1)}^S, \ldots, \mathcal{A}_{start(q_k)}^S) \subseteq \mathcal{F}_S(\mathcal{A}_{start(q_1)}^S, \ldots, \mathcal{A}_{start(q_k)}^S)$
(ii) For all $(S_1, \ldots, S_k) \subseteq S^k$ such that $(S_1, \ldots, S_k) \subseteq \mathcal{F}_S(S_1, \ldots, S_k)$ we have

$$(S_1, \ldots, S_k) \subseteq (\mathcal{A}_{start(q_1)}^S, \ldots, \mathcal{A}_{start(q_k)}^S).$$

We first prove (i). Recall that the i-th component of the tuple

$$\mathcal{F}_S(\mathcal{A}^S_{start(q_1)}, \ldots, \mathcal{A}^S_{start(q_k)})$$

is of the form

$$\|\tau_i(\mathcal{A}^S_{start(q_1)}/q_1, \ldots, \mathcal{A}^S_{start(q_k)}/q_k)\|_S.$$

Since τ_i was the formula equivalent to the automaton $\mathcal{A}_{start(q_i)free(U)}$ it is enough to show the following, for all states s in S:

$$\mathcal{A}_{start(q_i)} \text{ accepts } (\mathcal{S}, s) \quad \Rightarrow \quad \mathcal{A}_{start(q_i)free(U)} \text{ accepts } (\mathcal{S}', s) \tag{11.1}$$

where $\mathcal{S}'$ is $\mathcal{S}[q_1 \mapsto \mathcal{A}^S_{start(q_1)}, \ldots q_k \mapsto \mathcal{A}^S_{start(q_k)}]$. This is very similar to what we showed above when we proved (1); we leave the details as an exercise, see Exercise 11.4.

To prove (ii) let $(S_1, \ldots, S_k)$ satisfy the premise of (ii), and let $s_i \in S_i$. Since $s_i \in \|\tau_i(S_1, \ldots, S_k)\|_S$, by hypothesis about τ_i we have $s_i \in \mathcal{A}^{\mathcal{S}'}_{start(q_i)free(U)}$, where $\mathcal{S}'$ is $\mathcal{S}[q_1 \mapsto S_1, \ldots, q_k \mapsto S_k]$ (recall that τ_i is of the form $\tau_i(q_1, \ldots, q_k)$). So there is an accepting run of $\mathcal{A}_{start(q_i)free(U)}$ with the property that if it has a vertex (s_j, q_j) such that $q_j \in U$, then it is a leaf and we have $s_j \in S_j$. Hence we can reapply the premise of (ii) and construct a s_j-run of $\mathcal{A}_{start(q_j)free(U)}$, such that for all leaves of the form $(q_{j'}, s_{j'})$ with $q_{j'} \in U$ the premise of (ii) can be "re-"reapplied . Iterating this process, in the limit we get an accepting run of $\mathcal{A}_{start(q_i)}$ for s_i, since the following holds for all branches. If the branch is finite, then its end point is of the form (σ, s), where $\sigma \notin \{q_1, \ldots, q_k\}$. By assumption we have $s \in \lambda(\sigma) = \lambda'(\sigma)$ (where λ' is the valuation of $\mathcal{S}'$). For the infinite branches we have two cases. For the first case the infinite branch contains only finitely many states q which are in U. Then it easily follows that from the last appearance of a $q \in U$ on, this branch is the same as a branch of an accepting run of an automaton $\mathcal{A}_{start(q_i)free(U)}$. So the highest priority appearing infinitely often must be even, and the branch is accepted. For the other case, there are infinitely many states of U in the branch, and since U is the set where the priority function has its maximal value m and m is even, we again have an accepting branch. $\square$

Exercise 11.3. Carry out the details of the induction base.

Exercise 11.4. Carry out the details of the proof of the implication (11.1).

As a consequence of the above theorem and the results of the previous chapter, we note:

Corollary 11.7. *For every n,*

$$\Sigma_n^{\mu TR} = \Sigma_n^{TR} \quad \text{and} \quad \Pi_n^{\mu TR} = \Pi_n^{TR} .$$

We conclude this section by giving an example of an automaton and an equivalent μ-formula obtained with the construction described in the proof.

Example 11.8. Given an automaton $\mathcal{A} = (\{q_0, q_1, q_2\}, \{p_1, p_2\}, \delta, q_0, \Omega)$ such that $\delta(q_0) = \Box q_1$, $\delta(q_1) = q_2 \vee \Diamond q_0$ and $\delta(q_2) = p_1 \wedge \Box q_1$, and such that $\Omega(q_0) = 1$ (i.e. q_0 is not in the domain of Ω) and $\Omega(q_1) = \Omega(q_2) = 2$. We construct an equivalent μ-formula, following the proof of Theorem 11.6 (we use trivial equivalences of μ-formulae to get more compact representations).

We set $U = \{q_1, q_2\}$. By construction the formula φ equivalent to the automaton has the structure $\tau_0[\rho_1/q_1, \rho_2/q_2]$, where the formulae τ_0, ρ_1, ρ_2 are defined as follows:

- τ_0 is equivalent to $\mathcal{A}_{free(U)}$,
- ρ_1, ρ_2 are formulae such that for all S we have $(\|\rho_1\|_S, \|\rho_2\|_S) = \mathrm{GFP}(\mathcal{F}_1)$, where $\mathcal{F}_1$ is the functional

  $$\mathcal{F}_1 : (S_1, S_2) \mapsto \|\tau_1(S_1, S_2), \tau_2(S_1, S_2)\|_S,$$

  where $\tau_1(q_1, q_2)$ is the formula equivalent to $\mathcal{A}_{start(q_1)free(U)}$ and $\tau_2(q_1, q_2)$ is the formula equivalent to $\mathcal{A}_{start(q_2)free(U)}$.

By construction we also have for all transition systems S:

- $\mathcal{A}_{free(U)}$ is equivalent to $\mathrm{LFP}(\mathcal{F}_2)$ with

  $$\mathcal{F}_2 : S \mapsto \|\Box q_1\|_S.$$

- $\mathcal{A}_{start(q_1)free(U)}$ is equivalent to the second component of $\mathrm{LFP}(\mathcal{F}_3)$ with

  $$\mathcal{F}_3 : (S_0, S_1) \mapsto \|(\Box q_1, q_2 \vee \Diamond S_0)\|_S.$$

- $\mathcal{A}_{start(q_2)free(U)}$ is equivalent to the second component of $\mathrm{LFP}(\mathcal{F}_4)$ with

  $$\mathcal{F}_4 : (S_0, S_2) \mapsto \|(\Box q_1, p_1 \wedge \Box q_1)\|_S.$$

Putting all this together we obtain (Example 11.5 may be useful for a better understanding):

- $\tau_0 = \Box q_1$,
- $\tau_1 = q_2 \vee \Diamond \Box q_1$,
- $\tau_2 = p_1 \wedge \Box q_1$.

So we get

$$\mathcal{F}_1 : (S_1, S_2) \mapsto \|S_2 \vee \Diamond \Box S_1, p_1 \wedge \Box S_1\|_S$$

which gives us

$$(\rho_1, \rho_2) = (\nu X.((p_1 \wedge \Box X) \vee \Diamond \Box X), \nu Y.(p_1 \wedge \Box \nu X.(p_1 \wedge \Box X)))$$

and so we have

$$\varphi = \Box(\nu X.((p_1 \wedge \Box X) \vee \Diamond \Box X)).$$

11.5 Hierarchy Theorems

In this section we prove that the hierarchy of modal μ-calculus on transition systems is strict. We proceed similarly to Arnold in [5]. In the first subsection we show the strictness of the hierarchy induced by automata and then use this to get the main result in the second subsection.

11.5.1 Hierarchy Theorem for Automata

We assume that for all automata $\mathcal{A} \in \Sigma_n$ the range of the priority function is Ω_{Σ_n} and that for all automata $\mathcal{A} \in \Pi_n$ the range is Ω_{Π_n}, where Ω_{Σ_n} and Ω_{Π_n} are defined as follows.

- $n = 0$: If $\mathcal{A} \in \Sigma_n$ or $\mathcal{A} \in \Pi_n$ then $\Omega_{\Sigma_0} = \Omega_{\Pi_0} = \emptyset$.
- n even $(n \neq 0)$:
  - If $\mathcal{A} \in \Sigma_n$ then $\Omega_{\Sigma_n} = \{0, \dots, n-1\}$.
  - If $\mathcal{A} \in \Pi_n$ then $\Omega_{\Pi_n} = \{1, \dots, n\}$.
- n odd:
  - If $\mathcal{A} \in \Sigma_n$ then $\Omega_{\Sigma_n} = \{1, \dots, n\}$.
  - If $\mathcal{A} \in \Pi_n$ then $\Omega_{\Pi_n} = \{0, \dots, n-1\}$.

The assumptions we have made above are no real restriction, since all automata are equivalent to one fulfilling these assumptions (see Exercise 11.2).

For every natural number n we now introduce the **Σ_n-Test Automaton** T_{Σ_n} and the **Π_n-Test Automaton** T_{Π_n}. These test automata are designed to be "universal" in the sense that they accept encodings of arbitrary runs of automata in Σ_n and Π_n, respectively.

All T_{Σ_n} are of the form (where u is a new symbol)

$$T_{\Sigma_n} = (Q_{\Sigma_n}, P, q_u, \delta_{\Sigma_n}, \Omega)$$

and all T_{Π_n} are of the form

$$T_{\Pi_n} = (Q_{\Pi_n}, P, q_u, \delta_{\Pi_n}, \Omega)$$

where:

- $Q_{\Sigma_n} = \{q_i \mid i \in \Omega_{\Sigma_n}\} \cup \{q_u\}$,
- $Q_{\Pi_n} = \{q_i \mid i \in \Omega_{\Pi_n}\} \cup \{q_u\}$,
- $P = \{c_u\} \cup \{c_0, c_1, c_2, \dots\} \cup \{d_u\} \cup \{d_0, d_1, d_2, \dots\}$,
- for all states $q_j \in Q_{\Sigma_n}$ we have:

$$\delta(q_j) = \bigvee_{q_i \in Q_{\Sigma_n}} (c_i \wedge \Box q_i) \vee \bigvee_{q_i \in Q_{\Sigma_n}} (d_i \wedge \Diamond q_i),$$

- for all states $q_j \in Q_{\Pi_n}$ we have:

$$\delta(q_j) = \bigvee_{q_i \in Q_{\Pi_n}} (c_i \wedge \Box q_i) \vee \bigvee_{q_i \in Q_{\Pi_n}} (d_i \wedge \Diamond q_i),$$

- $\Omega(q_j) = j$ if $j \neq u$ and $\Omega(q_u) \uparrow$.

In the following, we only consider pointed transition systems which are rooted trees with degree at most 2, which we will call binary transition systems. This will be no restriction at all, because if formulas do not agree on such structures, then they will definitely not agree on all structures.

We reduce the problem of acceptance of a binary transition system S by a given automaton $\mathcal{A} \in \Sigma_n$ (resp. Π_n) to the acceptance of another binary transition system $G_{\mathcal{A},q}(S)$ by T_{Σ_n} (resp. T_{Π_n}). This transition system will in some sense be a representation of the game tree described in Chapter 9 and which was used to define acceptance of a tree.

To define this transition system, let us introduce a more compact notation for binary transition systems: In the sequel the symbols $t_1, t_2, \ldots$ stand for binary trees, when no confusion arises we also use them to denote binary transition systems. ϵ is the trivial binary tree (or transition system), that is, the one with no states. If t_1 and t_2 are two binary transition systems and a is a subset of the propositional variables then $a(t_1, t_2)$ denotes a binary transition system with a new root v such that exactly the variables in a are valid there and such that v has two edges to the roots of t_1 and t_2, respectively. (Observe that this means that we do not distinguish between $a(t_1, t_2)$ and $a(t_2, t_1)$.) If v should only have one son (resp. no son) we write $a(t_1, \epsilon)$ (resp. $a(\epsilon, \epsilon)$). If $a = \{p\}$ we also write $p(t_1, t_2)$. Obviously, for any binary transition system there are a, t_1, t_2 such that it is of the form $a(t_1, t_2)$ (when v is chosen in the right way).

Let $\mathcal{A} = (Q, P, q_1, \delta, \Omega) \in \Sigma_n$ (resp. Π_n) be an automaton and q a state of $\mathcal{A}$. With every binary transition system t we associate a new binary transition system $G_{\mathcal{A},q}(t)$. The definition of this transition system is inductive, according to the following rules.

- If $\delta(q) = q' \wedge q''$ and $\Omega(q) = i \in \omega$ then
$$G_{\mathcal{A},q}(a(t_1, t_2)) = c_i(G_{\mathcal{A},q'}(a(t_1, t_2)), G_{\mathcal{A},q''}(a(t_1, t_2))),$$

- if $\delta(q) = q' \vee q''$ and $\Omega(q) = i \in \omega$ then
$$G_{\mathcal{A},q}(a(t_1, t_2)) = d_i(G_{\mathcal{A},q'}(a(t_1, t_2)), G_{\mathcal{A},q''}(a(t_1, t_2))),$$

- if $\delta(q) = q'$ and $\Omega(q) = i \in \omega$ then
$$G_{\mathcal{A},q}(a(t_1, t_2)) = c_i(G_{\mathcal{A},q'}(a(t_1, t_2)), \epsilon),$$

- if $\delta(q) = \Diamond q'$, $\Omega(q) = i \in \omega$ and $t_1 \neq \epsilon$ or $t_2 \neq \epsilon$ then
$$G_{\mathcal{A},q}(a(t_1, t_2)) = d_i(G_{\mathcal{A},q'}(t_1), G_{\mathcal{A},q'}(t_2)),$$

- if $\delta(q) = \Box q'$, $\Omega(q) = i \in \omega$ and $t_1 \neq \epsilon$ or $t_2 \neq \epsilon$ then
$$G_{\mathcal{A},q}(a(t_1, t_2)) = c_i(G_{\mathcal{A},q'}(t_1), G_{\mathcal{A},q'}(t_2)),$$

- if $\delta(q) = q' \wedge q''$ and $\Omega(q) \uparrow$ then
$$G_{\mathcal{A},q}(a(t_1, t_2)) = c_u(G_{\mathcal{A},q'}(a(t_1, t_2)), G_{\mathcal{A},q''}(a(t_1, t_2))),$$

- if $\delta(q) = q' \vee q''$ and $\Omega(q) \uparrow$ then

$$G_{\mathcal{A},q}(a(t_1, t_2)) = d_u(G_{\mathcal{A},q'}(a(t_1, t_2)), G_{\mathcal{A},q''}(a(t_1, t_2))),$$

- if $\delta(q) = q'$ and $\Omega(q) \uparrow$ then

$$G_{\mathcal{A},q}(a(t_1, t_2)) = c_u(G_{\mathcal{A},q'}(a(t_1, t_2)), \epsilon),$$

- if $\delta(q) = \Diamond q'$, $\Omega(q) \uparrow$ and $t_1 \neq \epsilon$ or $t_2 \neq \epsilon$ then

$$G_{\mathcal{A},q}(a(t_1, t_2)) = d_u(G_{\mathcal{A},q'}(t_1), G_{\mathcal{A},q'}(t_2)),$$

- if $\delta(q) = \Box q'$, $\Omega(q) \uparrow$ and $t_1 \neq \epsilon$ or $t_2 \neq \epsilon$ then

$$G_{\mathcal{A},q}(a(t_1, t_2)) = c_u(G_{\mathcal{A},q'}(t_1), G_{\mathcal{A},q'}(t_2)),$$

- if $\delta(q) = \Diamond q'$ and $t_1 = t_2 = \epsilon$ then

$$G_{\mathcal{A},q}(a(t_1, t_2)) = \emptyset,$$

- if $\delta(q) = \Box q'$ and $t_1 = t_2 = \epsilon$ then

$$G_{\mathcal{A},q}(a(t_1, t_2)) = P,$$

- if $\delta(q) = \top$, or $\delta(q) = p$ and $p \in a$ then

$$G_{\mathcal{A},q}(a(t_1, t_2)) = P,$$

- if $\delta(q) = \bot$, or $\delta(q) = p$ and $p \notin a$ then

$$G_{\mathcal{A},q}(a(t_1, t_2)) = \emptyset.$$

It is easy to see that $G_{\mathcal{A},q}(a(t_1, t_2))$ is a binary transition system.

Example 11.9. Figure 11.1 shows a transition system S together with $G_{\mathcal{A},q_1}(S)$ and $G_{\mathcal{A},q_1}(G_{\mathcal{A},q_1}(S)) =: G^2_{\mathcal{A},q_1}(S)$. S is a binary transition system over a set of propositional variables $\{p_1, p_2\}$ of the form $p_1(t_1, t_2)$, where $t_1 = p_1(\epsilon, \epsilon)$ and $t_2 = p_2(\epsilon, \epsilon)$. Furthermore $\mathcal{A} = (\{q, q_2, q_3, q_4\}, \{p_1, p_2\}, \delta, q_1, \Omega)$ is an alternating Π_2-automaton with:

- $\delta(q_1) = \Box q_2$,
- $\delta(q_2) = q_4 \vee q_3$,
- $\delta(q_3) = p_1$,
- $\delta(q_4) = \Diamond q_1$,
- $\Omega(q_1) = \Omega(q_4) = 1$ and
- $\Omega(q_2) = \Omega(q_3) = 2$.

It can easily be seen that $G_{\mathcal{A},q}(S)$ is a representation of the game tree described in Chapter 9 (which there is called behaviour), where the choice nodes for player 0 are the d-nodes and the choice nodes for player 1 are the c-nodes. Furthermore, it follows easily from the definition that the Test Automaton accepts the game tree if and only if player 0 has a winning strategy. Since, as it is shown in Chapter 9, the existence of a winning strategy for player 0 implies acceptance we get the following lemma.

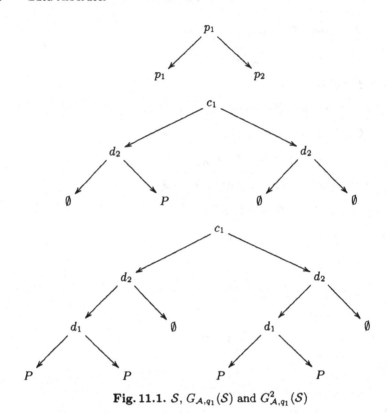

Fig. 11.1. S, $G_{\mathcal{A},q_1}(S)$ and $G_{\mathcal{A},q_1}^2(S)$

Lemma 11.10. *For any binary transition system S and any automaton $\mathcal{A}$ with initial state q, we have:*

- *If $\mathcal{A} \in \Sigma_n$:*

$$S \in \|\mathcal{A}\| \quad \Leftrightarrow \quad G_{\mathcal{A},q}(S) \in \|T_{\Sigma_n}\|.$$

- *If $\mathcal{A} \in \Pi_n$:*

$$S \in \|\mathcal{A}\| \quad \Leftrightarrow \quad G_{\mathcal{A},q}(S) \in \|T_{\Pi_n}\|.$$

The proof of the next lemma needs the notion of **limit tree**. Suppose we have a sequence of trees $(t_n)_{n\in\omega}$ which is monotone, that is, the following holds: For all $m \in \omega$ there is a $n(m) \in \omega$ such that for all $n', n'' \geq n(m)$ the trees $t_{n'}$ and $t_{n''}$ are identical up to depth m.

In that case we can define the limit tree $\lim((t_n)_{n\in\omega})$ of the sequence $(t_n)_{n\in\omega}$ such that for all natural numbers m the limit tree is identical to $t_{n(m)}$ up to depth m. Notice that $\lim((t_n)_{n\in\omega})$ is well defined since $(t_n)_{n\in\omega}$ is monotone.

Lemma 11.11. *Let $\mathcal{A} \in \Sigma_n (\in \Pi_n)$ be an automaton. There is an automaton $\mathcal{A}' \in \Sigma_n (\in \Pi_n)$ with initial state q' and a transition system $F_{\mathcal{A}',q}$ such that*

$$\|\mathcal{A}\| = \|\mathcal{A}'\| \quad \text{and} \quad G_{\mathcal{A}',q'}(F_{\mathcal{A}',q'}) = F_{\mathcal{A}',q'}.$$

Proof. Let $\mathcal{A}$ be an automaton of the form $(Q, P, q_1, \delta, \Omega)$. For the semantically equivalent automaton $\mathcal{A}'$ we take a new state q' and set

$$\mathcal{A}' = (Q \cup \{q'\}, P, q', \delta', \Omega')$$

where δ' is equal to δ on Q and $\delta'(q') = q_1 \wedge q_1$; and where Ω' is equal to Ω on Q and $\Omega'(q') \uparrow$. It can easily be seen that $\|\mathcal{A}\| = \|\mathcal{A}'\|$ and that if $\mathcal{A} \in \Sigma_n(\in \Pi_n)$ then $\mathcal{A}' \in \Sigma_n(\in \Pi_n)$.

Observe that the modification of the automaton ensures the following. Given two binary transition systems S and S' which are identical up to depth m, $G_{\mathcal{A}', q'}(S)$ and $G_{\mathcal{A}', q'}(S')$ are identical up to depth $m + 1$.

Let us construct the fixed point $F_{\mathcal{A}', q'}$. We first define a monotone sequence $(t_n)_{n \in \omega}$ of binary transition systems: t_0 is the binary transition system S of the form $c_u(\epsilon, \epsilon)$ and

$$t_{n+1} = G_{\mathcal{A}', q'}(t_n).$$

By induction on n, with the help of the claim, we can easily prove that for all n the trees t_n and t_{n+1} are identical up to depth n. From that, the monotonicity of $(t_n)_{n \in \omega}$ easily follows. We set

$$F_{\mathcal{A}', q'} = \lim((t_n)_{n \in \omega}).$$

By definition of the limit tree we see that $F_{\mathcal{A}', q'}$ is a fixed point of $G_{\mathcal{A}', q'}$, and this completes the proof.   □

We now prove the hierarchy theorem.

Theorem 11.12. *For all natural numbers n we have:*

(1) $\Sigma_{n+1}^{\mathrm{TR}} \neq \Sigma_n^{\mathrm{TR}}$,
(2) $\Pi_{n+1}^{\mathrm{TR}} \neq \Pi_n^{\mathrm{TR}}$.

Proof. 1. Proof by contradiction. Suppose $\Sigma_{n+1}^{\mathrm{TR}} = \Sigma_n^{\mathrm{TR}}$. By definition, it follows that $\Pi_n^{\mathrm{TR}} \subseteq \Sigma_n^{\mathrm{TR}}$. With Lemma 11.3 we get

$$\mathrm{TR} - \|T_{\Sigma_n}\| \in \Sigma_n^{\mathrm{TR}}.$$

So, there exists a Σ_n-automaton $\mathcal{A}$ such that $\mathrm{TR} - \|T_{\Sigma_n}\| = \|\mathcal{A}\|$. By Lemmas 11.10 and 11.11 there is a semantically equivalent automaton $\mathcal{A}' \in \Sigma_n$ and a transition system $F_{\mathcal{A}'}$ such that

$$F_{\mathcal{A}'} \in \|T_{\Sigma_n}\| \quad \Leftrightarrow \quad F_{\mathcal{A}'} \in \|\mathcal{A}'\|.$$

Since $\|\mathcal{A}'\| = \|\mathcal{A}\| = \mathrm{TR} - \|T_{\Sigma_n}\|$ we get

$$F_{\mathcal{A}'} \in \|T_{\Sigma_n}\| \quad \Leftrightarrow \quad F_{\mathcal{A}'} \in \mathrm{TR} - \|T_{\Sigma_n}\|$$

and hence a contradiction, which proves part 1 of the theorem.
   2. can be proven similarly to part 1.

11.5.2   Hierarchy Theorem for the μ-Calculus

We apply Theorem 11.12 to the modal μ-calculus. From Corollary 11.7 and Theorem 11.12, we immediately get:

Corollary 11.13. *For all natural numbers n we have:*

(1) $\Sigma_n^{\mu\,\mathrm{TR}} \neq \Sigma_{n+1}^{\mu\,\mathrm{TR}}$,
(2) $\Pi_n^{\mu\,\mathrm{TR}} \neq \Pi_{n+1}^{\mu\,\mathrm{TR}}$.

The theorem shows us that no finite part of the modal μ-hierarchy has the expressiveness of the whole calculus. In this sense, it can be seen as the evidence that the modal μ-calculus hierarchy is strict. Let us prove two corollaries before we illustrate the modal μ-calculus hierarchy.

Corollary 11.14. *For all natural numbers $n > 0$ we have*

$$\Sigma_n^{\mu\,\mathrm{TR}} \neq \Pi_n^{\mu\,\mathrm{TR}}.$$

Proof. We prove the contrapositive. Suppose that we have $\Sigma_n^{\mu\,\mathrm{TR}} = \Pi_n^{\mu\,\mathrm{TR}}$ for an $n > 0$. Now, let $\|\varphi\| \in \Sigma_{n+1}^{\mu\,\mathrm{TR}} \setminus \Sigma_n^{\mu\,\mathrm{TR}}$. So there is a $\psi \in \Sigma_{n+1}^{\mu}$ such that $\|\varphi\| = \|\psi\|$. Since $\Sigma_{n+1}^{\mu} = \mu(\Pi_n^{\mu})$, by definition of the operator μ there are formulae $\psi_1, \ldots, \psi_m, \neg\psi_{m+1}, \ldots, \neg\psi_{m+k}$ such that all $\psi_i \in \Pi_n^{\mu}$ and such that ψ is obtained from these formulae using $\wedge, \vee, \mu, \square, \diamond$ and substitution. Using this representation of ψ we show that the formula is equivalent to a formula $\psi' \in \Sigma_n^{\mu}$. Hence we have $\psi \in \Sigma_n^{\mu\,\mathrm{TR}}$, which is a contradiction to Corollary 11.13, since we have $\|\varphi\| = \|\psi\|$.

So, let us show the equivalence of ψ to a $\psi' \in \Sigma_n^{\mu}$. In the construction of ψ we started from formulae $\psi_1, \ldots, \psi_m, \neg\psi_{m+1}, \ldots, \neg\psi_{m+k}$ such that all $\psi_i \in \Pi_n^{\mu}$. Since by assumption $\Sigma_n^{\mu\,\mathrm{TR}} = \Pi_n^{\mu\,\mathrm{TR}}$, for all $i \in \{1, \ldots, m\}$ there are formulae $\psi_i' \in \Sigma_n^{\mu}$ which are equivalent to ψ_i. Further, by Lemma 11.2 for all $i \in \{m+1, \ldots, m+k\}$ there are formulae $\psi_i' \in \Sigma_n^{\mu}$ equivalent to $\neg\psi_i$. Hence ψ is equivalent to a formula constructed analogously starting from formulae $\psi_1', \ldots, \psi_m', \psi_{m+1}', \ldots, \psi_{m+k}'$, where all $\psi_i' \in \Sigma_n^{\mu}$, that is ψ is obtained from the ψ_i' by using $\wedge, \vee, \mu, \square, \diamond$ and substitution. Since Σ_n^{μ} is closed under these operations, we have $\Sigma_n^{\mu} = \mu(\Pi_{n-1}^{\mu})$. That means that $\psi' \in \Sigma_n^{\mu}$. Since ψ' is equivalent to ψ the proof is completed. $\square$

Corollary 11.15. *For all natural numbers n we have:*

(1) $\Sigma_n^{\mu\,\mathrm{TR}} \subsetneq \Pi_{n+1}^{\mu\,\mathrm{TR}}$,
(2) $\Pi_n^{\mu\,\mathrm{TR}} \subsetneq \Sigma_{n+1}^{\mu\,\mathrm{TR}}$.

Proof. 1. We prove the contrapositive. Suppose that $\Sigma_n^{\mu\,\mathrm{TR}} \subsetneq \Pi_{n+1}^{\mu\,\mathrm{TR}}$ does not hold. Since it is clear that $\Sigma_n^{\mu\,\mathrm{TR}} \subseteq \Pi_{n+1}^{\mu\,\mathrm{TR}}$ holds we then have $\Sigma_n^{\mu\,\mathrm{TR}} = \Pi_{n+1}^{\mu\,\mathrm{TR}}$. Now, suppose we have $\|\varphi\| \in \Sigma_{n+1}^{\mu\,\mathrm{TR}}$, by Lemma 11.2 we have $\|\neg\varphi\| \in \Pi_{n+1}^{\mu\,\mathrm{TR}}$ and with our assumption we get $\|\neg\varphi\| \in \Sigma_n^{\mu\,\mathrm{TR}}$ and by Lemma 11.2 $\|\varphi\| \in \Pi_n^{\mu\,\mathrm{TR}}$. Since φ was arbitrary we have $\Pi_n^{\mu\,\mathrm{TR}} = \Sigma_{n+1}^{\mu\,\mathrm{TR}}$. All together, this gives to us

$$\Sigma_n^{\mu\,\mathrm{TR}} = \Pi_{n+1}^{\mu\,\mathrm{TR}} \quad \text{and} \quad \Pi_n^{\mu\,\mathrm{TR}} = \Sigma_{n+1}^{\mu\,\mathrm{TR}}.$$

But then we easily get

$$\Sigma^{\mu\text{TR}}_{n+1} \subseteq \Pi^{\mu\text{TR}}_{n+1} \quad \text{and} \quad \Pi^{\mu\text{TR}}_{n+1} \subseteq \Sigma^{\mu\text{TR}}_{n+1}$$

which is not the case by Corollary 11.14.

2. is proven similarly. $\square$

We end with Figure 11.2 which illustrates the structure of the modal μ-calculus hierarchy.

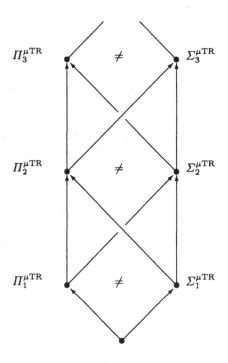

$$\Sigma^{\mu\text{TR}}_0 = \Pi^{\mu\text{TR}}_0$$

Fig. 11.2. The modal μ-calculus hierarchy. Notice that the arrows stand for strict inclusion and that $L^{\text{TR}}_\mu = \{\|\varphi\| \mid \varphi \in L_\mu\}$.

Notes on Part V

The modal μ-calculus L_μ as investigated here was introduced by Kozen [100] in 1983. Kozen proved that the satisfiability problem for L_μ is decidable, but his algorithm relied on a reduction to SωS and thus had non-elementary time complexity. Streett and Emerson [172] presented an automata-based decision procedure with an elementary complexity bound, and finally Emerson and Jutla [55] proved that the satisfiability problem for L_μ is complete for exponential time. In [57], Emerson, Jutla, and Sistla show that the modal μ-calculus model-checking problem is in NP $\cap$ co-NP, by a quadratic-time reduction to the emptiness problem for nondeterministic parity tree automata. In the same paper, they also show that the emptiness problem can be reduced in linear time to the modal μ-calculus model-checking problem. The intimate connection between the modal μ-calculus and (parity) tree automata was first made explicit in another paper by Emerson and Jutla [55], in 1991. As a textbook which develops the relation between μ-calculus model-checking and parity games we mention [169].

There has been quite a lot of work on improving the exact time complexity of the modal μ-calculus model checking problem. The straightforward algorithm (computing fixed points by approximation) gives rise to an algorithm polynomial in the number of states and length of the given formula and exponential in the "syntactic" alternation depth of the formula. The first improvement to this is due to Emerson and Lei [58], where also the right notion of alternation between least and greatest fixed points was introduced. Further improvements were obtained by Long, Brown, Clarke, Jha, and Marrero [116]; roughly, the exponent in the bound of the time complexity for their algorithm is half the alternation depth. An even better and simpler algorithm is due to Seidl [161], which, in its time complexity, is very similar to Jurdziński's algorithm [93] presented in Chapter 7.

The strictness of the modal μ-calculus alternation hierarchy was first independently proved by Bradfield [13, 14] and Lenzi [112]. Both proofs, the one by Bradfield, which made use of the arithmetic μ-calculus, and the one by Lenzi, which made use of topological arguments, are quite complicated. Subsequently, simpler proofs were presented. Bradfield himself published a follow-up in 1998 [15] and Arnold [5] gave the proof presented in this book. The fundamental insight on which Arnold's proof is based is due to Niwiński; he proved that the alternation hierarchy of modal μ-calculus corresponds exactly to the natural hierarchy on alternating parity tree automata. Arnold also used his method to prove the strictness of the weak alternation hierarchy, an alternation hierarchy exhausting the so-called alternation-free fragment of modal μ-calculus.

Now that we know that the alternation hierarchy is strict another question comes up: Can one, for a given modal μ-calculus formula, determine the smallest number of alternations that are needed to express it? This question has only been answered unsatisfactorily. Otto [140] proved that one can decide whether a property can be defined without using fixed-points, and Küsters and Wilke [108] show that definability with least fixed points only (or, symmetrically, greatest fixed points only) is decidable. That is, to date only Σ_0, Π_0, Σ_1, and Π_1 are decidable. See also [199].

In his paper [100] from 1983, Kozen already gave an axiomatization for the modal μ-calculus. Its completeness was open for quite a while. As a first step in the direction of a completeness proof, Walukiewicz proved completeness of a related axiomatization [193, 194] in 1993. Then, in 1995, he succeeded in proving the completeness of Kozen's original axiomatization [195, 197].

Modal μ-calculus is only one among many logics that are used to specify properties of programs or specification logics. Many of these logics have been dealt with in a similar fashion, using automata theory. For instance, PDLΔ and CTL* are dealt with in [54] and the alternation-free fragment of μ-calculus is dealt with in [10]. A very early paper is by Emerson and Lei [58]. For a survery, see [53]. See also [16] for a survey on modal logics and modal μ-calculus.

Natural extensions of modal logics are guarded logics. In particular, the modal μ-calculus can be generalized to guarded fixed points logics for expressing properties of arbitrary relational structures rather than just transition systems. Guarded logics will be treated in Chapters 18 and 19.

Note that the open problem from Part III, to determine the exact complexity of solving parity games, is equivalent to most important open problem related to the modal μ-calculus, namely to determine the model checking complexity of L_μ.

Part VI

Monadic Second-Order Logic

The first motivation for the study of automata over infinite strings and trees (around 1960) was to solve the decision problem for two basic mathematical theories, called S1S and S2S. S1S is the set of true sentences about the natural numbers with the successor function "+1", in which quantifiers over numbers and over sets of numbers are allowed. S2S is defined similarly, but referring to the branching structure of the infinite binary tree (with two successor functions).

Both systems are explained in detail in the first chapter, and (using results of previous chapters) are shown to be equivalent in expressive power to Büchi automata and Rabin's tree automata, respectively. As a first consequence, many theories can be shown to be decidable, starting with S1S and S2S. This is explained in detail for some important examples (monadic theory of countable orderings, Presburger arithmetic, modal μ-calculus). In the second chapter, the translation of monadic second-order formulas to finite automata is analyzed in detail. It is shown that the complexity of this translation cannot be bounded by any fixed iteration of the exponential function. Many results on high worst-case complexity of logical theories (or model-checking problems) rely on this fundamental theorem of Meyer and Stockmeyer (1970). A self-contained treatment was so far accessible only via Stockmeyer's PhD thesis. The last chapter provides an important bridge between monadic second-order logic and the modal μ-calculus, by a proof of the Theorem of Janin and Walukiewicz (1996): A monadic second-order property is expressible in the μ-calculus iff it is bisimulation-invariant.

12 Decidability of S1S and S2S

Mark Weyer

Institut für Mathematische Logik
Universität Freiburg

Overview

The purpose of this chapter is to prove the decidability of monadic second-order logic over infinite words and infinite binary trees, denoted S1S and S2S. It is organized as follows.

Section 12.1 tries to motivate the topic by showing its position relative to decidability questions of other logics. It may be regarded as an introduction, but it is not required for understanding the subsequent sections. In the Section 12.2 we define the logics and prove some expressibility lemmata, which will be needed later, and which familiarize the reader with the logics. In Section 12.3 we characterize the logics by means of automata. The decidability proofs are carried out in Section 12.4 based on material from earlier chapters. This section also contains a variety of corollaries concerning the decidability of other logics. In Section 12.5 we investigate special model properties of these logics, exploiting the structure of the decidability proofs.

We assume that the reader is familiar with the basic concepts of mathematical logic, as can be obtained by reading the central parts of [48].

12.1 Looking for Decidability

Inspired by an idea of Lullus, Leibniz hoped to develop a calculus for the decision of truth in the most general sense, allowing to settle even philosophical questions by computation (his terminology was different, though). Many discoveries of the 1930's (e.g., Gödel's Incompleteness Theorem [66]) implied that such a calculus can not exist. However, this left open the undecidablility of truth in special subtopics of mathematics. Charting the boundary between decidability and undecidability remained and still remains an important question in many areas. For instance, the undecidability result [121] for Hilbert's Tenth Problem [81] was not proved until 1970.

Proofs of undecidability of a logical formalism often work by encoding some computationally complete calculus in the logic (which implies that the logic itself is a computationally complete calculus). Suppose we choose Turing Machines. A run of a Turing Machine can be described by a coloured two-dimensional grid, where the configuration extends to the right and time extends downwards. Therefore, whenever a logic is expressive enough to encode infinite or arbitrarily large finite (coloured) grids, it is undecidable.

E. Grädel et al. (Eds.): Automata, Logics, and Infinite Games, LNCS 2500, pp. 207-230, 2002.

This applies to general first-order logic and first-order logic over finite structures because the vocabulary may be chosen to allow such an encoding rather directly. In fact, a single binary relation suffices. On the other hand, if the class of structures that the logic reasons about limits the interpretation of these relations, decidability may become possible again. An important example is Presburger arithmetic, i.e., the first-order theory of the structure $(\omega, +)$, which has been proved to be decidable in 1929 [146]. What about second-order logic? It is undecidable even over very limited classes of structures, because unrestricted binary relations can be created by second-order quantification. This even holds for universal and weak second-order logic. Hence logics with the expressiveness of first-order logic or above can only be decidable in cases where second-order quantification over binary relations is prohibited and no freely interpretable binary relations occur in the vocabulary. This leads to the investigation of monadic second-order logic.

Let us gather some results.

(1) The first-order theory of arithmetic $(\omega, +, \cdot)$ is undecidable, which is basically due to Gödel.

(2) The first-order theory of the field of reals $(\mathbb{R}, +, \cdot)$ is decidable, a result due to Tarski [174].

(3) The monadic second-order theory of $(\mathbb{R}, +, \cdot)$ is undecidable, because the set $\omega \subsetneq \mathbb{R}$ is definable and hence arithmetic may be embedded.

(4) The first-order theory of $(\omega, +)$ is decidable, as mentioned above.

(5) The monadic second-order theory of $(\omega, +)$ is undecidable: An $n \times k$ grid may be encoded by an appropriate subset of ω, using $+1$ and $+2k$ to move left and down.

This background leads us to monadic second-order logic over structures that are weaker than $(\omega, +)$. An obvious choice is (ω, S_0), where S_0 is the successor relation. We will show that the monadic second-order theory of this structure, often called S1S, is decidable. We instead use the name S1S for monadic second-order logic over ω-words. Decidability issues of both approaches are equivalent, because ω-words may be regarded as colourings of the structure (ω, S_0) and monadic second-order logic is able to reason about colourings.

The structure (ω, S_0) is free of rank one among the structures with one unary function. An obvious generalization is to admit more than one unary function. The structure that is free of rank one then is an infinite tree with fixed branching. We show decidability in that case as well.[1] Much of the research that is covered in other chapters has been initiated by the decidability question of S1S and such generalizations.

In Section 18.5 an extension of monadic second-order logic, called guarded second-order logic, will be introduced. Guarded second-order logic over usual

---

[1] The curious reader might ask about further generalizations. The monadic and weak monadic second-order theories of infinite free structures are decidable if, and only if, no higher arity than 1 occurs among the functions. The first-order theories of arbitrary free structures are decidable. However, that is not among the topics of this book.

structures is equivalent to monadic second-order logic over incidence structures. In the context of guarded second-order logic the connection between grids and decidability is even closer. By a theorem of Robertson and Seymour [155], a class of graphs contains arbitrarily large grids *as graph minors* if, and only if, it has unbounded tree-width (cf. Definition 18.14). The notion of graph minors is inexpressible in monadic second-order logic, but expressible in guarded second-order logic, which leads to the following result.

Theorem 12.1 (Seese [160]). *Guarded second-order logic over a class of graphs is undecidable if the class has unbounded tree-width.*

For monadic second-order logic, this is not true. The class of all cliques has unbounded tree-width but its monadic second-order theory is decidable. The converse of the theorem does not hold either. Undecidability of logics may have other origins, such as undecidability of pertainment to the class. But there are partial converses, such as the following.

Theorem 12.2. *For every natural number k, guarded second-order logic over the class of all structures that have tree-width at most k is decidable.*

This theorem is subsumed by Theorem 18.28, which is proved in Chapter 18.

12.2   MSO, S1S, and S2S

Monadic second-order logic (MSO for short) allows quantification over individuals and sets of individuals. Consider, for example, the formula

$$\forall P \left(\forall x \forall y \left((Px \wedge Exy) \rightarrow Py \right) \rightarrow \forall x \forall y \left(Px \leftrightarrow Py \right) \right).$$

Suppose that E is the edge relation of an undirected graph. Then the subformula

$$\forall x \forall y \left((Px \wedge Exy) \rightarrow Py \right)$$

states that the set P (which is a subset of the set of vertices) is closed under E. Hence it is the union of some of the graph's connected components. The subformula

$$\forall x \forall y \left(Px \leftrightarrow Py \right)$$

states that P does not separate any of the graph's vertices. So, the whole formula specifies that no union of connected components separates any vertices. This is equivalent to connectivity of the graph.

In this example two different versions of quantification were used: (first-order) quantification over vertices by $\forall x \dots$ and $\forall y \dots$ and (second-order) quantification over sets of vertices by $\forall P \dots$. We may equivalently replace quantification over individuals by quantification over sets containing exactly one individual (singleton sets). This leads us to a normal form of monadic second-order logic, which we use as a definition.

A **vocabulary** is a set of relational symbols, each of which has a specified arity. A symbol $R \in \sigma$ is called **monadic** if its arity is one, i.e., if it is used to denote sets.

Definition 12.3. The formulae of **monadic second-order logic** of vocabulary σ, denoted MSO $[\sigma]$, are defined simultaneously for all vocabularies σ by induction.

(1) If $R, S \in \sigma$ are monadic, then $R \subseteq S$ is in MSO $[\sigma]$.
(2) If $R_1, \ldots, R_k \in \sigma$ are monadic and $S \in \sigma$ has arity k, then $SR_1 \ldots R_k$ is in MSO $[\sigma]$.
(3) If φ and ψ are in MSO $[\sigma]$, then so are $\neg\varphi$, $\varphi \vee \psi$ and $\varphi \wedge \psi$.
(4) If φ is in MSO $[\sigma \uplus \{R\}]$ and R is monadic, then $\exists R\varphi$ and $\forall R\varphi$ are in MSO $[\sigma]$. Note that in this case the parameter σ changes.

The satisfaction relation $\models$ is defined for all vocabularies σ, all σ-structures $\mathfrak{A}$ and all $\varphi \in$ MSO $[\sigma]$ along the same induction.

(1) $\mathfrak{A} \models R \subseteq S$ iff $R^{\mathfrak{A}} \subseteq S^{\mathfrak{A}}$.
(2) $\mathfrak{A} \models SR_1 \ldots R_k$ iff $S^{\mathfrak{A}} \cap \left(R_1^{\mathfrak{A}} \times \cdots \times R_k^{\mathfrak{A}}\right) \neq \emptyset$ or in other words iff there are individuals $a_1 \in R_1^{\mathfrak{A}}, \ldots, a_k \in R_k^{\mathfrak{A}}$ such that $(a_1, \ldots, a_k) \in S^{\mathfrak{A}}$.
(3) $\mathfrak{A} \models \neg\varphi$ iff not $\mathfrak{A} \models \varphi$.
   $\mathfrak{A} \models \varphi \vee \psi$ iff at least one of $\mathfrak{A} \models \varphi$ and $\mathfrak{A} \models \psi$.
   $\mathfrak{A} \models \varphi \wedge \psi$ iff both $\mathfrak{A} \models \varphi$ and $\mathfrak{A} \models \psi$.
(4) $\mathfrak{A} \models \exists R\varphi$ iff $\mathfrak{B} \models \varphi$ for at least one $\sigma \uplus \{R\}$-expansion $\mathfrak{B}$ of $\mathfrak{A}$.
   $\mathfrak{A} \models \forall R\varphi$ iff $\mathfrak{B} \models \varphi$ for all $\sigma \uplus \{R\}$-expansions $\mathfrak{B}$ of $\mathfrak{A}$.

Definition 12.4. Weak monadic second-order logic (WMSO) has the same syntax as MSO, but quantification is restricted to finite sets. Hence, the satisfaction relation $\models_W$ is defined in the same way as $\models$, with the following exception:

(4) $\mathfrak{A} \models_W \exists R\varphi$ iff $\mathfrak{B} \models_W \varphi$ for at least one $\sigma \uplus \{R\}$-expansion $\mathfrak{B}$ of $\mathfrak{A}$ such that $R^{\mathfrak{B}}$ is finite.
   $\mathfrak{A} \models_W \forall R\varphi$ iff $\mathfrak{B} \models_W \varphi$ for all $\sigma \uplus \{R\}$-expansions $\mathfrak{B}$ of $\mathfrak{A}$ such that $R^{\mathfrak{B}}$ is finite.

Definition 12.5. We use the following shorthand notations for (W)MSO-formulae, where $I = \{i_1, \ldots, i_n\}$ is a finite set, x, P, and Q are arbitrary monadic relation symbols, and φ, ψ, $\varphi_{i_1}, \ldots, \varphi_{i_n}$ are arbitrary (W)MSO-formulae.

$$
\begin{array}{lll}
X = \emptyset & \text{for} & \forall Y\, X \subseteq Y \\
\mathrm{sing}\,(x) & \text{for} & \neg x = \emptyset \wedge \forall X\, (X \subseteq x \rightarrow (x \subseteq X \vee X = \emptyset)) \\
x \in P & \text{for} & \mathrm{sing}\,(x) \wedge x \subseteq P \\
P = Q & \text{for} & P \subseteq Q \wedge Q \subseteq P \\
\varphi \rightarrow \psi & \text{for} & \neg\varphi \vee \psi \\
\bigwedge_{i \in I} \varphi_i & \text{for} & \varphi_{i_1} \wedge \cdots \wedge \varphi_{i_n} \\
\bigvee_{i \in I} \varphi_i & \text{for} & \varphi_{i_1} \vee \cdots \vee \varphi_{i_n} \\
\exists x \in P\, \varphi & \text{for} & \exists x\, (x \in P \wedge \varphi) \\
\forall x \in P\, \varphi & \text{for} & \forall x\, (x \in P \rightarrow \varphi)
\end{array}
$$

Note that $\mathfrak{A} \models \mathrm{sing}\,(P)$ iff $P^{\mathfrak{A}}$ is a singleton set, i.e., contains exactly one element. Moreover, we use set theoretical operations that are clearly (W)MSO-definable such as $P \cup Q$, $P \cap Q$, $P \setminus Q$, and $P \uplus Q$.

Note. As above we use lowercase variable names $x, y, z, x_0, \ldots$ to denote monadic relation symbols that should be thought of as containing singletons.

ω-words and infinite binary trees as structures. Appropriate structures can be used to represent ω-words and infinite binary trees. Since the representation is not canonic, we have to explicate it. For this purpose let Σ be an alphabet.

Definition 12.6. Let $\mathfrak{W} = (W, S_0^{\mathfrak{W}}, (P_a^{\mathfrak{W}})_{a \in \Sigma})$ be a structure with vocabulary $\sigma = \{S_0\} \cup \{P_a \mid a \in \Sigma\}$. $\mathfrak{W}$ is called an **ω-word** with alphabet Σ, if

(1) S_0 is binary and all P_a are monadic,
(2) $W = \omega$ is the set of word positions,
(3) $S_0^{\mathfrak{W}} = \{(n, n+1) \mid n \in \omega\}$ is the successor relation, and
(4) the $P_a^{\mathfrak{W}}$ form a partition of W.

Let $\mathfrak{T} = (T, S_0^{\mathfrak{T}}, S_1^{\mathfrak{T}}, (P_a^{\mathfrak{T}})_{a \in \Sigma})$ be a structure with vocabulary $\sigma = \{S_0, S_1\} \cup \{P_a \mid a \in \Sigma\}$. $\mathfrak{T}$ is called an **infinite binary tree** with alphabet Σ, if

(1) S_0 and S_1 are binary while all P_a are monadic,
(2) $T = \{0, 1\}^*$ is the set of tree positions,
(3) $S_0^{\mathfrak{T}} = \{(w, w0) \mid w \in T\}$ and $S_1^{\mathfrak{T}} = \{(w, w1) \mid w \in T\}$ are the two successor relations, and
(4) the $P_a^{\mathfrak{T}}$ form a partition of T.

Vocabularies that satisfy Condition (1) are called **word vocabularies** or **tree vocabularies**, respectively. If Condition (1) to Condition (3) are satisfied, $\mathfrak{W}$ is called an **extended ω-word** and $\mathfrak{T}$ is called an **extended infinite binary tree**.

Note. We could push the analogy between ω-words and infinite binary trees one step further by identifying natural numbers $n \in \omega$ with words $0^n \in \{0\}^*$.

Definition 12.7. We define the following logics.

(1) S1S is the logic MSO over ω-words, i.e., the satisfaction relation $\models$ is restricted on the left-hand side to structures that are ω-words.
(2) WS1S is WMSO over ω-words.
(3) S2S is MSO over infinite binary trees.
(4) WS2S is WMSO over infinite binary trees.

For a more precise treatment of what a logic is, cf. Definition 12.28 and the subsequent remark and examples.

Definition 12.8. Define the orderings $<$ and $\prec$ of word or tree positions by:

$$\leq := \{(n, n+m) \mid n, m \in \omega\}$$
$$\preceq := \{(w, wv) \mid w, v \in \{0,1\}^*\}$$
$$< := \{(n, m) \in \leq \mid n \neq m\}$$
$$\prec := \{(w, v) \in \preceq \mid w \neq v\}$$

Thus $<$ is the transitive closure of the successor relation of ω-words. It intuitively specifies whether or not a position is closer to the initial position than another. Similarly, $\prec$ is the transitive closure of the union of both successor relations. It, in turn, specifies whether or not a position is closer to the root than another.

Exercise 12.1. Express in S1S that every occurrence of a is eventually followed by an occurrence of b. More precisely: find an S1S-formula φ such that for ω-words $\mathfrak{W}$ we have $\mathfrak{W} \models \varphi$ iff $\mathfrak{W}$ has the mentioned property. You may use the predicates $<$ and $\leq$ (due to Lemma 12.11).

Lemma 12.9 (Being initially closed is (W)S1S-expressible). *There is a formula* $\mathsf{Incl}_1(P) \in$ MSO *such that for all extended ω-words $\mathfrak{W}$ the following are equivalent.*

(1) $\mathfrak{W} \models \mathsf{Incl}_1(P)$,
(2) $\mathfrak{W} \models_w \mathsf{Incl}_1(P)$,
(3) $y \in P^{\mathfrak{W}}$ *implies* $x \in P^{\mathfrak{W}}$ *for all word positions* $x \leq y$.

Proof. Choose, for example,

$$\mathsf{Incl}_1(P) = \forall x \forall y \left(\left(\mathsf{sing}(x) \wedge S_0 xy \wedge y \in P \right) \rightarrow x \in P \right).$$

$\square$

Lemma 12.10. *Being initially closed is* (W)S2S-*expressible*

Proof. This time, choose

$$\mathsf{Incl}_2(P) = \forall x \forall y \left(\left(\mathsf{sing}(x) \wedge (S_0 xy \vee S_1 xy) \wedge y \in P \right) \rightarrow x \in P \right).$$

$\square$

Lemma 12.11. *The relations* $\leq$ *and* $<$ *are* (W)S1S-*expressible, the relations* $\preceq$ *and* $\prec$ *are* (W)S2S-*expressible.*

Proof. Observe that $a \leq b$ iff a is contained in all initially closed sets that contain b iff a is contained in all initially closed *finite* sets that contain b. The same holds for $a \preceq b$. Therefore we set

$$\begin{aligned} x \leq y &:= \mathsf{sing}(y) \wedge \forall P \left(\left(\mathsf{Incl}_1(P) \wedge y \in P \right) \rightarrow x \in P \right), \\ x \preceq y &:= \mathsf{sing}(y) \wedge \forall P \left(\left(\mathsf{Incl}_2(P) \wedge y \in P \right) \rightarrow x \in P \right), \\ x < y &:= x \leq y \wedge \neg x = y, \\ x \prec y &:= x \preceq y \wedge \neg x = y. \end{aligned}$$

$\square$

Lemma 12.12 (Lexicographic ordering is (W)S2S-expressible). *There is a formula* $\mathsf{Lex}(x, y)$ *such that for all extended infinite binary trees* $\mathfrak{T}$ *where* $x^{\mathfrak{T}}$ *and* $y^{\mathfrak{T}}$ *are singletons, say* $x^{\mathfrak{T}} = \{a\}$ *and* $y^{\mathfrak{T}} = \{b\}$, *the following holds.* $\mathfrak{T} \models \mathsf{Lex}(x, y)$ *iff* a *precedes* b *in the lexicographic ordering of tree positions (viewed as words with alphabet* $\{0, 1\}$).

Proof. We start by expressing that a common prefix of x and y is followed by 0 in x and by 1 in y:

$$\varphi := \exists z \exists z_0 \exists z_1 \left(\text{sing}\,(z) \wedge S_0 z z_0 \wedge S_1 z z_1 \wedge z_0 \preceq x \wedge z_1 \preceq y \right).$$

The lexicographic ordering is the union of this relation and the prefix relation. Hence we assemble

$$\text{Lex}\,(x, y) := \varphi \vee (x \prec y).$$

$\square$

Lemma 12.13 (Infiniteness is S1S- and S2S-expressible). *There are formulae* $\text{Inf}_1\,(P) \in \text{MSO}$ *and* $\text{Inf}_2\,(P) \in \text{MSO}$ *such that for ω-words $\mathfrak{W}$ respectively infinite binary trees $\mathfrak{T}$ we have* $\mathfrak{W} \models \text{Inf}_1\,(P)$ *respectively* $\mathfrak{T} \models \text{Inf}_2\,(P)$ *iff* $P^{\mathfrak{W}}$ *respectively* $P^{\mathfrak{T}}$ *is infinite.*

There are also formulae $\text{Fin}_1\,(P) \in \text{MSO}$ *and* $\text{Fin}_2\,(P) \in \text{MSO}$ *expressing finiteness of* $P^{\mathfrak{W}}$ *respectively* $P^{\mathfrak{T}}$.

Proof. We only construct $\text{Inf}_2\,(P)$.

We claim that a set S of tree positions is infinite iff there is a non-empty set S' of tree positions such that for all $a' \in S'$ there are $b \in S, b' \in S'$ with $a' \prec b$ and $a' \prec b'$. For the 'if' part suppose that S' is given. By recursively gathering the b' it follows that S' is infinite. Since every element in S may appear only finitely often as a b for some $a' \in S'$, S has to be infinite as well. For the 'only if' part suppose that S is infinite. Then there must be one child of the root such that S, restricted to the associated subtree, is still infinite. By recursion we define a path S' such that for all $a' \in S'$ there are still infinitely many $b \in S$ with $a' \prec b$. This set S' satisfies the condition.

Now we are able to define $\text{Inf}_2\,(P)$

$$\text{Inf}_2\,(P) = \exists P' \left(P' \neq \emptyset \ \wedge \ \forall x' \in P' \exists y \in P \exists y' \in P' \left(x' \prec y \wedge x' \prec y' \right) \right).$$

$\square$

Lemma 12.14. *Being a path is S2S-expressible.*

Proof. Observe that being a path is equivalent to being minimal among the infinite initially closed sets. Therefore we set

$$\text{Path}\,(P) := \text{Inf}_2\,(P) \wedge \text{Incl}_2\,(P) \wedge \forall Q \left(\left(\text{Inf}_2\,(Q) \wedge \text{Incl}_2\,(Q) \wedge Q \subseteq P \right) \rightarrow Q = P \right).$$

$\square$

12.3   Characterization of S1S and S2S

We intend to prove the decidability of S1S and S2S. For this purpose we characterize these logics by means of automata. The characterization is the content of the Theorems of Büchi and Rabin.

Theorem 12.15 (Büchi [18]).   *Büchi word automata and* S1S *are expressively equivalent. Moreover, the equivalence is effective.*

Theorem 12.16 (Rabin [148]).   *Muller tree automata and* S2S *are expressively equivalent. Moreover, the equivalence is effective.*

These theorems might need some explanation (for a precise formulation, see the next four lemmata). Automata and formulae both define languages of ω-words (infinite binary trees) over a certain alphabet. Automata do so by recognition, formulae by the satisfaction relation. Such languages are generally thought of as *properties* of ω-words (infinite binary trees) that are *expressed* by the automata or formulae. 'Expressive equivalence' means that the same languages may be defined by the two formalisms, and 'effectiveness' means that automata and formulae can be translated effectively into each other.

Example 12.17.   Consider the language T from Example 8.3 which is recognizable by a Muller tree automaton. We can also give a formula $\varphi \in$ S2S such that

$$T = \{\, \mathfrak{T} \mid \mathfrak{T} \text{ is an infinite binary tree and } \mathfrak{T} \models \varphi \,\},$$

namely

$$\varphi = \exists P \exists A \exists B \exists I \Big(\, \mathsf{Path}\,(P) \wedge P = A \cup B \cup I \wedge \mathsf{Incl}_2\,(I) \wedge \mathsf{Fin}_2\,(I) \wedge$$
$$A \subseteq P_a \wedge B \subseteq P_b \wedge \neg S_0 AA \wedge \neg S_1 AA \wedge \neg S_0 BB \wedge \neg S_1 BB \Big)$$

(cf. Lemma 12.10, Lemma 12.13 and Lemma 12.14). Rabin's Theorem states that this is no coincidence. Whenever there is an automaton describing some property of infinite binary trees there is also a formula describing the same property and vice versa.

The proofs of Theorem 12.15 and Theorem 12.16 are split into the following four lemmata. Instead of Büchi acceptance conditions we use Muller conditions.

Lemma 12.18.   *There is an algorithm that upon input of a Muller word automaton $\mathcal{A}$ produces a formula $\varphi_{\mathcal{A}} \in$ S1S such that for all ω-words $\mathfrak{W}$ we have $\mathfrak{W} \models \varphi_{\mathcal{A}}$ iff $\mathcal{A}$ accepts $\mathfrak{W}$.*

Lemma 12.19.   *There is an algorithm that upon input of an S1S-formula φ produces a Muller word automaton $\mathcal{A}_\varphi$ such that for all ω-words $\mathfrak{W}$ we have $\mathfrak{W} \models \varphi$ iff $\mathcal{A}_\varphi$ accepts $\mathfrak{W}$.*

Lemma 12.20.   *There is an algorithm that upon input of a Muller tree automaton $\mathcal{A}$ produces a formula $\varphi_{\mathcal{A}} \in$ S2S such that for all infinite binary trees $\mathfrak{T}$ we have $\mathfrak{T} \models \varphi_{\mathcal{A}}$ iff $\mathcal{A}$ accepts $\mathfrak{T}$.*

Lemma 12.21.   *There is an algorithm that upon input of an S2S-formula φ produces a Muller tree automaton $\mathcal{A}_\varphi$ such that for all infinite binary trees $\mathfrak{T}$ we have $\mathfrak{T} \models \varphi$ iff $\mathcal{A}_\varphi$ accepts $\mathfrak{T}$.*

Due to the the obvious similarities we only prove the latter two lemmata.

Proof (of Lemma 12.20). Let $\mathcal{A} = (Q, \Sigma, q_I, \Delta, \mathcal{F})$ be the given Muller tree automaton. We construct an equivalent MSO-formula $\varphi_\mathcal{A}$.

Note that the acceptance condition 'there is a tree of states satisfying the following conditions: ... ' already is in the form of existential second-order quantification. Monadic second-order symbols $\bar{R} = (R_q)_{q \in Q}$ are used to encode the 'tree of states' of $\mathcal{A}$. What remains is to express the 'conditions'.

The overall shape of $\varphi_\mathcal{A}$ is

$$\varphi_\mathcal{A} = \exists \bar{R} \, (\mathsf{Part} \wedge \mathsf{Init} \wedge \mathsf{Trans} \wedge \mathsf{Accept}) \, .$$

A tree of states that contains state q at position x is represented by a structure $\mathfrak{T}$ iff $x \in R_q^\mathfrak{T}$ and $x \notin R_{q'}^\mathfrak{T}$ for all $q' \neq q$. This is formalized by

$$\mathsf{State}_q \, (x) := x \in R_q \wedge \bigwedge_{q' \in Q \setminus \{q\}} \neg x \in R_{q'} \, .$$

Part expresses that the R_q form a partition, i.e., that the $\bar{R}$ indeed encode a tree of states.

$$\mathsf{Part} := \forall x \left(\mathsf{sing} \, (x) \rightarrow \bigvee_{q \in Q} \mathsf{State}_q \, (x) \right) \, .$$

Init formalizes the initial condition, i.e., that the root is in state q_I.

$$\mathsf{Init} := \exists x \left(\mathsf{State}_{q_I} \, (x) \wedge \forall y \, (\mathsf{sing} \, (y) \rightarrow x \preceq y) \right)$$

(cf. Lemma 12.11). Consistency of $\bar{R}$ with the transition relation is guaranteed by Trans.

$$\mathsf{Trans} := \forall x \forall y_0 \forall y_1 \Big(\big(\mathsf{sing} \, (x) \wedge \mathsf{sing} \, (y_0) \wedge \mathsf{sing} \, (y_1) \wedge S_0 x y_0 \wedge S_1 x y_1 \big) \rightarrow$$
$$\bigvee_{(q,a,q_0,q_1) \in \Delta} \big(\mathsf{State}_q \, (x) \wedge x \in P_a \wedge \mathsf{State}_{q_0} \, (y_0) \wedge \mathsf{State}_{q_1} \, (y_1) \big) \Big) \, .$$

In order to express the acceptance condition, we have to formalize infinite occurrence of states in paths. Let P be a monadic symbol that we think of as encoding a path. Then

$$\mathsf{InfOcc}_q \, (P) := \exists Q \, \big(Q \subseteq P \wedge Q \subseteq R_q \wedge \mathsf{Inf}_2 \, (Q) \big)$$

states that the state q occurs infinitely often within the path encoded by P (cf. Lemma 12.13). Using this, we express the Muller condition $\mathcal{F}$ for the path P by

$$\mathsf{Muller} \, (P) := \bigvee_{F \in \mathcal{F}} \left(\bigwedge_{q \in F} \mathsf{InfOcc}_q \, (P) \wedge \bigwedge_{q \notin F} \neg \mathsf{InfOcc}_q \, (P) \right)$$

and global acceptance by

$$\mathsf{Accept} := \forall P \, \big(\mathsf{Path} \, (P) \rightarrow \mathsf{Muller} \, (P) \big)$$

(cf. Lemma 12.14) □

Proof (of Lemma 12.21). We proceed using induction on φ. In order to apply induction, though, the statement has to be modified such that not only infinite binary trees, but also extended infinite binary trees are permitted. First we have to express how extended binary trees may be represented by trees. It is safe, though, to skip these technical details and resume at the following claim.

Let Σ be an alphabet and Σ' be an arbitrary set, disjoint from Σ. We define $[\Sigma, \Sigma']$ to be the alphabet $\Sigma \times \mathscr{P}(\Sigma')$. $[\Sigma, \Sigma']$ is a representation of the set of choices when exactly one element is to be picked from Σ and arbitrarily many from Σ'. When applied to extended infinite binary trees, the symbols P_a for $a \in \Sigma$ have to satisfy Condition (4) of Definition 12.6 (infinite binary trees), while the symbols P_a for $a \in \Sigma'$ do not (because they are bound by a quantifier).

For $a \in \Sigma \cup \Sigma'$ we use χ_a to denote the subset of $[\Sigma, \Sigma']$ which is formed by those encodings that express the choice of a.

$$\chi_a = \begin{cases} \{\, (a', S) \in [\Sigma, \Sigma'] \mid a = a' \,\} & \text{, if } a \in \Sigma, \\ \{\, (a', S) \in [\Sigma, \Sigma'] \mid a \in S \,\} & \text{, if } a \in \Sigma'. \end{cases}$$

Now, let σ be a tree vocabulary for the alphabet $\Sigma \cup \Sigma'$. An infinite binary tree $\mathfrak{T}$ with alphabet $[\Sigma, \Sigma']$ encodes a σ-structure $\tilde{\mathfrak{T}}$ being an extended infinite binary tree as follows.

$$P_a^{\tilde{\mathfrak{T}}} = \bigcup_{a' \in \chi_a} P_{a'}^{\mathfrak{T}}.$$

Obviously $\tilde{\mathfrak{T}}$ and $\mathfrak{T}$ are isomorphic if $\Sigma' = \emptyset$. Therefore Lemma 12.21 is subsumed by the following claim for $\Sigma' = \emptyset$.

Claim. There is an algorithm that upon input of Σ, Σ', and φ (which is an S2S-formula of appropriate vocabulary) produces a Muller tree automaton $\mathcal{A}_\varphi$ with alphabet $[\Sigma, \Sigma']$ such that for all infinite binary trees $\mathfrak{T}$ we have $\tilde{\mathfrak{T}} \models \varphi$ iff $\mathcal{A}_\varphi$ accepts $\mathfrak{T}$.

We proceed using induction on φ, simultaneously for all Σ'.

(1) To begin with, consider the formula $\varphi = P_a \subseteq P_b$. We have $\tilde{\mathfrak{T}} \models \varphi$ iff at every position x the following local condition holds: if a occurs at position x then so does b.

To illustrate what that means, suppose that $\Sigma = \{a, c\}$ and $\Sigma' = \{b, d\}$. The labels of $\mathfrak{T}$ that belong to a (i.e., the elements of χ_a) are

$$(a, \emptyset) \quad (a, \{b\}) \quad (a, \{d\}) \quad (a, \{b, d\})$$

and the labels that belong to b are

$$(a, \{b\}) \quad (a, \{b, d\}) \quad (c, \{b\}) \quad (c, \{b, d\})$$

Therefore the automaton $\mathcal{A}_\varphi$ verifies that the labels

$$(a, \emptyset) \quad (a, \{d\})$$

do not occur in $\mathfrak{T}$.

In general we set $\mathcal{A}_\varphi = (\{q\}, q, \Delta, \{\{q\}\})$, where

$$\Delta = \{ (q, a', q, q) \mid a' \notin \chi_a \setminus \chi_b \}.$$

(2) The construction of automata for the remaining base cases is left to the reader.

(3;4a) For formulae of the form $\neg\varphi$, $\varphi \vee \psi$, $\varphi \wedge \psi$, and $\exists P_a \varphi$, the induction step coincides with closedness of the class of Muller-recognizable tree languages under complementation, union, intersection and projection (cf. Chapter 8).

(4b) For the remaining case suppose that $\varphi = \forall P_a \psi$. Note that φ is equivalent to $\neg\exists P_a \neg\psi$, so we may set $\mathcal{A}_\varphi = \mathcal{A}_{\neg\exists P_a \neg\psi}$.

$\square$

Remark 12.22. A straightforward analysis of the size of the constructed automata reveals that the only expensive step is negation. By use of an appropriate normal form for formulae we may eliminate negation up to quantifier alternation. Then the automaton $\mathcal{A}_\varphi$ has at most

$$\left. 2^{2^{\cdot^{\cdot^{\cdot^{O(n)}}}}} \right\} q+1$$

states, where n is the length of φ and q is the number of quantifier changes in φ. In Chapter 13 it is proved that this is optimal.

Exercise 12.2. By combining the algorithms from the two proofs we obtain an algorithm that calculates a normal form for S2S. What is that normal form and what is its analogon for S1S?

At this point the reader is invited to a short digression that characterizes the cases of WMSO as well as the cases of finite words and finite trees.

Lemma 12.23. *Any language that is definable in* WS1S *(*WS2S*) is also definable in* S1S *(*S2S*).*

Proof. Suppose $n \in \{1,2\}$, $\varphi \in \text{WS}n\text{S}$, and φ defines the language L. Now replace every subformula of φ of the form $\exists R\psi$ or $\forall R\psi$ by $\exists R\,(\text{Fin}_n\,(R) \wedge \psi)$ or $\forall R\,(\text{Fin}_n\,(R) \rightarrow \psi)$ respectively, where $\text{Fin}_n\,(R)$ stems from Lemma 12.13. Let φ' be the resulting formula.

Clearly we have $\mathfrak{A} \models \varphi'$ iff $\mathfrak{A} \models_w \varphi$ for ω-words (or infinite binary trees) $\mathfrak{A}$.

$\square$

For WS1S and S1S, the converse is also true.

Theorem 12.24 (Büchi [18]). *For ω-languages L the following are effectively equivalent.*

(1) L *is Büchi-recognizable.*
(2) L *is* WS1S*-definable.*
(3) L *is* S1S*-definable.*

Proof. We add two more statements.

(4) L is Muller-recognizable.
(5) L is deterministic-Muller-recognizable.

Lemma 12.23 proves that (2) implies (3). Lemma 12.19 proves that (3) implies (4). Chapter 1 shows the effective equivalence of (1), (4), and (5). It remains to show that (5) implies (2). This parallels the proof of Lemma 12.20. Now, however, the automaton $\mathcal{A}$ is deterministic.

Due to the impossibility of representing a complete run using only finite sets, we restrict all investigations to initial segments of runs. Their domain is associated with the monadic symbol I. As in the proof of Lemma 12.20 we use a tuple $\bar{R} = (R_q)_{q \in Q}$ of monadic symbols to encode trees of states. This time the formulae are defined as

$$\mathsf{State}_q(x) := x \in R_q \wedge \bigwedge_{q' \in Q \setminus \{q\}} \neg x \in R_{q'},$$

$$\mathsf{Part} := \forall x \in I \bigvee_{q \in Q} \mathsf{State}_q(x),$$

$$\mathsf{Init} := \exists x \left(\mathsf{State}_{q_{\mathrm{I}}}(x) \wedge \forall y \left(\mathsf{sing}(y) \to x \le y \right) \right)$$

(cf. Lemma 12.11),

$$\mathsf{Trans} := \forall x \in I \forall y \in I \left(S_0 x y \to \bigvee_{(q,a,q') \in \Delta} \left(\mathsf{State}_q(x) \wedge x \in P_a \wedge \mathsf{State}_{q'}(y) \right) \right).$$

The fact that the one and only run is in state q at position x is expressed by the formula $\mathsf{Occ}_q(x)$.

$$\mathsf{Occ}_q(x) := \exists I \left(\mathsf{Incl}_1(I) \wedge x \in I \wedge \exists \bar{R} \left(\mathsf{Part} \wedge \mathsf{Init} \wedge \mathsf{Trans} \wedge \mathsf{State}_q(x) \right) \right)$$

(cf. Lemma 12.9). Now we may finish with

$$\mathsf{InfOcc}_q := \forall x \left(\mathsf{sing}(x) \to \exists y \left(x < y \wedge \mathsf{Occ}_q(y) \right) \right),$$

$$\mathsf{Accept} := \bigvee_{F \in \mathcal{F}} \left(\bigwedge_{q \in F} \mathsf{InfOcc}_q \wedge \bigwedge_{q \notin F} \neg \mathsf{InfOcc}_q \right),$$

because for ω-words $\mathfrak{W}$ we have $\mathfrak{W} \models \mathsf{Accept}$ iff $\mathcal{A}$ recognizes $\mathfrak{W}$.   □

This result raises the question whether or not WS2S = S2S. However, this is not the case. It is crucial for the proof just presented that the word automaton is deterministic. For tree automata this is not always possible: the automaton $\mathcal{A}_{\mathsf{sing}(P_a)}$ may serve as a counterexample. In fact WS2S is strictly weaker than S2S. We mention the following result without proof.

Theorem 12.25 (Rabin [149]).   *For languages L of infinite binary trees the following are equivalent.*

(1) *Both L and its complement are Büchi-recognizable.*
(2) *L is WS2S-definable.*

Using this theorem, it can easily be verified that the inclusion WS2S ⊆ S2S is strict. The language defined by 'there is a path containing infinitely many b', is Büchi-recognizable but its complement is not, cf. Chapter 8. Hence this language is S2S-expressible but not WS2S-expressible.

These examinations are also relevant in the finite case, where we have to replace the concept of

ω-word	by finite word
infinite binary tree	by finite binary tree
Muller word automaton	by finite automaton
Muller tree automaton	by bottom-up tree automaton

and obtain the following theorems.

Theorem 12.26 (Büchi [17], Elgot [51] and Trakhtenbrot [186]).   *For languages L of finite words the following are effectively equivalent.*

(1) *L is recognizable by a finite automaton.*
(2) *L is (W)MSO-definable within the class of finite words.*

Theorem 12.27 (Thatcher and Wright [176], Doner [45]).   *For languages L of finite binary trees the following are effectively equivalent.*

(1) *L is recognizable by a bottom-up tree automaton.*
(2) *L is (W)MSO-definable within the class of finite binary trees.*

The only part that needs further explanation is the notion of bottom-up tree automata. It differs from Muller tree automata in the following ways.

(1) The initial condition is situated at the frontier:
Whenever a child of a node is missing, the automaton acts as if the missing child was labelled with the state q_I.
(2) The acceptance condition $F \subseteq Q$ is situated at the root:
A run is called accepting if the state at the root is contained in F.
(3) The automaton may be imagined as visiting the leaves of the input tree first and making its way towards the root by merging information of siblings into their parent.
Due to this behaviour, the automaton is called 'bottom-up'.

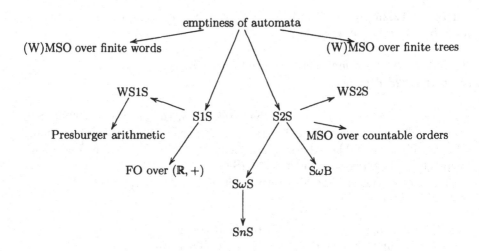

Fig. 12.1. A map through the decidability statements of Section 12.4

12.4 Decidability

An overview over the present section is given by Figure 12.1 that charts the decidability results ahead.

Definition 12.28. A **logic** is a triple $(\mathcal{C}, \models, \mathcal{L})$, where

(1) $\mathcal{C} = (\mathcal{C}[\sigma])_\sigma$ is a family of classes of structures indexed by vocabularies.
(2) $\mathcal{L} = (\mathcal{L}[\sigma])_\sigma$ is a family indexed by vocabularies, the language of the logic,
(3) $\models = (\models_\sigma)_\sigma$ is a family of binary relations indexed by vocabularies, the satisfaction relation of the logic.
(4) For all vocabularies σ it holds that $\models_\sigma \subseteq (\mathcal{C}[\sigma] \times \mathcal{L}[\sigma])$.

Remark 12.29. Despite the indexing, we will usually regard $\mathcal{C}$ and $\mathcal{L}$ as single classes and $\models$ as a single relation. Furthermore we will assume the union $\bigcup_\sigma \mathcal{L}[\sigma]$ to be disjoint and the index vocabulary to be computable from the formula. This can be achieved by replacing each $\varphi \in \mathcal{L}[\sigma]$ by (σ, φ).

Example 12.30. In the case of WS1S, $\mathcal{C}$ is the class of ω-words, $\models$ is $\models_W$, and $\mathcal{L}$ is the syntax of MSO for word vocabularies. (For other vocabularies $\mathcal{C}[\sigma]$, $\mathcal{L}[\sigma]$ and $\models_\sigma$ are empty.)

Example 12.31. In the case of modal μ-calculus, $\mathcal{C}$ is the class of pointed transition systems $(\mathcal{S}, s)$, $\models$ is as in Definition 10.5, and $\mathcal{L}$ is the set L_μ.

Definition 12.32. A logic $(\mathcal{C}, \models, \mathcal{L})$ is called **decidable** if there is an algorithm that decides upon input of a formula $\varphi \in \mathcal{L}[\sigma]$ whether or not φ is a tautology, i.e., whether or not $\mathfrak{A} \models \varphi$ for all structures $\mathfrak{A} \in \mathcal{C}[\sigma]$.

Note. Section 12.1 mentions that S1S and S2S sometimes are considered as theories rather than logics. Theories of structures may be regarded as the special cases of logics in which the class $\mathcal{C}$ contains only one structure. Then, decidability of tautology becomes decidability of truth in (or satisfaction by) that structure.

Theorem 12.33. (1) (W)MSO *over finite words is decidable [17, 51].*
(2) WS1S *is decidable [18].*
(3) S1S *is decidable [18].*
(4) (W)MSO *over finite binary trees is decidable [176, 45].*
(5) WS2S *is decidable [148].*
(6) S2S *is decidable [148].*

Proof. Part (2) and Part (5) are proved after Lemma 12.36 as an application of Lemma 12.23. For the other parts, suppose a formula φ is given. By one of Theorem 12.26, Theorem 12.15, Theorem 12.27 or Theorem 12.16 we may effectively construct an automaton $\mathcal{A}$ such that $\mathcal{A}$ accepts $\mathfrak{A}$ iff $\mathfrak{A} \models \neg\varphi$. The question whether or not $\mathfrak{A} \models \varphi$ always holds can be reduced to the question whether or not the language of $\mathcal{A}$ is empty. But emptiness of all these languages is decidable.

How do we decide emptiness of these automata?

For (1) and (4), there are simple algorithms for determining the reachable states. It suffices to check whether or not some final state is reachable.

For (6), emptiness of the automata is covered in Chapter 8. Let us recall this in more detail. In Section 8.3 it is indicated that a Muller tree automaton can be transformed into a parity tree automaton. In the proof of Theorem 8.19 it is shown how the emptiness question of this automaton can be rewritten into the winning question of some finite parity game. Decision of the latter is covered in Chapter 6 and Chapter 7.

For (3), we may proceed completely analogously. Some parts have already been established in other chapters: The transformation of the automata is indicated in Chapter 1. The decision of the winning question is the same as for (6) and is covered in Chapter 6 and Chapter 7.   □

These decidability results may be further exploited by reducing decidability questions of other logics to them.

Definition 12.34. Let $(\mathcal{C}_1, \models_1, \mathcal{L}_1)$ and $(\mathcal{C}_2, \models_2, \mathcal{L}_2)$ be logics. An **effective translation** from $(\mathcal{C}_1, \models_1, \mathcal{L}_1)$ to $(\mathcal{C}_2, \models_2, \mathcal{L}_2)$ is a tuple (v, R, f), where

(1) v is a mapping from vocabularies to vocabularies,
(2) $R = (R_\sigma)_\sigma$ is a family of relations $R_\sigma \subseteq \mathcal{C}_1[\sigma] \times \mathcal{C}_2[v(\sigma)]$ that are onto on both sides,
(3) $f = (f_\sigma)_\sigma$ is a family of mappings $f_\sigma : \mathcal{L}_1[\sigma] \to \mathcal{L}_2[v(\sigma)]$,
(4) the two-argument mapping $(\sigma, \varphi) \mapsto f_\sigma(\varphi)$ is effective and
(5) for all vocabularies σ, all formulae $\varphi \in \mathcal{L}_1[\sigma]$ and all structures $\mathfrak{A}_1 \in \mathcal{C}_1[\sigma]$, $\mathfrak{A}_2 \in \mathcal{C}_2[v(\sigma)]$ such that $(\mathfrak{A}_1, \mathfrak{A}_2) \in R_\sigma$ we have $\mathfrak{A}_1 \models_1 \varphi$ iff $\mathfrak{A}_2 \models_2 f_\sigma(\varphi)$.

Remark 12.35. As above for logics, we will usually neglect the indexing by vocabularies. We will regard R as a single relation and f as a single mapping. Furthermore the mapping v can be constructed from f and is omitted from the notation.

Lemma 12.36. *If $\mathcal{L}_2$ is decidable and if there is an effective translation (v, R, f) from $\mathcal{L}_1$ to $\mathcal{L}_2$, then $\mathcal{L}_1$ is decidable.*

Proof. As a decision procedure for $\mathcal{L}_1$, given a formula $\varphi \in \mathcal{L}_1[\sigma]$, apply the decision procedure for $\mathcal{L}_2$ to $f_\sigma(\varphi)$.

For the correctness of this decision procedure, recall that $f_\sigma(\varphi)$ is a tautology iff $\mathfrak{A}_2 \models_2 f_\sigma(\varphi)$ for all $\mathfrak{A}_2 \in \mathcal{C}_2[v(\sigma)]$. Since R_σ is onto on the right-hand side, this is the case iff $\mathfrak{A}_2 \models_2 f_\sigma(\varphi)$ for all $(\mathfrak{A}_1, \mathfrak{A}_2) \in R_\sigma$. By Condition (5) for effective translations this is the case iff $\mathfrak{A}_1 \models_1 \varphi$ for all $(\mathfrak{A}_1, \mathfrak{A}_2) \in R_\sigma$. Since R_σ is onto on the left-hand side, this is the case iff $\mathfrak{A}_1 \models_1 \varphi$ for all $\mathfrak{A}_1 \in \mathcal{C}_1[\sigma]$. $\square$

So far, the proofs of Part (2) and Part (5) of Theorem 12.33 have been omitted. Now we are able to prove these parts as a trivial application of the lemma.

Proof. We use the effective translation (R, f), where each R is the identity and f is as in the proof of Lemma 12.23. $\square$

Definition 12.37. Let $n > 2$. The logic SnS for infinite trees with branching of fixed arity n is defined in a completely analogous way to S2S.

The same holds for SωS, in which case there is one successor function S_i for every natural number i and hence ω-ary branching.

The logic SωB is different. It is MSO over structures $\mathfrak{T} = (T, S^{\mathfrak{T}}, (P_a^{\mathfrak{T}})_{a \in \Sigma})$ that are ω-ary branching unordered trees (of height ω), i.e., $S^{\mathfrak{T}}$ is the *one* successor relation (the union of all successor relations in former cases). Formally we might set

$$T = \omega^*$$
$$S^{\mathfrak{T}} = \{\, (v, v\alpha) \mid v \in \omega^*, \alpha \in \omega \,\}$$

Proposition 12.38. SωS *is decidable.*

Proof. Note that in an ω-ary tree, the n-th child of a node x is the n-th right sibling of the 0-th child of x. Instead of 0th child, first child, second child, etc. we may use the notions of leftmost child and next sibling. Instead of infinitely many successor relations we only need two relations to describe tree positions. These are identified with S_0 and S_1 respectively and the ω-ary tree can be embedded in a binary tree. This lifts to an embedding of SωS-structures in S2S-structures. cf. Figure 12.2 and Figure 12.3 for a visualization of an example with $\Sigma = \{a, b\}$.

More specifically, we state an effective translation (R, f) from SωS to S2S. For the relation R we give a bijection β from positions in ω-ary trees to the set B of binary tree positions not starting with 1. Note that B is S2S-expressible.

$$\beta(\varepsilon) := \varepsilon$$
$$\beta(vn) := \beta(v)\, 01^n$$

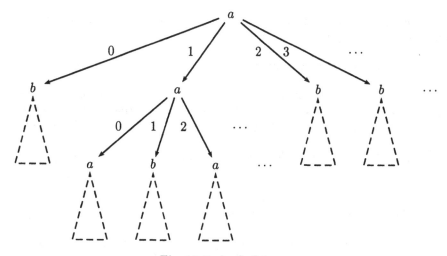

Fig. 12.2. An SωS-tree ...

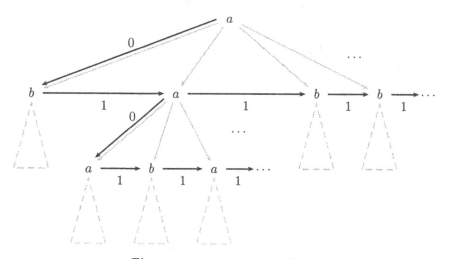

Fig. 12.3. ... viewed as an S2S-tree

Now, we can extend β to a one-to-many relation R between SωS-structures and S2S-structures. We label a position $\beta(x)$ in a binary tree equal to the position x in the ω-ary tree and all positions starting with 1 arbitrarily.

The mapping f applies the following replacements to atomic subformulae.

$$P \subseteq Q \mapsto P \cap B \subseteq Q \cap B$$
$$PX \mapsto P(X \cap B)$$
$$S_0 X Y \mapsto S_0 (X \cap B)(Y \cap B)$$
$$S_{n+1} X Y \mapsto \exists \bar{z} \left(\bigwedge_{0 \le i \le n} z_i \in B \wedge S_0 X z_0 \wedge \bigwedge_{0 \le i < n} S_1 z_i z_{i+1} \wedge S_1 z_n Y \right)$$

In addition to implementing the transformation due to β this also restricts the semantics to the tree positions in B.   □

Proposition 12.39. SωB *is decidable.*

Proof. We may use nearly the same effective translation as in the case of SωS. The only change is that SXY has to be translated to a formula stating 'There are $x \in X \cap B$ and $y \in Y$ such that y is of the form $x01^n$'. This can be done by

$$\forall Z \left(\forall x \forall x' \left(((x \in X \cap B \wedge S_0 x x') \vee (x \in Z \wedge S_1 x x')) \to Z x'\right) \to ZY\right).$$

□

Proposition 12.40. SnS *is decidable for all $n > 2$.*

Proof. It is clear that the concept of binary tree automaton can be adapted in such a way that all the results from Chapter 8 and Section 12.3 also hold for the case of SnS (for finite n). A proof of Proposition 12.40 might explicate this fact. More simply, one can find an effective translation (R, f) from SnS to SωS, because there is a trivial injection ι from positions of n-ary trees to positions of ω-ary trees. The proof works similar to the one of Proposition 12.38; here, ι assumes the role that β did formerly.   □

Definition 12.41. A structure $\mathfrak{O} = (O, <^{\mathfrak{O}})$ is called a **dense linear order without endpoints** if

(1) $<^{\mathfrak{O}}$ is a linear ordering of O.
(2) For all $x \in O$ there are $y, z \in O$ such that $y <^{\mathfrak{O}} x <^{\mathfrak{O}} z$.
(3) For all $x, y \in O$ such that $x <^{\mathfrak{O}} y$ there is $z \in O$ such that $x <^{\mathfrak{O}} z <^{\mathfrak{O}} y$.

Lemma 12.42 (Cantor [25]). *All countable dense linear orders without endpoints are isomorphic.*

Proof. Suppose $(O, <^{\mathfrak{O}})$ and $(P, <^{\mathfrak{P}})$ are dense linear orders without endpoints and β is a monotone bijection from a *finite* subset $O' \subsetneq O$ to a *finite* subset $P' \subsetneq P$. Suppose further that $o \in O \backslash O'$ is given. Due to the fact that $<^{\mathfrak{P}}$ is dense and without endpoints there is an element $p \in P \backslash P'$ such that $\beta \cup \{o \mapsto p\}$ is a monotone bijection between $O' \cup \{o\}$ and $P' \cup \{p\}$. Similar arguments succeed, if $p \in P \backslash P'$ is given.

Let $\eta : \omega \to O \cup P$ be an enumeration of $O \cup P$. By a naïve induction we can construct an increasing sequence $(\beta_n)_{n \in \omega}$ of monotone bijections between finite subsets of O and P, such that for all $n \in \omega$ it holds that $\eta(n)$ is in the domain or range of β_{n+1}: Let β_0 be the empty bijection. Let $\beta_{n+1} = \beta_n$ if $\eta(n)$ already is in the domain or range of β_n. Use the above extension otherwise. Then $\bigcup_{n \in \omega} \beta_n$ is a monotone bijection from O to P, i.e., an isomorphism from $\mathfrak{O}$ to $\mathfrak{P}$.

For a set-theoretical foundation of the naïve induction we have to use the Lemma of Zorn.   □

Lemma 12.43. MSO *is decidable over countable dense linear orders without endpoints.*

Proof. Since all countable dense linear orders without endpoints are isomorphic, it suffices to prove that $(\{\mathfrak{O}\}, \models, \text{MSO})$ is decidable for *one* countable dense linear order without endpoints $\mathfrak{O} = (O, <^{\mathfrak{O}})$. We will choose as O the set of binary tree positions and as $<^{\mathfrak{O}}$ the ordering from left to right. This ordering is S2S-definable because $x <^{\mathfrak{O}} y$ iff $x1$ precedes $y1$ in the lexicographic ordering of Lemma 12.12. It is straightforward to translate MSO over this order to S2S. It remains to prove that this order is dense and without endpoints.

For lack of endpoints let $x \in O$ be given. We have to construct $y, z \in O$ such that $y <^{\mathfrak{O}} x <^{\mathfrak{O}} z$. Choose $y = x0$, $z = x1$. For denseness let $x, y \in O$ be given such that $x <^{\mathfrak{O}} y$. We have to construct $z \in O$ such that $x <^{\mathfrak{O}} z <^{\mathfrak{O}} y$. Suppose first that x is at a larger depth in the tree than y. In this case choose $z = x1$, otherwise choose $z = y0$. □

Proposition 12.44. MSO *is decidable over countable linear orders.*

Proof. It is easy to see that every countable linear order is a suborder of a countable dense linear order without endpoints. Therefore all countable linear orders can be embedded in the structure $\mathfrak{O}$ of the previous lemma. This gives rise to an effective translation as follows.

Let R be the total relation. For the construction of f let us first fix a monadic symbol U. f works by relativizing all quantifications to U and adding $\forall U$ at the front. Then $\mathfrak{O} \models f(\varphi)$ iff $\mathfrak{P} \models \varphi$ for all linear orders $\mathfrak{P}$ that are suborders of $\mathfrak{O}$ iff $\mathfrak{P} \models \varphi$ for all countable linear orders. □

In first-order logic, or FO for short, quantification is permitted only over individuals.

Definition 12.45. Presburger arithmetic is first-order logic over the structure $(\omega, +)$ where
$$+ = \{ (a, b, c) \in \omega^3 \mid a + b = c \}.$$

Proposition 12.46 (Presburger [146]). *Presburger arithmetic is decidable.*

Proof. Again, we use an effective translation (R, f), this time to WS1S. R is the total relation. Consequently only the definition of f remains.

We will use binary number representation to interpret natural numbers in WS1S. A finite set $N \subseteq \omega$ of word positions encodes the natural number n given by
$$n = \sum_{i \in N} 2^i.$$

Let V be a set of variables (for natural numbers). An ω-word w with alphabet $\mathscr{P}(V)$ encodes a family $(n_v)_{v \in V}$ of natural numbers via the sets $N_v := \{ i < \omega \mid v \in w_i \}$. For example, the ω-word
$$\{a, c\} \{b, c\} \{a, b\} \{c\} \emptyset^\omega$$

encodes

$$N_a = \{0, 2\} \quad n_a = 5$$
$$N_b = \{1, 2\} \quad n_b = 6$$
$$N_c = \{0, 1, 3\} \, n_c = 11$$

Addition of numbers is specified most easily by an automaton implementing the blackboard addition algorithm. The automaton

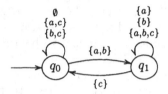

expresses that $n_a + n_b = n_c$. Let us see how it works. If the automaton is, e.g., in state q_1, then a carry of 1 has to be considered in addition to the digits of n_a and n_b. If these digits are 0 and 1 respectively, then n_c will have a digit 0 at the considered position. Hence, the position is labelled with b and neither with a nor c. Therefore the corresponding transition is labelled with $\{b\}$ and leads back to q_1 because the next carry is again 1. The automaton can be translated into a WS1S-formula. The remainder of the construction of f provides no more difficulties.   □

This technique extends to the addition of real numbers:

Proposition 12.47. FO *over the structure* $(\mathbb{R}, +)$ *(additive group of real numbers) is decidable.*

Proof. We identify real numbers r with pairs (n, x), where n is an integer, $0 \leq x < 1$, and $r = n + x$. By writing n in two's complement binary representation we can identify integers with $\{0, 1\}$-words not containing both 0 and 1 infinitely often. x can be written in normal binary representation, identifying fractional parts with $\{0, 1\}$-words containing 0 infinitely often. Examples: The real number π is represented by the two words $110000\ldots$ (for 3, the usual direction is $\ldots 000011$) and $001001000011111\ldots$ (for $0.1415\ldots$). The real number -6.25 is represented by the two words $1001111\ldots$ (for -7) and $1100000\ldots$ (for 0.75). Therefore a variable for $(\mathbb{R}, +)$ may be transformed into two monadic symbols of S1S. Specifying addition using this encoding can be done similar to the case of Presburger arithmetic.   □

Using a different proof technique, Tarski [174] proved in 1948 that even FO over $(\mathbb{R}, +, \cdot)$ is decidable.

12.5 Special Model Properties

Given a satisfiable formula in some logic, we are often interested in structures of particularly simple nature that satisfy the formula. For instance, the Löwenheim-Skolem-Tarski Theorem (cf. [83]) tells us that satisfiable first-order formulae have *countable* models. Therefore, we say that FO has the *countable model property*. We are interested in similar **special model properties** for other logics. These are closely related to the fact that the logics cannot identify every structure (up to isomorphism). Often the decidability of a logic can be established via a special model property.

The automata theoretic nature which underlies the proofs of many theorems in this chapter will yield special model properties for the logics that appeared in the previous section. It is known from Theorem 8.19 that every tree automaton recognizing a non-empty language accepts a *regular* tree. (Recall that an infinite binary tree is called regular if its labelling can be generated by a deterministic tree automaton with output (Chapter 8), or equivalently if it contains, up to isomorphism, only finitely many subtrees (Chapter 15).) The analogon for ω-words is treated in the following exercise.

Exercise 12.3. Prove that every word automaton (say with parity condition) with non-empty language accepts an eventually periodic ω-word. An ω-word v is called **eventually periodic**, if it is of the form $v_1 v_2^\omega$. You may want to look up the proof of Theorem 8.19.

By the equivalence of word and tree automata with S1S and S2S, we obtain special model properties of these logics.

Proposition 12.48 (Eventually periodic model property). *Each satisfiable S1S formula is satisfied by an eventually periodic ω-word.*

Proposition 12.49 (Regular model property). *Each satisfiable S2S formula is satisfied by a regular infinite binary tree.*

Exercise 12.4. Prove that model checking S2S over regular trees is decidable: On input of an S2S-formula φ and a regular binary tree $\mathfrak{T}$ (given by its generating automaton) it can be decided whether or not $\mathfrak{T} \models \varphi$.

Now, let us resume the investigation of countable linear orders. A **regular order** is an induced suborder of the infinite binary tree which is induced by a regular language (recall that tree positions are words).

Proposition 12.50. *Each MSO-formula that is satisfied by a countable linear order is also satisfied by a regular order.*

Proof. The proof of Proposition 12.44 shows that if φ is satisfiable by a countable order then $\exists U \varphi'$ is satisfied by the infinite binary tree, where φ' expresses that φ holds for the induced suborder of the infinite binary tree which is induced by U. Hence φ' holds for a suitable (extended) binary tree $(T, S_0^{\mathfrak{T}}, S_1^{\mathfrak{T}}, U^{\mathfrak{T}})$. We may conclude that φ' also holds for a regular (extended) binary tree, which finishes the proof. □

Of course, this is not satisfying in itself: The class of regular orders is not even closed under order-isomorphisms of the infinite binary branching tree. Instead, Proposition 12.52 will give an algebraic characterization.

Definition 12.51 (Läuchli and Leonard [111]). Let $\mathcal{O}$ be a minimal class of (linear) orders such that

(1) The one-point order is in $\mathcal{O}$.
(2) If $\mathfrak{O}_1$ and $\mathfrak{O}_2$ are orders in $\mathcal{O}$ then there is also an order in $\mathcal{O}$ that is isomorphic to $\mathfrak{O}_1 + \mathfrak{O}_2$.
(3) If $\mathfrak{O}$ is an order in $\mathcal{O}$ then there is also an order in $\mathcal{O}$ that is isomorphic to $(\omega, <) \times \mathfrak{O} = \mathfrak{O} + \mathfrak{O} + \dots$.
(4) If $\mathfrak{O}$ is an order in $\mathcal{O}$ then there is also an order in $\mathcal{O}$ that is isomorphic to $(\omega, >) \times \mathfrak{O} = \dots + \mathfrak{O} + \mathfrak{O}$.
(5) If $\bar{\mathfrak{O}}$ is a finite tuple (say of length n) of orders in $\mathcal{O}$ then there is also an order in $\mathcal{O}$ that is a countable dense shuffling without endpoints of $\bar{\mathfrak{O}}$.

In order to understand dense shufflings without endpoints, consider the following axioms, which are modifications of those for dense linear orders without endpoints.

(1) The tuple $\bar{S}$ of length n is a partition of S.
(2) $<$ is a linear ordering of S.
(3) For all $x \in S$, $0 \leq i < n$ there are $y, z \in S_i$ such that $y < x < z$.
(4) For all $x, y \in S$, $0 \leq i < n$ such that $x < y$ there is $z \in S_i$ such that $x < z < y$.

As before, there is up to isomorphisms only one countable structure $\mathfrak{S}$ satisfying these axioms. Take this structure and for all i replace every point of the colour S_i by a copy of $\mathfrak{O}_i$. Every order isomorphic to the resulting order is called a countable dense shuffling without endpoints of $\bar{\mathfrak{O}}$.

Proposition 12.52 (Heilbrunner [79]). *The regular orders coincide, up to isomorphisms, with the class $\mathcal{O}$.*

Corollary 12.53. MSO *over countable orders has the $\mathcal{O}$ model property.*

For FO over $(\mathbb{R}, +)$ we obtain:

Lemma 12.54. *Let φ be an FO-formula with free variables $\bar{x}, \bar{y}$ and let $\bar{c} \in \mathbb{Q}$. If there is a tuple $\bar{a} \in \mathbb{R}$ such that $(\mathbb{R}, +, \bar{a}, \bar{c}) \models \varphi$ then there is also a tuple $\bar{b} \in \mathbb{Q}$ such that $(\mathbb{R}, +, \bar{b}, \bar{c}) \models \varphi$.*

Proof. After applying the translation from Proposition 12.47, we have to prove that if an S1S-formula ψ is satisfied by an ω-word encoding real numbers $\bar{a}$ and rational numbers $\bar{c}$, then ψ is also satisfied by an ω-word encoding rational numbers $\bar{b}$ instead of $\bar{a}$ but the same rational numbers $\bar{c}$. Examining the encoding reveals that a *rational* number is encoded by two eventually periodic ω-words. These can be identified by suitable automata and hence be defined by suitable formulae. Therefore, we may eliminate $\bar{c}$ from the ω-word by a modification of ψ.

Suppose $\mathfrak{W} \models \psi$, where $\mathfrak{W}$ encodes any real numbers $\bar{a}$. By the eventually periodic model property of S1S, ψ is also satisfied by an eventually periodic ω-word $\mathfrak{V}$. But $\mathfrak{V}$ can only encode rational numbers. $\square$

The Lemma may be used to prove the following.

Proposition 12.55 $((\mathbb{R}, +)$ and $(\mathbb{Q}, +)$ are elementarily equivalent). *For every* FO-*formula φ we have* $(\mathbb{R}, +) \models \varphi$ *iff* $(\mathbb{Q}, +) \models \varphi$.

Proof. For an FO-formula φ, let φ' denote the formula that is obtained from φ by replacing all quantifiers $\exists x\,(\cdot)$ and $\forall x\,(\cdot)$ by $\exists x \in \mathbb{Q}\,(\cdot)$ and $\forall x \in \mathbb{Q}\,(\cdot)$. Since $\mathbb{Q}$ is not FO-definable in $(\mathbb{R}, +)$, φ' is *a priori* not equivalent over $(\mathbb{R}, +)$ to any FO-formula. Therefore we will interpret φ' in the structure $(\mathbb{R}, \mathbb{Q}, +)$. Obviously for $\bar{a} \in \mathbb{Q}$ we have $(\mathbb{R}, \mathbb{Q}, +, \bar{a}) \models \varphi'$ iff $(\mathbb{Q}, +, \bar{a}) \models \varphi$. As a consequence it suffices to show that $(\mathbb{R}, +, \bar{a}) \models \varphi$ iff $(\mathbb{R}, \mathbb{Q}, +, \bar{a}) \models \varphi'$ for $\bar{a} \in \mathbb{Q}$. This will be shown by induction on the formula φ.

The claim is trivial for quantifier-free φ because in that case $\varphi' = \varphi$. The induction steps $\varphi_1 \wedge \varphi_2$, $\varphi_1 \vee \varphi_2$, or $\neg\varphi_1$ are easy as well. Let us prove the case $\varphi = \exists x\psi$. The case $\varphi = \forall x\psi$ can be handled as $\neg\exists x\neg\psi$, since these two formulae are equivalent.

Suppose $(\mathbb{R}, +, \bar{a}) \models \varphi$ with $\bar{a} \in \mathbb{Q}$. Then there is an $a \in \mathbb{R}$ such that $(\mathbb{R}, +, \bar{a}, a) \models \psi$. Using Lemma 12.54 there is also a $b \in \mathbb{Q}$ such that $(\mathbb{R}, +, \bar{a}, b) \models \psi$. By the induction hypothesis we may conclude that $(\mathbb{R}, \mathbb{Q}, +, \bar{a}, b) \models \psi'$. Then $(\mathbb{R}, \mathbb{Q}, +, \bar{a}) \models \exists x \in \mathbb{Q}\psi'$ which is $(\mathbb{R}, \mathbb{Q}, +, \bar{a}) \models \varphi'$.

For the converse suppose $(\mathbb{R}, \mathbb{Q}, +, \bar{a}) \models \varphi'$. Then there is an $a \in \mathbb{Q}$ such that $(\mathbb{R}, \mathbb{Q}, +, \bar{a}, a) \models \psi'$. With the induction hypothesis we may conclude that $(\mathbb{R}, +, \bar{a}, a) \models \psi$. Since $a \in \mathbb{R}$ holds anyway we have $(\mathbb{R}, +, \bar{a}) \models \exists x\psi$ which is $(\mathbb{R}, +, \bar{a}) \models \varphi$. $\square$

The modal μ-calculus. It was proved already in Chapter 10 that the modal μ-calculus L_μ is decidable. In fact, this is closely related to special model properties of L_μ and to the embedding of L_μ into MSO (for details, see also Chapter 14).

Countable model property: Each satisfiable formula in L_μ has a countable model.

Tree model property: Each satisfiable formula in L_μ has a tree model.

The countable model property holds for fixed point logics in general (for a proof, see Chapter 18). The tree model property follows from the invariance of L_μ under bisimulation (see Chapter 14) and the possibility to unravel any transition system to a bisimilar tree model. Together, the two results imply that L_μ has the *countable tree model property*. Since every formula in L_μ can be translated into an equivalent MSO-formula, the decidability of L_μ follows from the decidability of SωB.

For a related result concerning the more powerful guarded fixed point logic μGF, see Chapter 18. Finally we prove that L_μ has the finite model property.

Proposition 12.56 (Finite model property). *Each satisfiable formula of the modal μ-calculus is satisfiable by a finite transition system.*

Proof. The essence of the proof is that the generating automaton of a regular tree already is a pointed finite transition system.

Let $\varphi \in L_\mu$ be satisfiable. We can transform φ first to a satisfiable formula $\varphi' \in S\omega B$ and from there, via the translation in the proof of Proposition 12.39, to a satisfiable formula $\varphi'' \in S2S$. We conclude that the latter possesses a regular model $\mathfrak{T}''$ with generating automaton $\mathcal{A}'' = (Q, \{0, 1\}, q_I, \delta'', f)$. Shifting $\mathfrak{T}''$ back through the translations, we obtain models $\mathfrak{T}'$ of φ' and $(\mathcal{S}, s)$ of φ. $\mathfrak{T}'$ is just the ω-ary tree that is generated by the automaton $\mathcal{A}' = (Q, \omega, q_I, \delta', f)$, where

$$\delta'(q, n) := \delta''(q, 01^n).$$

In order to understand $\mathcal{S} = (S, R, \lambda)$, observe that it is an induced subtree of the infinite ω-ary tree that is induced by $U^{\mathfrak{T}'}$ for some relational symbol U. Therefore $s = \varepsilon$, $S = U^{\mathfrak{T}'}$, $R = \{(v, vn) \mid vn \in U^{\mathfrak{T}'}\}$ and $\lambda = \alpha \circ f \circ \delta'(q_I, \cdot)$ for some coding function α.

Now consider the *finite* transition system $\mathcal{S}_0 = (Q_U, \Delta, \alpha \circ f)$, where

$$Q_U = \{q \in Q \mid f(q) \text{ does encode } U\}$$

$$\Delta = \{(q_1, q_2) \in Q_U \times Q_U \mid q_2 = \delta'(q_1, n) \text{ for some } n \in \omega\}.$$

Because S is non-empty and initially closed, we have $\varepsilon \in S$ and hence $q_I \in Q_U$. Furthermore it is straightforward to check that $(\mathcal{S}_0, q_I)$ and $(\mathcal{S}, s)$ are bisimilar (cf. Chapter 14 for a treatment of bisimulation) via the bisimulation relation

$$\{(q, v) \in Q_U \times S \mid q = \delta'(q_I, v)\}.$$

Hence $(\mathcal{S}_0, q_I) \models \varphi$.   □

Obviously, this proposition also establishes the finite model property of every modal or temporal logic that can be embedded into L_μ (such as LTL, CTL, CTL* etc.) We finally remark that using the translation of L_μ into alternating tree automata one obtains a stronger version of the tree model property and better complexity bounds (see Chapters 9 and 10).

Tree model property with bounded degree: Each satisfiable formula $\varphi \in L_\mu$ has a tree model of degree $\leq |\varphi|$.

Complexity: The satisfiability problem for L_μ is EXPTIME-complete.

For related results in the context of guarded logics, see Chapter 19.

13 The Complexity of Translating Logic to Finite Automata

Klaus Reinhardt

Wilhelm-Schickhard Institut für Informatik
Eberhard-Karls-Universität Tübingen

13.1 Introduction

The aim of this chapter is to show a non-elementary lower bound for the complexity of translating logic to finite automata.

Here a function is elementary if it is $\mathcal{O}(h_k(n))$ for one of the k-fold exponential functions h_k with $h_0(n) = n$ and $h_{k+1}(n) = 2^{h_k(n)}$.

The non-elementary lower bound is established directly by constructing a sequence of formulas which describe counters of binary numbers whose length is of non-elementary growth. This will show that the growth rate for corresponding finite automata is also non-elementary.

The main motivation for this result is the question how efficiently the decidability in Theorem 12.33 of Chapter 12 can be accomplished. The construction of a finite automaton using Lemma 12.19 can lead to an exponentiation in each step of recursion, where a negation forces to make the automaton deterministic (nondeterminism is caused by existential quantifiers). The following Section 13.2 shows that this blowup cannot be avoided for monadic second-order logic over finite words. This can be seen as an exercise for Section 13.3 which shows the same even for first-order logic with $<$ over finite words.

Furthermore, using the counters mentioned above, configurations of Turing machines are admeasured in Section 13.4, showing that the satisfiability problem (over word models) for first-order logic with $<$ and also for monadic second-order logic is complete for a non-elementary complexity class, which means that there is no principally better method of proving decidability of WS1S (Theorem 12.33 of Chapter 12), or the satisfiability of first-order logic with $<$ over words, than by the standard construction of the corresponding automata.

The kind of construction used in this chapter appears in [122, 123] and [170] in connection with picture languages and regular expressions.

13.2 Monadic Second-Order Logic

We use a method similar to the cyclically counting method in [122]. In the following we recursively define a formula φ_n^A describing the language

$$L_n = 0^* 10^{F(n)-1} 10^*$$

with the following non-elementary function F:

$$F(1) = 1, \quad F(n+1) = F(n)2^{F(n)}$$

E. Grädel et al. (Eds.): Automata, Logics, and Infinite Games, LNCS 2500, pp. 231-238, 2002.

This means that a word $w \in \{0,1\}^*$ is in L_n iff $\varphi_n^A(w)$ is true, where A is a predicate such that for a position x in the word $A(x)$ is true iff $w_x = 1$. Obviously any automaton recognizing the language $0^* 10^{F(n)-1} 10^*$ needs at least $F(n)$ states. (Otherwise a state would appear twice between the two 1's and allow pumping the number of 0's between the two 1's.)

The formula $\varphi_n(A)$ is constructed recursively over n. Let us start the inductive definition with

$$\varphi_1^A = \exists x (A(x) \wedge A(x+1) \wedge \forall y (y = x \vee y = x+1 \vee \neg A(y)))$$

describing the language $0^* 110^*$. The formula says that there are exactly 2 positions x and $x+1$ having a 1.

For the recursion we use φ_n^A to determine if two positions a and b have distance $F(n)$. This distance is now the *length* of a counter that is inremented from the binary number $0\ldots 0$ to $1\ldots 1$. The length is used to control the first and last counter counter value by means of two formulas InitializeC and FinalizeC, and the correct sequence of counter values is fixed by two formulas StartIncrement and Carry, by locally checking all corresponding bit positions in neighbor values. Recursively define

$$
\begin{aligned}
\varphi_{n+1}^A = \exists x \exists y (\; & A(x) \wedge A(y) \wedge \forall z \; z = x \vee z = y \vee \neg A(z) \wedge \\
& \exists B \exists C \; \forall a \forall b (\; (\exists A (\varphi_n^A \wedge a < b \leq y \wedge A(a) \wedge A(b)) \to \\
& \qquad (\text{InitializeC} \wedge \text{StartIncrement} \wedge \text{Carry} \wedge \text{FinalizeC})))
\end{aligned}
$$

Note that the syntax allows to reuse the variable A, which occurs twice under the scope of the existential quantifier, outside of the set quantifier; this makes it possible to define φ_n^A using only a finite number of variable-symbols. Here C contains blocks with consecutive counter representations and B marks the beginning of each block. The recursive use of the predicate A makes sure that a and b have exactly the distance of a block length. This means a complete counter sequence is used to admeasure the length of only one counter for the next n.

$$\text{InitializeC} := (a = x) \to (B(a) \wedge \neg C(a) \wedge \forall c(a < c < b \to (\neg C(c) \wedge \neg B(c))))$$

makes sure that the first block contains only zeros and exactly the beginning of the block (least significant bit) is marked by B.

$$\text{StartIncrement} := (B(a) \vee B(b)) \to (B(b) \wedge \neg (C(a) \leftrightarrow C(b)))$$

makes sure that the first (least significant) bit in each block changes each time and simultaneously takes care that B is continued which means that B also has a 1 at the next beginning of a block.

$$\text{Carry} := ((C(a) \wedge \neg C(b)) \leftrightarrow (\neg C(a+1) \leftrightarrow C(b+1))) \vee B(a+1)$$

makes sure that a 1 changes to a 0 exactly if in the corresponding bit in the following block, the next bit (if it was not the last in the block) must change.

$$\text{FinalizeC} := (b = y) \leftrightarrow (B(a) \wedge \forall c(a \leq c < b \to C(c)))$$

makes sure that the last block is the one containing only 1's.

Theorem 13.1. *The formula φ_n^A defined above has size $O(n)$ and defines the language $\{0^*10^{F(n)-1}10^*\}$, for which a finite automaton must have at least $F(n)$ states.*

Example:
The language $0^*10^{2047}10^*$ is described by φ_4^A, where the existentially quantified C contains all binary representations of numbers from 0 to 255 having length 8. In the figure below, a gap is inserted between these blocks to support readability. To check the correctness of C and the block-marks in B, the formula recursively uses φ_3^A describing $0^*10^710^*$, where the corresponding C contains all binary representations of numbers from 0 to 3 having length 2. This recursively uses φ_2^A describing 0^*1010^*, the corresponding C containing 0 and 1 finally using φ_1^A.

```
A: 0...0 10000000 00000000 00000000... 00000000 00000000 10...
C:       00000000 10000000 01000000... 01111111 11111111 00...
B:       10000000 10000000 10000000... 10000000 10000000 10...
A: 0...0 10000000 10...
C:       00100111 00...
B:       10101010 10...
A: 0...0 1010...
C:       0100...
B:       1110...
```

Exercise 13.1. Which language is described by φ_5^A?

Exercise 13.2. Assume we would replace Carry by the condition

$$((C(a) \vee C(a+1)) \leftrightarrow C(b+1)) \vee B(a+1);$$

which language would be described by φ_n^A now?

13.3   First-Order Logic with $<$

In the preceding section, we could concentrate on one level of recursion, since the counters on lower levels where guessed and stored in a existentially quantified predicate and thus hidden. Now, as in first-order logic we have only quantification on singletons available, we need to have all necessary informations of all levels to be present in the word. Therefore the counters have to work cyclically like in [122, 123] and [170], and furthermore each bit of a counter is followed by a counter on the next lower level containing the *position* of the bit. These counters can be used to identify corresponding positions in counters.

We use the non-elementary function G defined by

$$G(1) = 2, \quad G(n+1) = 2^{G(n)}$$

and the alphabets $\Sigma_k = \{\$_k, 0_k, 1_k\}$ for $k \leq n$, which allow us to represent counters on each level. Let $\Sigma_{<k} = \bigcup_{i=1}^{k-1} \Sigma_i$ and $\Sigma_{>k} = \bigcup_{i=k+1}^{n} \Sigma_i$, furthermore we use $\Sigma_{>k}(x)$ as abbreviation for the formula $\$_{k+1}(x) \vee 0_{k+1}(x) \vee ... \vee 1_n(x)$ meaning that the symbol at position x is $\$_{k+1}$ or 0_{k+1} or ... or 1_n.

The representations of the counters are defined inductively starting with $c_{1,0} := \$_1 0_1$, $c_{1,1} := \$_1 1_1$, representing 0 and 1 on the first alphabet. Then for example on the second alphabet $c_{2,0} := \$_2 0_2 c_{1,0} 0_2 c_{1,1}$, $c_{2,1} := \$_2 1_2 c_{1,0} 0_2 c_{1,1}$, $c_{2,2} := \$_2 0_2 c_{1,0} 1_2 c_{1,1}$ and $c_{2,3} := \$_2 1_2 c_{1,0} 1_2 c_{1,1}$ represent the numbers from 0 to 3. On the k-th alphabet $c_{k+1,0} := \$_{k+1} 0_{k+1} c_{k,0} 0_{k+1} c_{k,1} ... 0_{k+1} c_{k,G(k)-1}$ represents 0 and in general we have

$$c_{k+1,i} := \$_{k+1} x_0 c_{k,0} x_1 c_{k,1} ... x_{G(k)-1} c_{k,G(k)-1},$$

where the number i with $0 \leq i < G(k+1)$ is encoded in binary as

$$x_{G(k)-1} x_{G(k)-2} ... x_1 x_0 = h_{k+1}(bin(i));$$

here $h_{k+1}(0) = 0_{k+1}$ and $h_{k+1}(1) = 1_{k+1}$.

Now we inductively define formulas φ_k, which make sure that the counters count cyclically until the k-th level. On the first level we define the formula φ_1 for the language $(\Sigma_{>1}^* c_{1,0} \Sigma_{>1}^* c_{1,1})^+ \Sigma_{>1}^*$ as follows:

$$\varphi_1 := \exists x(\$_1(x) \wedge 0_1(x+1) \wedge \forall y < x\ \Sigma_{>1}(y)) \wedge$$
$$\forall x(0_1(x) \rightarrow \exists y > x(\$_1(y) \wedge 1_1(y+1) \wedge \forall z(x < z < y \rightarrow \Sigma_{>1}(z)))) \wedge$$
$$\forall x(1_1(x) \rightarrow \exists y > x(\$_1(y) \wedge 0_1(y+1) \wedge \forall z(x < z < y \rightarrow \Sigma_{>1}(z))) \vee$$
$$\forall z > x\ \Sigma_{>1}(z)).$$

Recursively for $k > 1$ we define the formula φ_k for the language

$$(\Sigma_{>k}^* c_{k,0} \Sigma_{>k}^* c_{k,1} ... \Sigma_{>k}^* c_{k,G(k)-1})^+ \Sigma_{>k}^*$$

as follows: First we use the formula φ_{k-1} to describe the necessary condition, that the word contains the counters on level $k-1$ in correct order. Now we can use these counters to identify corresponding positions in the counter on level k. This allows to define the equality of two counters starting on positions x and y by the identity of the digit before each sub-counter representation starting on position x' in the first counter with the digit before the equal sub-counter representation starting on position y' in the second counter:

$\text{Equal}_k(x,y) :=$
$\quad \forall\ x' > x((\$_{k-1}(x') \wedge \neg\exists u\ x < u < x' \wedge \$_k(u)) \rightarrow$
$\quad\quad \exists y' > y(\ \$_{k-1}(x') \wedge \text{Equal}_{k-1}(x',y') \wedge \neg\exists u\ y < u < y' \wedge \$_k(u) \wedge$
$\quad\quad (0_k(x'-1) \leftrightarrow 0_k(y'-1)))).$

Two counters are equal if the digit before equal sub-counter representations are equal, because they are ordered by recursion, the induction starts with $\text{Equal}_1(x,y) := (0_1(x+1) \leftrightarrow 0_1(y+1)))).$

Now we can define the neighbor relation $\text{Next}_k(x,y)$ expressing that the counter starting on position y contains the by one incremented number contained in the counter starting on position x. We proceed as follows (see the formula presented below): The first (least significant) bit always changes (line 2). For every but the first sub-counter starting on position x' (line 3) there is a corresponding sub-counter starting on position y', which represents the same number and and which is in the second counter (line 4). The previous bits (followed by sub-counters on the position x'' and y'' in line 5 such that there is no other sub-counter on position u described in line 6 or 7 between them) cause a change of the bit iff it changes from 1_k to 0_k (and thus causes a carry described in line 8).

(1) $\text{Next}_k(x, y) :=$
(2) $(0_k(x + 1) \leftrightarrow 1_k(y + 1))\wedge$
(3) $\forall\, x'((x + 2 < x' < y \wedge \$_{k-1}(x')) \rightarrow$
(4) $\exists y' > y\ (\$_{k-1}(y') \wedge \text{Equal}_{k-1}(x', y') \wedge \neg\exists u\ y < u < y' \wedge \$_k(u)\wedge$
(5) $\exists\, x'' < x', y'' < y'(\$_{k-1}(x'') \wedge \$_{k-1}(y'')\wedge$
(6) $\neg\exists u\ x'' < u < x' \wedge \$_{k-1}(u)\wedge$
(7) $\neg\exists u\ y'' < u < y' \wedge \$_{k-1}(u)\wedge$
(8) $((0_k(x' - 1) \leftrightarrow 1_k(y' - 1)) \leftrightarrow (1_k(x'' - 1) \wedge 0_k(y'' - 1)))))).$

The formula

$$\text{Initialize}_k(x) := \$_k(x) \wedge \exists y > x(\$_k(x) \wedge \neg\exists z(x < z < y \wedge (1_k(z) \vee \$_k(z))))$$

makes sure that the counter starting on position x is zero.

We now present the desired formula φ_k: It uses recursion (line 1) to ensure the correctness of the counters on level $k - 1$. The first counter has only zeros (line 2). In every counter exactly the first sub-counter has only zeros (line 3); this makes sure that each number is only once represented by a sub-counter which makes the choice of y' in $\text{Equal}_k(x, y)$ and $\text{Next}_k(x, y)$ unique. Every counter starting on position x ends at some position y and either there is a following counter starting on position z, which has the next binary number (line 4-6) or it is the last counter consisting only of 1's (line 7-8). Furthermore every digit of the counter must be followed by a sub-counter (line 9):

(1) $\varphi_k := \varphi_{k-1}\wedge$
(2) $\exists x(\text{Initialize}_k(x) \wedge \forall y < x\ \Sigma_{>k}(y))\wedge$
(3) $\forall x(\$_k(x) \leftrightarrow \text{Initialize}_{k-1}(x + 2))\wedge$
(4) $\forall x(\$_k(x) \rightarrow (\exists y > x(\ (\forall u(x < u \le y \rightarrow (\Sigma_{<k}(u) \vee 0_k(u) \vee 1_k(u)))\wedge$
(5) $\exists z > y(\ \$_k(z) \wedge \text{Next}_k(x, z)\wedge$
(6) $\forall u(y < u < z \rightarrow \Sigma_{>k}(u))))\vee$
(7) $(\forall u(x < u \le y \rightarrow (\Sigma_{<k}(u) \vee 1_k(u)))\wedge$
(8) $\forall u > y\ \Sigma_{>k}(u)))))\wedge$
(9) $\forall x((0_k(x) \vee 1_k(x)) \rightarrow \$_{k-1}(x + 1)).$

The length of the formula Equal_k and thus also the formula Next_k grows linear with k. Thus the length of φ_n is in $O(n^2)$. (If we count the representation of a variable indexed by n as having length $\log n$, we even have $O(n^2 \log n)$.) On the other hand a finite automaton recognizing the language described by φ_n

needs at least one state for each of the $G(n)$ counters. This means we have a sequence of formulas φ_n, where the growth rate for the size of equivalent finite automata is non-elementary.

Theorem 13.2. *The formula φ_n defined above has size $O(n^2 \log n)$ and defines the language $(\Sigma_{>n}^* c_{n,0} \Sigma_{>n}^* c_{n,1} \ldots \Sigma_{>n}^* c_{n,G(n)-1})^+ \Sigma_{>n}^*$, for which a finite automaton must have at least $G(n)$ states.*

Exercise 13.3. Give a better lower bound for the number of states in Theorem 13.2.

13.4   Simulation of a Turing Machine by Logic

Definition 13.3. Let DTIME($f(n)$) (resp. NTIME($f(n)$), DSPACE($f(n)$) or NSPACE($f(n)$)) be the class of languages, which can be recognized by a deterministic (resp. nondeterministic) Turing machine in time $f(n)$ time (resp. space) for inputs of length n (see [87]).

Remark 13.4. For G as defined above, we have

$$\bigcup_c \text{DTIME}(G(cn)) = \bigcup_c \text{NSPACE}(G(cn)),$$

since even a single increment in the input size already allows an exponential increase in time to simulate the NSPACE-machine.

Theorem 13.5. *The satisfiability problem for first-order logic with $<$ over finite words is complete for $\bigcup_c \text{DSPACE}(G(cn))$ under polynomial time reductions.*

Proof. For containment in the class see the proof of Lemma 12.21 (and the following Remark 12.22) in Chapter 12, where the given formula is translated to a finite automaton. The worst case for one step of recursion in this translation is an exponential blowup, which occurs when the automaton is made deterministic in order to translate negation by recognizing the complement.

To show hardness, we use the following reduction: Let L be recognized by a deterministic one-tape Turing machine $M = (\Sigma, Q, \delta, b, q_0, q_f)$ using $G(cn)$ space, with the blank symbol $b \in \Sigma$. A word $w = w_1 w_2 \cdots w_n$ is accepted by M if there is a sequence $w' = \$C_0 \$C_1 \$ \cdots \$C_f$ of configurations over $\Sigma \cup (\Sigma \times Q) \cup \{\$\}$ with the initial configuration $C_0 = (w_1, q_0)w_2 w_3 \cdots w_n b \cdots b$, a final configuration C_f starting with (b, q_f) (w.l.o.g M moves to the beginning, when it accepts,), $|\$C_i| = g(m)$ with $m := cn$ for $i \le f$ and $C_i \Rightarrow_M C_{i+1}$ for $i < f$. Since the k-th symbol in $\$C_{i+1}$ depends only on the $k-1$-th, k-th, and $k+1$-th symbol, we can construct a first-order formula $\varphi_\delta(x, y, z, y')$, which is true iff the symbol $\in \Sigma \cup (\Sigma \times Q) \cup \{\$\}$ at position y' is the correct consequence of (x, y, z) in the previous configuration (respecting the separation marker $\$$). Here y' corresponds to position y in the previous configuration. For example if $(q, a)(x)$ and $d(y)$ and $\delta(q, a) = (q', e, R)$, which means that the machine is in state q on the symbol a and the consequence is that it enters state q', writes a e and goes right, then $\varphi_\delta(x, y, z, y')$ is true iff $(q', d)(y')$, which means that in the following configuration the machine is in state q' on symbol d. Or if $(q, a)(y)$ and $\delta(q, a) = (q', e, R)$, then $\varphi_\delta(x, y, z, y')$ is true iff $e(y')$, which means that in the following configuration there is the e, which was written by the machine (but the machine has moved away). Since δ is finite, φ_δ is a finite formula as well.

Now we extend the construction in the previous section in the following way: Let $\Sigma_{m+1} := \Sigma \cup (\Sigma \times Q) \cup \{\$\}$ and $\Sigma_{>k} = \bigcup_{i=k+1}^{m+1} \Sigma_i$. Instead of describing

$$w' = \$w'_2 w'_3 \cdots w'_{g(m)} \$ \cdots w'_{t \cdot G(m)},$$

which would not enable the identification of corresponding positions, we describe

$$w'' = \$c_{m,0} w'_2 c_{m,1} w'_3 c_{m,2} \cdots w'_{G(m)} c_{m,G(m)-1} \$ c_{m,0} \cdots w'_{t \cdot G(m)} c_{m,G(m)-1},$$

where each symbol is followed by a counter containing its position. We use the following formula:

(1) $\varphi_{M(w)} := \varphi_m \wedge \$(1) \wedge \text{InitializeC}_w \wedge$
(2) $\quad \forall x(\$(x) \leftrightarrow \text{Initialize}_m(x+1)) \wedge$
(3) $\quad \forall x(\Sigma_{m+1}(x) \leftrightarrow \$_m(x+1)) \wedge$
(4) $\quad \forall x, y, z(\ (\Sigma_{m+1}(x) \wedge \Sigma_{m+1}(y) \wedge \Sigma_{m+1}(z) \wedge$
(5) $\quad\quad \neg \exists u(x < u < z \wedge u \neq y \wedge (\Sigma_{m+1}(u)) \rightarrow$
(6) $\quad\quad (\exists y' > z(\ \text{Equal}_m(y+1, y'+1) \wedge \varphi_\delta(x, y, z, y') \wedge$
(7) $\quad\quad\quad \neg \exists u(z < u < y' \wedge \text{Equal}_m(y+1, u))) \vee$
(8) $\quad\quad (\neg \exists y' > z(\text{Equal}_m(y+1, y'+1)) \wedge$
(9) $\quad\quad (\$(y) \rightarrow (b, q_f)(z)))),$

Here line 2 says that the separation marker $\$$ is exactly at those positions which are followed by the counter representation $c_{m,0}$. Line 3 says that each symbol of the configuration in followed by a counter, line 4 says that for all triples x, y, z of symbols of a configuration, which are (line 5) subsequent in the configuration, which means there are only symbols of the counter in-between, there is (line 6) a position y' followed by the same counter as y with the symbol, which is determined by δ. Line 7 makes sure that it is indeed the following configuration. The alternative of line 8 is that there is no following configuration and (line 9) the current configuration is a final configuration C_f. Line 1 makes sure that the counters work in the correct way according to the previous section and the first configuration is $\$C_0$, which is expressed by

$$\text{InitializeC}_w := \exists\ x_1 < x_2 < \ldots < x_n < y$$
$$(\ (w_1, q_0)(x_1) \wedge w_2(x_2) \wedge w_3(x_3) \wedge \ldots w_n(x_n) \wedge \$(y) \wedge$$
$$\forall u < y(\exists i\ u = x_i \vee \Sigma_{\leq m}(u) \vee (b(u) \wedge x_n < u)))$$

where line 1 and 2 define the positions occupied by the input symbols and line 3 says that all other symbols are either symbols of the counter or blank symbols filling the tape after the input w (this excludes the $\$$). Thus the size of InitializeC_w is linear. According to the previous section, the formula φ_m and thus also $\varphi_{M(w)}$ has a size of $O(m^2 \log m) = O(n^2 \log n)$ and can on input w be written in polynomial time. The machine M accepts w iff $\varphi_{M(w)}$ is satisfiable.

□

Corollary 13.6. *Satisfiability of first-order formulas with* $<$ *over finite words is in no elementary space-bounded complexity class.*

A word $w = w_0 \ldots w_{m-1}$ over the alphabet $\Sigma = \{a_1, \ldots, a_n\}$ can be coded by a partition of the initial segment $\{0, \ldots, m-1\}$ of the natural numbers into n sets (where the k-th set contains all i with $w_i = a_k$). Satisfiability of a first-order formula φ over finite words can thus be expressed by an WMSO-sentence over the set of natural numbers (applying existential quantification to the monadic letter predicates occurring in φ, adding a clause which says that these sets form a partition of an initial segment of ω). Thus we can conclude the following:

Corollary 13.7. *The theory WS1S, i.e., the set of* WMSO-*sentences which are true in the the structure* $(\omega, +1, <)$, *is complete for the class* $\bigcup_c \mathrm{DSPACE}(G(cn))$ *under polynomial time reduction, and thus is contained in no elementary space-bounded complexity class.*

Exercise 13.4. Schow that $\bigcup_c \mathrm{DSPACE}(G(cn)) = \bigcup_c \mathrm{DSPACE}(F(cn))$ (for F defined in Section 13.2).

14 Expressive Power of Monadic Second-Order Logic and Modal μ-Calculus

Philipp Rohde

Lehrstuhl für Informatik VII
RWTH Aachen

14.1 Introduction

We consider monadic second order logic (MSO) and the modal μ-calculus (L_μ) over transition systems (Kripke structures). It is well known that every class of transition systems which is definable by a sentence of L_μ is definable by a sentence of MSO as well. It will be shown that the converse is also true for an important fragment of MSO: every class of transition systems which is MSO-definable and which is closed under bisimulation – i.e., the sentence does not distinguish between bisimilar models – is also L_μ-definable. Hence we obtain the following expressive completeness result: the bisimulation invariant fragment of MSO and L_μ are equivalent. The result was proved by David Janin and Igor Walukiewicz. Our presentation is based on their article [91]. The main step is the development of automata-based characterizations of L_μ over arbitrary transition systems and of MSO over transition trees (see also Chapter 16). It turns out that there is a general notion of automaton subsuming both characterizations, so we obtain a common ground to compare these two logics. Moreover we need the notion of the ω-unravelling for a transition system, on the one hand to obtain a bisimilar transition tree and on the other hand to increase the possibilities of choosing successors.

We start with a section introducing the notions of transition systems and transition trees, bisimulations and the ω-unravelling. In Section 14.3 we repeat the definitions of MSO and L_μ. In Section 14.4 we develop a general notion of automaton and acceptance conditions in terms of games to obtain the characterizations of the two logics. In the last section we will prove the main result mentioned above.

14.2 Preliminary Definitions

Let $\mathrm{Prop} = \{p, p', \dots\} \cup \{\bot, \top\}$ be a set of unary predicate symbols (propositional letters) and $\mathrm{Rel} = \{r, r', \dots\}$ a set of binary predicate symbols (letters for relations). We consider a signature containing only symbols from Prop and Rel. Let $\mathrm{Var} = \{X, Y, \dots\}$ be a countable set of variables.

Definition 14.1. Let $S^{\mathcal{M}}$ be a non-empty set of states and $\mathrm{sr}^{\mathcal{M}}$ an element of $S^{\mathcal{M}}$. For each $r \in \mathrm{Rel}$ let $r^{\mathcal{M}}$ a binary relation on $S^{\mathcal{M}}$ and for each $p \in \mathrm{Prop}$

E. Grädel et al. (Eds.): Automata, Logics, and Infinite Games, LNCS 2500, pp. 239-257, 2002.
© Springer-Verlag Berlin Heidelberg 2002

let $p^{\mathcal{M}} \subseteq S^{\mathcal{M}}$ a subset of $S^{\mathcal{M}}$. A **transition system** $\mathcal{M}$ **with source sr$^{\mathcal{M}}$** – transition system for short – is the tuple

$$\left(S^{\mathcal{M}}, \mathrm{sr}^{\mathcal{M}}, \{\, r^{\mathcal{M}} \mid r \in \mathrm{Rel} \,\}, \{\, p^{\mathcal{M}} \mid p \in \mathrm{Prop} \,\} \right).$$

For every $r \in \mathrm{Rel}$ and state $s \in S^{\mathcal{M}}$ let

$$\mathrm{scc}_r^{\mathcal{M}}(s) := \{\, s' \in S^{\mathcal{M}} \mid (s, s') \in r^{\mathcal{M}} \,\}$$

be the set of r-successors of s.

A transition system $\mathcal{M}$ is called a **transition tree** if for every state $s \in S^{\mathcal{M}}$ there is a unique path to the root of the tree (alias the source of the system), i.e., a unique finite sequence $s_0, \ldots, s_n$ in $S^{\mathcal{M}}$ such that $s_0 = \mathrm{sr}^{\mathcal{M}}$, $s_n = s$ and for every $i \in \{0, \ldots, n-1\}$ we have $s_{i+1} \in \mathrm{scc}_{r_i}^{\mathcal{M}}(s_i)$ for exactly one $r_i \in \mathrm{Rel}$.

Definition 14.2. Two transition systems $\mathcal{M}$ and $\mathcal{N}$ are **bisimilar** – denoted by $\mathcal{M} \sim \mathcal{N}$ – if there is a **bisimulation relation** $R \subseteq S^{\mathcal{M}} \times S^{\mathcal{N}}$ such that for every $(s, t) \in R$, $p \in \mathrm{Prop}$ and $r \in \mathrm{Rel}$:

- $\left(\mathrm{sr}^{\mathcal{M}}, \mathrm{sr}^{\mathcal{N}} \right) \in R$,
- s satisfies p in $\mathcal{M}$ iff t satisfies p in $\mathcal{N}$, i.e., $s \in p^{\mathcal{M}} \Longleftrightarrow t \in p^{\mathcal{N}}$ holds,
- "Zig": for every r-successor s' of s in $\mathcal{M}$ there exists a r-successor t' of t in $\mathcal{N}$ such that $(s', t') \in R$,
- "Zag": for every r-successor t' of t in $\mathcal{N}$ there exists a r-successor s' of s in $\mathcal{M}$ such that $(s', t') \in R$.

Bisimulations are also known as *zigzagrelations*. For an example of a bisimulation see Fig. 14.1.

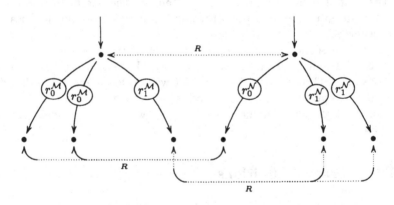

Fig. 14.1. Two bisimilar transition systems $\mathcal{M}$ and $\mathcal{N}$.

Let $\mathcal{C}$ be a class of transition systems. We say $\mathcal{C}$ is **bisimulation closed** if for all transition systems $\mathcal{M}$ and $\mathcal{N}$ the following holds:

$$\mathcal{M} \in \mathcal{C} \wedge \mathcal{N} \sim \mathcal{M} \Longrightarrow \mathcal{N} \in \mathcal{C}.$$

Exercise 14.1. Show that $\sim$ is an equivalence relation on the class of all transition systems.

Definition 14.3. Let $\mathcal{M}$ be a transition system and $s \in S^{\mathcal{M}}$. An ω-**path to** s is a finite sequence

$$s_0(a_1, r_1, s_1)(a_2, r_2, s_2) \ldots (a_n, r_n, s_n),$$

where $s_0 = \mathrm{sr}^{\mathcal{M}}$, $s_n = s$, $a_i \in \omega$ and each s_{i+1} is a r_i-successor of s_i, i.e., $s_{i+1} \in \mathrm{scc}^{\mathcal{M}}_{r_i}(s_i)$ holds for every $i \in \{0, \ldots, n-1\}$. The ω-**unravelling** $\widehat{\mathcal{M}}$ of $\mathcal{M}$ is the transition system defined as follows:

- $S^{\widehat{\mathcal{M}}}$ is the set of the ω-paths to the elements of $S^{\mathcal{M}}$,
- the sources are identical: $\mathrm{sr}^{\widehat{\mathcal{M}}} = \mathrm{sr}^{\mathcal{M}}$,
- for $u, v \in S^{\widehat{\mathcal{M}}}$ and $r \in \mathrm{Rel}$ we set $(u, v) \in r^{\widehat{\mathcal{M}}}$ iff v is a one-term extension of u, i.e., there are $a \in \omega$ and $s \in S^{\mathcal{M}}$ such that $v = u(a, r, s)$,
- for $v \in S^{\widehat{\mathcal{M}}}$ and $p \in \mathrm{Prop}$ we set $v \in p^{\widehat{\mathcal{M}}}$ iff either $v = \mathrm{sr}^{\widehat{\mathcal{M}}}$ and $\mathrm{sr}^{\mathcal{M}} \in p^{\mathcal{M}}$ or $v = u(a, r, s)$ for some $u \in S^{\widehat{\mathcal{M}}}$, $a \in \omega$, $r \in \mathrm{Rel}$ such that $s \in p^{\mathcal{M}}$.

For an example of an ω-unravelling see Fig. 14.2.

Exercise 14.2. Let $\mathcal{M}$ be a transition system. Show that:

(1) The ω-unravelling $\widehat{\mathcal{M}}$ is always unique and a transition tree,
(2) $\mathcal{M}$ and $\widehat{\mathcal{M}}$ are bisimilar.
    Hint: Consider the following relation $R \subseteq S^{\mathcal{M}} \times S^{\widehat{\mathcal{M}}}$:

$$(s, t) \in R :\Longleftrightarrow t \text{ is an } \omega\text{-path to } s.$$

The main property of the ω-unravelling for our purpose is, that we always have enough possibilities to choose a different r-successor for finitely many r-successors of an element in $\widehat{\mathcal{M}}$. In other words: Let t be an r-successor of s in $\mathcal{M}$ and let u be an ω-path to s. Then there are infinitely many r-successors of u in $\widehat{\mathcal{M}}$ which are bisimilar to t.

Definition 14.4. Let $\mathcal{M}$ and $\mathcal{N}$ be two transition systems. $\mathcal{M}$ is an **extension** of $\mathcal{N}$ – denoted by $\mathcal{M} \succeq \mathcal{N}$ – if there is a partial function $h : S^{\mathcal{M}} \to S^{\mathcal{N}}$ such that for every $s \in S^{\mathcal{M}}$, $r \in \mathrm{Rel}$ and $p \in \mathrm{Prop}$:

- the source in $\mathcal{M}$ is mapped to the source in $\mathcal{N}$: $h(\mathrm{sr}^{\mathcal{M}}) = \mathrm{sr}^{\mathcal{N}}$,
- s satisfies p in $\mathcal{M}$ iff $h(s)$ satisfies p in $\mathcal{N}$: $s \in p^{\mathcal{M}} \Longleftrightarrow h(s) \in p^{\mathcal{N}}$,
- s' is a r-successor of s in $\mathcal{M}$ if and only if $h(s')$ is a r-successor of $h(s)$ in $\mathcal{N}$: $h[\mathrm{scc}^{\mathcal{M}}_r(s)] = \mathrm{scc}^{\mathcal{N}}_r(h(s))$.

Exercise 14.3. Show that if $\mathcal{M}$ is an extension of $\mathcal{N}$ then $\mathcal{M}$ is bisimilar to $\mathcal{N}$, so the notion of bisimulation is more general than the notion of extension.

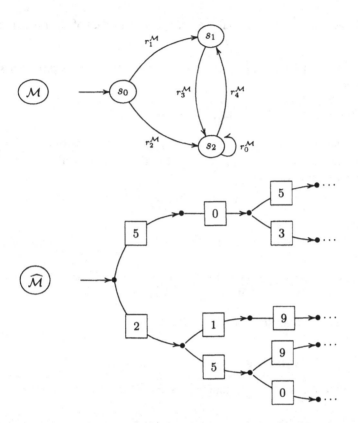

Fig. 14.2. A transition system $\mathcal{M}$ with source $s_0 = \mathrm{sr}^{\mathcal{M}}$ and a part of its ω-unravelling $\widehat{\mathcal{M}}$ (we suppressed the labelling of the nodes). Notice that in fact every node has infinitely many sons.

In fact we have:

Theorem 14.5 (Castellani 1987). *Two transition systems $\mathcal{M}_1$ and $\mathcal{M}_2$ are bisimilar iff there is a transition system $\mathcal{N}$ such that $\mathcal{M}_1 \succeq \mathcal{N}$ and $\mathcal{M}_2 \succeq \mathcal{N}$.*

The proof can be found in [27]. Notice that one direction is the statement of the last exercise. $\mathcal{N}$ can be seen as quotient of $\mathcal{M}_1$ and $\mathcal{M}_2$ under bisimulation relation, i.e., the minimal representative of the equivalence class $[\mathcal{M}_1]_\sim$.

In the countable case we obtain:

Exercise 14.4. Let M and $\mathcal{N}$ be transition systems such that $S^{\mathcal{M}}$ and $S^{\mathcal{N}}$ are countable. Show that:

- $\widehat{\mathcal{M}}$ is an extension of $\mathcal{M}$,
- If $\mathcal{M}$ and $\mathcal{N}$ are bisimilar then $\widehat{\mathcal{M}}$ and $\widehat{\mathcal{N}}$ are isomorphic.

14.3   Monadic Second Order Logic and the Modal μ-Calculus

These two logics will be interpreted over transition systems. There are several ways to define MSO over transition systems, for example by using two types of variables (first-order and second-order variables) or by introducing a new predicate sing(X) for singleton sets. We use the following definition:

Definition 14.6. The signature of **monadic second order logic (MSO)** over transition systems contains unary predicate symbols from Prop, binary predicate symbols from Rel, the constant symbol sr and variables from Var. Formulae of MSO are defined inductively by the following grammar. Let $p \in$ Prop, $r \in$ Rel and $X, Y \in$ Var:

- sr(X),
- $p(X)$,
- $r(X, Y)$,
- $X \subseteq Y$,
- $\neg\varphi$ for any formula φ,
- $\varphi \vee \psi$ for any formulae φ and ψ,
- $\exists X.\varphi(X)$ for any formula φ.

Other connectives, such as the conjunction $\wedge$, the implication $\Longrightarrow$ and the universal quantification $\forall$ are defined as abbreviations within this logic as usual. Furthermore we define the equality by $X = Y$ iff $X \subseteq Y \wedge Y \subseteq X$. A **sentence** is a formula without free variables. A formula resp. sentence of MSO is called a MSO-formula resp. MSO-sentence.

Note that 'monadic' refers to the fact that the only second-order quantification that is allowed is over monadic, i.e., unary predicates. Binary predicate symbols may occur in MSO-formulae, but only the unary ones may be quantified over.

For a given transition system $\mathcal{M}$ and an assignment $\beta : \text{Var} \to \mathscr{P}(S^{\mathcal{M}})$ the satisfaction relation $\models$ is defined inductively by:

$$(\mathcal{M}, \beta) \models \text{sr}(X) \qquad \text{iff } \beta(X) = \{\text{sr}^{\mathcal{M}}\},$$

$$(\mathcal{M}, \beta) \models p(X) \qquad \text{iff } \beta(X) \subseteq p^{\mathcal{M}},$$

$$(\mathcal{M}, \beta) \models r(X, Y) \qquad \text{iff there are } s, t \in S^{\mathcal{M}} \text{ such that } \beta(X) = \{s\},$$
$$\beta(Y) = \{t\} \text{ and } (s, t) \in r^{\mathcal{M}},$$

$$(\mathcal{M}, \beta) \models X \subseteq Y \qquad \text{iff } \beta(X) \subseteq \beta(Y),$$

$$(\mathcal{M}, \beta) \models \varphi \vee \psi \qquad \text{iff } (\mathcal{M}, \beta) \models \varphi \text{ or } (\mathcal{M}, \beta) \models \psi,$$

$$(\mathcal{M}, \beta) \models \neg\varphi \qquad \text{iff not } (\mathcal{M}, \beta) \models \varphi,$$

$$(\mathcal{M}, \beta) \models \exists X.\varphi(X) \qquad \text{iff there is a } T \subseteq S^{\mathcal{M}} \text{ such that}$$
$$(\mathcal{M}, \beta[X := T]) \models \varphi(X),$$

where $\beta[X := T]$ denotes the assignment such that $\beta[X := T](X) = T$ and $\beta[X := T](Y) = \beta(Y)$ for $Y \neq X$.

For a MSO-sentence φ we write $\mathcal{M} \models \varphi$ if $(\mathcal{M}, \beta) \models \varphi$ is true for an arbitrary assignment. A MSO-sentence φ defines a class of transition systems by

$$\mathcal{C}^{\mathrm{MSO}}(\varphi) := \{ \mathcal{M} \mid \mathcal{M} \text{ is a transition system and } \mathcal{M} \models \varphi \}.$$

Let $\mathcal{C}$ be a class of transition systems. $\mathcal{C}$ is **MSO-definable** if there is a MSO-sentence φ defining the class, i.e., $\mathcal{C} = \mathcal{C}^{\mathrm{MSO}}(\varphi)$ holds.

Remark 14.7. Not all MSO-definable classes of transition systems are bisimulation closed. Consider for example the MSO-sentence

$$\varphi := \exists X \exists Y.(\mathrm{sr}(X) \wedge r(X,Y) \wedge \forall Z.(r(X,Z) \Longrightarrow Y = Z)).$$

The sentence φ states that there is exactly one r-successor of the source. The class $\mathcal{C}^{\mathrm{MSO}}(\varphi)$ cannot be bisimulation closed because a bisimulation relation cannot fix any number of r-successors, i.e., if there is a r-successor in one transition system then there is one in all bisimilar systems, but there could be arbitrary many.

In the following we repeat the definition of the μ-calculus (cf. Chapter 10).

Definition 14.8. The signature of the **modal μ-calculus $\mathbf{L}_\mu$** over transition systems contains only unary predicate symbols from Prop, binary predicate symbols from Rel and variables from Var. Formulae are defined inductively by the following grammar. Let $p \in$ Prop, $r \in$ Rel and $X \in$ Var:

- X,
- p,
- $\neg\varphi$ for any formula φ,
- $\varphi \vee \psi$ for any formulae φ and ψ,
- $\langle r \rangle \varphi$ for any formula φ,
- $\mu X.\varphi(X)$ for any formula $\varphi(X)$ where X occurs only positively, i.e., under an even number of negations.

The dual of the modality $\langle r \rangle$ is denoted by $[r]$ and defined by $[r]\varphi := \neg\langle r \rangle\neg\varphi$. A formula resp. sentence of $\mathbf{L}_\mu$ is called a $\mathbf{L}_\mu$-formula resp. $\mathbf{L}_\mu$-sentence. For a given transition system $\mathcal{M}$ and an assignment $\beta : \text{Var} \to \mathscr{P}(S^{\mathcal{M}})$ we define inductively the set $\|\varphi\|_\beta^{\mathcal{M}}$ in which the $\mathbf{L}_\mu$-formula φ is true:

$$\|X\|_\beta^{\mathcal{M}} := \beta(X),$$
$$\|p\|_\beta^{\mathcal{M}} := p^{\mathcal{M}},$$
$$\|\neg\varphi\|_\beta^{\mathcal{M}} := S^{\mathcal{M}} - \|\varphi\|_\beta^{\mathcal{M}},$$
$$\|\varphi \vee \psi\|_\beta^{\mathcal{M}} := \|\varphi\|_\beta^{\mathcal{M}} \cup \|\psi\|_\beta^{\mathcal{M}},$$
$$\|\langle r \rangle\varphi\|_\beta^{\mathcal{M}} := \{ s \in S^{\mathcal{M}} \mid \mathrm{scc}_r^{\mathcal{M}}(s) \cap \|\varphi\|_\beta^{\mathcal{M}} \neq \emptyset \},$$
$$\|\mu X.\varphi(X)\|_\beta^{\mathcal{M}} := \bigcap \{ T \subseteq S^{\mathcal{M}} \mid \|\varphi(X)\|_{\beta[X:=T]}^{\mathcal{M}} \subseteq T \}.$$

Notice that we already used the Knaster-Tarski Theorem in the definition of $\|\mu X.\varphi(X)\|$ (cf. Theorem 20.4 in Chapter 20): due to the restriction that X may only occur positively in $\varphi(X)$, the operation $T \mapsto \|\varphi(X)\|_{\beta[X:=T]}^{\mathcal{M}}$ is monotone with respect to subset inclusion and the (existing) least fixed point of this map is exactly $\|\mu X.\varphi(X)\|_\beta^{\mathcal{M}}$. Monotone maps also have greatest fixed points. This is denoted by $\nu X.\varphi(X)$ and defined as $\neg\mu X.\neg\varphi[X := \neg X]$.

For a L_μ-sentence φ we write $(\mathcal{M}, s) \models \varphi$ if $s \in \|\varphi\|_\beta^{\mathcal{M}}$ holds for an arbitrary assignment. A L_μ-sentence φ defines a class $\mathcal{C}^{L_\mu}(\varphi)$ of transition systems by

$$\mathcal{C}^{L_\mu}(\varphi) := \big\{\, \mathcal{M} \mid \mathcal{M} \text{ is a transition system and } (\mathcal{M}, \mathrm{sr}^{\mathcal{M}}) \models \varphi \,\big\}.$$

Let $\mathcal{C}$ be a class of transition systems. $\mathcal{C}$ is $\mathbf{L_\mu}$-**definable** if there is a L_μ-sentence φ defining the class, i.e., $\mathcal{C} = \mathcal{C}^{L_\mu}(\varphi)$ holds.

As opposed to the situation of MSO we have:

Proposition 14.9. *Every L_μ-definable class is bisimulation closed.*

Proof. Let $\mathcal{M}$ and $\mathcal{N}$ be two transition systems and let R be a bisimulation relation between $\mathcal{M}$ and $\mathcal{N}$. It is easy to see that for any L_μ-sentence φ and for all $s \in S^{\mathcal{M}}$, $t \in S^{\mathcal{N}}$ with $(s,t) \in R$ the following holds:

$$s \in \|\varphi\|_\beta^{\mathcal{M}} \Longleftrightarrow t \in \|\varphi\|_{\beta^*}^{\mathcal{N}},$$

where β^* is an assignment for $\mathcal{N}$ derived from the assignment β for $\mathcal{M}$. Because we have $(\mathrm{sr}^{\mathcal{M}}, \mathrm{sr}^{\mathcal{N}}) \in R$ it follows:

$$(\mathcal{M}, \mathrm{sr}^{\mathcal{M}}) \models \varphi \wedge \mathcal{N} \sim \mathcal{M} \Longrightarrow (\mathcal{N}, \mathrm{sr}^{\mathcal{N}}) \models \varphi.$$

Hence $\mathcal{C}^{L_\mu}(\varphi)$ is bisimulation closed. $\qquad\square$

Remark 14.10. We consider only definability by sentences. For MSO it makes no difference because the quantification is available. But in the case of the μ-calculus it is a proper restriction. To show this we define for an arbitrary L_μ-formula φ:

$$\mathcal{C}_*^{L_\mu}(\varphi) := \big\{\, \mathcal{M} \mid \mathcal{M} \text{ is a transition system and}$$
$$\mathrm{sr}^{\mathcal{M}} \in \|\varphi\|_\beta^{\mathcal{M}} \text{ for all assignments } \beta \,\big\}.$$

A class $\mathcal{C}$ of transition systems is called $\mathbf{L_\mu}$-**formula-definable** if there is a L_μ-formula φ defining the class. There are L_μ-formula-definable classes which are not closed under bisimulation. Consider for example the following L_μ-formula where $r \in \mathrm{Rel}$:

$$\varphi := \neg(\langle r \rangle X \wedge \langle r \rangle \neg X).$$

Let $\mathcal{C} := \mathcal{C}_*^{L_\mu}(\varphi)$. For a transition system $\mathcal{M}$ and an arbitrary assignment β we have $\mathrm{sr}^{\mathcal{M}} \in \|\varphi\|_\beta^{\mathcal{M}}$ iff either the set $\beta(X)$ or the complement of $\beta(X)$ does not contain any r-successor of $\mathrm{sr}^{\mathcal{M}}$, i.e., for all $\mathcal{M}$ in $\mathcal{C}$ we have that either

$\mathrm{scc}_r^{\mathcal{M}}(\mathrm{sr}^{\mathcal{M}}) \cap \beta(X)$ is empty or $\mathrm{scc}_r^{\mathcal{M}}(\mathrm{sr}^{\mathcal{M}})$ is a subset of $\beta(X)$ for every assignment $\beta(X)$. In particular we obtain for the special case $\beta(X) := \{s\}$ with $s \in S^{\mathcal{M}}$ that there is at most one $s \in S^{\mathcal{M}}$ such that $s \in \mathrm{scc}_r^{\mathcal{M}}(\mathrm{sr}^{\mathcal{M}})$ for every $\mathcal{M} \in \mathcal{C}$. But there are transition systems without this property although they are bisimilar to $\mathcal{M}$, so $\mathcal{C}$ is not bisimulation closed (cf. Remark 14.7).

One direction of the expressive completeness result is the following:

Proposition 14.11. *Every* L_μ-*definable class is* MSO-*definable as well.*

Proof. For every L_μ-formula φ there is a MSO-formula $\varphi^*(X)$ where the variable X does not occur in φ and such that for every transition system $\mathcal{M}$ and every assignment β with $\beta(X) = \{s\}$ for some $s \in S^{\mathcal{M}}$:

$$(\mathcal{M}, \beta) \models \varphi^*(X) \Longleftrightarrow s \in \|\varphi\|_\beta^{\mathcal{M}}.$$

For that we define recursively:

- For $\varphi = Y$ let $\varphi^*(X) := X \subseteq Y$,
- For $\varphi = p$ let $\varphi^*(X) := \exists Y.\big(p(Y) \wedge X \subseteq Y\big)$,
- For $\varphi = \neg\psi$ let $\varphi^*(X) := \neg\psi^*(X)$,
- For $\varphi = \psi \vee \chi$ let $\varphi^*(X) := \psi^*(X) \vee \chi^*(X)$,
- For $\varphi = \langle r \rangle\psi$ let $\varphi^*(X) := \exists Y.\big(r(X,Y) \wedge \psi^*(Y)\big)$ where Y does not occur in ψ,
- For $\varphi = \mu Y.\psi(Y)$ let $\varphi^*(X)$ be a pure second order version of the statement

$$\forall Y.\big(\forall z(z \in \psi^*(Y) \longrightarrow z \in Y) \longrightarrow X \subseteq Y\big),$$

where z is an additional first order variable.

It is easy to check that φ^* satisfies the property above. We obtain for any assignment β:

$$
\begin{aligned}
\big(\mathcal{M}, \mathrm{sr}^{\mathcal{M}}\big) \models \varphi &\Longleftrightarrow \mathrm{sr}^{\mathcal{M}} \in \|\varphi\|_\beta^{\mathcal{M}} \\
&\Longleftrightarrow \big(\mathcal{M}, \beta[X := \{\mathrm{sr}^{\mathcal{M}}\}]\big) \models \varphi^*(X) \\
&\Longleftrightarrow (\mathcal{M}, \beta) \models \exists X.\big(\mathrm{sr}(X) \wedge \varphi^*(X)\big).
\end{aligned}
$$

For an arbitrary L_μ-sentence φ the formula $\tilde{\varphi} := \exists X.\big(\mathrm{sr}(X) \wedge \varphi^*(X)\big)$ is a MSO-sentence. Hence it follows $\mathcal{C}^{\mathrm{L}_\mu}(\varphi) = \mathcal{C}^{\mathrm{MSO}}(\tilde{\varphi})$. $\qquad\square$

14.4 μ-Automata and μ-Games

Definition 14.12. Let $\mathcal{U} = \{p_1, \ldots, p_n\}$ be a finite set of propositional letters and $\mathrm{Sent}(\mathcal{U})$ a set of sentences of the first order logic (possibly with equality predicate) over the signature consisting of the unary predicates $\{p_1, \ldots, p_n\}$. A **marking** of a set T is a function $m : \mathcal{U} \to \mathscr{P}(T)$.

In the sequel we consider structures of the form $(T, \{\, m(p) \mid p \in \mathcal{U} \,\})$, i.e., a structure with carrier T where each predicate $p \in \mathcal{U}$ is interpreted as $m(p)$. If a sentence $\varphi \in \text{Sent}(\mathcal{U})$ is satisfied in this structure we write as usual

$$(T, \{\, m(p) \mid p \in \mathcal{U} \,\}) \models \varphi.$$

In our situation we fix a transition system $\mathcal{M}$. Let Q be a finite set of states (distinct from the ones of $S^{\mathcal{M}}$) and let $\Sigma_R \subseteq \text{Rel}$ be a finite set of letters for relations. Then we let $\mathcal{U} := \Sigma_R \times Q$. So each predicate $p \in \mathcal{U}$ is of the form $p = (r, q)$ for $r \in \Sigma_R$ and $q \in Q$. We fix a state $s \in S^{\mathcal{M}}$ and consider the set T of the r-successors of s for all $r \in \Sigma_R$.

Example 14.13. Let $Q := \{q_1, q_2\}$ and $\Sigma_R := \{r\}$. Let $s \in S^{\mathcal{M}}$ and let $m(r, q_1)$ and $m(r, q_2)$ be sets of r-successors of s. In the structure $\mathcal{N}$ with carrier $\text{scc}_r^{\mathcal{M}}(s)$ the predicate p_1 will be interpreted as $m(r, q_1)$ and p_2 as $m(r, q_2)$. We consider the first order formula $\varphi := \exists x_1, x_2.\left(\bigwedge_{i=1,2} p_i(x_i) \wedge \forall y. \bigvee_{i=1,2} p_i(y) \right)$. Then we have:

$$\mathcal{N} \models \varphi \Longleftrightarrow m(r, q_1) \neq \emptyset \wedge m(r, q_2) \neq \emptyset \wedge m(r, q_1) \cup m(r, q_2) = \text{scc}_r^{\mathcal{M}}(s).$$

So φ is true in $\mathcal{N}$ iff $m(r, q_1)$ and $m(r, q_2)$ forms a partition of the set of r-successors of s into two non-empty (but not necessarily disjunct) sets.

We are now ready to define the notion of μ-automata:

Definition 14.14. Let Q be a finite set of states and $q_\text{I} \in Q$ an initial state. Let $\Sigma_P \subseteq \text{Prop}$ be a finite set of unary predicate symbols, $\Sigma_R \subseteq \text{Rel}$ a finite set of binary predicate symbols and $\delta : Q \times \mathscr{P}(\Sigma_P) \to \text{Sent}(\Sigma_R \times Q)$ a transition function. Finally let $\Omega : Q \to \omega$ be a parity function defining the acceptance condition. Then we call the tuple

$$(Q, \Sigma_P, \Sigma_R, q_\text{I}, \delta, \Omega)$$

an **μ-automaton $\mathcal{A}$**.

In fact this is the definition of an alternating parity automaton. Observe that the μ-automaton has two alphabets Σ_P and Σ_R, the first is for checking properties of states and the second is for checking the labels of taken transitions.

We will define the acceptance of arbitrary transition systems by the μ-automaton in terms of games. But we introduce first some abbreviations: for a given transition system $\mathcal{M}$ and a state $s \in S^{\mathcal{M}}$ let

$$L^{\mathcal{M}}(s) := \{\, p \in \Sigma_P \mid (\mathcal{M}, s) \models p \,\} = \{\, p \in \text{Prop} \mid s \in p^{\mathcal{M}} \,\} \cap \Sigma_P$$

be the set of all propositional letters p in Σ_P such that s satisfies p in $\mathcal{M}$ and

$$\text{SCC}^{\mathcal{M}}(s) := \bigcup_{r \in \Sigma_R} \text{scc}_r^{\mathcal{M}}(s)$$

the set of all r-successors of s for $r \in \Sigma_R$.

Definition 14.15. Let $\mathcal{M}$ be a transition system and let $\mathcal{A}$ be a μ-automaton. We consider the following μ-**game** $\mathcal{G}(\mathcal{M}, \mathcal{A})$:

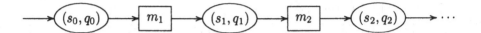

The initial position is $(s_0, q_0) = (\mathrm{sr}^{\mathcal{M}}, q_{\mathrm{I}})$. If the current position is (s_i, q_i) then Player 0 is to move. Player 0 chooses a marking m_{i+1} of $\mathrm{SCC}^{\mathcal{M}}(s_i)$ – i.e., a function $m_{i+1} : \Sigma_R \times Q \to \mathscr{P}(\mathrm{SCC}^{\mathcal{M}}(s_i))$ – such that:

- for every $r \in \Sigma_R$ and every $q \in Q$ the elements of $m_{i+1}(r, q)$ are r-successors of s_i,
- the structure $\mathcal{N} := \left(\mathrm{SCC}^{\mathcal{M}}(s_i), \{\, m_{i+1}(r, q) \mid r \in \Sigma_R, q \in Q \,\}\right)$ is a model of the first order sentence $\delta\left(q_i, L^{\mathcal{M}}(s_i)\right)$:

$$\mathcal{N} \models \delta\left(q_i, L^{\mathcal{M}}(s_i)\right).$$

If the current position is a marking m_i then Player 1 is to move and he chooses $r_i \in \Sigma_R$, $q_i \in Q$ and a state $s_i \in m_i(r_i, q_i)$. The pair (s_i, q_i) becomes the next position.

The criterion for winning the μ-game is as follows: one player wins if the other cannot make a move. Otherwise the play is infinite and we obtain the sequence

$$\left(\mathrm{sr}^{\mathcal{M}}, q_{\mathrm{I}}\right), m_1, (s_1, q_1), m_2, \ldots$$

Let $\pi = q_{\mathrm{I}} q_1 q_2 \ldots$ be the sequence of played states. Because of the finiteness of Q and the pigeonhole principle there is a $j \in \omega$ such that j appears infinitely often in the sequence $\Omega(q_{\mathrm{I}}), \Omega(q_1), \ldots$ Let $\min \mathrm{Inf}(\Omega(\pi))$ be the smallest number with this property. Then Player 0 wins the μ-game iff $\min \mathrm{Inf}(\Omega(\pi))$ is even. So $\mathcal{G}(\mathcal{M}, \mathcal{A})$ is in fact a sort of a parity game.

The transition system $\mathcal{M}$ is **accepted by the μ-automaton** $\mathcal{A}$ if there is a winning strategy f_0 for Player 0 in the μ-game $\mathcal{G}(\mathcal{M}, \mathcal{A})$. The class

$$L(\mathcal{A}) := \{\, \mathcal{M} \mid \mathcal{M} \text{ is a transition system accepted by } \mathcal{A} \,\}$$

is called the **language recognized by** $\mathcal{A}$.

We define for every $n \in \omega$ the formula **diff** of first order logic as follows:

$$\mathrm{diff}(x_1, \ldots, x_n) := \bigwedge_{1 \le i < j \le n} x_i \neq x_j.$$

The formula "diff" states that the values of $x_1, \ldots, x_n$ are pairwise different.

The main tool for our purpose is the following correspondence of μ-automata and formulae of L_μ and MSO respectively which was proved by Janin and Walukiewicz.

Theorem 14.16.

(1) *A class C of* **transition systems** *is* $\mathbf{L_\mu}$**-definable** *iff $C = L(A)$ for a μ-automaton $A = (Q, \Sigma_P, \Sigma_R, q_I, \delta, \Omega)$ such that $\mathrm{Sent}(\Sigma_R \times Q)$ contains only disjunctions of sentences of the form:*

$$\exists x_1, \ldots, x_m.\left(\bigwedge_{1 \le i \le m} p_{k_i}(x_i) \wedge \forall y. \bigvee_{1 \le i \le m} p_{k_i}(y)\right),$$

where $p_{k_i} \in \Sigma_R \times Q$ for $i \in \{1, \ldots, m\}$;

(2) *A class C of* **transition systems** *is* $\mathbf{L_\mu}$**-formula-definable** *iff $C = L(A)$ for a μ-automaton $A(Q, \Sigma_P, \Sigma_R, q_I, \delta, \Omega)$ such that $\mathrm{Sent}(\Sigma_R \times Q)$ contains only disjunctions of formulae of the form:*

$$\exists x_1, \ldots, x_m.\left(\bigwedge_{1 \le i \le m} p_{k_i}(x_i) \wedge \forall y.\chi(y)\right),$$

where $p_{k_i} \in \Sigma_R \times Q$ for $i \in \{1, \ldots, m\}$ and $\chi(y)$ is a disjunction of conjunctions of formulae of the form $p(y)$ for $p \in \Sigma_R \times Q$;

(3) *A class C of* **transition trees** *is* **MSO-definable** *iff $C = L(A)$ for a μ-automaton $A(Q, \Sigma_P, \Sigma_R, q_I, \delta, \Omega)$ such that $\mathrm{Sent}(\Sigma_R \times Q)$ contains only disjunctions of formulae of the form:*

$$\exists x_1, \ldots, x_m.\left(\bigwedge_{1 \le i \le m} p_{k_i}(x_i) \wedge \mathrm{diff}(x_1, \ldots, x_m) \wedge \right.$$
$$\left. \forall y.\left(\mathrm{diff}(y, x_1, \ldots, x_m) \longrightarrow \chi(y)\right)\right),$$

where $p_{k_i} \in \Sigma_R \times Q$ for $i \in \{1, \ldots, m\}$ and $\chi(y)$ is a disjunction of conjunctions of formulae of the form $p(y)$ for $p \in \Sigma_R \times Q$.

In all three cases empty disjunctions are allowed, i.e., the set $\mathrm{Sent}(\Sigma_R \times Q)$ may contain the sentence $\varphi = \bot$ (since we have $\bigvee \emptyset = \bot$).

In fact it can be shown that, if the μ-automaton A has the alphabets Σ_P and Σ_R then the corresponding formula which defines the class C is also in this language, i.e., only unary and binary predicate symbols of Σ_P and Σ_R respectively occur in the formula. The converse also holds: if C is defined by a formula φ such that the set of unary predicate symbols in φ is Σ_P and its set of binary predicate symbols is Σ_R then the corresponding μ-automata may be assumed to have the same alphabets Σ_P and Σ_R.

Item (1) is a reformulation of a result in [90] and the proof of item (2) can be found in [89]. For item (3) see Lemma 16.23 in Chapter 16.

Since most readers will not be familiar with μ-automata and the games played on them and since their transition function is unusual we will give an example here.

Example 14.17. We consider the L_μ-formula $\varphi := \langle r^* \rangle p$ which is equivalent to $\mu X.(p \vee \langle r \rangle X)$. So we have $(\mathcal{M}, s) \models \varphi$ iff there is a (possibly empty) r-path starting from s to a state in $\mathcal{M}$ where p holds. Let $\Sigma_P := \{p\}$, $\Sigma_R := \{r\}$ and $Q := \{q_1, q_2\}$. We define the μ-automaton

$$\mathcal{A} := (Q, \Sigma_P, \Sigma_R, q_1, \delta, \Omega),$$

where the parity function is defined as $\Omega(q_1) = 1$, $\Omega(q_2) = 0$ and the transition function as

$$\delta(q, P) := \begin{cases} \exists x_1, x_2. \left(\bigwedge_{i=1,2} p_i(x_i) \wedge \forall y. \bigvee_{i=1,2} p_i(y) \right) & \text{if } q = q_1 \text{ and } P = \emptyset, \\ \forall y. \bot \vee \exists x. (p_2(x) \wedge \forall y. p_2(y)) & \text{otherwise.} \end{cases}$$

Notice that since we have $\bigwedge \emptyset = \top$ and $\bigvee \emptyset = \bot$ the sentence

$$\exists x_1, \ldots, x_k. \left(\bigwedge_{1 \leq i \leq k} p_i(x_i) \wedge \forall y. \bigvee_{1 \leq i \leq k} p_i(y) \right) \tag{14.1}$$

is equivalent to $\forall y. \bot$ for $k = 0$. Hence the formulae $\delta(q, P)$ are disjunctions of sentences of the form (14.1) and therefore as stated in Theorem 14.16(1).

Let $\mathcal{M}$ be an arbitrary transition system. We consider the μ-game $\mathcal{G} := \mathcal{G}(\mathcal{M}, \mathcal{A})$. Notice that the game always starts with the position $(\text{sr}^{\mathcal{M}}, q_1)$. If the current position in $\mathcal{G}$ is (s, q_j) for $j = 1, 2$ and $s \in S^{\mathcal{M}}$ then a move of Player 0 is a marking $m : \Sigma_R \times Q \to \mathscr{P}(\text{scc}_r^{\mathcal{M}}(s))$. This move is legal if the structure with carrier $\text{scc}_r^{\mathcal{M}}(s)$ is a model of the formula $\delta(q_j, L^{\mathcal{M}}(s))$, where the predicate p_i is interpreted as the set $m(r, q_i)$ for $i = 1, 2$.

Claim. Assume that the current position in $\mathcal{G}$ is (s, q_2). Then Player 0 has a strategy to win.

Proof (of Claim). Player 0 plays the marking m defined as $m(r, q_1) = \emptyset$ and $m(r, q_2) = \text{scc}_r^{\mathcal{M}}(s)$. We have to check that m is indeed a legal move and that this move leads Player 0 toward winning the game.
Case 1. There is no r-successor of s in $\mathcal{M}$. Then the structure with carrier $\emptyset$ is a model of $\forall y. \bot$, hence the move is legal. Since both $m(r, q_1)$ and $m(r, q_2)$ are empty Player 1 cannot respond with any position and looses the game.
Case 2. The set $\text{scc}_r^{\mathcal{M}}(s)$ is non-empty. Since p_2 is interpreted as $m(r, q_2) = \text{scc}_r^{\mathcal{M}}(s)$ we have

$$(\text{scc}_r^{\mathcal{M}}(s), \{m(r, q_1), m(r, q_2)\}) \models \exists x. (p_2(x) \wedge \forall y. p_2(y)),$$

so the move is legal as well. Since $m(r, q_1)$ is empty Player 1 can only respond with a position (t, q_2) where t is a r-successor of s. To this position we can apply the same strategy again. If the resulting play is infinite then only q_2 is encountered infinitely often. So we have $\min \text{Inf}(\Omega(\pi)) = 0$ and therefore Player 0 wins the game. $\qquad \square$(Claim)

Now we prove that $\mathcal{C}^{\mathsf{L}_\mu}(\varphi) = L(\mathcal{A})$.

($\subseteq$) Let $\mathcal{M}$ be a transition system with $(\mathcal{M}, \text{sr}^{\mathcal{M}}) \models \varphi$, i.e., there is a sequence $s_0 = \text{sr}^{\mathcal{M}}, s_1, \ldots, s_n$ with $s_{i+1} \in \text{scc}_r^{\mathcal{M}}(s_i)$ for $i < n$ such that $(\mathcal{M}, s_n) \models p$. We may assume that $(\mathcal{M}, s_i) \not\models p$ for $i < n$.

If the current position is (s_i, q_1) with $i < n$ then Player 0 plays the marking m_{i+1} defined by $m_{i+1}(r, q_1) = \{s_{i+1}\}$ and $m_{i+1}(r, q_2) = \mathrm{scc}_r^{\mathcal{M}}(s_i)$. Since $L^{\mathcal{M}}(s_i) = \emptyset$ we have

$$\left(\mathrm{scc}_r^{\mathcal{M}}(s_i), \{m_{i+1}(r, q_1), m_{i+1}(r, q_2)\}\right) \models \delta(q_1, \emptyset),$$

so the move is legal. Then Player 1 must respond with the position (s_{i+1}, q_1), since otherwise he would loose the game by the claim above.

So eventually the position (s_n, q_1) is reached. Player 0 then plays the marking with $m_{n+1}(r, q_1) = \emptyset$ and $m_{n+1}(r, q_2) = \mathrm{scc}_r^{\mathcal{M}}(s_n)$. Now we have $L^{\mathcal{M}}(s_n) = \{p\}$ and the move is legal by

$$\left(\mathrm{scc}_r^{\mathcal{M}}(s_n), \{m_{n+1}(r, q_2), m_{n+1}(r, q_1)\}\right) \models \delta(q_1, \{p\}).$$

If Player 1 can make a move at all he can only respond with the position (t, q_2) for an r-successor t of s_n, so by the claim above he looses the game. This means that the strategy for Player 0 presented above is a winning strategy in the game $\mathcal{G}(\mathcal{M}, \mathcal{A})$ and therefore we obtain $\mathcal{M} \in L(\mathcal{A})$.

$(\supseteq)$ Let $\mathcal{M}$ be a transition system with $(\mathcal{M}, \mathrm{sr}^{\mathcal{M}}) \not\models \varphi$. Let (s, q_1) be the current position in the game $\mathcal{G}$. Since we have $\Sigma_R = \{r\}$ the states s_i of any prefix of a play in $\mathcal{G}$ form an r-path of $\mathcal{M}$ starting in $\mathrm{sr}^{\mathcal{M}}$. By the assumption we have $(\mathcal{M}, s) \not\models p$ and therefore $L^{\mathcal{M}}(s) = \emptyset$. Player 0 has to satisfy $\delta(q_1, \emptyset)$ in the structure with carrier $\mathrm{scc}_r^{\mathcal{M}}(s)$, so he must play two non-empty subsets $m(r, q_1)$ and $m(r, q_2)$ of $\mathrm{scc}_r^{\mathcal{M}}(s)$ such that the union is the whole set (cf. Example 14.13). Otherwise he would loose the game. If he can make a move at all then let $t \in m(r, q_1)$ be an r-successor of s. Player 1 responds with the position (t, q_1). By the assumption we have $(\mathcal{M}, t) \not\models p$ as well, so we can apply the same strategy again. With this strategy either Player 0 cannot make a move or an infinite game is played, where only q_1 is encountered infinitely often. Because $\Omega(q_1)$ is odd Player 1 wins the game. So we obtain a winning strategy for Player 1 and therefore we have $\mathcal{M} \notin L(\mathcal{A})$.

14.5 Expressive Completeness

Theorem 14.16 suggest a strong connection between monadic second order logic and the modal μ-calculus. But the basic sentences of MSO are more expressive. We are for example able to compare the number of r-successors of a state s with some constant by the use of the existential quantification together with the formula "diff(x)". On the other hand we conjecture that the equivalent μ-automaton for a MSO-definable and bisimulation closed class of transition systems should not use the formula "diff" and hence the class should be also L_μ-definable by the last theorem. In this section we will prove this conjecture. Notice that the considered μ-automata are non-deterministic, so the argument must deal with this fact, i.e., the μ-automaton may have only runs using instances of the formula "diff" but nevertheless the μ-automaton accepts a bisimulation closed class. This means that at last the acceptance of this class does not depend on the use of instances of the formula "diff" in the particular run.

Theorem 14.18. *Let C be a bisimulation closed class of transition systems, then*

C *is MSO-definable* $\Longleftrightarrow C$ *is L_μ-definable.*

For one direction we need the following lemma:

Lemma 14.19. *Let φ be a MSO-sentence. Then there is an effectively constructible L_μ-sentence $\widehat{\varphi}$ such that for every transition system M:*

$$\widehat{M} \models \varphi \Longleftrightarrow (M, \mathrm{sr}^M) \models \widehat{\varphi}.$$

Before proving the lemma let us show how it implies the theorem:

Proof (of Theorem 14.18). Let C be a bisimulation closed class of transition systems.

($\Leftarrow$) By Proposition 14.11 every L_μ-definable class is MSO-definable as well.

($\Rightarrow$) Let φ be a MSO-sentence defining the class C. Let M be an arbitrary transition system. By Exercise 14.2, M and $\widehat{M}$ are bisimilar. Since C is bisimulation closed we obtain $M \models \varphi \Longleftrightarrow \widehat{M} \models \varphi$. Let $\widehat{\varphi}$ be the L_μ-sentence given by Lemma 14.19, so

$$M \models \varphi \Longleftrightarrow \widehat{M} \models \varphi \Longleftrightarrow (M, \mathrm{sr}^M) \models \widehat{\varphi}.$$

In particular we have $C = C^{\mathrm{MSO}}(\varphi) = C^{L_\mu}(\widehat{\varphi})$ and so C is L_μ-definable. $\square$

It remains to prove the lemma:

Proof (of Lemma 14.19). For a formula ψ of the form

$$\exists x_1, \ldots, x_m. \left(\bigwedge_{1 \le i \le m} p_{k_i}(x_i) \wedge \mathrm{diff}(x_1, \ldots, x_m) \wedge \right.$$
$$\left. \forall y. (\mathrm{diff}(y, x_1, \ldots, x_m) \longrightarrow \chi(y)) \right) \quad (14.2)$$

we define the formula ψ^* by substituting "true" for "diff" in ψ:

$$\psi^* := \exists x_1, \ldots, x_m. \left(\bigwedge_{1 \le i \le m} p_{k_i}(x_i) \wedge \forall y. \chi(y) \right). \quad (14.3)$$

For a disjunction $\theta = \psi_1 \vee \cdots \vee \psi_l$ let $\theta^* := \psi_1^* \vee \cdots \vee \psi_l^*$.

Let φ be a MSO-sentence and let C be the class of transition trees defined by φ (notice that we consider transition *trees* here). By Theorem 14.16(3) there is a μ-automaton $A = (Q, \Sigma_P, \Sigma_R, q_1, \delta, \Omega)$ such that $C = L(A)$ and all formulae of $\mathrm{Sent}(\Sigma_R \times Q)$ have the form as stated in the theorem. In particular for every $q \in Q$ and $P \subseteq \Sigma_P$ the formula $\delta(q, P)$ is a disjunction of formulae of the form given by (14.2). Let $\delta^*(q, P) := (\delta(q, P))^*$. We define the μ-automaton A^* by

$$A^* = (Q, \Sigma_P, \Sigma_R, q_1, \delta^*, \Omega).$$

Claim. Let $\mathcal{M}$ be a transition system. Then $\mathcal{M}$ is accepted by $\mathcal{A}^*$ iff $\widehat{\mathcal{M}}$ is accepted by $\mathcal{A}$.

Before proving the claim let us show how it implies the lemma. By definition of the function δ^* the μ-automaton $\mathcal{A}^*$ has the required form of Theorem 14.16(2). Hence there is a L_μ-sentence $\widehat{\varphi}$ such that $L(\mathcal{A}^*) = \mathcal{C}^{L_\mu}(\widehat{\varphi})$. By Exercise 14.2 the ω-unravelling $\widehat{\mathcal{M}}$ is a transition tree for every transition system $\mathcal{M}$, hence we obtain by the claim

$$\widehat{\mathcal{M}} \in \mathcal{C} = L(\mathcal{A}) \iff \mathcal{M} \in L(\mathcal{A}^*) = \mathcal{C}^{L_\mu}(\widehat{\varphi}).$$

So we have

$$\widehat{\mathcal{M}} \models \varphi \iff (\mathcal{M}, \mathrm{sr}^{\mathcal{M}}) \models \widehat{\varphi}.$$

It remains to prove the claim:

Proof (of Claim). ($\Rightarrow$) Suppose that $\mathcal{M}$ is accepted by $\mathcal{A}^*$. We want to show that $\widehat{\mathcal{M}}$ is accepted by $\mathcal{A}$. We consider the μ-games $\mathcal{G}^* := \mathcal{G}(\mathcal{M}, \mathcal{A}^*)$ and $\mathcal{G} := \mathcal{G}(\widehat{\mathcal{M}}, \mathcal{A})$. By the assumption Player 0 has a winning strategy f_0^* in the game $\mathcal{G}^*$. We want to define inductively a winning strategy f_0 for Player 0 in the game $\mathcal{G}$. For that we play the games $\mathcal{G}^*$ and $\mathcal{G}$ simultaneously and transfer each move of Player 1 from $\mathcal{G}$ to $\mathcal{G}^*$. Then we transfer the suggested move of Player 0 by the given strategy f_0^* in the game $\mathcal{G}^*$ back to $\mathcal{G}$. Both games have the initial position $(\mathrm{sr}^{\mathcal{M}}, q_I)$. Let

$$(\mathrm{sr}^{\mathcal{M}}, q_I), m_1, (u_1, q_1), \ldots, m_n, (u_n, q_n)$$

be a prefix of a play in the game $\mathcal{G}$ according to the induction. Since we have that u_{i+1} is an r_{i+1}-successor of u_i for some $r_{i+1} \in \Sigma_R$ we may assume that $u_{i+1} = u_i(a_{i+1}, r_{i+1}, s_{i+1})$ holds for every $i < n$ with $a_{i+1} \in \omega$ and $s_{i+1} \in S^{\mathcal{M}}$. Consider the corresponding prefix

$$(\mathrm{sr}^{\mathcal{M}}, q_I), m_1^*, (s_1, q_1), \ldots, m_n^*, (s_n, q_n)$$

in the game $\mathcal{G}^*$ where s_{i+1} is an r_{i+1}-successor of s_i and the markings m_i^* are according to the strategy f_0^*. Let $m_{n+1}^* : \Sigma_R \times Q \to \mathscr{P}(\mathrm{SCC}^{\mathcal{M}}(s_n))$ be the marking suggested by f_0^* for the current position (s_n, q_n). We define the marking $m_{n+1} : \Sigma_R \times Q \to \mathscr{P}(\mathrm{SCC}^{\widehat{\mathcal{M}}}(u_n))$ by

$$m_{n+1}(r, q) := \bigcup_{a \in \omega} \{ u_n(a, r, t) \mid t \in m_{n+1}^*(r, q) \}.$$

In particular we have

$$m_{n+1}^* \neq \emptyset \implies m_{n+1} \neq \emptyset. \tag{14.4}$$

By definition of the ω-unravelling we have $m_{n+1}(r,q) \subseteq \mathrm{scc}_r^{\widehat{\mathcal{M}}}(u_n)$. Moreover it holds

$$s_n \in p^{\mathcal{M}} \iff u_n \in p^{\widehat{\mathcal{M}}}, \tag{14.5}$$

in particular $L^{\mathcal{M}}(s_n) = L^{\widehat{\mathcal{M}}}(u_n)$ and therefore

$$\delta^*\big(q_n, L^{\mathcal{M}}(s_n)\big) = \big(\delta(q_n, L^{\widehat{\mathcal{M}}}(u_n))\big)^*. \tag{14.6}$$

Next we define abbreviations for the two first order structures which occur in the rules of the games:

$$\mathcal{N} := (\mathrm{SCC}^{\mathcal{M}}(s_n), \{\, m_{n+1}^*(r,q) \mid r \in \Sigma_R, q \in Q \,\})$$

and

$$\widehat{\mathcal{N}} := \Big(\mathrm{SCC}^{\widehat{\mathcal{M}}}(u_n), \{\, m_{n+1}(r,q) \mid r \in \Sigma_R, q \in Q \,\}\Big).$$

By the fact that m_{n+1}^* is a legal move of Player 0 in the game $\mathcal{G}^*$ we have

$$\mathcal{N} \models \delta^*\big(q_n, L^{\mathcal{M}}(s_n)\big). \tag{14.7}$$

Let ψ^* be some satisfied disjunct of $\delta^*\big(q_n, L^{\mathcal{M}}(s_n)\big)$ of the form (14.3). We will show that

$$\widehat{\mathcal{N}} \models \psi,$$

where ψ has the original form given by (14.2). By (14.4) the 'existential part' of ψ is satisfied by the structure $\widehat{\mathcal{N}}$ as well. Because of the ω-indexing there are infinitely many elements in $m_{n+1}(r,q)$ corresponding to each single element in $m_{n+1}^*(r,q)$. Hence we can always choose pairwise different witnesses in $\widehat{\mathcal{N}}$, i.e., the formula $\mathrm{diff}(x_1,\ldots,x_m)$ is additionally satisfied.

Next we check that $\widehat{\mathcal{N}}$ is a model of $\forall y.\chi(y)$ as well, in particular the restriction $\forall y.\big(\mathrm{diff}(y, x_1,\ldots,x_m) \longrightarrow \chi(y)\big)$ and therefore ψ is satisfied by $\widehat{\mathcal{N}}$. To see this let $v = u_n(a,r,t)$ be an arbitrary element of $\mathrm{SCC}^{\widehat{\mathcal{M}}}(u_n)$. Then t is an r-successor of s_n and by (14.7) we have $\mathcal{N} \models \chi(t)$, i.e., $\mathcal{N}$ is a model of some appropriate predicates $p(t)$ occurring in χ. Since each p is interpreted as $m_{n+1}^*(r,q)$ for some $q \in Q$ it follows that $t \in m_{n+1}^*(r,q)$ and therefore $v \in m_{n+1}(r,q)$ by the definition of m_{n+1}. This means that $\widehat{\mathcal{N}}$ is a model of the same predicates $p(v)$ and therefore a model of $\chi(v)$.

In summary this means that taking m_{n+1} is indeed a legal move of Player 0 in the game $\mathcal{G}$. So we define the value of the strategy f_0 for the current position by m_{n+1}. From this position Player 1 chooses some $r_{n+1} \in \Sigma_R$, $q_{n+1} \in Q$ and a state $u_{n+1} \in m_{n+1}(r_{n+1}, q_{n+1})$ with $u_{n+1} = u_n(a, r_{n+1}, t)$. The pair (u_{n+1}, q_{n+1}) becomes the next position in the game $\mathcal{G}$. Now we let $s_{n+1} := t$ and continue the game $\mathcal{G}^*$ by the move (s_{n+1}, q_{n+1}) of Player 1. We arrive at prefixes of plays in $\mathcal{G}$ and $\mathcal{G}^*$ satisfying our initial assumption.

It is clear that if Player 1 gets stuck in the game $\mathcal{G}^*$ then he cannot make a move in the game $\mathcal{G}$ as well. On the other hand by the inductive definition of the strategy f_0 Player 0 can always make a move in $\mathcal{G}$. Hence he cannot lose in a finite number of rounds. For an infinite play the result is the sequence

$$\left(\mathrm{sr}^{\mathcal{M}}, q_{\mathrm{I}}\right), m_1, (u_1, q_1), \ldots, m_n, (u_n, q_n), \ldots$$

The corresponding play in $\mathcal{G}^*$ is infinite as well:

$$\left(\mathrm{sr}^{\mathcal{M}}, q_{\mathrm{I}}\right), m_1^*, (s_1, q_1), \ldots, m_n^*, (s_n, q_n), \ldots$$

Let $\pi = q_{\mathrm{I}} q_1 q_2 \ldots$ be the sequence of the played automaton states, which is the same for both games. Because the play in $\mathcal{G}^*$ is according to the winning strategy f_0^* the smallest integer appearing infinitely often in the sequence $\Omega(q_{\mathrm{I}})\Omega(q_1)\ldots$ is even. But the parity function Ω is identical for both automata and therefore the value of $\min \mathrm{Inf}(\Omega(\pi))$ is the same. It follows that Player 0 wins the game $\mathcal{G}$ as well. Hence f_0 is indeed a winning strategy for Player 0 and $\widehat{\mathcal{M}}$ is accepted by the μ-automaton $\mathcal{A}$.

($\Leftarrow$) Suppose now that $\widehat{\mathcal{M}}$ is accepted by $\mathcal{A}$ and let f_0 be a winning strategy for Player 0 in the game $\mathcal{G}$. The argument is analogous to the one above with interchanged roles of the games, i.e., now we want to define inductively a winning strategy f_0^* for Player 0 in the game $\mathcal{G}^*$. We use the same notations as before. Let

$$\left(\mathrm{sr}^{\mathcal{M}}, q_{\mathrm{I}}\right), m_1^*, (s_1, q_1), \ldots, m_n^*, (s_n, q_n)$$

be a prefix of a play in the game $\mathcal{G}^*$ according to the induction and let

$$\left(\mathrm{sr}^{\mathcal{M}}, q_{\mathrm{I}}\right), m_1, (u_1, q_1), \ldots, m_n, (u_n, q_n)$$

be the corresponding prefix in the game $\mathcal{G}$ where we have: if $s_{i+1} \in \mathrm{scc}_r^{\mathcal{M}}(s_i)$ holds for $r \in \Sigma_R$ then $u_{i+1} = u_i(a, r, s_{i+1})$ for some $a \in \omega$. The markings m_i are played according to the strategy f_0.

Let $m_{n+1} : \Sigma_R \times Q \to \mathscr{P}(\mathrm{SCC}^{\mathcal{M}}(u_n))$ be the marking suggested by f_0. We define the marking $m_{n+1}^* : \Sigma_R \times Q \to \mathscr{P}(\mathrm{SCC}^{\mathcal{M}}(s_n))$ by

$$m_{n+1}^*(r, q) := \left\{ t \in S^{\mathcal{M}} \mid \exists a \in \omega.\left(u_n(a, r, t) \in m_{n+1}(r, q)\right) \right\}.$$

Again we have $m_{n+1}^*(r, q) \subseteq \mathrm{scc}_r^{\mathcal{M}}(s_n)$ by the definition of the ω-unravelling. Since m_{n+1} is a legal move of Player 0 in the game $\mathcal{G}$ we have

$$\widehat{\mathcal{N}} \models \delta\left(q_n, L^{\widehat{\mathcal{M}}}(u_n)\right). \tag{14.8}$$

Let ψ be some satisfied disjunct of $\delta\left(q_n, L^{\widehat{\mathcal{M}}}(u_n)\right)$. We have to check that m_{n+1}^* is indeed a legal move of Player 0 in the game $\mathcal{G}^*$. By (14.6) it suffices to show that

$$\mathcal{N} \models \psi^*, \tag{14.9}$$

where ψ^* is the formula defined by (14.3). We may assume that the occurring predicates are $p_{k_i} = (r_i', q_i')$ with $r_i' \in \Sigma_R$ and $q_i' \in Q$ for every $i \in \{1, \ldots, m\}$. First we check that

$$m_{n+1}^*(r_i', q_i') \neq \emptyset \text{ for } i \in \{1, \ldots, m\}$$

and therefore

$$\mathcal{N} \models \exists x_1, \ldots, x_m. \bigwedge_{1 \leq i \leq m} p_{k_i}(x_i). \tag{14.10}$$

By (14.8) it follows that $\widehat{\mathcal{N}} \models \exists x_1, \ldots, x_m. \bigwedge_{1 \leq i \leq m} p_{k_i}(x_i)$, in particular $\widehat{\mathcal{N}} \models \exists x_i. p_{k_i}(x_i)$ for every $i \in \{1, \ldots, m\}$. Hence there is some $v \in \text{SCC}^{\widehat{\mathcal{M}}}(u_n)$ such that $v \in m_{n+1}(r_i', q_i')$. By the definition of successors in $\widehat{\mathcal{M}}$ and the fact that $m_{n+1}(r_i', q_i')$ contains only r_i'-successors of u_n in $\widehat{\mathcal{M}}$ we have $v = u_n(a, r_i', t)$ for some $a \in \omega$ and $t \in S^{\mathcal{M}}$. Hence $t \in m_{n+1}^*(r_i', q_i')$ by the definition of m_{n+1}^*. Next we check

$$\mathcal{N} \models \forall y. \chi(y). \tag{14.11}$$

Let $t \in \text{scc}_r^{\mathcal{M}}(s_n)$ for some $r \in \Sigma_R$. We use again the property of the ω-unravelling that there are infinitely many different r-successors of u_n in $\widehat{\mathcal{M}}$ corresponding to each r-successor of s_n in $\mathcal{M}$. Hence there exists an $a \in \omega$ such that for $v = u_n(a, r, t)$ we have $\widehat{\mathcal{N}} \models \text{diff}(v, x_1, \ldots, x_m)$. Therefore $\widehat{\mathcal{N}} \models \chi(v)$ holds by (14.8). Since χ is monotone in the predicates we obtain $\mathcal{N} \models \chi(t)$. To see this, notice that $\chi(v)$ has the form $\chi(v) = \bigvee_w \bigwedge_{w'} p_{w,w'}(v)$ with $p_{w,w'} \in \Sigma_R \times Q$. So we have $\widehat{\mathcal{N}} \models p_{w,w'}(v)$ for some appropriate pairs (w, w'), i.e., v is an element of $m_{n+1}(r, q_{w,w'})$. We obtain $t \in m_{n+1}^*(r, q_{w,w'})$ by the definition of m_{n+1}^* and therefore $\mathcal{N} \models p_{w,w'}(t)$ for the same predicates, i.e., $\mathcal{N} \models \chi(t)$ is true. By (14.10) and (14.11) and the definition of ψ^* we have $\mathcal{N} \models \psi^*$. This proves (14.9).

Taking m_{n+1}^* is therefore a legal move of Player 0 in the game $\mathcal{G}^*$. We define the value of the strategy f_0^* for the current position by m_{n+1}^* and arrive at the prefix

$$(\text{sr}^{\mathcal{M}}, q_{\text{I}}), m_1, (u_1, q_1), \ldots, m_n, (u_n, q_n), m_{n+1}$$

in the game $\mathcal{G}$ and the corresponding prefix

$$(\text{sr}^{\mathcal{M}}, q_{\text{I}}), m_1^*, (s_1, q_1), \ldots, m_n^*, (s_n, q_n), m_{n+1}^*$$

in the game $\mathcal{G}^*$. From this position in $\mathcal{G}^*$ Player 1 chooses some $r_{n+1} \in \Sigma_R$, $q_{n+1} \in Q$ and a state $s_{n+1} \in m_{n+1}^*(r_{n+1}, q_{n+1})$ and the pair (s_{n+1}, q_{n+1}) becomes the next position in $\mathcal{G}^*$. By definition of m_{n+1}^* there is an $a \in \omega$ such that $u_n(a, r_{n+1}, s_{n+1}) \in m_{n+1}(r_{n+1}, q_{n+1})$. We choose some $a_{n+1} \in \omega$ with this property and define

$$u_{n+1} := u_n(a_{n+1}, r_{n+1}, s_{n+1}).$$

Then (u_{n+1}, q_{n+1}) is a legal move of Player 1 in the game $\mathcal{G}$ and we continue it by this move. Again we arrive at prefixes of plays in $\mathcal{G}$ and $\mathcal{G}^*$ satisfying our initial assumptions.

We have to check that f_0^* is indeed a winning strategy for Player 0 in the game $\mathcal{G}^*$. By the inductive definition of f_0^* Player 0 can always make a move and hence he cannot lose in a finite number of rounds. As in the first case the played automaton states in any infinite play of $\mathcal{G}$ and in the corresponding infinite play of $\mathcal{G}^*$ are the same and the parity functions of both automata are identical. Since the play in $\mathcal{G}$ is according to the winning strategy f_0 of Player 0 the value of $\min \mathrm{Inf}(\Omega(\pi))$ is even. It follows that Player 0 wins the game $\mathcal{G}^*$ as well. Hence f_0^* is indeed a winning strategy for Player 0 and $\mathcal{M}$ is accepted by the μ-automaton $\mathcal{A}^*$.

This completes the proof of the Claim and of Lemma 14.19.   □

Since the branching time temporal logic CTL* is easily translatable into monadic second order logic over unwindings of transition systems and formulae resulting from this translation are bisimulation closed we obtain immediately a result of Dam shown in [44]:

Corollary 14.20. CTL* *is translatable into* L_μ.

Notes on Part VI

The origin of the study of monadic second-order theories is sketched in the introduction to Chapter 12. The observation that a tight connection between finite automata and monadic second-order logic can be used to show decidability results for arithmetical theories is first found in [17], [51], and [187], first for the weak theory of successor WS1S (where set variables range over finite sets), then in [18] for the theory S1S.

This decidability result on S1S, in particular the automata method presented there, was then extended in many directions. The most prominent step was Rabin's Tree Theorem on the decidability of S2S [148]. Precursor papers were [45] and [176], where the weak monadic theory WS2S of the binary tree was shown to be decidable.

Several of the many decidability results which can be inferred from Rabin's Tree Theorem are covered in Chapter 12, see also Rabin's survey [151]. In the subsequent part of the book, classes of infinite graphs which have a decidable monadic theory are presented. Here we mention some other tracks of research.

In [19, 20], Büchi started the analysis of monadic theories of transfinite ordinals (considered as linear orderings); it was shown that the ordinal ω_1 has a decidable monadic theory. Gurevich, Magidor and Shelah [78] showed that the monadic theories of ω_2 and of higher ordinals depend on set theoretic assumptions beyond the system ZFC.

Other extensions of Büchi's result on S1S were obtained by adding fixed predicates like "is a factorial number". First results were obtained by Elgot and Rabin [52]; for recent studies of such theories see [26] and [32].

An important and powerful alternative to the automata theoretic approach to monadic theories was developed in far-reaching work of Shelah [163]. The idea is to compose theories of linearly ordered models from theories of submodels which define intervals. An early survey of the applications of this model-theoretic method is [76]. A light introduction to the subject is given in [182].

Research on the complexity of logical theories and on the translation from monadic logic to automata started with Meyer's paper [127] (the original technical report dating from 1973), showing that the theory WS1S is not elementary recursive. This was sharpened by Stockmeyer in his PhD Thesis [170] who proved the same lower bound even for the first-order theory of the natural numbers with $<$ and (unquantified) monadic predicates. An overview of the work of the seventies on complexity of logical theories is given in [63]. Compton and Henson [39] develop a general method to obtain non-elementary and other lower bounds for theories. The presentation of Chapter 13 above uses ideas of Matz [122, 123]. A finer analysis of the model-checking problem, separating the parameters of formula complexity and length of the word model under consideration, is given in [64].

The logical characterization of bisimulation invariant properties was started by van Benthem [7] who showed that in modal logic one can express precisely the bisimulation invariant first-order properties. Rosen [156] showed that this holds even when only finite models are considered. The characterization of the bisimulation invariant monadic second-order properties in terms of the modal μ-calculus (Chapter 14 of this book) is due to Janin and Walukiewicz [90, 91]. A variant of this result, concerning "path logic" and the branching time logic CTL* as its bisimulation invariant fragment, appears in [130].

Part VII

Tree-like Models

Rabin's Tree Theorem says that the monadic second-order theory of the binary tree is decidable. This leads to the question which other classes of infinite graphs (besides the infinite tree) exist where this decidability result holds. In this part, such classes of infinite graphs are presented, all of them still tied in some way to the tree structure.

The first chapter introduces pushdown graphs (the infinite transition graphs of pushdown automata) and shows the Theorem of Muller and Schupp (1985): Any such graph has a decidable monadic second-order theory. For a slight generalization of these graphs (the prefix-recognizable graphs, proposed by Caucal in 1991), even more is shown: A graph belongs to this class iff it can be interpreted in the binary tree using certain automata theoretic operations, or equivalently using monadic second-order formulas. In the second chapter, a powerful method is exposed which allows a transfer of decidability results: If an infinite structure has a decidable monadic second-order theory, then the same holds for the tree unravelling of this structure. The last chapter is a study of parity games on pushdown graphs. The solution of these games is shown following a recent construction of Kupferman and Vardi.

15 Prefix-Recognizable Graphs and Monadic Logic

Martin Leucker*

Department of Computer Systems
Uppsala University

15.1 Introduction

In 1969, Rabin [148] showed that the monadic second-order theory (MSO-theory) of infinite binary trees is decidable (see Chapter 12 of this volume or [183]). Ever since, it has been an interesting goal to extend this result to other classes of objects.

Muller and Schupp [135] showed that the class of *pushdown graphs* has a decidable MSO-theory. This class is obtained by considering the configuration graphs of pushdown machines. The result was later extended to the class of *regular graphs* introduced by Courcelle [42], which are defined as solutions of graph-grammar equations.

Prefix-recognizable graphs were introduced by Caucal in [28]. They extend the pushdown graphs of Muller and Schupp and the regular graphs of Courcelle. Originally, Caucal introduced this class of graphs via transformations on the complete infinite binary tree. The decidability result of their MSO-theory was obtained by showing that these transformations are definable by MSO-formulas. Hereby, the decidability result of the MSO-theory of trees was transferred to the class of prefix-recognizable graphs. The approach can also be understood as interpreting prefix-recognizable graphs in the infinite binary tree by means of MSO-formulas. Barthelmann [6] and Blumensath [12] showed independently that Caucal's class of graphs coincides with the class of graphs MSO-interpretable in the infinite binary tree. In simple words, prefix-recognizable graphs provide a decidability proof of their MSO-theory via MSO-interpretations in the infinite binary tree.

The aim of this chapter is to present prefix-recognizable graphs and to show several of their representations. In contrast to Caucal's original outline, we start with graphs that are MSO-interpretable in the binary tree. In this way, we obtain a natural class of graphs which trivially have a decidable MSO-theory (see Section 15.3). We then provide several representations of these graphs in Section 15.3 and Section 15.5. We learn that prefix-recognizable graphs can be represented by means of prefix-transition systems, whose prefixes form regular languages, justifying the name of this class. Furthermore, we introduce Caucal's transformations on the binary tree and show that they induce the same class of graphs.

---

* Supported by European Research Training Network "Games".

E. Grädel et al. (Eds.): Automata, Logics, and Infinite Games, LNCS 2500, pp. 263-283, 2002.

Although the class of prefix-recognizable graphs is the largest *natural* class proving a decidability via interpretation in the binary tree, it should be mentioned that there are graphs which are not prefix-recognizable but have a decidable MSO-theory (see [12]). A different natural class of structures having a decidable MSO-theory is presented in Chapter 16.

This chapter is organized as follows. In Section 15.2, we fix our notation and introduce basic concepts. Section 15.3 introduces prefix-recognizable graphs as graphs which are MSO-interpretable in the infinite binary tree and provides a first representation. In Section 15.4 we present transformations on graphs and show some of their properties. Applying all these transformations on the binary tree will yield the same class of graphs. This is shown in Section 15.5. A characterization in terms of pushdown graphs in given in Section 15.6. We conclude by summarizing our results and by giving further representations.

15.2   Preliminaries

We denote alphabets by $\Sigma, \Gamma, \ldots$, and N. The most important alphabet considered in this chapter is the **binary alphabet** consisting of 0 and 1. It is denoted by $\mathbb{B} = \{0, 1\}$. As usual, a **language** over Σ is a subset of Σ^*, the set of finite sequences of elements of Σ. The elements of Σ^* are called **words**. The empty word is denoted by ε. Σ^+ denotes $\Sigma^* \setminus \{\varepsilon\}$. The class of **regular languages** over Σ is denoted by $\mathrm{REG}(\Sigma^*)$. For two sets of words U and V, we denote by UV their **language product**, i.e., $UV = \{uv \mid u \in U, v \in V\}$.

A **tree** over an alphabet N is a structure $\mathfrak{T} = (T, (\sigma_a)_{a \in N})$. Here, $T \subseteq N^*$ is prefix-closed and is called the **domain** of $\mathfrak{T}$. The a-successor relation σ_a contains all pairs (x, xa) for $xa \in T$. The **complete tree** over N is $\mathfrak{T}_N :=$ $(N^*, (\sigma_a)_{a \in N})$. It is sometimes convenient to regard trees as partial orders $(T, \preceq$ $, \sqcap)$, where $\preceq$ is the prefix-ordering and $x \sqcap y$ denotes the longest common prefix of x and y. Further, we identify a prefix-closed set $T \subseteq N^*$ with the tree $(T, (\sigma_a)_{a \in N})$. A Σ-**labelled tree** (Σ-tree for short) is either represented as a structure $(T, (\sigma_a)_{a \in N}, (P_a)_{a \in \Sigma})$ with $P_a \subseteq T$ or simply as a mapping $T \to \Sigma$. Finally, a **regular tree** is a tree with only finitely many subtrees up to isomorphism. In the following, by tree we will usually mean a complete infinite tree.

Figure 15.1 shows part of the infinite binary tree. Note that node 0 has successors 00 and 01. Hence, node s' is a descendant of s iff $s' = su$ for an appropriate word u. Sets of successors might therefore be represented by sets of suffixes. Originally, sets of descendants were identified by prefixes, yielding the notion of *prefix-recognizable graphs*. We follow the suffix approach because it simplifies our notation. It is clear that everything presented in this chapter can be turned into a "prefix" version by a simple "reversal" operator.

The kind of graphs we are going to consider are edge-labelled directed graphs. As for trees, the vertices will usually be words over some alphabet N, and the edge labels are from some alphabet Σ. Such a graph is also called Σ-**graph**. The edge set is partitioned into sets E_a collecting the edges labelled a. Thus

Fig. 15.1. A part of the binary tree

graphs will be represented in the form $\mathfrak{G} = (V, (E_a)_{a \in \Sigma})$. For convenience we allow graphs to be represented also in the form $\mathfrak{G} = (V, E)$ for $V \subseteq N^*$ and $E \subseteq N^* \times \Sigma \times N^*$. Sometimes, we simply use a ternary relation $E \subseteq N^* \times \Sigma \times N^*$ for a graph $\mathfrak{G}$, in which case we assume $V_{\mathfrak{G}}$ (the set of **nodes of $\mathfrak{G}$**) to be implicitly defined by $V_{\mathfrak{G}} = \{s \mid \exists a \in \Sigma, \exists t \in N^*.(s, a, t) \in E \text{ or } (t, a, s) \in E\}$. It is obvious that our notion of graphs subsumes that of trees.

Another key feature of our notion of graphs is that their nodes can be associated with words over some alphabet Σ. Hence, the nodes of graphs constitute languages. It is a traditional task to deal with finite representations of infinite languages by means of automata. Taking languages as the domain for our node sets, we provide the framework of automata theory for defining, characterizing, and modifying the corresponding graphs.

Let $\mathfrak{G} = (V, (E_a)_{a \in \Sigma})$ be a graph. An edge $(s, t) \in E_a$ is denoted by $s \xrightarrow[\mathfrak{G}]{a} t$, or, if $\mathfrak{G}$ is fixed, by $s \xrightarrow{a} t$. A **path** from s to t in $\mathfrak{G}$ via a word $u = a_1 \ldots a_k \in \Sigma^*$ is a sequence

$$s = p_1 \xrightarrow[\mathfrak{G}]{a_1} \cdots \xrightarrow[\mathfrak{G}]{a_k} p_{k+1} = t$$

for $s, t \in V$, and appropriate nodes $p_i \in V$. We write $s \xRightarrow[\mathfrak{G}]{u} t$ iff there is path from s to t via u. Again, we may omit the subscript $\mathfrak{G}$ if it is clear from the context. We write $s \xRightarrow{L} t$ to denote that there is path from s to t via a word u which is in L. A **root** of a graph is a node from which all other nodes are reachable, i.e., $r \in V$ is a root iff for all $s \in V$ there is a $u \in \Sigma^*$ such that there is path from r to s via u.

Given a sequence of edges, its sequence of labels is a word over the alphabet Σ. Given two nodes s and t of a graph $\mathfrak{G}$, we define the language $L(\mathfrak{G}, s, t)$ to be the union of all words which are obtained on paths from s to t in $\mathfrak{G}$ in the way described above. The union of $L(\mathfrak{G}, s, t)$ for arbitrary nodes s and t of $\mathfrak{G}$ is abbreviated by $L(\mathfrak{G})$.

A letter a can be associated with the set of a-labelled edges $\{p \xrightarrow{a} q\}$, while a word $w = a_1 \ldots a_n$ over Σ can be associated with the w-paths from a node p to a node q, $p = p_0 \xrightarrow{a_1} \cdots \xrightarrow{a_n} p_n = q$.

Given sets of words W, U, and V we denote by $W(U \xrightarrow{a} V)$ the set of edges $\{wu \xrightarrow{a} wv \mid w \in W, u \in U, v \in V\}$. In a similar manner, we define $U \xrightarrow{a} V$. A graph $\mathfrak{G}$ is called **recognizable** iff there are a natural number n and $a_1, \ldots, a_n \in \Sigma, U_1, V_1, \ldots, U_n, V_n \in \mathrm{REG}(\Sigma^*)$ such that $\mathfrak{G} = U_1 \xrightarrow{a_1} V_1 \cup \cdots \cup U_n \xrightarrow{a_n} V_n$.

Let us recall the automata theoretic notations from Chapter 1. We denote finite automata over words by tuples $\mathcal{A} = (Q, \Sigma, \Delta, q_0, F)$ with a set of states

Q, alphabet Σ, transition relation Δ, initial state q_0, and acceptance condition F. Sometimes, if the automaton is deterministic, Δ is replaced by a function δ. The language accepted by $\mathcal{A}$ is denoted by $L(\mathcal{A})$.

The power set of a set Σ is denoted by $\mathscr{P}(\Sigma)$.

Let us recall some basic definitions regarding monadic second-order logic. MSO-logic extends first-order logic FO by quantification over sets. First-order variables are usually denoted by $x, y, \ldots$ and second-order variables by $X, Y, \ldots,$ $X_1, \ldots$ We write $\varphi(x, y)$ to denote that φ has free variables among x and y. The **theory** of a structure comprises all formulas that hold in the structure. For a graph $\mathfrak{G}$, we denote by $\mathrm{MTh}(\mathfrak{G})$ its theory. For a thorough introduction to MSO-logic we refer to Chapter 12 of this volume.

15.3   Prefix-Recognizable Graphs

Given a structure $\mathfrak{B}$, an MSO-formula $\varphi(x)$ with a free first order variable x induces the set $B = \varphi^{\mathfrak{B}}(x) = \{b \mid \mathfrak{B} \models \varphi(b)\}$. We can specify a graph $\mathfrak{G} = (V, E)$ by providing MSO-formulas $\varphi(x)$ and $\psi(x, y)$ such that $V = \varphi^{\mathfrak{B}}(x)$ and $E = \psi^{\mathfrak{B}}(x, y)$ (defined analogously). In this case we say that $\mathfrak{G}$ is MSO-interpretable in $\mathfrak{B}$ via the formulas φ, ψ. Interpretations are a general tool for obtaining classes of finitely presented structures with sets of desired properties.

In this section we introduce a class of graphs via MSO-interpretations in the infinite binary tree. Since the latter has a decidable MSO-theory, we obtain a natural class of graphs with a decidable MSO-theory. Furthermore, we give a representation of these graphs in terms of prefix transition graphs whose prefixes form regular sets of words. This justifies the name *prefix-recognizable graphs*.

Let us make the notion of an MSO-interpretation precise:

Definition 15.1. Let $\mathfrak{A} = (A, R_1, \ldots, R_n)$ and $\mathfrak{B}$ be relational structures. A (one-dimensional) **MSO-interpretation** of $\mathfrak{A}$ in $\mathfrak{B}$ is a sequence

$$I = (\delta(x), \varepsilon(x, y), \varphi_{R_1}(\bar{x}), \ldots, \varphi_{R_n}(\bar{x}))$$

of MSO-formulas such that

$$\mathfrak{A} \cong (\delta^{\mathfrak{B}}(x), \varphi_{R_1}^{\mathfrak{B}}(\bar{x}), \ldots, \varphi_{R_n}^{\mathfrak{B}}(\bar{x}))/\varepsilon^{\mathfrak{B}}(x, y)$$

To make the previous structure well-defined, we require $\varepsilon^{\mathfrak{B}}$ to be a congruence of the structure $(\delta^{\mathfrak{B}}(x), \varphi_{R_1}^{\mathfrak{B}}(\bar{x}), \ldots, \varphi_{R_n}^{\mathfrak{B}}(\bar{x}))$.

We write $I : \mathfrak{A} \leq_{\mathrm{MSO}} \mathfrak{B}$ if I is an MSO-interpretation of $\mathfrak{A}$ in $\mathfrak{B}$. Since $\mathfrak{A}$ is uniquely determined by $\mathfrak{B}$ and I, we can regard I as a functor and denote $\mathfrak{A}$ by $I(\mathfrak{B})$. The **coordinate map** from $\delta^{\mathfrak{B}}(x)$ to A, the universe of $\mathfrak{A}$, is also denoted by I. We call I **injective** if the coordinate map is injective.

If I is clear from the context, or if we want to express that there is an interpretation of $\mathfrak{A}$ in $\mathfrak{B}$, we simply write $\mathfrak{A} \leq_{\mathrm{MSO}} \mathfrak{B}$. In the latter case, we also say that $\mathfrak{A}$ is MSO-interpretable in $\mathfrak{B}$.

Example 15.2. Words are MSO-interpretable in the binary tree. Intuitively, an infinite word can be obtained in the infinite binary tree by considering a single branch. First, observe that Root $(y) = \neg\exists x\, S_1 xy$ identifies the root of a tree. Let us take the path obtained by always considering the right successor. Then, the universe of a word is the minimal set of nodes that contains a root and all right successors. Thus we define

$$\delta(x) = \forall U(\exists y Uy \wedge \text{Root}\,(y) \wedge \forall p \forall q(Up \wedge S_1 pq \rightarrow Uq) \rightarrow Ux)$$

The successor relation is simply defined by $\varphi_{S_0}(x, y) = S_1 xy$ and every set of labels P_a can be defined by $\varphi_{P_a}(x) = P_a x$. It is now easy to see that $I = (\delta(x), \varepsilon(x, y), \varphi_{S_0}, (\varphi_{P_a})_{a \in \Sigma})$ is an MSO-interpretation of the word $\mathfrak{A}$ in $\mathfrak{B}$ where ε is assumed to express the identity relation of $\delta^{\mathfrak{A}}$.

Exercise 15.1. A structure $\mathfrak{A} = (A, <^{\mathfrak{A}})$ is called a *dense open order* if $<^{\mathfrak{A}}$ is a total order on A, if for all $x \in A$ there are $y, z \in A$ such that $y <^{\mathfrak{A}} x <^{\mathfrak{A}} z$, and if for all $x, y \in A$ such that $x <^{\mathfrak{A}} y$ there is a $z \in A$ such that $x <^{\mathfrak{A}} z <^{\mathfrak{A}} y$. Show that a dense open order can be interpreted in the infinite binary tree.

Theorem 15.3. *If* $\mathfrak{A} \leq_{\text{MSO}} \mathfrak{B}$ *and* $\mathfrak{B}$ *has a decidable MSO-theory then* $\mathfrak{A}$ *has a decidable MSO-theory.*

Proof. We give a sketch of the proof. The details are left as an exercise for the reader. Let $I = (\delta(x), \varepsilon(x, y), \varphi_{R_1}(\bar{x}), \dots, \varphi_{R_n}(\bar{x}))$ be an MSO-interpretation of $\mathfrak{A}$ in $\mathfrak{B}$. Consider a formula φ. Let φ' be obtained from φ in the following way: Replace every relational symbol R in φ by its defining formula φ_R. Furthermore, relativize every quantifier to $\delta(x)$, i.e. substitute $\exists x \varphi$ by $\exists x(\delta(x) \wedge \varphi)$ and $\forall x \varphi$ by $\forall x(\delta(x) \rightarrow \varphi)$. Now it is easy to see that $\mathfrak{A} \models \varphi$ iff $\mathfrak{B} \models \varphi'$.

Since we are interested in interpreting graphs with labelled edges in structures, we deal with interpretations of the form $I = (\delta(x), \varepsilon(x, y), (\varphi_{R_a}(x, y))_{a \in \Sigma})$.

The decidability of the monadic second-order theory of $\mathfrak{T}_{\mathbb{B}}$ was established by Rabin in [148]. Thus, if we consider MSO-interpretations in the binary tree we get structures with a decidable MSO-theory.

Corollary 15.4. *Every graph which is MSO-interpretable in the infinite binary tree* $\mathfrak{T}_{\mathbb{B}}$ *has a decidable monadic second-order theory.*

Let us now give a representation of the graphs which are MSO-interpretable in $\mathfrak{T}_{\mathbb{B}}$ in terms of prefix-transition graphs having regular prefixes.

Definition 15.5. Let Σ be an alphabet. A graph $\mathfrak{G} = (V, (E_a)_{a \in \Sigma})$ is called **prefix-recognizable** iff it is isomorphic to a graph of the form

$$\bigcup_{i=1}^{n} W_i(U_i \xrightarrow{a_i} V_i)$$

for some $n \geq 0$, $a_1, \dots, a_n \in \Sigma$ and languages $U_1, V_1, W_1, \dots, U_n, V_n, W_n \in \text{REG}(\mathbb{B}^*)$. The class of prefix-recognizable graphs with edge labels among Σ is denoted by $\text{PRG}(\Sigma)$ or PRG if Σ is fixed.

We will show in Section 15.5 that we can choose an arbitrary alphabet with at least two elements instead of $\mathbb{B}$.

Example 15.6. Let us consider the graph with edge labels a and b given by $\mathbb{B}^*((\varepsilon \xrightarrow{a} \mathbb{B}) \cup \mathbb{B}^*.(\mathbb{B}^+ \xrightarrow{b} \varepsilon))$. It is depicted in Figure 15.2. Note that this graph is (A^*, R_a, R_b) is isomorphic to $(\omega, \mathrm{succ}, >)$, where succ is the successor relation on the natural numbers.

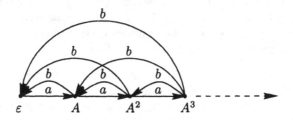

Fig. 15.2. A prefix-recognizable graph with infinite out-degree

This example shows that prefix-recognizable graphs may have nodes with infinite out-degree. The class of prefix-recognizable graphs is a strict extension of the class of regular graphs, since the latter have only a finite out-degree [42].

Every prefix-recognizable graph can be represented by a finite collection of **prefix-recognizable rewrite rules** $w.u \xrightarrow{a} v$ where w, u, and v are regular expressions. This way of representing prefix-recognizable graphs will be employed in Chapter 17.

Let us proceed to show that prefix-recognizable graphs coincide with graphs that are MSO-definable in $\mathfrak{T}_\mathbb{B}$. In our constructions, we need to code tuples of sets as labelled trees.

Definition 15.7. For sets $X_0, \ldots, X_{n-1} \subseteq \mathbb{B}^*$, abbreviated by $\bar{X}$, denote by $T_{\bar{X}}$ the $\mathbb{B}^n$-labelled binary tree such that the i-th component of the label $T_{\bar{X}}(y)$ for a node y is 1 iff $y \in X_i$. Singletons $X_i = \{x_i\}$ $(i = 0, \ldots, n-1)$ are also abbreviated by $\bar{x}$.

Furthermore, we employ Rabin's tree theorem which gives the relation between tree automata and MSO-logic: (see also Chapter 12 and [179])

Theorem 15.8. *For each $\varphi(\bar{X}, \bar{x}) \in$ MSO there is a tree-automaton $\mathcal{A}$ such that $L(\mathcal{A}) = \{T_{\bar{X}\bar{x}} \mid \mathfrak{T}_\mathbb{B} \models \varphi(\bar{X}, \bar{x})\}$.*

Let us establish the representation first for injective interpretations.

Proposition 15.9. *Let $\mathfrak{G}$ be a graph which is MSO-interpretable in $\mathfrak{T}_\mathbb{B}$ via an injective interpretation. Then $\mathfrak{G}$ is isomorphic to $\bigcup_{i=1}^n W_i(U_i \xrightarrow{a_i} V_i)$ for some $n \geq 0$; $a_1, \ldots, a_n \in \Sigma$; $U_1, V_1, W_1, \ldots, U_n, V_n, W_n \in \mathrm{REG}(\mathbb{B}^*)$.*

Proof. Let $I : \mathfrak{G} \leq_{\mathrm{MSO}} \mathfrak{T}_\mathbb{B}$ be an injective MSO-interpretation of $\mathfrak{G}$ in $\mathfrak{T}_\mathbb{B}$. Note that $\mathfrak{G} = (V, (E_a)_{a \in \Sigma})$ and every edge relation E is defined by a formula $\varphi(x, y)$. We have to show that every such edge relation E can be written as a finite union of $W(U \to V)$ where U, V, and W are regular. Let $\mathcal{A} = (Q, \mathbb{B}, \Delta, q_0, \Omega)$ be the tree-automaton associated with φ with respect to $\mathfrak{T}_\mathbb{B}$ (cf. Chapter 12). Thus $L(\mathcal{A}) = \{T_{xy} \mid \mathfrak{T}_\mathbb{B} \models \varphi(x, y)\}$. Note that every $T_{xy} \in L(\mathcal{A})$ is labelled by tuples in $\mathbb{B}^2$. Nearly all nodes are labelled by $[0, 0]$, except the node representing x, in which the first component of the tuple is 1 and the node representing y, in which the second component of the tuple is 1. Figure 15.3 shows a typical situation. Observe, that each pair x and y can be written as a wu and wv in the way described in the introductory section.

We construct languages U_q, V_q, and W_q such that $u \in U_q$, $v \in V_q$, and $w \in W_q$ if and only if there is an accepting run of $\mathcal{A}$ on $T_{\{wu\}\{wv\}}$ where the node w is labelled by q. Thus, $E = \bigcup_{q \in Q} W_q(U_q \to V_q)$. We show that every U_q, V_q, W_q is regular, and since Q is finite, we are done.

Let $Q_0 \subseteq Q$ be the subset of states from which $\mathcal{A}$ accepts the tree labelled by $[0, 0]$ everywhere. Note that this set is computable for $\mathcal{A}$. Obviously, wu or wv can only occur in a subtree not labelled by $[0, 0]$ everywhere. Hence, a node labelled by the state q from which wu and wv are reachable is in this subtree. Hence, we let W_q be the language recognized by the automaton $(Q, \mathbb{B}, \Delta_{W_q}, q_0, \{q\})$ where

$$
\begin{aligned}
\Delta_{W_q} := \ &\{\ (p, 0, p') \mid (p, [0, 0], p', p_0) \in \Delta, p_0 \in Q_0\} \\
&\cup \{\ (p, 1, p') \mid (p, [0, 0], p_0, p') \in \Delta, p_0 \in Q_0\}
\end{aligned}
$$

If the desired state q is reached, we have to look for a node labelled by $[1, \_]$ for an element of U_q and for a node labelled by $[\_, 1]$ for an element of V_q. Hence, we let $U_q := L((Q \cup \{q_f\}, \mathbb{B}, \Delta_{U_q}, q, \{q_f\}))$ where

$$
\begin{aligned}
\Delta_{U_q} := \ &\{\ (p, 0, p') \mid (p, [0, c], p', p_0) \in \Delta, p_0 \in Q_0, c \in \mathbb{B}\} \\
&\cup \{\ (p, 1, p') \mid (p, [0, c], p_0, p') \in \Delta, p_0 \in Q_0, c \in \mathbb{B}\} \\
&\cup \{\ (p, c, q_f) \mid (p, [1, d], p_0, p'_0) \in \Delta, p_0, p'_0 \in Q_0, c, d \in \mathbb{B}\}
\end{aligned}
$$

V_q is defined similar to U_q, only the tuples (labels) are switched.

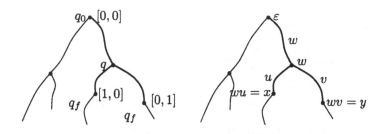

Fig. 15.3. A run of the tree automaton

Let us verify that it suffices to consider injective MSO-interpretations. Hence, we may assume that the equivalence classes with respect to $\varepsilon^{\mathfrak{B}}$ are singletons. Let us first show the following lemma:

Lemma 15.10. *Let* $D \subseteq \mathbb{B}^*$ *be regular and* $E \subseteq D \times D$ *an equivalence relation which is prefix-recognizable.[1] There is a regular language* $D' \subseteq D$ *such that* D' *contains exactly one element of each* E-*class.*

Proof. Denote the E-class of x by $[x]$, define $p_{[x]} := \inf_{\preceq}[x]$ and $s_x := (p_{[x]})^{-1}x$. Let $\varphi_p(x, y)$ be an MSO-definition of the function $x \mapsto p_{[x]}$. Finally, let s be the number of states of the tree automaton associated with E. We claim that each class $[x]$ has an element of length less than $|p_{[x]}| + s$. Thus, one can define

$$D' := \{x \in D \mid s_x \leq s_y \text{ for all } y \in [x]\}$$

where $\leq$ is the lexicographic ordering which is definable since the length of the words is bounded so that we only need to consider finitely many cases.

To prove the claim, choose $x_0, x_1 \in [x]$ such that $x_0 \sqcap x_1 = p_{[x]}$. Since $(x_0, x_1) \in E$ there are regular languages U, V, and W such that $x_0 = wu$, $x_1 = wv$ for $u \in U$, $v \in V$, and $w \in W$ with $w \preceq p_{[x]}$. If $|wu| \geq |p_{[x]}| + s$ then, by a pumping argument, there exists some $u' \in U$ such that $|p_{[x]}| \leq |wu'| \leq |p_{[x]}| + s$. Hence, $(wu', x_1) \in E$ is an element of the desired length.

Let us return to $\varepsilon^{\mathfrak{B}}$. Since it is a binary relation, it may be understood as the edge relation of a graph. By Proposition 15.9, this is prefix-recognizable, and by the previous lemma, there is a regular set D' which contains for every equivalence class with respect to $\varepsilon^{\mathfrak{B}}$ a single element. Since D' is regular, there is an MSO-formula $\delta'(x)$ defining D'. Hence, if $\mathfrak{A} \cong (\delta^{\mathfrak{B}}(x), \varphi_{R_1}^{\mathfrak{B}}(\bar{x}), \dots, \varphi_{R_n}^{\mathfrak{B}}(\bar{x}))/\varepsilon^{\mathfrak{B}}(x, y)$ then $\mathfrak{A}$ is also isomorphic to $(\delta'^{\mathfrak{B}}(x), \varphi_{R_1}^{\mathfrak{B}}(\bar{x}), \dots, \varphi_{R_n}^{\mathfrak{B}}(\bar{x}))$. Thus, the following corollary holds.

Corollary 15.11.

(1) PRG *is closed under prefix-recognizable congruences.*
(2) *Each graph MSO-interpretable in the binary tree has an injective MSO-interpretation in* $\mathfrak{T}_{\mathbb{B}}$.

Let us summarize the previous results:

Lemma 15.12. *Suppose* $\mathfrak{G}$ *is MSO-interpretable in* $\mathfrak{T}_{\mathbb{B}}$. *Then*

$$\mathfrak{G} \text{ is isomorphic to } \bigcup_{i=1}^{n} W_i(U_i \xrightarrow{a_i} V_i)$$

for some $n \geq 0$; $a_1, \dots, a_n \in \Sigma$; $U_1, V_1, W_1, \dots, U_n, V_n, W_n \in \mathrm{REG}(\mathbb{B}^*)$.

It is easy to see that also the converse holds.

---

[1] in the sense of E considered as a set of edges

Lemma 15.13. *Let $\mathfrak{G}$ be a graph isomorphic to*

$$\bigcup_{i=1}^{n} W_i(U_i \xrightarrow{a_i} V_i)$$

for some $n \geq 0$; $a_1, \ldots, a_n \in \Sigma$; $U_1, V_1, W_1, \ldots, U_n, V_n, W_n \in \mathrm{REG}(\mathbb{B}^*)$. Then $\mathfrak{G}$ is MSO-interpretable in $\mathfrak{T}_\mathbb{B}$.

Proof. We have to show that for each $a \in \{a_1, \ldots, a_n\}$ there is a formula $\varphi_{R_a}(x, y)$ interpreting the a-edges in $\mathfrak{T}_\mathbb{B}$. Clearly, the prefix-ordering $\preceq$ on binary strings is MSO-definable in $\mathfrak{T}_\mathbb{B}$. Further, for each regular language $L \subseteq \mathbb{B}^*$ there exists an MSO-formula $\varphi_L(u, v)$ stating the $u \preceq v$ and the labelling of the path from u to v in $\mathfrak{T}_\mathbb{B}$ is in L. The latter can be expressed by the formula $\mathrm{Path}_L(x, y)$ that can be defined inductively on L by:

$$
\begin{aligned}
\mathrm{Path}_{\emptyset}(x, y) &= \exists X(x \in X \wedge \neg(x \in X)) \quad \text{``false''} \\
\mathrm{Path}_{\{b\}}(x, y) &= S_b x y \\
\mathrm{Path}_{L+M}(x, y) &= \mathrm{Path}_L(x, y) \vee \mathrm{Path}_M(x, y) \\
\mathrm{Path}_{L.M}(x, y) &= \exists z(\mathrm{Path}_L(x, z) \wedge \mathrm{Path}_M(z, y)) \\
\mathrm{Path}_{L^*}(x, y) &= \forall X((x \in X \wedge \\
&\qquad \forall p \forall q((p \in X \wedge \mathrm{Path}_L(p, q)) \to q \in X)) \to y \in X)
\end{aligned}
$$

We now see that, $\bigcup_{\{i \mid a = a_i\}} W_i(U_i \xrightarrow{a_i} V_i)$ can be defined by

$$\varphi_{R_a}(x, y) = \bigvee_{\{i \mid a = a_i\}} \exists z \left(\varphi_{W_i}(\varepsilon, z) \wedge \varphi_{U_i}(z, x) \wedge \varphi_{V_i}(z, y) \right).$$

Combining the previous two lemmas we get

Theorem 15.14. *A graph $\mathfrak{G}$ is MSO-interpretable in $\mathfrak{T}_\mathbb{B}$ iff it is isomorphic to*

$$\bigcup_{i=1}^{n} W_i(U_i \xrightarrow{a_i} V_i)$$

for some $n \geq 0$; $a_1, \ldots, a_n \in \Sigma$; $U_1, V_1, W_1, \ldots, U_n, V_n, W_n \in \mathrm{REG}(\mathbb{B}^*)$.

In other words, a graph is MSO-interpretable in $\mathfrak{T}_\mathbb{B}$ iff it is prefix-recognizable.

Caucal introduced prefix-recognizable graphs employing transformations on the binary tree instead of MSO-interpretations. We will redevelop his approach in the next section, obtaining further representations of prefix-recognizable graphs.

15.4 Transformations on Graphs

In this section, we introduce several transformations on the complete infinite binary tree. For the first two transformations, we will prove that they are definable within MSO, giving rise to MSO-interpretations of graphs in $\mathfrak{T}_\mathbb{B}$. In other words, we obtain prefix-recognizable graphs by employing our transformations.

We will employ these transformations in the next section to obtain further representations of prefix-recognizable graphs.

The idea of the first transformation is to collapse paths within a given graph to a single edge with a new label in the new graph. To be able to deal with inverse edges of a graph, we introduce the notion of an inverse alphabet.

Definition 15.15. Let Σ be an alphabet. The **inverse alphabet** of Σ is the set $\overline{\Sigma} := \{\overline{a} \mid a \in \Sigma\}$ which is a disjoint copy of Σ. The **extended alphabet** of Σ is the union of Σ and its inverse alphabet and is denoted by $\hat{\Sigma}$.

Words over the extended alphabet of Σ may correspond to paths with inverse edges. For example, the word $\overline{a}bb$ may be understood as the set of pairs of nodes (p, q) such that there are p_1 and p_2 with $p_1 \xrightarrow{a} p$, $p_1 \xrightarrow{b} p_2$, and $p_2 \xrightarrow{b} q$.

We extend the notion of inverse letters to inverse words by defining for every $u = x_1 \ldots x_k \in \hat{\Sigma}^*$ the inverse $\overline{u}$ of u by $\overline{u} = \overline{x_k} \ldots \overline{x_1}$. Here, every x_i is an element of $\hat{\Sigma}$ and for $x_i = \overline{a}$, $a \in \Sigma$, $\overline{x_i}$ is identified with a.

Given a word u over $\hat{\Sigma}$, we assign to u a normal form $u\!\downarrow$ which is obtained by removing all pairs $\overline{a}a$ or $a\overline{a}$ in u. Formally, we could define for Σ a rewrite system $\downarrow_\Sigma \subseteq \hat{\Sigma}^* \times \hat{\Sigma}^*$ by $\downarrow_\Sigma := \{(\overline{a}a, \varepsilon), (a\overline{a}, \varepsilon) \mid a \in \Sigma\}$ and show that it is terminating and confluent. Hence, we can speak also about *the* normal form of u.

Let us now define our first transformation. It is based on the notion of an extended substitution.

Definition 15.16. Let Σ and Γ be two alphabets. An **extended substitution** from Γ to Σ is a homomorphism from Γ into the power set of words over the extended alphabet $\hat{\Sigma}$. More precisely, h is a mapping such that for every $b \in \Gamma$

$$h(b) \in \mathscr{P}(\hat{\Sigma}^*)$$

and furthermore $h(\varepsilon) = \{\varepsilon\}$ and $h(uv) = h(u)h(v)$.

h is called **regular** iff $h(b)$ is a regular set for all $b \in \Gamma$, and **finite** iff $h(b)$ is a finite set for all $b \in \Gamma$.

Sometimes, we silently assume an extended substitution to be extended to a mapping from $\hat{\Gamma}^*$ to $\mathscr{P}(\hat{\Sigma}^*)$ by $h(\overline{b}) = \overline{h(b)}$ for $b \in \Gamma$.

Now we are ready to make precise the notion of an inverse substitution of a graph.

Definition 15.17. Let $\mathfrak{G} = (V, E)$ be a graph with edge labels from a given alphabet Σ. Furthermore, let Γ be an alphabet, and let $h : \Gamma \to \mathscr{P}(\hat{\Sigma}^*)$ be an extended substitution. We define the **inverse substitution** $h^{-1}(\mathfrak{G})$ to be the graph $\mathfrak{G}' = (V, E')$ such that

$$s \xrightarrow[\mathfrak{G}']{b} t \text{ iff } \exists u \in h(b) \ s \xRightarrow[\mathfrak{G}]{u} t$$

for all $s, t \in V$. The inverse substitution is called **regular** (respectively **finite**) iff h is a regular (respectively finite) extended finite substitution.

Example 15.18. Let $\Sigma = \{a\}$ be a singleton alphabet. Consider the extended substitution given by $h(a) = \{\bar{0}1\}$. The corresponding inverse substitution of the infinite binary tree is shown in Figure 15.4.

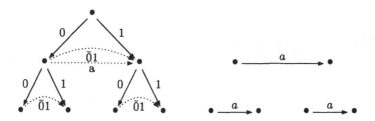

Fig. 15.4. A non-connected prefix-recognizable graph

For the graphs under consideration, we may assume without loss of generality that their nodes are words over some alphabet Σ. Hence, the nodes of our graphs constitute languages. A natural operation on languages is restriction. We will consequently also consider a second transformation on the binary tree called *restriction.*

Definition 15.19. Let $\mathfrak{G} = (V, E)$ be a graph with universe $V \subseteq N^*$ and edges $E \subseteq V \times \Sigma \times V$ for given alphabets N and Σ. Let L be a language over N. The **restriction** of $\mathfrak{G}$ with respect to L is defined to be the graph

$$(V \cap L, E \cap (L \times \Sigma \times L))$$

and is denoted by $\mathfrak{G}_{|L}$. The restriction is called **regular** (respectively **finite**) iff L is a regular (respectively finite) set.

A subgraph of a given graph $\mathfrak{G}$ can be identified by a restriction such that its nodes belong to the restricted language.

Let us show that regular restrictions of regular inverse substitutions are definable in MSO to obtain one of our main results:

Theorem 15.20. *Given a graph $\mathfrak{G}$ with a unique root r, a regular substitution h, and a regular label language $L \in \mathrm{REG}(\hat{N}^*)$, we have:*

$$\mathrm{MTh}(\mathfrak{G}) \; decidable \implies \mathrm{MTh}(h^{-1}(\mathfrak{G})_{|L_\mathfrak{G}}) \; decidable$$

where $L_\mathfrak{G} := \{s \mid r \overset{L}{\underset{\mathfrak{G}}{\Longrightarrow}} s\}$.

Proof. Let φ be an MSO-formula. Observe that an a-successor of $h^{-1}(\mathfrak{G})_{|L_\mathfrak{G}}$ corresponds to an $h(a)$-path in $\mathfrak{G}$. Furthermore, an element (a node) x exists in $h^{-1}(\mathfrak{G})_{|L_\mathfrak{G}}$ iff it is the starting point or end point of some path in $\mathfrak{G}$ and is not removed because of the restriction with respect to L. The latter means that the element is reached by some L-path from the root z of the graph. Hence, we define the formula $\varphi^{L,h,z}$ inductively:

$$
\begin{aligned}
S_a x y^{L,h,z} &= \text{Path}_{h(a)}(x,y) \\
(x \in X)^{L,h,z} &= x \in X \\
(\neg\varphi)^{L,h,z} &= \neg(\varphi^{L,h,z}) \\
(\varphi \wedge \psi)^{L,h,z} &= \varphi^{L,h,z} \wedge \psi^{L,h,z} \\
(\exists X\varphi)^{L,h,z} &= \exists X\varphi^{L,h,z} \\
(\exists x\varphi)^{L,h,z} &= \exists x\,(\text{Path}_L(z,x) \wedge \exists y(\text{Path}_M(x,y) \vee \text{Path}_M(y,x)) \\
&\quad \wedge \varphi^{L,h,z})
\end{aligned}
$$

where $M = \bigcup h(a)$ and $\text{Path}_L(x,y)$ is as in Lemma 15.13. It is easy to see that

$$
h^{-1}(\mathfrak{G})_{|L_\mathfrak{G}} \models \varphi \text{ iff } \mathfrak{G} \models \exists z\,(\forall y\,\text{Path}_{N^*}(x,y) \ \wedge \ \varphi^{L,h,z}).
$$

Note that the first conjunct assures that z is indeed a root of $\mathfrak{G}$.

The previous proof can easily be employed for defining an interpretation of a graph $h^{-1}(\mathfrak{G})_{|L_\mathfrak{G}}$ in $\mathfrak{G}$. The successor relations are explicitly given and the domain is easily defined using our ideas that led to the definition of the $\exists x$ case. The congruence $\varepsilon(x,y)$ can be defined to be equality. Thus, we see:

Corollary 15.21. *Regular restrictions of regular inverse substitutions of $\mathfrak{T}_\mathbf{B}$ yield prefix-recognizable graphs.*

We conclude that the graph shown in Example 15.18 is prefix-recognizable. Thus, we see that prefix-recognizable graphs are not necessarily connected. This distinguishes prefix-recognizable graphs from tree-like structures presented in Chapter 16.

As mentioned above, we will show in the next section that prefix-recognizable graphs are indeed the graphs obtained as regular restrictions of regular inverse substitutions of $\mathfrak{T}_\mathbf{B}$, establishing a further representation of the studied objects.

A further transformation considered is a *marking* of nodes belonging to a given set. To mark nodes of our graph, we introduce a new symbol $\# \notin \Sigma$, and, as we will see in the next section, add a $\#$-edge for nodes to be marked. Therefore, we consider also paths including this symbol $\#$. To simplify our notation, we write $\hat{\Sigma}_\#$ for an extended alphabet together with the symbol $\#$. Also, we consider normalizations which further reduce $\#$ to the empty word ε. For a word $u \in \hat{\Sigma}_\#^*$ its corresponding normal form is denoted by $u{\downarrow}_\#$.

Definition 15.22. Let $\mathfrak{G} = (V,E)$ be a graph with universe $V \subseteq N^*$ and edges $E \subseteq V \times \Sigma \times V$ for given alphabets N and Σ. Let L be a language over N. The **marking** of $\mathfrak{G}$, with respect to L, by a new symbol $\#$ not in Σ is defined to be the graph

$$
(V,E'), \text{ where } E' = E \cup \{s \xrightarrow{\#} s \mid s \in L\},
$$

and is denoted by $\#_L(\mathfrak{G})$. The marking is called **regular** (respectively **finite**) iff L is a regular (respectively finite) set.

Instead of $\hat{\Sigma}$, we sometimes consider $\hat{\Sigma}_{\#}$. All definitions extend to this case in the obvious way.

Let us collect some properties and interrelations of the transformations mentioned above.

Lemma 15.23. *Let Σ, Γ, and Ξ be alphabets, and $\mathfrak{G}$ be a Σ-graph. Let h be an extended substitution from Γ to Σ, and g one from Ξ to Γ. Then the following holds:*

(1) $s \underset{h^{-1}(\mathfrak{G})}{\overset{u}{\Longrightarrow}} t$ *iff* $s \overset{h(u)}{\underset{\mathfrak{G}}{\Longrightarrow}} t$ *for any* $u \in \Gamma^{+}$ *and* $s, t \in V_{\mathfrak{G}}$.

(2) $g^{-1}(h^{-1}(\mathfrak{G})) = ((g \circ h)^{-1}(\mathfrak{G}))_{|V_{h^{-1}(\mathfrak{G})}}$, *and if* $\varepsilon \notin g(\Xi)$ *then* $g^{-1}(h^{-1}(\mathfrak{G})) = ((g \circ h)^{-1}(\mathfrak{G}))$.

Definition 15.24. *A set L is called* **stable** *in a graph $\mathfrak{G}$, iff any path between vertices in L contains only vertices in L:*

If $s_0 \overset{}{\underset{\mathfrak{G}}{\longrightarrow}} s_1 \cdots s_{n-1} \overset{}{\underset{\mathfrak{G}}{\longrightarrow}} s_n$ and $s_0, s_n \in L$ then $s_1, \ldots, s_{n-1} \in L$.

For example, L is stable in $\mathfrak{G}_{|L}$. A simple but useful insight is that a restriction to any stable set commutes with any inverse substitution.

Lemma 15.25. *If L is stable in $\mathfrak{G}$ then*

$$h^{-1}(\mathfrak{G}_{|L}) = h^{-1}(\mathfrak{G})_{|L}.$$

Any restriction of an image of a graph is an image of a marking of the graph:

Lemma 15.26. *Let $\mathfrak{G} = (V, E)$ be a graph with universe $V \subseteq N^*$ and edges $E \subseteq V \times \Sigma \times V$ for given alphabets N and Σ. Let L be a language over N. Let $\#$ be a new symbol not in Σ. Furthermore, let h be an extended substitution from an alphabet Γ to Σ. Then*

$$(h^{-1}(\mathfrak{G}))_{|L} = g^{-1}(\#_L(\mathfrak{G})),$$

with $g(b) = \#h(b)\#$ for every $b \in \Gamma$.

Proof. By definition, $g^{-1}(\#_L(\mathfrak{G})) = \{s \overset{b}{\longrightarrow} t \mid \exists u \in g(b).s \underset{\#_L(\mathfrak{G})}{\overset{u}{\Longrightarrow}} t\}$. Since the words in the image under g are the ones under h with a $\#$ enclosing elements of L, we conclude that $\{s \overset{b}{\longrightarrow} t \mid \exists u \in g(b).s \underset{\#_L(\mathfrak{G})}{\overset{u}{\Longrightarrow}} t\} = \{s \overset{b}{\longrightarrow} t \mid \exists u' \in h(b).s \underset{\#_L(\mathfrak{G})}{\overset{u}{\Longrightarrow}} t$ and $s, t \in L\}$. The latter is equal to $\{s \overset{b}{\longrightarrow} t \mid \exists u' \in h(b).s \overset{u'}{\underset{\mathfrak{G}}{\Longrightarrow}} t$ and $s, t \in L\}$ since the words in the images of h do not contain the symbol $\#$. Thus, we obtain $g^{-1}(\#_L(\mathfrak{G})) = h^{-1}(G)_{|L}$.

We now show that the restriction to normal forms preserves regularity.

Lemma 15.27. *Let $L \in \text{REG}(N^*)$ and $M \in \text{REG}(\hat{N}^*_\#)$. Then we have in an effective way*

$$(L(\#_L(\mathfrak{T}_N)) \cap M)\!\downarrow_\# \in \text{REG}(N^*).$$

Proof. Let $M' = (L(\#_L(\mathfrak{T}_N)) \cap M)\!\downarrow_\#$. Let $\mathcal{A} = (Q, \hat{N}_\#, \delta, q_0, F)$ be a finite automaton recognizing M. We colour any vertex $u \in N^*$ of $\mathfrak{T}_N$ by the set $c(u)$ of states p such that (p, u) is a vertex of the product $Q \times \#_L(\mathfrak{T}_N)$ reachable from (q_0, ε):

$$c(u) = \{p \mid L((Q, \hat{N}_\#, \delta, q_0, \{p\})) \cap L(\#_L(\mathfrak{T}_N), \varepsilon, u) \neq \emptyset\}$$

Hence, $M' = \{u \in N^* \mid c(u) \cap F \neq \emptyset\}$. We show that M' is regular by proving that c is a regular colouring of $\#_L(\mathfrak{T}_N)$. We consider the following equivalence $\equiv$ on N^*:

$$u \equiv v \text{ iff } c(u) = c(v) \text{ and } u^{-1}L = v^{-1}L$$

Note that $u^{-1}L$ is an abbreviation for $\{w \in N^* \mid uw \in L\}$. As the image of c is finite and L is regular, the equivalence $\equiv$ is of finite index. Further, it is a simple matter to show that $\equiv$ is right-regular. So $H := \{[u] \xrightarrow{a} [ua] \mid u \in N^* \text{ and } a \in N\}$ is finite and $M' = L(H, [\varepsilon], \{[u] \mid c(u) \cap F \neq \emptyset\})$ is regular. Here, $[u]$ denotes the equivalence class of u with respect to $\equiv$.

To show the effectiveness of the construction of M', it suffices to show that H can be effectively constructed. The latter is clear if $c(u)$ is computable. This can be seen by recalling that

(1) $L(\mathcal{A})$ is regular,
(2) $L(\#_L(\mathfrak{T}_N), \varepsilon, u)$ is context-free for every $u \in N^*$,
(3) and the intersection of a regular and a context-free language is context-free.

Hence, the emptiness of $L(\mathcal{A}) \cap L(\#_L(\mathfrak{T}_N)), \varepsilon, u)$ is decidable.

Let us now show that instead of an arbitrary extended substitution, we can assume the image to be normalized in the following sense:

Proposition 15.28. *Let h be an extended substitution, yielding for each $a \in \Sigma$ a language over $\hat{N}_\#$, and $L \subseteq N^*$. Let $\mathfrak{G}$ be the graph with all edges of the form $w(\overline{u\!\downarrow_\#}) \xrightarrow{a} w(v\!\downarrow_\#)$ for $uv \in h(a)$, $\overline{u}, v \in L(\#_{w^{-1}L}(\mathfrak{T}_N))$, and $w \in N^*$. Then*

$$h^{-1}(\#_L(\mathfrak{T}_N)) = \mathfrak{G}.$$

Proof. We show that $h^{-1}(\#_L(\mathfrak{T}_N)) \subseteq \mathfrak{G}$. Let $s \xrightarrow[h^{-1}(\#_L(\mathfrak{T}_N))]{a} t$. Thus, there is a $z \in h(a)$, such that $s \xLeftrightarrow[\#_L(\mathfrak{T}_N)]{z} t$. Let $w = s \sqcap t$, $w \in N^*$. Hence, $s \xLeftrightarrow[\#_L(\mathfrak{T}_N)]{u} w \xLeftrightarrow[\#_L(\mathfrak{T}_N)]{v} t$, with $uv = z$, and w is the node "closest to the root". There are $x, y \in N^*$, such that $s = wx$ and $t = wy$, with $x \xLeftrightarrow[\#_{w^{-1}L}(\mathfrak{T}_N)]{u} \varepsilon \xLeftrightarrow[\#_{w^{-1}L}(\mathfrak{T}_N)]{v} y$. So, $\varepsilon \xLeftrightarrow[\#_{w^{-1}L}(\mathfrak{T}_N)]{\overline{u}} x$,

$\bar{u} \in L(\#_{w^{-1}L}(\mathfrak{T}_N))$, and $x = \bar{u}\downarrow_\# = \overline{u\downarrow_\#}$. Similarly, $v \in L(\#_{w^{-1}L}(\mathfrak{T}_N))$ and $y = v\downarrow_\#$. Thus, $s = wx = \overline{wu\downarrow_\#}$ and $t = wy = w(v\downarrow_\#)$. Finally, we have $s \xrightarrow{a}{}_{\mathfrak{G}} t$.

Let us now show the converse direction, i.e. $\mathfrak{G} \subseteq h^{-1}(\#_L(\mathfrak{T}_N))$. Consider $s \xrightarrow{a}{}_{\mathfrak{G}} t$. There are $uv \in h(a)$ and $w \in N^*$, such that $\bar{u}, v \in L(\#_{w^{-1}L}(\mathfrak{T}_N))$, $s = \overline{wu\downarrow_\#}$, $t = w(v\downarrow_\#)$. We must show that $s \xrightarrow[h^{-1}(\#_L(\mathfrak{T}_N))]{a} t$. Since $\bar{u} \in L(\#_{w^{-1}L}(\mathfrak{T}_N))$, we have $\varepsilon \xRightarrow[\#_{w^{-1}L}(\mathfrak{T}_N)]{\bar{u}} \bar{u}\downarrow_\# = \overline{u\downarrow_\#}$. So, $\overline{u\downarrow_\#} \xRightarrow[\#_{w^{-1}L}(\mathfrak{T}_N)]{u} \varepsilon$, $s = \overline{wu\downarrow_\#} \xRightarrow[\#_L(\mathfrak{T}_N)]{u} w$. In a similar manner, we show that $w \xRightarrow[\#_L(\mathfrak{T}_N)]{v} w(v\downarrow_\#) = t$. Thus, $s \xRightarrow[\#_L(\mathfrak{T}_N)]{uv} t$, $s \xRightarrow[\#_L(\mathfrak{T}_N)]{h(a)} t$, and $s \xrightarrow[h^{-1}(\#_L(\mathfrak{T}_N))]{a} t$.

Proposition 15.28 is rather technical, but allows a simple presentation if we introduce further notation.

Definition 15.29. Let Σ and N be alphabets, $L \subseteq N^*$, and $\mathfrak{G}$ a graph, whose edge relation is a subset of $N^* \times \Sigma \times N^*$. The **right concatenation** of $\mathfrak{G}$ by L is the graph

$$\mathfrak{G}.L := \{uw \xrightarrow{a} vw \mid u \xrightarrow{a}{}_{\mathfrak{G}} v \text{ and } w \in L\}$$

Similarly, we define their **left concatenation** $L.\mathfrak{G}$. For the sake of brevity, we also write $\mathfrak{G}L$ and $L\mathfrak{G}$ instead of $\mathfrak{G}.L$ and $L.\mathfrak{G}$, respectively.

It is folklore that a regular language $L \in \text{REG}(N^*)$ is the union of finitely many equivalence classes, given in the following form:

$$[u]_L := \{v \mid v^{-1}L = u^{-1}L\} \text{ and } [L] := \{[u]_L \mid u \in N^*\}$$

Now, Proposition 15.28 can be stated for regular extended substitutions in the following way:

Corollary 15.30. *For any substitution $h : \Sigma \to \hat{N}^*_\#$ and $L \in \text{REG}(N^*)$, we have that $h^{-1}(\#_L(\mathfrak{T}_N))$ equals*

$$\bigcup_{W \in [L]} W\{\overline{u\downarrow_\#} \xrightarrow{a} v\downarrow_\# \mid uv \in h(a) \text{ and } \bar{u}, v \in L(\#_{W^{-1}L}(\mathfrak{T}_N))\}.$$

If we further omit markings, we can simplify Proposition 15.28 to:

Corollary 15.31. *For any substitution $h : \Sigma \to \hat{N}^*$ we have that*

$$h^{-1}(\mathfrak{T}_N) = N^*\{u \xrightarrow{a} v \mid \overline{u}v \in h(a)\downarrow, u, v \in N^* \text{ and } a \in \Sigma\}.$$

15.5   Representations of Prefix-Recognizable Graphs

In Section 15.4, we introduced inverse substitution, restriction, and marking as transformations on graphs. Here, we introduce classes of graphs as regular restrictions of regular inverse substitutions on the complete binary tree. Furthermore, we show that these classes can be obtained by considering regular inverse substitutions of regular markings on the binary tree. Additionally, we prove that any complete tree can be employed instead of the binary one. Last but not least, we give a representation in terms of prefix-transition graphs which provides a link to Section 15.3.

Definition 15.32. Let Σ and N be alphabets. We define the classes $\mathrm{PRG}_N(\Sigma)_|$ and $\mathrm{PRG}_N^{\#}(\Sigma)$ of graphs with edge labels over Σ and nodes in N^*:

- $\mathfrak{G} \in \mathrm{PRG}_N(\Sigma)_|$ iff $\mathfrak{G}$ is isomorphic to $h^{-1}(\mathfrak{T}_N)_{|L}$ for a suitable regular extended substitution h from Σ to N and $L \in \mathrm{REG}(N^*)$.
- $\mathfrak{G} \in \mathrm{PRG}_N^{\#}(\Sigma)$ iff $\mathfrak{G}$ is isomorphic to $h^{-1}(\#_L(\mathfrak{T}_N))$ for a suitable regular extended substitution h from Σ to N and $L \in \mathrm{REG}(N^*)$.

Proposition 15.33. *For every alphabet N with $\mathbb{B} \subseteq N$, we have*

$$\mathrm{PRG}_N(\Sigma)_| \;=\; \mathrm{PRG}_\mathbb{B}(\Sigma)_| \;=\; \mathrm{PRG}_\mathbb{B}^{\#}(\Sigma) \;=\; \mathrm{PRG}_N^{\#}(\Sigma)$$

Proof. We show that $\mathrm{PRG}_N(\Sigma)_| \stackrel{(1)}{\subseteq} \mathrm{PRG}_N^{\#}(\Sigma) \stackrel{(2)}{\subseteq} \mathrm{PRG}_\mathbb{B}(\Sigma)_| \stackrel{(3)}{\subseteq} \mathrm{PRG}_N(\Sigma)_|$. This shows $\mathrm{PRG}_N(\Sigma)_| = \mathrm{PRG}_\mathbb{B}(\Sigma)_| = \mathrm{PRG}_N^{\#}(\Sigma)$. The last equation implies for $N = \mathbb{B}$ also $\mathrm{PRG}_\mathbb{B}(\Sigma)_| = \mathrm{PRG}_\mathbb{B}^{\#}(\Sigma)$.

(1) First we show $\mathrm{PRG}_N(\Sigma)_| \subseteq \mathrm{PRG}_N^{\#}(\Sigma)$. Let $\mathfrak{G} \in \mathrm{PRG}_N(\Sigma)_|$. So $\mathfrak{G}$ is isomorphic to $h^{-1}(\mathfrak{T}_N)_{|L}$ for a regular extended substitution h from Σ to N and $L \in \mathrm{REG}(N^*)$. By Lemma 15.26, $h^{-1}(\mathfrak{T}_N)_{|L} = g^{-1}(\#_L(\mathfrak{T}_N))$ with $g(a) = \#h(a)\#$ for all $a \in \Sigma$.

(2) We now show $\mathrm{PRG}_N^{\#}(\Sigma) \subseteq \mathrm{PRG}_\mathbb{B}(\Sigma)_|$. Let $\mathfrak{G} \in \mathrm{PRG}_N^{\#}(\Sigma)$. So $\mathfrak{G}$ is isomorphic to $h^{-1}(\#_L(\mathfrak{T}_N))$ for a regular extended substitution h from Σ to N and $L \in \mathrm{REG}(N^*)$.

Let $\mathcal{A}_L = (Q, N, \delta, q_0, F)$ be a finite and complete deterministic automaton recognizing L. Without loss of generality, we may assume that for $p, q \in Q$ we have that $\delta(p, a) = \delta(q, b)$ implies $a = b$.[2] Thus, every reachable state of Q has a unique "incoming" letter a. Let P denote the set of all sequences of states which can be obtained from the initial state q_0 via δ: $P = \{q_0 p_1 \ldots p_k \mid \exists k \geq 0, \exists a_1, \ldots, a_k \in N, \delta(q_0, a_1) = p_1, \delta(p_{i-1}, a_i) = p_i \text{ for all } i \in \{1, \ldots, k\}\}$. So every such sequence $q_0 p_1 \ldots p_k$ corresponds to a unique word $a_1 \ldots a_k$. Furthermore, it is easy to see that P is a regular set. Now consider the finite and therefore regular extended substitution f defined by

$$f(a) = \{\bar{p}pq \mid \delta(p, a) = q\}$$
$$f(\#) = \{\bar{p}p \mid p \in F\}$$

---

[2] Otherwise, duplicate states of $\mathcal{A}_L$ appropriately.

Then: $\#_L(\mathfrak{T}_N)$ is isomorphic to $f^{-1}(\mathfrak{T}_Q)_{|P}$. Instead of giving a formal proof, let us consider as an example the transition $s \xrightarrow[\#_L(\mathfrak{T}_N)]{\#} s$. Then $s = a_1 \ldots a_k \in L$. There is a unique sequence $q_0 p_1 \ldots p_k$ with $\delta(q_0, a_1) = p_1$, $\delta(p_{i-1}, a_i) = p_i$ for $i \in \{1, \ldots, k\}$, $p_k \in F$, and $q_0 p_1 \ldots p_k \in P$. Hence, there is a corresponding path from node q_0 to node $q_0 p_1 \ldots p_k$ in $f^{-1}(\mathfrak{T}_Q)_{|P}$ labelled by $a_1 \ldots a_k$. This situation is depicted in Figure 15.5.

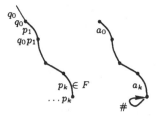

Fig. 15.5. Words vs. State

By definition, P is the vertex set of the connected component of $f^{-1}(\mathfrak{T}_Q)$ containing q_0. Hence, P is stable for $f^{-1}(\mathfrak{T}_Q)$.
We could now easily prove that $\mathfrak{G}$ (isomorphic to $h^{-1}(\#_L(\mathfrak{T}_N))$) is isomorphic to $h^{-1}(f^{-1}(\mathfrak{T}_Q))_{|P}$. However, we want to achieve such a result for $\mathbb{B}$ instead of Q. Therefore, we use a standard encoding of elements of Q by sequences of zeros and ones. Let $Q = \{p_1, \ldots, p_n\}$ and for $i \in \{1, \ldots, n\}$

$$g(p_i) = 01^{i-1}.$$

Furthermore, let $M = g(\{p_1, \ldots, p_n\}^*) = \{0, \ldots, 01^{n-1}\}^*$. Note that M is stable for $g^{-1}(\mathfrak{T}_B)$. Then we have

$$g[\mathfrak{T}_Q] = g^{-1}(\mathfrak{T}_B)_{|M}.$$

The latter means that $\mathfrak{T}_Q$ is isomorphic to $g^{-1}(\mathfrak{T}_B)_{|M}$ (via the isomorphism g). Figure 15.6 depicts an encoding of the ternary tree in the binary tree. The corresponding encoding function is given by:

$$g(a_0) = 0$$
$$g(a_1) = 01$$
$$g(a_2) = 011$$

Since $\#_L(\mathfrak{T}_N)$ is isomorphic to $f^{-1}(\mathfrak{T}_Q)_{|P}$, it is also isomorphic to the isomorphic image of $f^{-1}(\mathfrak{T}_Q)_{|P}$ via g. Hence, it is isomorphic to:

$$
\begin{aligned}
g[f^{-1}(\mathfrak{T}_Q)_{|P}] &= g[f^{-1}(\mathfrak{T}_Q)]_{|g(P)} \\
&= f^{-1}(g[\mathfrak{T}_Q])_{|g(P)} \\
&= f^{-1}(g^{-1}(\mathfrak{T}_B)_{|M})_{|g(P)} \\
&= f^{-1}(g^{-1}(\mathfrak{T}_B))_{|M \cap g(P)} \qquad \text{Lemma 15.25} \\
&= (f \circ g)^{-1}(\mathfrak{T}_B)_{|V_{g^{-1}(\mathfrak{T}_B)} \cap M \cap g(P)} \quad \text{Lemma 15.23} \\
&= (f \circ g)^{-1}(\mathfrak{T}_B)_{|g(P)}
\end{aligned}
$$

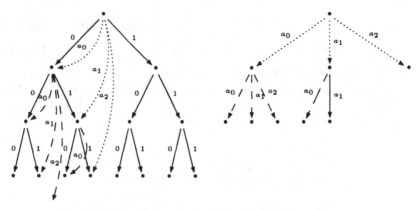

Fig. 15.6. Encoding a ternary tree in the binary tree

Note that $g(P)$ is stable for $(f \circ g)^{-1}(\mathfrak{T}_{\mathbf{B}})$, and, using Lemma 15.25, $\mathfrak{G}$ is isomorphic to:

$$h^{-1}((f \circ g)^{-1}(\mathfrak{T}_{\mathbf{B}})_{|g(P)})$$
$$= (h \circ f \circ g)^{-1}(\mathfrak{T}_{\mathbf{B}})_{|g(P)}$$
$$= ((h \circ f \circ g){\downarrow}_{\#})^{-1}(\mathfrak{T}_{\mathbf{B}})_{|g(P)}$$

where for any $x \in \Sigma$, $((h \circ f \circ g){\downarrow}_{\#})(x) = ((f \circ g)(h(x))){\downarrow}_{\#}$. As $f \circ g$ is a finite substitution, we have $((h \circ f \circ g){\downarrow}_{\#})$ is a regular extended substitution. Hence, $\mathfrak{G} \in \mathrm{PRG}_{\mathbf{B}}(\Sigma)_|$.

(3) Finally, we show $\mathrm{PRG}_{\mathbf{B}}(\Sigma)_| \subseteq \mathrm{PRG}_N(\Sigma)_|$. Let $\mathfrak{G} \in \mathrm{PRG}_{\mathbf{B}}(\Sigma)_|$. So $\mathfrak{G}$ is isomorphic to $h^{-1}(\mathfrak{T}_{\mathbf{B}})_{|L}$ for a regular extended substitution $h : \Sigma \to \mathbb{B}$ and $L \in \mathrm{REG}(\mathbb{B}^*)$. We have $\mathfrak{T}_{\mathbf{B}} = \iota^{-1}(\mathfrak{T}_N)_{|\mathbb{B}^*}$, where ι denotes the identity on $\mathbb{B}$. Note that $\mathbb{B}^*$ is stable for $\iota^{-1}(\mathfrak{T}_N)$. Hence, $\mathfrak{G}$ is isomorphic to:

$$h^{-1}(\iota^{-1}(\mathfrak{T}_N)_{|\mathbb{B}^*})_{|L} = (h^{-1}(\iota^{-1}(\mathfrak{T}_N)))_{|\mathbb{B}^*})_{|L} \qquad \text{by Lemma 15.25}$$
$$= (h \circ \iota)^{-1}(\mathfrak{T}_N)_{|V_{\iota^{-1}(\mathfrak{T}_N)} \cap \mathbb{B}^* \cap L} \qquad \text{by Lemma 15.23}$$
$$= (h \circ \iota)^{-1}(\mathfrak{T}_N)_{|\mathbb{B}^* \cap L}$$

Since $h \circ \iota$ is a regular extended substitution, we have $\mathfrak{G} \in \mathrm{PRG}_{\mathbf{B}}(\Sigma)_|$.

We now give three important representations of prefix-recognizable graphs.

Theorem 15.34 ([28]). *Given an alphabet N with at least two letters, the following properties are equivalent:*

(1) $\mathfrak{G}$ *is interpretable in* $\mathfrak{T}_{\mathbf{B}}$.
(2) $\mathfrak{G} \in \mathrm{PRG}_N(\Sigma)_|$.
(3) $\mathfrak{G}$ *is isomorphic to* $(N^*H)_{|L}$ *for some recognizable* $H \subseteq N^* \times \Sigma \times N^*$ *and* $L \in \mathrm{REG}(N^*)$.
(4) $\mathfrak{G}$ *is isomorphic to* $\bigcup_{i=1}^n W_i(U_i \xrightarrow{a_i} V_i)$ *for some* $n \geq 0$; $a_1, \ldots, a_n \in \Sigma$; $U_1, V_1, W_1, \ldots, U_n, V_n, W_n \in \mathrm{REG}(N^*)$.

Proof. (2) $\Rightarrow$ (3): Assume $\mathfrak{G} \in \mathrm{PRG}_N(\Sigma)_|$. So $\mathfrak{G}$ is isomorphic to $h^{-1}(\mathfrak{T}_N)_{|L}$ for an appropriate extended substitution h from Σ to N and $L \in \mathrm{REG}(N^*)$. By Corollary 15.31, we can write $h^{-1}(\mathfrak{T}_N)$ as N^*H for

$$H = \{\bar{u}v \in h(a)\!\downarrow \cap\, \overline{N}^* N^*, a \in \Sigma\}.$$

Since h is regular, $h(a)$ is a regular language, let us say C. We are done by showing that $C\!\downarrow \cap\, \overline{N}^* N^*$ is a finite union of the form UV for $U, V \in \mathrm{REG}(N^*)$. Let $\mathcal{A} = (Q, \hat{N}, \delta, q_0, F)$ be the automaton recognizing C. It is easy to see that $C\!\downarrow \cap\, \overline{N}^* N^*$ equals

$$\bigcup_{q \in Q} (\overline{L(Q, N, \delta, q_0, q)} \cap L(\mathfrak{T}_N))\!\downarrow(\overline{L(Q, N, \delta, q, F)} \cap L(\mathfrak{T}_N))\!\downarrow,$$

and regularity follows from Lemma 15.27.

(2) $\Rightarrow$ (4): Consider $\mathfrak{G} \in \mathrm{PRG}_N(\Sigma)_|$. Hence, $\mathfrak{G}$ is isomorphic to a $h^{-1}(\mathfrak{T}_N)_{|L}$ for a suitable regular extended substitution from Σ to N and $L \in \mathrm{REG}(N^*)$. For every $a \in \Sigma$, let $\mathcal{A}_a = (Q_a, \hat{N}_\#, \delta_a, q_{0a}, F_a)$ be the automaton recognizing $h(a)$. By Corollary 15.30 and similar arguments as in the previous case, we can write $h^{-1}(\mathfrak{T}_N)$ as

$$\bigcup_{\substack{W \in [L] \\ a \in \Sigma \\ q \in Q_a}} W(U(a, q) \xrightarrow{a} V(a, q)),$$

where

$$U(a, q) = \overline{(L(Q_a, \hat{N}_\#, \delta_a, q_{0a}, q) \cap L(\#_{W^{-1}L}(\mathfrak{T}_N)))}\!\downarrow_\#$$

and

$$V(a, q) = \overline{(L(Q_a, \hat{N}_\#, \delta_a, q, F_a) \cap L(\#_{W^{-1}L}(\mathfrak{T}_N)))}\!\downarrow_\#.$$

Regularity again follows from Lemma 15.27.

(3) $\Rightarrow$ (2): Let $H \subseteq N^* \times \Sigma \times N^*$ be a recognizable graph and $L \in \mathrm{REG}(N^*)$. By Corollary 15.31, $H = h^{-1}(\mathfrak{T}_N)$, such that $h(a) = \{\bar{u}v \mid u \xrightarrow{a}_H v\}$ for every $a \in \Sigma$.

(4) $\Rightarrow$ (2): Let $\mathfrak{G}$ be isomorphic to $\bigcup_{i=1}^n W_i(U_i \xrightarrow{a_i} V_i)$ for some $n \geq 1$; $a_1, \ldots, a_n \in \Sigma$; $U_1, V_1, W_1, \ldots, U_n, V_n, W_n \in \mathrm{REG}(N^*)$. Define L to be the regular language $L = \bigcup_{i=1}^n W_i a_i$, and let $h(a) = \bigcup\{\overline{U_i} a_i \# \overline{a_i} V_i \mid a_i = a\}$ for every $a \in \Sigma$ be a regular extended substitution. Then $\mathfrak{G} = h^{-1}(\#_L(\mathfrak{T}_N))$.

We have shown that (2) – (4) are equivalent. We had already shown in Theorem 15.14 that (1) implies (4) and (2) implies (1), using Proposition 15.33. Thus, all equivalences are shown.

15.6   Automata for Prefix-Recognizable Graphs

Let us conclude this chapter with a simple link from prefix-recognizable graphs to pushdown automata. The result is due to Stirling [168], and the proof is due to Caucal.[3]

Theorem 15.35. *Regular restrictions of the ε-closures of pushdown graphs are prefix-recognizable graphs.*

Proof. "$\Rightarrow$": Let us consider ε to be a new symbol. Then, the transition graph of a pushdown automaton with ε-transitions is a regular graph. The ε-closure of this graph can be obtained by an inverse regular mapping. Since regular graphs are a special kind of prefix-recognizable graphs and the class of prefix-recognizable graphs is closed with respect to regular inverse substitutions, we have that the latter is prefix-recognizable.

"$\Leftarrow$": Let $\mathfrak{G} = (\bigcup_{i=1}^{n}(U_i \overset{a_i}{\Longrightarrow} V_i)N^*)_{|L}$ be a prefix-recognizable graph with $U_1, V_1, \ldots, U_n, V_n, L \in \mathrm{REG}(N^*)$. For each U_i and V_i we have finite automata $\mathcal{A}_i^U = (Q_i^U, N, \delta_i^U, q_{0i}^U, F_i^U)$ and $\mathcal{B}_i^V = (Q_i^V, N, \delta_i^V, q_{0i}^V, F_i^V)$ recognizing U_i and V_i, respectively. Assume that these automata have pairwise disjoint state sets. Let $\#$ be a new symbol and construct the following rewriting system R:

$$
\begin{aligned}
\# &\overset{\varepsilon}{\Longrightarrow} q_{0i}^U \\
pa &\overset{\varepsilon}{\Longrightarrow} q \quad \text{if } q \in \delta_i^U(p,a) \\
p &\overset{\varepsilon}{\Longrightarrow} q \quad \text{if } p \in F_i^U \text{ and } q \in F_j^U \\
q &\overset{\varepsilon}{\Longrightarrow} pa \quad \text{if } q \in \delta_i^V(p,a) \\
q_{0i}^V &\overset{a_i}{\Longrightarrow} \#
\end{aligned}
$$

So $\mathfrak{G}$ is equal to the restriction to $\#_L$ of the ε-closure of the prefix transition graph of R.

15.7   Conclusion

In this chapter we introduced the class of prefix-recognizable graphs, originally introduced by Caucal (cf. [28]). We have shown that this class of graphs is the largest class of graphs providing a decidable MSO-theory provable by interpretation in the infinite binary tree.

Several further representations of prefix-recognizable graphs were given in the literature. Let us sum up (some) known results in the following theorem. Whenever the formal notions are not clear, we refer the reader to the citations given.

Theorem 15.36. *Let $\mathfrak{G}$ be a graph. The following statements are equivalent:*

(1) $\mathfrak{G} = h^{-1}(\mathfrak{T}_\mathbb{B})_{|C}$ *for a regular substitution h and a regular language C.*

(2) $\mathfrak{G}$ *is isomorphic to $\bigcup_{i=1}^{n} W_i(U_i \overset{a_i}{\longrightarrow} V_i)$ for some $n \geq 0$; $a_1, \ldots, a_n \in \Sigma$; $U_1, V_1, W_1, \ldots, U_n, V_n, W_n \in \mathrm{REG}(N^*)$.*

---

[3] private communication

(3) $\mathfrak{G} = h^{-1}(\#_C(\mathfrak{T}_\mathbf{B}))$ *for a regular substitution* h *and a regular marking* C.

(4) $\mathfrak{G}$ *is MSO-interpretable in the binary tree* $\mathfrak{T}_\mathbf{B}$.

(5) $\mathfrak{G}$ *is VR-equational.*

(6) $\mathfrak{G}$ *is a prefix-transition graph of Type-2.*

(7) $\mathfrak{G}$ *is the configuration graph of a pushdown automaton with* ε*-transitions.*

The equivalence of (1) – (3) was obtained by Caucal in [28]. (4) and (5) are shown in [6] and [12]. The last two characterizations are due to Stirling [168]. In this chapter, we have shown the equivalence of (1) – (4) and (7).

Two-player games for push-down graphs and prefix-recognizable are studied Chapter 17. A different natural class of objects providing a decidable MSO-theory is presented in Chapter 16.

16 The Monadic Theory of Tree-like Structures

Dietmar Berwanger and Achim Blumensath

Mathematische Grundlagen der Informatik
RWTH Aachen

16.1 Introduction

Initiated by the work of Büchi, Läuchli, Rabin, and Shelah in the late 60s, the investigation of monadic second-order logic (MSO) has received continuous attention. The attractiveness of MSO is due to the fact that, on the one hand, it is quite expressive subsuming – besides first-order logic – most modal logics, in particular the μ-calculus. On the other hand, MSO is simple enough such that model-checking is still decidable for many structures. Hence, one can obtain decidability results for several logics by just considering MSO.

For these reasons it is an important task to classify those structures for which MSO model-checking is decidable. So far, only partial results are known and it seems doubtful whether a complete characterisation can be obtained.

On the one hand, a useful tool to prove undecidability is the result that MSO model-checking for the grid $\omega \times \omega$ is undecidable. On the other hand, Rabin's famous tree theorem states that, for the complete binary tree, model-checking is decidable. Since many structures can be interpreted in the binary tree this provides a wide range of decidability results. Furthermore, we often only need to consider trees, as many modal logics have the tree-model property.

In this chapter we present a generalisation of Rabin's Tree Theorem. Given a structure $\mathfrak{A}$ we construct its *iteration* $\mathfrak{A}^*$ which is a tree whose vertices are finite sequences of elements of $\mathfrak{A}$. For each relation R of $\mathfrak{A}$ its iteration has the relation

$$R^* := \{ (wa_0, \ldots, wa_r) \mid \bar{a} \in R, \ w \in A^* \}.$$

Additionally, we include the successor relation son containing all pairs (w, wa) for $w \in A^*$, $a \in A$, and the clone relation cl consisting of all elements of the form waa. Muchnik's Theorem states that model-checking is decidable for $\mathfrak{A}$ if and only if it is so for $\mathfrak{A}^*$. The first published proof appears in Semenov [162]. It generalises an unpublished result of Stupp [173] described in Shelah [163] where the clone relation was left out. Our presentation follows Walukiewicz [200].

For the proof we employ the usual technique of translating formulae into automata and vice versa. Since, in general, we are operating on trees of infinite degree, a new type of automaton is needed where the transition function is defined by MSO-formulae. Furthermore, in order to handle the clone relation, the transition function has to depend on the current position in the input tree.

In the next section we introduce the kind of automaton we will use to prove Muchnik's Theorem but in a more general version than needed, and we prove that these automata are closed under boolean operations and projection.

E. Grädel et al. (Eds.): Automata, Logics, and Infinite Games, LNCS 2500, pp. 285-301, 2002.
© Springer-Verlag Berlin Heidelberg 2002

In Section 16.3 we will restrict the class of automata to those with MSO-definable transition function and the translation between automata and MSO-formulae is presented.

Finally, Section 16.4 contains the proof of Muchnik's Theorem.

16.2 Automata

To fix our notation, let $[n] := \{0, \dots, n-1\}$. By $\mathcal{B}^+(X)$ we denote the set of (infinitary) positive boolean formulae over X, i.e., all formulae constructed from X with disjunction and conjunction. An interpretation of a formula $\varphi \in \mathcal{B}^+(X)$ is a set $I \subseteq X$ of atoms we consider true. A Σ-**labelled** A-**tree** is a function $T : A^* \to \Sigma$ which assigns a label $T(w)$ to each vertex $w \in A^*$.

The main tool used for the investigation of MSO are automata on A-trees. Since A is not required to be finite we need a model of automaton which can work with trees of arbitrary degree. In addition the clone relation cl makes it necessary that the transition function depends on the current position in the input tree. Thus, we define a very general type of automaton which we will restrict suitably in the next section.

Definition 16.1. A **tree automaton** is a tuple

$$\mathcal{A} = (Q, \Sigma, A, \delta, q_\mathrm{I}, W)$$

where the input is a Σ-labelled A-tree, Q is the set of states, q_I is the initial state, $W \subseteq Q^\omega$ is the acceptance condition, and

$$\delta : Q \times \Sigma \to \mathcal{B}^+(Q \times A)^{A^*}$$

is the transition function which assigns to each state q and input symbol c a function $\delta(q,c) : A^* \to \mathcal{B}^+(Q \times A)$. Frequently we will write $\delta(q,c,w)$ instead of $\delta(q,c)(w)$.

Note that the transition function and acceptance condition of these automata are not finite. To obtain finite automata we will represent the transition function by an MSO-formula and consider only parity acceptance conditions in the next section. For simplicity all results in this section are stated and proved for the general model.

The language accepted by an automaton is defined by way of games. Recall that a game $\mathcal{G} = (V_0, V_1, E, W)$ consists of sets V_0 and V_1 of vertices associated to the respective players, an edge relation E, and the set of winning plays W.

Definition 16.2. Let $\mathcal{A} = (Q, \Sigma, A, \delta, q_\mathrm{I}, W)$ be an automaton and $T : A^* \to \Sigma$ a tree. The game $\mathcal{G}(\mathcal{A}, T)$ is defined as follows:

(a) The set of vertices is

$$(Q \cup \mathcal{B}^+(Q \times A)) \times A^*.$$

V_0 consists of all pairs $(q, w) \in Q \times A^*$ and all pairs of the form (φ, w) where φ is either atomic or a disjunction, and V_1 consists of all pairs where φ is a conjunction.

(b) The initial position is $(q_\mathrm{I}, \varepsilon)$.

(c) Each node (q, w) has the successor $(\delta(q, T(w), w), w)$. The successors of nodes $(\varphi \circ \psi, w)$ are (φ, w) and (ψ, w) where $\circ$ is either $\wedge$ or $\vee$. Finally, the successor of nodes $((q, a), w)$ with atomic formulae is (q, wa).

(d) Let $(\xi_i, w_i)_{i<\omega}$ be a play. Consider the subsequence $(\xi_{i_k}, w_{i_k})_{k<\omega}$ of positions where $\xi_{i_k} = q_k$ is a state. The play is winning if the sequence $q_0 q_1 \dots$ is in W.

The language $L(\mathcal{A})$ recognised by $\mathcal{A}$ is the set of all trees T such that player 0 has a winning strategy for the game $\mathcal{G}(\mathcal{A}, T)$.

Sometimes it is more convenient to use a simpler game where several moves of the same kind are replaced by a single one. Assume that δ is in disjunctive normal form. The abridged game $\check{\mathcal{G}}(\mathcal{A}, T)$ is defined by replacing (a) and (c) in the above definition by:

(a$'$) The set of vertices consists of $V_0 := Q \times A^*$ and $V_1 := \mathscr{P}(Q \times A) \times A^*$.

(c$'$) Each node $(q, w) \in V_0$ with $\delta(q, T(w), w) = \bigvee_i \bigwedge \Phi_i$ has the successors (Φ_i, w) for each i. The successors of some node $(\Phi, w) \in V_1$ are the nodes (q, wa) for $(q, a) \in \Phi$.

Both versions of the game are obviously equivalent. In the following sections we will consider only parity acceptance conditions.

Definition 16.3. A **parity condition** is given by a function $\Omega : Q \to [n]$ and defines the set of all sequences $(q_i)_{i<\omega} \in Q^\omega$ such that the least number appearing infinitely often in the sequence $(\Omega(q_i))_{i<\omega}$ is even.

In the remainder of this section we will prove that automata as defined above are closed under union, complement, and projection. This property is needed in the next section in order to translate formulae into automata. We start with the union.

Definition 16.4. Let $\mathcal{A}_i = (Q_i, \Sigma, A, \delta_i, q_i^\mathrm{I}, W_i)$, $i = 1, 2$, be tree automata. Their **sum** is the automaton

$$\mathcal{A}_0 + \mathcal{A}_1 := (Q_1 \cup Q_2 \cup \{q_\mathrm{I}\}, \Sigma, A, \delta, q_\mathrm{I}, W)$$

where

$$\delta(q, c, w) := \delta_i(q, c, w) \qquad \text{for } q \in Q_i,$$
$$\delta(q_\mathrm{I}, c, w) := \delta_0(q_0^\mathrm{I}, c, w) \vee \delta_1(q_1^\mathrm{I}, c, w),$$

and W consists of all sequences $q_0 q_1 q_2 \dots$ such that $q_0 = q_\mathrm{I}$ and $q_i^\mathrm{I} q_1 q_2 \dots \in W_i$ for some i.

Lemma 16.5. $L(\mathcal{A}_0 + \mathcal{A}_1) = L(\mathcal{A}_0) \cup L(\mathcal{A}_1)$.

Proof. Note that $\mathcal{G}(\mathcal{A}_0 + \mathcal{A}_1, T)$ consists of disjoint copies of $\mathcal{G}(\mathcal{A}_0, T)$ and $\mathcal{G}(\mathcal{A}_1, T)$, and a new initial position from which player 0 has to choose one of the two subgames. Obviously, each winning strategy for player 0 in $\mathcal{G}(\mathcal{A}_0, T)$ or $\mathcal{G}(\mathcal{A}_1, T)$ is also a winning strategy in $\mathcal{G}(\mathcal{A}_0 + \mathcal{A}_1, T)$. On the other hand, if σ is a winning strategy for player 0 in the compound game it is also winning in either $\mathcal{G}(\mathcal{A}_0, T)$ or $\mathcal{G}(\mathcal{A}_1, T)$ depending on which subgame player 0 chooses in his first move. □

Complementation is easy as well.

Definition 16.6. Let $\mathcal{A} = (Q, \Sigma, A, \delta, q_{\mathrm{I}}, W)$. $\bar{\mathcal{A}} := (Q, \Sigma, A, \bar{\delta}, q_{\mathrm{I}}, \bar{W})$ is the automaton with

$$\bar{\delta}(q, c, w) := \overline{\delta(q, c, w)} \quad \text{and} \quad \bar{W} := Q^\omega \setminus W.$$

Here $\bar{\varphi}$ denotes the dual of φ, i.e., the formula where each $\wedge$ is replaced by $\vee$ and vice versa.

Lemma 16.7. $T \in L(\bar{\mathcal{A}})$ iff $T \notin L(\mathcal{A})$.

Proof. Let $\mathcal{G}(\bar{\mathcal{A}}, T) = (\bar{V}_0, \bar{V}_1, \bar{E}, \bar{W})$. Note that in $\mathcal{G}(\bar{\mathcal{A}}, T)$ the roles of player 0 and 1 are exchanged. $\bar{V}_0$ consists of all former V_1-nodes, and $\bar{V}_1$ contains all V_0-nodes except for the atomic ones. Since the latter have exactly one successor it is irrelevant which player they are assigned to. Thus, each choice of player 0 in the old game is made by player 1 in the new one and vice versa. Hence, each winning strategy σ for player 0 in $\mathcal{G}(\mathcal{A}, T)$ is a strategy for player 1 in $\mathcal{G}(\bar{\mathcal{A}}, T)$ which ensures that the resulting play induces a sequence in $W = Q^\omega \setminus \bar{W}$. Thus, σ is winning for 1. The other direction follows by symmetry. □

The closure under projections is the hardest part to prove. The projection $\Pi(L)$ of a tree-language L is the set of all trees $T : A^* \to \Sigma$ such that there is a tree $T' : A^* \to \Sigma \times \{0, 1\}$ in L with $T'(w) = (T(w), i_w)$ for some $i_w \in \{0, 1\}$ and all $w \in A^*$.

The proof is split into several parts. We prove closure under projection for non-deterministic automata, and show that each alternating automaton can be transformed into an equivalent non-deterministic one.

Definition 16.8. An automaton $\mathcal{A} := (Q, \Sigma, A, \delta, q_{\mathrm{I}}, W)$ is **non-deterministic** if each formula $\delta(q, c, w)$ is in disjunctive normal-form $\bigvee_i \bigwedge_k (q_{ik}, a_{ik})$ where, for each fixed i, all the a_{ik} are different.

Definition 16.9. Let $\mathcal{A} = (Q, \Sigma \times \{0, 1\}, A, \delta, q_{\mathrm{I}}, W)$ be a non-deterministic automaton. Define $\mathcal{A}_\Pi := (Q, \Sigma, A, \delta_\Pi, q_{\mathrm{I}}, W)$ where

$$\delta_\Pi(q, c, w) := \delta(q, (c, 0), w) \vee \delta(q, (c, 1), w).$$

Lemma 16.10. $L(\mathcal{A}_\Pi) = \Pi(L(\mathcal{A}))$

Proof. ($\supseteq$) Let σ be a winning strategy for player 0 in $\mathcal{G}(\mathcal{A}, T)$. $\mathcal{G}(\mathcal{A}_\Pi, \Pi(T))$ contains additional vertices of the form $(\varphi_0 \vee \varphi_1, w)$ where $\varphi_i = \delta(q, (c, i), w)$. By defining

$$\sigma(\varphi_0 \vee \varphi_1, w) := \varphi_i \quad \text{for the } i \text{ with } T(w) = (c, i)$$

we obtain a strategy for player 0 in the new game. This strategy is winning since, if one removes the additional vertices from a play according to the extended strategy, a play according to σ in the original game is obtained which is winning by assumption.

($\subseteq$) Let σ be a winning strategy for player 0 in $\mathcal{G}(\mathcal{A}_\Pi, T)$. We have to define a tree $T' \in L(\mathcal{A})$ with $T = \Pi(T')$. Since $\mathcal{A}_\Pi$ is non-deterministic the game has the following structure: At each position $((q, a), w)$ with

$$\delta(q, T(w), w) = \bigvee_i \bigwedge_k (q_{ik}, a_{ik})$$

player 0 chooses some conjunction $\bigwedge_k (q_{ik}, a_{ik})$ out of which player 1 picks a successor (q_{ik}, a_{ik}). Thus, for each word $w \in A^*$ there is at most one state q such that a play according to σ reaches the position (q, w). Let $\sigma(\varphi_0 \vee \varphi_1, w) = (\varphi_i, w)$ where $\varphi_0 \vee \varphi_1 = \delta(q, T(w), w)$. We define T' by $T'(w) := (T(w), i)$. $\square$

It remains to show how to translate alternating automata to non-deterministic ones. To do so we need some notation to modify transition relations.

Definition 16.11. Let $\varphi \in \mathcal{B}^+(Q \times A)$.

(a) The **collection** of φ is defined as follows. Let $\bigvee_i \bigwedge_k (q_{ik}, a_{ik})$ be the disjunctive normal-form of φ.

$$\text{collect}(\varphi) := \bigvee_i \bigwedge_{a \in A} (Q_i(a), a) \in \mathcal{B}^+(\mathscr{P}(Q) \times A)$$

where $Q_i(a) := \{ q_{ik} \mid a_{ik} = a \}$.

(b) Let $q' \in Q'$. The **shift** of φ by q' is the formula $\text{sh}_{q'} \varphi \in \mathcal{B}^+(Q' \times Q \times A)$ obtained from φ by replacing all atoms (q, a) by (q', q, a).

(c) For $S \subseteq Q \times Q$ let

$$(S)_2 := \{ q \mid (q', q) \in S \text{ for some } q' \}.$$

The translation is performed in two steps. First, the alternating automaton is transformed into a non-deterministic one with an obscure non-parity acceptance condition. Then, the result is turned into a normal non-deterministic parity automaton. The construction used for the first step is the usual one. For each node of the input tree the automaton stores the set of states of the original automaton from which the corresponding subtree must be accepted. That is, for universal choices of the alternating automaton, all successors are remembered, whereas for existential choices, only one successor is picked non-deterministically. What makes matters slightly more complicated is the fact that, in order to define the acceptance condition, the new automaton has to remember not only the set of current states but their predecessors as well, i.e., its states are of the form (q', q) where q is the current state of the original automaton and q' is the previous one.

Definition 16.12. Let $\mathcal{A} = (Q, \Sigma, A, \delta, q_1, W)$ be an alternating automaton.

$$\mathcal{A}_n := \big(\mathscr{P}(Q \times Q), \Sigma, A, \delta_n, \{(q_1, q_1)\}, W_n\big)$$

is the automaton where

$$\delta_n(S, c, w) := \text{collect} \bigwedge_{q \in (S)_2} \text{sh}_q \, \delta(q, c, w).$$

A sequence $(q_i)_{i<\omega} \in Q^\omega$ is called a **trace** of $(S_i)_{i<\omega} \in \mathscr{P}(Q \times Q)^\omega$ if $(q_i, q_{i+1}) \in S_i$ for all $i < \omega$. W_n consists of all sequences $(S_i)_{i<\omega} \in \mathscr{P}(Q \times Q)^\omega$ such that every trace of $(S_i)_{i<\omega}$ is in W.

Lemma 16.13. *$\mathcal{A}_n$ is a non-deterministic automaton with $L(\mathcal{A}_n) = L(\mathcal{A})$.*

Proof. The definition of collect ensures that $\mathcal{A}_n$ is non-deterministic.

($\supseteq$) Let $T \in L(\mathcal{A})$ and let σ be the corresponding winning strategy for player 0 in $\check{\mathcal{G}}(\mathcal{A}, T)$. To define a strategy σ_n in $\check{\mathcal{G}}(\mathcal{A}_n, T)$ consider a position $(S, w) \in \check{\mathcal{G}}(\mathcal{A}, T)$. Let $\sigma(q, w) = (\Phi_q, w)$ for $q \in (S)_2$. We define $\sigma_n(S, w) := (\text{collect} \bigwedge \Phi, w)$ where

$$\Phi = \bigcup_{q \in (S)_2} \text{sh}_q \, \Phi_q.$$

This is valid since $(\text{collect} \bigwedge \Phi, w)$ is a successor of (q, w).

To show that σ_n is a winning strategy consider the result $(S_i)_{i<\omega}$ of a play according to σ_n. If $(\Phi, w) \in \sigma_n(S_i, w)$ and $(S_{i+1}, a) \in \Phi$, then for each $(q, q') \in S_{i+1}$ it holds that $(q', a) \in \Phi_q$. Thus, all traces of $(S_i)_{i<\omega}$ are plays according to σ and therefore winning.

($\subseteq$) Let σ_n be a – not necessarily memoryless – winning strategy for player 0 in $\check{\mathcal{G}}(\mathcal{A}_n, T)$. We construct a winning strategy for player 0 in $\check{\mathcal{G}}(\mathcal{A}, T)$ as follows. Let p_n be a play according to σ_n in $\check{\mathcal{G}}(\mathcal{A}_n, T)$ with last position (S, w), and let p be the play according to σ. By induction we ensure that the last position in p is of the form (q, w) for some $q \in (S)_2$. Let $(\Phi_n, w) = \sigma_n(p_n)$ and define

$$\Phi := \{ (q', a) \mid (S', a) \in \Phi_n \text{ and } ((q, q'), a) \in S' \text{ for some } S' \}.$$

Then $\bigwedge \Phi$ is a conjunction in $\delta(q, T(w), w)$, by definition of δ_n, and we can set $\sigma(p) := (\Phi, w)$. The answer of player 0 to this move consists of some position (q', wa) for $(q', a) \in \Phi$. Suppose that in $\check{\mathcal{G}}(\mathcal{A}_n, T)$ player 1 chooses the position (S_a, wa) where S_a is the unique state such that $(S_a, a) \in \Phi_n$. Since $(q, q') \in S_a$ the induction hypothesis is satisfied for the extended plays $p(\Phi, w)(q', wa)$ and $p_n(\Phi_n, w)(S_a, a)$.

It follows that each play p according to σ in $\check{\mathcal{G}}(\mathcal{A}, T)$ is a trace of some play p_n according to σ_n and therefore winning by construction of $\mathcal{A}_n$. $\qquad\square$

The automaton $\mathcal{A}_n$ constructed above does not have a parity acceptance condition. Since we intend to consider only parity automata in the next section, we have to construct a non-deterministic automaton with such an acceptance condition. It is easy to see that, provided that the original automaton does have a parity acceptance condition, there is some parity automaton on infinite words $\mathcal{B} = (P, \mathscr{P}(Q \times Q), \delta, p^0, \Omega)$ which recognises $W_n \subseteq \mathscr{P}(Q \times Q)^\omega$. Let $\mathcal{A}_p$ be the product automaton of $\mathcal{A}_n$ and $\mathcal{B}$, that is,

$$\mathcal{A}_p = (P \times \mathscr{P}(Q \times Q), \ \Sigma, \ A, \ \delta_p, \ (p^0, q_n^I), \ \Sigma_p)$$

where

$$\delta_p((p, S), c, w) = \mathrm{sh}_{p'} \ \delta_n(S, c, w) \qquad \text{for } p' := \delta(p, S)$$

and $\Omega_p(p, S) = \Omega(p)$.

Lemma 16.14. $\mathcal{A}_p$ *is a parity automaton with* $L(\mathcal{A}_p) = L(\mathcal{A}_n)$.

Proof. Let σ be a winning strategy for player 0 in $\check{\mathcal{G}}(\mathcal{A}_n, T)$. We define a corresponding strategy σ' in $\check{\mathcal{G}}(\mathcal{A}_p, T)$ by

$$\sigma'((p, S), w) := (\mathrm{sh}_{p'} \ \Phi, w)$$

where $(\Phi, w) = \sigma(S, w)$ and $p' = \delta(p, S)$. That way every play

$$((p_0, S_0), w_0)(\Phi'_0, w_0)((p_1, S_1), w_1)(\Phi'_1, w_1) \dots$$

in $\check{\mathcal{G}}(\mathcal{A}_p, T)$ according to σ' is induced by a play

$$(S_0, w_0)(\Phi_0, w_0)(S_1, w_1)(\Phi_1, w_1) \dots$$

in $\check{\mathcal{G}}(\mathcal{A}_n, T)$ according to σ. Further, $(p_i)_{i<\omega}$ is the run of $\mathcal{B}$ on $(S_i)_{i<\omega}$. Since the second play is winning, the first one is so as well, by definition of $\mathcal{B}$. Hence, σ' is a winning condition. The other direction is proved analogously. $\square$

In the next section we will define a restricted class of automata where we only allow transition-functions which are MSO-definable. In order to transfer the results of this section we need to extract the required closure properties of the set of allowed transition-functions from the above proofs.

Theorem 16.15. *Let* T *be a class of functions* $f : A^* \to B^+(Q \times A)$ *where* A *and* Q *may be different for each* $f \in T$. *If* T *is closed under disjunction, conjunction, dual, shift, and collection then the class of automata with transition functions* $\delta : Q \times \Sigma \to T$ *is closed under union, complement, and projection.*

16.3 Tree-like Structures

The type of automata defined in the previous section is much too powerful. In order to prove Muchnik's Theorem we have to find a subclass which corresponds exactly to MSO on the class of trees obtained from relational structures by the operation of iteration.

Definition 16.16. Let $\mathfrak{A} = (A, R_0, \dots)$ be a τ-structure. The **iteration** of $\mathfrak{A}$ is the structure $\mathfrak{A}^* := (A^*, \mathrm{son}, \mathrm{cl}, R_0^*, \dots)$ of signature $\tau^* := \tau \cup \{\mathrm{son}, \mathrm{cl}\}$ where

$$
\begin{aligned}
\mathrm{son} &:= \{\, (w, wa) \mid w \in A^*,\ a \in A \,\}, \\
\mathrm{cl} &:= \{\, waa \mid w \in A^*,\ a \in A \,\}, \\
R_i^* &:= \{\, (wa_0, \dots, wa_r) \mid w \in A^*,\ \bar{a} \in R_i \,\}.
\end{aligned}
$$

For simplicity we will use a variant of monadic second-order logic where all first-order variables are eliminated. That is, formulae are constructed from atoms of the form $X \subseteq Y$ and $RX_0 \dots X_r$ by boolean operations and set quantification. Using slightly non-standard semantics we say that $R\bar{X}$ holds if $\bar{a} \in R$ for some elements $a_i \in X_i$. Note that we do not require the X_i to be singletons. Obviously, each MSO-formula can be brought into this form.

Example 16.17. The iteration $\mathfrak{G}^* := (V^*, \mathrm{son}, \mathrm{cl}, E^*)$ of a graph $\mathfrak{G} = (V, E)$ consists of all finite sequences $w \in V^*$ of vertices. We will construct an MSO-definition of those sequences which are paths in the original graph $\mathfrak{G}$. A word $w \in V^*$ is a path in $\mathfrak{G}$ if for all prefixes of the form uab with $u \in V^*$ and $a, b \in V$ there is an edge $(a, b) \in E$. The prefix relation $\preceq$ is MSO-definable being the transitive closure of the son relation. Given a prefix $y := uab$ the word $z := uaa$ can be obtained using the clone relation as follows:

$$
\psi(y, z) := \exists u \big(\mathrm{son}(u, y) \wedge \mathrm{son}(u, z) \wedge \mathrm{cl}(z)\big).
$$

Thus, the set of paths in $\mathfrak{G}$ can be defined by

$$
\varphi(x) := \forall y \forall z (y \preceq x \wedge \psi(y, z) \to E^* yz).
$$

In order to evaluate MSO-formulae over the iteration of some structure we translate them into automata where the transition function is defined by MSO-formulae. This is done in such a way that the resulting class of automata is expressively equivalent to monadic second-order logic.

Definition 16.18. Let $\mathfrak{A}$ be a structure and fix some $n \in \omega$. The function

$$
\langle\!\langle \varphi \rangle\!\rangle_{\mathfrak{A}} : A^* \to \mathcal{B}^+([n] \times A)
$$

induced by $\varphi(C, \bar{Q}) \in \mathrm{MSO}$ on $\mathfrak{A}$ is defined by

$$
\langle\!\langle \varphi \rangle\!\rangle_{\mathfrak{A}}(\varepsilon) := \bigvee \Big\{ \bigwedge \{\, (q, b) \mid b \in S_q \,\} \ \Big|\ S_0, \dots, S_{n-1} \subseteq A \text{ such that }
$$
$$
\mathfrak{A} \models \varphi(\emptyset, \bar{S}) \Big\},
$$

$$
\langle\!\langle \varphi \rangle\!\rangle_{\mathfrak{A}}(wa) := \bigvee \Big\{ \bigwedge \{\, (q, b) \mid b \in S_q \,\} \ \Big|\ S_0, \dots, S_{n-1} \subseteq A \text{ such that }
$$
$$
\mathfrak{A} \models \varphi(\{a\}, \bar{S}) \Big\}.
$$

Let $T_{\mathfrak{A}}^n$ be the set of all such functions.

Definition 16.19. An **MSO-automaton** is a tuple $\mathcal{A} = (Q, \Sigma, \delta, q_\mathrm{I}, \Omega)$ where $Q = [n]$ for some $n \in \omega$ and $\delta : Q \times \Sigma \to$ MSO. $\mathcal{A}$ accepts a Σ-labelled structure $\mathfrak{A}^*$ if the automaton $\mathcal{A}_\mathfrak{A} := (Q, \Sigma, A, \delta_\mathfrak{A}, q_\mathrm{I}, \Omega)$ does so, where $\delta : Q \times \Sigma \to T_\mathfrak{A}^n$ is defined by $\delta_\mathfrak{A}(q, c) := \langle\!\langle \delta(q, c) \rangle\!\rangle_\mathfrak{A}$.

In order to translate formulae into automata, the latter must be closed under all operations available in the respective logic.

Proposition 16.20. MSO-*automata are closed under boolean operations and projection.*

Proof. By Theorem 16.15 it is sufficient to show closure under or, and, dual, shift, and collection. To do so we will frequently need to convert between interpretations $I \subseteq Q \times A$ of boolean formulae $\langle\!\langle \varphi \rangle\!\rangle_\mathfrak{A}(w) \in \mathcal{B}^+(Q \times A)$ and sets $\bar{Q}$ such that $\mathfrak{A} \models \varphi(C, \bar{Q})$. Given $I \subseteq Q \times A$ define

$$Q_i(I) := \{\, a \in A \mid (q_i, a) \in I \,\}$$

for $i < n$, and given $Q_0, \ldots, Q_{n-1} \subseteq A$ define

$$I(\bar{Q}) := \{\, (q_i, a) \mid a \in Q_i,\ i < n \,\}.$$

Note that $I(\bar{Q}(I)) = I$ and $Q_i(I(\bar{Q})) = Q_i$. Then

$$I \models \langle\!\langle \varphi \rangle\!\rangle_\mathfrak{A}(w) \quad \text{iff} \quad \mathfrak{A} \models \varphi(C, \bar{Q}(I))$$

and vice versa. (Here and below C denotes the set consisting of the last element of w.)

(or) For the disjunction of two MSO-definable functions we can simply take the disjunction of their definitions since

$$I \models \langle\!\langle \varphi_0 \rangle\!\rangle_\mathfrak{A}(w) \vee \langle\!\langle \varphi_1 \rangle\!\rangle_\mathfrak{A}(w)$$
iff $\ I \models \langle\!\langle \varphi_i \rangle\!\rangle_\mathfrak{A}(w)$ for some i
iff $\ \mathfrak{A} \models \varphi_i(C, \bar{Q}(I))$ for some i
iff $\ \mathfrak{A} \models \varphi_0(C, \bar{Q}(I)) \vee \varphi_1(C, \bar{Q}(I))$
iff $\ I \models \langle\!\langle \varphi_0 \vee \varphi_1 \rangle\!\rangle_\mathfrak{A}(w)$.

(dual) The definition of the dual operation is slightly more involved.

$$I \models \overline{\langle\!\langle \varphi \rangle\!\rangle_\mathfrak{A}(w)}$$
iff $\ Q \times A \setminus I \not\models \langle\!\langle \varphi \rangle\!\rangle_\mathfrak{A}(w)$
iff $\ J \models \langle\!\langle \varphi \rangle\!\rangle_\mathfrak{A}(w)$ implies $J \cap I \neq \emptyset$
iff $\ \mathfrak{A} \models \varphi(C, \bar{P})$ implies $P_i \cap Q_i(I) \neq \emptyset$ for some i
iff $\ \mathfrak{A} \models \forall \bar{P}\big(\varphi(C, \bar{P}) \to \bigvee_{i<n} P_i \cap Q_i \neq \emptyset\big)$

(and) follows from (or) and (dual).

(shift) For a shift we simply need to renumber the states. If the pair (q_i, q_k) is encoded as number $ni + k$ we obtain

$$\varphi(C, Q_{ni+0}, \ldots, Q_{ni+n-1}).$$

(collection) The collection of a formula can be defined the following way:

$I \models$ collect $\langle\!\langle \varphi \rangle\!\rangle_{\mathfrak{A}}(w)$

iff there are $Q'_S \subseteq Q_S(I)$ such that $\bar{Q}'$ partitions A and $\mathfrak{A} \models \varphi(C, \bar{P})$

where $a \in P_i$: iff $i \in S$ for the unique $S \subseteq [n]$ with $a \in Q'_S$

iff there are $\bar{Q}'$ partitioning A such that $\mathfrak{A} \models \varphi(C, \bar{P})$ where

$P_i := \bigcup_{S:i\in S} Q'_S$

iff $\mathfrak{A} \models \varphi(C, \bar{P})$ for some $P_i \subseteq \bigcup_{S:i\in S} Q_S$ with

$P_i \cap Q_S = \emptyset$ for all S with $i \notin S$

iff $\mathfrak{A} \models \exists \bar{P}(\varphi(C, \bar{P}) \wedge \bigwedge_{i<n} P_i \subseteq \bigcup_{S:i\in S} Q_S \wedge \bigwedge_{S\subseteq[n]} \bigwedge_{i\notin S} P_i \cap Q_S = \emptyset).\square$

Using the preceding proposition we can state the equivalence result. We say that an automaton $\mathcal{A}$ is **equivalent** to an MSO-formula $\varphi(X_0, \ldots, X_{m-1})$ if $L(\mathcal{A})$ consists of those structures whose labelling encode sets $\bar{U}$ such that $\varphi(\bar{U})$ holds. The encoding of $\bar{U}$ is the $\mathscr{P}([m])$-labelled tree T such that

$$T(w) = \{ i \in [m] \mid w \in X_i \}$$

for all $w \in \{0, 1\}^*$.

Theorem 16.21. *For every formula* $\varphi \in$ MSO *there is an equivalent MSO-automaton and vice versa.*

Proof. ($\Rightarrow$) By induction on $\varphi(\bar{X})$ we construct an equivalent MSO-automaton $\mathcal{A} := (Q, \mathscr{P}([m]), \delta, q_0, \Omega)$. Since or corresponds to union, negation to complement, and existential quantifiers to projection, and MSO-automata are closed under all of those operations we only need to construct automata for atomic formulae.

$(X_i \subseteq X_j)$ We have to check for every element w of the input tree T that $i \notin T(w)$ or $j \in T(w)$. Thus, we set $Q := \{q_0\}$ with $\Omega(q_0) := 0$ and define the transition function such that

$$\delta_{\mathfrak{A}}(q_0, c, w) = \begin{cases} \bigwedge_{a\in A}(q_0, a) & \text{if } i \notin c \text{ or } j \in c, \\ \text{false} & \text{otherwise.} \end{cases}$$

for each input structure $\mathfrak{A}^*$. This can be done by setting

$$\delta(q_0, c) := \begin{cases} \forall x Q_0 x & \text{if } i \notin c \text{ or } j \in c, \\ \text{false} & \text{otherwise.} \end{cases}$$

$(R^*(X_{i_1}, \ldots, X_{i_k}))$ Set $Q := \{q_0, \ldots, q_k\}$ and $\Omega(q_i) := 1$. The automaton guesses a node in the input tree while in state q_0 and checks whether its children are in the relation R. That is,

$$\delta_{\mathfrak{A}}(q_0, c, w) = \bigvee_{a \in A} (q_0, a) \vee \bigvee \{ (q_1, a_1) \wedge \cdots \wedge (q_k, a_k) \mid \bar{a} \in R^{\mathfrak{A}} \},$$

$$\delta_{\mathfrak{A}}(q_j, c, w) = \begin{cases} \text{true} & \text{if } j \in c, \\ \text{false} & \text{otherwise,} \end{cases} \qquad \text{for } 1 \leq j \leq k.$$

The corresponding MSO-definition is

$$\delta(q_0, c) := \exists x Q_0 x \vee \exists \bar{x} (R\bar{x} \wedge Q_1 x_1 \wedge \cdots \wedge Q_k x_k),$$

$$\delta(q_j, c) = \begin{cases} \text{true} & \text{if } i_j \in c, \\ \text{false} & \text{otherwise,} \end{cases} \qquad \text{for } 1 \leq j \leq k.$$

$(son(X_i, X_j))$ Let $Q := \{q_0, q_1\}$ and $\Omega(q_i) := 1$. We guess some element $w \in X_i$ having a successor in X_j.

$$\delta_{\mathfrak{A}}(q_0, c, w) = \begin{cases} \bigvee_{a \in A} (q_0, a) & \text{if } i \notin c, \\ \bigvee_{a \in A} ((q_0, a) \vee (q_1, a)) & \text{otherwise,} \end{cases}$$

$$\delta_{\mathfrak{A}}(q_1, c, w) = \begin{cases} \text{true} & \text{if } j \in c, \\ \text{false} & \text{otherwise.} \end{cases}$$

The corresponding MSO-definition is

$$\delta(q_0, c) := \begin{cases} \exists x Q_0 x & \text{if } i \notin c, \\ \exists x (Q_0 x \vee Q_1 x) & \text{otherwise,} \end{cases}$$

$$\delta(q_1, c) := \begin{cases} \text{true} & \text{if } j \in c, \\ \text{false} & \text{otherwise.} \end{cases}$$

$(cl(X_i))$ Let $Q := \{q_0, q_1\}$ and $\Omega(q_i) := 1$. We guess some element wa such that its successor waa is in X_i.

$$\delta_{\mathfrak{A}}(q_0, c, w) = \begin{cases} \bigvee_{a \in A} (q_0, a) & \text{if } w = \varepsilon, \\ \bigvee_{a \in A} (q_0, a) \vee (q_1, b) & \text{if } w = w'b, \end{cases}$$

$$\delta_{\mathfrak{A}}(q_1, c, w) = \begin{cases} \text{true} & \text{if } i \in c, \\ \text{false} & \text{otherwise.} \end{cases}$$

The corresponding MSO-definition is

$$\delta(q_0, c) := \exists x Q_0 x \vee \exists x (Cx \wedge Q_1 x),$$

$$\delta(q_1, c) := \begin{cases} \text{true} & \text{if } i \in c, \\ \text{false} & \text{otherwise.} \end{cases}$$

Note that this is the only place where the transition function actually depends on the current vertex.

($\Leftarrow$) Let $\mathcal{A} = (Q, \Sigma, \delta, 0, \Omega)$ be an MSO-automaton and fix an input structure $\mathfrak{A}^*$. W.l.o.g. assume that $\mathcal{A}$ is non-deterministic. $\mathfrak{A}^*$ is accepted by $\mathcal{A}$ if there is an accepting run $\varrho : A^* \to Q$ of $\mathcal{A}$ on $\mathfrak{A}^*$. This can be expressed by an MSO-formula $\varphi(\bar{X})$ in the following way: we quantify existentially over tuples $\bar{Q}$ encoding ϱ (i.e., $Q_i = \varrho^{-1}(i)$), and then check that at each position $w \in A^*$ a valid transition is used and that each path in ϱ is accepting. $\qquad\square$

Before proceeding to the proof of Muchnik's Theorem let us take a look at the case of empty signature. A structure with empty signature is simply a set A. Its iteration is the tree $(A^*, \text{son}, \text{cl})$. The clone relation is not very useful in this case, so we drop it. Hence, the transition formulae of MSO-automata do not depend on C and the following lemma implies that we can restrict our attention to MSO-automata with monotone formulae.

Lemma 16.22. *For every MSO-automaton there is an equivalent one where the formulae $\varphi(C, \bar{Q}) := \delta(q, c)$ are monotone in $Q_0, \ldots, Q_{n-1}$.*

Proof. Suppose that $\varphi(C, \bar{Q})$ is not monotone. We can replace it by

$$\varphi'(C, \bar{Q}) := \exists \bar{P}\Big(\bigwedge_{i<n} P_i \subseteq Q_i \wedge \varphi(C, \bar{P})\Big).$$

φ' is obviously monotone. Further it is easy to see that the automaton obtained in this way is equivalent to the original one by constructing an accepting run of the former from one of the latter and vice versa. $\qquad\square$

Let z be a first-order variable and $X_0, \ldots, X_{n-1}$ set variables. A **type** of z over $\bar{X}$ is a formula of the form

$$\tau(z; \bar{X}) := \bigwedge_{i \in S} X_i z \wedge \bigwedge_{i \notin S} \neg X_i z$$

for some $S \subseteq [n]$. Further, define

$$\text{diff}(\bar{x}) := \bigwedge_{i<k} x_i \neq x_k.$$

The next lemma provides a normalform for MSO-automata over the empty signature.

Lemma 16.23. *Every monotone MSO-formula $\varphi(\bar{X})$ over the empty signature is equivalent to a disjunction of FO-formulae of the form*

$$\exists \bar{y}\Big(\text{diff}(\bar{y}) \wedge \bigwedge_{i<n} \vartheta_i(y_i) \wedge \forall z\big(\text{diff}(\bar{y}, z) \to \bigvee_{i<m} \vartheta_i'(z)\big)\Big)$$

where the ϑ_i and ϑ_i' are the positive part of some type.

Proof. Using Ehrenfeucht-Fraïssé games it is easy to show that two structures are n-equivalent, i.e., indistinguishable by formulae of quantifier rank at most n, if, for every type $\tau(z; \bar{X})$, the number of elements satisfying τ are equal or both are greater than n. Thus, every first-order formula $\varphi(\bar{X})$ with n-quantifiers is equivalent to a disjunction of formulae of the form

$$\exists \bar{y}\Big(\mathrm{diff}(\bar{y}) \wedge \bigwedge_{i < n} \tau_i(y_i) \wedge \forall z\big(\mathrm{diff}(\bar{y}, z) \to \bigvee_{i < m} \tau'(z)\big)\Big)$$

each of which defines one of those n-equivalence classes where φ holds. If $\varphi(\bar{X})$ is monotone we can drop all negative atoms of the τ_i, τ'_i.

Analogously, one can show the claim also for MSO-formulae

$$Q_0 Y_0 \cdots Q_{n-1} Y_{n-1} \varphi(\bar{X}, \bar{Y})$$

with $\varphi \in$ FO, since the effect of set quantifiers amounts to splitting each type into two. □

16.4 Muchnik's Theorem

We are now ready to prove the main result of this chapter.

Theorem 16.24 (Muchnik). *For every sentence $\varphi \in$ MSO one can effectively construct a sentence $\hat{\varphi} \in$ MSO such that*

$$\mathfrak{A} \models \hat{\varphi} \quad \text{iff} \quad \mathfrak{A}^* \models \varphi$$

for all structures $\mathfrak{A}$.

Corollary 16.25. *Let $\mathfrak{A}$ be a structure. MSO model-checking is decidable for $\mathfrak{A}$ if and only if it is so for $\mathfrak{A}^*$.*

Before giving the proof let us demonstrate how Rabin's Tree Theorem follows from Muchnik's Theorem.

Example 16.26. Consider the structure $\mathfrak{A}$ with universe $\{0, 1\}$ and two unary predicates $L = \{0\}$ and $R = \{1\}$. MSO model-checking for $\mathfrak{A}$ is decidable since $\mathfrak{A}$ is finite. According to Muchnik's Theorem, model-checking is also decidable for $\mathfrak{A}^*$. $\mathfrak{A}^*$ is similar to the binary tree. The universe is $\{0, 1\}^*$, and the relations are

$$L^* = \{\, w0 \mid w \in \{0,1\}^* \,\},$$
$$R^* = \{\, w1 \mid w \in \{0,1\}^* \,\},$$
$$\mathrm{son} = \{\, (w, wa) \mid a \in \{0,1\},\ w \in \{0,1\}^* \,\},$$
$$\mathrm{cl} = \{\, waa \mid a \in \{0,1\},\ w \in \{0,1\}^* \,\}.$$

In order to prove that model-checking for the binary tree is decidable it is sufficient to define its relations in $\mathfrak{A}^*$:

$$S_0 xy := \mathrm{son}(x, y) \wedge L^* y, \qquad S_1 xy := \mathrm{son}(x, y) \wedge R^* y.$$

Similarly the decidability of SωS can be obtained directly without the need to interpret the infinitely branching tree into the binary one.

Example 16.27. Let $\mathfrak{A} := (\omega, \leq)$. The iteration $\mathfrak{A}^*$ has universe ω^* and relations

$$\leq^* = \{\, (wa, wb) \mid a \leq b,\ w \in \omega^* \,\},$$
$$\text{son} = \{\, (w, wa) \mid a \in \omega,\ w \in \omega^* \,\},$$
$$\text{cl} = \{\, waa \mid a \in \omega,\ w \in \omega^* \,\}.$$

The proof of Muchnik's Theorem is split into several steps. First, let $\mathcal{A} = (Q, \Sigma, \delta, q_{\mathrm{I}}, \Omega)$ be the MSO-automaton equivalent to φ. W.l.o.g. assume that $\Omega(i) = i$ for all $i \in Q = [n]$. Note that the input alphabet $\Sigma = \{\emptyset\}$ of $\mathcal{A}$ is unary since φ is a sentence. We construct a formula $\hat{\varphi}$ stating that player 0 has a winning strategy in the game $\check{\mathcal{G}}(\mathcal{A}, \mathfrak{A})$. Hence,

$$\mathfrak{A} \models \hat{\varphi} \quad \text{iff} \quad \mathfrak{A}^* \in L(\mathcal{A}) \quad \text{iff} \quad \mathfrak{A}^* \models \varphi.$$

A μ-calculus formula defining the winning set is given in Example 10.8 of Chapter 10. Translated into monadic fixed point logic it looks like

$$\mathrm{LFP}_{Z_n,x} \cdots \mathrm{GFP}_{Z_1,x} \bigvee_{i \leq n} \eta_i(x, \bar{Z})$$

with

$$\eta_i := S_i x \wedge [V_0 x \rightarrow \exists y (Exy \wedge Z_i y)] \wedge [V_1 x \rightarrow \forall y (Exy \rightarrow Z_i y)].$$

The game structure. In order to evaluate the above formula we need to embed $\check{\mathcal{G}}(\mathcal{A}, \mathfrak{A})$ in the structure $\mathfrak{A}$. First, we reduce the second component of a position (X, w) from $w \in A^*$ to a single symbol $a \in A$. Let $\mathcal{G}'(\mathcal{A}, \mathfrak{A})$ be the game obtained from $\check{\mathcal{G}}(\mathcal{A}, \mathfrak{A}^*)$ by identifying all nodes of the form (q, wa) and $(q, w'a)$, i.e.:

(a) Let $V_0 := Q \times A$. The vertices of player 0 are $V_0 \cup \{(q_0, \varepsilon)\}$, those of player 1 are $V_1 := \mathscr{P}(Q \times A)$.

(b) The initial position is (q_0, ε).

(c) Let $\langle\!\langle \delta(q, \emptyset) \rangle\!\rangle_{\mathfrak{A}}(a) = \bigvee_i \bigwedge \Phi_i$ for $a \in A \cup \{\varepsilon\}$. The node $(q, a) \in V_0$ has the successors Φ_i for all i. Nodes $\Phi \in V_1$ have their members $(q, a) \in \Phi$ as successors.

(d) A play $(q_0, a_0), \Phi_0, (q_1, a_1), \Phi_1, \ldots$ is winning if the sequence $(q_i)_{i<\omega}$ satisfies the parity condition Ω.

Lemma 16.28. *Player 0 has a winning strategy from the vertex (q, wa) in the game $\check{\mathcal{G}}(\mathcal{A}, \mathfrak{A}^*)$ if and only if he has one from the vertex (q, a) in the game $\mathcal{G}'(\mathcal{A}, \mathfrak{A})$.*

Proof. The unravelings of $\check{\mathcal{G}}(\mathcal{A}, \mathfrak{A}^*)$ and $\mathcal{G}'(\mathcal{A}, \mathfrak{A})$ from the respective vertices are isomorphic. □

In the second step we encode the game $\mathcal{G}'(\mathcal{A}, \mathfrak{A})$ as the structure

$$\mathfrak{B}(\mathcal{A}, \mathfrak{A}) := \bigl(V_0 \cup V_1,\ E,\ \mathrm{eq}_2,\ V_0,\ V_1,\ (S_q)_{q \in Q}, R_0, \ldots\bigr)$$

where (V_0, V_1, E) is the graph of the game,

$$
\begin{aligned}
&\text{eq}_2(q, a)(q', a') &&: \text{iff } a = a', \\
&S_q(q', a) &&: \text{iff } q = q', \\
&R_i(q_0, a_0) \ldots (q_r, a_r) &&: \text{iff } (a_0, \ldots, a_r) \in R_i^{\mathfrak{A}}.
\end{aligned}
$$

Note that these relations only contain elements of V_0. Let $\mathfrak{G}(\mathcal{A}, \mathfrak{A})|_{V_0}$ denote the restriction of $\mathfrak{G}(\mathcal{A}, \mathfrak{A})$ to V_0.

Finally, we can embed $\mathfrak{G}(\mathcal{A}, \mathfrak{A})|_{V_0}$ in $\mathfrak{A}$ via an interpretation.

Definition 16.29. Let $\mathfrak{A} = (A, R_0, \ldots, R_r)$ and $\mathfrak{B}$ be structures. An **interpretation** of $\mathfrak{A}$ in $\mathfrak{B}$ is a sequence

$$
\mathcal{I} := \langle k, (\vartheta_{\bar{\imath}}^R)_{R, \bar{\imath}} \rangle
$$

where, given R of arity r, the indices $\bar{\imath}$ range over $[k]^r$, such that

(i) $A \cong B \times [k]$,

(ii) $R_j \cong \{ ((a_1, i_1), \ldots, (a_r, i_r)) \mid \mathfrak{B} \models \vartheta_{\bar{\imath}}^{R_j}(\bar{a}) \}$.

The use of interpretations is made possible by the following property.

Lemma 16.30. *Let $\mathcal{I}$ be an interpretation and $\varphi \in \mathrm{MSO}$. There is a formula $\varphi^{\mathcal{I}}$ such that*

$$
\mathcal{I}(\mathfrak{A}) \models \varphi \quad \text{iff} \quad \mathfrak{A} \models \varphi^{\mathcal{I}}
$$

for every structure $\mathfrak{A}$.

To construct $\varphi^{\mathcal{I}}$ one simply replaces each relation in φ by its definition.

Lemma 16.31. *There is an interpretation $\mathcal{I}$ with $\mathfrak{G}(\mathcal{A}, \mathfrak{A})|_{V_0} = \mathcal{I}(\mathfrak{A})$ for all structures $\mathfrak{A}$.*

Proof. Let $\mathcal{I}$ be defined by

$$
\vartheta_{ik}^{\text{eq}_2}(X, Y) := X = Y,
$$

$$
\vartheta_k^{S_i}(X) \quad := \begin{cases} \text{true} & \text{if } i = k, \\ \text{false} & \text{otherwise,} \end{cases}
$$

$$
\vartheta_{\bar{k}}^{R_i}(\bar{X}) \quad := \begin{cases} R\bar{X} & \text{if } k_0 = \cdots = k_r, \\ \text{false} & \text{otherwise.} \end{cases} \qquad \square
$$

In order to speak about all of $\mathfrak{G}(\mathcal{A}, \mathfrak{A})$ in its restriction to V_0 we treat elements $\Phi \in V_1 = \mathcal{P}(V_0)$ as sets $\Phi \subseteq V_0$. All we have to do is to define the edge relation. We split E into three parts

$$
E_0 \subseteq V_0 \times V_1, \quad E_1 \subseteq V_1 \times V_0, \quad \text{and} \quad E_2 \subseteq \{(q_0, \varepsilon)\} \times V_1
$$

which we have to define separately by formulae $\varepsilon_0(x, Y)$, $\varepsilon_1(X, y)$, and $\varepsilon_2(Y)$.

Lemma 16.32. *There are formulae $\varepsilon_0(x, Y)$, $\varepsilon_1(X, y)$, and $\varepsilon_2(Y)$ defining the edge relations E_0, E_1 and E_2 respectively.*

Proof. Since $(\Phi, (q, a)) \in E_1$ iff $(q, a) \in \Phi$ we set

$$\varepsilon_1(Y, x) := Yx.$$

The definition of ε_0 is more involved. Let $\delta_q(C, \bar{Q}) := \langle\!\langle \delta(q, \emptyset) \rangle\!\rangle_{\mathfrak{A}}$. We have

$$((q, a), \Phi) \in E_0 \quad \text{iff} \quad \mathfrak{A} \models \delta_q(\{a\}, \bar{Q})$$

where $Q_i := \{ b \mid (i, b) \in \Phi \}$. In order to evaluate δ_q we need to define $\mathfrak{A}$ inside $\mathfrak{G}(\mathcal{A}, \mathfrak{A})$. Since the latter consists of $|Q|$ copies of $\mathfrak{A}$ with universes $(S_q)_{q \in Q}$, we pick one such copy and relativise δ_q to it. For simplicity we choose S_q corresponding to the first component of (q, a).

$$((q, a), \Phi) \in E_0 \quad \text{iff} \quad \mathfrak{G}(\mathcal{A}, \mathfrak{A})|_{V_0} \models \delta_q^{S_q}(\{(q, a)\}, \bar{Q}')$$

where $Q_i' := \{ (q, b) \mid (i, b) \in \Phi \}$. This condition can be written as

$$\mathfrak{G}(\mathcal{A}, \mathfrak{A})|_{V_0} \models \exists C \exists \bar{Q} \Big(\delta_q^{S_q}(C, \bar{Q}) \wedge C = \{(q, a)\}$$

$$\wedge \bigwedge_{i \in Q} Q_i = \{ (q, b) \mid (i, b) \in \Phi \} \Big).$$

Thus, we define

$$\varepsilon_0(x, Y) := \bigvee_{q \in Q} \left(S_q x \wedge \varepsilon_0^q(x, Y) \right)$$

where

$$\varepsilon_0^q(x, Y) := \exists C \exists \bar{Q} \Big(\delta_q^{S_q}(C, \bar{Q}) \wedge C = \{x\} \wedge \bigwedge_{i \in Q} Q_i = \{ (q, b) \mid (i, b) \in Y \} \Big).$$

Obviously, $Q_i = \{ (q, b) \mid (i, b) \in Y \}$ can be expressed by an MSO-formula using eq_2.

In the same way we define

$$\varepsilon_2(Y) := \exists \bar{Q} \Big(\delta_{q_0}^{S_{q_0}}(\emptyset, \bar{Q}) \wedge \bigwedge_{i \in Q} Q_i = \{ (q_0, b) \mid (i, b) \in Y \} \Big). \qquad \square$$

The winning set. It remains to evaluate the formula

$$\mathrm{LFP}_{Z_1, x} \cdots \mathrm{GFP}_{Z_n, x} \bigvee_{i \leq n} \eta_i(x, \bar{Z})$$

with

$$\eta_i := S_i x \wedge [V_0 x \rightarrow \exists y (E x y \wedge Z_i y)] \wedge [V_1 x \rightarrow \forall y (E x y \rightarrow Z_i y)]$$

which defines the winning set in the original game graph $\mathcal{G}'(\mathcal{A}, \mathfrak{A})$. Since in the given game the nodes of V_0 and V_1 are strictly alternating, we remain in V_0 if we take two steps each time.

$$\eta_i' := S_i x \wedge V_0 x \wedge \exists y \big(V_1 x \wedge E x y \wedge \forall z (E y z \rightarrow Z_i z) \big)$$

It is easy to prove the following result:

Lemma 16.33. *The formulae*

$$\mathrm{GFP}_{Z_1, x} \bigvee_{i \le n} \eta_i \quad and \quad \mathrm{GFP}_{Z_1, x} \bigvee_{i \le n} \eta'_i$$

define the same subset of V_0 in $\mathfrak{G}(\mathcal{A}, \mathfrak{A})$ for each assignment of the free variables.

Finally, interpreting elements of V_1 by subsets of V_0, as explained above, we obtain

$$\eta''_i := S_i x \wedge V_0 x \wedge \exists Y \big(Y \subseteq V_0 \wedge \varepsilon_0(x, Y) \wedge \forall z (\varepsilon_1(Y, z) \to Z_i z) \big)$$

Again, the equivalence of η'_i and η''_i is checked easily. Thus, we can state that player 0 has a winning strategy in $\mathcal{G}'(\mathcal{A}, \mathfrak{A})$ from position (q_0, ε) by

$$\hat{\varphi} := \exists Y \big[\varepsilon_2(Y) \wedge \forall x \big(\varepsilon_0(Y, x) \to \mathrm{LFP}_{Z_1, x} \cdots \mathrm{GFP}_{Z_n, x} \bigvee_{i \le n} \eta''_i \big) \big].$$

This concludes the proof of Theorem 16.24.

We end this chapter with an application of Muchnik's Theorem to algebraic trees. Trees are represented as structures $\mathfrak{T} = (T, (E_a)_{a \in \Sigma}, (P_c)_{c \in \Gamma})$ where Σ is a finite alphabet, $T \subseteq \Sigma^*$, $P_c \subseteq T$ are unary predicates, and the edge relations are

$$E_a := \{ (w, wa) \mid w \in T \}.$$

Such a tree is called **algebraic** if the set

$$\{ wc \in \Sigma^* \Gamma \mid w \in T, w \in P_c \} \subseteq \Sigma^* \Gamma$$

is a deterministic context-free language.

Algebraic trees can be obtained using a variant of iterations. The **unraveling** of a graph $\mathfrak{G} = (V, (E_a)_{a \in \Sigma}, (P_c)_{c \in \Gamma})$ is the tree $\widehat{\mathfrak{G}} := (T, (\widehat{E}_a)_{a \in \Sigma}, (\widehat{P}_c)_{c \in \Gamma})$ where T consists of all paths of $\mathfrak{G}$ and the relations are defined by

$$\widehat{E}_a := \{ wuv \in T \mid (u, v) \in E_a, w \in V^* \},$$
$$\widehat{P}_c := \{ wv \in T \mid v \in P_c, w \in V^* \}.$$

We have already seen that the set T of paths is definable in the iteration of a graph. Obviously, the predicates $\widehat{E}_a$ and $\widehat{P}_c$ are also definable. Thus, the unraveling of a graph can be interpreted in its iteration.

The following characterisation of algebraic trees was given by Courcelle [41, 42].

Proposition 16.34. *Every algebraic tree is the unraveling of an HR-equational graph.*

We omit the definition of HR-equational graphs. Their only property that is important in this context is that MSO-model-checking is decidable for them. Thus, we obtain the following result:

Theorem 16.35. MSO-*model-checking is decidable for algebraic trees.*

17 Two-Way Tree Automata Solving Pushdown Games

Thierry Cachat

Lehrstuhl für Informatik VII
RWTH Aachen

17.1 Introduction

Parity games (where the winner is determined by the parity of the maximal priority appearing infinitely often) were presented in Chapter 2 and algorithms solving parity games for the case of finite graphs in Chapter 7. In this paper we study parity games on a simple class of infinite graphs: the pushdown (transition) graphs. In [106], Kupferman and Vardi have given a very powerful method for the μ-calculus model checking of these graphs: the formalism of two-way alternating tree automata. This is a generalization of the (one-way) tree automata presented in Chapters 8 and 9.

The transition graph of the pushdown automaton defines the arena: the graph of the play and the partition of the vertex set needed to specify the parity winning condition. We know from Chapter 6 that such games are determined and that each of both players has a memoryless winning strategy on his winning region. The aim of this paper is to show how to compute effectively the winning region of Player 0 and a memoryless winning strategy. The idea of [106] is to simulate the pushdown system in the full W-tree, where W is a finite set of directions, and to use the expressive power of alternating two-way tree automata to answer these questions. Finally it is necessary to translate the 2-way tree automaton into an equivalent nondeterministic one-way tree automaton, with the construction from [190].

In the next section we define two-way alternating automata and the effective construction from [190] of equivalent one-way nondeterministic automata. In Section 17.3 we apply these results to solve parity games over pushdown graphs and to compute winning strategies. Section 17.4 presents an example. Some extensions and modifications are discussed in Section 17.5.

17.2 Reduction 2-way to 1-way

The formalism of alternating two-way parity tree automata is very "powerful", but we cannot handle directly these automata to answer our questions of nonemptiness (for the winning region) and strategy synthesis. We need the reduction presented in this section, which constructs step by step a one-way nondeterministic tree automaton that is equivalent to a given two-way alternating automaton $\mathcal{A}$, in the sense that they accept the same set of trees (finite or infinite).

E. Grädel et al. (Eds.): Automata, Logics, and Infinite Games, LNCS 2500, pp. 303-317, 2002.

17.2.1   Definition of Two-Way Automata

Given a finite set W of directions, a **W-tree** is a prefix closed set $T \subseteq W^*$, i.e., if $x.d \in T$, where $x \in W^*$ and $d \in W$, then also $x \in T$. We will sometimes forget the "." of the concatenation. The elements of T are called **nodes**, the empty word ϵ is the **root** of T. For every $x.d \in T, d \in W$ the node x is the unique **parent** of $x.d$, and $x.d$ is a **child** of x. The **direction** of a node $x.d$ ($\neq \epsilon$) is d. The **full infinite tree** is $T = W^*$. A **path** (branch) of a tree T is a sequence $\beta \in T^\infty$ such that $\beta = u_0 u_1 \cdots u_n$ or $\beta = u_0 u_1 u_2 \cdots$, $u_0 = \epsilon$ and $\forall i < n, \exists d \in W, u_{i+1} = u_i.d$. A path can be finite or infinite.

Given two finite alphabets W and Σ, a **Σ-labeled W-tree** is a pair $\langle T, l \rangle$ where T is a W-tree and $l : T \longrightarrow \Sigma$ maps each node of T to a letter in Σ. When W and Σ are not important or clear from the context, we call $\langle T, l \rangle$ a **labeled tree**.

We recall that for a finite set X, $\mathcal{B}^+(X)$ is the set of positive Boolean formulas over X (i.e., Boolean formulas built from elements in X using only $\wedge$ and $\vee$), where we also allow the formulas $\langle \text{true} \rangle$ and $\langle \text{false} \rangle$. For a set $Y \subseteq X$ and a formula $\theta \in \mathcal{B}^+(X)$, we say that Y **satisfies** θ iff assigning $\langle \text{true} \rangle$ to elements in Y and $\langle \text{false} \rangle$ to elements in $X \backslash Y$ makes θ true.

To navigate through the tree let $\text{ext}(W) := W \cup \{\epsilon, \uparrow\}$ be the extension of W: The symbol $\uparrow$ means "go to parent node" and ϵ means "stay on the present node". To simplify the notation we define $\forall u \in W^*, d \in W, u.\epsilon = u$ and $ud\uparrow = u$. The node $\epsilon\uparrow$ is not defined.

An **alternating two-way automaton** over Σ-labeled W-trees is a tuple $\mathcal{A} := (Q, \Sigma, \delta, q_{\mathrm{I}}, \text{Acc})$ where

  Q is a finite set of states,

  Σ is the input alphabet,

  $\delta : Q \times \Sigma \longrightarrow \mathcal{B}^+(\text{ext}(W) \times Q)$ is the transition function,

  q_{I} is the initial state, and

  Acc is the acceptance condition.

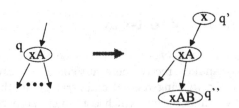

Fig. 17.1. Example of a transition $\delta(q, A) = (\uparrow, q') \wedge (B, q'')$, with the convention that the label is equal to the last letter of the node

The idea of a transition $\delta(q, l_1) = (\uparrow, q') \wedge (d, q'')$ is the following: if the automaton $\mathcal{A}$ is in state q on the node x of the labeled tree $\langle T, l \rangle$ and reads the input $l_1 = l(x)$, it will send a "copy" of $\mathcal{A}$ in state q' to the parent node of x and another copy in state q'' to xd. See Figure 17.1. After that the two copies are running independently. They may come again to the same node with two different states.

More precisely a run of an alternating two-way automaton $\mathcal{A}$ over a labeled tree $\langle W^*, l \rangle$ is *another* labeled tree $\langle T_r, r \rangle$ in which every node is labeled by an element of $W^* \times Q$. The latter tree is like the unfolding of the run, its structure is quite different from W^*. A node in T_r, labeled by (x, q), describes a "copy" of the automaton that is in state q and is situated at the node x of W^*. Note that many nodes of T_r can correspond to the same node of W^*, because the automaton can come back to a previously visited node. The label of a node and its successors have to satisfy the transition function. Formally, a run $\langle T_r, r \rangle$ is a Σ_r-labeled Γ-tree, for some (almost arbitrary) set Γ of directions, where $\Sigma_r := W^* \times Q$ and $\langle T_r, r \rangle$ satisfies the following conditions:

(a) $\epsilon \in T_r$ and $r(\epsilon) = (\epsilon, q_1)$

(b) Consider $y \in T_r$ with $r(y) = (x, q)$ and $\delta(q, l(x)) = \theta$. Then there is a (possibly empty) set $Y \subseteq \text{ext}(W) \times Q$, such that Y satisfies θ, and for all $\langle d, q' \rangle \in Y$, there is $\gamma \in \Gamma$ such that $y.\gamma \in T_r$ and the following holds: $r(y.\gamma) = (x.d, q')$.

Remember that $x.d$ can be $x.\epsilon$ or $x.\uparrow$, and the latter is defined only if $x \neq \epsilon$. So the run cannot go up from the root of the input tree. Note that it cannot use a transition $\delta(q, l(x)) = \langle \text{false} \rangle$ since the formula $\langle \text{false} \rangle$ cannot be satisfied.

A run $\langle T_r, r \rangle$ is accepting if all its infinite paths satisfy the acceptance condition Acc (the finite paths of a run end with a transition $\theta = \langle \text{true} \rangle$, which is viewed as successful termination). We consider here only **parity** acceptance conditions (see previous chapters): Acc is given by a priority function $\Omega : Q \longrightarrow [m]$. An infinite path $\beta \in T_r^\omega$ satisfies the acceptance condition iff the smallest priority appearing infinitely often in this path is even: $\min \text{Inf}(\Omega(r(\beta)))$ is even. Such a path in the run consists of following only one "copy" of the automaton. An automaton accepts a labeled tree if and only if there exists a run that accepts it. The tree language accepted by an automaton $\mathcal{A}$ is denoted $L(\mathcal{A})$. Two automata are equivalent if they accept the same tree language.

The automaton $\mathcal{A} = (Q, \Sigma, \delta, q_1, \Omega)$ and the input tree $\langle T, l \rangle$ are now fixed for the rest of the Section 17.2. In the next subsections we will study how the automaton $\mathcal{A}$ can accept the given tree. The strategy for $\mathcal{A}$ will give information about the transitions used by $\mathcal{A}$ (because $\mathcal{A}$ is not deterministic). Then the annotation will store the priorities seen during the detours of $\mathcal{A}$. With all these auxiliary tools, it is possible to construct a *one-way* tree automaton that checks whether $\mathcal{A}$ accepts a tree.

17.2.2 Strategy

In the same way as in Chapters 6, 4 and 8 of this book, $\mathcal{A}$ itself (as an alternating automaton) is equivalent to a two-player parity game. The initial configuration of this game is (ϵ, q_1) $(= r(\epsilon))$. From a configuration $(x, q), x \in T, q \in Q$, Player 0 chooses a set $Y \subseteq \text{ext}(W) \times Q$ that satisfies $\delta(q, l(x))$, then Player 1 chooses $\langle d, q' \rangle \in Y$, the new configuration is $(x.d, q')$ and so on. If $x.d$ is not defined or $\delta(q, l(x)) = \langle \text{false} \rangle$ then Player 1 wins immediately. If Y is empty ($\delta(q, l(x)) = \langle \text{true} \rangle$) then Player 0 wins immediately. If the play is infinite, then Player 0 wins iff the parity condition is satisfied. So Player 0 is trying to show that $\mathcal{A}$ accepts the input tree, and Player 1 is trying to challenge that.

Player 0 has a memoryless winning strategy iff $\mathcal{A}$ has an accepting run (see Chapter 6). In other words, if $\mathcal{A}$ has an accepting run, then it has an accepting run using a memoryless winning strategy: choosing always the same "transitions" from the same node and state. We decompose the run of $\mathcal{A}$ using this strategy.

Definition 17.1. A **strategy** for $\mathcal{A}$ and a given tree is a mapping

$$\tau : W^* \longrightarrow \mathscr{P}(Q \times \text{ext}(W) \times Q).$$

Intuitively $(q, d, q') \in \tau(x)$ means that if $\mathcal{A}$ is in state q on the node x, it has to send a copy in state q' to node xd. It is memoryless because it depends only on x. Note that the strategy does not read the labels, but it is defined for a fixed tree $\langle T, l \rangle$. See an example on Figure 17.2.

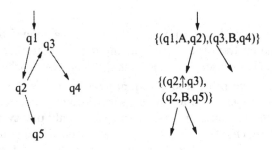

Fig. 17.2. Part of a run and the corresponding strategy

In this subsection we want to verify with a one-way automaton some simple conditions on the strategy τ of an alternating two way tree automaton $\mathcal{A}$. The first condition for a strategy to be correct (at node x) is to satisfy the transition of $\mathcal{A}$. The second condition is that the strategy can be followed: if $(q, d, q') \in \tau(x)$ then the strategy $\tau(xd)$ has to be defined in xd for the state q', such that the run can continue. Formally, both conditions are:

$\forall x \in W^*, \forall (q, d, q') \in \tau(x):$

$\{(d_2, q_2) \mid (q, d_2, q_2) \in \tau(x)\}$ satisfies $\delta(q, l(x))$, and $\qquad$ (17.1)

$\exists d_1, q_1, (q', d_1, q_1) \in \tau(xd)$ or $\emptyset$ satisfies $\delta(q', l(xd))$, $\qquad$ (17.2) and for the root:

$$\exists d_1, q_1, (q_I, d_1, q_1) \in \tau(\epsilon) \text{ or } \emptyset \text{ satisfies } \delta(q_I, l(\epsilon)). \tag{17.3}$$

Considering $St := \mathscr{P}(Q \times \text{ext}(W) \times Q)$ as an alphabet, a $(St \times \Sigma)$-labeled tree defines a memoryless strategy on the corresponding Σ-labeled tree. We will construct a *one-way* automaton $\mathcal{B}$ that checks that this strategy is correct according to the previous requirements. For $(q, d, q') \in \tau(x)$, if $d \in W$ it has just to check in the direction d downwards that the strategy is well defined for q', but if $d = \uparrow$, he must have *remembered* that the strategy *was* defined for q' in the parent-node. The states of $\mathcal{B}$ are pairs $\langle Q_1, Q_2 \rangle \in \mathscr{P}(Q) \times \mathscr{P}(Q)$, where $q' \in Q_1$ means that $\mathcal{B}$ has to check (down) that the strategy can be followed for q', and $q'' \in Q_2$ means that q'' is already allowed at the parent node.

$$\mathcal{B} := (\mathscr{P}(Q) \times \mathscr{P}(Q), St \times \Sigma, \delta_\mathcal{B}, \langle\{q_I\}, \emptyset\rangle, \langle\text{true}\rangle) \text{ where} \tag{17.4}$$

$$\delta_\mathcal{B}(\langle Q_1, Q_2 \rangle, \langle\tau_1, l_1\rangle) :=$$

IF $\forall q \in Q_1, \{(d_2, q_2) \mid (q, d_2, q_2) \in \tau_1\}$ satisfies $\delta(q, l_1)$, and $\tag{17.5}$

$\forall (q', \epsilon, q) \in \tau_1, \{(d_2, q_2) \mid (q, d_2, q_2) \in \tau_1\}$ satisfies $\delta(q, l_1)$, and $\tag{17.6}$

$\forall (q, \uparrow, q') \in \tau_1, q' \in Q_2 \tag{17.7}$

THEN $\displaystyle\bigwedge_{d \in W} \left(d, \langle\{q' \mid \exists (q, d, q') \in \tau_1\}, Q_2'\rangle\right) \tag{17.8}$

with $Q_2' := \{q'' \mid \exists d_1, q_1, (q'', d_1, q_1) \in \tau_1 \text{ or } \emptyset \text{ satisfies } \delta(q'', l_1)\}$, $\tag{17.9}$

ELSE $\langle\text{false}\rangle$. $\tag{17.10}$

The acceptance condition is easy to enunciate: it just requires that each path of $\mathcal{B}$ is infinite (*i.e.*, the transition is possible at each node). Note that although we have used the formalism of alternating automata, $\mathcal{B}$ is a *deterministic* one-way automaton: $\mathcal{B}$ sends exactly one copy to each son of the current node. It has $4^{|Q|}$ states.

In condition (17.5) there is no requirement on the $q \notin Q_1$, that's why the condition (17.1) above is stronger. This is not a problem for the following, as we are searching *some* winning strategy (one could define the *minimal* valid strategy as in [190]). If $\mathcal{A}$ follows the strategy, its run is "deterministic" on the input tree labeled by $St \times \Sigma$.

A **path** β in a strategy (tree) τ is a sequence $(u_0, q_0), (u_1, q_1), (u_2, q_2), \cdots$ of pairs from $W^* \times Q$ such that $(u_0, q_0) = (\epsilon, q_I)$ and for all $i \geqslant 0$, there is some $c_i \in \text{ext}(W)$ such that $(q_i, c_i, q_{i+1}) \in \tau(u_i)$ and $u_{i+1} = u_i c_i$. Thus, β just follows (nondeterministically) the "transitions" of τ. The parity condition for β is defined exactly the same way as for a path of (a run of) $\mathcal{A}$. We say that τ is accepting if all infinite paths in τ are accepting.

Proposition 17.2. *A two-way alternating parity automaton accepts an input tree iff it has an accepting strategy tree over the input tree.*

With the help of a so called annotation, we will check in the following subsections whether a strategy is accepting.

17.2.3   Annotation

The previous automaton $\mathcal{B}$ just checks that the strategy can be followed (ad infinitum) but forgets the priorities of $\mathcal{A}$. To check the acceptance condition, it is necessary to follow each path of $\mathcal{A}$ up and down, and remember the priorities appearing. Such a path can be decomposed into a *downwards* path and several finite *detours* from the path, that come back to their origin (in a loop). Because each node has a unique parent and $\mathcal{A}$ starts at the root, we consider only downwards detour (each move ↑ is in a detour). That is to say, if a node is visited more than once by a run β, we know that the first time it was visited, the run came from above. To keep track of these finite detours, we use the following annotation.

Definition 17.3. An **annotation** for $\mathcal{A}$ and a given tree is a mapping

$$\eta : W^* \longrightarrow \mathscr{P}(Q \times [m] \times Q). \tag{17.11}$$

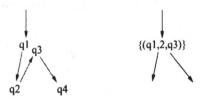

Fig. 17.3. Part of a run and the corresponding annotation, assuming that $\Omega(q_2) = 2, \Omega(q_3) = 3$

Intuitively $(q, f, q') \in \eta(x)$ means that from node x and state q there is a detour that comes back to x with state q' and the smallest priority seen along this detour is f. Figure 17.3 presents an example. By definition, the following conditions are required for the annotation η of a given strategy τ:

$$\forall\ q, q' \in Q,\ x \in W^*,\ d \in W,\ f, f' \in [m]:$$
$$(q, \epsilon, q') \in \tau(x) \Rightarrow (q, \Omega(q'), q') \in \eta(x), \tag{17.12}$$
$$(q_1, f, q_2) \in \eta(x), (q_2, f', q_3) \in \eta(x) \Rightarrow (q_1, \min(f, f'), q_3) \in \eta(x), \tag{17.13}$$
$$(q, d, q_1) \in \tau(x), (q_1, \uparrow, q') \in \tau(xd) \Rightarrow (q, \min(\Omega(q_1), \Omega(q')), q') \in \eta(x), \tag{17.14}$$

$$(q, d, q_1) \in \tau(x), (q_1, f, q_2) \in \eta(xd),\ (q_2, \uparrow, q') \in \tau(xd)$$
$$\Rightarrow (q, \min(\Omega(q_1), f, \Omega(q')), q') \in \eta(x). \tag{17.15}$$

Considering $An := \mathscr{P}(Q \times [m] \times Q)$ as an alphabet, the aim is to construct a *one-way* automaton $\mathcal{C}$ on $(An \times St)$-labeled trees that checks that the annotation satisfies these requirements. The conditions 17.12 and 17.13 above can be checked in each node (independently) without memory. For the last two, the automaton has to remember the whole $\eta(x)$ from the parent node x, and the part of $\tau(x)$ leading to the current node.

$$\mathcal{C} := (An \times \mathscr{P}(Q \times Q), An \times St, \delta_\mathcal{C}, \langle \emptyset, \emptyset \rangle, \langle \text{true} \rangle),$$

where

$\delta_\mathcal{C}(\langle \eta_0, \alpha \rangle, \langle \eta_1, \tau_1 \rangle) :=$

IF conditions 17.12 and 17.13 hold for η_1 and τ_1 AND

$\forall (q, q_1) \in \alpha, (q_1, \uparrow, q') \in \tau_1 \ \Rightarrow\ (q, \min(\Omega(q_1), \Omega(q')), q') \in \eta_0$

$\forall (q, q_1) \in \alpha, (q_1, f, q_2) \in \eta_1, (q_2, \uparrow, q') \in \tau_1$
$\qquad \Rightarrow\ (q, \min(\Omega(q_1), f, \Omega(q')), q') \in \eta_0$

THEN $\displaystyle\bigwedge_{d \in W} (d, \langle \eta_1, \{ (q, q_1) \mid \exists\, (q, d, q_1) \in \tau_1 \} \rangle)$

ELSE $\langle \text{false} \rangle$.

Similarly to $\mathcal{B}$, $\mathcal{C}$ is a *deterministic* one-way automaton with $2^{|Q|^2 m} \cdot 2^{|Q|^2} = 2^{|Q|^2 (m+1)}$ states, and the acceptance condition is very simple: each path has to be infinite. Note that if a part of the tree is not visited by the original automaton $\mathcal{A}$, the strategy and annotation can be empty on this part. The automaton $\mathcal{C}$ does not check that the annotation is minimal, but this is not a problem. With the help of the annotation one can determine if a path of $\mathcal{A}$ respects the acceptance condition or not, as showed in the next subsection.

17.2.4   Parity Acceptance

Up to now the automata $\mathcal{B}$ and $\mathcal{C}$ together just check that the strategy and annotation for the run of $\mathcal{A}$ are correct, but do not verify that the run of $\mathcal{A}$ is accepting, *i.e.*, that each path is valid. With the help of the annotation we can "simulate" (follow) a path of $\mathcal{A}$ with a one-way automaton, and determine the parity condition for this path. This one-way automaton does not go into the detours, but reads the smallest priority appearing in them.

$$\mathcal{D} := (Q \times [m], An \times St, \delta_\mathcal{D}, \langle q_1, 0 \rangle, \Omega_0),$$

$$\delta_\mathcal{D}(\langle q, i \rangle, \langle \eta_1, \tau_1 \rangle) := \bigvee_{(q,d,q') \in \tau_1, d \in W} (d, \langle q', \Omega(q') \rangle) \ \vee\ \bigvee_{(q,f,q') \in \eta_1} (\epsilon, \langle q', f \rangle).$$

At each step $\mathcal{D}$ either goes *down* following the strategy, or simulates a detour with an ϵ-move and the corresponding priority. The second component ($[m]$) of the states of $\mathcal{D}$ just remembers the last priority seen. We can transform $\mathcal{D}$ into a nondeterministic one-way automaton $\mathcal{D}'$ without ϵ-moves with the same state space. Note that $\mathcal{D}$ can possibly stay forever in the same node by using ϵ-transitions, either in an accepting run or not. This possibility can be checked by $\mathcal{D}'$ just by reading the current annotation, with a transition $\langle \text{true} \rangle$ or $\langle \text{false} \rangle$.

We will use $\mathcal{D}$ and $\mathcal{D}'$ to find the *invalid* paths of the run of $\mathcal{A}$, just by changing the acceptance condition: $\Omega_0(\langle q, i \rangle) := i + 1$.

Proposition 17.4. *The one-way tree automaton $\mathcal{D}'$ accepts a $(An \times St)$-labeled tree iff the corresponding run of $\mathcal{A}$ is not accepting.*

But $\mathcal{D}'$ is not deterministic, and accepts a tree if $\mathcal{D}'$ has *some* accepting run. We can view $\mathcal{D}'$ as a word automaton: it follows just a branch of the tree. For this reason it is possible to co-determinize it: determinize and complement it in a singly exponential construction (see Chapter 8 and 9) to construct the automaton $\overline{\mathcal{D}}$ that accepts those of the $(An \times St)$-labeled trees that represent the accepting runs of $\mathcal{A}$.

We will define the product $\mathcal{E} := \mathcal{B} \times \mathcal{C} \times \overline{\mathcal{D}}$ of the previous automata, that accepts a $(An \times St \times \Sigma)$-labeled input tree iff the corresponding run of $\mathcal{A}$ is accepting. Let

$$\mathcal{E} := (Q_{\mathcal{B}} \times Q_{\mathcal{C}} \times Q_{\overline{\mathcal{D}}}, An \times St \times \Sigma, \delta_{\mathcal{E}}, q_{\mathrm{I},\mathcal{E}}, \mathrm{Acc}),$$

$$\delta_{\mathcal{E}}(\langle q_{\mathcal{B}}, q_{\mathcal{C}}, q_{\overline{\mathcal{D}}} \rangle, \langle \eta_1, \tau_1, l_1 \rangle) :=$$
$$\langle \delta_{\mathcal{B}}(q_{\mathcal{B}}, \langle \tau_1, l_1 \rangle), \delta_{\mathcal{C}}(q_{\mathcal{C}}, \langle \eta_1, \tau_1 \rangle), \delta_{\overline{\mathcal{D}}}(q_{\overline{\mathcal{D}}}, \langle \eta_1, \tau_1 \rangle) \rangle,$$

where $Q_{\mathcal{B}}$ is the state space of $\mathcal{B}$, and so on. The acceptance condition of $\mathcal{E}$ is then exactly the one of $\overline{\mathcal{D}}$.

We define the automaton $\mathcal{E}'$ to be the "projection" of $\mathcal{E}$ on the input alphabet Σ: $\mathcal{E}'$ nondeterministically guesses the labels from $An \times St$. Finally $\mathcal{E}'$ is a nondeterministic one-way tree-automaton on Σ-labeled trees that is equivalent to $\mathcal{A}$: it accepts the same trees. The strategy and annotation depended on the input tree, now after the projection, $\mathcal{E}'$ can search the run of $\mathcal{A}$ for each input tree. The automaton $\mathcal{E}$ is deterministic and has (like $\mathcal{E}'$) $4^{|Q|} \cdot 2^{|Q|^2(m+1)} \cdot 2^{c|Q|m} = 2^{|Q|^2(m+1)} \cdot 2^{|Q|(2+cm)}$ states.

Theorem 17.5 ([190]). *To every alternating two-way parity tree automaton $\mathcal{A}$ there exists an equivalent nondeterministic one-way tree automaton $\mathcal{E}$, in the sense that they recognize the same tree language: $L(\mathcal{A}) = L(\mathcal{E})$.*

Corollary 17.6 ([190]). *The emptiness problem for alternating two-way tree automata is in* EXPTIME.

17.3   Application: Pushdown Games

We use alternating two-way automata to solve parity games on pushdown graphs. Thanks to the previous section the results are effective.

17.3.1   Definition of the Game

We first recall the definition of two player parity games. The **arena** $\mathcal{A} := (V_0, V_1, E)$ is a graph, composed of two disjoint sets of vertices, V_0 and V_1, and a set of edges $E \subseteq V \times V$, where $V = V_0 \uplus V_1$. To define a **parity game** $\mathcal{G} := (\mathcal{A}, \Omega_{\mathcal{G}})$ we need a mapping $\Omega_{\mathcal{G}} : V \longrightarrow [m], m < \omega$ which assigns a priority to each vertex. Then the **initialized game** $(\mathcal{G}, v_{\mathrm{I}})$ is given with an initial vertex $v_{\mathrm{I}} \in V$.

A **play** of $(\mathcal{G}, v_I)$ proceeds as follows:

(a) $v_0 = v_I$ is the first "current state" of the play,
(b) from state $v_i, i \geqslant 0$, if $v_i \in V_0$ (resp. $v_i \in V_1$) then Player 0 (resp. Player 1) chooses a successor $v_{i+1} \in v_i E$, which is the new current state.

The play is then the sequence $\pi = v_0 v_1 \cdots \in V^\infty$. This sequence is maximal: it is finite only if no more move is possible. We consider min-parity games:

$$\text{Player 0 wins } \pi \text{ iff } \min \text{Inf}(\Omega_\mathcal{G}(\pi)) \text{ is even.}$$

These definitions are essentially the same for finite and infinite arena. We consider now pushdown graphs: (V, E) is the (possibly infinite) transition graph of a pushdown system, which is an unlabeled pushdown automaton.

Definition 17.7. A **pushdown system** (PDS) is a tuple $\mathcal{Z} := (P, W, \Delta)$ where:

(a) P is a finite set of (control) states,
(b) W is a finite (stack) alphabet,
(c) $\Delta \subseteq P \times W \times P \times W^*$ is a *finite* transition relation.

A stack content is a word from W^*. Unlike standard notation we write the top of the stack at the right of the word (we are considering suffix rewriting as in Chapter 15). A **configuration** is a stack content and a control state: (w, p), shortly wp, where $w \in W^*, p \in P$. The **transition graph** of $\mathcal{Z}$ is (V, E) where $V = W^* P$ is the whole set of configurations and $\forall u, w \in W^*, \forall a \in W, \forall p, p' \in P$

$$(uap)E(uwp') \Leftrightarrow (p, a, p', w) \in \Delta.$$

This defines a vertex labeled graph: each vertex is labeled by his name, the edges have no label. We use the name pushdown system, like in [61] because the transitions are not labeled: we are not interested in the language recognized by the pushdown automaton but in the underlying transition graph. To obtain a parity game, it remains to define the sets V_0 and V_1, associating the vertices to the two players, and the priorities of the configurations. One fixes a disjoint union $P = P_0 \uplus P_1$, then $V_0 = W^* P_0$ and $V_1 = W^* P_1$. The mapping $\Omega_\mathcal{G}$ is first defined on P, then $\Omega_\mathcal{G}(wp) = \Omega_\mathcal{G}(p), \forall w \in W^*$ and $p \in P$. So the player and the priority only depend on the control states of $\mathcal{Z}$, like in [196] and [198]. These restrictions will be discussed later in Section 17.5.1.

The **pushdown game** is completely defined if we also fix an initial configuration $v_I \in V$: $v_I = w_I p_I$.

17.3.2   Winning Region

We construct an alternating two-way automaton $\mathcal{A}$ that determines if Player 0 can win the game $(\mathcal{G}, v_I)$, i.e., wins every play, whatever Player 1 does. The automaton $\mathcal{A}$ will simulate the transitions of the pushdown system $\mathcal{Z}$ on the full

W-tree, guess nondeterministically the best moves of Player 0 and follow each possible move of Player 1 using alternation.

As an example, the transition $(p, a, p', bc) \in \Delta$ from a configuration uap of the pushdown system can be simulated by a two-way automaton over the full W-tree from the node ua by the following sequence of moves: $\uparrow, b, c$ because $ua{\uparrow}bc = ubc$. We have chosen suffix rewriting rather than prefix to conform with the notation of the tree. The control states of $\mathcal{Z}$ are represented in the states of $\mathcal{A}$.

For our particular application, we simplify the definition of two-way automata a little. The full W-tree will not be labeled by an input alphabet Σ, and the automaton will "read" the last letter of the node, almost the same way as a pushdown automaton (as remarked in [106], another solution is to check that each label is equal to the last letter of its node).

To simulate with many steps a transition of $\mathcal{Z}$, $\mathcal{A}$ has to remember in its states the letters it has to write (see Figure 17.4). Let

$$\text{tails}(\Delta) := \{\, u \in W^* \mid \exists v, a, p, p'\ (p, a, p', vu) \in \Delta \vee vu = v_\mathrm{I} \,\},$$
$$\mathcal{A} := (P \times \text{tails}(\Delta), W, \delta, \langle p_\mathrm{I}, v_\mathrm{I} \rangle, \Omega),$$
$$\forall\, b, l_1 \in W, x \in W^*, p \in P:$$

$$\delta_{\mathcal{A}}(\langle p, b.x \rangle, l_1) := (b, \langle p, x \rangle), \tag{17.16}$$

$$\delta_{\mathcal{A}}(\langle p, \epsilon \rangle, l_1) := \bigvee_{(p, l_1, p', w) \in \Delta} (\uparrow, \langle p', w \rangle) \quad \text{if } p \in P_0, \tag{17.17}$$

$$\delta_{\mathcal{A}}(\langle p, \epsilon \rangle, l_1) := \bigwedge_{(p, l_1, p', w) \in \Delta} (\uparrow, \langle p', w \rangle) \quad \text{if } p \in P_1. \tag{17.18}$$

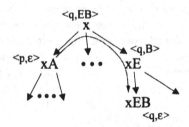

Fig. 17.4. Transition (p, A, q, EB) of the PDS (long arrow) simulated by the two-way automaton

From a state $\langle p, bx \rangle$ ($bx \neq \epsilon$ because $b \in W$) the automaton goes down in direction b, that is to say writes b, whatever it reads, and remembers the (sub)word x it still has to write and the state p of the pushdown system. These intermediate states just simulate a transition of $\mathcal{Z}$, they do not correspond to a particular configuration of the game. Only a state $\langle p, \epsilon \rangle$ on a node $w \in W^*$ corresponds to a configuration wp of the game. If $p \in P_1$ then $wp \in V_1$ and $\mathcal{A}$

executes all the possible moves of Player 1, to ensure that Player 0 can win after each of these moves. But if $p \in P_0$, $\mathcal{A}$ chooses nondeterministically a move of Player 0 and tries to make Player 0 win.

The "winning" condition of $\mathcal{A}$ is almost the same as the one of $\mathcal{G}$: $\Omega(\langle p, x \rangle) = \Omega_\mathcal{G}(p)$. The initial state of $\mathcal{A}$ causes it to go "deterministically" to the initial configuration of the game.

Theorem 17.8. *Player 0 has a winning strategy in $(\mathcal{G}, v_I)$ iff $\mathcal{A}$ accepts the full infinite tree W^*.*

Proof. By definition, $\mathcal{A}$ accepts W^* iff there exists an accepting run $\langle T_r, r \rangle$. Each path in $\langle T_r, r \rangle$ describes a play of the game, with the same winning condition. If each path is accepting, then each play is winning for Player 0, and every possible answer of Player 1 is in $\langle T_r, r \rangle$. That describes a winning strategy for Player 0. Conversely a winning strategy for Player 0 determines a tree of all the plays that follow it, which is an accepting run for $\mathcal{A}$.

These strategies are not necessarily memoryless as presented, but the result of Chapter 6 holds for both formalisms: there is a memoryless winning strategy if there is a winning strategy.

17.3.3 Winning Strategy

Once the automaton $\mathcal{E}$ of Theorem 17.5 is defined, we know from Chapter 8, Theorem 8.19, that we can solve the emptiness problem and generate a regular tree in $L(\mathcal{E})$ if $L(\mathcal{E}) \neq \emptyset$. Implicitly in that tree the states of $\mathcal{E}$ describe a strategy for $\mathcal{A}$ (Section 17.2.2), *i.e.*, for the game $(\mathcal{G}, v_I)$. If we follow a path (branch) of that tree, $\mathcal{E}$ corresponds to a deterministic word automaton $\mathcal{F}$ that can output the moves of Player 0. Finally $\mathcal{F}$ defines a memoryless winning strategy for Player 0 in $(\mathcal{G}, v_I)$ under the assumption that $L(\mathcal{E}) \neq \emptyset$, *i.e.*, if Player 0 wins the game.

More precisely $\mathcal{F}$ accepts all configurations in the winning region connected to v_I and each final state of $\mathcal{F}$ is labeled by a move of player 0, such that the strategy defined in this way is winning. This result from [106] is stronger (and more general, see Section 17.5.2) than the result of [196] that prove the existence of a pushdown strategy. The finite automaton $\mathcal{F}$ can easily be simulated with a pushdown automaton that defines a strategy like in [196].

Since we have considered an initial configuration v_I, the previous results do not define the memoryless winning strategy over the whole winning region of Player 0, but only over the nodes that can be reached by the play starting from v_I.

17.4 Example

We present here a simple example of pushdown game to illustrate the results of this chapter. Using notations of section 17.3, let

$$W = \{a, \bot\}, P_0 = \{p_0\}, P_1 = \{p_1, p_3\},$$
$$\Delta = \{(p_1, \bot, p_1, \bot a), (p_1, a, p_1, aa), (p_1, a, p_0, a), (p_0, a, p_0, \epsilon), (p_0, \bot, p_1, \bot),$$
$$(p_0, \bot, p_3, \bot), (p_3, \bot, p_3, \bot)\},$$
$$\Omega_G(p_1) = 0, \Omega_G(p_0) = \Omega_G(p_3) = 1.$$

The game graph looks as follows:

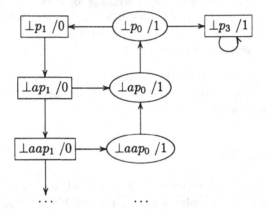

We consider the initial position $q_I = \langle p_I, v_I \rangle = \langle p_1, \bot \rangle$. For the automaton $\mathcal{A}$ we get $\text{tails}(\Delta) = \{\epsilon, \bot, \bot a, a, aa\}$. Transitions are

$$\delta_{\mathcal{A}}(\langle p_1, \epsilon \rangle, a) := (\uparrow, \langle p_1, aa \rangle) \wedge (\uparrow, \langle p_0, a \rangle), \qquad \text{(Player 1)}$$
$$\delta_{\mathcal{A}}(\langle p_0, \epsilon \rangle, \bot) := (\uparrow, \langle p_3, \bot \rangle) \vee (\uparrow, \langle p_1, \bot \rangle). \qquad \text{(Player 0)}$$

As a shortcut we consider

$$\delta_{\mathcal{A}}(\langle p_1, \epsilon \rangle, a) := (\epsilon, \langle p_1, a \rangle) \wedge (\epsilon, \langle p_0, \epsilon \rangle),$$
$$\delta_{\mathcal{A}}(\langle p_0, \epsilon \rangle, \bot) := (\epsilon, \langle p_3, \epsilon \rangle) \vee (\epsilon, \langle p_1, \epsilon \rangle).$$

Other transition rules are straightforward. The strategy τ is only relevant at the node $\bot p_0$, where Player 0 has a real choice: he must go to $\bot p_1$, otherwise Player 1 wins. We put

$$\tau(\bot) = \{(p_0, \epsilon, p_1), (p_1, a, p_1), (p_3, \epsilon, p_3)\}.$$

Other values are forced:

$$\forall i > 0, \tau(\bot a^i) = \{(p_1, a, p_1), (p_1, \epsilon, p_0), (p_0, \uparrow, p_0)\}.$$

Following the rules for the annotation we get for all $i \geq 0$:

$$(p_0, \epsilon, p_1) \in \tau(\perp) \Rightarrow (p_0, 0, p_1) \in \eta(\perp) \qquad \text{cf 17.12}$$

$$(p_1, \epsilon, p_0) \in \tau(\perp a^{i+1}) \Rightarrow (p_1, 1, p_0) \in \eta(\perp a^{i+1}) \qquad \text{cf 17.12}$$

$$(p_1, a, p_1) \in \tau(\perp a^i), (p_1, 1, p_0) \in \eta(\perp a^{i+1}), (p_0, \uparrow, p_0) \in \tau(\perp a^{i+1})$$
$$\Rightarrow (p_1, \min(0, 1, 1), p_0) \in \eta(\perp a^i) \Rightarrow (p_1, 0, p_0) \in \eta(\perp a^i) \qquad \text{cf 17.15}$$

$$(p_1, 0, p_0) \in \eta(\perp), (p_0, 0, p_1) \in \eta(\perp)$$
$$\Rightarrow (p_0, 0, p_0) \in \eta(\perp), (p_1, 0, p_1) \in \eta(\perp) \qquad \text{cf 17.13}$$

Now we can see that $\mathcal{D}$ can not find an accepting path, *i.e.*, a winning path for Player 1. Player 0 win the game from q_I, provided he never moves to the vertex $\perp p_3$. Unlike finite graphs, we can have here arbitrary long paths with (minimal) priority 1, but no infinite path winning for Player 1.

Exercise 17.1. Complete the solution of this example, and compute the strategy according to section 17.3.3.

17.5   Discussion, Extension

We discuss here some conventions and hypotheses we have made, sometimes implicitly.

17.5.1   Discussion on the Conventions

We have assumed that the priority of a configuration depends only on the control state. Another possibility is to define regular set of states for each priority, or equivalently a finite automaton with output (over the alphabet $W \cup P$) that accepts each configuration and outputs its priority. That wouldn't be more general: this automaton can be simulated by the states of the one-way automaton $\mathcal{E}$ (or by $\mathcal{A}$ with new labels on the tree). Otherwise it can be simulated by $\mathcal{Z}$ by extending the stack alphabet. The same ideas apply for the definition of V_0 and V_1 in V.

A usual convention for an arena (V_0, V_1, E) is that $E \subseteq V_0 \times V_1 \cup V_1 \times V_0$, *i.e.*, Player 0 and 1 alternate. This convention may clarify the situation but is not essential for us. If a pushdown system $\mathcal{Z}$ does not satisfy it, we can add "dummy" states to obtain a new pushdown game $\mathcal{Z}'$ which is equivalent to $\mathcal{Z}$ and satisfies the condition that in the new states there is only one possible move (choice).

The usual convention is also that a player who cannot move has lost. This is convenient with our formalism if we consider (see equations 17.17 and 17.18) that an empty disjunction is false and an empty conjunction is true (analogously it agrees with the definitions of $\Box$ and $\Diamond$ in μ-calculus). With pushdown games we can simulate another convention. We know in which configuration no transition is possible: if the stack is empty, or if there are no q', u with $(q, a, q', u) \in \Delta$.

We can add new transitions to a particular state for the second case, and for the first case we can use a new symbol as the "bottom" of the stack, that can neither be put nor removed, and new transitions for this symbol.

17.5.2 Extensions

One can easily extend the results presented in this paper to any suffix (resp. prefix) rewrite system, either by simulating it with a pushdown automaton (up to bisimilarity) or by adapting our construction to allow $\mathcal{A}$ to go up along a fixed word (stored in its memory). In contrast one could restrict the pushdown system so that a transition consists just of pushing *or* popping one letter, which is equivalent to the general model.

In [106] other results are obtained with the help of two-way automata: the model checking procedure is extended to any μ-calculus formula (Theorem 2) over any context-free or even prefix recognizable graph (Theorem 5). In the present paper we have just considered the problem of solving parity games. On the other hand, each μ-calculus formula on a pushdown system is equivalent to a parity game. To simulate the prefix recognizable rewrite rules (see Chapter 15), the two-way automaton simulates the finite automata that recognize the different parts of the word (the prefix, the old suffix and the new suffix) using alternation and guessing the correct rule.

17.6 Conclusion

After some technical work to make the two-way automata "usable", it was possible to compute winning regions and winning strategies. This formalism is very powerful and hopefully comprehensible.

Its expressive power is the same as the μ-calculus on trees and on the transition systems that can be simulated on trees: pushdown systems and prefix recognizable graphs.

Chapter 15 of this book deals with another result about model checking: it is shown that Monadic Second Order logic (MSO) is decidable on prefix recognizable graphs. It is well known (see Chapter 14) that MSO is at least as expressive as μ-calculus, so implicitly the model-checking problem for μ-calculus on prefix-recognizable graphs was already solved by Caucal in [28]. It is natural to define parity games on prefix-recognizable graphs the same way as we have done: a configuration (node of the game graph) is a word, for clarity we suppose that the priority and the player (V_0 and V_1) are given by the first letter of the word. In fact we can define in MSO the winning region of Player 0 (resp. Player 1).

But if we compare both approaches in more detail, important differences show up: the MSO formula describes the whole winning region: the decision procedure gives a finite automaton that recognizes the whole set of winning vertices of Player 0 (resp. 1). On the contrary, the construction presented in the present chapter just checks one at a time if a given "initial" configuration is in the winning region. On the other hand, it is proved in [106] that his technique generates a winning strategy for this initialized game, represented by a finite automaton.

A similar result could be obtained by the methods introduced in Chapter 15, if a strategy could be defined in MSO. Unfortunately, this is not possible over the given arena. Indeed, a strategy is a binary relation, or a function from the vertices to the vertices, and it is not allowed in MSO to quantify about (non monadic) relations. Note that a strategy provides more information than a winning region does. It is possible to stay forever in the winning region and not win (never reach the "goal"). One cannot quantify about paths: they are not uniquely defined by their set of nodes. Finally, if the prefix-recognizable graph is a directed tree, and the game played from the root (top-down), the situation is much simpler: the strategy is a subtree with some good conditions, and is MSO-definable. (This gives an answer to a question of [180].) But in general the unraveling tree of a prefix-recognizable graph from a given vertex is not a prefix-recognizable graph (it is an algebraic tree, but this is outside the scope of this book).

Notes on Part VII

As mentioned in Chapter 15, the subject of pushdown graphs was opened by Muller and Schupp [135]; they proved that the MSO-theory of a pushdown graph is decidable. These graphs play an important role in the theory of concurrency, as configuration graphs of **context-free processes** or **context-free graphs**. The decidability of their MSO-theory encouraged several authors to develop model-checking procedures for other logics, in particular the modal μ-calculus (cf. [24, 23]).

Prefix-recognizable graphs were introduced by Caucal in [28]. An extended version of his approach can be found in [29] and [30]. In [31] configuration graphs of Turing machines are characterized. Many of the proofs in Chapter 15 are taken from [28] and an extended unpublished version of [31].

The characterization of prefix-recognizable graphs as the graphs MSO-interpretable in the binary tree is due to [6] and [12]. The approach of interpretations can be extended to arbitrary relational structures; cf. [12]. Model-checking of prefix-recognizable graphs and the μ-calculus employing the automata-theoretic approach is studied in [106].

With respect to modelling system behaviour, the behaviour of transition graphs is often considered modulo *bisimulation*. Stirling discusses in [168] several classes of graphs (including prefix-recognizable graphs) with respect to bisimulation equivalence and decidability of bisimulation equivalence.

The operation of unraveling of a structure (and the question how the MSO-theory of the unraveling can be obtained from the original MSO-theory) was first studied by Stupp [173], taking up ideas of Shelah. Muchnik (in unpublished work) and Walukiewicz [200] extended these results, as presented in Chapter 16. Other related references are [42, 43, 32].

The solution of infinite games over pushdown graphs was given by Walukiewicz [196]. The technique of reducing two-way to one-way automata is due to Vardi [190] and was applied in μ-calculus model-checking games in [106].

Part VIII

Guarded Logics

Guarded logics are generalizations of modal logics (such as propositional multi-modal logic or the modal μ-calculus) to reason about arbitrary relational structures rather than just transition systems. While they are much more expressive than modal logics, they preserve — and to a certain extent explain — their good algorithmic and model-theoretic properties. Semantically, guarded logics are fragments of first-order logic, fixed point logic or second-order logic in which formulae can simultaneously refer to a collection of elements in a structure only if all these elements are "close together". Syntactically this means all quantifiers are relativised by guard formulae in an appropriate way.

In Chapter 18, a survey on guarded logics is given. It is shown that fundamental concepts for modal logics, like bisimulation and the tree model property, generalize in a natural way to guarded logics. A general decidability criterion is established, which is based on the decidability of the monadic theory of trees and on the fact that satisfiable guarded formulae have models of small tree width. The criterion implies the decidability of guarded fixed point logic. In Chapter 19, the idea of unravelling a structure and encoding it by a labelled tree is refined, and an automata based decision procedure for guarded fixed point logic is presented. It is proved that it provides optimal complexity bounds.

18 Introduction to Guarded Logics

Thoralf Räsch

Institut für Mathematik
Universität Potsdam

18.1 Introduction

Guarded logics are a family of logical formalisms that generalize certain desirable properties of modal logics from transition systems to the setting of arbitrary relational structures. Modal logics are widely used in a number of areas in computer science, particularly for the specification and verification of hardware and software systems, for knowledge representation, in databases, and in artificial intelligence. The most basic modal logic is propositional modal logic ML, which is just the fixed-point free part of the μ-calculus (see Chapter 10). But modal logics, broadly conceived, form a family of many different formalisms, including temporal logics, description logics, process logics, etc, many of which are also closely related to automata. An important reason for the successful applications of modal logics is their good balance between expressive power and computational complexity. This means that on the one hand, the relevant statements for many applications are expressible in these logics, and on the other hand, the usual reasoning tasks are decidable and admit reasonably efficient algorithms.

In particular, the satisfiability problem is decidable for most modal logics, including the modal μ-calculus (for instance via automata based methods). This in sharp contrast with first-order logic where even quite simple fragments are undecidable. Vardi [189] explicitly formulated the question, to find reasons for the robust decidability properties of modal logics. Note, however, that satisfiability problems tend to be of relatively high complexity. Even for plain propositional logic satisfiability is NP-complete and for more powerful logics it quickly becomes PSPACE- or EXPTIME-hard. For instance the satifiability problems for propositional modal logic ML and the modal μ-calculus are PSPACE-complete [109] and EXPTIME-complete [54].

There is a standard translation of ML into first-order logic (FO), inductively taking a modal formula φ to a first-order formula φ^*. This translation takes $\langle a \rangle \varphi$ to $\exists y(E_a xy \wedge \varphi^*(y))$ and $[a]\varphi$ to $\forall y(E_a xy \rightarrow \varphi^*(y))$. The first-order formulae that correspond to ML-formulae under this translation form what in [4] is called the *modal fragment* of first-order logic. It has been shown that this fragment has interesting properties, in particular a semantic characterisation via *bisimulation*: The properties definable in ML are precisely the properties that are first-order definable and invariant under bisimulation (see Chapter 14). Another important feature is the so-called *tree model property* which was already considered in [189]. We will look at a generalisation of this property in Section 18.4.

E. Grädel et al. (Eds.): Automata, Logics, and Infinite Games, LNCS 2500, pp. 321-341, 2002.

Both bisimulation invariance and the tree model property are important for the analysis of modal logics. In the following we will use these ideas for investigating *guarded logics*.

To understand guarded logics let us come back to the question of Vardi mentioned above: What are the reasons for the good algorithmic properties of modal logics? Looking at a typical formula of the modal fragment, say $\exists y(E_a xy \wedge \varphi^*(y))$, we note that we only need at most binary predicates and two variables. This strong restriction might be an answer but there is another observation: We only use quantifiers that are somehow restricted or *guarded* by the predicate E. Let us look at this property in a more general context.

In [4], Andréka, van Benthem and Németi have introduced the *guarded fragment* GF of first-order logic which we will define in the next section. Roughly, the idea is to consider arbitrary first-order languages but only allow guarded quantifiers. The concept of a guarded quantifier needs to be defined and we will see that there are several different ways to do it. Even a rather liberal notion of guardedness, *clique-guarded quantification*, leads to decidable extensions of propositional modal logic and the μ-calculus. Moreover, these clique-guarded logics will give us the possibility to prove general statements about guarded logics. In fact, we prove in Theorem 18.23 a general decidability result for various logics, particularly for guarded logics.

With this goal in mind we will define in Section 18.2 the guarded logics GF and CGF, and their fixed point extensions μGF and μCGF (that correspond to thew modal μ-calculus). In Section 18.3 we shall prove some basic properties of these logics, e.g., that GF can define precisely the model classes that are first-order definable and closed under guarded bisimulation. We will prove that even our the most liberal guarded fixed point logic μCGF has a (generalised) tree model property (Theorem 18.17). In Section 18.5 we define guarded second-order logics, GSO and CliqueSO, which generalize monadic second-order MSO. We shall then be prepared to prove the general decidability result, Theorem 18.23), in Section 18.6.

Note that this decidability result is based on the decidability of monadic theory of trees and therefore does not provide good complexity bounds for guarded logics. For complexity issues and decision procedures for guarded logics that are based automata-theoretic methods we refer to Chapter 19. Further information on guarded logics can be found in [65, 67, 69, 68, 71, 72, 73, 74, 75, 86]. The exposition in this chapter is based on [67, 72, 73, 74].

18.2   Guarded Logics

In general the concept of guarded logics can be defined by restricting quantification not only in first-order logic but also in second-order logic, fixed point logic or infinitary logics in such a way that, semantically speaking, each formula can 'speak' only about elements that are 'very close together' or 'guarded'. Syntactically, this means that all first-order quantifiers must be relativised by certain 'guard formulae' that tie together all free variables in the scope of a quantifier. Quantification appears in one of the form

$$\exists \bar{y}(\,\alpha(\bar{x},\bar{y}) \wedge \varphi(\bar{x},\bar{y})\,) \quad \text{or} \quad \forall \bar{y}(\,\alpha(\bar{x},\bar{y}) \rightarrow \varphi(\bar{x},\bar{y})\,),$$

where quantifiers may range over a tuple $\bar{y}$ of variables, 'guarded' by a formula α that must contain *all* free variables of the formula φ. The guard formulae are of a simple syntactic form (in the basic version, they are just atoms). Depending on the conditions imposed on guard formulae, one has logics with different levels of 'closeness' or 'guardedness'.

The Guarded Fragment

Let us start with the classical guarded logic, the so-called *guarded fragment* (GF) defined by induction as follows:

Definition 18.1. The **guarded fragment** (GF) is the smallest collection of formulae with the following properties.

(i) Every atomic formulae belongs to GF.
(ii) GF is closed under propositional connectives $\neg$, $\vee$, $\wedge$, $\rightarrow$, $\leftrightarrow$.
(iii) If $\bar{x}$ and $\bar{y}$ are tuples of variables, $\alpha(\bar{x},\bar{y})$ is an atomic formula, and $\varphi(\bar{x},\bar{y})$ is a formula in GF such that free$(\varphi) \subseteq$ free$(\alpha) = \{\bar{x},\bar{y}\}$, then the formulae $\exists \bar{y}(\,\alpha(\bar{x},\bar{y}) \wedge \varphi(\bar{x},\bar{y})\,)$ and $\forall \bar{y}(\,\alpha(\bar{x},\bar{y}) \rightarrow \varphi(\bar{x},\bar{y})\,)$ belong to GF.

For short we write

$$(\exists \bar{y}.\alpha(\bar{x},\bar{y})\,)\varphi(\bar{x},\bar{y}) \quad \text{for} \quad \exists \bar{y}(\,\alpha(\bar{x},\bar{y}) \wedge \varphi(\bar{x},\bar{y})\,) \quad \text{and}$$
$$(\forall \bar{y}.\alpha(\bar{x},\bar{y})\,)\varphi(\bar{x},\bar{y}) \quad \text{for} \quad \forall \bar{y}(\,\alpha(\bar{x},\bar{y}) \rightarrow \varphi(\bar{x},\bar{y})\,).$$

Let us stress that *all* free variables of the formula must be contained in the guard. Note that we just have generalised the modal concept we have spoken about in the first section. Clearly, the aforementioned translation of modal logics into first-order logic uses only guarded quantification, so we see immediately that the modal fragment is contained in GF. The guarded fragment generalises the modal fragment by dropping the restrictions to use only two variables and only monadic and binary predicates, and retains the restriction that quantifiers must be guarded.

Definition 18.2. Let $\mathfrak{A}$ be a structure with universe A and vocabulary τ. A set $X = \{a_1, \ldots, a_n\} \subseteq A$ is **guarded** in $\mathfrak{A}$ if there exists an atomic formula $\alpha(x_1, \ldots, x_n)$ such that $\mathfrak{A} \models \alpha(a_1, \ldots, a_n)$. A tuple $(b_1, \ldots, b_n) \in B^n$ is guarded if $\{b_1, \ldots, b_n\} \subseteq X$ for some guarded set X.

The Clique-Guarded Fragment

We next consider a more liberal notion of guarded quantification and define the clique-guarded fragment CGF of first-order logic. Although we will have more freedom to take formulae, CGF still has the nice properties we are expecting from a suitable generalisation of ML.

Definition 18.3. The **Gaifman graph** of a relational structure $\mathfrak{A}$ is the undirected graph $G(\mathfrak{A}) = (A, E^{\mathfrak{A}})$ where

$$E^{\mathfrak{A}} := \{(a, a') \mid a \neq a', \text{there exists a guarded set } X \subseteq A \text{ such that } a, a' \in X\}.$$

A set of nodes in a graph is called a *clique* if every node of that set is adjacent to any other node of it.

Definition 18.4. A set X of elements of a structure $\mathfrak{A}$ is **clique-guarded** in $\mathfrak{A}$ if it induces a clique in $G(\mathfrak{A})$.

Obviously, guarded sets are also clique-guarded. To see that the converse is false, consider the structure $\mathfrak{A} = (A, R)$ with universe $A = \{a_1, a_2, a_3, b_{12}, b_{23}, b_{13}\}$ and one ternary relation R containing the triangles (a_1, a_2, b_{12}), (a_2, a_3, b_{23}), (a_1, a_3, b_{13}). Then the set $\{a_1, a_2, a_3\}$ is not guarded but induces a clique in $G(\mathfrak{A})$.

Note that, for each finite vocabulary τ and each $k \in \mathbb{N}$ there is a positive, existential first-order formula $clique(x_1, \ldots, x_k)$ such that for every τ-structure $\mathfrak{A}$ and all $a_1, \ldots, a_k \in A$ the following holds.

$$\mathfrak{A} \models \text{clique}(a_1, \ldots, a_k) \iff a_1, \ldots, a_k \text{ induce a clique in } G(\mathfrak{A}).$$

Definition 18.5. The **clique-guarded fragment**, denoted CGF, is defined in the same way as GF (see Definition 18.1), except that the quantifier rule is changed as follows.

(c'') If $\varphi(\bar{x}, \bar{y})$ is in CGF, then $\exists \bar{y}(\text{clique}(\bar{x}, \bar{y}) \wedge \varphi(\bar{x}, \bar{y}))$ and $\forall \bar{y}(\text{clique}(\bar{x}, \bar{y}) \to \varphi(\bar{x}, \bar{y}))$ belong to CGF where $\text{free}(\psi) \subseteq \text{free}(\text{clique}) = \{\bar{x}, \bar{y}\}$.

For short we write

$$(\exists \bar{y}.\text{clique}(\bar{x}, \bar{y}))\varphi(\bar{x}, \bar{y}) \quad \text{for} \quad \exists \bar{y}(\text{clique}(\bar{x}, \bar{y}) \wedge \varphi(\bar{x}, \bar{y})) \qquad \text{and}$$
$$(\forall \bar{y}.\text{clique}(\bar{x}, \bar{y}))\varphi(\bar{x}, \bar{y}) \quad \text{for} \quad \forall \bar{y}(\text{clique}(\bar{x}, \bar{y}) \to \varphi(\bar{x}, \bar{y})).$$

Guarded Fixed Point Logics

So far we have defined guarded fragments of first-order logics, which generalize propositional modal logic. But now we can go on and generalize also the modal μ-calculus to obtain guarded variants of least fixed fixed point logic.

Definition 18.6. The guarded fixed point logics μGF and μCGF are obtained by adding to GF and CGF, respectively, the following rules for constructing fixed point formulae.

Let W be a k-ary relation symbol, $\bar{x} = (x_1, \ldots, x_k)$ a k-tuple of distinct variables and $\varphi(W, \bar{x})$ be a guarded formula that contains only positive occurrences of W, no free first-order variables other than $x_1, \ldots, x_k$ and where W is not used in guards.
Then we can build the formulae $\text{LFP}_{W,\bar{x}}(\varphi)(\bar{x})$ and $\text{GFP}_{W,\bar{x}}(\varphi)(\bar{x})$.

The semantics of the fixed point formulae is the following. Given a structure $\mathfrak{A}$ providing interpretations for all free second-order variables in φ except W, let $\varphi^{\mathfrak{A}}$ be the operator on k-ary relations $W \subseteq A^k$ defined by

$$W \mapsto \varphi^{\mathfrak{A}}(W) := \{\bar{a} \in A^k \mid \mathfrak{A} \models \varphi(W, \bar{a})\}.$$

Since W occurs only positively in φ, this operator is monotone — i.e., $W \subseteq W'$ implies $\varphi^{\mathfrak{A}}(W) \subseteq \varphi^{\mathfrak{A}}(W')$ — and therefore has a least fixed point $\mathrm{LFP}(\varphi^{\mathfrak{A}})$ and a greatest fixed point $\mathrm{GFP}(\varphi^{\mathfrak{A}})$. The semantics of least fixed point formulae is defined by

$$\mathfrak{A} \models \mathrm{LFP}_{W,\bar{x}}(\varphi(W,\bar{x}))(\bar{a}) \iff \bar{a} \in \mathrm{LFP}(\varphi^{\mathfrak{A}})$$

and similarly for GFP-formulae.

An instructive example of a guarded fixed point sentence is

$$\exists xy Fxy \wedge \forall xy(\, Fxy \to \exists x Fyx\,) \wedge \forall xy(\, Fxy \to \mathrm{LFP}_{W,x}(\,\forall y(Fyx \to Wy)\,)(x)).$$

Here, the first two conjuncts say that there exists an F-edge and that every F-edge can be extended to an infinite path. The third conjunct asserts that each point x on an F-edge is in the least fixed point of the the operator $W \mapsto \{w \mid$ all F-predecessors of w are in $W\}$. This least fixed point is the set of points that have only finitely many F-predecessors. Hence, the sentence says that there is an infinite forward F-chain but no infinite backward F-chain. This means in particular that F does not cycle. Thus, this sentence is only satisfiable in infinite models. This shows that, contrary to the μ-calculus, guarded fixed point logics do not have the finite model property.

Least and greatest fixed points can be defined inductively as we have already seen in Chapter 10. For a formula $\varphi(W, \bar{x})$ with k-ary relation variable W a structure $\mathfrak{A}$, for ordinals α, and limit ordinals λ set

$$W^0 := \varnothing \qquad\qquad \tilde{W}^0 := A^k$$
$$W^{\alpha+1} := \varphi^{\mathfrak{A}}(W^\alpha) \qquad \tilde{W}^{\alpha+1} := \varphi^{\mathfrak{A}}(\tilde{W}^\alpha)$$
$$W^\lambda := \bigcup_{\alpha<\lambda} W^\alpha \qquad \tilde{W}^\lambda := \bigcap_{\alpha<\lambda} \tilde{W}^\alpha$$

The relations W^α and $\tilde{W}^\alpha$ are called the **stages** of the LFP- or GFP-induction, respectively, of $\varphi(W, \bar{x})$ on $\mathfrak{A}$. Since the operator $\varphi^{\mathfrak{A}}$ is monotone, we have $W^0 \subseteq W^1 \subseteq \cdots \subseteq W^\alpha \subseteq W^{\alpha+1} \subseteq \cdots$ and $\tilde{W}^0 \supseteq \tilde{W}^1 \supseteq \cdots \supseteq \tilde{W}^\alpha \supseteq \tilde{W}^{\alpha+1} \supseteq \cdots$ and there exist ordinals α, α' such that $W^\alpha = \mathrm{LFP}(\varphi^{\mathfrak{A}})$ and $\tilde{W}^{\alpha'} = \mathrm{GFP}(\varphi^{\mathfrak{A}})$. These are called the **closure ordinals** of the LFP- or GFP-induction, respectively, of $\varphi(W, \bar{x})$ on $\mathfrak{A}$.

Countable Models

While the finite model property fails for guarded fixed point logics we recall that the so-called Löwenheim-Skolem property holds even for the (unguarded) least fixed point logic (FO + LFP), i.e., every satisfiable fixed point sentence has a countable model.

Lemma 18.7 ([73]). *Every satisfiable sentence in* (FO+LFP), *and hence every satisfiable sentence in* μGF, *and* μCGF, *has a model of countable cardinality.*

Proof. We only have to look at fixed point formulae. Therefore, let us consider $\psi(\bar{x}) := \text{LFP}_{R,\bar{x}}(\,\varphi(R,\bar{x})\,)(\bar{x})$, with first-order formula φ such that $\mathfrak{A} \models \psi(\bar{a})$ for some infinite $\mathfrak{A}$.

For any ordinal α, let R^α be the α-th stage of the least fixed point induction of φ on $\mathfrak{A}$. Expand $\mathfrak{A}$ by a monadic relation U, a binary relation $<$, and an $(m+1)$-ary relation S (where m is the arity of R) such that

(i) $(U, <)$ is a well-ordering of length $\gamma + 1$, and $<$ is empty outside U.
(ii) S describes the stages of $\varphi^{\mathfrak{A}}$ in the following way:

$$S := \{(u, \bar{b}) \mid \text{ for some ordinal } \alpha \leq \gamma,\ u \text{ is the } \alpha\text{-th element of } (U, <),\ \bar{b} \in R^\alpha\}.$$

In the expanded structure $\mathfrak{A}^* := (\mathfrak{A}, U, <, S)$, the stages of the operator $\varphi^{\mathfrak{A}}$ are defined by the sentence:

$$\eta := \forall u \forall \bar{x}(\, Su\bar{x} \longleftrightarrow \exists z(\, z < u \wedge \varphi[\, R\bar{y}/\exists z(z < u \wedge Sz\bar{y})\,](\bar{x})\,)\,).$$

Here, $\varphi[\, R\bar{y}/\exists z(z < u \wedge Sz\bar{y})\,](\bar{x})$ is the formula obtained from $\varphi(R,\bar{x})$ by replacing all occurrences of subformula $R\bar{y}$ by $\exists z(\, z < u \wedge Sz\bar{y}\,)$.

Now, let $\mathfrak{B}^* := (\mathfrak{B}, U^{\mathfrak{B}}, <^{\mathfrak{B}}, S^{\mathfrak{B}})$ be a countable elementary substructure of $\mathfrak{A}^*$, containing the tuple $\bar{a}$. Since $\mathfrak{A}^* \models \eta$, also $\mathfrak{B}^* \models \eta$ and therefore $S^{\mathfrak{B}}$ encodes the stages of $\varphi^{\mathfrak{B}}$. Since also $\mathfrak{B}^* \models \exists u Su\bar{a}$, it follows that $\bar{a}$ is contained in the least fixed point of $\varphi^{\mathfrak{B}}$, i.e., $\mathfrak{B} \models \psi(\bar{a})$.

A straightforward iteration of this argument gives the desired result for arbitrary nesting of fixed point operators, and hence for the entire fixed point logic (FO+LFP). $\qquad\square$

Infinitary Guarded Logics

Fixed point logics have a close relationship to infinitary logics (with bounded number of variables). In order to formulate general statements we will consider the following logics.

Definition 18.8. GF^∞ and CGF^∞ are the canonical infinitary variants of the guarded fragments GF and CGF, respectively. For instance, GF^∞ extends GF by the following rule for building new formulae: If $\Phi \subseteq \text{GF}^\infty$ is any set of formulae, then also $\bigvee \Phi$ and $\bigwedge \Phi$ are formulae of GF^∞. The definition for CGF^∞ is analogous.

In the following we explicitly talk about the clique-guarded case only, i.e., about μCGF and CGF^∞ but all results apply to the guarded as well. The following simple observation relates μCGF and CGF^∞. Recall that the **width** of a formula is the the maximal number of free variables in its subformulae.

Lemma 18.9 ([73]). *For each $\varphi \in \mu$CGF of width k and each cardinal γ, there is a $\varphi' \in$ CGF$^\infty$, also of width k, which is equivalent to φ on all structures of cardinality up to γ.*

Proof. Consider a typical fixed point formula LFP$_{R,\bar{x}}(\varphi(R, \bar{x}))(\bar{x})$. For every ordinal α there is a formula $\varphi^\alpha \in$ CGF$^\infty$ that defines the stage α of the fixed point induction of φ. Indeed, let $\varphi^0 := \bot$, let $\varphi^{\alpha+1} := \varphi[R\bar{y}/\varphi^\alpha(\bar{y})](\bar{x})$, that is, the formula that one obtains from $\varphi(R, \bar{x})$ if one replaces each atom $R\bar{y}$ (for any $\bar{y}$) by the formula $\varphi^\alpha(\bar{y})$, and for limit ordinals λ, let $\varphi^\lambda := \bigvee_{\alpha < \lambda} \varphi^\alpha(\bar{x})$.

But on structures of bounded cardinality, also the closure ordinal of any fixed point formula is bounded. Hence, for every cardinal γ there is an ordinal α such that LFP$_{R,\bar{x}}(\varphi(R, \bar{x}))(\bar{x})$ is equivalent to $\varphi^\alpha(\bar{x})$ on structures of cardinality at most γ. □

18.3   Guarded Bisimulations

One of the main tools for the analysis of the modal μ-calculus is the notion of bisimulation. We are going to generalise this idea now in the context of guarded logics.

For GF, the so-called *guarded bisimulations* play a fundamental role for characterising the expressive power, in the same way as bisimulation is crucial for understanding modal logics. For instance, the characterisation theorem by van Benthem, saying that a property is definable in propositional modal logic if and only if it is first-order definable and invariant under bisimulation, has a natural analogue for the guarded fragment.

Lemma 18.10 ([4]). *GF can define precisely the model classes that are first-order definable and closed under guarded bisimulations.*

We are going to consider *clique-bisimulations* and prove a similar result for the clique-guarded fragment CGF. The notions of guarded bisimulations can be defined analogously.

Definition 18.11. A **clique-k-bisimulation** between two τ-structures $\mathfrak{A}$ and $\mathfrak{B}$ is a non-empty set I of finite partial isomorphisms $f : X \to Y$ from $\mathfrak{A}$ to $\mathfrak{B}$ where $X \subseteq A$ and $Y \subseteq B$ are clique-guarded sets of size at most k such that the following 'back and forth' conditions are satisfied: For every $f : X \to Y$ in I,

(forth)   for every clique-guarded set $X' \subseteq A$ of size at most k there exists a partial isomorphism $g : X' \to Y'$ in I such that f and g agree on $X \cap X'$;

(back)   for every clique-guarded set $Y' \subseteq B$ of size at most k there exists a partial isomorphism $g : X' \to Y'$ in I such that f^{-1} and g^{-1} agree on $Y \cap Y'$.

More generally, a **clique-bisimulation** is defined in the same way but without the restriction on the size of the sets X, X', Y, Y'. Finally, we say that two structures are **clique-(k-)bisimilar** if there exists a clique-(k-)bisimulation between them. Furthermore, two structures are **clique-bisimilar** if and only if they are clique-k-bisimilar for all k. One can describe clique-k-bisimilarity also via a guarded variant of the infinitary Ehrenfeucht-Fraissé game with k pebbles. One just has to impose that after every move, the set of all pebbled elements induces a clique in the Gaifman graph of each of the two structures. Then $\mathfrak{A}$ and $\mathfrak{B}$ are clique-k-bisimilar if and only if the second player has a winning strategy for this guarded game.

Adapting basic and well-known model-theoretic techniques to the present situation one obtains the following result.

Theorem 18.12 ([73]). *For all τ-structures $\mathfrak{A}$ and $\mathfrak{B}$ the following two conditions are equivalent.*

(i) *$\mathfrak{A}$ and $\mathfrak{B}$ are clique-k-bisimilar.*
(ii) *For all sentences $\varphi \in \mathrm{CGF}^\infty$ of width at most k, $\mathfrak{A} \models \varphi \iff \mathfrak{B} \models \varphi$.*

Proof. To prove the direction from (i) to (ii) let I be a clique-k-bisimulation between $\mathfrak{A}$ and $\mathfrak{B}$, let $a_1, \ldots, a_n \in \mathfrak{A}$ and $b_1, \ldots, b_n \in \mathfrak{B}$ and also $\varphi(x_1, \ldots, x_n)$ be a formula in CGF^∞ of width at most k such that $\mathfrak{A} \models \varphi(a_1, \ldots, a_n)$ and $\mathfrak{B} \models \neg\varphi(b_1, \ldots, b_n)$. We are going to show by induction on φ that there is no partial isomorphism $f \in I$ with $f(a_1) = b_1, \ldots, f(a_n) = b_n$. By setting $n = 0$, this proves the claim.

If φ is atomic this is obvious, and the induction steps for the formulae $\varphi = \bigvee \Phi$ and $\varphi = \neg\psi$ are immediate. Hence the only interesting case concerns formulae of the form:

$$\varphi(\bar{x}) := (\,\exists \bar{y}.\mathrm{clique}(\bar{x}, \bar{y})\,)\psi(\bar{x}, \bar{y}).$$

Since $\mathfrak{A} \models \varphi(\bar{a})$, there exists a tuple $\bar{a}'$ in $\mathfrak{A}$ such that $\mathfrak{A} \models \mathrm{clique}(\bar{a}, \bar{a}') \wedge \psi(\bar{a}, \bar{a}')$. Suppose—towards a contradiction—that some $f \in I$ takes the tuples $\bar{a}$ to $\bar{b}$. Since the set $\{a_1, \ldots, a_n, a'_1, \ldots, a'_m\}$ is clique-guarded there exists a partial isomorphism $g \in I$, taking $\bar{a}$ to $\bar{b}$ and $\bar{a}'$ to some tuple $\bar{b}'$ in $\mathfrak{B}$. But then the set $\{b_1, \ldots, b_n, b'_1, \ldots, b'_m\}$ must be clique-guarded as well and $\mathfrak{B} \models \neg\psi(\bar{b}, \bar{b}')$, which contradicts the induction hypothesis.

For the direction from (ii) to (i), let I be the set of all partial isomorphisms $\bar{a} \mapsto \bar{b}$, taking a clique-guarded tuple $\bar{a}$ in $\mathfrak{A}$ to a clique-guarded tuple $\bar{b}$ in $\mathfrak{B}$ such that for all formulae $\varphi(\bar{x}) \in \mathrm{CGF}^\infty$ of width at most k, $\mathfrak{A} \models \varphi(\bar{a})$ if and only if $\mathfrak{B} \models \varphi(\bar{b})$. Since $\mathfrak{A}$ and $\mathfrak{B}$ cannot be distinguished by sentences of width k in CGF^∞, I contains the empty map and is therefore non-empty. It remains to show that I satisfies the 'back and forth' properties.

For the 'forth' property, take any partial isomorphism $f : X \to Y$ in I and any clique-guarded set X' in $\mathfrak{A}$ of size at most k. Let $X' = \{a_1, \ldots, a_n, a'_1, \ldots, a'_m\}$ where $X \cap X' = \{a_1, \ldots, a_n\}$. We only have to show that there exists $g \in I$, defined on X' that coincides with f on $X \cap X'$.

Suppose that we cannot find such g. For $\bar{a} := (a_1, \ldots, a_n)$, $\bar{a}' := (a_1', \ldots, a_m')$, and $\bar{b} := f(\bar{a})$, let T be the set of all tuples $\bar{b}' := (b_1', \ldots, b_m')$ such that $\{b_1, \ldots, b_n, b_1', \ldots, b_m'\}$ is clique-guarded in $\mathfrak{B}$. Since there is no appropriate $g \in I$ there exists for every tuple $\bar{b}' \in T$ a formula $\psi_{\bar{b}'}(\bar{x}, \bar{y}) \in \mathrm{CGF}^\infty$ such that $\mathfrak{A} \models \psi_{\bar{b}'}(\bar{b}, \bar{b}')$. But then we can construct the formula

$$\varphi(\bar{x}) := (\, \exists \bar{y}.\mathrm{clique}(\bar{x}, \bar{y})\,) \bigwedge \{\psi_{\bar{b}'}(\bar{x}, \bar{y}) \mid \bar{b}' \in T\}.$$

Clearly, $\mathfrak{A} \models \varphi(\bar{a})$ but also $\mathfrak{B} \models \neg\varphi(\bar{b})$ which is impossible knowing that $f \in I$ maps $\bar{a}$ to $\bar{b}$. The proof for the 'back' property is analogous. □

In particular, this shows that clique-(k-)bisimilar structures cannot be separated by $\mu\mathrm{CGF}$-sentences (of width k, respectively).

We show next that we can find a similar characterisation for CGF and clique-guarded bisimulation as we have already seen in Chapter 14 for the propositional modal logic as bisimulation-invariant fragments of first-order logic. The proof is a straightforward adaption of van Benthem's proof for modal logic. Recall that every structure has an ω-saturated elementary extension.

Theorem 18.13 ([73]). *A first-order sentence is invariant under clique-guarded bisimulation if and only if it is equivalent to a CGF-sentence.*

Proof. We have already established that CGF-sentences (in fact, even sentences from CGF^∞) are invariant under clique-guarded bisimulation. For the converse, suppose that ψ is a satisfiable first-order sentence that is invariant under clique-guarded bisimulation. Let $\varPhi$ be the set of sentences $\varphi \in \mathrm{CGF}$ such that $\psi \models \varphi$. It suffices to show that $\varPhi \models \psi$.

Indeed, then by the compactness theorem, already a finite conjunction of sentences from $\varPhi$ will then imply, and hence be equivalent to, ψ.

Since ψ was assumed to be satisfiable, so is $\varPhi$. Take any model $\mathfrak{A} \models \varPhi$. We have to prove that $\mathfrak{A} \models \psi$. Let $T_{\mathrm{CGF}}(\mathfrak{A})$ be the CGF-theory of $\mathfrak{A}$, i.e., the set of all CGF-sentences that hold in $\mathfrak{A}$.

Claim. $T_{\mathrm{CGF}}(\mathfrak{A}) \cup \{\psi\}$ is satisfiable.

Otherwise, there were sentences $\varphi_1, \ldots, \varphi_n \in T_{\mathrm{CGF}}(\mathfrak{A})$ such that $\psi \models \neg(\varphi_1 \wedge \cdots \wedge \varphi_n)$. Hence $\neg(\varphi_1 \wedge \cdots \wedge \varphi_n)$ is a CGF-sentence implied by ψ and is therefore contained in $\varPhi$. But then $\mathfrak{A} \models \neg(\varphi_1 \wedge \cdots \wedge \varphi_n)$ which is impossible since $\varphi_1, \ldots, \varphi_n \in T_{\mathrm{CGF}}(\mathfrak{A})$. This proves the claim.

Now, take any model $\mathfrak{B} \models T_{\mathrm{CGF}}(\mathfrak{A}) \cup \{\psi\}$, and let $\mathfrak{A}^+$ and $\mathfrak{B}^+$ be ω-saturated elementary extensions of $\mathfrak{A}$ and $\mathfrak{B}$, respectively.

Claim. $\mathfrak{A}^+$ and $\mathfrak{B}^+$ are clique-bisimilar.

In order to prove the claim, let I be the set of partial isomorphisms $f : X \to Y$ from clique-guarded subsets of $\mathfrak{B}^+$ such that, for all formulae $\varphi(\bar{x})$ in CGF and all tuples $\bar{a}$ from X, we have that $\mathfrak{A}^+ \models \varphi(\bar{a})$ if and only if $\mathfrak{B}^+ \models \varphi(f\bar{a})$.

The fact that $\mathfrak{A}^+$ and $\mathfrak{B}^+$ are ω-saturated implies that the 'back and forth' conditions for the clique-guarded bisimulations are satisfied by I. Indeed, let $f \in I$, and let X' be any clique-guarded set in $\mathfrak{A}^+$, with $X \cap X' = \{a_1, \ldots, a_r\}$ and $X' \setminus X = \{a'_1, \ldots, a'_s\}$. Let Φ be the set of all formulae in CGF of the form $\varphi(fa_1, \ldots, fa_r, y_1, \ldots, y_s)$ such that $\mathfrak{A}^+ \models \varphi(a_1, \ldots, a_r, a'_1, \ldots, a'_s)$.

For every formula $\varphi(f\bar{a}, \bar{y}) \in \Phi$, we have $\mathfrak{A}^+ \models (\exists \bar{y}.\mathrm{clique}(\bar{a}, \bar{y}))\varphi(\bar{a}, \bar{y})$ and therefore also $\mathfrak{B}^+ \models (\exists \bar{y}.\mathrm{clique}(f\bar{a}, \bar{y}))\varphi(f\bar{a}, \bar{y})$. Hence, Φ is a consistent type of $(\mathfrak{B}^+, f\bar{a})$ which—by ω-saturation—is realised in $\mathfrak{B}^+$ by some fixed tuple $\bar{b}$ such that $(f\bar{a}, \bar{b})$ is clique-guarded. And so, the function g taking $\bar{a}$ to $f\bar{a}$ and $\bar{a}'$ to $\bar{b}$ is a partial isomorphism with domain X' that coincides with f on $X \cap X'$.

The 'back' property is proved in the same way, exploiting that $\mathfrak{A}^+$ is ω-saturated.

We can now complete the proof of the theorem: Since $\mathfrak{B} \models \psi$ and $\mathfrak{B}^+$ is an elementary extension of $\mathfrak{B}$, we have that $\mathfrak{B}^+ \models \psi$. By assumption, ψ is invariant under clique-guarded bisimulation, so $\mathfrak{A}^+ \models \psi$ and therefore also $\mathfrak{A} \models \psi$.   □

An analogous result applies to clique-k-bisimulations and CGF-sentences of width k, for any $k \in \mathbb{N}$.

18.4   Tree Model Property

We will now define the notion of *tree width* which is an important tool in graph theory as well. It measures how closely a structure resembles a tree. Informally, a structure has tree width $\leq k$ if it can be covered by (possibly overlapping) substructures of size at most $k + 1$ which are arranged in a tree-like manner. So, forests will have tree width 1 and cycles tree width 2 (cf. Figure 18.1).

Definition 18.14. A structure $\mathfrak{A}$ has **tree width** k if k is the minimal natural number satisfying the following condition: There exists a directed tree $T = (V, E)$ and a function $F : V \to \{X \subseteq A \,;\, |X| \leq k + 1\}$, assigning to every node v of T a set $F(v)$ of at most $k + 1$ elements of $\mathfrak{A}$ such that the following two conditions hold:

(i) For every guarded set X in $\mathfrak{A}$ there exists a node v of T with $X \subseteq F(v)$.
(ii) For every element b of $\mathfrak{A}$, the set of nodes $\{v \in V : b \in F(v)\}$ is connected (and hence induces a subtree of T).

For each node v of T, $F(v)$ induces a substructure $\mathfrak{F}(v) \subseteq \mathfrak{A}$ of cardinality at most $k + 1$. We call $(T, (\mathfrak{F}(v) \mid v \in T))$ a **tree decomposition** of width k of $\mathfrak{A}$.

Lemma 18.15 ([73]). *Guarded and clique-guarded sets are contained in some $F(v)$ of a tree decomposition $(T, (\mathfrak{F}(v) \mid v \in T))$.*

Proof. By definition for guarded sets this is true. We show that it also holds for a general clique-guarded set X. For each $a \in X$, let V_a be the set of nodes v such that $a \in F(v)$. By definition of a tree decomposition, each V_b induces a subtree

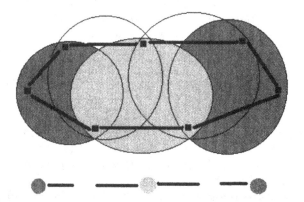

Fig. 18.1. The upper part shows a graph (circle) with seven nodes divided into clusters of size '2 + 1' whereas the lower one gives us the arrangement of these clusters in a tree-like manner. Note, each edge of the circle is contained in at least one cluster and the arrangement is in the sense of (ii) of Definition 18.14.

of T. For all $a, a' \in X$ the intersection $V_a \cap V_{a'}$ is non-empty, since b and b' are adjacent in $G(\mathfrak{A})$ and must therefore coexist in some atomic fact that is true in $\mathfrak{A}$. It is known that any collection of pairwise overlapping subtrees of a tree has a common node (*cf.* [154, p. 94]). Hence there is a node v of the tree T such that $F(v)$ contains all elements of X. □

With this in mind we can define a general notion of the so-called *tree model property*.

Definition 18.16. Let L be a logic and C a class of structures. We say that L has the **generalised tree model property** on C if there exists a computable function t, assigning to every sentence $\varphi \in L$ a natural number $t(\varphi)$ such that, whenever φ is satisfiable on C, then there also exists a model $\mathfrak{A} \models \varphi$ such that $\mathfrak{A} \in C$ and $\mathfrak{A}$ has tree width at most $t(\varphi)$. In the case where C is the class of all structures, we simply say that L has the generalised tree model property.

The definition is very general since it only requires that the bound $t(\varphi)$ on the tree width of a model for φ must be computable from φ.

We can prove the tree model property for the logics we are considering.

Theorem 18.17 ([73]). *Every satisfiable sentence in μCGF with width k has a countable model of tree width at most $k - 1$. In particular, μCGF has the generalised tree model property.*

Proof. We can *unravel* any given structure to get a bisimilar tree-like structure. The idea is to look at the local situation of the structure and paste copies of small parts of it together, arranged as a tree.

The k-unravelling $\mathfrak{A}^{(k)}$ of a structure $\mathfrak{A}$ is defined inductively. We build a tree T together with functions F and G such that for each node v of T, $F(v)$ induces a clique-guarded substructure $\mathfrak{F}(v) \subseteq \mathfrak{A}$, and $G(v)$ induces a substructure $\mathfrak{G} \subseteq \mathfrak{A}^{(k)}$ that is isomorphic to $\mathfrak{F}(v)$. Furthermore, $(T, (\mathfrak{G}(v) \mid v \in T))$ will be a tree decomposition of $\mathfrak{A}^{(k)}$.

The root of T is λ, with $F(\lambda) = G(\lambda) = \varnothing$. Given a node v of T with $F(v) = \{a_1, \ldots, a_r\}$ and $G(v) = \{a_1', \ldots, a_r'\}$ we create for every clique-guarded set $\{b_1, \ldots, b_s\}$ in $\mathfrak{A}$ with $s \leq k$ a successor node w of v such that $F(w) = \{b_1, \ldots, b_s\}$ and $G(w)$ is the set $\{b_1', \ldots, n_s'\}$ which is defined as follows: For those i, such that $b_i = a_j \in F(v)$, put $b_i' = a_j'$ such that $G(w)$ has the same overlap with $G(v)$ as $F(w)$ has with $F(v)$. The other b_i' in $G(w)$ are fresh elements.

Let $f_w : F(w) \to G(w)$ be the bijection taking b_i to b_i' for $i = 1, \ldots, s$. For $\mathfrak{F}(w)$ being the substructures of $\mathfrak{A}$ induced by $F(w)$, define $\mathfrak{G}(w)$ such that f_w is an isomorphism from $\mathfrak{F}(w)$ to $\mathfrak{G}(w)$.

Finally, $\mathfrak{A}^{(k)}$ is the structure with the tree decomposition $(T, (\mathfrak{G}(v) \mid v \in T))$. Note that the k-unravelling of a structure has tree width at most $k - 1$.

Claim. $\mathfrak{A}$ and $\mathfrak{A}^{(k)}$ are k-bisimilar.

This is witnessed by the set I, consisting of all functions $f_v : F(v) \to G(v)$ for all nodes v of T.

Thus, it follows that no sentence of width k in CGF^∞, and hence no sentence of width k in $\mu\mathrm{CGF}$ distinguishes between a structure and its k-unravelling. Since every satisfiable sentence in $\mu\mathrm{CGF}$ has a model of at most countable cardinality—by Lemma 18.7—and since the k-unravelling of a countable model is again countable, our claim is proved. $\qquad\square$

18.5 Guarded Second-Order Logic

At this point we want to discuss another generalisation of GF. Let us consider the natural second-order extension of the guarded fragment.

Definition 18.18. Guarded second-order logic (GSO) is second-order logic, where second-order quantification appears only in the following form:

$$(\exists X.\forall \bar{y}(X\bar{y} \to \mathrm{guarded}(\bar{y}))\varphi(X) \quad \text{and} \quad (\forall X.\forall \bar{y}(X\bar{y} \to \mathrm{guarded}(\bar{y}))\varphi(X).$$

Here, $\mathrm{guarded}(\bar{y})$ is a first-order formula expressing that $\bar{y}$ is a guarded tuple. More explicitly, on structures with relations $R_1, \ldots, R_n$ let $\mathrm{guarded}(\bar{y}) := \bigvee_{i_1}^{n} \exists \bar{x}(R_i \bar{y} \wedge \bigwedge_j \bigvee_l y = j = x_l)$. Obviously, GSO includes full first-order logic and so GSO is undecidable and, unlike GF and μGF, not invariant under guarded bisimulation. Also note that, as singletons are always guarded, the monadic version of guarded second-order logic coincides with full MSO. Consequently, since MSO is strictly more expressive than FO, the same is true for GSO. Furthermore, Lemma 18.20 below shows that GSO collapses to MSO over words. So, we can get the analogue embeddings as in the case of modal logic—cf. Figure 18.2.

The robustness of GSO is underlined by the following statement.

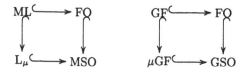

Fig. 18.2. Embeddings around ML and GF

Lemma 18.19 ([74]). *The following fragments of second-order logic are equally expressive.*

(i) *The extension of* GF *by full second-order quantification.*
(ii) *The extension of* GF *by second-order quantification with guarded semantics.*
(iii) *Guarded second-order logic* GSO.

Proof. It obviously suffices to present translations from (i) and (iii) to (ii).

For the direction from (i) to (ii) consider a second-order variable X in a formula according to (i) which is meant to range over arbitrary rather than guarded relations. Consider first the case of sentences. For any atom X occurring in the scope of a guarded quantification $(Q\bar{y}.\alpha(\bar{y}\bar{z}))\varphi$ where the occurrence of $\bar{x}$ is free in φ, the $\bar{x}$ all occur in α. It follows that only truth values of $X\bar{x}$ for guarded tuples have an influence on the truth value of φ.

For formulae with free variables the quantifier-free part (w.r.t. first-order quantification) may depend on truth-values for unguarded tuples. However, since the number of free variables is fixed, there is only a fixed number of possibilities for the second-order variables that can be explicitly enumerated.

So, if $\exists X \varphi(\bar{x})$ is a subformula of the given formula type (i) that occurs outside of any first-order quantifier we translate it into type (ii) as follows: Let $H = H(X, \bar{x})$ be the set of all $\{X\}$-structures with universe $\bar{x}$. For this transformation we assume that no variable in φ is reused in quantifications. Replace $\exists X \varphi(\bar{x})$ with $\exists X \bigvee_{\mathfrak{A} \in H} \varphi^{\mathfrak{A}}(\bar{x})$ where $\varphi^{\mathfrak{A}}$ is obtained from φ by substituting all atoms $X\bar{y}$ where $\bar{y} \subseteq \bar{x}$ with $\bot$ if $\mathfrak{A} \models X\bar{y}$, and with $\top$ otherwise.

For the direction from (iii) to (ii) it suffices to show that unrestricted first-order quantification can be simulated by guarded second-order quantification over GF ranging over monadic variables: Each element variable x is replaced by a set-variable X, and we use the following rules for translating formulae:

$$x = y \quad \mapsto \quad \forall x (Xx \leftrightarrow Yx)$$

$$R\bar{x} \quad \mapsto \quad (\exists \bar{x}.R\bar{x}) \bigwedge_i X_i x_i$$

$$Z\bar{x} \quad \mapsto \quad (\exists \bar{x}.\text{guarded}(\bar{x}))(\bigwedge_i X_i x_i \wedge Z\bar{x})$$

$$\exists x \varphi(x, \bar{y}) \quad \mapsto \quad \exists X (\varphi(X, \bar{y}) \wedge \text{singleton}(X))$$

where 'guarded($\bar{x}$)' for vocabulary $\tau = \{R_1, \ldots, R_n\}$ is the following formula:

$$\text{guarded}(x_1, \ldots, x_n) := \bigvee_{i=1}^{t} \exists \bar{y}(R_i \bar{y} \wedge \bigwedge_l \bigvee_j x_l = y_j)$$

and 'singleton(X)' states that X contains exactly one element:

$$\text{singleton}(X) := \exists x X x \wedge \forall Y (\forall x (Y x \to X x) \to (\forall x \neg Y x \vee (\forall x Y x \leftrightarrow X x))).$$

Note that these translations — particularly singleton(X)—are in GF, since first-order quantification over a single first-order variable x is always guarded (by $x = x$). □

Lemma 18.20 ([74]). *Guarded second-order logic* (GSO) *lies strictly between monadic second-order logic* (MSO) *and full second-order logic* (SO).

Proof. Obviously, we have MSO $\subseteq$ GSO $\subseteq$ SO. We now show that both inclusions are strict.

First we consider *Hamiltonicity* of graphs, i.e. the question whether a given graph contains a closed walk that contains every vertex exactly once. This property can be expressed by the following GSO-formula:

$$\exists H (\forall x \forall y (H x y \to E x y) \wedge \forall x (\exists^{=1} y H x y \wedge \exists^{=1} y H y x) \wedge$$
$$\forall X [(\exists x X x \wedge \forall x \forall y (H x y \wedge X x \to X y)) \to \forall x X x]$$

Evaluated on a graph $G = (V, E)$ the formula says that there exists a $H \subseteq E$ with unique successors and predecessors such that (V, H) is connected. This means that G has a Hamilton cycle. As Hamiltonicity is known not to be expressible in MSO (see [47]), this shows that GSO is more expressive than MSO.

In order to prove the second part we show that GSO collapses to MSO over words. Hence, GSO is not more expressive than MSO over words, i.e., able to define exactly the regular languages. On the other hand, full second-order logic is known to capture the polynomial-time hierarchy and, hence, much stronger than MSO.

We represent words $w = w_1 \cdots w_{n-1} \in A^*$ by word structures $(\{0, \ldots, n-1\}, S, (P_a \mid a \in A))$ where $S = \{(i, i+1) \mid i < n-1\}$ and P_a is the set of positions in the word carrying the letter a, i.e., $P_a = \{i < n \mid w_i = a\}$. The predicate of maximal arity in a word structure is the successor relation, so a guarded set is either a singleton or a set $\{i, i+1\}$. As guarded n-ary relation therefore contains only n-tuples $(a_1, \ldots, a_n)$ such that $\{a_1, \ldots, a_n\} \subseteq \{i, i+1\}$ for some i and can therefore be encoded by a sequence of monadic relations. For instance a guarded n-ary relation X can be represented by $(X_u \mid u \in \{0,1\}^n)$, where for each $u = (u_0, \ldots, u_{n-1})$, $X_u := \{i < n-1 \mid (i+u_0, \ldots, i+u_{n-1}) \in X\}$. This was all we needed for our goal. □

Similarly to GSO, we now can apply this idea to the clique-guarded case.

Definition 18.21. Clique-guarded second-order logic (CliqueSO) is full second-order logic with clique-guarded semantics for the second-order quantifiers.

As in the case of GSO it should be clear that the semantic restrictions for the second-order quantifiers could also be captured purely syntactically, by admitting second-order quantifications similarly to the GSO case only of the form

$$(\exists X.\forall \bar{y}(X\bar{y} \to \text{clique}(\bar{y}))\varphi(X) \quad \text{and} \quad (\forall X.\forall \bar{y}(X\bar{y} \to \text{clique}(\bar{y}))\varphi(X).$$

The proof of Lemma 18.19 carries over immediately to the analogous result for CGF and CliqueSO. It is also not difficult to prove that CliqueSO is a proper subset of full second-order logic, for instance on words. To summarise, we have the following hierarchy of logics:

$$\text{GF} \subsetneq \text{LGF} \subsetneq \text{CGF} \subsetneq \text{FO} \subsetneq \text{MSO} \subsetneq \text{GSO} \subseteq \text{CliqueSO} \subsetneq \text{SO}.$$

We can go one step further and consider the relation between the μ-calculus and monadic second-order logic: Being able to embed the former into the latter one we can now try to do the same with μGF and GSO.

Lemma 18.22 ([74]). μGF $\subsetneq$ GSO, *i.e., we can embed the guarded fixed point logic into the guarded second order logic and. Moreover, the last one is strictly more powerful.*

Proof. First of all we consider the following restriction of the definition the guarded fixed point logic: Let us only allow least (or greatest) fixed points over variable-guarded formulae, or fixed points like $\text{LFP}_{X,\bar{x}}(\varphi(X,\bar{x}) \wedge \text{guarded}(\bar{x}))$. We refer to these as *strictly guarded fixed points*.

Claim. Any formula of μGF is logically equivalent to one in which all fixed points are strictly guarded.

So the restriction of μGF to strictly guarded fixed points does not diminish its expressive power.

Assuming the claim, we may—without loss of generality—consider μGF formulae whose fixed point applications are strictly guarded such that these fixed points are themselves guarded relations. It is clear that such fixed points are definable within GSO by means of the usual second-order characterisation of least and greatest fixed points:

$$\text{LFP}_{X,\bar{x}}(\varphi(X,\bar{x})) \iff \forall X[(\forall \bar{y}.\text{guarded}(\bar{y}))(\varphi(X,\bar{y}) \to X\bar{x})].$$

Is is also clear that GSO is strictly more powerful than μGF: For instance as GSO includes all of MSO, it is neither decidable nor invariant under guarded bisimulation.

It remains to prove the claim now. Consider a least fixed point expression of the form $\text{LFP}_{X,\bar{x}}(\varphi(X,\bar{x}))$. Inductively, we assume that all fixed points within φ are in strictly guarded form. Looking at X-atoms in $\varphi(X,\bar{x})$, we distinguish the following cases:

(i) X-atoms in the scope of guarded first-order quantification.
(ii) X-atoms in the scope of least or greatest fixed point operators.
(iii) X-atoms at quantifier-free level, $X\bar{z}$, $\bar{z} \subseteq \bar{x}$.

For occurrences of type (i) or (iii) we may replace X by its guarded part throughout the fixed point iteration. For type (ii) occurrences that are not of the type (i) this relies on the inductive assumption that fixed points within φ are strictly guarded. As far as guarded tuples are concerned, even an atom of type (iii) can evaluate to true for a guarded instantiation of $\bar{x}$ in $\varphi(\bar{x})$ only if it would also evaluate to true for the guarded part of X. Hence, inductively, we find that the guarded part $(\mathrm{LFP}_X(\varphi))^g$ of the fixed point $\mathrm{LFP}_{X,\bar{x}}(\varphi(X,\bar{x}))$ is definable as a strictly guarded fixed point:

$$(\mathrm{LFP}_X(\varphi))^g := \mathrm{LFP}_{X,\bar{x}}(\varphi(X,\bar{x}) \wedge \mathrm{guarded}(\bar{x})).$$

Let $\varphi((\mathrm{LFP}_X(\varphi))^g, X, \bar{x})$ be the result of substituting

$$\mathrm{LFP}_{X,\bar{x}}(\varphi(X,\bar{x}) \wedge \mathrm{guarded}(\bar{x}))$$

for all occurrences of X apart from those of type (iii). As $(\mathrm{LFP}_X(\varphi))^g \subseteq \mathrm{LFP}_{X,\bar{x}}(\varphi(X,\bar{x}))$ and by monotonicity, we clearly have

$$\mathrm{LFP}_{X,\bar{x}}(\varphi(X,\bar{x})) = \mathrm{LFP}_{X,\bar{x}}(\varphi((\mathrm{LFP}_X(\varphi))^g, X, \bar{x})).$$

Note that, the only remaining free occurrences of X in $\varphi((\mathrm{LFP}_X(\varphi))^g, X, \bar{x})$ are at the quantifier free level. It follows that the fixed point iteration in

$$\mathrm{LFP}_{X,\bar{x}}(\varphi((\mathrm{LFP}_X(\varphi))^g, X, \bar{x}))$$

is bounded in the sense that the fixed point is attained within an uniformly bounded finite number of iterations, since there are only finitely many quantifier free types over a vocabulary enriched by names for all the X-free constituents of $\varphi((\mathrm{LFP}_X(\varphi))^g, X, \bar{x})$ which are static for the fixed point process in question. By unravelling this finite number of iterations within GF we can conclude that $\mathrm{LFP}_{X,\bar{x}}(\varphi(X,\bar{x}))$ is GF-definable from strictly guarded fixed points. $\square$

18.6   A Criterion for Decidability

In this section we prove the general criterion for decidability that we promised earlier.

Theorem 18.23 ([67]). *Let L be a logic, C a class of structures such that the following two conditions are satisfied.*

(i) *L has the generalised tree model property on C.*
(ii) *Every sentence $\varphi \in L$ can be effectively translated to a sentence of CliqueSO that is equivalent to φ on C.*

Then *$Sat_C(L)$, the satisfiability problem for L on C, is decidable.*

The proof is based on the following powerful decidability result which can be found in [163, 185]:

Theorem 18.24 (Shelah, LeTourneau). *The monadic second-order theory of the class of all trees is decidable.*

From Chapter 12 we know that $S\omega S$ the MSO-theory of countable trees is decidable. So, we are going to reduce the given logic L to the CliqueSO-theory of trees with bounded tree width which we will further reduce to $S\omega S$ where we know that satisfiability is decidable.

Let $C_k(\tau)$ be the class of all τ-structures of tree width at most k. We are going to prove the statement by reducing, for every $k \in \mathbb{N}$, the CliqueSO-theory of $C_k(\tau)$ to the monadic second-order theory of trees.

Tree Representation of Structures

We first need to represent structures of bounded tree width by ordinary trees with a finite set of labels.

Towards this let τ be a finite relational vocabulary, and let $(T, (\mathfrak{F}(v) \,|\, v \in T))$ be a tree decomposition of width k of a τ-structure $\mathfrak{D}$ with universe D. We fix a set K of $2(k+1)$ constants and choose a function $f : D \to K$ assigning to each element d of $\mathfrak{D}$ a constant $a_d \in K$ such that the following condition is satisfied:

If v and w are adjacent nodes of T, then distinct elements of $\mathfrak{F}(v) \cup \mathfrak{F}(w)$ are always mapped to distinct constants of K.

For each constant $a \in K$, let Q_a be the set of those nodes $v \in T$ at which the constant a occurs, i.e., for which there exists an element $d \in \mathfrak{F}(v)$ such that $f(d) = a$. Further, we introduce for each m-ary relation R of $\mathfrak{D}$ a tuple $\bar{R} := (R_{\bar{a}} \,|\, \bar{a} \in K^m)$ of monadic relations on T with

$$R_a := \{ \, v \in T \mid \text{there exist } d_1, \ldots, d_m \in \mathfrak{F}(v) \text{ such that}$$
$$\mathfrak{F}(v) \models Rd_1 \cdots d_m \text{ and } f(d_1) = a_1, \ldots, f(d_m) = a_m \, \}.$$

Here, the tree $T = (V, E)$ together with the monadic relations Q_a and R_a—for $R \in \tau$—is called the *tree structure* $T(\mathfrak{D})$ *associated with* $\mathfrak{D}$ (strictly speaking, with its tree decomposition and with K and f). Note that two occurrences of a constant $a \in K$ at nodes u and v of T represent the same element of $\mathfrak{D}$ if and only if a occurs in the label of all nodes on the link between u and v. Recall, the *link* between two nodes u and v in a tree T is the smallest connected subgraph of T containing both u and v.

An arbitrary tree $T = (V, E)$ with monadic relations Q_a and $\bar{R}$ does define a tree decomposition of width k of some structure $\mathfrak{D}$, providing that the following axioms are satisfied:

(i) At each node v, at most $k + 1$ of the predicates Q_a are true.
(ii) Neighbouring nodes agree on their common elements. For all m-ary relation symbols $R \in \tau$ we have the axiom

$$\text{consistent}(\bar{R}) := \bigwedge_{\bar{a} \in K^m} \forall x \forall y ((Exy \wedge \bigwedge_{a \in \bar{a}} (Q_a x \wedge Q_a y)) \rightarrow (R_{\bar{a}} x \leftrightarrow R_{\bar{a}} y)).$$

The conjunction over all these conditions forms a first-order axiom θ over the vocabulary $\tau^* := \{E\} \cup \{Q_a \mid a \in K\} \cup \{R_{\bar{a}} \mid \bar{a} \in K^m\}$. Given a tree structure $\mathcal{T}$ with underlying tree $T = (V, E)$ and monadic predicates Q_a and $R_{\bar{a}}$ satisfying θ, we obtain a structure $\mathfrak{D}$ such that $\mathcal{T}(\mathfrak{D}) = \mathcal{T}$ as follows:

For every constant $a \in K$, we call two nodes u and w of T a-equivalent if $\mathcal{T} \models Q_a v$ for all nodes v on the link between u and w. Clearly, this is an equivalence relation on $Q_a^\mathcal{T}$. We write $[v]_a$ for an a-equivalence class of the node v. The universe of $\mathfrak{D}$ is the set of all a-equivalence classes of T for a $a \in K$, i.e., $D := \{ [v]_a \mid v \in T, a \in K, \mathcal{T} \models Q_a v \}$. For every m-ary relation symbol R in τ, we then define

$$R^{\mathfrak{D}} := \{ ([v_1]_{a_1}, \ldots, [v_m]_{a_m}) \mid \mathcal{T} \models R_{a_1 \cdots a_m} v \text{ for some}$$
$$\text{(and hence all) } v \in [v_1]_{a_1} \cap \cdots \cap [v_m]_{a_m} \}.$$

The Translation

For every formula $\varphi(x_1, \ldots, x_m) \in \text{CliqueSO}(\tau)$ and every tuple $\bar{a} = (a_1, \ldots, a_m)$ over K, we now construct a monadic second-order formula $\varphi_{\bar{a}}(\bar{z})$ of vocabulary τ^*, with one free variable. The formula $\varphi_a(z)$ describes in the associated tree structure $\mathcal{T}(\mathfrak{D})$ the same properties of guarded tuples as $\varphi(\bar{x})$ does in $\mathfrak{D}$. We will make this statement more precise below. To define this translation we exploit the fact that clique-guarded tuples in $\mathfrak{D}$ are somehow *local* in $\mathcal{T}(\mathfrak{D})$, i.e., they coexist at some node of $\mathcal{T}(\mathfrak{D})$—*cf.* Lemma 18.15.

On a directed tree $T = (V, E)$ we can express that U contains all nodes on the link between x and y by the formula

$$\text{connect}(U, x, y) := Ux \wedge Uy \wedge \exists r (Ur \wedge \forall z (Ezr \rightarrow \neg Uz)$$
$$\wedge \forall w \forall z (Ewz \wedge Uz \wedge z \neq r \rightarrow Uw)).$$

For any set $\bar{a} \subseteq K$ we can then construct a monadic second-order formula

$$\text{link}_{\bar{a}}(x, y) := \exists U (\text{connect}(U, x, y) \wedge \forall z (Uz \rightarrow \bigwedge_{a \in \bar{a}} Q_a z))$$

saying that the tuple $\bar{a}$ occurs at all nodes on the link between x and y.

Lemma 18.25. *For every tuple* $\bar{a} \in K^m$, *let*

$$\text{clique}_{\bar{a}}(z) := \bigwedge_{a, a' \in \bar{a}} \exists y (\text{link}_{a, a'}(y, z) \wedge \bigvee_{R \in \tau} \bigvee_{\bar{b}: a, a' \in \bar{b}} R_{\bar{b}} y).$$

Let v *be a node of* $\mathcal{T}(\mathfrak{D})$, *let* $\bar{d}$ *be the tuple in* $\mathfrak{F}(v)$ *with* $f(\bar{d}) = \bar{a}$. *Then*

$$\mathcal{T}(\mathfrak{D}) \models \text{clique}_{\bar{a}}(v) \quad \text{if and only if} \quad \bar{d} \text{ is clique-guarded in } \mathfrak{D}.$$

Proof. The formula $\text{clique}_{\bar{a}}(v)$ says that for any pair a, a' of components of $\bar{a}$, there is a node w such that:

- The nodes a and a' occur at all nodes on the link from v to w and hence represent the same elements d and d' at w as they do at v.
- $T(\mathfrak{D}) \models R_{\bar{b}} w$ for some predicate R and some tuple $\bar{b}$ that contains both a and a'. By induction hypothesis, this means that d and d' are components of some tuple $\bar{d}'$ such that $\mathfrak{D} \models R\bar{d}'$.

Hence $T(\mathfrak{D}) \models \text{clique}_{\bar{a}}(v)$ if and only if the tuple $\bar{d}$ induces a clique in the Gaifman graph $G(\mathfrak{D})$.   □

A clique-guarded relation $X \subseteq D^m$ consists only of local tuples. Therefore, X can be represented in the same way as the basic relations of $\mathfrak{D}$ by a tuple $\bar{X} = (X_{\bar{a}} \mid \bar{a} \in K^m)$ of monadic predicates on $T(\mathfrak{D})$. So, we define

$$\text{clique-guarded}(\bar{X}) := \text{consistent}(\bar{X}) \wedge \bigwedge_{\bar{a} \in K^m} \forall y (X_{\bar{a}} y \rightarrow \text{clique}_{\bar{a}}(y)).$$

Lemma 18.26. *For any $\mathfrak{D}$, a tuple $\bar{X} := (X_{\bar{a}} \mid \bar{a} \in K^m)$ of monadic predicates on $T(\mathfrak{D})$ encodes a clique-guarded m-ary relation on $\mathfrak{D}$ if and only if $T(\mathfrak{D}) \models \text{clique-guarded}(\bar{X})$.*

With Lemma 18.25 the proof is straightforward.

Since first-order quantification on CliqueSO can be assumed to be of the form $(\exists \bar{y}. \text{clique}(\bar{x}, \bar{y})) \eta(\bar{x}, \bar{y})$. Without loss of generality we can define the translation as follows.

(i) If $\varphi(\bar{x})$ is an atom $S x_{i_1} \cdots x_{i_m}$ (where S is either a relation symbol $R \in \tau$ or a relation variable X), then $\varphi_{\bar{a}}(z) := S_{\bar{b}} z$ where $\bar{b} := (a_{i_1}, \ldots, a_{i_m})$.
(ii) If $\varphi = (x_i = x_j)$, let $\varphi_{\bar{a}}(z) = \top$ if $a_i = a_j$ and $\varphi_{\bar{a}}(z) = \bot$ otherwise.
(iii) If $\varphi = (\eta \wedge \theta)$, let $\varphi_{\bar{a}}(z) = (\eta_{\bar{a}}(z) \wedge \theta_{\bar{a}}(z))$.
(iv) If $\varphi = \neg\theta$, let $\varphi_{\bar{a}}(z) = \neg\theta_{\bar{a}}(z)$.
(v) If $\varphi = (\exists \bar{y}. \text{clique}(\bar{x}, \bar{y})) \eta(\bar{x}, \bar{y})$, let

$$\varphi_{\bar{a}}(z) := \exists y (\eta_{\bar{a}}(y, z) \wedge \bigvee_{\bar{b}} (\bigwedge_{b \in \bar{b}} Q_b y \wedge \text{clique}_{\bar{a}\bar{b}}(y) \wedge \eta_{\bar{a}\bar{b}}(y))).$$

(vi) If $\varphi = \exists Y \theta$ for some m-ary relation variable Y, let

$$\varphi_{\bar{a}}(z) := \exists \bar{Y} (\text{clique-guarded}(\bar{Y}) \wedge \theta_{\bar{a}}(z)).$$

Here, $\bar{Y}$ is a tuple $(Y_{\bar{b}} \mid \bar{b} \in K^m)$ of set variables.

The translation takes a sentence $\varphi \in \text{CliqueSO}$ to a formula $\varphi_{\varnothing}(z)$ without introducing new constants.

The Showdown

We are now well-prepared to bring it all together using techniques from [73] with the following two theorems:

Theorem 18.27. *For each structure $\mathfrak{D} \in C_k(\tau)$, with tree representation $T(\mathfrak{D})$, and for every sentence $\varphi \in$ CliqueSO we have*

$$\mathfrak{D} \models \varphi \qquad \text{if and only if} \qquad T(\mathfrak{D}) \models \forall z \varphi_\varnothing(z).$$

Proof. By induction, we will prove a slightly more general statement.

Let $\varphi(\bar{x}, Y_1, \ldots, Y_m)$ be a formula in CliqueSO with free first- and second-order variables as displayed, with translation $\varphi_{\bar{a}}(\bar{Y}_1, \ldots, \bar{Y}_m, z)$. Let $\mathfrak{D}$ be a structure, expanded by clique-guarded relations $J_1, \ldots, J_m$ and let $T(\mathfrak{D})$ be the associated tree structure, expanded by the representations $\bar{J}_1, \ldots, \bar{J}_m$ of the relations $J_1, \ldots, J_m$.

Claim. For every node v of $T(\mathfrak{D})$ and every tuple $\bar{d} \subseteq \mathfrak{F}(v)$ with $f(\bar{d}) = \bar{a}$,

$$\mathfrak{D} \models \varphi(\bar{d}, J_1, \ldots, J_m) \qquad \text{if and only if} \qquad T(\mathfrak{D}) \models \varphi_{\bar{a}}(v, \bar{J}_1, \ldots, \bar{J}_m).$$

The only cases that need to be discussed here are first-order and second-order quantifications. If $\varphi(\bar{x}) = (\exists \bar{y}\,.\text{clique}(\bar{x}, \bar{y}))\eta(\bar{x}, \bar{y})$ and $\mathfrak{D} \models \varphi(\bar{d})$, then there exists a tuple $\bar{d}'$ such that $\mathfrak{D} \models \text{clique}(\bar{d}, \bar{d}') \wedge \eta(\bar{d}, \bar{d}')$.

By Lemma 18.15, there exists a node w of T such that all components of $\bar{d} \cup \bar{d}'$ are contained in $\mathfrak{F}(w)$. Let $f(\bar{d}') = \bar{b}$. By induction hypothesis, it follows that

$$T(\mathfrak{D}) \models \bigwedge_{b \in \bar{b}} Q_b w \wedge \text{clique}_{\bar{a}\bar{b}}(w) \wedge \eta_{\bar{a}\bar{b}}(w).$$

Let U be the set of nodes on the link between v and w. Then, the tuple $\bar{d}$ occurs in $\mathfrak{F}(u)$ for all nodes $u \in U$. It follows that $T(\mathfrak{D}) \models \text{link}_{\bar{a}}(v, w)$. Hence, $T(\mathfrak{D}) \models \varphi_{\bar{a}}(v)$.

Conversely, if $T(\mathfrak{D}) \models \varphi_{\bar{a}}(v)$, then there exists a node w such that the constants $\bar{a}$ occur at all nodes on the link between v and w (and hence correspond to the same tuple $\bar{d}$) and such that $T(\mathfrak{D}) \models \text{clique}_{\bar{a}\bar{b}}(w) \wedge \eta_{\bar{a}\bar{b}}(w)$ for some tuple $\bar{b}$. By induction hypothesis this implies that $\mathfrak{D} \models \text{clique}(\bar{d}, \bar{d}') \wedge \eta(\bar{d}, \bar{d}')$ for some tuple $\bar{d}'$, hence $\mathfrak{D} \models \varphi(\bar{d})$.

With $\varphi(\bar{x}) = \exists Y \theta$ the claim follows immediate from the induction hypothesis and from Lemma 18.26. $\qquad\qquad\square$

Theorem 18.28. *For each $k \in \mathbb{N}$, the CliqueSO-theory of C_k is decidable.*

Proof. Let φ be a sentence in CliqueSO of vocabulary τ. We translate φ into a monadic second-order sentence φ^* such that φ belongs to the CliqueSO-theory of C_k if and only if φ^* is in the monadic theory of all trees.

Fix a set K of $2k + 1$ constants and let $\bar{Q}$ be the tuple of monadic relations Q_a for $a \in K$. Further, for each m-ary relation symbol $R \in \tau$, let $\bar{R}$ be the tuple of monadic relation $R_{\bar{a}}$ where $\bar{a} \in K^m$. The desired monadic second-order sentence has the form:

$$\varphi^* := (\forall \bar{Q})(\forall \bar{R})(\,\theta \to \forall x \varphi_\varnothing(x)\,).$$

Here, θ is the first-order axiom expressing that the tree T expanded by the relations $\bar{Q}$ and $\bar{R}$ is a tree structure $\mathcal{T}(\mathfrak{D})$ associated to some τ-structure $\mathfrak{D}$. By Theorem 18.27, $\mathcal{T}(\mathfrak{D}) \models \forall x \varphi_\varnothing(x)$ if and only if $\mathfrak{D} \models \varphi$. Hence φ is true on all structures of tree width at most k if and only if φ^* is true on all trees. $\square$

Theorem 18.23 now follows immediately: Given an arbitrary sentence we test satisfiability via the tree model property by testing satisfiability of its translation into CliqueSO on trees. In this way we obtain an equivalent satifiability problem, which is decidable by Theorem 18.28.

19 Automata for Guarded Fixed Point Logics

Dietmar Berwanger and Achim Blumensath

Mathematische Grundlagen der Informatik
RWTH Aachen

19.1 Introduction

The guarded fixed point logics μGF and μCGF introduced in the previous chapter extend the guarded fragments of first-order logic GF and CGF on the one hand and the modal μ-calculus on the other hand. Thereby, the expressive power of the underlying formalisms is increased considerably. On transition systems, for instance, μGF already subsumes the μ-calculus with backwards modalities. Hence, the question arises, whether these logics are still manageable algorithmically. In this chapter we will study the complexity of their satisfiability problems.

As a consequence of the general criterion stated in Theorem 18.23, it follows that the satisfiability problems for μGF and μCGF are decidable. Yet, the argument does not allow us to derive precise complexity bounds for the decision problem. A lower bound can be obtained from the respective results for L_μ and GF. For L_μ the satisfiability problem is EXPTIME-complete [54], whereas for GF it is complete for 2EXPTIME [73]. However, if we consider formulae of bounded width, i.e., with a bounded number of variables, it becomes EXPTIME-complete as well.

Following Grädel and Walukiewicz [75, 73] we will prove that even for μCGF, the strongest logic considered, the satisfiability problem is still in 2EXPTIME in the general case, and in EXPTIME for formulae of bounded width. In other words, the fixed point extensions of guarded logics are almost for free in terms of complexity of the satisfiability problem.

Given the expressive power of these logics, this result is rather surprising. For instance, in contrast to L_μ, already the weakest guarded fixed point logic μGF lacks the finite model property. An example of a formula with only infinite models was given in the previous chapter:

$$(\exists xy.Exy) \wedge (\forall xy.Exy)(\exists z.Eyz)[\mathrm{LFP}_{Z,z}(\forall y.Eyz)Zy](z).$$

A crucial model theoretic aspect of guarded logics is their (generalised) tree model property stated in Theorem 18.16. Informally, this asserts that models of guarded formulae can be represented as trees. In [189, 71] Vardi and Grädel emphasise that the tree model property seems to be the key feature responsible for the good algorithmic behavior of modal logics because it makes them amenable to automata-theoretic techniques for solving satisfiability and model-checking problems. The generalised tree model property allows us to lift these techniques to guarded logics. In order to decide whether a given formula ψ is satisfiable one can construct two automata: the first one, called *model checking automaton*,

E. Grädel et al. (Eds.): Automata, Logics, and Infinite Games, LNCS 2500, pp. 343-355, 2002.

takes an appropriate representation of a structure as input and accepts if and only if the structure satisfies ψ; the other automaton recognises the set of all appropriate representations. Then, the formula is satisfiable iff the product of these automata recognises a non-empty language.

This scheme outlines the plan of the present chapter. First, we introduce appropriate tree representations of structures in Section 19.2 together with a suitable automata model. For a better understanding we will proceed on two tracks. On the one hand, we define the *unravelling tree* of a structure. The nodes of this tree are associated to the guarded sets of the structure, in such a way that every node has all guarded sets represented in its successors. This rich encoding allows checking of the encoded model by rather simple automata. Moreover, the underlying technique was already discussed in the previous chapter, in the proof of Theorem 18.17. On the other hand, we introduce *decomposition trees* which, being more compact representations, require more sophisticated two-way automata for model checking.

Section 19.3 is dedicated to the construction of the model checking automaton. Starting from input structures encoded as unravelling trees, we define a one-way automaton which, when viewed as a two-way automaton, still recognises the same structures, but in a different encoding, as decomposition trees. At that point, the two tracks of our exposition converge.

Finally, Section 19.4 concludes the reduction by presenting an automaton which recognises valid decomposition trees. Putting all pieces together we are able to derive the desired complexity bounds for the satisfiability problem.

19.2 Requisites

19.2.1 Clique Guarded Fixed Point Formulae

When speaking of formulae we always mean μCGF-formulae as introduced in the previous chapter. To simplify our notation we will, however, omit the clique guards, i.e., instead of $(\exists \bar{x}.\text{clique}(\bar{x}))\eta(\bar{x})$ we will write $\exists \bar{x}.\eta(\bar{x})$ and accordingly for universal formulae.

Furthermore, we will assume that all formulae are *well named* and in *negation normal form*, that is, fixed point variables are defined at most once and negation applies to atomic formulae only. Clearly, every μCGF-formula can be rewritten to meet these requirements.

A crucial parameter of a formula is its **width** which is defined as the greatest number of free variables occurring in a subformula. Equivalently, a formula has width k iff it can be transformed, by renaming of variables, so that it uses only k variables. In the following we will always assume that every formula of width k is written with the variables $\{x_0, x_1, \ldots, x_{k-1}\}$.

19.2.2 Tree Representations

In order to use tree automata for model checking and satisfiability we encode structures by trees. Recall that every subformula of a formula of width k can

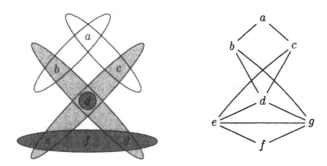

Fig. 19.1. A structure with relations of arity 1, 2, and 3 and its Gaifman graph

refer to at most k structure elements at the same time, which, moreover, have to be guarded. On account of this, we associate to a given structure $\mathfrak{A}$ a tree whose nodes are labelled by the substructures of $\mathfrak{A}$ induced by at most k guarded elements. In addition, the overlap of two adjacent nodes is stored in the label of their common edge.

Let us fix some notation for the remainder of this chapter. The set of guarded subsets of size at most k of a σ-structure $\mathfrak{A}$ is denoted by

$$\Gamma_k(\mathfrak{A}) := \{\, K \subseteq A \mid K \text{ is } k\text{-clique-guarded in } \mathfrak{A} \,\}.$$

The substructures induced by these sets are mapped onto the fixed universe $[k] = \{0, \ldots, k-1\}$ and then arranged to form a tree while keeping track of overlaps along the edges. Thus, the nodes of the resulting trees are labelled by the alphabet

$$\Sigma_k := \{\, \mathfrak{C} \mid \mathfrak{C} \text{ is a } \sigma\text{-structure over a universe } C \subseteq [k] \,\}$$

while the edges are labelled by subsets of $[k]$. We call trees labelled by these alphabets shortly **k-type trees**. When we speak about a D-edge, we mean an edge labelled with $D \subseteq [k]$, and a D-neighbour or D-successor of a node is a neighbour respectively a successor along some D-edge.

Definition 19.1. For a given width k, the **k-unravelling tree** of a structure $\mathfrak{A}$ is the k-type tree T over the set of nodes $\Gamma_k(\mathfrak{A})^*$ labelled as follows:

(i) The root of T is labelled with the empty structure $(\emptyset, \sigma)$ and all outgoing edges are labelled with $\emptyset$.

(ii) Every node $v \in \Gamma_k(\mathfrak{A})^* K$ is labelled with an isomorphic copy $\mathfrak{C}$ of $\mathfrak{A}|_K$, the restriction of $\mathfrak{A}$ to $K \in \Gamma_k(\mathfrak{A})$.

(iii) If $\pi : \mathfrak{A}|_K \to \mathfrak{C}$ and $\pi' : \mathfrak{A}|'_K \to \mathfrak{C}'$ are isomorphisms labelling, respectively, a node $v \in \Gamma_k(\mathfrak{A})^* K$ and its successor $v' = vK'$, then π and π' agree on $K \cap K'$ and the edge (v, v') is labelled with $\pi(K \cap K')$.

Remark 19.2. It is easy to see that for every D-edge (v, v') of an unravelling tree T the following conditions hold:

(i) **Consistency:** the labels $\mathfrak{C}$ of v and $\mathfrak{C}'$ of v' agree on D, that is, $\mathfrak{C}|_D = \mathfrak{C}'|_D$.

(ii) **Completeness:** for any $H \subseteq [k]$ the H-successors of v and v' agree on $D \cap H$, i.e., there is a one-to-one map assigning to each H-successor w of v an H-successor w' of v' such that the labels of w and w' agree on $D \cap H$.

Generally, we call a k-type tree **consistent**, if it satisfies the first condition. Let us now look at the relationship between a tree representation and the encoded structure.

Definition 19.3. Given a consistent k-type tree T, consider the disjoint sum of its node labels,

$$\mathfrak{D} := \bigcup \cdot \{ (\mathfrak{C}, v) \mid \mathfrak{C} \text{ is the label of } v \in T \}.$$

Let $\sim$ be the least equivalence relation on the universe of $\mathfrak{D}$ with

$$(i, v) \sim (i, v') \quad \text{if } v' \text{ is a successor of } v \text{ and } i \text{ is in the label of } (v, v').$$

Then, by consistency of T, $\sim$ is a congruence relation on $\mathfrak{D}$. We call the quotient $\mathfrak{D}/_\sim$ the structure **recovered** from T.

Definition 19.4. The k-**unravelling** $\mathfrak{A}^{(k)}$ of a structure $\mathfrak{A}$ is the structure recovered from the k-unravelling tree of $\mathfrak{A}$.

Since μCGF is invariant under guarded bisimulation (see [73]), it follows that sentences of width up to k cannot distinguish between a structure $\mathfrak{A}$ and its k-unravelling $\mathfrak{A}^{(k)}$.

Proposition 19.5. *Every structure $\mathfrak{A}$ is k-clique bisimilar to its k-unravelling $\mathfrak{A}^k$. That is, for all μCGF-sentences ψ of width at most k we have*

$$\mathfrak{A} \models \psi \quad \text{iff} \quad \mathfrak{A}^{(k)} \models \psi.$$

If we recall the notion of tree decomposition of a structure introduced in the previous chapter we can easily establish the following connection.

Proposition 19.6. *A k-type tree T is a tree decomposition of some structure $\mathfrak{A}$ iff the structure recovered from T is isomorphic to $\mathfrak{A}$.*

This relationship suggests tree decompositions as candidates for structure representations.

Definition 19.7. For a given width k, a k-**decomposition tree** of a structure $\mathfrak{A}$ is a k-type tree T where

(i) for every $K \in \Gamma_k(\mathfrak{A})$ there is a node labelled with (an copy of) $\mathfrak{A}|_K$;

(ii) the labels of any two nodes connected by a D-edge agree on D;

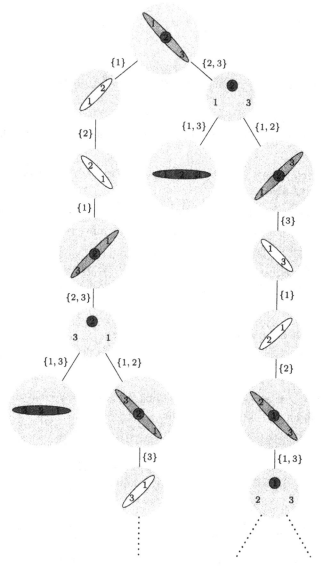

Fig. 19.2. A k-decomposition tree of the structure in Fig. 19.2.2

(iii) every node v is labelled with $\mathfrak{A}|_K$ for some $K \in \Gamma_k(\mathfrak{A})$ via an isomorphism π. Moreover, for each $K' \in \Gamma_k(\mathfrak{A})$ there is a node v' labelled with $\mathfrak{A}|_{K'}$, such that all edges on the path between v and v' include $\pi(K \cap K')$ in their labels.

Remark 19.8.   (i) The k-unravelling tree of a structure is also a k-decomposition tree of that structure.

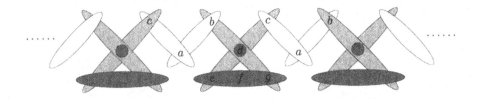

Fig. 19.3. The structure recovered from the decomposition tree in Fig. 19.2.2

(ii) Each k-decomposition tree of a structure $\mathfrak{A}$ induces a subtree in the k-unravelling tree of $\mathfrak{A}$.

It is an easy exercise to show that the process of k-decomposing a structure preserves its properties up to bisimulation, yielding a more compact representation than unravelling does.

Proposition 19.9. *Given a structure $\mathfrak{A}$, let $\mathfrak{A}'$ be the structure recovered from a k-decomposition tree of $\mathfrak{A}$. Then $\mathfrak{A}$ and $\mathfrak{A}'$ are clique-k-bisimilar.*

19.2.3 The Automata Model

We employ alternating automata that work on trees where nodes and edges are labelled.

Definition 19.10. An **alternating tree automaton** over a node alphabet Σ and an edge alphabet Δ is given by a tuple

$$\mathcal{A} = (Q, \Sigma, \Delta, \delta, q_{\mathrm{I}}, \Omega)$$

where $Q = Q_0 \cup Q_1$ is the set of universal and existential states, q_{I} designates the initial state, $\Omega : Q \to \omega$ is a parity condition and

$$\delta : Q \times \Sigma \to \mathscr{P}(\Delta \times Q)$$

is the transition function. The pairs $(d, q) \in \Delta \times Q$ are called transitions.

We define the behaviour of such automata by way of games.

Definition 19.11. Let $\mathcal{A} = (Q, \Sigma, \Delta, \delta, q_{\mathrm{I}}, \Omega)$ be an automaton and T an appropriately labelled tree. The game $\mathcal{G}(\mathcal{A}, T)$ associated to $\mathcal{A}$ and T is the parity game with positions $Q \times T$ and acceptance condition Ω played as follows.

Every play starts in state q_{I} at the root of T. Assume that the play reached some position (q, v) where the node v is labelled with c. If q belongs to Q_0, Player 0 can move to a position (q', v') if

(i) there is a transition $(d, q') \in \delta(q, c)$ and
(ii) v' is a d-successor of v.

The moves of Player 1 are defined analogously.

The language $L(\mathcal{A})$ accepted by a tree automaton $\mathcal{A}$ is the set of all trees T, such that Player 0 has a winning strategy in the game $\mathcal{G}(\mathcal{A}, T)$.

Usually, automata are defined as devices scanning their input only in one direction. However, for our purpose it is convenient to allow them to move backwards and remain still as well.

Definition 19.12. An **alternating two-way tree automaton** is given in the same way as a (one-way) alternating automaton,

$$\mathcal{A}^2 = (Q, \Sigma, \Delta, \delta, q_{\mathrm{I}}, \Omega)$$

where acceptance is defined in a different way. The game $\mathcal{G}(\mathcal{A}^2, T)$ associated to a two-way automaton $\mathcal{A}^2$ and a tree T is the parity game obtained as in Definition 19.11, but replacing rule (2) with

(ii') either $v' = v$ or v' is a d-neighbour of v.

The language $L(\mathcal{A}^2)$ accepted by a two-way tree automaton $\mathcal{A}^2$ is the set of all trees T such that Player 0 has a winning strategy in the game $\mathcal{G}(\mathcal{A}^2, T)$.

19.3 Model Checking

The results presented in Chapter 14 and 10 reveal a close relationship between alternating automata and games on the one side, and logical formalisms on the other side. The automaton constructed in Section 10.3 for L_μ translates first-order operations into state transitions, while fixed point predicates are encoded as priorities.

In a similar way, we will construct automata for μCGF. But unlike L_μ, where a formula is evaluated at a single node of a transition system, a μCGF-formula with several free variables may involve several structure elements. Since these elements have to be clique-guarded, they appear together in the label of some node in the unravelling (or, decomposition) tree. To allow our automaton to access the structure in the node labels of the input tree, its states will contain two components: a subformula, and an assignment of the variables appearing free therein.

The *closure* $\mathrm{cl}(\psi)$ of a formula ψ is the set consisting of all subformulae of ψ together with the formulae true and false.

Definition 19.13. To any formula $\psi \in \mu$CGF of width k we associate the automaton $\mathcal{A}_\psi = (Q, \Sigma_k, \mathscr{P}([k]), \delta, q_{\mathrm{I}}, \Omega)$ over k-type trees where the state set

$$Q := \{ (\varphi, \beta) \mid \varphi \in \mathrm{cl}(\psi) \text{ and } \beta : \{x_0 \ldots x_{k-1}\} \to [k] \}$$

is partitioned into existential and universal states by

$$Q_0 := \{ (\varphi, \beta) \mid \varphi = \text{false, or } \varphi = \eta \vee \vartheta, \text{ or } \varphi = \exists \bar{y}.\eta \}, \text{ and}$$
$$Q_1 := Q \setminus Q_0.$$

The initial state is $q_{\mathrm{I}} = (\psi, \emptyset)$ where $\emptyset$ stands for the void assignment.

It remains to specify the transition function. To simplify our notation we use expressions $\langle H \rangle S$ with $H \subseteq [k]$ and $S \subseteq Q$ to denote the set of transitions $\{ D \subseteq [k] \mid H \subseteq D \} \times S$. In particular, when we refer to the universe of $\mathfrak{C}$ we write $\langle \cdot \rangle S$ instead of $\langle C \rangle S$. Furthermore, omitting parenthesis, we simply write $\delta(\varphi, \beta, \mathfrak{C})$ instead of $\delta((\varphi, \beta), \mathfrak{C})$.

(i) If $\varphi =$ true or $\varphi =$ false then $\delta(\varphi, \beta, \mathfrak{C}) = \emptyset$.

(ii) If φ is a σ-atom or a negated σ-atom then

$$\delta(\varphi, \beta, \mathfrak{C}) = \begin{cases} \langle \cdot \rangle \{(\text{true}, \emptyset)\} & \text{if } \mathfrak{C}, \beta \models \varphi, \\ \langle \cdot \rangle \{(\text{false}, \emptyset)\} & \text{if } \mathfrak{C}, \beta \not\models \varphi. \end{cases}$$

(iii) If $\varphi = \eta \wedge \vartheta$ or $\varphi = \eta \vee \vartheta$ then

$$\delta(\varphi, \beta, \mathfrak{C}) = \langle \cdot \rangle \{(\eta, \beta), (\vartheta, \beta)\}.$$

(iv) If $\varphi(\bar{x}) = \mathrm{FP}_{T\bar{y}}(\eta)(\bar{x})$ then

$$\delta(\varphi, \beta, \mathfrak{C}) = \langle \cdot \rangle \{(\eta, \beta)\}.$$

(v) If $\varphi(\bar{x}) = T\bar{x}$ and $\mathrm{FP}_{T\bar{y}}(\eta)(\bar{x})$ it the unique definition of T in ψ then

$$\delta(\varphi, \beta, \mathfrak{C}) = \langle \cdot \rangle \{(\eta, \beta)\}.$$

(vi) If $\varphi(\bar{x}) = \exists \bar{y}.\eta(\bar{x}, \bar{y})$ or $\varphi(x) = \forall \bar{y}.\eta(\bar{x}, \bar{y})$ then

$$\delta(\varphi, \beta, \mathfrak{C}) = \langle \cdot \rangle \{ (\eta, \beta') \mid \beta'|_{\bar{x}} = \beta|_{\bar{x}} \} \cup \langle \beta(\bar{x}) \rangle \{(\varphi, \beta)\}.$$

Finally, if the fixed point variables of ψ occur in the order $Z_1, \ldots, Z_n$ the parity condition is given by

$$\Omega(\varphi, \beta) := \begin{cases} 2i & \varphi = Z_i \bar{x} \text{ and } Z_i \text{ is a GFP-variable,} \\ 2i + 1 & \varphi = Z_i \bar{x} \text{ and } Z_i \text{ is an LFP-variable,} \\ 2n + 4 & \varphi = \forall \bar{y}.\eta, \\ 2n + 3 & \varphi = \exists \bar{y}.\eta, \\ 2n + 2 & \text{otherwise.} \end{cases}$$

The automaton works in a similar way as the L_μ-automata defined in Section 10.3: disjunctions are decomposed by Player 0, conjunctions by Player 1 and fixed points are regenerated. Atomic statements are verified locally and terminate the run. Acceptance of infinite runs is determined by the priority function which reflects the nesting and type of fixed point definitions. Note that, except when dealing with quantifiers, the automaton changes only the formula component of its states, while the variable assignment remains the same. Moreover, the $\langle \cdot \rangle$-transitions allow to move only to successors that retain the structure information of the current node.

To understand the handling of quantification, consider, e.g., an existential formula $\varphi(\bar{x}) = \exists \bar{y}.\eta(\bar{x}, \bar{y})$. Player 0 may use a transition from $\langle \beta(\bar{x}) \rangle \{(\varphi, \beta)\}$

to proceed to a successor that retains the structure living on elements currently assigned to the free variables $\bar{x}$. In this way, he can reassign the quantified variables $\bar{y}$ to elements of the chosen successor. After such a move, the formula in the new state is still φ and Player 0 is again in turn to move. But, as existential formulae have odd priority, he can reiterate these moves only finitely many times and must then take a transition of the form $\langle\cdot\rangle\{(\eta,\beta')\mid\beta'|_{\bar{x}}=\beta|_{\bar{x}}\}$.

Given an input tree that k-unravels a structure $\mathfrak{A}$, the structures labelling the nodes are all induced by k-cliques in $\mathfrak{A}$. Moreover, from each node (a copy of) every other k-clique of $\mathfrak{A}$ is accessible within one move.

It remains to prove that our construction is correct, that is, that we can use the automaton defined above to solve the model checking problem for μCGF.

Proposition 19.14. *Given a formula ψ of width k and a structure $\mathfrak{A}$, the automaton $\mathcal{A}_\psi$ accepts the k-unravelling tree of $\mathfrak{A}$ iff $\mathfrak{A}\models\psi$.*

Proof. It is convenient to argue in terms of games. Model checking games for μCGF were introduced in [11] as a generalisation of the model checking games for L_μ. Although defined for finite structures, the extension of these games to the transfinite case is straightforward.

Let T be the k-unravelling tree of the structure $\mathfrak{A}$. We will show that the game which determines acceptance of T by the automaton $\mathcal{A}_\psi$ is essentially the model checking game associated to $\mathfrak{A}$ and ψ.

Let $\mathcal{G}$ be the acceptance game $\mathcal{G}(\mathcal{A}_\psi, T)$. We can simplify this game by collapsing positions which share the same formula and map its free variables to the same part of the structure.

Recall that any node v of T is labelled via some isomorphism π. Furthermore, at every position (φ,β,v) in a play of $\mathcal{G}$, the image of π includes the image of the assignment β. Thus, we can define a mapping from the positions of $\mathcal{G}$ to $\{(\varphi,\chi)\mid\varphi\in\mathrm{cl}(\psi)$ and $\chi:\{x_0\ldots x_{k-1}\}\to A\}$ as follows:

$$\hat{\cdot}:(\varphi,\beta,v)\mapsto(\varphi,\pi^{-1}\circ\beta).$$

By the construction of $\mathcal{G}$, we can easily verify that this mapping induces a congruence relation $\hat{\approx}$ among the positions of $\mathcal{G}$,

$$(\varphi,\beta,v)\hat{\approx}(\varphi,\beta,v')\quad\text{iff}\quad\widehat{(\varphi,\beta,v)}=\widehat{(\varphi,\beta,v')},$$

which is also a bisimulation on $\mathcal{G}$.

Consider now the (strong homomorphic) image $\hat{\mathcal{G}}$ of $\mathcal{G}$ under $\hat{\cdot}$. On the one hand, $\mathcal{G}$ and $\hat{\mathcal{G}}$ are bisimilar via $\hat{\cdot}$ and, consequently, the same player has a winning strategy in both plays. On the other hand, $\hat{\mathcal{G}}$ is almost the model checking game $\mathcal{G}'=\mathcal{G}(\mathfrak{A},\psi)$ as defined in [11]. The only difference arises at positions (φ,χ) where φ is an existential or universal formula, say $\varphi=\exists\bar{y}\eta(\bar{x},\bar{y})$. Then, the model checking game allows moves to (η,χ') with χ' such that

(i) χ and χ' agree on the values of $\bar{x}$ and
(ii) $\mathfrak{A},\chi'\models\mathrm{clique}(\bar{x},\bar{y})$,

whereas in $\hat{\mathcal{G}}$ the legal moves go either to (φ,χ') with χ' as above, or to (η,χ).

Nevertheless, we will show that the same player wins both $\mathcal{G}'$ and $\widehat{\mathcal{G}}$. If Player 0 has a winning strategy in the model checking game $\mathcal{G}'$, he can also play this strategy in $\widehat{\mathcal{G}}$, as long as no existential formula is met. Otherwise, at positions (φ, χ) as above, he can imitate the move to the position (η, χ') he would perform in $\mathcal{G}'$ by taking two steps:

(i) move to (φ, χ'); this is possible since, for every χ' agreeing with χ on the free variables of φ, the position (φ, χ') is reachable from (φ, χ) in one step.
(ii) At (φ, χ') it's still Player 0 turn: move to (η, χ').

Towards a contradiction, let us assume that Player 1 wins this play. Then, after any universal formula $\varphi = \forall \bar{y} \eta(\bar{x}, \bar{y})$ occurring in the play, there can follow only finitely many positions with φ until Player 1 chooses some position (η, χ'); otherwise he would lose with the highest even priority. But then, Player 1 also wins by choosing (φ, χ') right from position (φ, χ) and proceeding with (η, χ'). However, these two moves translate into one move in the corresponding play of $\mathcal{G}'$ which leads Player 1 to a win in $\mathcal{G}$ despite Player 0's winning strategy, which is not possible. This concludes our proof that a player has a winning strategy in the model checking game iff he has one in the acceptance game.

The correctness of our construction relies on the fact that the input trees are complete in the sense of Remark 19.2 (ii). That is, if the current node is labelled by a k-clique of the represented structure, then every other k-clique appears in the label of some successor node. Unfortunately, it is very hard to check whether a given tree satisfies this property. By letting $\mathcal{A}_\psi$ run as a two-way automaton $\mathcal{A}_\psi^2$, we can relax this requirement and claim instead that every k-clique shall be reachable via a finite path from the current node.

Proposition 19.15. *Given a formula ψ of width k and a structure $\mathfrak{A}$, let T be a k-decomposition tree of $\mathfrak{A}$. Then the automaton $\mathcal{A}_\psi^2$ accepts T iff $\mathfrak{A} \models \psi$.*

Proof. The idea is to show that $\mathcal{A}_\psi^2$ runs on T in a similar way as its one-way variant does on the k-unravelling tree T' of $\mathfrak{A}$. Towards this we will transform the acceptance game $\mathcal{G}(\mathcal{A}_\psi^2, T)$ by introducing shortcuts into a game which is bisimilar to the acceptance game $\mathcal{G}(\mathcal{A}, T')$ of the one-way automaton.

Let $\mathcal{G}^*$ be the least game extending $\mathcal{G} := \mathcal{G}(\mathcal{A}_\psi^2, T)$ by new transitions in such a way that, whenever there are two transitions

$$(\varphi, \beta, v) \to (\varphi, \beta, v') \to (\varphi, \beta, v'')$$

in $\mathcal{G}^*$, the shortcut $(\varphi, \beta, v) \to (\varphi, \beta, v'')$ is also a transition in $\mathcal{G}^*$.

Observe that the new transitions just shortcut a sequence of steps in the original game, all performed by the same player. To see that this does not change the winning partitions, assume, towards a contradiction, that Player 1 has a winning strategy for $\mathcal{G}^*$ while Player 0 has one for $\mathcal{G}$. All moves in $\mathcal{G}$ are still available in $\mathcal{G}^*$, so Player 0 can apply his winning strategy for $\mathcal{G}$ in the play π of $\mathcal{G}^*$ against the winning strategy of Player 1. Let us now look at the play in $\mathcal{G}$ in which both players move like in π except at positions (φ, β, v) where

Player 1 used a shortcut to, say (φ, β, v'), for φ a universal formula. At that point, Player 1 can move step by step via finitely many positions (φ, β, w) along the path leading to the destination of the shortcut. From there, the play proceeds like in π. Clearly, Player 1 wins this play in $\mathcal{G}$ in contradiction to our assumption on Player 0's winning strategy.

The mapping $\widehat{}$ which was defined in the proof of Proposition 19.14 can be applied to the positions of $\mathcal{G}^*$. It induces a congruence relation on $\mathcal{G}^*$ and, as such, a bisimulation between $\mathcal{G}^*$ and its strong homomorphic image $\widehat{\mathcal{G}}^*$. This image is precisely the game $\widehat{\mathcal{G}}(\mathfrak{A}_\psi, T')$ which is bisimilar to $\mathcal{G}(\mathfrak{A}_\psi, T')$.

Accordingly, the automaton $\mathcal{A}_\psi^2$ accepts the k-decomposition tree T iff $\mathcal{A}_\psi$ accepts the k-unravelling tree T'.

19.4 Satisfiability

The model checking automata introduced above operate correctly on inputs which represent structures. But in order to solve the satisfiability problem this does not suffice. We need to make sure that all inputs which do not represent structures are rejected.

Checking representation validity. From a given a k-type tree T, we can recover a structure according to Definition 19.3, only if T is consistent, that is, if every node agrees with its D-neighbours on the D-part of its label.

Provided T is consistent, let $\mathfrak{A}$ be the recovered structure. Now T is a k-decomposition tree of $\mathfrak{A}$ iff every node label of T induces a clique in $\mathfrak{A}$. This is crucial, since the model-checking automaton assumes that all elements appearing in the label of its input represent clique-guarded elements of the structure. Another way to formulate this condition is: For every node v and every pair of elements $\{i, j\} \subseteq [k]$ in its label, there is a node v' in which i and j are guarded by an atom and all edges on the path between v and v' include $\{i, j\}$ in their labels.

Now, we build an automaton that checks the above two conditions.

Definition 19.16. For every width k, we construct a two-way automaton $\mathcal{A}_k^2 = (Q, \Sigma_k, \mathscr{P}([k]), \delta, \text{check}, \Omega)$ over k-type trees whose set of states is partitioned into

$$Q_0 = \{\text{false}\} \cup [k]^2 \quad \text{and}$$
$$Q_1 = \{\text{true}, \text{check}\} \cup \{ R\bar{a} \mid R \in \sigma,\ \bar{a} \subseteq [k] \}.$$

In state check the automaton allows Player 1 to move freely on the input tree to reach a node where either the consistency or the guardedness condition may be violated. At that event, state $R\bar{a}$ records the loss of the atom $R\bar{a}$ along an edge that preserves $\bar{a}$ while the states $(i, j) \in [k]^2$ indicate the search for witnesses to the guardedness of i and j. The transitions are as follows.

$$\delta(\text{check}, \mathfrak{C}) = \langle \emptyset \rangle \{\text{check}\} \cup \bigcup \{ \langle \bar{a} \rangle \{R\bar{a}\} \mid \mathfrak{C} \models R\bar{a} \}$$
$$\cup \langle \cdot \rangle \{ (i, j) \mid \mathfrak{C} \not\models \text{clique}(i, j) \}.$$

At a node where the elements i and j are not guarded, Player 1 can challenge his opponent to find a node where $\{i,j\}$ appear guarded, along a path where these elements persist in the edge labels.

$$\delta((i,j),\mathfrak{C}) = \begin{cases} \langle\cdot\rangle\{\text{true}\} & \mathfrak{C} \models \text{clique}(i,j), \\ \langle\{i,j\}\rangle\{(i,j)\} & \text{otherwise.} \end{cases}$$

Also, Player 1 may pick a currently valid atomic fact to check whether it is indeed preserved along the edges that contain all involved elements in their label.

$$\delta(R\bar{a},\mathfrak{C}) = \begin{cases} \langle\cdot\rangle\{\text{true}\} & \mathfrak{C} \models R\bar{a}, \\ \langle\cdot\rangle\{\text{false}\} & \text{otherwise.} \end{cases}$$

If the player agree on a local test, the run is finite: $\delta(\text{true}) = \delta(\text{false}) = \emptyset$.

On an infinite run, the automaton assumes forever either the state check or some state (i,j). Since in the first case Player 0 should win, we set $\Omega(\text{check}) = 0$. In the second case, instead, Player 0 should lose, because he does not provide a witness to the guardedness of i and j after a finite number of steps. To enforce that, we set $\Omega((i,j)) = 1$ for all $(i,j) \in [k]^2$.

It is easy to see that the above checks ensure the consistency and the guardedness of the input tree.

Lemma 19.17. *The automaton $\mathcal{A}_k^2$ recognises the set of k-decomposition trees of all σ-structures.*

Reduction to the emptiness problem. After having constructed an automaton $\mathcal{A}_\psi^2$ for the model checking of a tree representation and an automaton $\mathcal{A}_k^2$ to check the validity of the input tree, we can build the product automaton $\mathcal{B}_\psi^2 := \mathcal{A}_\psi^2 \times \mathcal{A}_k^2$ which recognises precisely the set of k-decomposition trees of all models of ψ. In this way, the satisfiability problem for ψ is reduced to the emptiness problem for $\mathcal{B}_\psi^2$.

Proposition 19.18. *A μCGF formula ψ is satisfiable iff $L(\mathcal{B}_\psi) \neq \emptyset$.*

Emptiness of two-way automata. In order to establish the complexity of the emptiness problem for our automata model we will reduce it to the two-way automata introduced by Vardi [190] defined for input trees of bounded branching degree.

Lemma 19.19. *Any two-way automaton recognising a non-empty language, accepts some tree whose degree is bounded by the size of its state set.*

Proof. Let $\mathcal{A}^2$ be a two-way automaton accepting some input tree T. Hence, Player 0 has a winning strategy in the parity game $\mathcal{G}(\mathcal{A}^2, T)$ and, by [55, 132], even a memoryless one: $f : Q_0 \times T \to Q \times T$. For any node $v \in T$, let $S(v)$ be the set of nodes targeted by f at some position with v:

$$S(v) := \{ v' \in T \mid f(q,v) \in Q \times \{v'\} \text{ for some } q \in Q_0 \}.$$

Consider now the tree T' obtained from T by discarding at every node v those successors which are not in $S(v)$. Since $|S(v)| \leq |Q_0|$, this yields a tree of branching degree bounded by $|Q_0| \leq |Q|$. Moreover, f is still a winning strategy in $\mathcal{G}(\mathcal{A}^2, T')$. In other words, the automaton $\mathcal{A}^2$ also accepts T'.

19.5   Complexity

Since Vardi's automata work on trees with unlabelled edges, we have to remove the edge labels and place them into their target node. Then, our automaton has to verify the validity of taken transitions, thus, requiring a blow-up of its state set by the size of the edge alphabet. Taking into account this modification, we can transfer the complexity of the emptiness test of Vardi's automata to our model.

Theorem 19.20. *The emptiness of a two-way alternating automaton with s states and t edge symbols can be decided in time $2^{O((st)^2)}$.*

For the computations in the remainder of this chapter, let us fix a formula ψ of size n and width k. Note that, the number of states of the automata $\mathcal{A}^2_\psi$ and $\mathcal{A}^2_k$ is bounded by $O(n \cdot k^k)$. Accordingly, their product $\mathcal{B}^2_\psi$ has at most $O(n^2 k^{2k})$ states. From Lemma 19.19 we can now infer a stronger variant of the tree model property for μCGF.

Proposition 19.21. *Any satisfiable μCGF-formula of width k has a model with a tree decomposition of width at most $k - 1$ and branching degree bounded by $O(n^2 k^{2k})$.*

By Theorem 19.20, the reduction of the satisfiability problem for ψ to the emptiness of $\mathcal{B}^2_\psi$ yields the following complexity bounds:

$$2^{O((n \cdot k^k)^4)} = 2^{O(n^4 2^{4k \log k})} = 2^{2^{O(n)}}.$$

When k is bounded by a constant, the above expression boils down to $2^{O(n^4)}$.

Since the complexity results on CGF quoted in the introduction of this chapter imply hardness of this bounds, we can state:

Theorem 19.22. *The satisfiability problem for μCGF is 2EXPTIME-complete in the general case. For clique guarded fixed point sentences of bounded width it is EXPTIME-complete.*

Notes on Part VIII

Guarded logics, and in particular the guarded fragment GF of first-order logic, were introduced by Andréka, van Benthem, and Németi [4]. They proved that the satisfiability problem for GF is decidable, introduced the notion of guarded bisimulation, and investigated the model-theoretic properties of GF. They also stated, without proof, that GF has the finite model property. Complexity results and a proof of the finite model property of GF were given by Grädel [71]. He also established the tree model property of GF.

The results in [4, 71] led to a systematic study of guarded logics generalising GF in several directions. On the one side, different notions of guarded quantification were investigated, leading to loosely guarded logics [8], action guarded logics [9, 67, 82], packed logics [120], and clique guarded logics [70, 73]. On the other side, guarded variants of more powerful logics than first-order logic have been studied, in particular guarded fixed point logics [75] and guarded second-order logic (GSO) [74].

Grädel and Walukiewicz [75] proved that guarded fixed point logic is decidable and determined its complexity (see Chapter 18 for a model-theoretic decidability proof and Chapter 19 for an automata based decision procedure giving optimal complexity bounds).

Recall from Chapter 14 that the Janin-Walukiewicz Theorem characterises the modal μ-calculus as the bisimulation-invariant fragment of monadic second-order logic. Grädel, Hirsch, and Otto [74] lifted this characterisation theorem to the world of guarded logics, showing that guarded fixed point logic μGF is semantically equivalent to the guarded bisimulation invariant fragment of GSO.

Further information on algorithmic and model-theoretic issues of guarded logics (decision procedures, games, model checking problems, automata, characterisation theorems, finite model property, tree model property, interpolation, etc.) can be found in [11, 65, 67, 69, 68, 71, 72, 73, 74, 75, 82, 84, 86, 141].

Part IX

Appendices

20 Some Fixed Point Basics

Carsten Fritz

Institut für Informatik und Praktische Mathematik
Christian-Albrechts-Universität zu Kiel

This chapter is intended to give the reader a brief overview of some basic notations and theorems regarding fixed points of monotone functions on complete lattices. The main results stated and proved here are the Knaster-Tarski Theorem [175] (Theorem 20.4), and Theorem 20.12 on the characterization of simultaneous fixed points. That is, this chapter provides proofs and some additional insights to propositions introduced in Chapter 10.

Therefore, our main interest is the μ-calculus dealing with fixed points of monotone functions on the complete lattice of subsets of the states of a Kripke structure. Consequently, power set lattices will be our main models of complete lattices, but our approach will be somewhat more general.

20.1 Preliminaries

We fix a **complete lattice** $\mathfrak{L} = (L, \leq, \top, \bot)$, i.e.

(1) L is a non-empty set,
(2) $\leq$ is a partial order on L such that every subset $M \subseteq L$ has a supremum and an infimum,
(3) $\top, \bot \in L$ are the greatest and least elements, respectively, of L, i.e., for every $x \in L$, $\bot \leq x \leq \top$ holds.

Note that $\inf \emptyset = \top$, $\sup \emptyset = \bot$. Our main instance of a complete lattice is the **power set lattice** $(\mathscr{P}(A), \subseteq, A, \emptyset)$ of an arbitrary set A. For a subset $M \subseteq \mathscr{P}(A)$, we have $\inf M = \bigcap M$, $\sup M = \bigcup M$.

Let On be the class of ordinals. For a cardinal c, let c^+ be the least ordinal such that $|c^+| > c$.

Definition 20.1. Let $f : L \to L$ be a function.

(1) $x \in L$ is a **fixed point** of f iff $f(x) = x$.
(2) x is the **least (greatest) fixed point** of f iff x is a fixed point of f and $x \leq y$ ($y \leq x$) holds for all fixed points y of f.
(3) f is **monotone** iff for all $x, y \in L$, $x \leq y$ implies $f(x) \leq f(y)$.
(4) f is **inflationary** iff $x \leq f(x)$ holds for all $x \in L$.
(5) We inductively define a sequence $(f^\alpha)_{\alpha \in \mathrm{On}}$ of elements $f^\alpha \in L$ by

$$f^0 := \bot,$$
$$f^{\alpha+1} := f(f^\alpha),$$
$$f^\lambda := \sup_{\alpha < \lambda} f^\alpha \qquad \text{for limit ordinals } \lambda.$$

(6) f is **inductive** iff $f^\beta \leq f^\alpha$ holds for all $\alpha, \beta \in \mathrm{On}, \beta < \alpha$.

E. Grädel et al. (Eds.): Automata, Logics, and Infinite Games, LNCS 2500, pp. 359–364, 2002.
© Springer-Verlag Berlin Heidelberg 2002

The following lemma connects these notions.

Lemma 20.2.   (i) *If f is monotone or inflationary, it also is inductive.*
(ii) *If f is inductive, there is an inflationary function $g : L \to L$ such that $g^\alpha = f^\alpha$ for all $\alpha \in \mathrm{On}$.*
(iii) *If f is inductive, there is an $\alpha \in \mathrm{On}$ such that $|\alpha| \le |L|$ and $f^{\alpha+1} = f^\alpha$ (i.e., f^α is a fixed point of f). If $\mathcal{L}$ is the power set lattice of a set A, there is an $\alpha \in \mathrm{On}$ such that f^α is a fixed point of f and $|\alpha| \le |A|$.*

Proof.   (i) First, let f be monotone. To show that f is inductive, we use induction on α:
($\alpha = 0$): Trivial.
($\alpha \to \alpha + 1$): Using the monotonicity of f and the induction hypothesis, we have $f^{\alpha+1} = f(f^\alpha) \ge f(f^\beta) = f^{\beta+1}$ for all $\beta < \alpha$. Thus $f^\beta \le f^{\alpha+1}$ for all $\beta < \alpha + 1$.
(α a limit ordinal): Immediately by the definition of f^α.
The proof for inflationary f is trivial.
(ii) Let f be inductive and define $g : L \to L, x \mapsto \sup\{x, f(x)\}$. Obviously, g is inflationary. By induction, we show $\forall \alpha \in \mathrm{On}(g^\alpha = f^\alpha)$:
($\alpha = 0$): $g^0 = \bot = f^0$
($\alpha \to \alpha + 1$): The induction hypothesis yields $g^{\alpha+1} = g(g^\alpha) = g(f^\alpha) = \sup\{f^\alpha, f(f^\alpha)\}$. Since f is inductive, $\sup\{f^\alpha, f(f^\alpha)\} = f^{\alpha+1}$.
(α a limit ordinal): By induction hypothesis, $g^\alpha = \sup_{\beta<\alpha} g^\beta = \sup_{\beta<\alpha} f^\beta = f^\alpha$.
(iii) Assume that there is no such α. Then, for every $\alpha < \beta < |L|^+$, $f^\alpha \ne f^\beta$. That is, the set $\{ f^\alpha \in L \mid \alpha < |L|^+ \} \subseteq L$ has cardinality $\||L|^+| > |L|$. Contradiction. If $\mathcal{L}$ is the power set lattice of a set A, there is an $x_\alpha \in f^{\alpha+1} \setminus f^\alpha$ for every $\alpha < |A|^+$. Thus $X := \{ x_\alpha \mid \alpha < |A|^+ \}$ is a subset of A, but $|X| = \||A|^+| > |A|$. Contradiction.

Definition 20.3. The least $\alpha \in \mathrm{On}$ such that $f^{\alpha+1} = f^\alpha$ is the **closure ordinal** of f. Notation: $\mathrm{cl}(f)$. For monotone f, we define $f^! := f^{\mathrm{cl}(f)}$.

20.2   Least and Greatest Fixed Points

The Knaster-Tarski Theorem [175] asserts the existence of a least and a greatest fixed point of any monotone function on a complete lattice. More precisely, these fixed points are the infimum and supremum, respectively, of certain subsets of the complete lattice and can be generated inductively.

Theorem 20.4 (Knaster and Tarski). *Let $f : L \to L$ be monotone. Then there is a least fixed point $\mathrm{LFP}(f)$ and a greatest fixed point $\mathrm{GFP}(f)$ of f. These are*

$$\mathrm{LFP}(f) = \inf\{ x \in L \mid f(x) \le x \}$$
$$\mathrm{GFP}(f) = \sup\{ x \in L \mid x \le f(x) \}.$$

Proof. Let $\varPhi := \{\, x \in L \mid f(x) \le x \,\}$ and $y := \inf \varPhi$. We first show that y is a fixed point of f.

$(f(y) \le y)$: For all $x \in \varPhi$, $y \le x$ holds. Since f is monotone, we have (using the definition of $\varPhi$) $\forall x \in \varPhi (f(y) \le f(x) \le x)$. Thus $f(y) \le \inf \varPhi = y$.

$(y \le f(y))$: Using $f(y) \le y$ and the monotonicity of f, we have $f(f(y)) \le f(y)$, i.e., $f(y) \in \varPhi$. Thus $y = \inf \varPhi \le f(y)$.

This shows that y is a fixed point of f. Since y is the infimum of $\varPhi$, in particular $y \le x$ holds for all $x \in L$ such that $f(x) = x$. Thus y is the least fixed point of f.

The proof for the greatest fixed point is similar.

Now we show that the least fixed point of a monotone $f : L \to L$ is contained in the sequence $(f^{\alpha})_{\alpha \in \mathrm{On}}$ and can thus be computed inductively.

Lemma 20.5. *Let* $f : L \to L$ *be a monotone function. Then* $\mathrm{LFP}(f) = f^{!}$.

Proof. Again, let $\varPhi := \{\, x \in L \mid f(x) \le x \,\}$. By definition, $f^{!}$ is a fixed point, thus $\mathrm{LFP}(f) \le f^{!}$. To show the reverse, it suffices to establish

$$\forall \alpha \in \mathrm{On}, x \in \varPhi (f^{\alpha} \le x),$$

using induction on α.

$(\alpha = 0)$: $f^{0} = \bot \le x$ for all $x \in L$.

$(\alpha \to \alpha + 1)$: Let $x \in \varPhi$. By induction hypothesis, $f^{\alpha} \le x$. Thus we have $f^{\alpha+1} = f(f^{\alpha}) \le f(x) \le x$, using the monotonicity of f.

$(\alpha$ a limit ordinal$)$: By induction hypothesis, $f^{\beta} \le x$ holds for all $\beta < \alpha$, $x \in \varPhi$, which implies $f^{\alpha} = \sup_{\beta < \alpha} f^{\beta} \le x$.

To generate the greatest fixed point in the same fashion, we introduce a dual sequence $(f^{*\alpha})_{\alpha \in \mathrm{On}}$.

Definition 20.6. *For a function* $f : L \to L$, *the sequence* $(f^{*\alpha})_{\alpha \in \mathrm{On}}$ *of elements* $f^{*\alpha} \in L$ *is defined inductively as follows:*

$$f^{*0} = \top$$
$$f^{*(\alpha+1)} = f(f^{*\alpha})$$
$$f^{*\lambda} = \inf_{\alpha < \lambda} f^{*\alpha} \qquad \text{for limit ordinals } \lambda.$$

Note that $(f^{*\alpha})_{\alpha \in \mathrm{On}}$ is a decreasing sequence for monotone f. We define $f^{*!} := f^{*\alpha}$ for the least α such that $f^{*(\alpha+1)} = f^{*\alpha}$.

Lemma 20.7. *Let* $f : L \to L$ *be monotone. Then* $\mathrm{GFP}(f) = f^{*!}$.

Proof. Dual to the proof of Lemma 20.5.

In the case of power set lattices – which is our main interest – we can exploit the duality of least and greatest fixed points.

For the remainder of this section, let $\mathfrak{L}$ be the power set lattice of a set A.

Definition 20.8. For every function $f : \mathscr{P}(A) \to \mathscr{P}(A)$, the **dual function** $f' : \mathscr{P}(A) \to \mathscr{P}(A)$ of f is defined by $f'(X) := \overline{f(\overline{X})}$ where $\overline{X} := A \setminus X$.

Note that $f'' = f$.

Lemma 20.9. *Let* $f : \mathscr{P}(A) \to \mathscr{P}(A)$ *be monotone.*

(i) f' *is monotone.*
(ii) $\mathrm{LFP}(f) = \overline{\mathrm{GFP}(f')}$ *and* $\mathrm{GFP}(f) = \overline{\mathrm{LFP}(f')}$

Proof. (i) Let $X, Y \in \mathscr{P}(A)$, $X \subseteq Y$. Thus $\overline{Y} \subseteq \overline{X}$, and $f(\overline{Y}) \subseteq f(\overline{X})$ by the monotonicity of f, which implies $\overline{f(\overline{X})} \subseteq \overline{f(\overline{Y})}$.

(ii) At first, we note that the first claim implies the second: If $\mathrm{LFP}(f) = \overline{\mathrm{GFP}(f')}$ then $\overline{\mathrm{LFP}(f')} = \overline{\overline{\mathrm{GFP}(f'')}} = \mathrm{GFP}(f)$.

To prove the first claim, we show by induction that $f^{\alpha} = \overline{f'^{*\alpha}}$ holds for all $\alpha \in \mathrm{On}$.

$(\alpha = 0)$: $f^0 = \emptyset = \overline{A} = \overline{f'^{*0}}$
$(\alpha \to \alpha + 1)$: We have

$$
\begin{aligned}
f^{\alpha+1} &= f(f^{\alpha}) \\
&= f(\overline{f'^{*\alpha}}) & \text{(Ind. Hyp.)} \\
&= \overline{f'(f'^{*\alpha})} & \text{(by Def. 20.8)} \\
&= \overline{f'^{*(\alpha+1)}} & \text{(by Def. 20.6)}
\end{aligned}
$$

$(\alpha$ a limit ordinal): Here we have $f^{\alpha} = \bigcup_{\beta < \alpha} f^{\beta} = \overline{\bigcap_{\beta < \alpha} \overline{f^{\beta}}} = \overline{\bigcap_{\beta < \alpha} f'^{*\beta}} = \overline{f'^{*\alpha}}$,

using the induction hypothesis for the third equation.

20.3   Simultaneous Fixed Points

Let $n \in \omega$ and $\mathfrak{L}_0 = (L_0, \leq_0, \top_0, \bot_0), \ldots, \mathfrak{L}_{n-1} = (L_{n-1}, \leq_{n-1}, \top_{n-1}, \bot_{n-1})$ be complete lattices.

Define $L := L_0 \times \ldots \times L_{n-1}$ and

$$
\mathfrak{L} := (L, \leq, (\top_0, \ldots, \top_{n-1}), (\bot_0, \ldots, \bot_{n-1})),
$$

where $\leq$ is defined by

$$
(x_0, \ldots, x_{n-1}) \leq (y_0, \ldots, y_{n-1}) \text{ :iff } \forall i \in [n](x_i \leq_i y_i).
$$

It is easy to see that $\mathfrak{L}$ is a complete lattice, the **product lattice** of $\mathfrak{L}_0, \ldots, \mathfrak{L}_{n-1}$. We will also write $\mathfrak{L} = \mathfrak{L}_0 \times \ldots \times \mathfrak{L}_{n-1}$.

Now let $f_0 : L \to L_0, \ldots, f_{n-1} : L \to L_{n-1}$ be monotone functions. Obviously,

$$
f : L \to L, (x_0, \ldots, x_{n-1}) \mapsto (f_0(x_0, \ldots, x_{n-1}), \ldots, f_{n-1}(x_0, \ldots, x_{n-1}))
$$

is a monotone function as well and thus has a least and a greatest fixed point (Theorem 20.4). These are called the **simultaneous** (least and greatest) **fixed points** of $f_0, \ldots, f_{n-1}$.

We now wish to compute the least and greatest fixed points of f by generating nested fixed points of monotone functions defined on the lattices $L_0, \ldots, L_{n-1}$. For the sake of brevity (and clarity), we restrict ourselves to the case $n = 2$ and the computation of the least fixed point, but the generalization is straightforward.

Let $g : L \to L_0$ and $h : L \to L_1$ be monotone functions, and let $f : L \to L, (x_0, x_1) \mapsto (g(x_0, x_1), h(x_0, x_1))$. Let $\mathrm{LFP}(f) =: ((f^!)_0, (f^!)_1) \in L_0 \times L_1$ denote the least fixed point of f, i.e., $(f^!)_i = \mathrm{pr}_i(f^!)$ $(i = 0, 1)$. For $\alpha \in \mathrm{On}$, we define $f_i^\alpha := \mathrm{pr}_i(f^\alpha)$ $(i = 0, 1)$.

The following lemmas give us a computation recipe at hand:

For every $x \in L_0$, we define $h_x : L_1 \to L_1, y \mapsto h(x, y)$. The monotonicity of h implies the monotonicity of h_x, so we can generate, for every $x \in L_0$, the least fixed point $\mathrm{LFP}(h_x) = h_x^! \in L_1$ (cf. Lemma 20.5).

Lemma 20.10. *The function* $e : L_0 \to L_0, x \mapsto g(x, h_x^!)$ *is monotone. We have* $(e^!, h_{e^!}^!) = ((f^!)_0, (f^!)_1)$.

Proof. We first show that e is monotone. To do so, it suffices to show that $x \mapsto h_x^!$ is monotone. Indeed, if $x \mapsto h_x^!$ is monotone, then

$$x \leq_0 x' \Rightarrow e(x) = g(x, h_x^!) \leq_0 g(x', h_{x'}^!) = e(x')$$

since g is monotone.

Hence we show $\forall \alpha \in \mathrm{On}(\forall x, x' \in L_0(x \leq_0 x' \to h_x^\alpha \leq_1 h_{x'}^\alpha))$ by induction on α:

$(\alpha = 0)$: Trivial.

$(\alpha \to \alpha + 1)$: Let $x \leq_0 x'$. We have $h_x^{\alpha+1} = h(x, h_x^\alpha) \leq_1 h(x', h_{x'}^\alpha) = h_{x'}^{\alpha+1}$.

$(\alpha$ a limit ordinal$)$: Let $x \leq_0 x'$. $h_x^\alpha = \sup_{\beta < \alpha} h_x^\beta \leq_1 \sup_{\beta < \alpha} h_{x'}^\beta = h_{x'}^\alpha$.

Next, we show that $(f^!)_1$ is a fixed point of $h_{(f^!)_0}$; this implies $h_{(f^!)_0}^! \leq_1 (f^!)_1$:

$h_{(f^!)_0}((f^!)_1) = h((f^!)_0, (f^!)_1) = \mathrm{pr}_1(f((f^!)_0, (f^!)_1)) = (f^!)_1$, since $((f^!)_0, (f^!)_1)$ is a fixed point of f.

Now we show $e^! \leq_0 (f^!)_0$. This implies $h_{e^!}^! \leq_1 h_{(f^!)_0}^!$, since $x \mapsto h_x^!$ is monotone.

$(e^! \leq_0 (f^!)_0)$: Using $h_{(f^!)_0}^! \leq_1 (f^!)_1$ and the monotonicity of g, we have $e((f^!)_0) = g((f^!)_0, h_{(f^!)_0}^!) \leq_0 g((f^!)_0, (f^!)_1) = \mathrm{pr}_0(f((f^!)_0, (f^!)_1)) = (f^!)_0$, that is, $(f^!)_0 \in \{x \in L_0 \mid e(x) \leq_0 x\}$. Now since $e^! = \inf\{x \in L_0 \mid e(x) \leq x\}$, we have $e^! \leq_0 (f^!)_0$.

We now know that $h_{e^!}^! \leq_1 h_{(f^!)_0}^! \leq_1 (f^!)_1$ and $e^! \leq_0 (f^!)_0$.

To show that $f^! = ((f^!)_0, (f^!)_1) \leq (e^!, h_{e^!}^!)$ and hence $(e^!, h_{e^!}^!) = \mathrm{LFP}(f)$, it suffices to establish $\forall \alpha \in \mathrm{On}(f^\alpha \leq (e^!, h_{e^!}^!))$, as usual by induction on α.

$(\alpha = 0)$: Trivial.

$(\alpha \to \alpha + 1)$: Using the induction hypothesis, we have $f^{\alpha+1} = f(f_0^\alpha, f_1^\alpha) = (g(f_0^\alpha, f_1^\alpha), h(f_0^\alpha, f_1^\alpha)) \leq (g(e^!, h_{e^!}^!), h(e^!, h_{e^!}^!))$. By the definitions of $e!$ and $h_{e^!}$, $(g(e^!, h_{e^!}^!), h(e^!, h_{e^!}^!)) = (e(e^!), h_{e^!}(h_{e^!}^!)) = (e^!, h_{e^!}^!)$.

$(\alpha$ a limit ordinal$)$: We use the definition of $\leq$ and the induction hypothesis, getting $f^\alpha = \sup_{\beta < \alpha}(f_0^\beta, f_1^\beta) = (\sup_{\beta < \alpha} f_0^\beta, \sup_{\beta < \alpha} f_1^\beta) \leq (e^!, h_{e^!}^!)$.

In other words,

$$\mathrm{pr}_0(\mathrm{LFP}(f)) = \mathrm{LFP}(x \mapsto g(x, \mathrm{LFP}(y \mapsto h(x, y)))).$$

In the same manner, we can show

Lemma 20.11. *Let $g_y : L_0 \to L_0, x \mapsto g(x, y)$, for every $y \in L_1$, and let $e : L_1 \to L_1, y \mapsto h(g_y^!, y)$. The functions g_y and e are monotone, and we have $((f^!)_0, (f^!)_1) = (g_{e^!}^!, e^!)$.*

These lemmas imply

Theorem 20.12. *Let $\mathfrak{L} = \mathfrak{L}_0 \times \mathfrak{L}_1$ be the product lattice of the lattices $\mathfrak{L}_0 = (L_0, \leq_0, \top_0, \bot_0)$ and $\mathfrak{L}_1 = (L_1, \leq_1, \top_1, \bot_1)$, and let $g : L \to L_0, h : L \to L_1$ be monotone functions. Let $f : L \to L, (x_0, x_1) \mapsto (g(x_0, x_1), h(x_0, x_1))$. Then*

$$\mathrm{pr}_0(\mathrm{LFP}(f)) = \mathrm{LFP}(x \mapsto g(x, \mathrm{LFP}(y \mapsto h(x, y)))),$$
$$\mathrm{pr}_1(\mathrm{LFP}(f)) = \mathrm{LFP}(y \mapsto h(\mathrm{LFP}(x \mapsto g(x, y)), y)).$$

Literature

1. Martín Abadi, Leslie Lamport, and Pierre Wolper, *Realizable and unrealizable specifications of reactive systems*, Proceedings of the 16th International Colloquium on Automata, Languages and Programming, ICALP '89, Lecture Notes in Computer Science, vol. 372, Springer-Verlag, 1989, pp. 1–17. [40]
2. Luca de Alfaro and Thomas A. Henzinger, *Concurrent omega-regular games*, Proceedings of the 15th IEEE Symposium on Logic in Computer Science, LICS 2000, IEEE Computer Society Press, 2000, pp. 141–154. [40]
3. Luca de Alfaro, Thomas A. Henzinger, and Freddy Y. C. Mang, *The control of synchronous systems*, Proceedings of the 11th International Conference on Concurrency Theory, CONCUR 2000, Lecture Notes in Computer Science, vol. 1877, Springer-Verlag, 2000, pp. 458–473. [40]
4. Hajnal Andréka, István Németi, and Johan van Benthem, *Modal logic and bounded fragments of predicate logic*, Journal of Philosophical Logic **27** (1998), no. 3, 217–274. [321, 322, 327, 356]
5. André Arnold, *The μ-calculus alternation-depth hierarchy is strict on binary trees*, Theoretical Informatics and Applications **33** (1999), no. 4–5, 329–340. [185, 195, 202]
6. Klaus Barthelmann, *When can an equational simple graph be generated by hyperedge replacement?*, Proceedings of the 23rd International Symposium on Mathematical Foundations of Computer Science, MFCS '98, Lecture Notes in Computer Science, vol. 1450, Springer-Verlag, 1998, pp. 543–552. [263, 283, 318]
7. Johan van Benthem, *Modal correspondence theory*, Ph.D. thesis, Instituut voor Logica en Grondslagenonderzoek van Exacte Wetenschappen, Universiteit van Amsterdam, The Netherlands, 1976. [258]
8. ———, *Dynamic bits and pieces*, Tech. Report LP-97-01, Institute for Logic, Language and Computation, University of Amsterdam, The Netherlands, 1997. [356]
9. ———, *Modal logic in two gestalts*, Advances in Modal Logic, Volume II (Stanford, California), CSLI Publications, 1998, pp. 73–100. [356]
10. Orna Bernholtz, Moshe Y. Vardi, and Pierre Wolper, *An automata-theoretic approach to branching-time model checking*, Proceedings of the 6th International Conference on Computer Aided Verification, CAV '94, Lecture Notes in Computer Science, vol. 818, Springer-Verlag, 1994, pp. 142–155. [203]
11. Dietmar Berwanger and Erich Grädel, *Games and model checking for guarded logics*, Proceedings of the 8th International Conference on Logic for Programming, Artificial Intelligence and Reasoning, LPAR 2001, Lecture Notes in Artificial Intelligence, vol. 2250, Springer-Verlag, 2001, pp. 70–84. [351, 356]
12. Achim Blumensath, *Prefix-recognizable graphs and monadic second order logic*, Tech. Report AIB-06-2001, RWTH Aachen, Germany, 2001. [263, 264, 283, 318]
13. Julian C. Bradfield, *The modal mu-calculus alternation hierarchy is strict*, Proceedings of the 7th International Conference on Concurrency Theory, CONCUR '96, Lecture Notes in Computer Science, vol. 1119, Springer-Verlag, 1996, pp. 232–246. [185, 202]
14. ———, *The modal μ-calculus alternation hierarchy is strict*, Theoretical Computer Science **195** (1998), no. 2, 133–153. [202]

15. _____, *Simplifying the modal mu-calculus alternation hierarchy*, Proceedings of the 15th Annual Symposium on Theoretical Aspects of Computer Science, STACS '98, Lecture Notes in Computer Science, vol. 1373, Springer-Verlag, 1998, pp. 39–49. [202]

16. Julian C. Bradfield and Colin Stirling, *Modal logics and mu-calculi: an introduction*, Handbook of Process Algebra (Jan A. Bergstra, Alban Ponse, and Scott A. Smolka, eds.), Elsevier, 2001, pp. 293–332. [203]

17. J. Richard Büchi, *Weak second-order arithmetic and finite automata*, Zeitschrift für mathematische Logik und Grundlagen der Mathematik **6** (1960), 66–92. [3, 153, 219, 221, 258]

18. _____, *On a decision method in restricted second order arithmetic*, International Congress on Logic, Methodology and Philosophy of Science, Stanford University Press, 1962, pp. 1–11. [39, 61, 92, 214, 217, 221, 258]

19. _____, *Decision methods in the theory of ordinals*, Bulletin of the American Mathematical Society **71** (1965), 767–770. [258]

20. _____, *The monadic theory of ω_1*, Decidable Theories II, Lecture Notes in Mathematics, vol. 328, Springer-Verlag, 1973, pp. 1–127. [258]

21. _____, *Using determinacy to eliminate quantifiers*, Fundamentals of Computation Theory, Lecture Notes in Computer Science, vol. 56, Springer-Verlag, 1977, pp. 367–378. [95, 108, 135]

22. J. Richard Büchi and Lawrence H. Landweber, *Solving sequential conditions by finite-state strategies*, Transactions of the American Mathematical Society **138** (1969), 295–311. [39]

23. Olaf Burkart, *Automatic verification of sequential infinite-state processes*, Lecture Notes in Computer Science, vol. 1354, Springer-Verlag, 1997. [318]

24. Olaf Burkart and Bernhard Steffen, *Model checking for context-free processes*, Proceedings of the 3rd International Conference on Concurrency Theory, CONCUR '92, Lecture Notes in Computer Science, vol. 630, Springer-Verlag, 1992, pp. 123–137. [318]

25. Georg Cantor, *Beiträge zur Begründung der transfiniten Mengenlehre*, Mathematische Annalen **46** (1895), 481–512. [224]

26. Olivier Carton and Wolfgang Thomas, *The monadic theory of morphic infinite words and generalizations*, Information and Computation **176** (2002), 51–76. [258]

27. Ilaria Castellani, *Bisimulations and abstraction homomorphisms*, Journal of Computer and System Sciences **34** (1987), no. 2–3, 210–235. [242]

28. Didier Caucal, *On infinite transition graphs having a decidable monadic theory*, Proceedings of the 23rd International Colloquium on Automata, Languages and Programming, ICALP '96, Lecture Notes in Computer Science, vol. 1099, Springer-Verlag, 1996, pp. 194–205. [263, 280, 282, 283, 316, 318]

29. _____, *Sur des graphes infinis réguliers*, Institut de Formation Supérieure en Informatique et en Communication, L'Université des Rennes 1, 1998, Habilitation thesis. [318]

30. _____, *On infinite transition graphs having a decidable monadic theory*, Theoretical Computer Science (2001), To appear. [318]

31. _____, *On the transition graphs of Turing machines*, Proceedings of the 3rd International Conference Machines, Computations, and Universality, MCU '01, Lecture Notes in Computer Science, vol. 2055, Springer-Verlag, 2001, pp. 177–189. [318]

32. _____, *On infinite terms having a decidable monadic theory*, Proceedings of the 27th International Symposium on Mathematical Foundations of Computer

Science, MFCS '02, Lecture Notes in Computer Science, Springer-Verlag, 2002, pp. 165–176. [258, 318]

33. Ashok K. Chandra, Dexter Kozen, and Larry J. Stockmeyer, *Alternation*, Journal of the ACM **28** (1981), no. 1, 114–133. [168]

34. Yaacov Choueka, *Theories of automata on omega-tapes: A simplified approach*, Journal of Computer and System Sciences **8** (1974), no. 2, 117–141. [92]

35. Alonzo Church, *Logic, arithmetic, and automata*, Proceedings of the International Congress of Mathematicians (Stockholm, Sweden), 1962. [39]

36. Rina S. Cohen and Arie Y. Gold, *Theory of ω-languages I & II*, Journal of Computer and System Science **15** (1977), no. 2, 169–208. [4]

37. _____, *ω-computations on deterministic pushdown machines*, Journal of Computer and System Science **16** (1978), no. 3, 275–300. [4]

38. _____, *ω-computations on turing machines*, Theoretical Computer Science **6** (1978), 1–23. [4]

39. Kevin J. Compton and C. Ward Henson, *A uniform method for proving lower bounds on the computational complexity of logical theories*, Annals of Pure and Applied Logic **48** (1990), no. 1, 1–79. [258]

40. Anne Condon, *The complexity of stochastic games*, Information and Computation **96** (1992), no. 2, 203–224. [111]

41. Bruno Courcelle, *The monadic second order logic of graphs, II: Infinite graphs of bounded width*, Mathematical System Theory **21** (1989), no. 4, 187–222. [301]

42. _____, *The monadic second order logic of graphs, IX: Machines and their behaviours*, Theoretical Computer Science **151** (1995), no. 1, 125–162. [263, 268, 301, 318]

43. Bruno Courcelle and Igor Walukiewicz, *Monadic second-order logic, graph converings and unfoldings of transition systems*, Annals of Pure and Applied Logic **92** (1998), no. 1, 35–62. [318]

44. Mads Dam, *CTL* and ECTL* as fragments of the modal μ-calculus*, Theoretical Computer Science **126** (1994), no. 1, 77–96. [257]

45. John Doner, *Tree acceptors and some of their applications*, Journal of Computer and System Sciences **4** (1970), no. 5, 406–451. [219, 221, 258]

46. Stefan Dziembowski, Marcin Jurdziński, and Igor Walukiewicz, *How much memory is needed to win infinite games?*, Proceedings of the 12th Annual IEEE Symposium on Logic in Computer Science, LICS '97, IEEE Computer Society Press, 1997, pp. 99–110. [39]

47. Heinz-Dieter Ebbinghaus and Jörg Flum, *Finite model theory*, Perspectives in Mathematical Logic, Springer-Verlag, 1995. [334]

48. Heinz-Dieter Ebbinghaus, Jörg Flum, and Wolfgang Thomas, *Mathematical logic*, Undergraduate texts in mathematics, Spinger-Verlag, 1984. [207]

49. Andrzej Ehrenfeucht and Jan Mycielski, *Positional strategies for mean payoff games*, International Journal of Game Theory **8** (1979), 109–113. [109, 110, 113, 114]

50. Samuel Eilenberg, *Automata, languages and machines*, vol. A, Academic Press, New York, 1974. [92]

51. Calvin C. Elgot, *Decision problems of finite automata design and related arithmetics*, Transactions of the American Mathematical Society **98** (1961), 21–51. [219, 221, 258]

52. Calvin C. Elgot and Michael O. Rabin, *Decidability and undefinability of second (first) order theory of (generalized) successor*, Journal of Symbolic Logic **31** (1966), 169–181. [258]

·

53. E. Allen Emerson, *Temporal and modal logic*, Handbook of Theoretical Computer Science (Jan van Leeuwen, ed.), vol. B: Formal Models and Sematics, Elsevier, 1990, pp. 995–1072. [203]

54. E. Allen Emerson and Charanjit S. Jutla, *The complexity of tree automata and logics of programs (exteded abstract)*, Proceedings of the 29th Annual Symposium on Foundations of Computer Science, FoCS '88, IEEE Computer Society Press, 1988, pp. 328–337. [130, 168, 203, 321, 343]

55. _____, *Tree automata, mu-calculus and determinacy (extended abstract)*, Proceedings of the 32nd Annual Symposium on Foundations of Computer Science, FoCS '91, IEEE Computer Society Press, 1991, pp. 368–377. [39, 95, 103, 108, 130, 135, 138, 202, 354]

56. E. Allen Emerson, Charanjit S. Jutla, and A. Prasad Sistla, *On model-checking for fragments of μ-calculus*, Proceedings of the 5th International Conference on Computer Aided Verification, CAV '93, Lecture Notes in Computer Science, vol. 697, Springer-Verlag, 1993, pp. 385–396. [95, 104, 108]

57. _____, *On model checking for the μ-calculus and its fragments*, Theoretical Computer Science **258** (2001), no. 1–2, 491–522. [202]

58. E. Allen Emerson and Chin-Laung Lei, *Efficient model checking in fragments of the propositional mu-calculus (extended abstract)*, Proceedings of the Symposium on Logic in Computer Science, LICS '86, IEEE Computer Society Press, 1986, pp. 267–278. [202, 203]

59. E. Allen Emerson and A. Prasad Sistla, *Deciding full branching time logic*, Information and Control **61** (1984), no. 3, 175–201. [92]

60. Joost Engelfriet and Hendrik Jan Hoogeboom, *X-automata on ω-words*, Theoretical Computer Science **110** (1993), 1–51. [39]

61. Javier Esparza, David Hansel, Peter Rossmanith, and Stefan Schwoon, *Efficient algorithms for model checking pushdown systems*, Proceedings of the 12th International Conference on Computer Aided Verification, CAV 2000, Lecture Notes in Computer Science, vol. 1855, Springer-Verlag, 2000, pp. 232–247. [311]

62. Shimon Even, *Graph algorithms*, Pitman Publishing, London, 1979. [55]

63. Jeanne Ferrante and Charles W. Rackoff, *The computational complexity of logical theories*, Lecture Notes in Mathematics, vol. 718, Springer-Verlag, 1979. [258]

64. Markus Frick and Martin Grohe, *The complexity of first-order and monadic second-order logic revisited*, Proceedings of the 17th IEEE Symposium on Logic in Computer Science, LICS '02, IEEE Computer Society Press, 2002, pp. 215–224. [258]

65. Harald Ganziger, Christoph Meyer, and Margus Veanes, *The two-variable guarded fragment with transitive relations*, Proceedings of the 14th IEEE Symposium on Logic in Computer Science, LICS '99, IEEE Computer Society Press, 1999, pp. 24–34. [322, 356]

66. Kurt Gödel, *Über formal unentscheidbare Sätze der Principia Mathematica und verwandter Systeme I*, Monatshefte für Mathematik und Physik **38** (1931), 173–198. [207]

67. Elisabeth Gonçalves and Erich Grädel, *Decidability issues for action guarded logics*, Proceedings of the 2000 International Workshop on Description Logics, DL 2000, 2000, pp. 123–132. [322, 336, 356]

68. Georg Gottlob, Erich Grädel, and Helmut Veith, *Datalog LITE: A deductive query language with linear time model checking*, ACM Transactions on Computional Logic **3** (2002), no. 1, 42–79. [322, 356]

69. Erich Grädel, *The decidability of guarded fixed point logic*, JFAK. Essay Dedicated to Johan van Benthem on the occasion of his 50th Birthday, CD-ROM (Jelle Gerbrandy, Maarten Marx, Maarten de Rijke, and Yde Venema, eds.), Amsterdam University, 1999. [322, 356]

70. _____, *Decision procedures for guarded logics*, Proceedings of 16th International Conference on Automated Deduction, CADE '99, Lecture Notes in Artificial Intelligence, vol. 1632, Springer-Verlag, 1999, pp. 31–51. [356]

71. _____, *On the restrainning power of guards*, Journal of Symbolic Logic **64** (1999), 1719–1742. [322, 343, 356]

72. _____, *Why are modal logics so robustly decidable?*, Current Trends in Theoretical Computer Science, Entering the 21st Century (Gheorghe Paun, Grzegorz Rozenberg, and Arto Salomaa, eds.), World Scientific, 2001, pp. 393–498. [322, 356]

73. _____, *Guarded fixed point logics and the monadic theory of countable trees*, Theoretical Computer Science **288** (2002), 129 – 152. [322, 326, 327, 328, 329, 330, 331, 339, 343, 346, 356]

74. Erich Grädel, Colin Hirsch, and Martin Otto, *Back and forth between guarded and modal logics*, ACM Transactions on Computional Logic **3** (2002), no. 3, 418–463. [322, 333, 334, 335, 356]

75. Erich Grädel and Igor Walukiewicz, *Guarded fixed point logic*, Proceedings of the 4th Annual IEEE Symposium on Logic in Computer Science, LICS '99, IEEE Computer Society Press, 1999, pp. 45–54. [322, 343, 356]

76. Yuri Gurevich, *Monadic second-order theories*, Model-Theoretical Logics (Jon Barwise and Solomon Feferman, eds.), Springer-Verlag, 1985, pp. 479–506. [258]

77. Yuri Gurevich and Leo Harrington, *Trees, automata and games*, Proceedings of the 14th Annual ACM Symposium on Theory of Computing, STOC '82, ACM Press, 1982, pp. 60–65. [39, 95, 108, 135, 141]

78. Yuri Gurevich, Menachem Magidor, and Saharon Shelah, *The monadic theory of ω_2*, Jounal of Symbolic Logic **48** (1983), 387–398. [258]

79. Stephan Heilbrunner, *An algorithm for the solution of fixed-point equations for infinite words*, R.A.I.R.O. Informatique théorique/Theoretical Informatics **14** (1980), no. 2, 131–141. [228]

80. B. Herwig, *Zur Modelltheorie von L_μ*, Ph.D. thesis, Universität Freiburg, Germany, 1989. [130]

81. David Hilbert, *Mathematische Probleme. Vortrag, gehalten auf dem internationalen Mathematiker-Kongress zu Paris 1900*, Nachrichten von der Königl. Gesellschaft der Wissenschaften zu Göttingen, Mathematisch-Physikalische Klasse (1900), 253–297. [207]

82. Colin Hirsch, *Guarded logics: Algorithms and bisimulation*, Ph.D. thesis, RWTH Aachen, Germany, 2002. [356]

83. Wilfrid Hodges, *Model theory*, Encyclopedia of Mathematics and its Applications, Cambridge University Press, 1993. [226]

84. Ian Hodkinson, *Loosely guarded fragment has finite model property*, Studia Logica **70** (2002), 205–240. [356]

85. A. Hoffmann and Richard M. Karp, *On nonterminating stochastic games*, Management Science **12** (1966), 359–370. [108, 125]

86. Eva Hoogland, Maarten Marx, and Martin Otto, *Beth definability for the guarded fragment*, Proceedings of the 6th International Conference on Logic for Programming and Automated Reasoning, LPAR '99), Lecture Notes in Computer Science, vol. 1705, Springer-Verlag, 1999, pp. 273–285. [322, 356]

87. John E. Hopcroft and Jeffrey D. Ullman, *Introduction to automata theory, languages, and computation*, Addison-Wesley, 1979. [44, 63, 236]

88. Robert Hossley and Charles W. Rackoff, *The emptiness problem for automata on infinite trees*, Proceedings of the 13th Annual Symposium on Switching and Automata Theory, IEEE Computer Society Press, 1972, pp. 121–124. [168]

89. David Janin, *Propriérés logiques du non-déterminisme et μ-calcul modal*, Ph.D. thesis, LaBRI – Université de Bordeaux I, France, 1995. [249]

90. David Janin and Igor Walukiewicz, *Automata for the modal mu-calculus and related results*, Proceedings of the 20th International Symposium on Mathematical Foundations of Computer Science, MFCS '95, Lecture Notes in Computer Science, vol. 969, Springer-Verlag, 1995, pp. 552–562. [249, 259]

91. _____, *On the expressive completeness of the propositional mu-calculus with respect to monadic second order logic*, Proceedings of the 7th International Conference on Concurrency Theory, CONCUR '96, Lecture Notes in Computer Science, vol. 1119, Springer-Verlag, 1996, pp. 263–277. [239, 259]

92. Marcin Jurdziński, *Deciding the winner in parity games is in UP ∩ co-UP*, Information Processing Letters **68** (1998), no. 3, 119–124. [96, 103, 104, 108, 110, 112, 115, 130]

93. _____, *Small progress measures for solving parity games*, Proceedings of the 17th Annual Symposium on Theoretical Aspects of Computer Science, STACS 2000, Lecture Notes in Computer Science, vol. 1770, Springer-Verlag, 2000, pp. 290–301. [96, 103, 106, 108, 109, 117, 119, 124, 130, 151, 153, 202]

94. Charanjit S. Jutla, *Determinization and memoryless winning strategies*, Information and Computation **133** (1997), no. 2, 117–134. [80]

95. Alexander S. Kechris, *Classical descriptive set theory*, Graduate Texts in Mathematics, Springer-Verlag, 1995. [30]

96. Bakhadyr Khoussainov and Anil Nerode, *Automata theory and its applications*, Progress in Computer Science and Applied Logic, vol. 21, Birkhäuser, 2001. [39]

97. Nils Klarlund, *Progress measures for complementation of omega-automata with applications to temporal logic*, Proceedings of the 32nd Annual Symposium on Foundations of Computer Science, FoCS '91, IEEE Computer Society Press, 1991, pp. 358–367. [61, 62, 63]

98. _____, *Progress measures, immediate determinacy, and a subset construction for tree automata*, Annals of Pure and Applied Logic **69** (1994), no. 2–3, 243–268. [39]

99. Nils Klarlund, Madhavan Mukund, and Milind A. Sohoni, *Determinizing Büchi asynchronous automata*, Proceedings of the 15th Conference on Foundations of Software Technology and Theoretical Computer Science, FSTTCS '95, Lecture Notes in Computer Science, no. 1026, Springer-Verlag, 1995, pp. 456–470. [44]

100. Dexter Kozen, *Results on the propositional mu-calculus*, Theoretical Computer Science **27** (1983), 333–354. [95, 108, 171, 202, 203]

101. Orna Kupferman, P. Madhusudan, P. S. Thiagarajan, and Moshe Y. Vardi, *Open systems in reactive environments: Control and synthesis*, Proceedings of the 11th International Conference on Concurrency Theory, CONCUR 2000, Lecture Notes in Computer Science, vol. 1877, Springer-Verlag, 2000, pp. 92–107. [40]

102. Orna Kupferman and Moshe Y. Vardi, *Weak alternating automata are not that weak*, Proceedings of the Fifth Israel Symposium on Theory of Computing and Systems, ISTCS '97, IEEE Computer Society Press, 1997, pp. 147–158. [61, 77]

103. _____, *Weak alternating automata and tree automata emptiness*, Proceedings of the 30th Annual ACM Symposium on Theory of Computing, STOC '98, ACM Press, 1998, pp. 224–233. [168]

104. ———, *Chruch's problem revisted*, The Bulletin of Symbolic Logic **5** (1999), no. 2, 245–263. [40]

105. ———, *The weakness of self-complementation*, Proceedings of the 16th Annual Symposium on Theoretical Aspects of Computer Science, STACS '99, Lecture Notes in Computer Science, vol. 1563, Springer-Verlag, 1999, pp. 455–466. [168]

106. ———, *An automata-theoretic approach to reasoning about infinite-state systems*, Proceedings of the 12th International Conference on Computer Aided Verification, CAV 2000), Lecture Notes in Computer Science, vol. 1855, Springer-Verlag, 2000. [303, 312, 313, 316, 317, 318]

107. ———, *Weak alternating automata are not that weak*, ACM Transactions on Computational Logic **2** (2001), no. 3, 408–429. [61, 77]

108. Ralf Küsters and Thomas Wilke, *Determinizing Büchi asynchronous automata*, Proceedings of the 22th Conference on Foundations of Software Technology and Theoretical Computer Science, FSTTCS '02, Lecture Notes in Computer Science, Springer-Verlag, 2002, To appear. [202]

109. Richard E. Ladner, *The computational complexity of provability in systems of propositinal modal logic*, SIAM Journal on Computing **6** (1977), no. 3, 467–480. [321]

110. Lawrence H. Landweber, *Decision problems for ω-automata*, Mathematical Systems Theory **3** (1969), no. 4, 376–384. [20, 39]

111. H. Läuchli and J. Leonard, *On the elementary theory of linear order*, Fundamenta Mathematicae **59** (1966), 109–116. [228]

112. Giacomo Lenzi, *A hierarchy theorem for the mu-calculus*, Proceedings of the 23rd International Colloquium on Automata, Languages and Programming, ICALP '96, Lecture Notes in Computer Science, vol. 1099, Springer-Verlag, 1996, pp. 87–97. [185, 202]

113. Matti Linna, *On ω-sets associated with context-free languages*, Information and Control **31** (1976), no. 3, 272–293. [4]

114. Christof Löding, *Optimal bounds for the transformation of omega-automata*, Proceedings of the 19th Conference on Foundations of Software Technology and Theoretical Computer Science, FSTTCS '99, Lecture Notes in Computer Science, vol. 1738, Springer-Verlag, 1999, pp. 97–109. [16, 17, 18, 19, 39, 79, 87, 88, 89]

115. Christof Löding and Wolfgang Thomas, *Alternating automata and logics over infinite words*, Proceedings of the IFIP International Conference on Theoretical Computer Science, IFIP TCS 2000, Lecture Notes in Computer Science, vol. 1872, Springer-Verlag, 2000. [61, 68]

116. David E. Long, Anca Browne, Edmund M. Clarke, Somesh Jha, and Wilfredo R. Marrero, *An improved algorithm for the evaluation of fixpoint expressions*, Proceedings of the 6th International Conference on Computer Aided Verification, CAV '94, Lecture Notes in Computer Science, vol. 818, Springer-Verlag, 1994, pp. 338–350. [202]

117. Walter Ludwig, *A subexponential randomized algorithm for the simple stochastic game problem*, Information and Computation **117** (1995), no. 1, 151–155. [111, 125, 130]

118. P. Madhusudan and P.S. Thiagarajan, *Distributed controller synthesis for local specifications*, Proceedings of the 28th International Colloquium on Automata, Languages and Programming, ICALP '01, Lecture Notes in Computer Science, vol. 2076, Springer-Verlag, 2001, pp. 396–407. [40]

119. Donald A. Martin, *Borel determinacy*, Annals of Mathematics **102** (1975), 363–371. [30, 95, 130]

120. Maarten Marx, *Tolerance logic*, Tech. Report IR-469, Faculteit der Exacte Wetenschappen, Vrije Universiteit Amsterdam, The Netherlands, 1999. [356]

121. Yuri Matiyasevich, *Diophantine nature of enumerable sets (Russian)*, Doklady Akademija Nauk SSSR **191** (1970), no. 2, 279–282. [207]

122. Oliver Matz, *Dot-depth and monadic quantifier alternation over pictures*, Ph.D. thesis, RWTH Aachen, Germany, 1999, Aachener Informatik Berichte 99-08. [231, 233, 258]

123. ———, *Dot-depth, monadic quantifier alternation, and first-order closure over grids and pictures*, Theoretical Computer Science **270** (2002), no. 1–2, 1–70. [231, 233, 258]

124. Robert McNaughton, *Finite-state infinite games*, Tech. report, Project MAC, Massachusetts Institute of Technology, USA, 1965. [39]

125. ———, *Testing and generating infinite sequences by a finite automaton*, Information and Control **9** (1966), no. 5, 521–530. [39, 43, 61, 92]

126. ———, *Infinite games played on finite graphs*, Annals of Pure and Applies Logic **65** (1993), no. 2, 149–184. [39, 96, 108, 130]

127. A. R. Meyer, *Weak monadic second order theory of successor is not elementary-recursive*, Proceedings of the Boston University Logic Colloquium, Springer-Verlag, 1975, pp. 132–154. [258]

128. Max Michel, *Complementation is more difficult with automata on infinite words*, Manuscript, CNET, Paris, 1988. [16, 39]

129. Satoru Miyano and Takeshi Hayashi, *Alternating finite automata on ω-words*, Theoretical Computer Science **32** (1984), 321–330. [76]

130. Faron Moller and Alexander Rabinovich, *On the expressive power of CTL**, Proceedings of the 14th IEEE Symposium on Logic in Computer Science, LICS '99, IEEE Computer Society Press, 1999, pp. 360–369. [259]

131. Andrzej Wlodzimierz Mostowski, *Regular expressions for infinite trees and a standard form of automata*, Computation Theory, Lecture Notes in Computer Science, vol. 208, Springer-Verlag, 1984, pp. 157–168. [39, 130]

132. ———, *Games with forbidden positions*, Tech. Report 78, Instytut Matematyki, Uniwersytet Gdański, Poland, 1991. [39, 95, 130, 354]

133. David E. Muller, *Infinite sequences and finite machines*, Proceedings of the 4th IEEE Symposioum on Switching Circuit Theory and Logical Design, 1963, pp. 3–16. [3, 39, 43, 92, 168]

134. David E. Muller, Ahmed Saoudi, and Paul E. Schupp, *Alternating automata, the weak monadic theory of the tree, and its complexity*, Proceedings of the 13th International Colloquium on Automata, Languages and Programming, ICALP '86, Lecture Notes in Computer Science, vol. 226, Springer-Verlag, 1986, pp. 275–283. [168]

135. David E. Muller and Paul E. Schupp, *The theory of ends, pushdown automata, and second-order logic*, Theoretical Computer Science **37** (1985), 51–75. [263, 318]

136. ———, *Alternating automata on infinite trees*, Theoretical Computer Science **54** (1987), 267–276. [68, 168]

137. ———, *Simulating alternating tree automata by nondeterministic automata: New results and new proofs of the theorems of Rabin, McNaughton and Safra*, Theoretical Computer Science **141** (1995), no. 1–2, 69–107. [43, 92, 154, 162]

138. Damian Niwiński, *On fixed-point clones (extended abstract)*, Proceedings of the 13th International Colloquium on Automata, Languages and Programming, ICALP '86, Lecture Notes in Computer Science, vol. 226, Springer-Verlag, 1986, pp. 464–473. [176]

139. _____, *Fixed point characterization of infinite behavior of finite-state systems*, Theoretical Computer Science **189** (1997), no. 1–2, 1–69. [171, 185]

140. Martin Otto, *Eliminating recursion in the μ-calculus*, Proceedings of the 16th Annual Symposium on Theoretical Aspects of Computer Science, STACS '99, Lecture Notes in Computer Science, vol. 1563, Springer-Verlag, 1999, pp. 531–540. [202]

141. _____, *Modal and guarded characterisation theorems over finite transition systems*, Proceedings of the 17th IEEE Symposium on Logic in Computer Science, LICS 2002, IEEE Computer Society Press, 2002, pp. 371–380. [356]

142. Christos H. Papadimitriou, *Complexity theory*, Addison Wesley, 1994. [108, 115]

143. Dominique Perrin and Jean-Eric Pin, *Infinite words*, available on `http://www.liafa.jussieu.fr/~jep/Resumes/InfiniteWords.html`. [39]

144. Amir Pnueli and Roni Rosner, *On the synthesis of a reactive module*, Proceedings of the Sixteenth Annual ACM Symposium on Principles of Programming Languages, POPL '89, ACM Press, 1989, pp. 179–190. [40, 168]

145. _____, *Distributed reactive systems are hard to synthesize*, Proceedings of the 31st Annual Symposium on Foundations of Computer Science, FoCS '90, IEEE Computer Society Press, 1990, pp. 746–757. [40]

146. Mojzesz Presburger, *Über die Vollständigkeit eines gewissen Systems der Arithmetik ganzer Zahlen, in welchem die Addition als einzige Operation hervortritt*, Comptes Rendus du Ier Congrès des Mathématiciens des Pays Slaves, Warszawa (1929), 92–101. [208, 225]

147. Anuj Puri, *Theory of hybrid systems and discrete event systems*, Ph.D. thesis, University of California, Berkeley, 1995. [110, 125, 130]

148. Michael O. Rabin, *Decidability of second-order theories and automata on infinite trees*, Transactions of the American Mathematical Society **141** (1969), 1–35. [95, 108, 135, 146, 168, 214, 221, 258, 263, 267]

149. _____, *Weakly definable relations and special automata*, Mathematical Logic and Foundations of Set Theory, North-Holland, 1970, pp. 1–23. [139, 168, 219]

150. _____, *Automata on infinite objects and Church's problem*, American Mathematical Society (1972). [39, 92, 168]

151. _____, *Decidable theories*, Handbook of Mathematical Logic (Jon Barwise, ed.), North-Holland, 1977, pp. 595–629. [258]

152. Peter J. Ramadge and W. Murray Wonham, *The control of discrete event systems*, Proceedings of the IEEE **77** (1989), no. 1, 81–98. [40]

153. Roman R. Redziejowski, *Construction of a deterministic ω-automaton using derivatives*, Theoretical Informatics and Applications **33** (1999), no. 2, 133–158. [43]

154. Bruce Reed, *Tree width and tangles: A new conectivity measure and some applications*, Surveys in Combinatorics (Rosemary A. Bailey, ed.), Cambridge University Press, 1997, pp. 87–162. [331]

155. Neil Robertson and Paul D. Seymour, *Graph minors. V. Excluding a planar graph*, Journal of Combinatorial Theory, Series B **41** (1986), 92–114. [209]

156. Eric Rosen, *Modal logic over finite structures*, Journal of Logic, Language, and Information **6** (1997), 427–439. [258]

157. Bertrand Le Saec, Jean-Eric Pin, and Pascal Weil, *A purely algebraic proof of McNaughton's theorem on infinite words*, Proceedings of the 11th Conference on Foundations of Software Technology and Theoretical Computer Science, FSTTCS '91, Lecture Notes in Computer Science, no. 560, Springer-Verlag, 1991, pp. 141–151. [92]

158. Shmuel Safra, *On the complexity of omega-automata*, Proceedings of the 29th Annual Symposium on Foundations of Computer Science, FoCS '88, IEEE Computer Society Press, 1988, pp. 319–327. [16, 43, 61, 92]

159. ———, *Exponential determinization for omega-automata with strong-fairness acceptance condition (extended abstract)*, Proceedings of the 24th Annual ACM Symposium on the Theory of Computing, STOC '92, ACM Press, 1992, pp. 275–282. [18, 79, 80, 86, 92]

160. Detlef Seese, *The structure of the models of decidable monadic theories of graphs*, Annals of Pure and Applied Logic **53** (1991), no. 2, 169–195. [209]

161. Helmut Seidl, *Fast and simple nested fixpoints*, Information Processing Letters **59** (1996), no. 6, 303–308. [117, 130, 202]

162. Alexei L. Semenov, *Decidability of monadic theories*, Proceedings of the 11th International Symposium on Mathematical Foundations of Computer Science, MFCS '84, Lecture Notes in Computer Science, vol. 176, Springer-Verlag, 1984, pp. 162–175. [285]

163. Saharon Shelah, *The monadic second order theory of order*, Annals of Mathematics **102** (1975), 379–419. [258, 285, 337]

164. Ludwig Staiger, *Research in the theory of ω-languages*, Journal of Information Processing Cybernetics EIK **23** (1987), 415–439. [39]

165. ———, *ω-languages*, Handbook of Formal Language Theory, vol. III, Springer-Verlag, 1997, pp. 339–387. [4, 39]

166. Ludwig Staiger and Klaus W. Wagner, *Automatentheoretische und Automatenfreie Charakterisierungen Topologischer Klassen Regulärer Folgenmengen*, Elektronische Informationsverarbeitung und Kybernetik EIK **10** (1974), 379–392. [20]

167. Colin Stirling, *Local model checking games*, Proceedings of the 6th International Conference on Concurrency Theory, CONCUR '95, Lecture Notes in Computer Science, vol. 962, Springer-Verlag, 1995, pp. 1–11. [130]

168. ———, *Decidability of bisimulation equivalence for pushdown processes*, Tech. Report EDI-INF-RR-0005, School of Informatics, University of Edinburgh, Scottland, 2000. [282, 283, 318]

169. ———, *Modal and temporal properties of processes*, Texts in Computer Science, Springer-Verlag, 2001. [202]

170. Larry J. Stockmeyer, *The complexity of decision problems in automata theory and logic*, Ph.D. thesis, Deptartment of Electrical Engineering, MIT, Boston, Massachusetts, 1974. [231, 233, 258]

171. Robert S. Streett, *Propositional dynamic logic of looping and converse is elementary decidable*, Information and Control **54** (1982), no. 1–2, 121–141. [39, 79]

172. Robert S. Streett and E. Allen Emerson, *An automata theoretic decision procedure for the propositional mu-calculus*, Information and Computation **81** (1989), no. 3, 249–264. [202]

173. Jonathan Stupp, *The lattice-model is recursive in the original model.*, Tech. report, Institute of Mathematics, The Hebrew University, Jerusalem, Israel, 1975. [285, 318]

174. Alfred Tarski, *A decision method for elementary algebra and geometry*, Tech. report, Rand Corporation, Santa Monica, California, 1948. [208, 226]

175. ———, *A lattice-theoretical fixpoint theorem and its applications*, Pacific Journal of Mathematics **5** (1955), 285–309. [122, 359, 360]

176. James W. Thatcher and Jesse B. Wright, *Generalized finite automata theory with an application to a decision problem of second-order logic*, Mathematical Systems Theory **2** (1968), no. 1, 57–81. [219, 221, 258]

177. John G. Thistle and W. Murray Wonham, *Supervision of infinite behavior of discrete-event systems*, SIAM Journal on Control and Optimization **32** (1994), no. 4, 1098–1113. [40]

178. Wolfgang Thomas, *A combinatorial approach to the theory of ω-automata*, Information and Control **48** (1981), 261–283. [92]

179. ———, *Automata on infinite objects*, Handbook of Theoretical Computer Science, vol. B: Formal Models and Semantics, Elsevier, 1990, pp. 133–192. [39, 92, 268]

180. ———, *On the synthesis of strategies in infinite games*, Proceedings of the 12th Annual Symposium on Theoretical Aspects of Computer Science, STACS '95, Lecture Notes in Computer Science, vol. 900, Springer-Verlag, 1995, pp. 1–13. [39, 130, 317]

181. ———, *Languages, automata and logic*, Tech. Report 9607, Institut für Informatik und Praktische Mathematik, Christian-Albrechts-Universität Kiel, Germany, 1996. [130]

182. ———, *Ehrenfeucht games, the composition method, and the monadic theory of ordinal words*, Structures in Logic and Computer Science, Lecture Notes in Computer Science, vol. 1261, Springer-Verlag, 1997, pp. 118–143. [258]

183. ———, *Languages, automata, and logic*, Handbook of Formal Language Theory, vol. III, Springer-Verlag, 1997, pp. 389–455. [39, 62, 108, 130, 135, 263]

184. ———, *Complementation of Büchi automata revisited*, Jewels are Forever, Contributions on Theoretical Computer Science in Honor of Arto Salomaa, Springer-Verlag, 1999, pp. 109–120. [61, 68, 75]

185. John Joseph Le Tourneau, *Decision problems related to the concept of operation*, Ph.D. thesis, University of California, Berkeley, 1968. [337]

186. Boris A. Trakhtenbrot, *Finite automata and the logic of monadic predicates*, Dokl. Akad. Nauk SSSR **140** (1961), 326–329. [219]

187. ———, *Finite automata and the logic of one-place predicates*, Sibirian Mathematical Journal **13** (1962), 103–131, (in Russian). [258]

188. Boris A. Trakhtenbrot and Y.M. Barzdin, *Finite automata: Behavior and synthesis*, North-Holland, 1973. [39]

189. Moshe Y. Vardi, *Why is modal logic so robustly decidable?*, Descriptive Complexity and Finite Models: Proceedings of a DIMACS Workshop, vol. 31, American Mathematical Society, 1996, pp. 149–184. [321, 343]

190. ———, *Reasoning about the past with two-way automata.*, Proceedings of the 25th International Colloquium on Automata, Languages and Programming, ICALP '98, Lecture Notes in Computer Science, vol. 1443, Springer-Verlag, 1998, pp. 628–641. [303, 307, 310, 318, 354]

191. Jens Vöge and Marcin Jurdziński, *A discrete strategy improvement algorithm for solving parity games*, Proceedings of the 12th International Conference on Computer Aided Verification, CAV 2000, Lecture Notes in Computer Science, vol. 1855, Springer-Verlag, 2000, pp. 202–215. [108, 125, 129, 130]

192. Klaus W. Wagner, *On ω-regular sets*, Information and Control **43** (1979), 123–177. [39]

193. Igor Walukiewicz, *A complete deductive system for the mu-calculus*, Ph.D. thesis, Institute of Informatics, Warsaw University, Poland, 1993. [203]

194. ———, *On completeness of the mu-calculus*, Proceedings of the 8th Annual IEEE Symposium on Logic in Computer Science, LICS '93, IEEE Computer Society Press, 1993, pp. 136–146. [203]

195. ———, *Completeness of Kozen's axiomatisation of the propositional μ-calculus*, Proceedings of the 10th Annual IEEE Symposium on Logic in Computer Science, LICS '95, IEEE Computer Society Press, 1995, pp. 14–24. [203]

196. ———, *Pushdown processes: Games and model checking*, Proceedings of the 8th International Conference on Computer Aided Verification, CAV '96, Lecture Notes in Computer Science, vol. 1102, Springer-Verlag, 1996, pp. 62–74. [311, 313, 318]

197. ———, *Completeness of Kozen's axiomatisation of the propositional mu-calculus*, Information and Computation **157** (2000), no. 1–2, 142–182. [203]

198. ———, *Pushdown processes: Games and model checking*, Information and Computation **164** (2001), no. 2, 234–263. [311]

199. ———, *Deciding low levels of tree-automata hierarchy*, Electronic Notes in Theoretical Computer Science **67** (2002). [202]

200. ———, *Monadic second-order logic on tree-like structures*, Theoretical Computer Science **275** (2002), no. 1–2, 311–346. [285, 318]

201. Thomas Wilke, *Klarlund's optimal complementation procedure for Büchi automata*, Unpublished Note, 2000. [61]

202. ———, *Alternating tree automata, parity games, and modal μ-calculus*, Bull. Soc. Math. Belg. **8** (2001), no. 2. [95, 153, 154, 161, 171, 185]

203. Wieslaw Zielonka, *Infinite games on finitely coloured graphs with applications to automata on infinite trees*, Theoretical Computer Science **200** (1998), no. 1–2, 135–183. [39, 96, 99, 108, 130, 135]

204. Uri Zwick and Mike Paterson, *The complexity of mean payoff games on graphs*, Theoretical Computer Science **158** (1996), no. 1–2, 343–359. [109, 110, 111, 112, 115, 130]

Symbol Index

Index

Lecture Notes in Computer Science

For information about Vols. 1–2476

please contact your bookseller or Springer-Verlag